W9-CID-737

FOR REFERENCE

Do Not Take From This Room

MILESTONE DOCUMENTS
IN WORLD HISTORY

Exploring the Primary Sources
That Shaped the World

Volume 4
1942–2000

Brian Bonhomme
Editor in Chief

Cathleen Boivin
Consulting Editor

Schlager Group
Dallas, Texas

Milestone Documents in World History
Copyright © 2010 by Schlager Group Inc.

All rights reserved. No part of this book may be reproduced or utilized in any form or by any means, electronic or mechanical, including photocopying, recording, or by any information storage or retrieval systems, without permission in writing from the publisher. For information, contact:

Schlager Group Inc.
2501 Oak Lawn Avenue, Suite 440
Dallas, Tex. 75219
USA

You can find Schlager Group on the World Wide Web at
http://www.schlagergroup.com
Text and cover design by Patricia Moritz

Printed in the United States of America

10 9 8 7 6 5 4 3 2 1

ISBN: 978-0-9797758-6-4

This book is printed on acid-free paper.

CONTENTS

VOLUME 2: 1082–1833

MILESTONE DOCUMENTS
IN WORLD HISTORY

Exploring the Primary Sources
That Shaped the World

Mahatma Gandhi (AP/Wide World Photos)

Mahatma Gandhi's Speech to the All India Congress Committee

"We shall either free India or die in the attempt."

Overview

On the evening of August 8, 1942, Mahatma Gandhi, the father of modern India, made a historic appeal calling for a mass civil-disobedience movement in support of the greatest cause of his life: the struggle for India's freedom from the yoke of British imperialism. Gandhi finished delivering his address, commonly known as the Quit India Speech, shortly before midnight at Gowalia Tank Maidan, a park in Bombay (now Mumbai). Earlier that day the All India Congress Committee (AICC)—the main organizational wing of the Indian National Congress—endorsed the Quit India Resolution, which demanded an immediate end to British rule in India; this endorsement provided the occasion for Gandhi's speech. Three weeks earlier, on July 14, the Working Committee of the AICC had passed the Quit India Resolution. To this day, the AICC is made up of delegates from the Indian National Congress. The Congress, as it is simply called, is India's largest and oldest democratic organization (having been founded in 1885), which Gandhi had reorganized as its spiritual and political leader beginning in 1918.

Context

The chain of events that led to Gandhi's speech and the Quit India Movement began with the resignation of Congress ministries in 1939 following the unilateral decision of the British government to bring India into World War II. After enactment of the Government of India Act of 1935 (which made provisions for the formation of elected government), an election was held in provinces across the country in 1937. The Indian National Congress emerged as the single largest party, and by September 1938 it had formed ministries in as many as eight states. With the unilateral decision of the British government to join World War II, the members of the Congress ministries resigned. Efforts at further dialogue between the Indian National Congress and British authorities proved to be unsuccessful. In reaction to this political stalemate, Gandhi in October 1940 called for members of the Congress to begin personal campaigns based on satyagraha.

Satyagraha, which literally means "truthful request," was a protest method Gandhi devised that used acts of nonviolent resistance, including peaceful violation of laws, mass arrests, workers' strikes (*hartals*), and long marches. Satyagraha was grounded in Gandhi's deep faith in the core principles of truth (*satya*) and nonviolence (ahimsa), as articulated in his 1909 pamphlet *Hind Swaraj* (Indian Home Rule). During the 1920s and 1930s civil-disobedience satyagraha campaigns had been huge collective undertakings. During the satyagraha of October 1940 to December 1941, however, only individual Congress members defied British wartime regulations, such as those that limited the right of free speech. The Congress leadership remained deeply divided about launching any kind of movement in defiance of the British in a time of war. At its annual session held at Ramgarh in 1940, the Congress emphasized organizational preparation and moderation in action. The president of the Congress, Jawarhalal Nehru, was deeply concerned that any broad-based movement protesting British authority could harm the Allied forces in their fight against Fascism. Nehru gave his consent to further mass civil-disobedience movements only after much persuasion from Gandhi himself.

Japan entered World War II on December 7, 1941, with the attack on the U.S. naval fleet at Pearl Harbor, Hawaii. In less than three months, Japan would become a major threat to the British Empire in South Asia. By March 1942 the Japanese army had made huge inroads into Burma, and its ships and military aircraft had advanced as far as the Bay of Bengal. Japanese conquests elsewhere brought disturbing news of instances of racism toward Indians. Europeans had fled Malaysia, Singapore, and Burma but left Indians living in those areas at the mercy of the Japanese military. Within India itself, the stresses of war were all too apparent; trains were packed with wounded Indian soldiers who had fought for the British, war-weary plantation laborers coming home from Assam on the Burmese border, and hordes of migrant workers returning to their villages in northern India from Calcutta on the Bay of Bengal. All these factors led to widespread predictions of the imminent collapse of the British government. People began to withdraw their savings from banks and started hoarding gold, silver, and coins in their homes. Many had lost confidence

1940

- **October**
Mahatma Gandhi
and many of his
colleagues in the
Indian National
Congress begin to
defy wartime regu-
lations with individ-
ual acts of civil dis-
obedience; the defi-
ance continues to
December 1941.

1941

- **December 7**
Japan attacks
the United
States and offi-
cially enters
World War II,
after having
allied with Ger-
many and Italy
in 1940.

1942

- **March 23**
Sir Stafford Cripps,
a minister of
Churchill's war cab-
inet, arrives in India
to win public sup-
port for the British
war effort in
exchange for the
promise of full
dominion status for
India within the
British Empire after
the war.

- **July 14**
The All India
Congress Working
Committee issues
the Quit India
Resolution, which
calls for a new
satyagraha
campaign and
demands that
British rule in India
end immediately.

- **August 8**
The All India Congress
Committee approves
the Quit India
Resolution and
sanctions the
implementation of a
resistance movement
under the leadership of
Gandhi, who delivers
his Quit India speech
that evening.

in the British system of governance, and their faith in law and order was at its lowest ebb. In this historical context, Gandhi's desperation was at its peak. Yet he still wanted India's freedom regardless and gave it precedence despite growing tensions between religious groups and the Fascist threat to democracy.

An astute reader of the popular pulse, Gandhi well understood the growing wartime discontent over the rising price of food, shortages of staples such as rice and salt, and the economic dislocation of the peasantry. Also, the British government failed to check black-marketing operations on the Indian Subcontinent. Food hoarding and profiteering grew out of control in the early 1940s and directly led to one of the most horrible famines in Indian history, the Bengal famine of 1943. British wartime measures also includ-ed the seizure and destruction of boats in the eastern states of Bengal and Orissa in order to ward off the Japanese. Gandhi correctly observed that depriving people in East Bengal of their boats was like cutting off their limbs.

U.S. president Franklin Delano Roosevelt expressed his concern about the situation in India during talks with British prime minister Winston Churchill in Washington, D.C., in December 1941. In February 1942 during a visit to India, Chinese Nationalist leader Chiang Kai-shek expressed his sympathy for India's aspiration for freedom. Owing to pressure from Britain's allies and the need to win Indian support for the Allied war effort, Churchill dis-patched Sir Stafford Cripps, a Socialist politician and war cabinet minister, to India in March 1942 with a proposal for the postwar creation of a new Indian union with full dominion status in the British Empire. Under the terms of the Cripps Mission proposal, India would have created its own constitution, and all British members of the ruling Executive Council would have been replaced with Indians. Still, India would have remained part of the British Empire, and the British monarch would have remained its ultimate head of state; moreover, individual provinces would have had the option not to join the union. The opt-out stipulation was included partly in response to the demands of Muslim League leader Mohammed Ali Jinnah for a separate Muslim state. (Jinnah would eventually get his wish with the creation of the Muslim state of Pakistan, of which he would be the first governor-general.) Gandhi and other Congress leaders rejected the Cripps Mission proposal in April 1942.

In the wake of the Cripps Mission's failure, the Con-gress's Working Committee resolved in a meeting at Ward-ha on July 14, 1942, to launch a new satyagraha campaign to be known by the slogan Quit India. Gandhi's speech of August 8, 1942, was made on the occasion of the AICC's approval of the Quit India Resolution. Upon passage of this resolution in July, the Working Committee had originally emphasized the policy of "nonembarrassment" the Con-gress had pursued since the outbreak of the war. To keep the spirit of national struggle alive without actually ham-pering British war efforts, Gandhi had made it clear to the government that he did not wish to embarrass the British state. Hence he launched a program of individual acts of satyagraha instead of mass civil disobedience. Because of this policy, the Congress's leadership had preferred to keep the campaign individually based and deliberately symbolic in nature. But in unambiguous terms, Gandhi also appealed directly to the British on behalf of the Congress that "British rule in India must end immediately" not only because its imperialist subjection of India must cease but also "because India in bondage can play no effective part in defending herself and in affecting the fortunes of the war that is desolating humanity" (Mahatma Gandhi, p. 451). In case Gandhi's appeal failed, the Congress leadership had also agreed to inaugurate a nonviolent civil-disobedience movement on the broadest scale under Gandhi's leadership. Gandhi had already made his stance clear when in May 1942 he said in an interview that the "orderly disciplined anarchy" of British governance should end and "if as a result there is complete lawlessness I would risk it" (Mahatma Gandhi, p. 114).

It was in this context that Gandhi made his influential speech on August 8, 1942. In the early morning of August 9, just a few hours after the speech, British authorities arrested and imprisoned Gandhi together with all the prominent leaders of the Indian National Congress, though they were later released. However, the slogan "Quit India" had already won broad-based popular support and soon gave rise to mass civil disobedience that would last until negotiations for the transfer of power from British to Indian self-rule were finalized in 1947. In the opinion of Victor Alexander John Hope, the 2nd Marquis of Linlithgow, who served as viceroy and governor general of India from 1936 to 1943, the Quit India Movement was the most serious threat to British rule in India since the Indian Rebellion of 1857—a failed revolt against Britain that was begun by Indian soldiers in the service of the East India Company but which soon gathered strength and spread through the country.

After the arrests, the British government declared the Congress illegal and sealed its offices and seized its printing presses. These measures only stoked popular sentiment against the British. Public property and sites of British authority soon became prime targets of the people's discontent. Police stations were attacked, and in different regions parallel governments independent of British governance came into existence. The intensity and violence of the demonstrations distinguish the Quit India Movement from earlier civil-disobedience campaigns of the 1920s and 1930s. The Quit India Movement accelerated the process toward India's independence on August 15, 1947.

About the Author

Mahatma Gandhi was born Mohandas Karamchand Gandhi in the northwestern Indian state of Gujarat on October 2, 1869, and was educated in both India and England. His activism first came to prominence during his career as a lawyer for an Indian firm in Durban, South Africa, from 1893 to 1914. His fight against racial discrim-

Time Line

1942

- **August 9**
  Gandhi and all prominent Congress leaders are arrested, and the organization is declared illegal. Clashes with authorities erupt as soon as the public learns about the arrests.

- **August 10**
  Hartals (massive workers' strikes, closure of shops and offices) commence in Delhi and other northern Indian cities; massive nationwide demonstrations soon occur, many of them violent.

- **December 17**
  Jatiya Sarkar, the first of several parallel regional governments independent of British authority, is established in Tamluk, Bengal, and remains in operation until September 1944.

1943

- **February 10**
  While in jail, Gandhi begins a twenty-one day fast; he refuses to condemn the severity of demonstrations across India and criticizes the British for having unleashed violence.

1944

- **May 6**
  Gandhi is released from jail on medical grounds.

1945

- **June 14**
  The release of all imprisoned Congress members is ordered.

1945

■ **June 25**
The Shimla Conference meets to discuss Indian self-rule and a new constitution; talks later break down because of Mohammed Ali Jinnah's demand that the Muslim League be granted the exclusive right to represent India's Muslims.

1946

■ **March–June**
The Cabinet Mission carries on negotiations with Indian political leaders about self-rule and drafts a provisional constitution.

■ **August 16**
The Muslim League withdraws its acceptance of the Cabinet Mission plan for Indian self-rule; violence between Hindus, Muslims, and Sikhs erupts.

1947

■ **June 3**
Viceroy Lord Louis Mountbatten announces that the Congress, the Muslim League, and Sikh leaders have accepted his plan providing for two nations, India and Pakistan.

■ **July 18**
The Indian Independence Act is ratified by the British Parliament and the Crown.

■ **August 15**
British India is partitioned, creating the newly independent countries of India and Pakistan.

ination in South Africa began with prayers and petitions, but by 1907 he had invented the strategy of passive resistance, which he called satyagraha. Hardly a slave to tradition, he believed in changing and modifying his satyagraha techniques. Because of the evolution of his ideology, he titled his autobiography *An Experiment with Truth*. However, his core belief in truth, nonviolence, and the goal of swaraj (political self-determination for India) remained unchanged throughout his life.

Soon after his return to India in 1914, he started working toward unification of the then-divided Indian National Congress. First, he championed the cause of indigo plantation workers in the northern state of Bihar and the plight of textile mill workers in Ahmadabad in his native Gujarat. During the 1920s he successfully reorganized the Congress as a mass-based political organization, and he expanded its social composition by bringing in the peasantry as members. By combining the struggle against British imperialism with social and economic justice, he emerged as Mahatma, which literally means "great soul."

In 1921 and 1930, Gandhi launched two countrywide civil-disobedience movements that focused on social reconstruction measures. He also endeavored, albeit with limited success, to keep India's diverse religious and ethnic groups unified, despite nascent forces of religious and cultural separatism. Because of the growing strength of these separatist forces in the early 1940s, it is not surprising much of his Quit India speech directly addressed discord between Hindus and Muslims.

Gandhi did not live to see the final fruits of his efforts. Just six months later, on January 30, 1948, he was taking his nightly walk in New Delhi when he was shot and killed by an assassin, a Hindu nationalist named Nathuram Godse. Later that year Godse and a co-conspirator were executed for the crime. Gandhi's birthday, October 2, is a national holiday in India, and the United Nations has proclaimed October 2 the International Day of Non-Violence.

Explanation and Analysis of the Document

The Quit India speech is one of Gandhi's longest addresses. He delivered it first in Hindi and then in a shortened English version. The document reproduced here is a translation of the full Hindi text. The speech was the second made by Gandhi during the two-day All India Congress Committee meeting in Bombay. The earlier speech was given on August 7, before the AICC's endorsement of the Quit India Resolution. The speeches of August 7 and August 8 complement each other in content; both are passionate pleas for initiating the largest civil-disobedience movement in Indian history. In the first speech, Gandhi expressed his faith in nonviolent resistance, while barely touching upon issues such as the separatist politics of Hindu extremists or Mohammad Ali Jinnah. Instead, he emphasized the need for religious unity in order to foster true democracy, "the like of which has not been so witnessed" (Mahatma Gandhi, p. 380).

◆ **Paragraphs 1–21**

Gandhi begins his speech of August 8 by congratulating the committee for its approval of the Quit India Resolution. He then also congratulates those thirteen members who had voted against the resolution. In his earlier speech on August 7, Gandhi had appealed to committee members to vote in favor of the resolution *only* if they believed in its truthfulness. He had also warned them that in case of the resolution's failure he was not prepared at his advanced age to remain leader of the Congress. In the opening paragraphs of the speech of August 8, Gandhi also names Maulana Abul Kalam Azad and Jawaharlal Nehru, two Congress leaders who had questioned the timing of the Quit India Movement and had agreed to launch it only after much persuasion from Gandhi. By mentioning their names, Gandhi publicly conveys their consent.

After addressing internal voices of dissent, Gandhi turns to India's Muslim community. Jinnah had recently emerged as the chief spokesman for India's Muslims, and the Muslim League under Jinnah opposed joining with the Congress in any mass movement against colonial rule, particularly since the British Government had been wooing the league since 1940. (Gandhi uses the word *Mussalman*, an antique usage for "Muslim.") Jinnah believed that the Muslim League should be recognized as the only representative of the Muslim community and be treated at par with the Congress in any negotiation for the transfer of authority from the Crown to Indian subjects. Gandhi viewed Muslim participation in the movement as essential to its success, and it was imperative for him to counter Jinnah's growing popularity as well as the two-nation theory, which held that Hindus and Muslims constituted two distinct religious and cultural groups. With his reference to Maulana Muhammad Ali and Maulana Shaukat Ali, brothers who had been prominent Muslim activists and allies of the Congress, Gandhi recalls the joint Hindu/Muslim movements of the early 1920s as the golden moment of interfaith unity, when Muslim leaders had worked hand in hand with the Congress.

Gandhi perceived religious and cultural conflict as arising from the fundamentalist Hindu Mahasabha organization as well as Jinnah's separatist faction within the Muslim League. Neither Mahasabha nor the Muslim League officially supported a united front involving all Indians. Gandhi criticizes two important Hindu fundamentalist leaders—Dr. B. S. Moonje and Vinayak Damodar Savarkar, the latter an ideologue who advocated forming an exclusively Hindu nation—for their opposition to the Quit India Resolution as well as their promotion of hatred and violence toward other religious communities. Despite these reservations, Gandhi insists that "freedom cannot now wait for the realization of communal unity" (paragraph 16). He had always considered conflicts about religious faith and caste to be internal issues, though he never would have wanted the price of political freedom to include religious strife. Therefore, Gandhi eagerly appeals here to Hindus and Muslims to unite in the fight for India's freedom and not pay much heed to demands for a separate Muslim state. Gandhi's statement that "the Congress must win

freedom or be wiped out in the effort" (paragraph 16) reflects his determination as well as his growing anxiety over Jinnah's rise to power.

Gandhi then briefly alludes to the possibility of a Japanese attack on India. Here his disappointment with British rule is palpable. His close disciple, Mirabehn, born Madeleine Slade, had been traveling in the state of Orissa in eastern India and personally confirmed reports that British authorities were destroying Indian-owned boats. Gandhi was well aware of popular anger about repressive British wartime measures, which made his call for mass action all the more urgent: "If today I sit quiet and inactive, God will take me to task" (paragraph 21).

◆ **Paragraphs 22–35**

After again invoking the need for united immediate action, Gandhi shifts to his time-tested method of inviting the British government to respond to his demands first. He thus makes clear that the Quit India Movement has not yet begun. Gandhi preferred to wait for the viceroy's response to the demands, and by his calculation that meant a window of two to three weeks. This was important because Gandhi launched civil-disobedience movements only after careful planning. This organizational drill was still necessary, even though the Quit India Resolution had been issued three weeks earlier and the proposed movement had already attracted considerable buzz.

As a preparatory measure in anticipation of the movement, Gandhi had prepared detailed instructions for civil resisters and presented them for consideration by the Congress Working Committee. The committee discussed these instructions on August 8, 1942, and approval was expected on August 9. Because of the arrest of Gandhi and all of the Congress's committee members on the morning of August 9, further discussion of the instructions and their approval was postponed indefinitely. Gandhi's instructions were meant to provide a discipline for resisters and thus ensure the movement's nonviolent character. Gandhi conceived of the movement as including a series of fasts, passive resistance to British coercive measures, and persuasion of movement nonsupporters to reconsider their political stance. On the day of a *hartal*, or national strike, no processions or meetings were to take place. Along with these instructions, Gandhi also encouraged people to follow a constructive program, aspects of which he describes in his speech. This program included efforts toward religious unity, the prohibition of intoxicants, and the propagation of homespun cotton cloth known as *khaddar* or *khadi*. It also advocated removal of "untouchability," a reference to the Indian caste system that relegated—and continues to relegate—millions of poor Indians to the lowest rung on the social order and subjects them to discrimination and violence entirely because of their birth.

While Gandhi asks his listeners to wait for Viceroy Linlithgow's response and to meanwhile follow the constructive program, he also encourages them to consider themselves free men and women. Gandhi viewed the opposites of freedom and servitude as the outcome of a mental com-

Muslim refugees sit on the roof of an overcrowded railway train coach as they try to flee India on September 19, 1947. (AP/Wide World Photos)

promise between the ruler and the ruled. For this reason, he urges all Indians to break free from the mindset of British rule and remain "no longer under the heel of this imperialism" (paragraph 22). Gandhi was determined to translate this mental freedom into political reality. He announces that he will not be "satisfied with anything short of complete freedom" (paragraph 24).

Gandhi had no illusion about how daunting the movement would be or how long it might last, despite his insistence that Indians should already view themselves as free. Unlike during earlier civil-disobedience movements, he asks that his followers neither fill the prisons nor leave their occupations. Instead, he instructs different social groups on courses of action they ought to follow. In these instructions the core principles remained truth and nonviolence. These instructions were doomed to be misinterpreted and ignored, once British authorities had arrested all Congress Party committee members at the central, provincial, and district levels during the months following the speech.

Audience

The first group Gandhi addressed in his speech was India's Muslim population. The Cripps Mission had reaffirmed British willingness to recognize the demands of Jinnah for a separate Muslim province. Political developments since the Lahore Resolution of 1940, which had demanded adequate and effective safeguards for Muslims to protect their rights and interests as a minority community, had elevated Jinnah to the position of spokesman for nearly all Muslims in India and had significantly impaired the ability of the Congress to represent the entire nation. For Gandhi, a messenger of religious brotherhood, the unity of religious communities was crucial for the success of any nationwide anti-British agitation. He vociferously criticized Jinnah as well as Hindu extremists like B. S. Moonje and Vinayak Damodar Savarkar for having preached and encouraged the doctrine of violence against followers of other faiths. Gandhi stressed the need for the unity of hearts and a joint effort by Hindus and Muslims in the fight for freedom. Religion divisions, in Gandhi's view, were not to stand in the way of Indian independence.

Another audience consisted of the committee members who had voted on the Quit India Resolution—both for and against it. Clearly, he was appreciative of those who voted in favor of the resolution, but he also commends those who voted against it, as long as they were voting their conscience. At the same time, he was addressing such figures as Maulana Abul Kalam Azad and Jawaharlal Nehru, who objected to the timing of the resolution in light of ongoing hostilities in World War II. In this sense, Gandhi was walking a fine line between continuing his calls for Indian independence but doing so in a way that would not undermine the British fight against Fascism.

Gandhi directly appealed to specific groups such as journalists, princes, landlords, soldiers, government officials, and students to follow broad lines of action in resistance to British authority. He did not ask them, as he had in earlier civil-disobedience movements, to boycott their classes, courts, or offices. Instead, he entrusted them to continue their work while at the same time openly declaring themselves Congress members and free subjects.

Impact

A broad cross section of Indian society participated in the Quit India Movement as a result of Gandhi's careful planning since 1939 as well as widespread dissatisfaction with British wartime policies. The Muslim League, the Communist Party of India, and Hindu fundamentalist parties did not officially support the movement, in the belief that it could weaken the Allied forces and inadvertently help the Axis powers. However, at the local and regional levels, members of these parties often either participated in the movement or at worst were neutral toward it. This allowed for considerable communal harmony. Despite Communist nonparticipation, members of other left-wing organizations shaped the movement's militancy, especially the systematic targeting of public property and communication networks. Socialists such as Jaya Prakash Narayan and Ram Manohar Lohia and other left-wing leaders were particularly active in directing attacks on British installations.

The Quit India Movement began on the morning of August 9, 1942—the day after Gandhi's speech—in Bombay, where a large number of people had gathered to await further instructions from the central leadership of the Indian National Congress. The news of the arrests of Congress leaders sparked the first incidents of unrest. Bombay remained the epicenter during the movement's first few days, with striking laborers playing a leading role in the demonstrations. By the following day, August 10, 1942, *hartals* were under way in Delhi and other northern Indian cities.

Within a week, massive protests occurred in the eastern United Provinces and the states of Bihar and Bengal, especially around the town of Tamluk in the Midnapur district, where the Jatiya Sarkar regional parallel government was formed in December 1942. In the town of Talcher in Orissa, a regional peasant-labor government known as a *chasi-maula raj* was established. Large-scale attacks on infrastructure and public property occurred in western India and southern India. Local regional governments similar to those established in Bengal and Orissa also came into being in these areas. Some of these governments proved to be quite effective and implemented economic and administrative reforms. The Jatiya Sarkar government functioned until late September 1944 and had its own armed fighting unit, Vidut Vahini. It also created its own legal system, administered schools and relief activities, and implemented egalitarian measures such as taking away agrarian crops and money from rich peasants and landlords and redistributing them to poor peasants.

In reaction to the Quit India Movement and nationalist activities in the sixteen districts of eastern United Provinces and Bihar, the British government implemented a mass mobilization of the military and police, though underground guerrilla activities still continued sporadically for some time in the frontier regions bordering Nepal. In Orissa, the British resorted to aerial bombardment of movement strongholds in order to thwart guerrilla attacks that continued until May 1943.

One of the major reasons for the scale of the violence against the British was the widespread but erroneous belief that India had already achieved freedom as of Gandhi's speech on August 8. Regardless of Gandhi's advocacy of passive resistance, violence exploded across India in the months following the Quit India speech. From 1942 to 1944, 208 police stations, 332 railway stations, and 945 post offices or telegraph lines were damaged or destroyed. This same period witnessed 664 guerrilla bomb explosions, in which 1,060 civilians and sixty-three policemen were officially reported as casualties. British authorities responded with an unprecedentedly brutal campaign, carried out mainly by the police and army, with measures that included torture, murder, and rape of the movement's participants as well as aerial bombardment and indiscriminate gunfire on civilians. While in prison with other members of the Congress, Gandhi refused to condemn the violence unleashed by the resisters and instead blamed the government as ultimately responsible, and in February 1943 he launched a twenty-one-day hunger strike. By the time India achieved independence, this legacy of violence had acquired the semblance of legitimacy. After independence, public property would be repeatedly targeted in demonstrations against the state.

The Quit India Movement necessitated the transfer of power from British colonial rule to Indian self-rule. The global context of international war had allowed the British to mobilize extraordinary military force against the movement. In the period immediately following World War II, the likelihood of renewed guerrilla violence remained, in part because of difficulties encountered by the British in releasing prisoners, a sharp increase in unemployment, and general social unrest. Viceroy Archibald Wavell (1943–1947) clearly communicated to the British government his apprehension about further violence in India. In 1945 a new Labour government sympathetic to the cause of Indian self-rule came to power in Britain, and negotiations regarding the transfer of power in India began soon afterward.

Within the Congress, the Quit India Movement helped reestablish the dominance of the Socialists, who had figured strongly in the movement and guerrilla activities, and also right-wing figures, who had become increasingly marginalized owing to their conservative pro-British attitudes. The Communists, on the other hand, lost much of their appeal, since they had prioritized the fight against Fascism over the struggle for Indian independence. One may conclude that the Quit India Movement, despite its mass following, facilitated the consolidation of power in the hands of the Indian bourgeoisie.

> "I, therefore, want freedom immediately, this very night, before dawn, if it can be had. Freedom cannot now wait for the realization of communal unity."
>
> (Paragraph 16)

> "India is without doubt the homeland of all the Mussalmans [Muslims] inhabiting this country. Every Mussalman should therefore cooperate in the fight for India's freedom. The Congress does not belong to any one class or community; it belongs to the whole nation."
>
> (Paragraph 19)

> "Here is a mantra.... You may imprint it on your hearts and let every breath of yours give expression to it. The mantra is: 'Do or Die.' We shall either free India or die in the attempt; we shall not live to see the perpetuation of our slavery."
>
> (Paragraph 25)

> "Let every man and woman live every moment of his or her life hereafter in the consciousness that he or she eats or lives for achieving freedom and will die, if need be, to attain that goal."
>
> (Paragraph 25)

Events unfolded quickly beginning in 1945. In June and July of that year, the Shimla Conference was held to discuss Indian self-rule and a new constitution, but the conference broke down because of Mohammed Ali Jinnah's insistence that the Muslim League be granted the exclusive right to represent India's Muslims. From March to June 1946 the Cabinet Mission—a diplomatic initiative formed by British prime minister Clement Attlee—took on the task of conducting negotiations with Indian political leaders about self-rule and drafted a provisional constitution. In August the Muslim League withdrew its acceptance of the Cabinet Mission plan for Indian self-rule, resulting in violence between Hindus, Muslims, and Sikhs. Finally, on June 3, 1947, Indian viceroy Lord Louis Mountbatten announced that the Congress, the Muslim League, and Sikh leaders had accepted his plan providing for two nations, India and Pakistan.

On July 18, 1947, the British Parliament and the Crown ratified the Indian Independence Act, setting August 15, 1947, as the date for partitioning British India and creating the newly independent countries of India and Pakistan. What followed was horror. The partition led to simultaneous mass exoduses of Muslims from India to Pakistan and non-Muslims from Pakistan to India. The number of refugees was at least fifteen million and perhaps as many as twenty-five million. Worse, the partition provoked religious riots in which as many as two million people—Muslims, Hindus, and Sikhs—lost their lives and perhaps 75,000 women were raped. Meanwhile, the border between India and Pakistan was somewhat ill defined, and still in the twenty-first century the two nations continue to square off against each other over the province of Kashmir, each claiming it for its own.

The most ironic outcome of the Quit India Movement, other than the violence that accompanied Indian independence, had to do with Gandhi himself, who was released early from jail for health reasons in 1944. During the three years following his release, negotiations involving the transfer of power took place, but he was largely marginalized from the negotiation process. Worse, Gandhi's trusted political allies, armed with the conviction that independence was imminent, began to desert him, and he was left as a lone warrior who sought to advance nonviolence and communal harmony. Still, Gandhi's policy of nonviolent passive resistance has a global legacy and political struggles in the second half of the twentieth century across the globe (from the antiapartheid movement in South Africa, led by Nelson Mandela, to the civil rights movement, led Martin Luther King, in the United States) has carried strong footprints of his ideology.

Further Reading

■ Books

Gandhi, Mahatma. *Collected Works of Mahatma Gandhi*. Vol. 76: *April 1, 1942–December 17, 1942*. 2nd rev. ed. New Delhi, India: Ministry of Information and Broadcasting, Government of India, 1969.

Gandhi, Rajmohan. *Mohandas: A True Story of a Man, His People, and an Empire*. New York: Penguin Books, 2006.

Gupta, Partha Sarathi, ed. *Towards Freedom: Documents on the Movement for Independence in India, 1943–44*. Delhi, India: Oxford University Press, 1997.

Harcourt, Max. "Kisan Populism and Revolution in Rural India: The 1942 Disturbances in Bihar and East United Provinces." In *Congress and the Raj: Facets of the Indian Struggle, 1917–47*, ed. D. A. Low. Columbia, Mo.: South Asia Books, 1977.

Henningham, Stephen. "Quit India Revolt, 1942." In his *Peasant Movements in Colonial India: North Bihar, 1917–1942*. Canberra: Australian National University, 1982.

Hutchins, Francis G. *Spontaneous Revolution: The Quit India Movement*. Delhi, India: Manohar Book Service, 1971.

Pandey, Gyanendra, ed. *The Indian Nation in 1942*. Kolkata, India: K. P. Bagchi, 1988.

Sarkar, Sumit. *Modern India, 1885–1947*. Chennai, India: Macmillan, 1983.

■ Web Sites

"Congress and the Freedom Movement." Indian National Congress Web site.
http://www.aicc.org.in/new/congress-the-freedom-movement.php.

Lal, Vinay. "Gandhi—A Select Bibliographic Guide." Manas Web site.
http://www.sscnet.ucla.edu/southasia/History/Gandhi/Gandhi biblio.html.

Questions for Further Study

1. Compare the independence movement that Gandhi led with similar independence movements as reflected in the entries on the Dutch Declaration of Independence, Simón Bolívar's Cartagena Manifesto, the Proclamation of the Provisional Government of the Irish Republic, or the Proclamation of the Algerian National Liberation Front. What similar goals did the independence movements have? How were their methods and outcomes similar, and how did they differ?

2. Refer to the entry Government of India Act of 1919. Examine the extent to which the 1919 act, contrary to British expectations, gave momentum to the Indian independence movement and would result in India's achieving its independence in 1947.

3. Why do you think so much violence accompanied the partition of India and Pakistan, given that the achievement of independence from an imperial power should be a cause for celebration?

4. In the twenty-first century, India and Pakistan, both nuclear powers, have threatened to go to war with each other, in large part over disputes about who owns the Kashmir province. To what extent to you think this hostility can be traced to events that preceded the independence of the two nations from British rule?

5. The name of Mahatma Gandhi survives as a virtual synonym for nonviolent resistance to oppressive rule. In this way his name has achieved iconic status. What other major historical figures who played a role in the creation of milestone documents enjoy similar iconic status in the twenty-first century? Why?

"Some of the Highlights of the 1942 Quit India Movement, Gowalia Tank Maidan, Bombay" Mahatma Gandhi Information Web site.

http://gandhi-manibhavan.org/activities/quit_India.htm.

—Sadan Jha

Mahatma Gandhi's Speech to the All India Congress Committee

I congratulate you on the resolution that you have just passed. I also congratulate the three comrades on the courage they have shown in pressing their amendments to a division, even though they knew that there was an overwhelming majority in favour of the resolution, and I congratulate the thirteen friends who voted against the resolution. In doing so, they had nothing to be ashamed of. For the last twenty years we have tried to learn not to lose courage even when we are in a hopeless minority and are laughed at. We have learned to hold on to our beliefs in the confidence that we are in the right. It behooves us to cultivate this courage of conviction, for it ennobles man and raises his moral stature. I was, therefore, glad to see that these friends had imbibed the principle which I have tried to follow for the last fifty years and more.

Having congratulated them on their courage, let me say that what they asked this Committee to accept through their amendments was not the correct representation of the situation. These friends ought to have pondered over the appeal made to them by the Maulana to withdraw their amendments; they should have carefully followed the explanations given by Jawaharlal. Had they done so, it would have been clear to them that the right which they now want the Congress to concede has already been conceded by the Congress.

Time was when every Mussalman claimed the whole of India as his motherland. During the years that the Ali Brothers were with me, the assumption underlying all their talks and discussions was that India belonged as much to the Mussalmans as to the Hindus. I can testify to the fact that this was their innermost conviction and not a mask; I lived with them for years. I spent days and nights in their company. And I make bold to say that their utterances were the honest expression of their beliefs. I know there are some who say that I take things too readily at their face value, that I am gullible. I do not think I am such a simpleton, nor am I so gullible as these friends take me to be. But their criticism does not hurt me. I should prefer to be considered gullible rather than deceitful.

What these Communist friends proposed through their amendments is nothing new. It has been repeated from thousands of platforms. Thousands of Mussalmans have told me that if the Hindu-Muslim question was to be solved satisfactorily, it must be done in my lifetime. I should feel flattered at this; but how can I agree to a proposal which does not appeal to my reason? Hindu-Muslim unity is not a new thing. Millions of Hindus and Mussalmans have sought after it. I consciously strove for its achievement from my boyhood. While at school, I made it a point to cultivate the friendship of Muslim and Parsi fellow students. I believed even at that tender age that the Hindus in India, if they wished to live in peace and amity with the other communities, should assiduously cultivate the virtue of [good] neighbourliness. It did not matter, I felt, if I made no special effort to cultivate the friendship with Hindus, but I must make friends with at least a few Mussalmans. It was as counsel for a Mussalman merchant that I went to South Africa. I made friends with other Mussalmans there, even with the opponents of my client, and gained a reputation for integrity and good faith. I had among my friends and co-workers Muslims as well as Parsis. I captured their hearts and when I left finally for India, I left them sad and shedding tears of grief at the separation.

In India, too, I continued my efforts and left no stone unturned to achieve that unity. It was my lifelong aspiration for it that made me offer my fullest co-operation to the Mussalmans in the Khilafat movement. Muslims throughout the country accepted me as their true friend.

How then is it that I have now come to be regarded as so evil and detestable? Had I any axe to grind in supporting the Khilafat movement? True, I did in my heart of hearts cherish a hope that it might enable me to save the cow. I am a worshipper of the cow. I believe the cow and myself to be the creation of the same God, and I am prepared to sacrifice my life in order to save the cow. But, whatever my philosophy of life and my ultimate hopes, I joined the movement in no spirit of bargain. I co-operated in the struggle for the Khilafat solely in order to discharge my obligation to my neighbour who, I saw, was in distress. The Ali Brothers, had they been alive today, would have testified to the truth of this assertion. And so would many others bear me out in that it was not a bargain on my part for saving the cow. The cow, like the Khilafat, stood on her own merits.

As an honest man, a true neighbour and a faithful friend, it was incumbent on me to stand by the Mussalmans in the hour of their trial.

In those days I shocked the Hindus by dining with the Mussalmans, though with the passage of time they have now got used to it. Maulana Bari told me, however, that though he would insist on having me as his guest, he would not allow me to dine with him, lest some day he should be accused of a sinister motive. And so, whenever I had occasion to stay with him, he called a Brahmin cook and made special arrangements for separate cooking. Firangi Mahal, his residence, was an old-styled structure with limited accommodation; yet he cheerfully bore all hardships and carried out his resolve from which I could not dislodge him. It was the spirit of courtesy, dignity and nobility that inspired us in those days. The members of each community vied with one another in accommodating members of sister communities. They respected one another's religious feelings, and considered it a privilege to do so. Not a trace of suspicion lurked in anybody's heart. Where has all that dignity, that nobility of spirit, disappeared now? I should ask all Mussalmans, including Qaid-e-Azam Jinnah, to recall those glorious days and to find out what has brought us to the present impasse. Qaid-e-Azam Jinnah himself was at one time a Congressman. If today the Congress has incurred his wrath, it is because the canker of suspicion has entered his heart. May God bless him with long life, but when I am gone, he will realize and admit that I had no designs on Mussalmans and that I had never betrayed their interests. Where is the escape for me if 1 injure their cause or betray their interests? My life is entirely at their disposal. They are free to put an end to it, whenever they wish to do so. Assaults have been made on my life in the past, but God has spared me till now, and the assailants have repented for their action. But if someone were to shoot me in the belief that he was getting rid of a rascal, he would kill not the real Gandhi, but the one that appeared to him a rascal.

To those who have been indulging in a campaign of abuse and vilification I would say, "Islam enjoins you not to revile even an enemy. The Prophet treated even enemies with kindness and tried to win them over by his fairness and generosity. Are you followers of that Islam or of any other? If you are followers of the true Islam, does it behoove you to distrust the words of one who makes a public declaration of his faith? You may take it from me that one day you will regret the fact that you distrusted and killed one who was a true and devoted friend of yours." It cuts me to the quick to see that the more I appeal and the more the Maulana importunes, the more intense does the campaign of vilification grow. To me, these abuses are like bullets. They can kill me, even as a bullet can put an end to my life. You may kill me. That will not hurt me. But what of those who indulge in abusing? They bring discredit to Islam. For the fair name of Islam, I appeal to you to resist this unceasing campaign of abuse and vilification.

Maulana Saheb is being made a target for the filthiest abuse. Why? Because he refuses to exert on me the pressure of his friendship. He realizes that it is a misuse of friendship to seek to compel a friend to accept as truth what he knows is an untruth.

To the Qaid-e-Azam I would say: "Whatever is true and valid in the claim for Pakistan is already in your hands. What is wrong and untenable is in nobody's gift, so that it can be made over to you. Even if someone were to succeed in imposing an untruth on others, he would not be able to enjoy for long the fruits of such coercion. God dislikes pride and keeps away from it. God would not tolerate a forcible imposition of an untruth."

The Qaid-e-Azam says that he is compelled to say bitter things but that he cannot help giving expression to his thoughts and his feelings. Similarly I would say: I consider myself a friend of the Mussalmans. Why should I then not give expression to the things nearest to my heart, even at the cost of displeasing them? How can I conceal my innermost thoughts from them? I should congratulate the Qaid-e-Azam on his frankness in giving expression to his thoughts and feelings, even if they sound bitter to his hearers. But even so why should the Mussalmans sitting here be reviled, if they do not see eye to eye with him? If millions of Mussalmans are with you, can you not afford to ignore the handful of Mussalmans who may appear to you to be misguided? Why should one with the following of several millions be afraid of a majority community, or of the minority being swamped by the majority? How did the Prophet work among the Arabs and the Mussalmans? How did he propagate Islam? Did he say he would propagate Islam only when he commanded a majority? I, therefore, appeal to you for the sake of Islam to ponder over what I say. There is neither fair play nor justice in saying that the Congress must accept a thing even if it does not believe in it and even if it goes counter to principles it holds dear.

Rajaji said: "I do not believe in Pakistan. But Mussalmans ask for it, Mr. Jinnah asks for it, and it has become an obsession with them. Why not then say 'yes' to them just now? The same Mr. Jinnah will later on realize the disadvantages of Pakistan and will forgo the demand." I said: "It is not fair to accept as true a thing which I hold to be untrue and ask others to do so in the belief that the demand will not be pressed when the time comes for settling it finally. If I hold the demand to be just, I should concede it this very day. I should not agree to it merely in order to placate Jinnah Saheb. Many friends have come and asked me to agree to it for the time being to placate Mr. Jinnah, disarm his suspicions and to see how he reacts to it. But I cannot be party to a course of action with a false promise. At any rate, it is not my method."

The Congress has no sanction but the moral one for enforcing its decisions. It believes that true democracy can only be the outcome of non-violence. The structure of a world federation can be raised only on a foundation of non-violence, and violence will have to be totally abjured from world affairs. If this is true, the solution of the Hindu-Muslim question, too, cannot be achieved by resort to violence. If the Hindus tyrannize over the Mussalmans, with what face will they talk of a world federation? It is for the same reason that I do not believe in the possibility of establishing world peace through violence as the English and American statesmen propose to do. The Congress has agreed to submitting all the differences to an impartial international tribunal and to abide by its decisions. If even this fairest of proposals is unacceptable, the only course that remains open is that of the sword, of violence. How can I persuade myself to agree to an impossibility? To demand the vivisection of a living organism is to ask for its very life. It is a call to war. The Congress cannot be party to such a fratricidal war. Those Hindus who, like Dr. Moonje and Shri Savarkar, believe in the doctrine of the sword may seek to keep the Mussalmans under Hindu domination. I do not represent that section. I represent the Congress. You want to kill the Congress which is the goose that lays golden eggs. If you distrust the Congress, you may rest assured that there is to be a perpetual war between the Hindus and the Mussalmans, and the country will be doomed to continue warfare and bloodshed. If such warfare is to be our lot, I shall not live to witness it.

It is for that reason that I say to Jinnah Saheb, "You may take it from me that whatever in your demand for Pakistan accords with considerations of justice and equity is lying in your pocket; whatever in the demand is contrary to justice and equity you can take only by the sword and in no other manner."

There is much in my heart that I would like to pour out before this assembly. One thing which was uppermost in my heart I have already dealt with. You may take it from me that it is with me a matter of life and death. If we Hindus and Mussalmans mean to achieve a heart unity, without the slightest mental reservation on the part of either, we must first unite in the effort to be free from the shackles of this Empire. If Pakistan after all is to be a portion of India, what objection can there be for Mussalmans against joining this struggle for India's freedom? The Hindus and Mussalmans must, therefore, unite in the first instance on the issue of fighting for freedom. Jinnah Saheb thinks the war will last long. I do not agree with him. If the war goes on for six months more, how shall we be able to save China?

I, therefore, want freedom immediately, this very night, before dawn, if it can be had. Freedom cannot now wait for the realization of communal unity. If that unity is not achieved, sacrifices necessary for it will have to be much greater than would have otherwise sufficed. But the Congress must win freedom or be wiped out in the effort. And forget not that the freedom which the Congress is struggling to achieve will not be for the Congressmen alone but for all the forty crores of the Indian people. Congressmen must forever remain humble servants of the people.

The Qaid-e-Azam has said that the Muslim League is prepared to take over the rule from the Britishers if they are prepared to hand it over to the Muslim League, for the British took over the Empire from the hands of the Muslims. This, however, will be Muslim raj. The offer made by Maulana Saheb and by me does not imply establishment of Muslim raj or Muslim domination. The Congress does not believe in the domination of any group or any community. It believes in democracy which includes in its orbit Muslims, Hindus, Christians, Parsis, Jews— every one of the communities inhabiting this vast country. If Muslim raj is inevitable, then let it be; but how can we give it the stamp of our assent? How can we agree to the domination of one community over the others?

Millions of Mussalmans in this country come from Hindu stock. How can their homeland be any other than India? My eldest son embraced Islam some years back. What would his homeland be— Porbander or the Punjab? I ask the Mussalmans: "If India is not your homeland, what other country do you belong to? In what separate homeland would you put my son who embraced Islam?" His mother wrote him a letter after his conversion, asking him if he had on embracing Islam given up drinking which Islam forbids to its followers. To those who gloated over the conversion, she wrote to say: "I do not mind his becoming a Mussalman so much as his drinking. Will you, as pious Mussalmans, tolerate his drinking even after his conversion? He has reduced himself to the state of a rake by drinking. If you are going to make a man of him again, his conversion will have been turned to good account. You will, therefore, please see that he as a Mussalman abjures wine and women. If that change does not come about, his conversion goes in vain and our non-cooperation with him will have to continue."

India is without doubt the homeland of all the Mussalmans inhabiting this country. Every Mussalman should therefore cooperate in the fight for India's freedom. The Congress does not belong to any one class or community; it belongs to the whole nation. It is open to Mussalmans to take possession of the Congress. They can, if they like, swamp the Congress by their numbers, and can steer it along the course which appeals to them. The Congress is fighting not on behalf of the Hindus but on behalf of the whole nation, including the minorities. It would hurt me to hear of a single instance of a Mussalman being killed by a Congressman. In the coming revolution, Congressmen will sacrifice their lives in order to protect the Mussalman against a Hindu's attack and *vice versa*. It is a part of their creed, and is one of the essentials of non-violence. You will be expected on occasions like these not to lose your heads. Every Congressman, whether a Hindu or a Mussalman, owes this duty to the organization to which he belongs. The Mussalman who will act in this manner will render a service to Islam. Mutual trust is essential for success in the final nation-wide struggle that is to come.

I have said that much greater sacrifices will have to be made this time in the wake of our struggle because of the opposition from the Muslim League and from Englishmen. You have seen the secret circular issued by Sir Frederick Puckle. It is a suicidal course that he has taken. It contains an open incitement to organizations which crop up like mushrooms to combine to fight the Congress. We have thus to deal with an Empire whose ways are crooked. Ours is a straight path which we can tread even with our eyes closed. That is the beauty of satyagraha.

In satyagraha, there is no place for fraud or falsehood, or any kind of untruth. Fraud and untruth today are stalking the world. I cannot be a helpless witness to such a situation. I have travelled all over India as perhaps nobody in the present age has. The voiceless millions of the land saw in me their friend and representative, and I identified myself with them

to an extent it was possible for a human being to do. I saw trust in their eyes, which I now want to turn to good account in fighting this Empire upheld on untruth and violence. However gigantic the preparations that the Empire has made, we must get out of its clutches. How can I remain silent at this supreme hour and hide my light under the bushel? Shall I ask the Japanese to tarry a while? If today I sit quiet and inactive, God will take me to task for not using up the treasure He had given me, in the midst of the conflagration that is enveloping the whole world. Had the condition been different, I should have asked you to wait yet awhile. But the situation now has become intolerable, and the Congress has no other course left for it.

Nevertheless, the actual struggle does not commence this moment. You have only placed all your powers in my hands. I will now wait upon the Viceroy and plead with him for the acceptance of the Congress demand. That process is likely to take two or three weeks. What would you do in the mean while? What is the programme, for the interval, in which all can participate? As you know, the spinning-wheel is the first thing that occurs to me. I made the same answer to the Maulana. He would have none of it, though he understood its import later. The fourteen-fold constructive programme is, of course, there for you to carry out. What more should you do? I will tell you. Every one of you should, from this moment onwards, consider yourself a free man or woman, and act as if you are free and are no longer under the heel of this imperialism.

It is not a make-believe that I am suggesting to you. It is the very essence of freedom. The bond of the slave is snapped the moment he considers himself to be a free being. He will plainly tell the master: "I was your bondslave till this moment, but I am a slave no longer. You may kill me if you like, but if you keep me alive, I wish to tell you that if you release me from the bondage of your own accord, I will ask for nothing more from you. You used to feed and clothe me, though I could have provided food and clothing for myself by my labour. I hitherto depended on you instead of on God, for food and raiment. God has now inspired me with an urge for freedom and I am today a free man and will no longer depend on you."

You may take it from me that I am not going to strike a bargain with the Viceroy for ministries and the like. I am not going to be satisfied with anything short of complete freedom. Maybe, he will propose the abolition of salt tax, the drink evil, etc. But I will say: "Nothing less than freedom."

Here is a *mantra*, a short one, that I give you. You may imprint it on your hearts and let every breath of yours give expression to it. The *mantra* is: "Do or Die." We shall either free India or die in the attempt; we shall not live to see the perpetuation of our slavery. Every true Congressman or [Congress] woman will join the struggle with an inflexible determination not to remain alive to see the country in bondage and slavery. Let that be your pledge. Keep jails out of your consideration. If the Government keep me free, I will spare you the trouble of filling the jails. I will not put on the Government the strain of maintaining a large number of prisoners at a time when it is in trouble. Let every man and woman live every moment of his or her life hereafter in the consciousness that he or she eats or lives for achieving freedom and will die, if need be, to attain that goal. Take a pledge with God and your own conscience as witness, that you will no longer rest till freedom is achieved and will be prepared to lay down your lives in the attempt to achieve it. He who loses his life will gain it; he who will seek to save it shall lose it. Freedom is not for the coward or the faint-hearted.

A word to the journalists. I congratulate you on the support you have hitherto given to the national demand. I know the restrictions and handicaps under which you have to labour. But I would now ask you to snap the chains that bind you. It should be the proud privilege of the newspapers to lead and set an example in laying down one's life for freedom. You have the pen which the Government can't suppress. I know you have large properties in the form of printing-presses, etc., and you would be afraid lest the Government should attach them. I do not ask you to invite an attachment of the printing-press voluntarily. For myself, I would not suppress my pen, even if the press was to be attached. As you know my press was attached in the past and returned later on. But I do not ask from you that final sacrifice. I suggest a middle way. You should now wind up your Standing Committee, and you may declare that you will give up writing under the present restrictions and take up the pen only when India has won her freedom. You may tell Sir Frederick Puckle that he can't expect from you a command performance, that his Press notes are full of untruth, and that you will refuse to publish them. You will openly declare that you are whole-heartedly with the Congress. If you do this, you will have changed the atmosphere before the fight actually begins.

From the Princes I ask with all respect due to them a very small thing. I am a well-wisher of the Princes. I was born in a State. My grandfather refused to salute with his right hand any Prince other than his own. But he did not say to the Prince, as I feel he ought to have said, that even his own master could not compel him, his minister, to act against his conscience. I have eaten the Princes' salt and I would not be false to it. As a faithful servant, it is my duty to warn the Princes that if they will act while I am still alive, the Princes may come to occupy an honourable place in free India. In Jawaharlal's scheme of free India, no privileges or the privileged classes have a place. Jawaharlal considers all property to be State-owned. He wants planned economy. He wants to reconstruct India according to plan. He likes to fly; I do not. I have kept a place for the Princes and the zamindars in India that I envisage. I would ask the Princes in all humility to enjoy through renunciation. The Princes may renounce ownership over their properties and become their trustees in the true sense of the term. I visualize God in the assemblage of people. The Princes may say to their people: "You are the owners and masters of the State and we are your servants." I would ask the Princes to become servants of the people and render to them an account of their own services. The Empire too bestows power on the Princes, but they should prefer to derive power from their own people; and if they want to indulge in some innocent pleasures, they may seek to do so as servants of the people. I do not want the Princes to live as paupers. But I would ask them: "Do you want to remain slaves for all time? Why should you, instead of paying homage to a foreign power, not accept the sovereignty of your own people?" You may write to the Political Department: "The people are now awake. How are we to withstand an avalanche before which even the large Empires are crumbling? We, therefore, shall belong to the people from today onwards. We shall sink or swim with them." Believe me, there is nothing unconstitutional in the course I am suggesting. There are, so far as I know, no treaties enabling the Empire to coerce the Princes. The people of the States will also declare that though they are the Princes' subjects, they are part of the Indian nation and that they will accept the leadership of the Princes, if the latter cast their lot with the People, but not otherwise. If this declaration enrages the Princes and they choose to kill the people, the latter will meet death bravely and unflinchingly, but will not go back on their word.

Nothing, however, should be done secretly. This is an open rebellion. In this struggle secrecy is a sin. A free man would not engage in a secret movement. It is likely that when you gain freedom you will have a C.I.D. of your own, in spite of my advice to the contrary. But in the present struggle, we have to work openly and to receive the bullets on our chest, without taking to heels.

I have a word to say to the Government servants also. They may not, if they like, resign their posts yet. The late Justice Ranade did not resign his post, but he openly declared that he belonged to the Congress. He said to the Government that though he was a judge, he was a Congressman and would openly attend the sessions of the Congress, but that at the same time he would not let his political views warp his impartiality on the bench. He held Social Reform Conference in the very pandal of the Congress. I would ask all the Government servants to follow in the footsteps of Ranade and to declare their allegiance to the Congress as an answer to the secret circular issued by Sir Frederick Puckle.

This is all that I ask of you just now. I will now write to the Viceroy. You will be able to read the correspondence not just now but when I publish it with the Viceroy's consent. But you are free to aver that you support the demand to be put forth in my letter. A judge came to me and said: "We get secret circulars from high quarters. What are we to do?" I replied, "If I were in your place, I would ignore the circulars. You may openly say to the Government: 'I have received your secret circular. I am, however, with the Congress. Though I serve the Government for my livelihood, I am not going to obey these secret circulars or to employ underhand methods.'"

Soldiers too are covered by the present programme. I do not ask them just now to resign their posts and leave the army. Soldiers come to me, Jawaharlal and to the Maulana and say: "We are wholly with you. We are tired of the governmental tyranny." To these soldiers I would say: "You may say to the Government, 'Our hearts are with the Congress. We are not going to leave our posts. We will serve you so long as we receive your salaries. We will obey your just orders, but will refuse to fire on our own people.'"

To those who lack the courage to do this much I have nothing to say. They will go their own way. But if you can do this much, you may take it from me that the whole atmosphere will be electrified. Let the Government then shower bombs, if they like. But no

Glossary

Ali Brothers	Mohammad and Shaukat Ali, who were allied with the Indian National Congress during the days of the Khilafat movement
brahmachari	a figurative way to describe a man who does not expend vital energies on passing fancies
Justice Ranade	Mahadev Govind Ranade; a founder of the Indian National Congress
Khilafat movement	efforts by Muslims in India to secure favorable treatment from the British government (1919–1924)
Maulana Bari	Abdul Bari, a leader of the Khilafat movement
Maulana Jawaharlal	Jawaharlal Nehru, later India's first prime minister; as a gesture of ecumenism, Gandhi uses Maulana, a title accorded Muslim leaders (literally, "our lord," "our master" in Arabic), to describe his fellow Hindu.
Maulana Saheb	Abdul Kalam Azad; a Muslim leader and friend of Gandhi's who was much respected in tribal India
Qaid-e-Azam Jinnah	Muhammed Ali Jinnah; the title means "great leader" in Urdu
Rajaji	Gandhi's name (meaning "keeper of my conscience") for his close associate Chakravarthi Rajagopalachari
Sir Frederick Puckle	director-general of the Central Board of Information of British India
[the] Viceroy	Victor Alexander John Hope, 2nd Marquis of Linlithgow

power on earth will then be able to keep you in bondage any longer.

If the students want to join the struggle only to go back to their studies after a while, I would not invite them to it. For the present, however, till the time that I frame a programme for the struggle, I would ask the students to say to their professors: "We belong to the Congress. Do you belong to the Congress or to the Government? If you belong to the Congress, you need not vacate your posts. You will remain at your posts but teach us and lead us unto freedom." In all fights for freedom, the world over, the students have made very large contributions.

If in the interval that is left to us before the actual fight begins, you do even the little I have suggested to you, you will have changed the atmosphere and will have prepared the ground for the next step.

There is much I should yet like to say. But my heart is heavy. I have already taken up much of your time. I have yet to say a few words in English also. I thank you for the patience and attention with which you have listened to me even at this late hour. It is just what true soldiers would do. For the last twenty-two years, I have controlled my speech and pen and have stored up my energy. He is a true *brahmachari* who does not fritter away his energy. He will, therefore, always control his speech. That has been my conscious effort all these years. But today the occasion has come when I had to unburden my heart before you. I have done so, even though it meant putting a strain on your patience; and I do not regret having done it. I have given you my message and through you I have delivered it to the whole of India.

Ho Chi Minh (AP/Wide World Photos)

DECLARATION OF INDEPENDENCE OF THE DEMOCRATIC REPUBLIC OF VIETNAM

"Viet-Nam has the right to be a free and independent country — and in fact it is so already."

Overview

On the afternoon of September 2, 1945, speaking to an enthusiastic crowd of about four hundred thousand Vietnamese and an attentive handful of foreign observers in Hanoi's Ba Dinh Square, the president of the provisional government, Ho Chi Minh, proclaimed the independence of the Democratic Republic of Vietnam. The Vietnamese Declaration of Independence came at the high point of the August Revolution, staged in the weeks following the surrender of imperial Japan on August 15, 1945, which ended World War II. Seizing the opportune moment, the Vietminh had taken control of the major cities of Vietnam, replaced the short-lived Japanese-backed Tran Trong Kim government, and pressured Emperor Bao Dai, who had ruled for almost twenty years, to abdicate.

The independence declaration was a defining moment in Vietnamese history. It signaled the long-awaited close of more than eighty years of French colonial domination and also the end point of the Vietnamese monarchy as a political institution. Internationally, however, it failed to have the same importance because the administration of U.S. president Harry Truman had already accepted France's intent to return to colonial power in Southeast Asia. This discrepancy eventually led to the unleashing of destructive forces that would engulf the eastern half of the Indochinese peninsula in three decades of civil and international warfare.

The enduring appeal of the Vietnamese Declaration of Independence, as with the declarations produced by the Dutch in 1581 and the American colonists in 1776, is that this most public challenge to the colonial masters was not defeated but eventually led to victory. Coming in the immediate aftermath of World War II, the declaration also signaled the onset of a major wave of decolonization. In the present-day Socialist Republic of Vietnam, the Communist Party regards the document, despite its many different versions, as a key foundational text and its issuance as a legitimizing event. In the context of world history, Ho Chi Minh's presentation of the declaration continues to fascinate owing to the hybrid nature of the event, text in translation, and speech and the author's means of addressing various audiences.

Context

In mid-1945 the opportune moment that Vietnamese nationalists had been awaiting for so long seemed to finally arrive in the shape of a double power vacuum. First, on March 9, 1945, the Japanese troops garrisoned in French Indochina since 1940 destroyed the French-Indochinese military apparatus and brought down the administration of Jean Decoux, which was aligned with France's Vichy government (and so with Nazi Germany, since the Vichy government was the puppet regime that collaborated with the Nazis). Eighty or so years of French colonial domination were thus effectively ended within a day. Five months later, following the Soviet offensive in Manchuria and the devastation of the U.S. atomic bombs dropped on Hiroshima and Nagasaki, on August 15 the Japanese imperial government surrendered—as such leaving a dangerous void of authority in French Indochina. While the Japanese troops remained in Indochina to be disarmed by the Allies and the French were yet held captive by the Japanese, the Japanese-backed government of the conservative scholar and politician Tran Trong Kim resigned. The international and domestic race for political control of Vietnam had begun in earnest.

After being ousted, the French government proved intent on reoccupying Indochina, though they were willing to grant more autonomy within the framework of the Indochina federation the French had formed in 1893 and that encompassed the regions of Vietnam, Cambodia, and later Laos; officials of the Truman administration repeatedly signaled consent to this goal. In early June, French president Charles de Gaulle instructed General Philippe Leclerc to organize a French Far East Expeditionary Corps, which would arrive in October. Meanwhile, the close of World War II was orchestrated by the Potsdam Agreement of July 24 and Allied General Order No. 1 of September 2 (which established U.S. control of Japan following the Japanese surrender). In Vietnam, Chinese Nationalist troops (from the Republic of China, now known as Taiwan) were to disarm the Japanese north of latitude 16° north, and British forces were to do the same to the south. In late August, some two hundred thousand of General Lu Han's Chinese Nationalist troops were entering Tonkin, while the vanguard of General Douglas Gracey's twenty-six thousand

1893

- Completing a piecemeal process of conquest begun in 1859, the French set up the Indochinese Union, including the states of Tonkin, Annam, and Cochinchina as well as Cambodia and Laos.

1941

- The Indochinese Communist Party sets up the Vietminh and the National Salvation Army, precursor to the Vietnamese Liberation Army.

1945

- **March 9**
  A Japanese coup overthrows the Jean Decoux administration in French Indochina and incapacitates its military forces.

- **August 19–30**
  After the Japanese-backed government dissolves, the Vietminh seize control of major cities in the August Revolution, and Emperor Bao Dai is forced to abdicate.

- **September 2**
  In Hanoi, Ho Chi Minh delivers the Declaration of Independence of the Democratic Republic of Vietnam.

- **November 11**
  The ICP officially self-dissolves, although it continues to exist underground.

British Indian troops arrived in Saigon on September 12, three days after Lu Han's first men marched into Hanoi.

Domestically, Vietnamese political groups of various orientations were harboring hopes of filling the power vacuum. Only the Indochinese Communist Party (ICP), however, was able to fully exploit the limited time frame of about three weeks between the Japanese surrender in mid-August and the arrival of the British and Chinese troops in early September. Drawing on the lessons of more than fifteen years of anticolonial mobilization, it had begun its preparations immediately after the Japanese coup of March 9. Indeed, the ICP was the most well-prepared and decisive of all Vietnamese political forces and the only one capable of operating countrywide. As early as May 1941, on Ho Chi Minh's advice, the party had set up a broad Communist-led front, the Viet Nam Doc Lap Dong Minh (Vietnam Independence League, or Vietminh). It was to be useful as a cover to project the image of a unity government and to integrate non-Communist groups and individuals, whereas its branch committees and mass organizations throughout Vietnam would mobilize the population and garner public support. The ICP had also created the National Salvation Army and the Armed Propaganda Brigade, which merged in May 1945 into the Vietnamese Liberation Army. Although at this stage it was merely a fledgling guerrilla force of not more than several hundred men, it had cultivated contacts with the U.S. Office of Strategic Services (OSS; the forerunner of the Central Intelligence Agency), the British, and to some extent the French. In particular, its friendly and openly visible relations with U.S. representatives were an invaluable asset in convincing the Vietnamese population and rival political organizations that the Vietminh had the blessing of the Truman administration.

As the opportune moment arrived with the impending Japanese surrender, Ho Chi Minh gave the final call for a general insurrection on August 13, 1945. The rapid mobilization of the Vietminh's military, paramilitary, and popular forces allowed it to take control of cities, towns, and villages throughout the country within twelve days. Among major cities, Hanoi was secured on August 19, Hue on August 23, and Saigon on August 25; cities in the south were taken over in coalition with other political forces. At last the Vietminh pressured Emperor Bao Dai to abdicate, which he did on August 30, thus irrevocably sealing the fate of the Vietnamese monarchy. Also in late August and into September, the Vietminh began to abduct thousands of people perceived as obstacles to the revolution or as traitors, many of whom were never to return. Tens of thousands more were neutralized by being placed under arrest.

It was in this rapidly evolving international and domestic context that preparations for the independence declaration were made. In the evening of August 25, Ho Chi Minh was secretly ushered into Hanoi. His presence and identity were kept secret to all but a trusted few, for reasons of safety, security, and surprise. On August 27, in consultation with cabinet members, he decided to command countrywide preparations for Independence Day, to be held on September 2. With the main event to be held in Hanoi, formal observance was to be organized in as many places as possible. Ho then apparently drafted the independence declaration. On August 30, he showed a typewritten draft with many handwritten corrections and numerous marginal notes to Major Archimedes Patti, the senior OSS representative in Hanoi. When it was translated, Patti was surprised to find that the opening passage quoted from the American Declaration of Independence.

With only five days to organize nationwide Independence Day celebrations, preparations were challenging. Hanoi's Ba Dinh Square, then known as the Place Puginier and located next to the palace of the governor-general of French Indochina, was chosen because it could easily accommodate the expected mass audience. A high wooden platform had to be erected and a public address system installed. Security measures were taken, and live audio transmissions to other parts of the country were set up, though they eventually failed because Japanese roadblocks obstructed the transmitter vehicle.

On Sunday, September 2, Vietnamese Liberation Army guards secured the platform by keeping the arriving crowds about twenty yards away, while self-defense units were positioned in strategic places. Many Buddhists and Catholics arrived in groups led by their head monks and priests, respectively, while schoolteachers performed the same function for their pupils. Entire villages from the Hanoi countryside were guided by their elders and Vietminh organizers, and ethnic minorities also descended from the hills. Several American OSS members under Major Patti were present, as was the French representative, Jean Sainteny. Wearing white rubber sandals and a high-collared khaki jacket, similar in style to the ones worn by the Communist leaders Joseph Stalin and Mao Zedong, Ho briskly led his cabinet up the platform. The national anthem was played, followed by a flag-raising ceremony and Ho's introduction by General Vo Nguyen Giap. Waving his hands to the crowds for several minutes, Ho eventually raised his palms to command silence and then read out the declaration.

About the Author

The Declaration of Independence of the Democratic Republic of Vietnam was authored by Ho Chi Minh, who played a crucial role in the founding of the Vietnamese Communist movement. Ho was born as Nguyen Sinh Cung in the province of Nghe An, now in central Vietnam, in 1890. His father, a relatively poor scholar-official, inculcated in him patriotic and anti-French views. In 1911 he sailed to France but failed to be admitted to the École Coloniale in Paris, thereafter earning his living aboard ships. After a short time in London, at the end of World War I he arrived in Paris and circulated in the Vietnamese expatriate community and in French Socialist circles. He adopted a new name, Nguyen Ai Quoc (Nguyen the Patriot), and became a founding member of the French Communist Party in 1921. During this period he worked as a writer, journalist, and newspaper publisher.

Time Line

1946

■ **October 30**
Following breakthroughs in Jean Sainteny's negotiations with Ho Chi Minh, a Franco-Vietnamese modus vivendi comes into force.

■ **December 19**
The First Indochina War breaks out when the Vietminh attack the French in Hanoi.

1954

■ **July 21**
The Geneva Accords temporarily divide Vietnam along the seventeenth parallel, with the Communist-led Democratic Republic of Vietnam to the north and the State of Vietnam to the south.

1959

■ **September 26**
The Second Indochina War, also known as the Vietnam War, breaks out.

1975

■ **April 30**
The Republic of Vietnam, known as South Vietnam, is defeated.

1976

■ **July 2**
Postwar unification is formally completed with the creation of the Socialist Republic of Vietnam.

Trained as a Comintern (Communist International) agent in Moscow in 1923, Ho was assigned positions in southern China and Southeast Asia beginning in 1925. He created the proto-Communist Youth League (Thanh Nien) in Guangzhou (Canton), China, in 1925, while on assignment for the Comintern. In February 1930, in Hong Kong, he helped prevent a permanent fissure within the movement by reconciling two rival factions, along with another party, into the Vietnamese Communist Party. That party was soon reconfigured against Ho's wishes as the ICP, which shows that he was not uncontested in his leadership. After he was arrested because of his Communist militancy in Hong Kong in 1931, he was released by the British authorities in 1933 and returned to the Soviet Union. He went to China in 1938 and reestablished contact with the ICP, founding the Vietminh in 1941. At about the same time, he adopted the name Ho Chi Minh (He Who Enlightens). He served as the Democratic Republic of Vietnam's first president until his death on September 2, 1969. Although he had wished to have his ashes distributed in four urns in the four corners of Vietnam, his body lies embalmed and on public display in the Ho Chi Minh Mausoleum, which is symbolically located at the head of Ba Dinh Square.

Explanation and Analysis of the Document

Although it is a relatively short document of less than 950 words and composed in clear language that avoids using difficult political jargon or legal terms, the Vietnamese Declaration of Independence nevertheless poses several explanatory and analytical challenges. It is hard to separate the text from the event—Ho Chi Minh even recorded an audio version about ten years later in a studio. Moreover, as it was made at a quickly shifting juncture of Vietnamese as well as world history and addressed to two distinct audiences, there are different Vietnamese versions and even more slightly different translations into English.

The primary aim of the declaration is clear, namely, to announce to the Vietnamese and to the world the birth of an independent Vietnamese state and its new government. The Vietnamese audience was told that the new state would be the Democratic Republic of Vietnam, whereas early translations into English—such as the one derived from the Hanoi-based French-language newspaper *La république* of October 1, 1945—coyly dropped the "Democratic," suggesting that the provisional government thought that a simple "republic" would receive a more favorable international response. It is arguably for this reason, too, that Ho Chi Minh highlighted that his government was a "provisional" one, knowing that he might have to negotiate the nature of the government in the months to come. Indeed, the Japanese forces were yet to be disarmed, while the Chinese, British, and French forces that would soon make their presence felt on Vietnamese soil would all favor Vietnamese political groups other than the ICP.

The secondary aim of the independence declaration was to gain domestic and international acceptance for the new Democratic Republic of Vietnam and its provisional government. It was also the right time to present the Vietminh as the nation's major political force and to announce a radical rupture with the past. The period of time when Vietnam was ruled by foreigners—the French having encroached on Vietnamese sovereignty from 1859, to be briefly replaced by the Japanese in early 1945—was finally over. The abdication of Emperor Bao Dai represented a radical break with Vietnam's indigenous past, as it constituted the end to a centuries-old political institution and the associated feudal order. While the Vietminh had achieved the twin goals of ending imperialism and feudalism, the declaration also makes clear that these achievements would have to be defended.

While the aims of the Vietnamese Declaration of Independence were clear, its proclamation was also an opportunity to win over the hearts and minds of the Vietnamese and international audiences by explaining why the new state and government were legitimate and deserved to be supported and recognized. In part drawing on the argument and structure of the American Declaration of Independence, Ho Chi Minh nevertheless gave the Vietnamese declaration an original touch.

Ho's words of address, "the compatriots of the entire country," are inclusive and set the tone for the speech, allowing him to connect to his audience as equals rather than keeping as much distance as possible between government and governed, as had been the preference of the Vietnamese imperial tradition. The term *compatriots* also allowed the speaker to give his address broader historical and mythical meaning. Moreover, the inclusive phrase, literally meaning "from the same sack of eggs," allowed Ho to make much larger mythical claims. The phrase refers to offspring of the country's mythical progenitors, the water-based dragon Lac Long Quan and the mountain-based fairy goddess Au Co, whose eggs gave rise to the first Vietnamese people and the first of the nation's kings.

Having united his entire audience in Hanoi by reference to their common origins, Ho tried to find common ground for his global audience in referring to the international lineage of Vietnam's August Revolution. He adroitly omits reference to the Russian October Revolution of 1917 (the second phase of the Russian Revolution of that year, which brought the Communists to power); doing so would not have won him friends in the capitalist West, among General Lu Han's Chinese Nationalist forces, or among Vietnamese conservative nationalists. Ho suggests that the August Revolution was a continuation of the American and French revolutions and their ideologies. In a later section, the declaration also refers to the 1943 Tehran Conference (among U.S. president Franklin Roosevelt, British prime minister Winston Churchill, and Soviet premier Joseph Stalin, which, among other matters, pledged to recognize Iran's independence) and the 1945 United Nations Conference on International Organization, held in San Francisco, invoking the norms of the newly emergent U.S.-led inter-

An Algerian unit of French colonial forces move through a swamp in the countryside of Indochina during the First Indochinese War. (AP/Wide World Photos)

national society of states, particularly the "equality of nations." In this context, it is unclear to what extent Ho actually subscribed to the notions of inborn and "inalienable" rights of individuals promulgated in the 1776 American Declaration of Independence and the 1789 French Declaration of the Rights of Man and of the Citizen, or whether he rather believed in the inalienable collective right of peoples to form independent nations.

Regardless of Ho's beliefs in individual or collective rights or both, the Vietnamese experience of French rule clearly contradicted the ideals of the French Republic. As the Americans had summarized their grievances in 1776, Ho recalls the suffering of the Vietnamese, though in language far more modern and evocative—almost headline style—and everyone in his audience could have related to at least some of his points. Politically, French rule had been oppressive, inhumane, and divisive and had weakened the Vietnamese race. Economically, French domination had led to the exploitation of Vietnam's natural resources and its people. Ho does not refrain from reminding the French of their painful failure to live up to their colonial and protectorate obligations to defend the Vietnamese against Japanese occupation.

Given all these shortcomings, which blatantly contradicted the very ideals of the American and French revolutions, it followed that the French did not have any legitimate right to rule over Vietnam. If, in fact, they ever had, they had lost it, and so had the Japanese through their surrender. Instead, a combination of popular and morally superior actions had earned the Vietnamese the right to independence and the Vietminh the legitimacy to govern the country. With Emperor Bao Dai's abdication, there would be no return to the traditional monarchical and feudal order; the Vietnamese were finally free of foreign and domestic oppression.

The last few paragraphs, like the American Declaration of Independence, announce the rupture with the French colonial past and appeal to the Allied powers to recognize Vietnamese independence. All French treaties and privileges are considered annulled. While Ho threatened to fight any French attempt to return to power, the provisional government also indirectly suggested that it was willing to entertain relations with a nonimperialist France on equal terms. As the Allies had already recognized the equality of peoples at the 1943 Tehran and 1945 San Francisco conferences, Ho expresses his conviction that they should recognize Vietnam's independence as the Vietnamese people's right; even if they would not, the clock could not be turned back because Vietnam was already "free and independent." In view of the decades of warfare to come, Ho's final words were almost prophetic: "To safeguard their independence and liberty," the Vietnamese were "determined to mobilize all their physical and mental strength" and "to sacrifice their lives and property." These words were also a final bow to the Americans, whose support his triumphant and yet fledgling government greatly needed in the face of external threats and domestic political rivals who had different visions of Vietnam's future.

The Vietnamese Declaration of Independence originally closed with the signatures of Ho and his fourteen provisional government members. Most of them belonged to the ICP, which formally self-dissolved on November 11, 1945; this might be why later versions usually do not feature the signatures. It is equally plausible that the divergent political fortunes of some—Vo Nguyen Giap, for example, was repeatedly sidelined by party rivals—made it opportune to omit all signatures.

Audience

The newly founded Democratic Republic of Vietnam needed full patriotic support from all Vietnamese—regardless of political inclination, ethnicity, or social station—in order to maintain independence. It also nonetheless required the recognition of the international society of states, most notably the United States and France.

Ho Chi Min's Vietnamese audience responded enthusiastically to the proclamation, as they wanted to be independent and in charge of their own national destiny. His inclusive message, which did not outline any Communist policies, appealed to all. In Hanoi and many other places, families welcomed Independence Day by lighting incense on the family altars and informing their ancestors of independence. Led by well-placed party members, the crowd of four hundred thousand, regardless of age, gender, class, ethnicity, or religion, cheered Ho and repeatedly chanted "Independence" as he waved to them, even though few really knew who he was. A few sentences into his proclamation, Ho achieved an intimate and lasting bond with the crowd when they responded as one to his question—not part of the text—"Do you hear me distinctly, fellow countrymen?"

In contrast to the proclamation's reception by the immediate Vietnamese audience—beyond Hanoi, the population was able to read the speech in the newspaper and on posters or hear it read aloud on the radio the next day—the international response was far more muted. Ho had tried to court the Americans and sway the French with the speech, and he knew that American and French representatives were attending and closely observing. Yet Major Patti, the senior OSS representative in Hanoi, had declined Ho's invitation to stand on the platform alongside the provisional government, instead positioning himself in front of the platform among local dignitaries—though this did not

prevent him from saluting the Vietnamese flag. Patti reported that Ho reached the audience owing to his "powerful emotional delivery" (p. 251). He had the Vietnamese text version translated and sent to OSS headquarters in Kunming, China, which duly delivered it to the OSS director in Washington. The reports were passed on as mementos to the secretary of state but appear to have been ignored in light of more urgent matters needing attention. Perhaps determining the level of American interest in the event was the fact that by this time the U.S. State Department had already signaled to Charles de Gaulle that it would accept France's return to Indochina.

Jean Sainteny, France's commissioner for the protectorates of Annam and Tonkin, also had the speeches translated. Although he must have swallowed hard regarding Ho's account of French colonialism, Sainteny recognized a willingness to negotiate—but he failed to get instructions from Paris to open formal discussions. As with the Truman administration, it seems that Paris simply ignored Vietnamese independence, probably because preparations were well under way to regain a position of strength in Indochina, though perhaps on different terms than previously.

Impact

While the independence declaration does not directly touch on inopportune issues such as Russia's October Revolution or the policies that the provisional government stood for, the remainder of the Independence Day ceremony made Ho Chi Minh's intentions for Vietnam clear. He was handed Bao Dai's golden seal and sword, and after an oath sworn by his cabinet members and several more speeches, he declared that the sword would be used to sever the heads of traitors. When two American planes suddenly flew over the crowd, it was announced that they demonstrated U.S. support for the democratic republic. The ceremony concluded with the recitation of an oath in support of the provisional government and its president. The audience was also sworn to defending the nation at all cost.

The most obvious significance of the Declaration of Independence of the Democratic Republic of Vietnam was that it symbolized Vietnamese aspirations toward independence. It also boosted the legitimacy of the provisional government and the Vietminh; no other political organization would have been able to profit from the vacuum of authority to seize power on a nationwide level. Historically, the declaration precipitated a series of events that led to the First Indochina War (1946–1954), the Second Indochina War (1959–1975), and arguably even the Third Indochina War (1979). As the first successful Communist-led pro-independence movement in the third world, it also represented a major turning point in the history of early post–World War II anticolonialism.

In terms of its immediate impact on Vietnamese politics and society, the proclamation demonstrated, at least temporarily, the political leadership of the Vietminh and, behind it, of the ICP. Still, while other political contenders,

"All men are created equal; they are endowed by their Creator with certain inalienable Rights; among these are Life, Liberty, and the pursuit of Happiness. This immortal statement was made in the Declaration of Independence of the United States of America in 1776. In a broader sense, this means: All the peoples on the earth are equal from birth, all the peoples have a right to live, to be happy and free."

(Paragraphs 1–2)

"The Declaration of the Rights of Man and Citizen of the French Revolution made in 1791 also states: All men are born free and with equal rights, and must always remain free and have equal rights."

(Paragraph 3)

"Those are undeniable truths. Nevertheless, for more than eighty years, the French imperialists, abusing the standard of Liberty, Equality, and Fraternity, have violated our Fatherland and oppressed our fellow citizens. They have acted contrary to the ideals of humanity and justice."

(Paragraphs 4–5)

"A people who have courageously opposed French domination for more than eighty years, a people who have fought side by side with the Allies against the fascists during these last years, such a people must be free and independent!"

(Paragraph 26)

"Viet-Nam has the right to be a free and independent country—and in fact it is so already. The entire Vietnamese people are determined to mobilize all their physical and mental strength, to sacrifice their lives and property in order to safeguard their independence and liberty."

(Paragraph 28)

most at the regional level, had lost out in the short term, Vietminh hegemony was far from dominant, despite the assassinations and arrests of those considered political rivals or even traitors, and in November 1945 the ICP officially self-dissolved, although it continued to exist under-ground. In the north, where the Vietminh were strongest, Ho Chi Minh had to be mindful of and accommodate his Chinese-backed competitors in the Vietnamese Revolutionary League, at least as long as the two hundred thousand Chinese Nationalist troops were present. In contrast, the Vietminh's hold on power in the south was far more tenuous, as Saigon could be taken in alliance only with other parties, while the existence of influential religious sects such as the Hoa Hao and Cao Dai further complicated the political landscape.

These regional differences would be further accentuated by Ho's unsuccessful courting of the United States and his fruitless appeal to the French to live up to French republican ideals. The Potsdam Agreement had tasked neither of these nation's forces but rather British troops to the south of the sixteenth parallel and Chinese Nationalist troops to the north to accept Japan's surrender and disarm its troops. Ho would find a modus vivendi (an expression used in diplomacy to refer to a temporary accommodation) with General Lu Han in the north and profit from the fact that French troops who had retreated into southern China as a result of the Japanese coup were held up by Chinese authorities until early 1946; but General Gracey's troops in the south acted sternly against the Vietminh, liberated the French prisoners of war, and prepared for the arrival of the French Far East Expeditionary Corps under General Leclerc in October.

Despite various attempts by France and Vietnam to attain peaceful resolution over the next fifteen months—including the Ho-Sainteny Agreement of March 1946, the Da Lat conferences, the Fontainebleau negotiations, and the eventual coming into force of a Franco-Vietnamese modus vivendi on October 30, 1946—Franco-Vietnamese relations soon turned sour. After a relatively minor dispute over customs in Haiphong harbor on November 20 appeared to be settled two days later, the French fleet bombarded the city's indigenous quarters on November 23, killing up to six thousand people. Less than a month later, the outbreak of the First Indochina War came on December 19 with a Vietminh counterattack in Hanoi. Nearly ten conflict-ridden years later, the French defeat and the Geneva Accords of 1954 led to the temporary partition of Vietnam along the seventeenth parallel, with the Communist Democratic Republic of Vietnam in the north and the State of Vietnam in the south. The accords provided only limited reprieve from warfare, as the elections scheduled for 1956 did not materialize owing to southern fears of a Communist electoral victory; these fears spurred the preemptive formation of the Republic of Vietnam in the south in 1955, thus sowing the seeds for the Second Indochina War, also called the Vietnam War. This war ended with the fall of Saigon and the southern regime's surrender on April 30, 1975. On July 2, 1976—two days before the two hundredth anniversary of the American Declaration of Independence—the Socialist Republic of Vietnam was inaugurated. Meanwhile, by this time a Cambodian-Vietnamese conflict was already under way, which would lead to the Vietnamese invasion of Cambodia of late 1978, triggering the brief Third Indochina War, or Sino-Vietnamese War, of 1979.

Questions for Further Study

1. The text makes reference to the Dutch Declaration of Independence of 1581. Consult that entry and prepare a list of the similarities between the Dutch Declaration and the Declaration of Independence of the Democratic Republic of Vietnam.

2. Vietnamese independence was part of a broader movement toward decolonization that was taking place in the 1940s and beyond. In particular, France was losing its colonies, both in Vietnam and Algeria. Compare this document with the Proclamation of the Algerian National Liberation Front of 1954. What similar—or differing—impulses motivated the Vietnamese and the Algerians?

3. Vietnam eventually became a Communist nation. To what extent did Vietnam realize the aspirations expressed in documents by other prominent Communists, such as Cuba's Fidel Castro (*History Will Absolve Me*), China's Mao Zedong ("Report on an Investigation of the Peasant Movement in Hunan"), or Russia's Vladimir Lenin (*What Is to Be Done?*)?

4. From the early to mid-1960s to the mid-1970s, the United States was embroiled in a highly divisive war in Vietnam. Would the history of those years have been any different if the Truman administration had acted differently in the years following the Vietnamese Declaration of Independence? Explain.

5. The Japanese played an important role in the history of Asia in the 1940s. How did its role in Vietnam resemble its earlier role in Korea, leading to the Korean Declaration of Independence in 1919?

If not for the ensuing several decades of civil war and international conflict and if not for the eventual success of the Vietnamese Communists in their bid for independence, the Declaration of Independence of the Democratic Republic of Vietnam would have been a curious footnote in world history. Today, the declaration remains one of the most interesting independence proclamations of all time, issued at a crucial juncture when the European-dominated society of nations was being recrafted by a new hegemonic power, the United States. It was one of the first declarations of independence to come from the third world or from Asia. The intriguing content, with a staunch Communist quoting the 1776 U.S. Declaration of Independence and the 1789 French Declaration of the Rights of Man and of the Citizen, makes for an excellent study in decolonization, the Vietnam War, and world history.

The declaration remains a key document for a state ruled by a Communist Party that seeks to maintain its political domination through reference to foundational documents and events that give it continued legitimacy in times of rapid economic and social change. With the number of adults who can remember the heady days of the August Revolution and the birth of the Vietnamese Declaration of Independence fast diminishing, modern-day Vietnamese schoolchildren are required to read and memorize the document. It remains to be seen whether a Vietnamese reinterpretation of the declaration, such as with particular attention focused on individual rather than collective liberty and rights, might eventually be used to change the Communist Party of Vietnam from within or to challenge the existing regime.

Further Reading

▪ Articles

Bradley, Mark Philip. "Making Revolutionary Nationalism: Vietnam, America and the August Revolution of 1945." *Itinerario* 23, no. 1 (1999): 23–51.

Huynh Kim Khanh. "The Vietnamese August Revolution Reinterpreted." *Journal of Asian Studies* 30, no. 4 (August 1971): 761–782.

▪ Books

Bradley, Mark Philip. *Imagining Vietnam and America: The Making of Postcolonial Vietnam, 1919–1950*. Chapel Hill: University of North Carolina Press, 2000.

Charlton, Michael, and Anthony Moncrieff. *Many Reasons Why: The American Involvement in Vietnam*. New York: Hill and Wang, 1989.

Dommen, Arthur J. *The Indochinese Experience of the French and the Americans: Nationalism and Communism in Cambodia, Laos, and Vietnam*. Bloomington: Indiana University Press, 2001.

Duiker, William J. *Ho Chi Minh: A Life*. New York: Hyperion, 2000.

Ho Chi Minh. *Selected Writings, 1920–1969*. Hanoi, Vietnam: Foreign Languages Publishing House, 1977.

Huynh Kim Khanh. *Vietnamese Communism, 1925–1945*. Ithaca, N.Y.: Cornell University Press, 1982.

Isaacs, Harold R., ed. *New Cycle in Asia: Selected Documents on Major International Developments in the Far East, 1943–1947*. New York: Macmillan, 1947.

Marr, David G. "Ho Chi Minh's Independence Declaration." In *Essays into Vietnamese Pasts*, ed. Keith W. Taylor and John K. Whitmore. Ithaca, N.Y.: Cornell University Southeast Asia Program Publications, 1995.

———. *Vietnam 1945: The Quest for Power*. Berkeley: University of California Press, 1995.

Patti, Archimedes L. A. *Why Viet Nam? Prelude to America's Albatross*. Berkeley: University of California Press, 1980.

Porter, Gareth, ed. *Vietnam: The Definitive Documentation of Human Decisions*, Vol. 1. Stanfordville, N.Y.: Earl M. Coleman Enterprises, 1979.

———. *Vietnam: A History in Documents*. New York: Meridian, 1981.

Tønnesson, Stein. *The Vietnamese Revolution of 1945: Roosevelt, Ho Chi Minh and de Gaulle in a World at War*. London: Sage, 1991.

—Tobias Rettig

DECLARATION OF INDEPENDENCE OF THE DEMOCRATIC REPUBLIC OF VIETNAM

The compatriots of the entire country,

All men are created equal; they are endowed by their Creator with certain inalienable Rights; among these are Life, Liberty, and the pursuit of Happiness.

This immortal statement was made in the Declaration of Independence of the United States of America in 1776. In a broader sense, this means: All the peoples on the earth are equal from birth, all the peoples have a right to live, to be happy and free.

The Declaration of the Rights of Man and Citizen of the French Revolution made in 1791 also states: *All men are born free and with equal rights, and must always remain free and have equal rights.*

Those are undeniable truths.

Nevertheless, for more than eighty years, the French imperialists, abusing the standard of Liberty, Equality, and Fraternity, have violated our Fatherland and oppressed our fellow citizens. They have acted contrary to the ideals of humanity and justice.

In the field of politics, they have deprived our people of every democratic liberty.

They have enforced inhuman laws; they have set up three distinct political regimes in the North, the Center, and the South of Viet-Nam in order to wreck our national unity and prevent our people from being united.

They have built more prisons than schools. They have mercilessly slain our patriots; they have drowned our uprisings in rivers of blood.

They have fettered public opinion; they have practiced obscurantism against our people.

To weaken our race they have forced us to use opium and alcohol.

In the field of economics, they have fleeced us to the backbone, impoverished our people and devastated our land.

They have robbed us of our rice fields, our mines, our forests, and our raw materials. They have monopolized the issuing of bank notes and the export trade.

They have invented numerous unjustifiable taxes and reduced our people, especially our peasantry, to a state of extreme poverty.

They have hampered the prospering of our national bourgeoisie; they have mercilessly exploited our workers.

In the autumn of 1940, when the Japanese fascists violated Indochina's territory to establish new bases in their fight against the Allies, the French imperialists went down on their bended knees and handed over our country to them.

Thus, from that date, our people were subjected to the double yoke of the French and the Japanese. Their sufferings and miseries increased. The result was that, from the end of last year to the beginning of this year, from Quang Tri Province to the North of Viet-Nam, more than two million of our fellow citizens died from starvation. On March 9 [1945], the French troops were disarmed by the Japanese. The French colonialists either fled or surrendered, showing that not only were they incapable of "protecting" us, but that, in the span of five years, they had twice sold our country to the Japanese.

On several occasions before March 9, the Viet Minh League urged the French to ally themselves with it against the Japanese. Instead of agreeing to this proposal, the French colonialists so intensified their terrorist activities against the Viet Minh members that before fleeing they massacred a great number of our political prisoners detained at Yen Bai and Cao Bang.

Notwithstanding all this, our fellow citizens have always manifested toward the French a tolerant and humane attitude. Even after the Japanese Putsch of March, 1945, the Viet Minh League helped many Frenchmen to cross the frontier, rescued some of them from Japanese jails, and protected French lives and property.

From the autumn of 1940, our country had in fact ceased to be a French colony and had become a Japanese possession.

After the Japanese had surrendered to the Allies, our whole people rose to regain our national sovereignty and to found the Democratic Republic of Viet-Nam.

The truth is that we have wrested our independence from the Japanese and not from the French.

The French have fled, the Japanese have capitulated, Emperor Bao Dai has abdicated. Our people have broken the chains which for nearly a century have fettered them and have won independence for the Fatherland. Our people at the same time have overthrown the monarchic regime that has reigned supreme for dozens of centuries. In its place has been established the present Democratic Republic.

For these reasons, we, members of the Provisional Government, representing the whole Vietnamese people, declare that from now on we break off all relations of a colonial character with France; we repeal all the international obligation that France has so far subscribed to on behalf of Viet-Nam, and we abolish all the special rights the French have unlawfully acquired in our Fatherland.

The whole Vietnamese people, animated by a common purpose, are determined to fight to the bitter end against any attempt by the French colonialists to reconquer the country.

We are convinced that the Allied nations, which at Tehran and San Francisco have acknowledged the principles of self-determination and equality of nations, will not refuse to acknowledge the independence of Viet-Nam.

A people who have courageously opposed French domination for more than eighty years, a people who have fought side by side with the Allies against the fascists during these last years, such a people must be free and independent!

For these reasons, we, members of the Provisional Government of the Democratic Republic of Viet-Nam, solemnly declare to the world that:

Viet-Nam has the right to be a free and independent country—and in fact it is so already. The entire Vietnamese people are determined to mobilize all their physical and mental strength, to sacrifice their lives and property in order to safeguard their independence and liberty.

Winston Churchill (Library of Congress)

WINSTON CHURCHILL'S "THE SINEWS OF PEACE"

1946

"An iron curtain has descended across the Continent."

Overview

 On March 5, 1946, following World War II, former British prime minister Winston Churchill made one of his greatest speeches at Westminster College in Fulton, Missouri, entitled "The Sinews of Peace," more commonly known as the "Iron Curtain" Speech. As soldiers returned home from Europe and the Pacific in 1945 and 1946, often to devastation in their own home countries, there seemed to be even more hope than in 1919, after World War I, that a lasting world peace was at hand. Coexistence between the capitalist democracies and the Communist dictatorship in the Soviet Union had been demonstrated during the war. This state of affairs did not last. Communist parties and politicians were elected or appointed to positions of power in Eastern European countries, none of whom ever proved willing to pursue democratic electoral processes again. Other Communist parties in East Asia seemed poised to attain power as well; in China, Communists would, in fact, rise to power in 1949. Instead of a new world peace, by 1950 the postwar world was divided into political camps, each threatening the others with atomic bombs. The "hot war" with the Nazis had evolved into a "cold war" between the wartime allies: the British Empire and the United States on the one hand and the Soviet Union and the People's Republic of China on the other.

Most of Churchill's speech outlined his own hopes for the future of the United Nations and the "special relationship" he defined as existing between Britain and the United States. But the speech became famous for its proclamation that an "iron curtain" had settled between Western capitalist democracies and Eastern European Communist dictatorships. Although many people questioned Churchill's judgment in 1946, he proved to be right in the end, even as many more ignored the rest of his message of international cooperation.

Context

As a seasoned politician in the Liberal Party and the British coalition government in 1917 and 1918, Winston

Churchill had definite opinions on the rise of Communism in Russia—he wanted it ended. The distinguishing characteristic of Bolshevik Communism as a utopian vision, in his opinion, was its reliance on violence in order to achieve its ends, and this violence had to be curtailed. As Allied troops were sent to the northern Russian ports of Archangel and Murmansk to support the forces in opposition to the Bolshevik Red Army, Churchill insisted that they have a clear purpose: to destroy the Bolsheviks before their ideology and power could spread. Yet Europeans and Americans seemed opposed to the idea, and politicians in the British coalition government dismissed Churchill's concerns. Partly this was because of earlier failures in military strategy perpetuated by Churchill during World War I, which had lessened his reputation for levelheaded decision making; partly it was the result of Churchill's bombastic denunciations of the Bolshevik regime, which seemed hysterical. Arthur Balfour, the British coalition government's foreign secretary, once remarked to Churchill sarcastically, "I admire the exaggerated way you tell the truth" (MacMillan, p. 67).

Eventually, Allied troops were withdrawn, and the Red Army overran the Russian Empire's former territories to form the Union of Soviet Socialist Republics (USSR) in 1922. Because of war, famine, disease, and political executions, some ten million people had died in the five years since the Bolshevik revolution began. The late 1920s and 1930s brought the First Five-Year Plan, which saw the "liquidation"—murder—of millions of successful peasants, particularly in the Ukraine. When Churchill asked the Soviet premier Joseph Stalin for his own approximation of how many had died, Stalin estimated another ten million. Finally, in the late 1930s, Stalin launched purges of the Communist Party and the army, which likely led to the death of yet another one and a half million.

In other words, Churchill had been right about the Bolsheviks, yet by the 1930s virtually no one in British politics much cared. His rhetoric in speeches had made the Soviets appear to be a deadly menace, but he had applied the same language of vituperation to the rise of the Labour Party in Britain and to other political events, especially the Indian independence movement led by Mohandas Gandhi. Basically, Churchill had little sense of political or rhetorical moderation; everything he opposed took on the aura of

1922

- **December 28**
  The Union of Soviet Socialist Republics is created.

1928

- **October**
  Joseph Stalin announces the Soviet Union's First Five-Year Plan; the collectivization of farms leads to the murder or starvation of millions of peasants for perceived resistance.

1934

- **December**
  Stalin begins a four-year "purge" of Soviet bureaucracy to remove any perceived threats to his own leadership.

1939

- **March 15**
  The German army invades Czechoslovakia.

- **August 23**
  The Soviet Union signs a nonaggression pact with Germany.

- **September 1**
  Germany invades Poland, beginning World War II.

1940

- **May 10**
  Winston Churchill becomes prime minister of Britain.

1941

- **June 22**
  The German Army invades the Soviet Union; Britain and Churchill offer an alliance to the Soviet Union.

---

imminent danger and evil in his speeches. His long-standing reputation for impulsiveness and poor judgment was only fortified by the literate and forceful orations he made in defense of his opinions.

Thus, when another menace to parliamentary democracy and freedom arose in the form of Nazism in Germany, most British politicians ignored Churchill's warnings against the British government's policies of military disarmament and appeasement of the German chancellor Adolf Hitler as an aggressor. Churchill outlined his rigid political opposition to Nazi expansion in a magnificent speech at the time of the Munich agreement in October 1938, which permitted Germany to annex Czechoslovakia's Sudetenland; as usual, his words were met mostly with hostility. Then Hitler's armies invaded the whole of Czechoslovakia, and opinion began to turn in Churchill's direction. By September 1939, Britain was at war with Germany for the second time in twenty-five years, and suddenly Churchill seemed like a prophet as opposed to a pariah.

Churchill became prime minister in May 1940; the man had finally met his hour. As the American journalist Edward R. Murrow put it, Churchill "mobilized the English language, and sent it into battle" (Churchill, 1989, p. 11); for once, no matter how strident his claims about the nation's enemies, they were all true. As director of the British government and the war effort, Churchill proved more pragmatic than he had been in past political situations. Most critically, when Nazi armies invaded the Soviet Union in June 1941, Churchill offered an immediate alliance to Stalin's government.

As the war continued and Churchill met with Stalin, he found that they had much in common. Being a nineteenth-century imperialist himself, he understood Stalin's desire to reacquire old territories in Eastern Europe and to secure for himself a buffer against further German aggression in the future. In Moscow in October 1944, he sat down with Stalin at a dinner table and, on a cocktail napkin, drew up a list of names of European countries with percentages listed next to them that were linked to the names "Britain" and "Russia." In essence, he divided Eastern Europe into spheres of influence so successfully that Stalin took out a blue pencil and placed a large check mark on it to signify his approval. Thus was the rough draft of the fate of Eastern Europe determined as a Communist bloc.

At the end of the war, the United States, Britain, and the Soviet Union created a formal division of Europe along geographic lines, based mostly on where their armies had met on the battlefield. The Soviets controlled Eastern Europe, as Churchill had projected; the United States and Britain controlled Western Europe. Germany was divided into four zones (including a French-occupied zone), and the capital, Berlin, sitting in the Soviet zone, was split four ways as well. According to agreements made at the wartime Tehran, Yalta, and Potsdam conferences, free elections were to be held in every European country, and Germany would be reunited under a single government. In 1946 this still seemed like a reasonable expectation as Europe rebuilt itself and was confronted with the details

---

of the Holocaust, confirming all of Churchill's rhetoric about the Nazis.

Churchill himself was turned out of office in July 1945 by the British electorate, to the shock of the rest of the world. Perhaps he had been a great wartime leader, but in the effort to rebuild Britain from the ashes of the war, most British voters saw him as entirely unsuitable; his election loss was the second-largest parliamentary turnaround of the twentieth century. His long-term career as a politician had not been forgotten by the British people—but neither had his wartime heroism, and that had gained him an even larger and deserved status as the visionary who had foreseen victory over evil. To that end, he was invited to deliver the seventh John Findley Green lecture at Westminster College in Fulton, Missouri, in 1946. In it, he would surprise his audience by returning briefly to discussion of an old menace, Communism, which many Americans did not truly consider a threat in 1946. They would find soon after that Churchill's rhetoric had once again described an enemy whose dangers could not be exaggerated.

About the Author

Winston Churchill was born in 1874, the son of a prominent British Conservative Party politician and an American heiress and socialite. After making a poor showing in school as a youngster, he was not accepted to university—as most young men of his social status would have been—and he ended up in the British army, where he proved to be a brave soldier on campaigns in Africa. In a later job as a journalist, he was captured by the enemy during the South African War (also known as the Boer War) and made a daring escape from a prisoner of war camp that made him famous in Britain overnight. He rode his fame to election in the House of Commons in 1900, where he embarked on the career that would make him a somewhat unlikely world hero during World War II.

By March 1946, Churchill was seventy-one years old. He had attained status as a war leader and hero against the Nazis that had made him a "statesman of the world," a phrase repeatedly applied to his postwar career. In some respects, this was ironic, as Churchill was manifestly a man with a nineteenth-century temperament—he was an imperialist, a chauvinist, and a blind patriot. Yet in his speech "The Sinews of Peace" he richly earned his newfound status as an icon of internationalism, showing that he had perhaps learned the lessons of two world wars better than any other Western politician of the twentieth century. In September 1946, just six months later, he made another of his greatest speeches in Zurich, Switzerland, in favor of the possibility of establishing a future "United States of Europe"; he thus helped lend vision and credibility to the project of creating what is today the European Union. In 1951 he would return to the British prime minister's position and preside in a largely ceremonial position over Britain's return to postwar economic prosperity while other

Time Line

1943

- **November 28**
  The Tehran Conference of Stalin, Churchill, and Franklin Roosevelt begins and lasts until December 1; there Churchill negotiates with Stalin to move Polish borders westward.

1944

- **October 9**
  Churchill and Stalin start a series of meetings in Moscow, the site of the famous "napkin agreement."

1945

- **February 4**
  The Yalta Conference, at which Eastern European hegemony is ceded to the Soviet Union, begins, continuing until February 11.

- **May 8**
  World War II ends in Europe with the surrender of Germany.

- **July 17**
  The Potsdam Conference begins, with the goal of establishing a postwar order; it lasts until August 2.

- **July 26**
  Churchill resigns as prime minister after his party's defeat in a general election.

1946

- **February 9**
  Stalin makes a speech on the eve of elections to the Supreme Soviet, claiming that Communism and capitalism are incompatible.

1946

- **March 5**
  Winston Churchill delivers "The Sinews of Peace," an address containing the phrase *iron curtain* in reference to Soviet hegemony in Eastern Europe.

1948

- **February**
  In a coup d'état, the Czechoslovakian government falls to the Communists.

- **June 24**
  The Soviet blockade of West Berlin and the Berlin airlift begin; the blockade continues until May 24, 1949.

1949

- **May 23**
  The Federal Republic of Germany—capitalist West Germany—is created.

- **October**
  The Chinese Communist Party wins a civil war with Nationalists and the People's Republic of China is established.

- **October 7**
  The German Democratic Republic, Communist East Germany, is created.

ministers ran the country. Churchill himself was most interested in negotiating the terms of the cold war that he himself had helped define at Westminster College in 1946. He retired in 1955 and died on January 24, 1965.

Explanation and Analysis of the Document

The John Findley Green Foundation lecture series at Westminster College was meant to showcase speakers talk-ing about current political and economic events. Churchill was its seventh and most prominent speaker since the series began in 1937. President Harry Truman had persuaded him to come to the United States in lieu of a vacation trip to North Africa with the promise that if Churchill spoke at Westminster in Truman's home state of Missouri, Truman himself would introduce him. The introduction of a private citizen by a president of the United States was a clear sign of Truman's esteem for Churchill, as he made clear at the podium. Postwar enmities between the United States and the Soviet Union had not set in yet in March 1946.

◆ Paragraphs 1–13

Churchill opens with a joke, saying that the name "Westminster"—the area of London that is the seat of gov-ernment—seems familiar to him, and he thanks the presi-dent for the honor of his introduction. Then he asserts that he will discuss the problems of the postwar world and ways to preserve the peace. The United States, in his opinion, is in a position to remake the entire world in its own image, with the help of Britain, maintaining a continued union of the "English-speaking peoples." In opposition to their designs are the two old adversaries Churchill mentions in paragraph 7, "war and tyranny," which threaten the ability of the average person to achieve happiness, freedom from want, and progress.

The United Nations was the means to keep the peace and spread prosperity, and Churchill is determined that it have the opportunity to become—unlike the prewar League of Nations—"a force for action, and not merely a frothing of words," as he says in paragraph 10. To him that meant that the United Nations needed the capability to use force in the defense of international justice. He states his belief, in paragraph 12, that the United Nations should have at its disposal a combined world air force, as donated by its member nations. Oddly and perhaps significantly, Churchill never says here how such an international mili-tary force would be deployed. In point of fact, the United Nations has had international military forces, but only in the Korean War has it had any sort of aggressive capacity to keep the peace.

On the other hand, the United Nations Atomic Energy Commission had just been formed two months earlier, and Churchill did not believe it should have access to the "secret knowledge" behind the making of an atomic bomb, at least until the United Nations had demonstrated its sta-bility and progress toward world peace. This was a contro-versial issue at the time. Many of the scientists involved in the Manhattan Project (the U.S. project to design and build the atomic bomb), among them its head, J. Robert Oppenheimer, thought nuclear research should be shared across the nations so that the further use of such weapons would be impossible without threatening the annihilation of humanity.

◆ Paragraphs 14–22

Churchill then turns from war to tyranny, asserting in paragraph 15 that "the liberties enjoyed by individual citizens throughout the United States and throughout the British Empire are not valid in a considerable number of countries, some of which are very powerful." Choosing "the British Empire" as a home of civil liberties was somewhat deceptive, since India at the time was trying to force its way out of the British Empire for just such reasons, in the opinion of the leadership of the Indian National Congress. Nevertheless, Churchill's targets were different: namely, authoritarian states that still did not allow their peoples freedom of speech, equal justice before the law, and free elections.

How could war be prevented, tyranny opposed, and the United Nation's expansive power promoted? In paragraph 20, Churchill calls for recognition of what he termed for the first time the "special relationship between the British Commonwealth and Empire and the United States of America." In 1946 Churchill envisioned a simple continuation of wartime collaboration between militaries and military bases. He puts forward the hope that in future years collaboration would be extended to the rest of the British Commonwealth—in Churchill's eyes, the white dominions—and there might one day even be an exchange of citizenship rights among them all. Churchill's vision has yet to reach fruition: The United States has long since outdistanced Britain as a major world power, and Britain's involvement in the European Union has revised any conception of Commonwealth citizenship. But in 1946 the British Empire was still largely intact, and Britain had the technical knowledge to build its own atomic bomb. The idea of Britain and the United States as equals on the world stage did not seem implausible at the time. Such a relationship would, in Churchill's opinion, guarantee the security and power of the United Nations, to whose development both nations were dedicated, as he states in paragraph 16.

◆ **Paragraphs 23–27**

In fact, Churchill notes in paragraph 23 that the creation of such a formal relationship was a close necessity: "Beware, I say; time may be short." The reason that time might be short was that despite goodwill toward the Soviet Union, an "iron curtain" had fallen across Eastern Europe, the nations the Soviet Red Army had invaded during the war. This phrase, coined by Churchill, would color the entire cold war era. At the time, Communist parties, while small in membership in Eastern Europe, had gained public credibility and support as the vanguard of the Soviet soldiers who had freed these nations from Nazi control. Furthermore, nothing had happened publicly since the war to reaffirm the idea that Stalin's Soviet Union was bent upon worldwide revolution and domination. Yet a mere month before Churchill's speech, Stalin had made a speech little heard in the Western world, claiming that Communism and capitalism were incompatible. Churchill, the venerable anti-Communist, was simply reminding many that Soviet Communist aims in the world had never changed and would return to the fore sooner or later. In point of fact, since Churchill himself had drawn up the "iron curtain" as spheres of influence on a napkin in front of Stalin in October 1944, he could hardly have been in a better place to define where it lay.

Churchill also discusses the settlement in Germany, where the Soviets occupied the territory east of the Elbe River, and the United States, Britain, and France occupied the territory west of the river. He notes in paragraph 26 that the Soviets favored German leftist politicians, expecting that they were trying to establish a Communist government in a united Germany too. Here is an example of the forcefully one-sided nature of Churchill's rhetoric, especially in the notion that the Germans could ever possibly have "the power of putting themselves up to auction between the Soviets and the Western democracies" (paragraph 27). In point of fact, the Americans and British were naturally trying just as hard to find prewar democratic politicians to establish a provisional government.

◆ **Paragraphs 28–31**

"The safety of the world," says Churchill, "requires a new unity in Europe." There are "causes for anxiety." He warns that the Communist parties in Italy and France were well formed and organized: "Communist fifth columns are established and work in complete unity and absolute obedience to the directions they receive from the Communist center." This assertion—not entirely unfounded but certainly exaggerated—would transfer itself to politicians in the United States over the next eight years. He also addressed the situation in China, one that would come to haunt American domestic politics into the 1950s. The danger in Manchuria that Churchill refers to in paragraph 30 was a civil war between the Chinese Communist Party and the nominally democratic Nationalist Party. Three years later, the Communists would win the civil war and establish the People's Republic of China in October 1949. Thus, the world's largest population would be firmly placed in the Communist camp. Anyone like Churchill who believed—wrongly, as it turned out—that Communism was a monolithic political movement directed from Moscow had to be frightened by the prospect. In the next paragraph, Churchill compares the world political situation unfavorably to the period in 1919, when the world had high hopes for the League of Nations; the League had failed miserably to keep the peace, and Churchill feared similar results now.

◆ **Paragraphs 32–35**

Even so, Churchill ends on a message of hope. A new war is not inevitable, he declares; the Soviets did not want it, and it could be prevented with the same strong diplomatic measures against aggression that had been lacking in the era of appeasement. The United Nations offered the opportunity to unite the majority of the world against the designs of the Soviets. Churchill calls upon its members to hear his message as they had not in the late 1930s, to stand strong against Soviet aggression and flex "the Sinews of Peace."

Audience

Winston Churchill wrote his speeches with the expectation that they would be read and studied, similarly to how he

Backed up by barbed wire and tank barriers, an East German police officer stands guard while a bricklayer repairs damage to the Berlin Wall in 1961. (AP/Wide World Photos)

had read and studied speeches as a young student at Harrow. Besides his audience at Westminster College, he clearly expected that other informed people would read his words and react to them. The Westminster College audience received Churchill's words with warm appreciation, interrupting him several times for applause. This made sense; they heard the tenor of the entire speech, which was far less focused on the coming diplomatic breakdown with the Soviet Union, and far more centered on the future of the United Nations and the continuation of the wartime alliance between the United States and Britain. However, the speech was mainly reported for its stunning notion that an "iron curtain" had settled over Europe just ten months after V-E (Victory in Europe) Day; as a result, initial commentary was mostly unfavorable. While members of Churchill's own political party, the Conservatives, hailed further evidence of their leader's genius, several Labour members of Parliament denounced the speech as warmongering. American newspapers scoffed at Churchill's notion that the wartime alliance with the Soviets had already broken down, and Stalin himself denounced the speech, even though he had made a similar one just weeks before. Only as public opinion changed and fear of Soviet expansionism grew would the speech be read as a prescient vision of the coming cold war—and even then it was due to a mere half-reading of its thesis.

Impact

Churchill tends to be credited for recognizing the changing nature of the relationship between the Western democracies and the Soviet Union; because he helped design the "iron curtain" to a minor extent, such is hardly a surprise. The "sinews of peace" was a concept for which he deserved far greater credit, though few people read or heard the entire speech. In effect, the last nineteenth-century imperialist transformed himself into the first credible twentieth-century internationalist.

The "special relationship" Churchill defined as central to the "sinews of peace" was hardly the given that Americans see it as today. In the nineteenth century, cultural affinities between Britain and the United States were recognized, especially as immigration changed the nature of American citizenship and intellectuals began to define the world in terms of "races." Yet at the same time, no American forgot that the United States was originally a rebellious colony that had freed itself from the mighty and hegemonic British Empire. Well into the 1930s, Roosevelt's first vice president, John Nance Garner, claimed that he would like to meet the British king and punch him in the nose, and many a senator and representative, especially those of Irish origin, made a political name by

"Neither the sure prevention of war, nor the continuous rise of world organization will be gained without what I have called the fraternal association of the English-speaking peoples. This means a special relationship between the British Commonwealth and Empire and the United States of America."

(Paragraph 20)

"An iron curtain has descended across the Continent. Behind that line lie all the capitals of the ancient states of Central and Eastern Europe. Warsaw, Berlin, Prague, Vienna, Budapest, Belgrade, Bucharest and Sofia, all these famous cities and the populations around them lie in what I must call the Soviet sphere, and all are subject in one form or another, not only to Soviet influence but to a very high and, in many cases, increasing measure of control from Moscow."

(Paragraph 25)

"In a great number of countries, far from the Russian frontiers and throughout the world, Communist fifth columns are established and work in complete unity and absolute obedience to the directions they receive from the Communist center. Except in the British Commonwealth and in the United States where Communism is in its infancy, the Communist parties or fifth columns constitute a growing challenge and peril to Christian civilization."

(Paragraph 29)

"There never was a war in all history easier to prevent by timely action than the one which has just desolated such great areas of the globe."

(Paragraph 34)

denouncing British imperialism. The most contentious arguments between Roosevelt and Churchill during the war had been over the idea that fighting for world freedom involved the ending of colonialism.

For Churchill to decide at the end of the war that a "special relationship" with the United States needed to be maintained and enhanced to the point of exchanging citizenship rights was not merely a concession to the inevitable; it was to some extent also a bold prophecy. His notion that such a

relationship would support the growth in power of the new United Nations proved to have greater limits. So far, no nation on earth has willingly surrendered its national interest in the name of a greater internationalism.

Meanwhile, "The Sinews of Peace" is known mainly for its prediction of the coming cold war, and Churchill's outlining of the next forty years of diplomatic conflict could not have been more correct. One year after the speech, in March 1947, President Truman was concerned enough about a possible Communist win in the civil war in Greece that he called on Congress to lend a massive sum of money to support the non-Communist (and Fascist-sympathetic) monarchy. Then, too, Churchill noted several times that Europe was desperate, impoverished, starving, and despairing at the end of the war. In June 1947, Secretary of State George C. Marshall outlined the details of the European Recovery Program, which came to be referred to as the Marshall Plan, a $13 billion stimulus package meant to allow Europe to rebuild its nations' economies. The result was just the sort of internationalist integration Churchill had asked for in his speech.

Soon after, the cold war solidified in Europe and around the world. In 1946, Churchill claimed that behind the "iron curtain" only Czechoslovakia maintained a "true democracy." The Czech Communist Party was still popular, and several of its members achieved elected office. But as events unfolded in the rest of Eastern Europe, the Czech voting population became more uncomfortable with the intentions of its own Communist politicians and ministers. Before they could vote the Communist Party out of government, a coup took place in February 1948. The Communist Party formed a one-party government, and as if to underscore the shocking nature of the change, the Czech foreign minister was found dead in his pajamas beneath a window in the Foreign Ministry, an apparent suicide, though many still believe that he was murdered. His death at least provided symbolic entry into the era of Communist domination of the Eastern European states.

In Germany, where Churchill accused the Soviets of trying to promote their own politicians, the British and U.S. zones introduced their own currency in early 1948, the first violation of the postwar agreement over the provisional arrangements made before Germany was reunited. The western zones' currency was much stronger than that in the eastern Soviet zone; along with the Marshall Plan, it seemed as if it was put forward specifically to show up the Soviets' poorer economic reach. Stalin decided he would challenge the West's commitment to Germany. Overnight in June 1948, all roads were cut off to the joint U.S., British, and French zone in West Berlin; in the midst of rebuilding, the people of the city faced starvation. Effectively, Stalin expected the West to abandon Berlin to the eastern zone after this show of force. Instead, the Truman administration organized an airlift to bring supplies to Berlin, daring the Soviets to shoot down the planes. This game of diplomatic chicken lasted an entire year; by the end of it, permanent governments were in the making in West Germany and East Germany, and the two halves would remain divided for the rest of the cold war.

Finally, in August 1949, the world was shocked to discover that the Soviet Union had tested its first atomic bomb. Churchill warned that nuclear technology should not be shared between nations or come under the control of the United Nations; now, the point was moot. Using plans cribbed by Klaus Fuchs, a German-born British physicist, the Soviets had matched the U.S. trump card in the military competition between the two powers. In October the Communist Party took power in China as well, and suddenly the "special relationship" was resisted by two Communist powers as opposed to just one. In June 1950 the cold war turned hot, not in Eastern Europe but in Korea, when the Communist north invaded the U.S.-supported south and nuclear war seemed right around the cor-

Questions for Further Study

1. Winston Churchill had earlier warned the West about the "Red menace" in the Soviet Union, but no one took him seriously. Why do you think political leaders ignored his warnings in the 1920s and 1930s?

2. Historians might argue that Churchill himself was at least partly responsible for the "iron curtain" and the conditions that created it. On what basis could they make that argument?

3. Perhaps the most prominent development in geopolitics during the second half of the twentieth century was the cold war. Define the phrase *cold war* and explain how it developed, particularly in light of the cooperation between the Western democracies and the Soviet Union during World War II.

4. Churchill's speech is remembered primarily for his coining of the term *iron curtain*. Yet Churchill had other purposes in the speech as well. What were those purposes?

5. Compare the world situation at the end of World War I (using, for example, the entries on the Treaty of Versailles, the Treaty of Lausanne, and the Covenant of the League of Nations) with that prevailing at the end of World War II. How were they similar? How did they differ? What were the prospects for peace following each war?

ner. Churchill's warnings could not have seemed timelier. Not only did an "iron curtain" fall over Eastern Europe, but a Communist bloc had been created as well, and only a united international opposition, forged in the democracy that Churchill championed, seemed capable of stopping it.

Further Reading

■ Articles

Reynolds, David. "Rethinking Anglo-American Relations." *International Affairs* 65, no. 1 (Winter 1988–89): 89–111.

■ Books

Archer, Ian W., and Arthur Burns. *Transactions of the Royal Historical Society*, sixth series, Vol. 11. Cambridge, U.K.: Cambridge University Press, 2001.

Churchill, Winston. *Memoirs of the Second World War*. Boston: Houghton Mifflin, 1959.

———. *Blood, Toil, Tears and Sweat: The Speeches of Winston Churchill*, ed. David Cannadine. Boston: Houghton Mifflin, 1989.

Gaddis, John Lewis. *The Cold War: A New History*. New York: Penguin, 2005.

Harbutt, Fraser J. *The Iron Curtain: Churchill, America, and the Origins of the Cold War*. New York: Oxford University Press, 1986.

MacMillan, Margaret. *Paris 1919: Six Months That Changed the World*. New York: Random House, 2001.

Malia, Martin E. *The Soviet Tragedy: A History of Socialism in Russia, 1917–1991*. New York: Free Press, 1994.

■ Web Sites

"The Cold War Files: Interpreting History through Documents." Woodrow Wilson Center for International Scholars Web site. http://www.wilsoncenter.org/coldwarfiles/index.cfm?fuseaction=home.flash.

—David Simonelli

Winston Churchill's "The Sinews of Peace"

President McCluer, ladies and gentlemen, and last but certainly not least, the President of the United States of America:

I am very glad indeed to come to Westminster College this afternoon, and I am complimented that you should give me a degree from an institution whose reputation has been so solidly established. The name "Westminster" somehow or other seems familiar to me. I feel as if I have heard of it before. Indeed now that I come to think of it, it was at Westminster that I received a very large part of my education in politics, dialectic, rhetoric, and one or two other things. In fact we have both been educated at the same, or similar, or, at any rate, kindred establishments.

It is also an honor, ladies and gentlemen, perhaps almost unique, for a private visitor to be introduced to an academic audience by the President of the United States. Amid his heavy burdens, duties, and responsibilities—unsought but not recoiled from—the President has traveled a thousand miles to dignify and magnify our meeting here today and to give me an opportunity of addressing this kindred nation, as well as my own countrymen across the ocean, and perhaps some other countries too. The President has told you that it is his wish, as I am sure it is yours, that I should have full liberty to give my true and faithful counsel in these anxious and baffling times. I shall certainly avail myself of this freedom, and feel the more right to do so because any private ambitions I may have cherished in my younger days have been satisfied beyond my wildest dreams. Let me however make it clear that I have no official mission or status of any kind, and that I speak only for myself. There is nothing here but what you see.

I can therefore allow my mind, with the experience of a lifetime, to play over the problems which beset us on the morrow of our absolute victory in arms, and to try to make sure with what strength I have that what has been gained with so much sacrifice and suffering shall be preserved for the future glory and safety of mankind.

Ladies and gentlemen, the United States stands at this time at the pinnacle of world power. It is a solemn moment for the American Democracy. For with primacy in power is also joined an awe-inspiring accountability to the future. If you look around you, you must feel not only the sense of duty done but also you must feel anxiety lest you fall below the level of achievement. Opportunity is here and now, clear and shining for both our countries. To reject it or ignore it or fritter it away will bring upon us all the long reproaches of the after-time. It is necessary that constancy of mind, persistency of purpose, and the grand simplicity of decision shall rule and guide the conduct of the English-speaking peoples in peace as they did in war. We must, and I believe we shall, prove ourselves equal to this severe requirement.

President McCluer, when American military men approach some serious situation they are wont to write at the head of their directive the words "overall strategic concept." There is wisdom in this, as it leads to clarity of thought. What then is the overall strategic concept which we should inscribe today? It is nothing less than the safety and welfare, the freedom and progress, of all the homes and families of all the men and women in all the lands. And here I speak particularly of the myriad cottage or apartment homes where the wage-earner strives amid the accidents and difficulties of life to guard his wife and children from privation and bring the family up the fear of the Lord, or upon ethical conceptions which often play their potent part.

To give security to these countless homes, they must be shielded from the two gaunt marauders, war and tyranny. We all know the frightful disturbance in which the ordinary family is plunged when the curse of war swoops down upon the bread-winner and those for whom he works and contrives. The awful ruin of Europe, with all its vanished glories, and of large parts of Asia glares us in the eyes. When the designs of wicked men or the aggressive urge of mighty States dissolve over large areas the frame of civilized society, humble folk are confronted with difficulties with which they cannot cope. For them is all distorted, all is broken, all is even ground to pulp.

When I stand here this quiet afternoon I shudder to visualize what is actually happening to millions now and what is going to happen in this period when famine stalks the earth. None can compute what has been called "the unestimated sum of human pain." Our supreme task and duty is to guard the homes of the common people from the horrors and miseries of another war.

We are all agreed on that.

Our American military colleagues, after having proclaimed their "over-all strategic concept" and computed available resources, always proceed to the next step—namely, the method. Here again there is widespread agreement. A world organization has already been erected for the prime purpose of preventing war. UNO, the successor of the League of Nations, with the decisive addition of the United States and all that that means, is already at work. We must make sure that its work is fruitful, that it is a reality and not a sham, that it is a force for action, and not merely a frothing of words, that it is a true temple of peace in which the shields of many nations can someday be hung up, and not merely a cockpit in a Tower of Babel. Before we cast away the solid assurances of national armaments for self-preservation we must be certain that our temple is built, not upon shifting sands or quagmires, but upon a rock. Anyone can see with his eyes open that our path will be difficult and also long, but if we persevere together as we did in the two world wars—though not, alas, in the interval between them—I cannot doubt that we shall achieve our common purpose in the end.

I have, however, a definite and practical proposal to make for action.

Courts and magistrates may be set up but they cannot function without sheriffs and constables. The United Nations Organization must immediately begin to be equipped with an international armed force. In such a matter we can only go step by step, but we must begin now. I propose that each of the Powers and States should be invited to dedicate a certain number of air squadrons to the service of the world organization. These squadrons would be trained and prepared in their own countries, but would move around in rotation from one country to another. They would wear the uniforms of their own countries but with different badges. They would not be required to act against their own nation, but in other respects they would be directed by the world organization. This might be started on a modest scale and it would grow as confidence grew. I wished to see this done after the First World War, and I devoutly trust that it may be done forthwith.

It would nevertheless, ladies and gentlemen, be wrong and imprudent to entrust the secret knowledge or experience of the atomic bomb, which the United States, Great Britain, and Canada now share, to the world organization, while it is still in its infancy. It would be criminal madness to cast it adrift in this still agitated and un-united world. No one in any country has slept less well in their beds because this knowledge and the method and the raw materials to apply it, are present largely retained in American hands. I do not believe we should all have slept so soundly had the positions been reversed and some Communist or neo-Fascist State monopolized for the time being these dread agencies. The fear of them alone might easily have been used to enforce totalitarian systems upon the free democratic world, with consequences appalling to human imagination. God has willed that this shall not be and we have at least a breathing space to set our house in order before this peril has to be encountered. And even then, if no effort is spared, we should still possess so formidable a superiority as to impose effective deterrents upon its employment, or threat of employment, by others. Ultimately, when the essential brotherhood of man is truly embodied and expressed in a world organization with all the necessary practical safeguards to make it effective, these powers would naturally be confided to that world organization.

Now I come to the second of the two marauders, to the second danger which threatens the cottage homes, and ordinary people—namely, tyranny.

We cannot be blind to the fact that the liberties enjoyed by individual citizens throughout the United States and throughout the British Empire are not valid in a considerable number of countries, some of which are very powerful. In these States control is enforced upon the common people by various kinds of all-embracing police governments to a degree which is overwhelming and contrary to every principle of democracy. The power of the State is exercised without restraint, either by dictators or by compact oligarchies operating through a privileged party and a political police. It is not our duty at this time when difficulties are so numerous to interfere forcibly in the internal affairs of countries which we have not conquered in war. But we must never cease to proclaim in fearless tones the great principles of freedom and the rights of man which are the joint inheritance of the English-speaking world and which through Magna Carta, the Bill of Rights, the Habeas Corpus, trial by jury, and the English common law find their most famous expression in the American Declaration of Independence.

All this means that the people of any country have the right, and should have the power by constitutional action, by free unfettered elections, with secret ballot, to choose or change the character or form of government under which they dwell; that freedom of speech and thought should reign; that courts of justice, independent of the executive, unbiased by any party, should administer laws which have received the broad assent of large majorities or are consecrated by time and custom. Here are the title deeds of freedom which should lie in every cottage home. Here is the message of the British and American peoples to mankind. Let us preach what we practice—let us practice what we preach.

Though I have now stated the two great dangers which menace the home of the people, war and tyranny, I have not yet spoken of poverty and privation which are in many cases the prevailing anxiety. But if the dangers of war and tyranny are removed, there is no doubt that science and cooperation can bring in the next few years, certainly in the next few decades, to the world, newly taught in the sharpening school of war, an expansion of material well-being beyond anything that has yet occurred in human experience.

Now, at this sad and breathless moment, we are plunged in the hunger and distress which are the aftermath of our stupendous struggle; but this will pass and may pass quickly, and there is no reason except human folly or sub-human crime which should deny to all the nations the inauguration and enjoyment of an age of plenty. I have often used words which I learn fifty years ago from a great Irish-American orator, a friend of mine, Mr. Bourke Cockran, "There is enough for all. The earth is a generous mother; she will provide in plentiful abundance food for all her children if they will but cultivate her soil in justice and in peace."

And so far I feel that we are in full agreement.

Now, while still pursuing the method—the method of realizing our overall strategic concept, I come to the crux of what I have traveled here to say. Neither the sure prevention of war, nor the continuous rise of world organization will be gained without what I have called the fraternal association of the English-speaking peoples. This means a special relationship between the British Commonwealth and Empire and the United States of America. Ladies and gentlemen, this is no time for generalities, and I will venture to be precise. Fraternal association requires not only the growing friendship and mutual understanding between our two vast but kindred systems of society, but the continuance of the intimate relations between our military advisers, leading to common study of potential dangers, the similarity of weapons and manuals of instruction, and to the interchange of

officers and cadets at technical colleges. It should carry with it the continuance of the present facilities for mutual security by the joint use of all Naval and Air Force bases in the possession of either country all over the world. This would perhaps double the mobility of the American Navy and Air Force. It would greatly expand that of the British Empire forces and it might well lead, if and as the world calms down, to important financial savings. Already we use together a large number of islands; more may well be entrusted to our joint care in the near future.

The United States has already a Permanent Defense Agreement with the Dominion of Canada, which is so devotedly attached to the British Commonwealth and the Empire. This Agreement is more effective than many of those which have been made under formal alliances. This principle should be extended to all the British Commonwealths with full reciprocity. Thus, whatever happens, and thus only, shall we be secure ourselves and able to work together for the high and simple causes that are dear to us and bode no ill to any. Eventually there may come—I feel eventually there will come—the principle of common citizenship, but that we may be content to leave to destiny, whose outstretched arm many of us can already clearly see.

There is however an important question we must ask ourselves. Would a special relationship between the United States and the British Commonwealth be inconsistent with our overriding loyalties to the world organization? I reply that, on the contrary, it is probably the only means by which that organization will achieve its full stature and strength. There are already the special United States relations with Canada which I have just mentioned, and there are the relations between the United States and the South American Republics. We British have also our twenty years Treaty of Collaboration and Mutual Assistance with Soviet Russia. I agree with Mr. Bevan, the Foreign Secretary of Great Britain, that it might well be a fifty years treaty so far as we are concerned. We aim at nothing but mutual assistance and collaboration with Russia. The British have an alliance with Portugal unbroken since the year 1384, and which produced fruitful results at a critical moment in the recent war. None of these clash with the general interest of a world agreement, or a world organization; on the contrary, they help it. "In my father's house are many mansions." Special associations between members of the United Nations which have no aggressive point against any other country, which harbor no design incompatible with the Charter of the United Nations, far from being harmful, are beneficial and, as I believe, indispensable.

I spoke earlier, ladies and gentlemen, of the Temple of Peace. Workmen from all countries must build that temple. If two of the workmen know each other particularly well and are old friends, if their families are intermingled, if they have "faith in each other's purpose, hope in each other's future and charity towards each other's shortcomings"—to quote some good words I read here the other day—why cannot they work together at the common task as friends and partners? Why can they not share their tools and thus increase each other's working powers? Indeed they must do so or else the temple may not be built, or, being built, it may collapse, and we should all be proved again unteachable and have to go and try to learn again for a third time in a school of war incomparably more rigorous than that from which we have just been released. The dark ages may return, the Stone Age may return on the gleaming wings of science, and what might now shower immeasurable material blessings upon mankind, may even bring about its total destruction. Beware, I say; time may be short. Do not let us take the course of allowing events to drift along until it is too late. If there is to be a fraternal association of the kind of I have described, with all the express strength and security which both our countries can derive from it, let us make sure that that great fact is known to the world, and that it plays its part in steadying and stabilizing the foundations of peace. There is the path of wisdom. Prevention is better than the cure.

A shadow has fallen upon the scenes so lately light by the Allied victory. Nobody knows what Soviet Russia and its Communist international organization intends to do in the immediate future, or what are the limits, if any, to their expansive and proselytizing tendencies. I have a strong admiration and regard for the valiant Russian people and for my wartime comrade, Marshal Stalin. There is deep sympathy and goodwill in Britain—and I doubt not here also—towards the peoples of all the Russias and a resolve to persevere through many differences and rebuffs in establishing lasting friendships. We understand the Russian need to be secure on her western frontiers by the removal of all possibility of German aggression. We welcome Russia to her rightful place among the leading nations of the world. We welcome her flag upon the seas. Above all, we welcome, or should welcome, constant, frequent and growing contacts between the Russian people and our own people on both sides of the Atlantic. It is my duty however, for I am sure you would wish me to state the facts as I see them to you. It is my duty to place before you certain facts about the present position in Europe.

From Stettin in the Baltic to Trieste in the Adriatic an iron curtain has descended across the Continent. Behind that line lie all the capitals of the ancient states of Central and Eastern Europe. Warsaw, Berlin, Prague, Vienna, Budapest, Belgrade, Bucharest and Sofia, all these famous cities and the populations around them lie in what I must call the Soviet sphere, and all are subject in one form or another, not only to Soviet influence but to a very high and, in some cases, increasing measure of control from Moscow. Athens alone—Greece with its immortal glories—is free to decide its future at an election under British, American and French observation. The Russian-dominated Polish government has been encouraged to make enormous and wrongful inroads upon Germany, and mass expulsions of millions of Germans on a scale grievous and undreamed-of are now taking place. The Communist parties, which were very small in all these Eastern States of Europe, have been raised to preeminence and power far beyond their numbers and are seeking everywhere to obtain totalitarian control. Police governments are prevailing in nearly every case, and so far, except in Czechoslovakia, there is no true democracy.

Turkey and Persia are both profoundly alarmed and disturbed at the claims which are being made upon them and at the pressure being exerted by the Moscow government. An attempt is being made by the Russians in Berlin to build up a quasi-Communist party in their zone of occupied Germany by showing special favors to groups of left-wing German leaders. At the end of the fighting last June, the American and British armies withdrew westward, in accordance with an earlier agreement, to a depth at some points of 150 miles upon a front of nearly four hundred miles, in order to allow our Russian allies to occupy this vast expanse of territory which the Western democracies had conquered.

If now the Soviet government tries, by separate action, to build up a pro-Communist Germany in their areas, this will cause new serious difficulties in the American and British zones, and will give the defeated Germans the power of putting themselves up to auction between the Soviets and the Western democracies. Whatever conclusions may be drawn from these facts—and facts they are—this is certainly not the liberated Europe we fought to build up. Nor is it one which contains the essentials of permanent peace.

The safety of the world, ladies and gentlemen, requires a new unity in Europe, from which no nation should be permanently outcast. It is from the quarrels of the strong parent races in Europe that the world wars we have witnessed, or which occurred in former times, have sprung. Twice in our own lifetime we have seen the United States, against their wishes and their traditions, against arguments, the force of which it is impossible not to comprehend, twice we have seen them drawn by irresistible forces, into these wars in time to secure the victory of the good cause, but only after frightful slaughter and devastation have occurred. Twice the United State has had to send several millions of its young men across the Atlantic to find the war; but now war can find any nation, wherever it may dwell between dusk and dawn. Surely we should work with conscious purpose for a grand pacification of Europe, within the structure of the United Nations and in accordance with our Charter. That I feel opens a course of policy of very great importance.

In front of the iron curtain which lies across Europe are other causes for anxiety. In Italy the Communist Party is seriously hampered by having to support the Communist-trained Marshal Tito's claims to former Italian territory at the head of the Adriatic. Nevertheless the future of Italy hangs in the balance. Again one cannot imagine a regenerated Europe without a strong France. All my public life I worked for a strong France and I never lost faith in her destiny, even in the darkest hours. I will not lose faith now. However, in a great number of countries, far from the Russian frontiers and throughout the world, Communist fifth columns are established and work in complete unity and absolute obedience to the directions they receive from the Communist center. Except in the British Commonwealth and in the United States where Communism is in its infancy, the Communist parties or fifth columns constitute a growing challenge and peril to Christian civilization. These are somber facts for anyone to have [to] recite on the morrow a victory gained by so much splendid comradeship in arms and in the cause of freedom and democracy; but we should be most unwise not to face them squarely while time remains.

The outlook is also anxious in the Far East and especially in Manchuria. The Agreement which was made at Yalta, to which I was a party, was extremely favorable to Soviet Russia, but it was made at a time when no one could say that the German war might not extend all through the summer and autumn of 1945 and when the Japanese war was expected by the best judges to last for a further 18 months from the end of the German war. In this country you [are] all so well-informed about the Far East, and such devoted friends of China, that I do not need to expatiate on the situation there.

I have, however, felt bound to portray the shadow which, alike in the west and in the east, falls upon the world. I was a minister at the time of the Versailles Treaty and a close friend of Mr. Lloyd-George, who was the head of the British delegation at Versailles. I did not myself agree with many things that were done, but I have a very strong impression in my mind of that situation, and I find it painful to contrast it with that which prevails now. In those days there were high hopes and unbounded confidence that the wars were over and that the League of Nations would become all-powerful. I do not see or feel that same confidence or even the same hopes in the haggard world at the present time.

On the other hand, ladies and gentlemen, I repulse the idea that a new war is inevitable, still more that it is imminent. It is because I am sure that our fortunes are still in our own hands and that we hold the power to save the future, that I feel the duty to speak out now that I have the occasion and the opportunity to do so. I do not believe that Soviet Russia desires war. What they desire is the fruits of war and the indefinite expansion of their power and doctrines. But what we have to consider here today while time remains, is the permanent prevention of war and the establishment of conditions of freedom and democracy as rapidly as possible in all countries. Our difficulties and dangers will not be removed by closing our eyes to them. They will not be removed by mere waiting to see what happens; nor will they be removed by a policy of appeasement. What is needed is a settlement, and the longer this is delayed, the more difficult it will be and the greater our dangers will become.

From what I have seen of our Russian friends and Allies during the war, I am convinced that there is nothing they admire so much as strength. And there is nothing for which they have less respect than for weakness, especially military weakness. For that reason the old doctrine of a balance of power is unsound. We cannot afford, if we can help it, to work on narrow margins, offering temptations to a trial of strength. If the Western democracies stand together in strict adherence to the principles of the United Nations Charter, their influence for furthering those principles will be immense and no one is likely to molest them. If, however, they become divided or falter in their duty and if these all-important years are allowed to slip away, then indeed catastrophe may overwhelm us all.

Last time I saw it all coming and I cried aloud to my own fellow-countrymen and to the world, but no one paid any attention. Up till the year 1933 or even 1935, Germany might have been saved from the awful fate which has overtaken her and we might all have been spared the miseries Hitler let loose upon mankind. There never was a war in history easier to prevent by timely action than the one which has just desolated such great areas of the globe. It could have been prevented in my belief without the firing of a single shot, and Germany might be powerful, prosperous and honored today; but no one would listen and one by one we were all sucked into the awful whirlpool. We surely, ladies and gentlemen, I put it to you, surely, we must not let that happen again. This can only be achieved by reaching now, in 1946, by reaching a good understanding on all points with Russia under the general authority of the United Nations Organization and by the maintenance of that good understanding through many peaceful years, by the whole strength of the English-speaking world and all its connections. There is the solution which I respectfully offer to you in this address to which I have given the title, "The Sinews of Peace."

Let no man underrate the abiding power of the British Empire and Commonwealth. Because you see the 46 millions in our island harassed about their food supply, of which they only grow one half, even in war-time, or because we have difficulty in restarting our industries and export trade after six years of passionate war effort, do not suppose we shall not come through these dark years of privation as we have come through the glorious years of agony. Do not suppose that half a century from now you will not see 70 or 80 millions of Britons spread about the world united in defense of our traditions, and our way of life, and of the world causes which you and we espouse. If the population of the English-speaking Commonwealths be added to that of the United States with all that such cooperation implies in the air, on the sea, all over the globe and in science and in industry, and in moral force, there will be no quivering, precarious balance of power to offer its temptation to ambition or adventure. On the contrary there will be an overwhelming assurance of security. If we adhere faithfully to the Charter of the United Nations and walk forward in sedate and sober strength seeking no one's land or treasure, seeking to lay no arbitrary control upon the thoughts of men; if all British moral and material forces and convictions are joined with your own in fraternal association, the highroads of the future will be clear—not only for us but for all, not only for our times but for a century to come.

Glossary

Marshal Tito	Josip Broz Tito (1892–1980), Yugoslavian resistance leader who was the country's prime minister in 1946
Marshal Stalin	Joseph Stalin (1878–1953), long-time leader of the Soviet Union
Mr. Bevin	Aneurin Bevan (1897–1960), British left-wing politician and National Health Service founder
Mr. Lloyd George	David Lloyd George (1863–1945), British prime minister during World War I
President McCluer	Franc McCluer, president of Westminster College
Treaty of Versailles	the settlement between Germany and the Allied powers, signed in 1919, which ended World War I

"The Japanese people forever renounce war as a sovereign right of the nation."

Overview

Japan's unconditional surrender on August 15, 1945, under the terms of the Potsdam Declaration, precipitated the American occupation of Japan after World War II. The Potsdam Declaration specified that the occupation of Japan should result in "a peacefully inclined and responsible government" under "the freely expressed will of the Japanese people." In the opening years of this occupation, which ended in 1952, the 1947 Constitution of Japan was quickly written by the American occupiers. General Douglas MacArthur, as supreme commander for the Allied powers, was unhappy with two drafts of a new constitution proposed by Japanese governmental elites, which he considered mere rewrites of the 1889 Constitution of the Empire of Japan, known as the Meiji Constitution. As shaped by MacArthur's offices, the focus of the 1947 constitution is the determination for Japan to remain a peaceful country that will not ever again fall into "the horrors of war through the action of government."

The 1947 Constitution—considered by historians to be one of the most liberal constitutions in the world and also known as the Peace Constitution—thus replaced the 1889 Meiji Constitution, under which the emperor technically had had absolute control. Under the 1947 constitution, the emperor became the symbol of the state and of the unity of the people, a far cry from being constitutionally considered sacred and inviolable. Thirty-nine articles of the 1947 document guarantee fundamental human rights, among other provisions allowing labor to organize, specifying universal adult suffrage, giving women marriage and property rights, and renouncing war or the creation of armed forces. The Japanese, including women who were casting ballots for the first time, voted overwhelmingly in the fall of 1946 for candidates who supported the new constitution. It came into effect on May 3, 1947, and has not been amended since its promulgation.

Context

The Japanese government began spiraling toward anarchy on May 15, 1932, when junior naval officers and army cadets assassinated Prime Minister Inukai Tsuyoshi. His successors were chosen from military men, sparking struggles for power that increasingly led to the suppression of dissent and more assassinations. In November 1936, Japan and Germany signed the Anti-Comintern Pact in opposition to the Communist International (Comintern) organization and the Soviet Union. On July 7, 1937, the Imperial Japanese Army invaded China at the Marco Polo Bridge, near Beijing, under the pretense that the Chinese had fired on the Japanese; this event marked the beginning of the Second Sino-Japanese War and, more broadly, the Pacific War. In line with its aggression, Japan proclaimed the Greater East Asia Co-prosperity Sphere around 1938. This concept was a reaction against Western imperialism in Asia, stipulating that Japan would be the leader of Asian nations and that the Western powers who had control over nine of the ten Southeast Asian countries were to leave Asia. Within two years, Japan dissolved political parties and in September 1940 signed the Tripartite Pact with Germany and Italy, an alliance for cooperation in international matters, with Germany in a leading role.

As initiated by the conflict fought between Japan and China from 1937 onward, the Pacific War took place in eastern Asia and the islands of the Pacific. This war became part of the larger conflict of World War II after the 1941 Japanese attack on the American base at Pearl Harbor, Hawaii, a desperate and ultimately losing gamble. Japanese military leaders, as well as Emperor Hirohito, believed that the United States was strangling Japan financially and territorially. For example, in September 1940 America imposed a scrap-metal boycott on Japan, which hindered Japanese shipbuilding. In July 1941, the United States demanded that Japan pull out of China and stop advancing to the south. Japan had already invaded the northern part of French Indochina (later to become North Vietnam); when Japan invaded the southern part of French Indochina (South Vietnam) later that month, America froze Japanese assets in the United States and imposed an oil boycott on Japan. Australia, Great Britain, and the Dutch government in exile (operating from London following Germany's invasion of the Netherlands) joined America in these sanctions and discontinued the selling of iron ore, steel, and oil to Japan. At the time, Japan was dependent

1890

■ **November 29**
The Meiji Constitution comes into effect, stipulating in Article 3, "The Emperor is sacred and inviolable."

1937

■ **July 7**
Japan invades and begins occupying China.

1941

■ **December 7**
Japan bombs Pearl Harbor, Hawaii, and brings the United States into World War II.

1945

■ **July 26**
The Potsdam Declaration is issued, setting out the Allies' demands regarding a new Japanese constitution, including respect of human rights and freedom of speech, religion, and thought.

■ **August 15**
Emperor Hirohito broadcasts the Japanese surrender, and the Japanese Imperial Army and Imperial Navy, seven million men in number, begin disarming and demobilizing.

■ **October 9**
A new Japanese cabinet is formed following the resignation of the former cabinet.

■ **October 11**
Prime Minister Kijuro Shidehara, head of the new cabinet, meets for the first time with General Douglas MacArthur, the Allies' supreme commander, and is instructed by MacArthur to begin constitutional reforms.

upon imported oil for about 80 percent of its oil needs, such that the sanctions led Japan to feel encircled by these four countries.

The plan to attack the U.S. Pacific Fleet at Pearl Harbor—a plan ratified by a Japanese imperial conference held on December 1, 1941—was part of a larger scheme to also attack the Philippines, an American colony, and the British colonies of Hong Kong and Singapore as well as to isolate Australia. Japanese military thinking held that even if provoked by the surprise bombing of Pearl Harbor, the United States would aid its European allies first before counterattacking Japan, which was then forming its Greater East Asia Co-prosperity Sphere. America did direct primary assistance to Great Britain and its European allies, but it still possessed the resources to then turn to the Pacific to deal with Japan in the hope of bringing freedom to Asian countries that had been invaded and occupied by Japan. On April 18, 1942, the American lieutenant colonel James Doolittle led sixteen B-25 bombers in striking military and industrial targets in Tokyo. The turning point of the Pacific War in favor of the United States was the Battle of Midway of June 4–7, 1942. Japan was overextended, suffering from insufficient military forces, petroleum, and food and supply lines for its Greater East Asia Co-prosperity Sphere as well as severe food shortages on the main islands of Japan.

Japan was devastated by the end of the Pacific War, even before the infamous atomic bombings of Hiroshima and Nagasaki. The United States dropped the first atomic bomb, code-named Little Boy, on Hiroshima on August 6, 1945. Two days later the Soviet Union declared war on Japan and invaded Manchuria, in northern China. Then, on August 9, America dropped the second atomic bomb, code-named Fat Man, on Nagasaki. This second bombing finally caused Emperor Hirohito to break a deadlock among his advisers, three of whom wanted to continue the war and three of whom wanted to surrender; Emperor Hirohito decided to make peace, agreeing to an unconditional surrender on August 15, 1945. Some two million Japanese—almost a third of them civilians—had died during the war, and more than fifteen million Japanese were homeless as the result of the extensive conventional bombings of the main islands of Japan that had preceded the dropping of the two atomic bombs. (The American incendiary bombing of Tokyo on the night of March 9, 1945, caused upwards of eighty-eight thousand deaths and forty-three thousand injuries and rendered 1.5 million homeless.) In addition, repatriation of the more than six million disarmed Japanese soldiers and civilians scattered throughout the Pacific and Asia began in mid-September 1945, and at the peak of repatriation in mid-1946 almost two hundred thousand people were coming back to Japan every week. Starvation remained a real threat for many Japanese before and after the surrender and early on during the American occupation.

Throughout this grim situation, the Japanese were surprised that the American occupation following the Pacific War did not prove vindictive and harsh, especially considering the way the Japanese military had treated prisoners of war and combatants during the war. In fact, it was statistically more dangerous to be a prisoner of the Japanese during the war than to fight the Japanese during the war. According to the judgment of the Tokyo War Crimes Tribunal, about 27 percent of British and American prisoners of war of the Japanese did not survive—far more than the 4 percent of Allied prisoners of war of the Germans and Italians who died.

This relief at the lack of vindictiveness on the part of the Americans led to a spirit of cooperation that enabled the ultimate public acceptance of a constitution that would not have been formulated in Japan under other circumstances. However, the elite who continued to serve as leaders after the surrender were not anxious for reform. Most were bureaucrats who had been in office before the war, and radical change was not high on their agenda. They attempted to simply modify the 1889 Meiji Constitution, intending to preserve what was left of the old order.

In October 1945, Prince Fumimaro Konoe, a member of the Japanese cabinet, met with General MacArthur to discuss issues of postwar administration, at which time MacArthur encouraged Konoe to work on a revision of the constitution. MacArthur had hoped that the Japanese would draft an acceptable constitution embodying the ideas of democracy and revising the emperor-centered political system; he wanted the Japanese leaders to initiate democratic reforms on their own. However, the Japanese elites, including Prime Minister Kijuro Shidehara, preferred a more conservative document than what MacArthur and the Americans had in mind. Shidehara appointed the Matsumoto Commission in late 1945, and it submitted its recommendations for a new constitution in February 1946. When the American occupiers read the Japanese proposals, they were unhappy with the minimal degree of change from the 1889 Meiji Constitution, in particular with regard to the status of the emperor, who under these Japanese drafts was designated "supreme and inviolable," not much of a change from the Meiji "sacred and inviolable" designation (Inoue, p. 121).

The unsatisfactory Japanese response inspired MacArthur to direct his staff to draft a completely new document. Courtney Whitney, chief of the Government Section, and the lawyer Milo Rowell authored much of it, while Beate Sirota, a translator on MacArthur's staff, dealt with women's issues. The new draft embodied democratic ideals, more equality of the sexes, and a revised political system allowing the emperor limited powers and under which he would not be considered divine. It also abolished the designation of Shintoism as the state religion, extended the franchise to women, encouraged labor unions, liberalized education, abolished the powerful Zaibatsu conglomerates (large family-controlled banking and industrial groups), and outlawed war. In drafting the constitution, the American authors included most of the American Bill of Rights as well as the right of labor to organize and many marriage and property rights for women. American women received the right to obtain an abortion in 1973; Japanese women were given this right in 1948. On February 13,

Time Line

1946

- **January 1**
  Emperor Hirohito disavows his own divinity.

- **February 3**
  MacArthur orders Courtney Whitney and his staff to prepare a draft of a constitution, which they finish in ten days.

- **February 13**
  Whitney and three steering committee members present the American constitutional draft to the Japanese foreign minister Shigeru Yoshida.

- **June 25**
  Yoshida introduces the draft for the new Japanese constitution to the newly elected representatives, who form a special committee that debates the document in detail until July 23.

- **July 25**
  A special subcommittee begins fourteen meetings over a month's time to discuss the draft constitution and negotiate various amendments.

- **August 24**
  The entire House of Representatives convenes for a final vote, and the new Constitution of Japan is approved by a vote of 429 to eight.

1947

- **May 3**
  The Constitution of Japan is enacted.

1946, Whitney and three staff members met with and presented the proposed constitution to the Japanese foreign minister Shigeru Yoshida (with the interactions requiring extensive translation and interpretation between the English and Japanese languages). The Japanese officials, according to all accounts, were surprised and dismayed at the liberal and radical constitution, which gave the Japanese more rights than Americans had.

On February 18, Whitney, further frustrated with Japanese delays, threatened to publish the U.S. draft on February 20 and appeal to Japanese public opinion if the Japanese representatives continued to delay. However, MacArthur would tolerate many more delays on the part of the Japanese representatives between June and December 1946, to give the impression that the Americans were not forcing a constitution on the Japanese.

On June 25, 1946, Foreign Minister Yoshida introduced the draft of the new Japanese constitution to the newly elected representatives, who formed a special committee of seventy-two members; they debated the document in detail until July 23. On July 25, 1946, a special subcommittee began a series of fourteen meetings over a month's time to discuss the constitution—with special attention given to the language of both the English and Japanese drafts—and negotiate various amendments. On August 24, the entire House of Representatives convened for a final vote, and the new constitution was approved by a vote of 429 to eight; five of the eight opposition votes came from Communist members who wanted the constitution to go further to promote individual rights and liberties. On November 3, 1946, the new Constitution of Japan was promulgated by the National Diet of Japan, and on May 3, 1947, the constitution was officially enacted.

About the Author

There is no listed author of the Japanese Constitution, but the Government Section of General MacArthur's headquarters prepared the draft, under Courtney Whitney, with the aid of Milo Rowell and Beate Sirota. Major General Courtney Whitney (1897–1969), a lawyer and staff officer for MacArthur during the American occupation of Japan, had enlisted in the U.S. Army in 1917 and served as a pilot during World War I. In 1927 he received a law degree from George Washington University and left the army to begin the practice of law in Manila. In 1940 he returned to active duty with the military and served in China and the Philippines. After the Japanese surrender, he accompanied MacArthur to Japan and became chief of the Government Section. He served under MacArthur during the Korean War and in 1956 wrote a biography of MacArthur entitled *MacArthur: His Rendezvous with History*.

Lieutenant Colonel Milo E. Rowell (1903–1977), who was also a lawyer and staff officer for MacArthur, graduated from Stanford University and Harvard Law School and practiced law in the United States until he enlisted in the army in 1943. He served under MacArthur in the Philippines and accompanied him to Japan during the occupa-

tion to serve as chief of judicial affairs. Rowell's area of expertise was a comparison of the existing Meiji Constitution of Japan and the new constitution for Japan.

Beate Sirota (1923–) was born in Vienna, Austria, and moved to Japan with her family, where her father taught at the Imperial Academy of Music in Tokyo. She lived in Tokyo for ten years and was fluent in Japanese. When she was sixteen, her parents sent her to Mills College in California. During World War II, she was cut off from her parents, who stayed in Japan. After graduation, she worked in the United States and then returned to Japan in 1945 as the first American civilian to enter postwar Japan. MacArthur's staff hired her to work as a translator, and she then was assigned to the civil rights subcommittee working on the constitution. She concentrated on the legal equality of men and women when she worked on Articles 14 and 24. She returned to the United States in 1947 and lives in New York City.

Explanation and Analysis of the Document

In the preamble, which summarizes the intents of the constitution, the authors stress peaceful cooperation with all nations, emphasize that power in the country rests with the people, and reject any earlier constitutions or political documents that conflict with these notions. The word *peace* occurs five times in the preamble, and the Japanese people pledge their national honor to achieve the high ideals described. The idealistic and ambitious reforms of the Americans are prominent in the constitution, which served to abolish Shintoism as the state religion, extend the vote to women, encourage labor unions, liberalize education, end (at least temporarily) the powerful Zaibatsu conglomerates, and outlaw war. Many Japanese who were not part of the elite class that had held power for generations genuinely welcomed the American reforms. Yet when the Japanese National Diet promulgated the constitution, it did not refer to American contributions, which is what MacArthur wanted. It is significant that through the first decade of the twenty-first century, the 1947 Japanese Constitution was not amended.

◆ **Chapter I: The Emperor**

In Article 1 of the first chapter, the emperor is characterized as "the symbol of the State and of the unity of the people." This description diverges from the terms of Article 3 of the 1889 Meiji Constitution, under which the emperor was "sacred and inviolable." While the emperor's role is thus reduced, Article 2 retains the system of dynastic succession, and Japan's emperorship remains the longest-lasting continuous dynasty in the world today. Both Russia and England advocated for Emperor Hirohito to be tried as a war criminal at the end of the Pacific War, but MacArthur as supreme commander maintained that Emperor Hirohito's presence was necessary for the stability of the occupation. The remaining articles of this chapter require the advice and approval of the cabinet for the emperor's acts, permit the emperor to appoint the prime minister as designated by the diet (parliament), and allow the emperor, with

General Douglas MacArthur (seated) and members of his staff, including Courtney Whitney (far left) (AP/Wide World Photos)

the advice and approval of the cabinet, to act in an array of ceremonial and functionary duties on behalf of the people.

◆ Chapter II: Renunciation of War

In Article 9 the Japanese people "forever renounce war as a sovereign right of the nation" and establish that "land, sea, and air forces, as well as other war potential, will never be maintained. The right of belligerency of the state will not be recognized." This peace-oriented segment of the Japanese Constitution is directly attributable to the American occupation and the reaction to Japanese military aggression prior to and during the Pacific War. This renunciation of war is in great contrast with Articles 11–13 of the 1889 Meiji Constitution, by which the emperor, as commander of the army and navy, was entitled to declare war, make peace, and conclude treaties. In line with the emperor's having renounced his divinity, he also lost the right to declare war, part of the emphasis on peace of the 1947 constitution.

◆ Chapter III: Rights and Duties of the People

In Articles 11, 12, and 13, the constitution guarantees fundamental human rights, including the rights to "life, liberty, and the pursuit of happiness," in phrasing very familiar to Americans from the U.S. Declaration of Independence. In Article 11, fundamental human rights are guaranteed for present and future generations of Japanese. Article 12 further stresses human freedoms and rights and prohibits any abuses of the same.

In Article 14, the prohibition of discrimination based on race, creed, sex, social status, or family origin marks an attempt to refashion Japanese society without the entrenched elites having so much power. Japanese society had remained stratified since the Meiji Restoration of 1868, such as through the power of the genro, elder statesmen who served as advisers to the emperor and who had a great deal of power. The House of Peers, as delineated in the Meiji Constitution, consisted of members of the emperor's family, nobles by birth, and anyone that the emperor wished to appoint. In turn, the House of Representatives was elected, but members had to be male and meet property qualifications. Article 14 speaks to the formerly sanctioned Japanese discrimination against *burakumin* citizens, previously called *eta*, who are descendants of leather workers, executioners, undertakers, and the like. Traditionally such people were discriminated against and forced to live in their own villages. Articles 15 and 16 establish the right of the people to choose public officials, with adult voting rights being universal, and allow citizens to petition to remove public officials or repeal laws. Under the Meiji Constitution, voting rights were severely limited by birth or property ownership, and no women were allowed to vote.

In Articles 18–20, the 1947 constitution prohibits involuntary servitude, guarantees freedom of thought and religion, and replaces the Meiji Constitution designation of Shintoism as the state religion with a prohibition of any state religious education or activity. The Meiji oligarchs used the state Shinto establishment to foster support for their policies by making the emperor the formal head of Shinto. However, they did not force Shinto doctrines on people. Once Emperor Hirohito disavowed his own divinity in 1946, Shintoism and the state were separated, although the Americans still wanted the new constitution to include the prohibition of any state religion. Article 21 guarantees freedom of assembly, speech, and press with no censorship, terms very different from those of the 1930s, when right-wing patriotism and press censorship dominated the political climate in Japan.

Articles 22 and 23 impart the right to change residence and occupation and guarantee academic freedom. Article 24 focuses on the rights of women entering into marriage, a reaction against marriages being arranged without women having a choice. Under the Meiji Civil Code, the father had complete authority over the lives of all family members. Women had no rights with regard to marriage, divorce, or inheritance; they also could not vote. The rights of women quickly came into play in postwar Japan, with more than thirteen million women registering to vote in the general election of April 10, 1946. In repudiating the complete control of the father, the 1947 constitution effectively opened the job market to women.

Articles 25–40 deal with additional freedoms, including those related to public health, equal education, working conditions, right of workers to organize, the right to own property, legal protection of life and liberty, speedy trials, and protection against unreasonable search and seizure or double jeopardy. The Meiji Constitution protected citizens from having one's house searched or entered but did not specify any guarantees of public health, equal education, fair working conditions, rights of workers to organize, or speedy trials or against double jeopardy.

◆ Chapter IV: The Diet

Articles 41–64 set up the National Diet of Japan (called the Kokkai in Japanese), with a lower house called the House of Representatives and an upper house called the House of Councillors. This is quite similar to the legislative structure set up by the 1889 Meiji Constitution, which was based on the Prussian and English models. Under the Meiji Constitution, the upper house was limited to members of the imperial family, nobles, and members appointed by the emperor; the lower house membership was male only, and there were property restrictions. Under Chapter IV of the 1947 constitution, both houses are to be elected, with no discrimination or property-ownership qualifications. The diet has the sole authority to make law. In accord with the change in the status of the emperor, the diet diverges a great deal from the Meiji model. For example, Article 44 guarantees no discrimination because of race, creed, sex, social status, family origin, education, prop-

erty, or income. Under Article 50, no member of either house may be apprehended (arrested) while the diet is in session.

◆ Chapter V: The Cabinet

Articles 65–75 describe the cabinet, which consists of the prime minister and ministers of state, all of whom are appointed by the prime minister. All cabinet members have to be civilians (a departure from prewar years, when the cabinet was dominated by the military), and a majority have to be members of the diet. The cabinet has executive power, but the entire cabinet must resign if the House of Representatives passes a no-confidence resolution. The cabinet manages foreign affairs and concludes treaties, as long as the House of Representatives approves the treaties.

◆ Chapter VI: Judiciary

Articles 76–82 delineate the nature of the judiciary, as marked by the removal of the Meiji Constitution statement that the courts operate in the name of the emperor. Article 78 protects judges from being removed except if the public impeaches them or if they prove mentally or physically incompetent. Article 79 provides for the cabinet to appoint all judges except the chief judge and for the House of Representatives to review the judges after they are first appointed and then every ten years. Article 81 makes the Supreme Court responsible for determining the constitutionality of laws, and Article 82 makes trials public.

◆ Chapter VII: Finance

In Articles 83–91, the constitution specifies that the National Diet of Japan authorizes all spending (Article 85), that the cabinet submits the budget (Article 86), and that the property of the imperial family belongs to the state and that the state will support the imperial family (Article 88). It also clearly states in Article 89 that no state support is to be allowed for religious institutions.

◆ Chapter VIII: Local Self-Government

Local self-government is laid out in four brief statements (Articles 92–95). Local governments are given the power to establish laws for organizing and regulating public entities in cities and prefectures of Japan and to autonomously manage their property and affairs. All local officials are to be elected by direct popular vote.

◆ Chapter IX: Amendments

The single article of this chapter makes the Constitution difficult to amend. It requires any amendments to be initiated by two-thirds of the diet and ratified by a majority of the electorate.

◆ Chapter X: Supreme Law

Articles 97–99 underscore the absolute authority of the constitution. It is described as the "supreme law of the nation," disallowing the "validity" of any act or edict contrary to its positions. Moreover, the human rights of the people are declared "inviolate," and all public officials are called on to uphold the constitution.

American soldiers stand guard in a prison van taking Japanese prisoners to trial for war crimes. (AP/Wide World Photos)

◆ **Chapter XI: Supplementary Provisions**

Articles 100–103 speak to the beginning stages of adoption of the new constitution. The articles specify enforcement within six months of promulgation while allowing the House of Councillors to be elected before the six-month period is over. Article 101 specifies that the House of Representatives will initially function as the diet if the House of Councillors has not yet been elected. Article 102 sets the three-year first term of office for the House of Councillors, and Article 103 protects officials in power at the time of promulgation of the constitution as long as the positions are recognized under the new constitution. However, existing officials in power may be replaced when successors are elected or appointed.

Audience

The 1947 Constitution of Japan was primarily addressed to the Japanese people. Not surprisingly—given the civilian

and military losses of the war—they accepted it from the beginning. In September 1951, fifty-one nations met in San Francisco to make a peace accord with Japan. After Japan's becoming an international outlaw in league with Adolf Hitler's Germany and Benito Mussolini's Italy under the Tripartite Pact as of September 1940, the global audience's viewing of this peaceful constitution was important to the acceptance of Japan as a respected citizen of the world once more. The American audience was particularly important, since after fighting Japan as an enemy through World War II, the United States became its occupying power; Japan's adoption of a peaceful constitution gave the Americans the desired guarantee that it would not pursue war ever again.

Impact

In 1952, when Japan had provided for the peaceful and responsible government specified in the 1945 Potsdam Declaration, jointly issued by the U.S., British, and

"We, the Japanese people, acting through our duly elected representatives in the National Diet, determined that we shall secure for ourselves and our posterity the fruits of peaceful cooperation with all nations and the blessings of liberty throughout this land, and resolved that never again shall we be visited with the horrors of war through the action of government, do proclaim that sovereign power resides with the people and do firmly establish this Constitution."

(Preface)

"The Emperor shall be the symbol of the State and of the unity of the people, deriving his position from the will of the people with whom resides sovereign power."

(Article 1)

"Aspiring sincerely to an international peace based on justice and order, the Japanese people forever renounce war as a sovereign right of the nation and the threat or use of force as a means of settling international disputes."

(Article 9)

Chinese leaders, the United States ended its occupation. The 1947 constitution was the first step in achieving this goal; and the fact that the document had not been amended as of early 2010 certainly speaks to its sustained relevancy and impact. Immediately following the end of the American occupation, there was a move by conservatives and nationalists to revise the constitution to make it more Japanese and less foreign and American. However, amendment is very difficult, with the requirement for the assent of two-thirds of the members of both houses of the diet, followed by a referendum to the people, as specified by Article 96. In the 1990s, when voices of the right in Japan became more fashionable, there were more calls to amend the constitution, particularly Article 9, the renunciation of war and the limiting of a military to self-defense forces. Some historians believe that the difficulty of amending the constitution has been the primary reason it has not been amended, but others believe that the Japanese have shown in public opinion polls that they do not want amendments.

The issue of Article 9 came before the Japanese Supreme Court in 1952, when the court ruled that judicial review was limited to concrete cases, as the American

Supreme Court works, rather than permitting determination of the constitutionality of prospective events. Another legal challenge to Article 9 came in 1959, when the Supreme Court deferred further challenges to the cabinet and legislature while ruling that American forces stationed in Japan did not violate Article 9. In 1982 the Supreme Court declined to rule on the constitutionality of Japan's military forces, the Japan Self-Defense Forces, under Article 9. That article has remained problematical for Japan when it has wanted to or has been pressured by the United States to participate in UN peacekeeping operations. Between 1989 and 1991, following the collapse of the Soviet Union, the Persian Gulf War brought various debates about the peace clause, the most since the 1950s. Those who sought to revise Article 9 wanted the Japan Self-Defense Forces to participate in collective-security actions; various Japanese leaders questioned whether Japan would otherwise be able to meet its international responsibilities under the UN Charter. Japan contributed approximately $1 billion at the beginning of the Persian Gulf War and eventually gave $13 billion to the coalition fighting there. Japanese leaders did not feel authorized, under Article 9, to send combat troops and so compromised by sending logistical and humanitarian support, staff to monitor elections, and aid to civilian administration. Japan refused to monitor cease-fires, disarm combatants, or patrol buffer zones. In September 1992, several hundred Japanese personnel, primarily engineers, joined the UN peacekeeping effort in Cambodia. Although some Japanese leaders, including the successive prime ministers Junichiro Koizumi and Shinzo Abe, have publically advocated amending Article 9, nationwide polls in 1991 and 1994 showed very little public support for such revision.

The Japan Self-Defense Forces originated in 1950 with the outbreak of the Korean War and General MacArthur's belief that Japan needed protection as the United States withdrew so many U.S. troops to fight in Korea. Founded as the National Police Reserve, the body was renamed the Japan Self-Defense Forces in 1954, and its members are technically civilians. During the 1980s, increases in government appropriations for the Self-Defense Forces averaged over 5 percent per year, and by 1990 Japan had the world's third-largest military, in terms of defense expenditures, behind only the United States and Russia.

There remains a division of political opinion about armed forces in Japan, with more conservative citizens and politicians desiring a full-fledged twenty-first-century military that participates in UN peacekeeping forces and U.S. military actions around the world, while more liberal and pacifist citizens and politicians desire at the most the limited nonaggressive forces allowed by Article 9. A flashpoint of controversy between the right-wing politicians and citizens and other Japanese politicians and citizens has been the Yasukuni Shrine in Tokyo. In 1978 the Shinto priests at Yasukuni secretly enshrined the fourteen class-A war criminals who had been executed following the Tokyo war-crimes trials. The successive emperors and prime ministers had before felt comfortable officially visiting Yasukuni Shrine; after 1987, the emperors declined any official state visits, as did all prime ministers with the exception of Prime Minister Koizumi, who officially, with great press fanfare, visited the shrine six times. These actions pleased the conservative Japanese factions while greatly angering Chinese and South Korean citizens.

In May 2007 the Japanese National Diet passed legislation to allow for a national referendum in 2010 to revise the constitution and amend Article 9. Two-thirds of diet members would need to initiate this referendum, and a majority of voters would need to approve it. As North Korea has continued to engage in saber rattling and the launching of missiles that could imperil Japan, the Japanese government has considered whether a preemptive strike option would fall under the nation's self-defense rights under its constitution.

Questions for Further Study

1. Compare the Japanese Constitution of 1947 with the Meiji Constitution of 1889. How do the two documents differ? Despite their differences, how does each reflect the cultural history of Japan?

2. Typically, most nations would resist having a constitution imposed on them by a victorious adversary in war. The Japanese, however, have accepted the constitution to the point of never even amending it. Why were the Japanese willing to accept a constitution written by Americans? Why did the Japanese do such an abrupt about-face after their militarism of the 1920s through World War II?

3. If in fact the Japanese constitution is among the most liberal constitutions in the world, what provisions make it so?

4. The Japanese Constitution of 1947 renounces war and the maintenance of war-making capacity. However, in the intervening decades, Japan has faced potential threats (notably from Communist North Korea) and, as an American ally, has come under pressure to support U.S. war efforts in Afghanistan and Iraq. Further, Japan could be called on to provide troops for UN peacekeeping missions. Do you believe that any nation, including Japan, should constitutionally forfeit the right to maintain a military to preempt attacks and to defend democratic values?

5. On December 7, Americans pause to remember the Japanese attack on Pearl Harbor in 1941. Similarly, the Japanese pause every year to remember the atomic bombings of Hiroshima and Nagasaki in August 1945. Despite the bitterness of these events, the United States and Japan are close allies and trading partners. Why do you think both sides have been able to put aside so thoroughly the animosity of the war years?

Further Reading

▪ Articles

Amakawa Akira. Review of *The Japanese Constitution: A Documentary History of Its Framing and Adoption*, ed. Ray A. Moore and Donald L. Robinson. *Journal of Japanese Studies* 26, no. 2 (Summer 2000): 526–529.

Satoh, Haruko. "Japan Seeks Its Constitutional Soul." *Far Eastern Economic Review* 168, no. 7 (July 2005): 30–35.

▪ Books

Bix, Herbert P. *Hirohito and the Making of Modern Japan*. New York: HarperCollins Publishers, 2000.

Dower, John W. *War without Mercy: Race and Power in the Pacific War*. New York: Pantheon Books, 1986.

———. *Embracing Defeat: Japan in the Wake of World War II*. New York: W. W. Norton, 1999.

Gordon, Andrew, ed. *Postwar Japan as History*. Berkeley: University of California Press, 1993.

Henderson, Dan Fenno, ed. *The Constitution of Japan: Its First Twenty Years, 1947–67*. Seattle: University of Washington Press, 1968.

Higuchi, Yoichi. *Five Decades of Constitutionalism in Japanese Society*. Tokyo: University of Tokyo Press, 2001.

Inoue, Kyoko. *MacArthur's Japanese Constitution: A Linguistic and Cultural Study of Its Making*. Chicago: University of Chicago Press, 1991.

McClain, James L. *Japan: A Modern History*. New York: W. W. Norton, 2002.

Moore, Ray A., and Donald L. Robinson. *Partners for Democracy: Crafting the New Japanese State under MacArthur*. Oxford, U.K.: Oxford University Press, 2002.

▪ Web Sites

Kawasaki, Akira. "Article 9's Global Impact." Foreign Policy in Focus Web site.
    http://www.fpif.org/fpiftxt/4426.

Martin, Craig. "The Case against 'Revising Interpretations' of the Japanese Constitution." Asia-Pacific Journal: Japan Focus Web site.
    http://www.japanfocus.org/-Craig-Martin/2434.

"The Postwar Constitution." Japan: Country Studies Web site.
    http://countrystudies.us/japan/110.htm.

"Potsdam Declaration." Birth of the Constitution of Japan Web site.
    http://www.ndl.go.jp/constitution/e/etc/c06.html.

—Carole Schroeder

JAPANESE CONSTITUTION

We, the Japanese people, acting through our duly elected representatives in the National Diet, determined that we shall secure for ourselves and our posterity the fruits of peaceful cooperation with all nations and the blessings of liberty throughout this land, and resolved that never again shall we be visited with the horrors of war through the action of government, do proclaim that sovereign power resides with the people and do firmly establish this Constitution. Government is a sacred trust of the people, the authority for which is derived from the people, the powers of which are exercised by the representatives of the people, and the benefits of which are enjoyed by the people. This is a universal principle of mankind upon which this Constitution is founded. We reject and revoke all constitutions, laws, ordinances, and rescripts in conflict herewith.

We, the Japanese people, desire peace for all time and are deeply conscious of the high ideals controlling human relationships, and we have determined to preserve our security and existence, trusting in the justice and faith of the peace-loving peoples of the world. We desire to occupy an honored place in an international society striving for the preservation of peace, and the banishment of tyranny and slavery, oppression and intolerance for all time from the earth. We recognize that all peoples of the world have the right to live in peace, free from fear and want.

We believe that no nation is responsible to itself alone, but that laws of political morality are universal; and that obedience to such laws is incumbent upon all nations who would sustain their own sovereignty and justify their sovereign relationship with other nations.

We, the Japanese people, pledge our national honor to accomplish these high ideals and purposes with all our resources.

Chapter I: The Emperor

Article 1. The Emperor shall be the symbol of the State and of the unity of the people, deriving his position from the will of the people with whom resides sovereign power.

Article 2. The Imperial Throne shall be dynastic and succeeded to in accordance with the Imperial House law passed by the Diet.

Article 3. The advice and approval of the Cabinet shall be required for all acts of the Emperor in matters of state, and the Cabinet shall be responsible therefor.

Article 4. The Emperor shall perform only such acts in matters of state as are provided for in this Constitution and he shall not have powers related to government

(2) The Emperor may delegate the performance of his acts in matters of state as may be provided by law.

Article 5. When, in accordance with the Imperial House law, a Regency is established, the Regent shall perform his acts in matter of state in the Emperor's name. In this case, paragraph one of the article will be applicable.

Article 6. The Emperor shall appoint the Prime Minister as designated by the Diet.

(2) The Emperor shall appoint the Chief Judge of the Supreme Court as designated by the Cabinet.

Article 7. The Emperor, with the advice and approval of the Cabinet, shall perform the following acts in makers of state on behalf of the people:

(i) Promulgation of amendments of the constitution, laws, cabinet orders and treaties;

(ii) Convocation of the Diet;

(iii) Dissolution of the House of Representatives;

(iv) Proclamation of general election of members of the Diet;

(v) Attestation of the appointment and dismissal of Ministers of State and other officials as provided for by law, and of full powers and credentials of Ambassadors and Ministers;

(vi) Attestation of general and special amnesty, commutation of punishment, reprieve, and restoration of rights;

(vii) Awarding of honors;

(viii) Attestation of instruments of ratification and other diplomatic documents as provided for by law;

(ix) Receiving foreign ambassadors and ministers;

(x) Performance of ceremonial functions.

Article 8. No property can be given to, or received by, the Imperial House, nor can any gifts be made therefrom, without the authorization of the Diet.

Chapter II: Renunciation of War

Article 9. Aspiring sincerely to an international peace based on justice and order, the Japanese people forever renounce war as a sovereign right of the nation and the threat or use of force as a means of settling international disputes.

(2) In order to accomplish the aim of the preceding paragraph, land, sea, and air forces, as well as other war potential, will never be maintained. The right of belligerency of the state will not be recognized.

Chapter III: Rights and Duties of the People

Article 10. The conditions necessary for being a Japanese national shall be determined by law.

Article 11. The people shall not be prevented from enjoying any of the fundamental human rights. These fundamental human rights guaranteed to the people by this Constitution shall be conferred upon the people of this and future generations as eternal and inviolate rights.

Article 12. The freedoms and rights guaranteed to the people by this Constitution shall be maintained by the constant endeavor of the people, who shall refrain from any abuse of these freedoms and rights and shall always be responsible for utilizing them for the public welfare.

Article 13. All of the people shall be respected as individuals. Their right to life, liberty, and the pursuit of happiness shall, to the extent that it does not interfere with the public welfare, be the supreme consideration in legislation and in other governmental affairs.

Article 14. All of the people are equal under the law and there shall be no discrimination in political, economic or social relations because of race, creed, sex, social status or family origin.

(2) Peers and peerage shall not be recognized.

(3) No privilege shall accompany any award of honor, decoration or any distinction, nor shall any such award be valid beyond the lifetime of the individual who now holds or hereafter may receive it.

Article 15. The people have the inalienable right to choose their public officials and to dismiss them.

(2) All public officials are servants of the whole community and not of any group thereof.

(3) Universal adult suffrage is guaranteed with regard to the election of public officials.

(4) In all elections, secrecy of the ballot shall not be violated. A voter shall not be answerable, publicly or privately, for the choice he has made.

Article 16. Every person shall have the right of peaceful petition for the redress of damage, for the removal of public officials, for the enactment, repeal or amendment of law, ordinances or regulations and for other matters, nor shall any person be in any way discriminated against sponsoring such a petition.

Article 17. Every person may sue for redress as provided by law from the State or a public entity, in case he has suffered damage through illegal act of any public official.

Article 18. No person shall be held in bondage of any kind. Involuntary servitude, except as punishment for crime, is prohibited.

Article 19. Freedom of thought and conscience shall not be violated.

Article 20. Freedom of religion is guaranteed to all. No religious organization shall receive any privileges from the State nor exercise any political authority.

(2) No person shall be compelled to take part in any religious acts, celebration, rite or practice.

(3) The state and its organs shall refrain from religious education or any other religious activity.

Article 21. Freedom of assembly and association as well as speech, press and all other forms of expression are guaranteed.

(2) No censorship shall be maintained, nor shall the secrecy of any means of communication be violated.

Article 22. Every person shall have freedom to choose and change his residence and to choose his occupation to the extent that it does not interfere with the public welfare.

(2) Freedom of all persons to move to a foreign country and to divest themselves of their nationality shall be inviolate.

Article 23. Academic freedom is guaranteed.

Article 24. Marriage shall be based only on the mutual consent of both sexes and it shall be maintained through mutual cooperation with the equal rights of husband and wife as a basis.

(2) With regard to choice of spouse, property rights, inheritance, choice of domicile, divorce and other matters pertaining to marriage and the family, laws shall be enacted from the standpoint of individual dignity and the essential equality of the sexes.

Article 25. All people shall have the right to maintain the minimum standards of wholesome and cultured living.

(2) In all spheres of life, the State shall use its endeavors for the promotion and extension of social welfare and security, and of public health.

Article 26. All people shall have the right to receive an equal education correspondent to their ability, as provided by law.

(2) All people shall be obligated to have all boys and girls under their protection receive ordinary educations as provided for by law. Such compulsory education shall be free.

Article 27. All people shall have the right and the obligation to work.

(2) Standards for wages, hours, rest and other working conditions shall be fixed by law.

(3) Children shall not be exploited.

Article 28. The right of workers to organize and to bargain and act collectively is guaranteed.

Article 29. The right to own or to hold property is inviolable.

(2) Property rights shall be defined by law, in conformity with the public welfare.

(3) Private property may be taken for public use upon just compensation therefor.

Article 30. The people shall be liable to taxations as provided by law.

Article 31. No person shall be deprived of life or liberty, nor shall any other criminal penalty be imposed, except according to procedure established by law.

Article 32. No person shall be denied the right of access to the courts.

Article 33. No person shall be apprehended except upon warrant issued by a competent judicial officer which specifies the offense with which the person is charged, unless he is apprehended, the offense being committed.

Article 34. No person shall be arrested or detained without being at once informed of the charges against him or without the immediate privilege of counsel; nor shall he be detained without adequate cause; and upon demand of any person such cause must be immediately shown in open court in his presence and the presence of his counsel.

Article 35. The right of all persons to be secure in their homes, papers and effects against entries, searches and seizures shall not be impaired except upon warrant issued for adequate cause and particularly describing the place to be searched and things to be seized, or except as provided by Article 33.

(2) Each search or seizure shall be made upon separate warrant Issued by a competent judicial officer.

Article 36. The infliction of torture by any public officer and cruel punishments are absolutely forbidden.

Article 39. In all criminal cases the accused shall enjoy the right to a speedy and public trial by an impartial tribunal.

(2) He shall be permitted full opportunity to examine all witnesses, and he shall have the right of compulsory process for obtaining witnesses on his behalf at public expense.

(3) At all times the accused shall have the assistance of competent counsel who shall, if the accused is unable to secure the same by his own efforts, be assigned to his use by the State.

Article 38. No person shall be compelled to testify against himself.

(2) Confession made under compulsion, torture or threat, or after prolonged arrest or detention shall not be admitted in evidence.

(3) No person shall be convicted or punished in cases where the only proof against him is his own confession

Article 39. No person shall be held criminally liable for an act which was lawful at the time it was committed, or of which he has been acquitted, nor shall he be placed in double jeopardy.

Article 40. Any person, in case he is acquitted after he has been arrested or detained, may sue the State for redress as provided by law.

Chapter IV: The Diet

Article 41. The Diet shall be the highest organ of state power, and shall be the sole law-making organ of the State.

Article 42. The Diet shall consist of two Houses, namely the House of Representatives and the House of Councillors.

Article 43. Both Houses shall consist of elected members, representative of all the people.

(2) The number of the members of each House shall be fixed by law.

Article 44. The qualifications of members of both Houses and their electors shall be fixed by law. However, there shall be no discrimination because of race, creed, sex, social status, family origin, education, property or income.

Article 45. The term of office of members of the House of Representatives shall be four years. However, the term shall be terminated before the full term is up in case the House of Representatives is dissolved.

Article 46. The term of office of members of House of Councillors shall be six years, and election for half the members shall take place every three years.

Article 47. Electoral districts, method of voting and other matters pertaining to the method of election of members of both Houses shall be fixed by law.

Article 48. No person shall be permitted to be a member of both Houses simultaneously.

Article 49. Members of both Houses shall receive appropriate annual payment from the national treasury in accordance with law.

Article 50. Except in cases provided by law, members of both Houses shall be exempt from apprehension while the Diet is in session, and any members apprehended before the opening of the session shall be freed during the term of the session upon demand of the House.

Article 51. Members of both Houses shall not be held liable outside the House for speeches, debates or votes cast inside the House.

Article 52. An ordinary session of the Diet shall be convoked once per year.

Article 53. The Cabinet may determine to convoke extraordinary sessions of the Diet. When a quarter or more of the total members of either house makes the demand, the Cabinet must determine on such convocation.

Article 54. When the House of Representatives is dissolved, there must be a general election of members of the House of Representatives within forty (40) days from the date of dissolution, and the Diet must be convoked within thirty (30) days from the date of the election.

(2) When the House of Representatives is dissolved, the House of Councillors is closed at the same time. However, the Cabinet may in time of national emergency convoke the House of Councillors in emergency session.

(3) Measures taken at such session as mentioned in the proviso of the preceding paragraph shall be provisional and shall become null and void unless agreed to by the House of Representatives within a period of ten (10) days after the opening of the next session of the Diet.

Article 55. Each House shall judge disputes related to qualifications of its members. However, in order to deny a seat to any member, it is necessary to pass a resolution by a majority of two-thirds or more of the members present.

Article 56. Business cannot be transacted in either House unless one third or more of total membership is present.

(2) All matters shall be decided, in each House, by a majority of those present, except as elsewhere provided in the Constitution, and in case of a tie, the presiding officer shall decide the issue.

Article 57. Deliberation in each House shall be public. However, a secret meeting may be held where a majority of two-thirds or more of those members present passes a resolution therefor.

(2) Each House shall keep a record of proceedings. This record shall be published and given general circulation, excepting such parts of proceedings of secret session as may be deemed to require secrecy.

(3) Upon demand of one-fifth or more of the members present, votes of the members on any matter shall be recorded in the minutes.

Article 58. Each house shall select its own president and other officials.

(2) Each House shall establish its rules pertaining to meetings, proceedings and internal discipline, and may punish members for disorderly conduct. However, in order to expel a member, a majority of two-thirds or more of those members present must pass a resolution thereon.

Article 59. A bill becomes a law on passage by both Houses, except as otherwise provided by the Constitution.

(2) A bill which is passed by the House of Representatives, and upon which the House of Councillors makes a decision different from that of the House of Representatives, becomes a law when passed a second time by the House of Representatives by a majority of two-thirds or more of the members present.

(3) The provision of the preceding paragraph does not preclude the House of Representatives from calling for the meeting of a joint committee of both Houses, provided for by law.

(4) Failure by the House of Councillors to take final action within sixty (60) days after receipt of a bill passed by the House of Representatives, time in recess excepted, may be determined by the House of Representatives to constitute a rejection of the said bill by the House of Councillors.

Article 60. The Budget must first be submitted to the House of Representatives.

(2) Upon consideration of the budget, when the House of Councillors makes a decision different from that of the House of Representatives, and when no agreement can be reached even through a joint committee of both Houses, provided for by law, or in the case of failure by the House of Councillors to take final action within thirty (30) days, the period of recess excluded, after the receipt of the budget passed by the House of Representatives, the decision of the House of Representatives shall be the decision of the Diet.

Article 61. The second paragraph of the preceding article applies also to the Diet approval required for the conclusion of treaties.

Article 62. Each House may conduct investigations in relation to government, and may demand the presence and testimony of witnesses, and the production of records.

Article 63. The Prime Minister and other Ministers of State may, at any time, appear in either House for the purpose of speaking on bills, regardless of whether they are members of the House or not. They must appear when their presence is required in order to give answers or explanations.

Article 64. The Diet shall set up an impeachment court from among the members of both Houses for the purpose of trying judges against whom removal proceedings have been instituted.

(2) Matters relating to impeachment shall be provided by law.

Chapter V: The Cabinet

Article 65. Executive power shall be vested in the Cabinet.

Article 66. The Cabinet shall consist of the Prime Minister, who shall be its head, and other Ministers of State, as provided for by law.

(2) The Prime Minister and other Minister of State must be civilians.

(3) The Cabinet, in the exercise of executive power, shall be collectively responsible to the Diet.

Article 67. The Prime Minister shall be designated from among the members of the Diet by a resolution of the Diet. This designation shall precede all other business.

(2) If the House of Representatives and the House of Councillors disagree and if no agreement can be reached even through a joint committee of both Houses, provided for by law, or the House of Councillors fails to make designation within ten (10) days, exclusive of the period of recess, after the House of Representatives has made designation, the decision of the House of Representatives shall be the decision of the Diet.

Article 68. The Prime Minister shall appoint the Ministers of State. However, a majority of their number must be chosen from among the members of the Diet.

(2) The Prime Minister may remove the Ministers of State as he chooses.

Article 69. If the House of Representatives passes a non-confidence resolution, or rejects a confidence resolution, the Cabinet shall resign en masse, unless the House of Representatives is dissolved within ten (10) days.

Article 70. When there is a vacancy in the post of Prime Minister, or upon the first convocation of the Diet after a general election of members of the House of Representatives, the Cabinet shall resign en masse.

Article 71. In the cases mentioned in the two preceding articles, the Cabinet shall continue its functions until the time when a new Prime Minister is appointed.

Article 72. The Prime Minister, representing the Cabinet, submits bills, reports on general national affairs and foreign relations to the Diet and exercises control and supervision over various administrative branches.

Article 73. The Cabinet, in addition to other general administrative functions, shall perform the following functions:

(i) Administer the law faithfully; conduct affairs of state;

(ii) Manage foreign affairs;

(iii) Conclude treaties. However, it shall obtain prior or, depending on circumstances, subsequent approval of the Diet;

(iv) Administer the civil service, in accordance with standards established by law;

(v) Prepare the budget, and present it to the Diet;

(vi) Enact cabinet orders in order to execute the provisions of this Constitution and of the law. However, it cannot include penal provisions in such cabinet orders unless authorized by such law.

(vii) Decide on general amnesty, special amnesty, commutation of punishment, reprieve, and restoration of rights.

Article 74. All laws and cabinet orders shall be signed by the competent Minister of state and countersigned by the Prime Minister.

Article 75. The Ministers of state, during their tenure of office, shall not be subject to legal action without the consent of the Prime Minister. However, the right to take that action is not impaired hereby.

Chapter VI: Judiciary

Article 76. The whole judicial power is vested in a Supreme Court and in such inferior courts as are established by law.

(2) No extraordinary tribunal shall be established, nor shall any organ or agency of the Executive be given final judicial power.

(3) All judges shall be independent in the exercise of their conscience and shall be bound only by this Constitution and the laws.

Article 77. The Supreme Court is vested with the rule-making power under which it determines the rules of procedure and of practice, and of matters relating to attorneys, the internal discipline of the courts and the administration of judicial affairs.

(2) Public procurators shall be subject to the rule-making power of the Supreme Court.

(3) The Supreme Court may delegate the power to make rules for inferior courts to such courts.

Article 78. Judges shall not be removed except by public impeachment unless judicially declared mentally or physically incompetent to perform official duties. No disciplinary action against judges shall be administered by any executive organ or agency.

Article 79. The Supreme Court shall consist of a Chief Judge and such number of judges as may be determined by law; all such judges excepting the Chief Judge shall be appointed by the Cabinet.

(2) The appointment of the judges of the Supreme Court shall be reviewed by the people at the first general election of members of the House of Representatives following their appointment, and shall be reviewed again at the first general election of members of the House of Representatives after a lapse of ten (10) years, and in the same manner thereafter.

(3) In cases mentioned in the foregoing paragraph, when the majority of the voters favors the dismissal of a judge, he shall be dismissed.

(4) Matters pertaining to review shall be prescribed by law.

(5) The judges of the Supreme Court shall of retired upon the attainment of the age as fixed by law.

(6) All such judges shall receive, at regular stated intervals, adequate compensation which shall not be decreased during their terms of office.

Article 80. The judges of the inferior courts shall be appointed by the Cabinet from a list of persons nominated by the Supreme Court. All such judges shall hold office for a term of ten (10) years with privilege of reappointment, provided that they shall be retired upon the attainment of the age as fixed by law.

(2) The judges of the inferior courts shall receive, at regular stated intervals, adequate compensation which shall not be decreased during their terms of office.

Article 81. The Supreme Court is the court of last resort with power to determine the constitutionality of any law, order, regulation or official act.

Article 82. Trials shall be conducted and judgment declared publicly.

(2) Where a court unanimously determines publicity to be dangerous to public order or morals, a trial may be conducted privately, but trials of political offenses, offenses involving the press or cases wherein the rights of people as guaranteed in Chapter III of this Constitution are in question shall always be conducted publicly.

Chapter VII: Finance

Article 83. The power to administer national finances shall be exercised as the Diet shall determine.

Article 84. No new taxes shall be imposed or existing ones modified except by law or under such conditions as law may prescribe.

Article 85. No money shall be expended, nor shall the State obligate itself, except as authorized by the Diet.

Article 86. Cabinet shall prepare and submit to the Diet for its consideration and decision a budget for each fiscal year.

Article 87. In order to provide for unforeseen deficiencies in the budget, a reserve fund may be authorized by the Diet to be expended upon the responsibility of the Cabinet.

(2) The Cabinet must get subsequent approval of the Diet for all payments from the reserve fund.

Article 88. All property of the Imperial Household shall belong to the State. All expenses of the Imperial Household shall be appropriated by the Diet in the budget.

Article 89. No public money or other property shall be expended or appropriated for the use, benefit or maintenance of any religious institution or association or for any charitable, educational benevolent enterprises not under the control of public authority.

Article 90. Final accounts of the expenditures and revenues of State shall be audited annually by a Board of Audit and submitted by the Cabinet to the Diet, together with the statement of audit, during the fiscal year immediately following the period covered.

(2) The organization and competency of the Board of Audit shall determined by law.

Article 91. At regular intervals and at least annually the Cabinet shall report to the Diet and the people on the state of national finances.

Milestone Documents

Chapter VIII: Local Self-Government

Article 92. Regulations concerning organization and operations of local public entities shall be fixed by law in accordance with the principle of local autonomy.

Article 93. The local public entities shall establish assemblies as their deliberative organs, in accordance with law.

(2) The chief executive officers of all local public entities, the members of their assemblies, and such other local officials as may be determined by law shall be elected by direct popular vote within their several communities.

Article 94. Local entities shall have the right to manage their property, affairs and administration and to enact their own regulations within law.

Article 95. A special law, applicable to one local public entity, cannot be enacted by the Diet without the consent of the majority of the voters of the local public entity concerned, obtained in accordance with law.

Chapter IX: Amendments

Article 96. Amendment to this Constitution shall be initiated by the Diet, through a concurring vote of two-thirds or more of all the members of each House and shall thereupon be submitted to the people for ratification which shall require the affirmative vote of a majority of all votes cast thereon, at special referendum or at such election as the Diet shall specify.

(2) Amendments when so ratified shall immediately be promulgated by the Emperor in the name of the people, as an integral part of this Constitution.

Chapter X: Supreme Law

Article 97. The fundamental human rights by this Constitution guaranteed to the people of Japan are fruits of the age-old struggle of man to be free; they have survived the many exacting tests for durability and are conferred upon this and future generations in trust, to be held for all time inviolate.

Article 98. This Constitution shall be the supreme law of the nation and no law, ordinance, imperial rescript or other act of government, or part thereof, contrary to the provisions hereof, shall have legal force or validity.

(2) The treaties concluded by Japan and established laws of nations shall be faithfully observed.

Article 99. The Emperor or the Regent as well as Ministers of State, members of the Diet, judges, and all other public officials have the obligation to respect and uphold this Constitution.

Chapter XI: Supplementary Provisions

Article 100. This Constitution shall be enforced as from the day when the period of six months will have elapsed counting from the day of its promulgation.

(2) The enactment of laws necessary for the enforcement of this Constitution, the election of members of the House of Councillors, and the procedure for the convocation of the Diet and other preparatory procedures for the enforcement of this Constitution may be executed before the day prescribed in the preceding paragraph.

Article 101. If the House of Councilors is not constituted before the effective date of this Constitution, the House of Representatives shall function as the Diet until such time as the House of Councilors shall be constituted.

Article 102. The term of office for half the members of the House of Councillors serving in the first term under this Constitution shall be three years. Members falling under this category shall be determined in accordance with law.

Article 103. The Ministers of State, members of the House of Representatives, and judges in office on the effective date of this Constitution, and all other public officials, who occupy positions corresponding to such positions as are recognized by this Constitution shall not forfeit their positions automatically on account of the enforcement of this Constitution unless otherwise specified by law. When, however, successors are elected or appointed under the provisions of this Constitution, they shall forfeit their positions as a matter of course.

Jawaharlal Nehru (AP/Wide World Photos)

"At the stroke of the midnight hour, when the world sleeps, India will awake to life and freedom."

Overview

Jawaharlal Nehru's speech "Tryst with Destiny," delivered to the Constituent Assembly on the eve of Indian independence on August 14, 1947, and the address "The Appointed Day," given to the nation the next day, together constitute a visionary statement regarding the future of India and the Indian Subcontinent. These speeches on freedom derive their fundamental justification from the principle of swaraj, or self-rule. They mark the end of British rule in India, which began in the mid-eighteenth century and ended with independence. "Tryst with Destiny" includes a pledge to be taken by all members of the Constituent Assembly of dedication "to the service of India and her people," but the speech's main body outlines certain principles that were integral to the freedom struggle in India as well as hope for the continued functioning of the best of these principles in an independent India.

Context

India came under British rule after the failure of the Indian Rebellion of 1857 (also known as the Sepoy Mutiny), in which diverse princely states of the Indian Subcontinent united to resist British occupation (mainly through the British East India Company) of Indian territory. Power transferred to the British Crown soon thereafter, in November 1859, and Queen Victoria was crowned empress of India in the Delhi Durbar of 1877.

The foundation of the Indian National Congress (INC) in 1885 was the first step in organized political resistance to British rule in India. Although the INC was initially formed by groups seeking reform within the framework of British governance, those groups were gradually estranged by a series of repressive acts and policies that ran counter to the welfare of the citizens. The watershed moment was the partition of Bengal in 1905 into the East (Muslim dominated) and the West (Hindu dominated), ostensibly for administrative purposes but in reality an extension of the British policy of "divide and rule." Although the partition

was revoked in 1911 after it caused widespread discontent and resistance, it had engendered three major strands in the national struggle. First, the revolutionary *swadeshi* ("own country") movement, with military and ideological dimensions, provided a framework for different revolutionary movements as well as a phenomenon identifiable as Hindu nationalism (including nation worship in the form of a goddess), which furthered a rift between Hindus and Muslims in the country. Second, the foundation of the Muslim League in 1906 in support of the partition and the interests of the Muslim community in India established the success of the divide-and-rule policy by centering communalism as a key theme of the national struggle. Third, the immediate outcome of the partition was the INC's adoption of swaraj ("self-rule") as a goal.

The subsequent history of the national struggle may be seen as developments of these three strands. The revolutionary movement, which adopted violence and counterterrorism (as opposed to the state-sponsored terrorism that was dominant in the colonial hierarchy) as a means of procuring freedom, spawned several incidents of skirmish and resistance. Armed military movements, such as Jugantar and Anushilan Samiti, in the two sides of the partitioned Bengal, led by the ideologies of Bipin Chandra Pal and Sri Aurobindo Ghose, asked people to avenge the violence inflicted on their motherland. Other significant events in the revolutionary protest that left a deep impression on the public mind included the Ashe murder case (1911), in which the district magistrate (Robert W. D. E. Ashe) of Tinnevelly (Tirunelveli), Pondicherry, was killed as part of a political conspiracy; the Buribalam incident, in which an Indian revolutionary leader fought against the British police force and was martyred (1915); the Rampa Rebellion, which was a tribal uprising against British occupation (1922); the Delhi Central Assembly Hall bombings by Indian revolutionaries (1929); the Chittagong armory raid, in which revolutionary youth seized arms and ammunition (1930); and the Azad park shootout between police and the revolutionary Chandrashekar Azad (1931).

The activities of the revolutionaries provided both sentimental value to the freedom movement and iconic value to the struggle, and revolutionary heroes assumed demigod status in the imagination of the masses. Moreover, the

1877

■ **January 1**
Queen Victoria, the British monarch, is crowned empress of India.

1885

■ **December 28**
The Indian National Congress (INC) is founded.

1905

■ **October 16**
Bengal is partitioned into East Bengal (Muslim dominated) and West Bengal (Hindu dominated).

1906

■ **December 26–29**
The INC session in Calcutta adopts swaraj, or self-rule, as its goal.

■ **December 30**
The Muslim League is established to protect and advance the political interests of Muslims in India.

1929

■ **December 29–31**
During the INC session at Lahore, under the leadership of President Jawaharlal Nehru, the INC declares complete independence as its goal.

1940

■ **March 22**
The Muslim League holds a session at Lahore; on the following day the league passes a resolution for separate sovereign states for Muslims.

---

repression that was brought to bear upon the revolutionaries and Indians in order to counter militancy further spawned mass discontent. One of the more famous instances of repression, the Jallianwala Bagh massacre (1919), in which a British general massacred 379 unarmed men, women, and children who had gathered in a park in Amritsar for a peaceful protest, led to widespread and international condemnation. In a symbolic gesture of protest, the Nobel laureate and poet of the masses Rabindranath Tagore rejected the knighthood conferred upon him by the British monarch. The revolutionary movement also revealed a rift between the moderates (led by Gopal Krishna Gokhale in the initial stages) and the extremists (led by such leaders as Bal Gangadhar Tilak and, later, Subhas Chandra Bose) within the INC. The moderates were more inclined toward a freedom struggle based on political negotiation, while the extremists wanted noninterference from the British in matters of Indian culture and religion and espoused the idea of armed revolutionary struggle. The revolutionary dimension of the freedom struggle is one of the major issues in the two speeches by Nehru.

The Muslim League, which negotiated between the British government and a section of the Muslim community in India, supported the partition and condemned INC support for the *swadeshi* movement. The revocation of the partition was viewed by the league as a betrayal of trust, and the fortunes of the league dwindled. It was revived from this state by Mohammed Ali Jinnah. Initially a member of the INC and a supporter of Hindu-Muslim unity, Jinnah later came to adopt the two-nation theory, namely that a separate nation for Muslims was necessary for the protection of Muslim interests, as Muslims were a minority in India. In the Lahore Resolution (1940), the Muslim League resolved to demand autonomy within territories with a Muslim majority, namely, the northwestern territories (the future West Pakistan) and the eastern territories (the future East Pakistan), an idea that led to the formation of the independent nation of Pakistan in 1947.

The INC found its most powerful leader in Mohandas Karamchand Gandhi. Gandhi, who first came to prominence in South Africa with his method of nonviolent resistance inspired by the Transcendentalist writer Henry David Thoreau's theory of civil disobedience, termed *satyagraha* ("the appeal or force of truth"), returned to India in 1915 and found the time ready for a mass civil resistance–based freedom struggle. Gandhi started his first *satyagraha* campaign at Champaran in 1917. (*Satyagraha* refers to Gandhi's philosophy and practice of nonviolent resistance, which he deployed in a variety of ways meant to pressure the British to grant Indian independence.) From the 1920s the INC increasingly relied upon civil disobedience as a means of struggle—one of the reasons for its splintering. Both Bose and Jinnah had been members of the INC before their differences of opinion with the Gandhian mode of passive resistance. The crisis came to a head with the start of World War II. The initial victories of the Axis powers were condemned by the INC, which opposed illegal occupation of foreign territory. Thus the INC's support for

---

the Allies was explicit, though guarded. The leaders of the INC felt that the Allies were in the right, although the Allies were themselves invaders of Indian territory. The INC refused to support the Allied war effort without an assurance of Indian independence. Sir Stafford Cripps, a senior British politician and government minister in the war cabinet, was sent to India in March of 1942 to secure India's cooperation in the war. India was promised dominion status by the British after the war, which was intended as a compromise, but this plan was rejected by the INC on the ground that it did not promise complete independence. In the same year, on August 8, the All India Congress Working Committee passed the Quit India Resolution, which resulted in swift retaliation by the British government. All of the major leaders of the INC were arrested the next day and imprisoned.

At the same time, the war also afforded militant nationalists the opportunity to develop an organized army wing. This wing was led by Subhas Chandra Bose. Bose had resigned the presidency of the INC over differences of opinion with Gandhi and left to form his own party, Forward Bloc, in 1939. Bose saw the war as an opportunity to rid the country of the British, and for this purpose he took the support of the Axis powers. He left for Germany in 1941 and in 1943 assumed the leadership of the Indian independence movement from Rash Behari Bose in Tokyo. Thereafter he organized the Indian National Army and started a march toward India to fight the British. However, the movement collapsed in May 1945 as the Axis powers lost the war. Bose himself died under mysterious circumstances in a plane crash on August 18, 1945.

The war had brought about all but the complete collapse of British rule in India. The deteriorating economy of Great Britain, the mounting communal tension within India, the loss of military resources in the East at the end of the war, and the hardships faced by Indians that had given rise to a militant desperation all contributed to the swift collapse of the British raj after the war. In 1945 the Labour Party claimed victory in Great Britain. Their focus was on reform of the economic depression, unemployment, and other internal social ills. At the same time, they lacked a definite program on how to deal with the colonies. Thus, their victory further accelerated the process of Indian independence. The Cabinet Mission Plan was announced on June 16, 1946, granting complete independence to India while accommodating Muslim demands for regional autonomy. On this basis, a constituent assembly was convened to draw up a constitution, and in the meantime the viceroy formed an interim government.

On September 2, 1946, the interim government of Nehru was sworn in. However, differences of opinion between the INC and the Muslim League led to nationwide communal violence, which the British failed to control. Lord Louis Mountbatten, who assumed the position of viceroy of India on March 24, 1947, announced a quick plan for British withdrawal from the Indian Subcontinent in August as well as a plan to partition the subcontinent into India and Pakistan. The partition of India plan, known

Time Line

1942

- **March 12–23**
  The Cripps Mission to India promises India dominion status after World War II.

- **August 8**
  The Quit India Resolution is passed by the All India Congress Working Committee in Bombay.

1944

- **March 19**
  The Indian National Army of Subhas Chandra Bose crosses over to Indian territory and hoists the national flag on Indian soil.

1946

- **June 16**
  The Cabinet Mission statement announces a plan for the British to leave India once suitable institutions for government are put in place; in the meantime, the viceroy was to form an interim government.

1947

- **March 24**
  Lord Louis Mountbatten takes over as viceroy of India.

- **June 3**
  Mountbatten announces a plan for partition of the Indian Subcontinent into India and Pakistan and for the British withdrawal in August.

- **August 14**
  Pakistan comes into being. Nehru delivers his "Tryst with Destiny" speech.

- **August 15**
  India wins independence. Nehru delivers his "Appointed Day" speech to the press.

as the Radcliffe Plan, orchestrated a territorial division on communal lines and also necessitated a movement of Hindus and Muslims across borders. One of the largest mass migrations in recent history, it was a source of unbridled suffering as people were uprooted from their ancestral lands and moved to a new territory as the result of political exigency. On August 14, 1947, Pakistan emerged as a free state, and on August 15, 1947, India won independence.

About the Author

The author of the two speeches was Pandit Jawaharlal Nehru, born in 1889 into a wealthy and prominent political family. Nehru received a predominantly Western education: He went to Harrow School in London and, at age sixteen, graduated from Trinity College, Cambridge. Thereafter, he studied law at the Inner Temple in London. Nehru returned to India in 1912 and soon joined the political fray. The Jallianwala Bagh incident drove Nehru to hard-line politics within the INC. He participated in several struggles and movements for independence, including the Salt March to Dandi on March 12, 1930—the first act of organized opposition to British rule after the INC's declaration of independence. He was first elected as INC president in 1931 and served as president four times prior to independence. In 1937, during his third term as president, Nehru made a tactical mistake in estranging the Muslim League by articulating his belief that the policies of the INC alone reflected the needs of Indians and by adopting the Gandhian noncooperation policy as a solution for Indian independence. In January 1942, Gandhi publicly declared Nehru as his successor, and in August, Nehru moved the famous Quit India Resolution. Soon after, Nehru and the other leaders of the INC were imprisoned for participating in anti–Cripps Mission agitation and for passing the Quit India Resolution. After his release from jail in 1945, he was elected president of the INC for the fourth time and was invited by the Cabinet Mission to form the interim government. Nehru became the first prime minister of India following independence on August 15, 1947.

Explanation and Analysis of the Document

On August 14, 1947, on the eve of Indian independence from British rule, as the first prime minister of India, Nehru delivered a speech titled "Tryst with Destiny" to the Constituent Assembly in the Parliament House in New Delhi. In this speech Nehru recollects the struggles and dreams leading up to India's freedom and also outlines a path for India following the attainment of independence. In the subsequent address to the press on August 15, 1947, titled "The Appointed Day," Nehru spoke further to the people of India about the nature and meaning of freedom and the responsibilities that freedom entails. A key element of the two speeches is the vision that Nehru had for the Indian Subcontinent and its role in world affairs. The idea

of destiny that he evokes throughout the speeches is derived from the ideals of the *swadeshi* movement, particularly the notion of a unique Indian destiny to be found in the writings of Sri Aurobindo Ghose. Nehru began as a follower of the extremist faction under Bal Gangadhar Tilak, and although he later grew close to the moderate faction under Gandhi, Nehru attempts to find in this speech a synthesis of the two approaches.

"Tryst with Destiny" includes reminiscences of the freedom struggle as well as a pledge to be taken by all members of the Constituent Assembly to dedicate themselves to the service of the country and to work toward its further glory. "The Appointed Day" expresses similar reminiscences, but its focus is on the fundamental principles that would later be enshrined in the constitution, including secularism, democracy, and sovereignty.

◆ "Tryst with Destiny"

The opening paragraph sets the tone for the rest of the speech, which shifts among three different time lines: the past, which includes the history of the subcontinent and the country from ancient times to the latest freedom struggle; the immediate future as present, which is the moment of Indian independence and the transfer of power to the Indian government at midnight on August 15 as well as its political emergence as a unified nation; and the future, which involves certain commitments on the part of those involved in the freedom struggle and the members of the first government of the free India with a view to the larger interests of the nation and its role in the world. The second paragraph, with its evocation of the long journey of India toward the present, lends coherence to the objectives of the freedom struggle, namely, the ideal of freedom itself and the opportunities afforded by independence. This and the next paragraph also distinguish between political freedom and the circumspect use of that freedom toward better rule of the self (swaraj). As independence in this case involved not a period of anarchy but instead the transfer of power from an imposed government to a representative one, the onus was on the latter to fulfill the needs that gave it birth. Thus the speech introduces a note of caution with the theme of responsibility, even as it celebrates the end of a period of tribulation.

The fourth paragraph brings to view certain realities and problems of the subcontinent: overpopulation, poverty, and caste- and class-based inequalities. A reference to Gandhi is made at this juncture, as Gandhi's role in uniting the different castes and communities had been pivotal during the freedom struggle. There is a subtle shift of tone in referring to Gandhi, underscoring the difference between ideals and the realization of those ideals in pragmatic terms in the context of national development.

The next paragraph speaks of the connected nature of world politics that was increasingly evident during World War II. The war had revealed how national policies led to global ramifications, just as the end of the war and the formation of the United Nations in 1945 had raised hopes of a more permanent peace among the nations. The later emergence of the

An Indian Border Security Force soldier patrols the India-Pakistan border area of Golpattan, near Jammu.
(AP/Wide World Photos)

nonaligned movement, or nonadherence to any power bloc, is evident within the vision of Nehru outlined here.

The final section consists of a call to resolve differences among the different political groups in the independent India in order to achieve the development objectives. The pledge that concludes the speech, to be taken by all members of the Constituent Assembly, is toward this end. The pledge reiterates the idea of a unique destiny for India in world history, of which the moment of independence was a first step.

◆ "The Appointed Day"

"The Appointed Day" is often considered a companion piece to "Tryst with Destiny" because it is similar in tone and style, though it is addressed to a different audience and differs somewhat in content. The speech consists of three main sections. The opening section is a statement on the history and the idea of destiny. The second section invokes the architects of India's freedom as well as the costs it had incurred in the struggle for independence. The third section speaks of the responsibilities attendant on freedom.

Nehru's belief in a Marxist view of history is evident in the opening section. The dialectical model of history, with its ceaseless movement of conflicts and new resolutions and equilibriums, is invoked by Nehru when he speaks of the past as a finished process leading to the present, which in turn consists of new conflicts and struggles: The histor-

ical process in which people live and act is always received and recorded by the future as complete. This view of history is combined with the notion of the present as the necessary outcome of a particular destiny, an idea that is also evident in the earlier speech.

In the second paragraph, Nehru compares the moment of India's independence to the birth of a new star in the East, a metaphor borrowed from the speech of Rabindranath Tagore on nationalism in Japan, delivered in 1916. The inherent contradiction in this metaphor—the comparison of a preexisting nation to the birth of a new star—is resolved if we consider that the geopolitical unification of modern India, from diverse states united by common cultural roots but segregated by diverse political affiliations, happened after independence.

In paragraph 4, Nehru first pays homage to Gandhi, "the Father of our Nation," who embodied the principles of nonviolence and gave currency through his speeches and deeds to some of the cultural values present in the philosophical texts of the Indian tradition, particularly the Bhagavad Gita and the Upanishads. Nehru then speaks of the revolutionaries and soldiers who gave up their lives during the freedom struggle. A particular reference here is to the soldiers of the Indian National Army, formed by Subhas Chandra Bose as the first army of independent India. The much-publicized Indian National Army trials were a major

"*Long years ago we made a tryst with destiny, and now the time comes when we shall redeem our pledge, not wholly or in full measure, but very substantially. At the stroke of the midnight hour, when the world sleeps, India will awake to life and freedom.*"

("Tryst with Destiny," Paragraph 1)

"*And so we have to labour and to work, and work hard, to give reality to our dreams. Those dreams are for India, but they are also for the world, for all the nations and peoples are too closely knit together today for any one of them to imagine that it can live apart.*"

("Tryst with Destiny," Paragraph 5)

"*It is a fateful moment for us in India, for all Asia and for the world. A new star rises, the star of freedom in the East, a new hope comes into being, a vision long cherished materializes. May the star never set and that hope never be betrayed!*"

("The Appointed Day," Paragraph 2)

"*All of us, to whatever religion we may belong, are equally the children of India with equal rights, privileges and obligations. We cannot encourage communalism or narrow-mindedness, for no nation can be great whose people are narrow in thought or in action.*"

("The Appointed Day," Paragraph 8)

catalyst in the demand for freedom in the final stages of the freedom struggle. These trials were the courts-martial for treason of a number of officers who had been part of the British Indian Army and had later joined the Indian National Army and fought alongside the Japanese in Burma. Nehru invokes a recent memory in order to further the unity of the nation.

In the next paragraph, Nehru refers to the partition of India, which entailed the separation of people from the same country by political boundaries that resulted from communal tension. Nehru does not refer to the freedom of Pakistan but only to the fact that Pakistan does not share the freedom of India, in part because of the belief shared by Nehru and Gandhi that the partition was only a temporary process that would eventually be revoked once the commu-

nal tension subsided. It is one of the reasons that Nehru emphasizes secular values in his speech and that until his death refused to let India be declared a Hindu nation.

In the closing paragraphs Nehru outlines the immediate concerns to be addressed by the political parties after independence as well as the ideologies that were to drive the process of nation building. The dimensions of nation building formed an interconnected network of infrastructural development, psychical reorientation, and social emancipation, which allowed individuals to experience the social opportunities derived from freedom and fully express themselves. The speech concludes by stressing the fundamental values of the Indian nation that would eventually be part of the constitution: secularism and democracy. As a nation that had been vivisected by communal tension and seen its independence sacrificed partially on the altar of political convenience, the call of secularism appears as a plea for unity as well as a potent warning to prevent further dismembering. The speech ends with the words "Jai Hind," or "victory to Hind (India)."

Audience

The audience of "Tryst with Destiny" included members of the Constituent Assembly and the interim government. The Constituent Assembly had come into being as part of the Cabinet Mission Plan. The Cabinet Mission Plan was crafted by the Labour Party once Britain had decided to leave Indian soil. The plan conceived of three different group constituencies within India—section A with Madras, Bombay, Uttar Pradesh, Bihar, Orissa, and Central Provinces (Madhya Pradesh); section B with Punjab, the North-West Frontier Province, and Sind; and section C with Bengal and Assam—with one controlling center handling foreign affairs, defense, and communications. This controlling center, the Constituent Assembly, consisted of members elected from the provincial Legislative Assemblies. Most of the general seats had been won by the INC,

and a majority of the Muslim seats had been won by the Muslim League in these elections. The Constituent Assembly formed the interim government before Indian independence, headed by the viceroy. On June 3, 1947, the newly elected viceroy announced the plan for India's independence. The Constituent Assembly in turn became the first parliament of independent India.

"The Appointed Day" was a message to the press on the day of Indian independence, August 15, 1947. This companion speech was addressed to the political leaders of the Constituent Assembly and to the people of India. The message was also intended for the people of Pakistan, East as well as West, the separate nation that had been carved out by the leadership of the Muslim League. The speech served as a vision of unity among the different newly independent nations, and the concluding part of the speech foreshadows the politics of the nonaligned movement, one of the major strategic decisions of Nehru.

Impact

The speeches are largely rhetorical and were intended to satisfy psychical and social more than political needs.

Questions for Further Study

1. A prominent theme of Nehru's speeches is the concept of self-rule. Compare Nehru's conception of Indian self-rule with similar aspirations in other countries. Possible entries to consult include Nelson Mandela's Inaugural Address, the Proclamation of the Algerian National Front, Patrice Lumumba's Speech at the Proclamation of Congolese Independence, or the Proclamation of the Provisional Government of the Irish Republic.

2. A significant number of Milestone Documents have to do with India; among them are the British Regulating Act, Queen's Victoria's Proclamation concerning India, the Government of India Act of 1919, Mahatma Gandhi's Speech to the All India Congress Committee, the Constitution of India, and the Lahore Resolution—as well as Nehru's speeches. Why do you think historians regard the history of India and its relationship with the British Empire as so important? What themes in this history have worldwide resonance? Explain.

3. Jawaharlal Nehru and Mahatma Gandhi are arguably the two most important and well-known figures in modern Indian history. Compare their speeches, consulting the entry Mahatma Gandhi's Speech to the All India Congress Committee. What similar rhetorical devices do they use? How do they appeal to their audiences? Who do you think was the most effective writer?

4. In his speeches about the granting of Indian independence from British rule, Nehru does not mention the British. Why?

5. Nehru gave considerable emphasis to the concept of secularism. In contrast, a figure such as the Ayatollah Khomeini from Iran, in his *Islamic Government: Governance of the Jurist*, argues for government based on the principles of Islam. Which of the two forms of government is likely to be more successful in the modern world? Explain your reasoning.

The immediate intended impact was to stem the tide of communal hatred that had occurred during the last months of British rule and that were a major cause of violence during the process of partition. The speeches thus focus on the principles of secularism and communal harmony that were to be a major feature of the Indian Constitution. They also functioned as a morale boost to a country that had suffered for a century under an oppressive colonial regime. However, Nehru's remarks do not focus so much on the hardships of the freedom struggle. Instead, they outline a history of India and the subcontinent that accommodated hardship as a reality that led to higher cultural growth. Consequently, the speeches do not even once mention the British and the immediate colonial context but speak of Indian tradition and culture as imbued with a unique destiny that spans millennia, of which the immediate past is a fragment. Thus Nehru's addresses have an agenda of cultural decolonization intended to serve the masses as a means to overcome the trauma of colonization and partition. In terms of political impact, the speeches signaled the birth of a new nation and at the same time its intention to reach out to other nations, including Pakistan as well as other newly independent nations.

As a visionary statement, the speeches have stood the test of time. The value of secularism, in particular, has been crucial in shaping Indian identity as a nation. India has managed to remain one of the largest democracies in the world, while the nations carved off its territory have faced persistent problems in maintaining a democratic identity. Nonetheless, some of the intentions expressed by Nehru were unrealized or only partially realized during his stints as prime minister. Nehru's belief in amicable relations with Pakistan soon soured, as two months after independence, in October 1947, Pakistan invaded the princely territory of Jammu and Kashmir, which had a Muslim majority. While Indian armies managed to drive out the invaders when the ruler of the state acceded to India, a small portion of Kashmir remained in the hands of Pakistan, known as Pakistan-Occupied Kashmir, a region that has witnessed many violent conflicts and continues to be a source of militancy movements to this day.

Further Reading

■ Books

Brown, Judith M. *Nehru: A Political Life*. New Haven, Conn.: Yale University Press, 2003.

Chandra, Bipan, et al. *India's Struggle for Independence, 1857–1947*. New York: Penguin Books, 1989.

Madhava, K. G. Vasantha. *History of the Freedom Movement in India (1857–1947)*. New Delhi, India: Navrang, 1995.

Nehru, Jawaharlal. *Jawaharlal Nehru's Speeches*. New Delhi, India: Publications Division, Ministry of Information and Broadcasting, 1983.

Zachariah, Benjamin. *Nehru*. London: Routledge, 2004.

■ Web Sites

"History of the Indian National Congress." All India Congress Committee Web site.
    http://www.aicc.org.in/new/history.php.

—Bodhisattva Chattopadhyay

JAWAHARLAL NEHRU'S SPEECHES ON THE GRANTING OF INDIAN INDEPENDENCE

Tryst with Destiny

Long years ago we made a tryst with destiny, and now the time comes when we shall redeem our pledge, not wholly or in full measure, but very substantially. At the stroke of the midnight hour, when the world sleeps, India will awake to life and freedom. A moment comes, which comes but rarely in history, when we step out from the old to the new, when an age ends, and when the soul of a nation, long suppressed, finds utterance. It is fitting that at this solemn moment we take the pledge of dedication to the service of India and her people and to the still larger cause of humanity.

At the dawn of history India started on her unending quest, and trackless centuries are filled with her striving and the grandeur of her success and her failures. Through good and ill fortune alike she has never lost sight of that quest or forgotten the ideals which gave her strength. We end today a period of ill fortune and India discovers herself again. The achievement we celebrate today is but a step, an opening of opportunity, to the greater triumphs and achievements that await us. Are we brave enough and wise enough to grasp this opportunity and accept the challenge of the future?

Freedom and power bring responsibility. The responsibility rests upon this Assembly, a sovereign body representing the sovereign people of India. Before the birth of freedom we have endured all the pains of labour and our hearts are heavy with the memory of this sorrow. Some of those pains continue even now. Nevertheless, the past is over and it is the future that beckons to us now.

That future is not one of ease or resting but of incessant striving so that we may fulfil the pledges we have so often taken and the one we shall take today. The service of India means the service of the millions who suffer. It means the ending of poverty and ignorance and disease and inequality of opportunity. The ambition of the greatest man of our generation has been to wipe every tear from every eye. That may be beyond us, but as long as there are tears and suffering, so long our work will not be over.

And so we have to labour and to work, and work hard, to give reality to our dreams. Those dreams are for India, but they are also for the world, for all the nations and peoples are too closely knit together today for any one of them to imagine that it can live apart. Peace has been said to be indivisible; so is freedom, so is prosperity now, and so also is disaster in this One World that can no longer be split into isolated fragments.

To the people of India, whose representatives we are, we make an appeal to join us with faith and confidence in this great adventure. This is no time for petty and destructive criticism, no time for ill-will or blaming others. We have to build the noble mansion of free India where all her children may dwell.

I beg to move, Sir,

That it be resolved that:

(1) After the last stroke of midnight, all members of the Constituent Assembly present on this occasion do take the following pledge:

"At this solemn moment when the people of India, through suffering and sacrifice, have secured freedom, I,........., a member of the Constituent Assembly of India, do dedicate myself in all humility to the service of India and her people to the end that this ancient land attain her rightful place in the world and make her full and willing contribution to the promotion of world peace and the welfare of mankind";

(2) Members who are not present on this occasion do take the pledge (with such verbal changes as the President may prescribe) at the time they next attend a session of the Assembly.

The Appointed Day

The appointed day has come—the day appointed by destiny—and India stands forth again, after long slumber and struggle, awake, vital, free and independent. The past clings on to us still in some measure and we have to do much before we redeem the pledges we have so often taken. Yet the turning point is past, and history begins anew for us, the history which we shall live and act and others will write about.

It is a fateful moment for us in India, for all Asia and for the world. A new star rises, the star of freedom in the East, a new hope comes into being, a vision long cherished materializes. May the star never set and that hope never be betrayed!

We rejoice in that freedom, even though clouds surround us, and many of our people are sorrow-stricken and difficult problems encompass us. But freedom brings responsibilities and burdens and we have to face them in the spirit of a free and disciplined people.

On this day our first thoughts go to the architect of this freedom, the Father of our Nation, who, embodying the old spirit of India, held aloft the torch of freedom and lighted up the darkness that surrounded us. We have often been unworthy followers of his and have strayed from his message, but not only we but succeeding generations will remember this message and bear the imprint in their hearts of this great son of India, magnificent in his faith and strength and courage and humility. We shall never allow that torch of freedom to be blown out, however high the wind or stormy the tempest.

Our next thoughts must be of the unknown volunteers and soldiers of freedom who, without praise or reward, have served India even unto death.

We think also of our brothers and sisters who have been cut off from us by political boundaries and who unhappily cannot share at present in the freedom that has come. They are of us and will remain of us whatever may happen, and we shall be sharers in their good [or] ill fortune alike.

The future beckons to us. Whither do we go and what shall be our endeavour? To bring freedom and opportunity to the common man, to the peasants and workers of India; to fight and end poverty and ignorance and disease; to build up a prosperous, democratic and progressive nation, and to create social, economic and political institutions which will ensure justice and fullness of life to every man and woman.

We have hard work ahead. There is no resting for any one of us till we redeem our pledge in full, till we make all the people of India what destiny intended them to be. We are citizens of a great country, on the verge of bold advance, and we have to live up to that high standard. All of us, to whatever religion we may belong, are equally the children of India with equal rights, privileges and obligations. We cannot encourage communalism or narrow-mindedness, for no nation can be great whose people are narrow in thought or in action.

To the nations and peoples of the world we send greetings and pledge ourselves to co-operate with them in furthering peace, freedom and democracy.

And to India, our much-loved motherland, the ancient, the eternal and the ever-new, we pay our reverent homage and we bind ourselves afresh to her service. JAI HIND.

David Ben-Gurion (AP/Wide World Photos)

Declaration of the Establishment of the State of Israel

"The State of Israel will be open to the immigration of Jews from all countries of their dispersion."

Overview

On Friday, May 14, 1948, at four o'clock in the afternoon, David Ben-Gurion, leader of Palestine's Workers Party and head of the Jewish Agency, read a statement declaring the inauguration of an independent Jewish state in Palestine that night, as thirty years of British Mandate over the country came to an end. The declaration had two main aims. The first aim was legal. The declaration was meant to close a possible legal gap, as neither the British Mandate authorities nor the United Nations had designated a specific successor or a complete legal apparatus for transferring power to a new state. The second aim was practical: Knowing that the British departure might encourage neighboring states to invade the borders of the anticipated Jewish state as planned by the UN resolution, Ben-Gurion wanted to establish Israel's legitimacy. And, indeed, the new state soon gained international recognition.

The declaration of independence involved more than a focused transfer of power or a change of regime. Through the first decade of the twenty-first century the constituent and later legislative authorities of Israel have failed to write a constitution. Thus, the declaration of independence has remained the basis for the nation's constitutional and legal operation. Therefore, its significance and impact are not limited to a certain point in time: The declaration is still a vital constituent document for the state of Israel.

Context

At the middle of the nineteenth century, the Hebrew-speaking population of Palestine was almost nonexistent. Hebrew was used during religious sermons, in communicating the teachings of scripture, and for correspondence with Jewish communities around the world. Meanwhile, on the political front, it took decades until modern nationalism, as developed in Europe in the aftermath of the French Revolution and the Napoleonic Wars, reached the eastern provinces of the Ottoman Empire, where Palestine was located.

But two parallel processes that occurred during the second half of the nineteenth century soon changed this situation. The spread of nationalism throughout central and eastern Europe and the formation of independent nation-states there led many Jewish scholars and intellectuals to contemplate the possibility of making a new nation out of the Jewish religious community. The best known among them was Eliezer Ben-Jehuda, who, in an article published in 1879, called for the revival of Hebrew nationhood in Palestine. The second process was the technological innovations that improved transportation and communication between Europe and Palestine.

Three years after Ben-Jehuda published his article, in 1882, a wave of Jewish immigration from Yemen and eastern Europe (Poland, Russia, and Ukraine) to Palestine laid the foundations for a Hebrew-speaking community. Subsequent waves of immigration followed, encouraged by the emergence of European Zionism and the founding of the World Zionist Organization as an organized political movement in August 1897. The significance of this event was summarized by its leader and first president, Theodor Herzl, who wrote afterward that no one would believe him, but in Basel (Switzerland) he had created the state of the Jews. Encouraged by the success of the Hebrew renaissance in Palestine, the aim of the Zionist Organization was to build, as the Israeli independence proclamation would state, a "National Home" for Jewish people there.

The increasing immigration and the spread of the Hebrew language among natives in Palestine contributed to the steady growth of the Jewish population—some eighty thousand people on the eve of World War I. The importance of this community, however, went far beyond its numbers. Living in a region governed by conservative Islamic rulers, having strong connections with modern European culture, and with no other modern cultural community emerging in its vicinity (as attempts to modernize the Arabic world had had limited success), the Jewish community was the locomotive that drove not only the country's technological and economic modernization but also its cultural and social progress. It gained support from Britain, expressed in the Balfour Declaration of 1917. In a letter to the Zionist Federation of Great Britain and Ireland, Britain's foreign secretary, Lord Arthur James Balfour, stated that the British gov-

Time Line

1879

- **March 8**
  Eliezer Ben-Jehuda publishes "A Burning Question," calling for the renaissance of the Hebrew language and the founding of a new Hebrew society in Palestine.

1897

- **August 29**
  The World Zionist Organization is founded in Basel, Switzerland.

1917

- **November 2**
  The Balfour Declaration is issued, expressing British support for a Jewish homeland.

1918

- **September**
  British forces defeat Ottoman and German troops east of Haifa, completing the British conquest of Palestine.

1922

- **August 12**
  The League of Nations approves a British memorandum separating its mandate territory into Arab and Jewish zones.

1939

- **September 1**
  World War II begins in Europe.

1945

- **October**
  The Hebrew Rebellion Movement is formed.

---

ernment would support the establishment in Palestine of a national home for the Jewish people. This statement would be the basis for Zionist organizations' claims for their right to establish a Jewish state there.

The hardships of World War I were a passing episode. The conquering of the land by British forces in September 1918 was followed by the enactment of British civil occupation rule in 1920. On September 11, 1922, the League of Nations made Palestine an official British Mandate. According to Article 22 of the Covenant of the League of Nations (accepted on June 28, 1919), the territories conquered by the victorious Allies and inhabited by peoples unable to rule themselves (effectively meaning non-Europeans) would be entrusted to advanced nations (meaning the victorious European powers) until the local people could conduct their own affairs.

The mandate regime was not limited in time. Soon, many local political activists came to believe that they were able and ready to rule themselves. Nationalist sentiments were not limited to the Jewish community; the tightening ties with Europe and the increasing diffusion of ideas from Europe to the Middle East affected the Arab-speaking populations as well. Consequently, the 1920s and 1930s saw the emergence of two competing national movements in Palestine: a Zionist, or Jewish, movement and an Arab, or Palestinian, movement. The mandate period was marked by alternating cooperation and clashes with the British regime. Zionists were particularly disappointed with a British memorandum detailing how Britain proposed to organize the British Mandate of Palestine, a plan that was approved by the League of Nations on September 23, 1922. The memorandum separated the eastern and western parts of the British Mandate unequally into Transjordan (77 percent) and Palestine (23 percent), respectively. Transjordan was granted to Prince Abdullah from the House of Hashem, and transfer of administration over that territory took place over a period of five years (though Britain's mandate did not end there until 1946, when the territory became the Hashemite Kingdom of Jordan). Many Zionist activists had hoped that Britain would make all of Palestine a national Jewish home. This disappointment prompted armed struggle against the British occupier.

After a period of relative calm during World War II, the demand for Jewish statehood reemerged with greater force. Britain was victorious but exhausted after the war and could not maintain its global empire. In 1945 armed Hebrew factions united to combat the British government, forming the Hebrew Rebellion Movement, often called the Jewish Resistance Movement. This movement was halted in 1946 after the various factions failed to agree on whether to increase attacks against the British government or to come to terms with it. The gradual British withdrawal from Palestine was only a part of the global process of decolonization and reshaping of the world's map, as the old superpowers (mainly Britain and France) gave up their territorial assets and cleared the stage for other forces, mainly the United States and the Soviet Union.

A secondary but not unimportant factor that contributed to the demand for an independent Jewish state in Palestine was the almost total annihilation of Zionism in Europe during the Nazi-perpetrated Holocaust. The loss of Jewish lives in Europe left Palestine the center of Zionism. Therefore, Zionists saw great importance in fortifying this center and gaining total control of it. The Holocaust, combined with the global process of decolonization, led to the UN decision to end mandate rule in Palestine and create separate Arab and Jewish states in Palestine west of the Jordan River. On November 29, 1947, the UN General Assembly approved Resolution 181 about "the future Government of Palestine," making August 1, 1948, the target date for British withdrawal and the inauguration of the two states. The next morning, a civil war broke out between Jews and Arabs in Palestine, as neither side was entirely happy with the partition of the country. Understanding the futility of continuing its presence in Palestine, the British government decided not to wait until August and to withdraw its forces earlier, on May 15, 1948. That became the new target date for founding an independent Jewish state in Palestine.

The writing of the declaration began on April 23, 1948, three weeks before the due date for the end of British Mandate. Pinchas Rosen, Israel's first minister of justice, together with his assistant, Mordechaj Bühm, wrote a draft that was highly inspired by the U.S. Declaration of Independence and with a clear religious inclination, mentioning God several times. This draft was then edited by Zvi Berenson, the legal councilor of the World Zionist Organization (later a member of Israel's Supreme Court), who added a paragraph defining the state as Jewish, free, independent, and democratic and explicitly mentioning the rights of minorities. Because of pressure from religious circles, this "democratic" paragraph was deleted from the declaration's final version, which included only the word "Jewish."

In turn, nonreligious and atheist members of the People's Council opposed the mentioning of God in the declaration. Another draft was written by Moshe Sharett (later foreign minister and prime minister). When this version was also rejected, Ben-Gurion wrote a fourth draft, where he added a sentence stating that the "members of the National Council, representing the Jewish people in Palestine and the World Zionist Movement," were assembled by "natural and historic right" to declare independence. The controversy regarding the mentioning of God, however, was still unsolved. While secular members of the council insisted on deleting the phrase "Rock of Israel," their religious counterparts wanted to write "the Rock of Israel and its Saviour." Finally, the phrase "Rock of Israel," first suggested by Rosen and Bühm, remained as it was. The final version was authorized by the People's Council in a long session, which began on Wednesday, May 12, and continued almost until dawn of the following day.

About the Author

Several men had a significant hand in the drafting of the declaration of independence. Pinchas Rosen was born Felix Rosenblüth on May 1, 1887, in Berlin, Germany. He immi-

Time Line

1946

- **August**
  The Hebrew Rebellion Movement is dismantled.

1947

- **November 29**
  The United Nations General Assembly approves Resolution 181 about the future government of Palestine.

1948

- **May 14**
  David Ben-Gurion reads aloud the Declaration of the Establishment of the State of Israel in the main hall of the Tel Aviv Museum.

- **May 15**
  Syrian, Lebanese, Egyptian, Jordanian, and Iraqi armies invade Palestine west of the Jordan River.

1949

- **January 25**
  Elections for the Constituent Assembly, with the task of forming a constitution, are held in Israel.

- **February 24**
  The first of the Armistice Agreements between Israel and its Arab opponents is signed with Egypt.

- **July 20**
  The last of the Armistice Agreements between Israel and its Arab opponents is signed with Syria.

grated to Palestine in 1926 and spent most of his adult life in politics. After Israel declared its independence, he was elected to the Knesset—the Israeli parliament—and he was the nation's first minister of justice. He died on May 3, 1978. Later drafts were the work of several figures, including Rosen. One was David Remez, born David Drabkin in the Russian Empire (in what is now Belarus) in 1886. He immigrated to Palestine in 1913 and worked in a variety of government and trade union posts. He was Israel's first minister of transportation before his death on May 19, 1951. Haim-Moshe Shapira, too, was born in the Russian Empire (Belarus), on March 26, 1902. He immigrated to Palestine in 1925 and was active in the Zionist movement. After Israeli independence, he served in a variety of ministries until his death on July 16, 1970. Moshe Sharett was born Moshe Shertok in the Russian Empire (in today's Ukraine) on October 10, 1894. He immigrated to Palestine in 1906. He was Israel's second prime minister and died on July 7, 1965. Aharon Zisling, born in the Russian Empire (Belarus) on February 26, 1901, immigrated to Palestine in 1914. He served in the Knesset after independence and died on January 16, 1964.

The chief architect of Israeli independence and the leading signer of the declaration was David Ben-Gurion, the nation's first prime minister (who served a second term after Sharett). Ben-Gurion was born David Grün in the Russian Empire (in today's Poland) on October 16, 1886. An ardent Zionist, he was expelled from Palestine for his political activities in 1915. He then moved to New York City, though he returned to Palestine after World War I to continue his involvement in Zionist activities. Chief among these activities was his service as the chairman of the executive committee of the Jewish Agency for Palestine, essentially the Jewish government in Palestine prior to Israeli independence. After independence, he served two terms as Israel's prime minister (1948–1953 and 1955–1963). He died on December 1, 1973.

Explanation and Analysis of the Document

It is important to note what the Declaration of the Establishment of the State of Israel did and what it did not do. It established an internationally recognized sovereign state. It promised a constitution and set a timetable for drawing it. It also provided general guidelines for running the state. It did not, however, portray the exact future mechanisms and organs of the state. It left those details to be defined by the anticipated constitution, which was never written.

The declaration makes a clear distinction between the terms *Jewish* and *Hebrew*, using *Jewish* in reference to the international community of Jews and *Hebrew* when addressing or mentioning the population of Palestine. This is an important point: Whereas the term *Jewish* was (and still is) used to denote a nonterritorial ethnic or religious social group, *Hebrew* was the name given to the young territorial nation in Palestine. The latter group is secular and does not have any ethnic or religious conditions for admis-

sion, thus enabling a relatively easy and quick integration of all citizens, regardless of any religious or ethnic affiliation. The use of the term *Jewish* in the twelfth and thirteenth paragraphs was probably a result of the wish to fully adhere to the words of UN General Assembly Resolution 181, which required the establishment of a "Jewish" state.

◆ Paragraphs 1–10

The twenty paragraphs of the declaration can be divided into four parts. The first part (paragraphs 1 to 10) is meant to set the background and provide justification for the act of inaugurating the state in a way that would support a Zionist version of the story. Therefore, it not only refers to twentieth-century resolutions of the League of Nations and the United Nations but also depicts a long and specific historical narrative, namely, a Zionist one.

The declaration actually opens with a small misstatement, for Palestine was not the birthplace of the Jewish people: Their national identity was rather formed by Judeans going into exile, as correctly mentioned in paragraph 2. The assertion in paragraph 3 that "Jews strove throughout the centuries to go back to the land of their fathers" can also be disputed. For generations, Jews have lived and still live all around the world, embedded in many countries and societies. This assertion was probably made to establish historical precedent for the aspirations of modern Zionism. The text, however, maintains the Zionist ethos of pioneering success by claiming that only now has the "wilderness" been "reclaimed."

Paragraphs 4 and 5 describe the recent history of Palestine as seen by Zionists. Referring to the First Zionist Congress summoned in Basel in 1897 and to the Balfour Declaration of 1917, the declaration draws a straight historical line from ancient independence through generations of exile to the modern return to Palestine. Paragraphs 6 and 7 continue the narrative by referencing the horrors of the Nazi genocide of European Jews during World War II, just a few years before the declaration. Ben-Gurion uses the Holocaust as a strong argument for the establishment of the Jewish state, which would serve as a safe haven for Jews in the future, where they could lead "a life of dignity, freedom and honest toil in their ancestral land." Paragraph 7 uses the phrase "Eretz-Yisrael," which is the anglicized translation of a Hebrew phrase meaning simply "Land of Israel."

Paragraph 8 raises another argument for independence, claiming a reward for the Hebrew community in Palestine for taking part in Britain's war efforts. This claim was not unique to Palestine: It was raised by many other nations all around the declining British Empire. In England, Prime Minister Winston Churchill was a committed Zionist sympathizer and backed cooperation between British and Jewish Palestinian forces. Ironically, the training that Britain gave these forces in sabotage, demolitions, and guerrilla warfare would be used against Britain after the war as Israel fought for its independence. However, UN General Assembly Resolution 181, mentioned in paragraph 9, decreed the establishment not of a Hebrew but of a Jewish state in Palestine. The diplomats who phrased the resolution were unaware of the different meanings of "Hebrew" and "Jewish" in the Palestinian context. Accordingly, paragraph 10 states the "natural right of the Jewish people" to have a sovereign state.

◆ **Paragraphs 11–13**

The second part of the declaration, consisting of paragraphs 11 through 13, makes the actual declaration of the founding of the new state. Here again, the term *Hebrew* is used to describe the people in Palestine, whereas *Jewish* is used only when referring to Resolution 181. Paragraph 11 names the organs establishing the state of Israel: the National Council together with the World Zionist Movement. Paragraph 12 declares the establishment of the state. Paragraph 13 is the legislative core of the declaration. It sets the timetable for independence (May 15, 1948, at midnight) and for drawing a constitution (October 1, 1948) by a constituent assembly. It also states that a provisional government and provisional council will rule the state until elections to the legislative authority are held.

Paragraph 13 mostly remained a dead letter. The all-out war that broke out the day after the declaration was read postponed the elections for a constituent assembly to January 25, 1949. In what actually can be regarded as a coup d'état, in its opening session a month later, the assembly declared itself (by a vote of 118 to 2) to be the Knesset, a regular parliament (the word *Knesset* means literally "gathering" or "assembly"). As a result, a constitution was never written for the state of Israel. The Defence Emergency Regulations, enacted by the British Mandate regime in September 1945, are still in force in the twenty-first century.

◆ **Paragraphs 14–19**

The third part (paragraphs 14 to 19) specifies the basic guidelines according to which the new state should act and calls upon others to cooperate with it. The fourteenth paragraph has probably been the one most frequently quoted by Israeli courts throughout the years. It promises that the state would be "based on the principles of liberty, justice and peace," that it would grant "full social and political equality," and that it would guarantee "freedom of religion, conscience, education and culture." For many years, until the passage of Basic Law: Human Dignity and Liberty by the Knesset in March 1992, this paragraph was the closest thing the Israeli citizens had to a bill of rights. Although its explicit negation of any "distinction of religion, race or sex" was breached many times, it still portrays an ideal to which many Israelis aspire.

Paragraph 14 ends with a commitment to uphold the principles of the UN Charter, continued by a clear appeal to join that organization, stated in paragraphs 15 and 16. Paragraph 17 promises "full and equal citizenship" to the Arab inhabitants of the country. Some observers argue that this promise was not fulfilled. They note that from October 21, 1948, until December 1, 1966, Arab Israelis were officially subjected to a military regime. A few months after that regime was abolished, in June 1967, Israel occupied Judea, Samaria, Gaza, Sinai, and the Golan Heights after

The ship Jewish State *docks at the port of Haifa October 3, 1947, carrying Jewish settlers and Holocaust survivors from Europe.* (AP/Wide World Photos)

launching a preemptive attack against a coalition of Arab states that had massed troops on the Israeli border (the Six-Day War). The Arab inhabitants of Judea, Samaria, and Gaza still live under Israeli rule.

Paragraph 18, offering "peace and neighbourliness" to neighboring states, represented an effort to comply with the bylaws of the United Nations and to avoid war with surrounding nations. However, the statement was also directed to dissident Hebrew armed factions, mainly the National Military Organization ("Etzel" in Hebrew) and the Fighters for the Freedom of Israel, or the "Lehi," also known as the "Stern Gang," who doubted Ben-Gurion's authority over their demands for further conquests and a continuation of the war until more territories were gained.

The authors of the declaration knew that the majority of the world's Jews were neither Palestinian nor active Zionists. Therefore, their call to "the Jewish people all over the world to rally to our side in the task of immigration and development" in paragraph 19 was an attempt to appeal along two lines. The first was spiritual, a call for the "redemption" of Israel. In a more practical vein, it expressed the Zionists' immediate need for external material support for establishing and fortifying the new state.

◆ **Paragraph 20**

The fourth part (paragraph 20) officially approves the previous parts and prepares the declaration for signing by the members of the council. The term "Rock of Israel" used in referring to God was adopted as a compromise between religious Jews and "secular" Zionists. The reading and signing of the declaration on Friday afternoon was probably not

"In the Second World War the Jewish people in Palestine made their full contribution to the struggle of the freedom-loving nations against the Nazi evil. The sacrifices of their soldiers and their war effort gained them the right to rank with the nations which founded the United Nations."

(Paragraph 8)

"On November 29, 1947, the General Assembly of the United Nations adopted a Resolution requiring the establishment of a Jewish State in Palestine. The General Assembly called upon the inhabitants of the country to take all the necessary steps on their part to put the plan into effect. This recognition by the United Nations of the right of the Jewish people to establish their independent State is unassailable."

(Paragraph 9)

"We hereby proclaim the establishment of the Jewish State in Palestine, to be called Medinath Yisrael (The State of Israel)."

(Paragraph 12)

"We hereby declare that, as from the termination of the Mandate at midnight, the 14th–15th May, 1948, … the National Council shall act as the Provisional State Council, and that the National Administration shall constitute the Provisional Government of the Jewish State, which shall be known as Israel."

(Paragraph 13)

"The State of Israel will be open to the immigration of Jews from all countries of their dispersion; will promote the development of the country for the benefit of all its inhabitants: will be based on the principles of liberty, justice and peace as conceived by the Prophets of Israel: will uphold the full social and political equality of all its citizens, without distinction of religion, race, or sex."

(Paragraph 14)

a coincidence. Trying to grant the event a unique symbolic meaning, Ben-Gurion scheduled the ceremony so it would end just before Friday's sunset—a clear parallel to the creation of the world.

Audience

The immediate audience of the declaration of independence were the members of the People's Council and the dignitaries assembled at the Tel Aviv Museum, as well as the thousands of people gathered in the boulevard and the adjacent streets. But Ben-Gurion aimed the declaration to much larger audiences. The phrasing was the outcome of a compromise, an attempt to satisfy all parts of the Hebrew-speaking community. Additionally, though, the declaration had three other main audiences.

First was the international community. Assuming that the Hebrew community of Palestine would not be able to repel an Arab attack on it, Ben-Gurion emphasized the appeal for international recognition and support. This was in line with the long-standing policy of the Palestinian Workers Party of maintaining good relations with at least one superpower. Hence, under mandate rule Ben-Gurion usually opposed demands to directly confront the British government. Later, during the 1950s, he relied mostly on alliances with Great Britain and France; during the 1960s his successors allied with the United States.

Second were the people living in Palestine. The message for this audience was less in the content of the declaration and more in the fact that it was delivered by Ben-Gurion, leader of the largest political party, and signed by members of many other parties and factions—from the nationalist right to the Communist Party—including representatives of religious Jewish groups. By that, Ben-Gurion managed to show his authority, which later on helped him maintain power as prime minister for more than a decade. It is still contested how serious and sincere was Ben-Gurion's' call for the Arab inhabitants to take part in the building of the land, given that on the day of the declaration a de facto civil war had already been raging for some six months.

A third audience was made up of Jewish communities abroad. Facing considerable opposition to Zionism among many Jewish communities, the authors of the declaration did not forget to address Jews all around the world, with the hope of harnessing them to their efforts.

Impact

The first and most obvious impact of the Declaration of the Establishment of the State of Israel was that it established the basis for the state, which immediately took control over vast parts of western Palestine. Within less than two decades, Israel would become a regional military power.

A second impact was that on the Hebrew community in Palestine. Israel became an independent nation, recognized as such by the international community and an equal member in the family of nations. This is not a minor matter, for the world after World War II and during the cold

Questions for Further Study

1. How did the wave of nationalism that swept over Europe in the nineteenth century contribute to the formation of the state of Israel in the twentieth century?

2. How might the troubled modern history of Palestine have been different if the region had not become a British Mandate after World War I? What effect would that have had on the quest for Jewish nationhood?

3. Compare the Declaration of the Establishment of the State of Israel with the entry Theodor Herzl's "A Solution to the Jewish Question." What would Herzl's reaction have been to the declaration? To what extent was the declaration a realization of Herzl's vision?

4. Does it strike you as surprising that in a declaration establishing a state in which Judaism would be the dominant religion there would be controversy about the inclusion of the word "God" in the document? Why do you think such a controversy arose?

5. Compare the Declaration of the Establishment of the State of Israel and the events surrounding it with the Palestinian National Charter and the events leading to (and following) the formation of the Palestine Liberation Organization. What has been the source of the continuing hostility and conflict in the region? Do you think that conflict will ever be resolved in the near future?

war was shaped and formed by nation-states. Israel became a power economically, technologically (with five of its universities ranked among the world's best five hundred), and culturally (every year, more new books are printed in Israel than in all of its neighboring countries combined).

A third impact was on all the inhabitants of Palestine who came under the rule of a Jewish state. While some Jewish states have existed in various places around the world during the last two millennia, the last time a Jewish state existed in Palestine was nineteen hundred years ago, during the zenith of the Roman Empire. Generally, Judaism evolved for centuries without any relation to a specific state. Lacking a constitution and with only vague notions of what "a Jewish state" means in practice, the people of Israel now live in a state with a very fluid shape, governmental apparatus, and boundaries.

In a similar vein, the declaration had an indirect impact on Jewish communities around the world. The Zionist proclamation of Israel as a Jewish state posed a challenge to the mere notion of Judaism and what it actually means, because for millennia Judaism has thrived and evolved by adhering to the principle of remaining detached from states. A Jewish state is confusing in a tradition based on this principle. Second, the Zionist aspiration and claim to represent all Jews worldwide while practicing politically contested policies made Jews around the world, in the eyes of some observers, a scapegoat and a target for hatred, hostility, and violence.

Further Reading

■ Articles

Friling, Tuvia, and Ilan Troen. "Proclaiming Independence: Five Days in May from Ben-Gurion's Diary." *Israel Studies* 3, no. 1 (1998): 170–194.

■ Books

Evron, Boas. *Jewish State or Israeli Nation?* Bloomington: Indiana University Press, 1995.

Gerner, Deborah J. *One Land, Two Peoples: The Conflict over Palestine*, 2nd ed. Denver, Colo.: Westview Press, 1994.

Hertzberg, Arthur, ed. *The Zionist Idea: A Historical Analysis and Reader*. New York: Atheneum, 1981.

Morris, Benny. *1948 and After: Israel and the Palestinians*. Oxford, U.K.: Clarendon Press, 1990.

Segev, Tom. *1949: The First Israelis*. New York: Henry Holt, 1998.

———. *One Palestine, Complete: Jews and Arabs under the British Mandate*. New York: Henry Holt, 2000.

Sheffer, Gabriel. *Moshe Sharett: Biography of a Political Moderate*. New York, Oxford University Press, 1996.

■ Web Sites

Gorali, Moshe. "How God and Democracy Were Left Out." Haaretz.com Web site.
    www.haaretz.com/hasen/pages/ShArt.jhtml?itemNo=290261&contrassID=2&subContrassID=5&sbSubContrassID=0&listSrc=Y.

"Resolution 181 (II): Future Government of Palestine." United Nations General Assembly Web site.
    http://unispal.un.org/UNISPAL.NSF/8d0125d24ffa6a5d85256b97004d9b37/7f0af2bd897689b785256c330061d253?OpenDocument.

—Dan Tamir

DECLARATION OF THE ESTABLISHMENT OF THE STATE OF ISRAEL

The Land of Israel was the birthplace of the Jewish people. Here their spiritual, religious and national identity was formed. Here they achieved independence and created a culture of national and universal significance. Here they wrote and gave the Bible to the world.

Exiled from the Land of Israel the Jewish people remained faithful to it to in all the countries of their dispersion, never ceasing to pray and hope for their return and the restoration of their national freedom.

Impelled by this historic association. Jews strove throughout the centuries to go back to the land of their fathers and regain their statehood. In recent decades they returned in their masses. They reclaimed the wilderness, revived their language, built cities and villages, and established a vigorous and ever-growing community, with its own economic and cultural life. They sought peace, yet were prepared to defend themselves. They brought the blessings of progress to all inhabitants of the country and looked forward to sovereign independence.

In the year 1897 the First Zionist Congress, inspired by Theodor Herzl's vision of the Jewish State, proclaimed the right of the Jewish people to national revival in their own country.

This right was acknowledged by the Balfour Declaration of November 2, 1917, and re-affirmed by the Mandate of the League of Nations, which gave explicit international recognition to the historic connection of the Jewish people with Palestine and their right to reconstitute their National Home.

The recent holocaust, which engulfed millions of Jews in Europe, proved anew the need to solve the problem of the homelessness and lack of independence of the Jewish people by means of the re-establishment of the Jewish State, which would open the gates to all Jews and endow the Jewish people with equality of status among the family of nations.

The survivors of the disastrous slaughter in Europe, and also Jews from other lands, have not desisted from their efforts to reach Eretz-Yisrael, in face of difficulties, obstacles and perils, and have not ceased to urge their right to a life of dignity, freedom and honest toil in their ancestral land.

In the Second World War the Jewish people in Palestine made their full contribution to the struggle of the freedom-loving nations against the Nazi evil. The sacrifices of their soldiers and their war effort gained them the right to rank with the nations which founded the United Nations.

On November 29, 1947, the General Assembly of the United Nations adopted a Resolution requiring the establishment of a Jewish State in Palestine. The General Assembly called upon the inhabitants of the country to take all the necessary steps on their part to put the plan into effect. This recognition by the United Nations of the right of the Jewish people to establish their independent State is unassailable.

It is the natural right of the Jewish people to lead, as do all other nations, an independent existence in its sovereign State.

Accordingly we, the members of the National Council, representing the Jewish people in Palestine and the World Zionist Movement, are met together in solemn assembly today, the day of termination of the British Mandate for Palestine: and by virtue of the natural and historic right of the Jewish people and of the Resolution of the General Assembly of the United Nations.

We hereby proclaim the establishment of the Jewish State in Palestine, to be called Medinath Yisrael (The State of Israel).

We hereby declare that, as from the termination of the Mandate at midnight, the 14th–15th May, 1948, and pending the setting up of the duly elected bodies of the State in accordance with a Constitution, to be drawn up by the Constituent Assembly not later than the 1st October, 1948, the National Council shall act as the Provisional State Council, and that the National Administration shall constitute the Provisional Government of the Jewish State, which shall be known as Israel.

The State of Israel will be open to the immigration of Jews from all countries of their dispersion; will promote the development of the country for the benefit of all its inhabitants: will be based on the principles of liberty, justice and peace as conceived by the Prophets of Israel: will uphold the full social and political equality of all its citizens, without distinction of religion, race, or sex: will guarantee freedom of religion, conscience, education and culture: will safeguard the Holy Places of all religions; and will loyally uphold the principles of the United Nations Charter.

The State of Israel will be ready to co-operate with the organs and representatives of the United Nations in the implementation of the Resolution of the Assembly of November 29, 1947, and will take steps to bring about the Economic Union over the whole of Palestine.

We appeal to the United Nations to assist the Jewish people in the building of its State and to admit Israel into the family of nations.

In the midst of wanton aggression, we yet call upon the Arab inhabitants of the State of Israel to preserve the ways of peace and play their part in the development of the State, on the basis of full and equal citizenship and due representation in all its bodies and institutions—provisional and permanent.

We extend our hand in peace and neighbourliness to all the neighbouring states and their peoples, and invite them to co-operate with the independent Jewish nation for the common good of all. The State of Israel is prepared to make its contribution to the progress of the Middle East as a whole.

Our call goes out to the Jewish people all over the world to rally to our side in the task of immigration and development, and to stand by us in the great struggle for the fulfillment of the dream of generations for the redemption of Israel.

With trust in the Rock of Israel, we set our hand to this Declaration, at this Session of the Provisional State Council, on the soil of the Homeland, in the city of Tel-Aviv, on this Sabbath eve, the fifth of Iyar, 5708, the fourteenth of May, 1948.

"Everyone has the right to freedom of thought, conscience and religion."

Overview

The Universal Declaration of Human Rights (UDHR) was adopted unanimously by the General Assembly of the United Nations on December 10, 1948. Eight countries abstained: Saudi Arabia, South Africa, Byelorussia, Czechoslovakia, Poland, Ukraine, the Soviet Union, and Yugoslavia. The document had been drafted by the Commission on Human Rights, chaired by Eleanor Roosevelt, the widow of U.S. president Franklin D. Roosevelt. In a speech before the General Assembly she described the declaration as the "international Magna Carta of all men everywhere" (http://www.americanrhetoric.com/speeches/eleanorrooseveltdeclarationhumanrights.htm). The former secretary-general of the United Nations, Kofi Annan, is not alone in his belief that "the principles enshrined in the Declaration are the yardstick by which we measure progress. They lie at the heart of all that the United Nations aspires to achieve in its global mission of peace and development" (qtd. in Danieli et al., p. v).

The declaration has been translated into more than 350 languages and was written so that ordinary people could understand it. It reflects the complex state of international relations at a particular historical moment—immediately after World War II and at the beginning of the cold war (the state of tension between the United States and its allies and the Soviet bloc). It has formed the basis of many conventions and treaties and has influenced more than two dozen national constitutions. It continues to be upheld as a universal standard of morality and is widely recognized as international common law. The declaration is the founding document of the International Bill of Human Rights, which was completed by the addition of the International Covenant on Civil and Political Rights and the International Covenant on Economic, Social and Cultural Rights in 1966.

Context

The declaration was the product of nearly two years of intense and often conflicted discussion among members of the newly formed UN Commission on Human Rights. The United Nations had faced enormous pressure from individuals, nongovernmental organizations (NGOs), and international conferences calling for the United Nations to prioritize human rights in its charter. Instead of including a bill of human rights in its charter, the United Nations established the eighteen-member Commission on Human Rights.

The declaration was written soon after World War II. In 1941, U.S. president Franklin Roosevelt had met with Winston Churchill, the prime minister of England, to discuss the international postwar balance of power. Their major concern was international peace and security. Later, various meetings took place as the circle was enlarged to include the third Allied leader, Josef Stalin of the Soviet Union. Finally, in 1945, fifty nations met in San Francisco. Dominated by the Big Three, who had invited France and China to join them, the assembled nations drafted the UN charter. The charter was intended to provide a mechanism to prevent future aggression, resolve disputes, and ensure that national borders would be kept intact. The principle of national sovereignty was built into the charter, and from the beginning this principle was in tension with the potential for the United Nations to intervene or "interfere" in a nation's internal affairs.

As the horrors of the Nazi genocide against Jews and other "undesirables" became known across the world, global voices demanding attention to human rights grew louder. A shared determination to prevent the rise again of Nazism or Fascism was critical to the drafting of the UDHR. Other effects of the war were also influential, including the plight of refugees and national security concerns. The horrors of the war provided the catalyst that enabled people from so many diverse cultural, political, social, and economic backgrounds to develop a shared moral code.

The declaration was also influenced by the League of Nations, formed after World War I, which had failed to prevent World War II. The league had not mentioned human rights, but the authors of the UDHR wanted to ensure that international security would include the protection of human rights. Many wanted the document to include the means for implementing its proposals, but the document became a statement of shared beliefs in human rights on which more action-based treaties or conventions could be

1945

■ **June 25**
The San Francisco Conference unanimously approves the charter of the United Nations.

■ **August 15**
Japan surrenders, ending World War II.

■ **October 24**
The United Nations is created with the ratification of its charter.

1946

■ **June**
The UN Commission on Human Rights and UN Commission on the Status of Women are established.

1948

■ **December 10**
The UN General Assembly adopts the Universal Declaration of Human Rights.

■ The Convention on the Freedom of Association and Protection of the Right to Organize, the Declaration of the Rights of Man by the Organization of American States, and the Convention on the Prevention and Punishment of the Crime of Genocide are adopted.

built. (A treaty is a specific agreement between or among nations; a convention is a more general agreement on principles that does not necessarily require specific action.)

Few Asian and African countries were represented in the United Nations and on the commission because so many (other than Japan, which was excluded) were European colonies. A few had gained independence after the war, and these countries played an important role in the process. The delegate from France, René Cassin, sat face to face with the delegate from a former French colony, Charles Malik of Lebanon. (This was also the case with the United States and the Philippines and with Great Britain and its colonies, India and Pakistan.) The question of the human rights of colonized people would be a source of tension, and the word *colony* or its derivations would not appear in the document.

Another contentious issue was the treatment of minorities and the eradication of racism. Although the war had destroyed the moral basis of scientific racism, for example, a number of countries had not yet internalized this lesson. The Soviet Union, for example, was subjected to sharp criticism of its human rights record.

Women's human rights would also present a challenge. Many UN member nations had not granted women full political rights, let alone cultural, social, or economic equality. Two women served on the commission: Eleanor Roosevelt and Hansa Mehta of India. Roosevelt argued that the word "men" included "women," but Mehta insisted on specifically including women in the declaration. The UN Commission on the Status of Women played an important role. No mandate was given for these two commissions to work together, but representatives of the Commission on the Status of Women regularly attended committee meetings and provided crucial input, helping to ensure the removal of sexist language and the full inclusion of women in the category of "men." In several regards, then, the commission had to develop a moral agenda that challenged many of the delegates' own countries' human rights records at that very moment.

NGOs also played a critical role in pushing human rights onto the international agenda. Many people and organizations developed international bills of human rights; even the pope called for such a document. When the commission began its work, it invited and welcomed comments and suggestions, and NGOs maintained pressure throughout.

International events that help to contextualize the committee's work include the beginnings of decolonization in such countries as the Philippines, Lebanon, India, and Pakistan; the continuation of colonial rule in both Asia and Africa; apartheid laws passed in South Africa the same year as the declaration; Britain's relinquishment of its mandate over Palestine and the formation of Israel; Jewish and Palestinian refugees; and the transition to a Communist government in China. These were the early years of the cold war between the Soviet bloc and the West. It is remarkable that delegates from both sides of the Iron Curtain and across many religious, political, and ideological divides could work together so intensely to develop a shared commitment to a global moral blueprint for human rights. There were seven distinct stages in the drafting process. Small subcommittees worked on the document and then brought it to the entire eighteen-member commission for a vote. This continued for nearly two years. In the process of drafting this document, every word and sentence attracted scrutiny and revision, and the entire committee voted on every article until it was finally adopted in December of 1948.

About the Author

The UDHR has no single author. The UN's Economic and Social Council was responsible for the formation of a permanent Commission on Human Rights, established in June 1946. Eleanor Roosevelt, who had worked tirelessly as a social and political activist during her years as first lady and who had been appointed as a delegate to the United Nations by her husband's successor, Harry Truman, chaired the commission as it worked on its first, critical, task: to draft an international bill of human rights.

The Human Rights Commission comprised eighteen members. The United States, the Soviet Union, the United Kingdom, France, and China would be permanent members. The other thirteen seats would rotate among the other UN member nations at three-year intervals; at the time, the additional thirteen countries were Australia, Belgium, Byelorussia, Chile, Egypt, India, Iran, Lebanon, Panama, Philippines, Ukraine, Uruguay, and Yugoslavia. The first director of the Human Rights Division of the UN Secretariat (the UN organ headed by the secretary-general) was a Canadian, John Humphrey, a legal scholar and human rights activist who would play a critical role.

The entire commission may be considered the author of this document, but certain delegates played particularly important roles. Following intensive research, Humphrey drafted the original text on which the declaration was based. The commission then had to revise this document. A subcommittee of four quickly realized that this task would be best conducted by one individual. René Cassin, a French legal expert, revised the document and provided a valuable structure. In addition to Roosevelt, Humphrey, and Cassin, key authors included Charles Malik of Lebanon, a prominent philosopher, diplomat, and later Lebanon's minister of foreign affairs and member of that nation's National Assembly, and Peng-chun Chang, a well-known Chinese diplomat and playwright who was likely selected as vice-chair of the commission because of his Western education at Princeton University, his English fluency, and his recognized ability to bridge Asian and Western culture. However, everyone had the opportunity to speak and be heard as the document went through many revisions. NGOs, other UN members, and individuals attended the meetings and lobbied for their positions on human rights.

Explanation and Analysis of the Document

The declaration is a product of a specific time and place, yet it has often also been described as a living document. The authors chose not to define several concepts, from "the family" to "torture," so ambiguity is built into the UDHR. The authors believed that human rights are universal. In other words, nations cannot pick and choose certain rights and ignore others. Countries that voted to adopt the declaration were accepting the whole package. The division of the document into thirty separate articles may make it

Sculpture of Eleanor Roosevelt on display in the main lobby of the United Nations in Geneva, Switzerland
(AP/Wide World Photos)

difficult to remember that they are all interconnected and interdependent.

The declaration was given a particular structure by Cassin, and the basic structure still stands. The foundation, or core values, consists of dignity, liberty, equality, and brotherhood. The preamble leads to the four pillars of the declaration: life, liberty and personal security (Articles 3–11); rights in civil society (Articles 12–17); rights in the polity (political rights; Articles 18–21); and economic, social, and cultural rights (Articles 22–27). The final three articles (28–30) deal with duties, limits, and order. The UDHR does not specifically discuss the human rights of soldiers or civilians during wartime; it focuses on the rights that must be upheld in order to preserve peace.

◆ Preamble

The preamble introduces the declaration and summarizes its core values. First, international peace and security are not just a matter of diplomacy. They are a function of human rights. Then, dignity is "inherent," a vital part of being human. All people have the right to respect and share certain rights that cannot be taken away. Finally, these rights are shared equally: All people have the same rights, and no one has more of one right than anyone else.

In the preamble's reference to "barbarous acts," the authors clearly had in mind World War II, but they do not mention the war, for they wanted the document to focus on the future. The second paragraph alludes to the "four freedoms" that were articulated by President Roosevelt in a 1941 speech. Although Roosevelt was speaking as an American, the delegates agreed that these are the "highest aspiration of the common people": freedom from fear and want (or poverty) and freedom of speech and belief. This list includes social, economic, political, and cultural rights. In a sense, the UDHR is an expansion of the four freedoms.

Recalling the American Declaration of Independence, the preamble warns governments to protect human rights so as to avoid "rebellion against tyranny and oppression." Such rebellion might be inevitable if human rights are not inscribed in the rule of law. There is a clear, if subtle, warning that national peace can be ensured only through the protection of human rights. The preamble then shifts to a reminder that protecting human rights is a vital aspect of the international peace process and essential for "social progress" or development. The preamble ends with a pledge by member states to ensure the implementation of the UDHR by means of education that will promote respect for human rights and to introduce various measures to "secure their universal and effective recognition and observance." The final sentence includes colonies, people without political, social, or economic rights, though the word *colony* does not appear. Instead, reference is made to "territories" under the "jurisdiction" of the member states.

◆ Articles 1 and 2

The first two articles spell out the core values of the UDHR. The preamble tells us that we are all members of the "human family," and the first article declares that we should act "in brotherhood." The implication is that a shared humanity is more important than being members of different countries, religions, or other belief systems. The preamble suggests that if we can understand that we are all part of one family, world peace may be possible.

Article 2 states that no one can be discriminated against on any basis. The list begins with physiological markers. Race and color are listed separately to ensure the greatest protection for minorities and others previously denied their rights on the basis of skin color. Sex is the other genetic marker. The article goes on to cover freedom of belief and opinion and ends with social and economic factors, including national and social status (class or caste). Finally, UN members are reminded that colonized people share these rights. The question arises as to whether a country that colonized other countries *could* adhere to the UDHR. It is a challenge to find an article in this document that does not raise this question.

◆ Articles 3–11

The individual rights included in Article 3 are absolute. No conditions are attached to the right to life, liberty, and personal security. The right to life is not limited by national or international interests. There is no differentiation or hierarchy of rights: The right to life has the same value as the right to personal security. This implies that both capital punishment and wartime killing may be defined as violations of human rights. These rights might conflict, as in the case of self-defense or national security. The French Declaration of the Rights of Man and of the Citizen included a contradiction between individual rights to liberty and national security concerns. This contradiction remains pertinent today and is recognized in the final set of articles in the UDHR.

Article 4 prohibits slavery and states that no one can be held in "servitude." Forced labor is outlawed. This connects with Article 9 (against arbitrary arrest) and to Article 23, which protects the right to choose one's work.

Article 5 continues the theme of personal security. It deals with the right to protection of the body from torture, or "cruel, inhuman or degrading treatment or punishment." Read with the third article, one might again argue that capital punishment is a violation of human rights. A similar argument has been made about interrogation. Note the inclusion of the word "punishment": Even convicted criminals have the right to humane punishment. "Torture" is an excellent example of how the failure to define a term allows governments to redefine their policies or actions as "not torture" when others claim they are indeed torturous acts. At the same time, it underscores the moral power of the declaration, because governments do not claim the right to torture. This article demonstrates both the weakness and the strength of the declaration. Because it did not define its terms clearly, there is room for maneuvering, which may be used either to demand protection of human rights (normally by NGOs or individuals) or withhold human rights (normally by governments). Later conventions seek to address these kinds of shortcomings.

Articles 6–11 relate the individual to national legal systems. The UDHR states the moral obligation to create laws that protect human rights. These articles assume that such laws and constitutions are in place (see particularly Article 8). Article 6 ensures that every person has a right to fair treatment under the law, whereas Article 7 details the right to equality before the law. Not only is discrimination prohibited, but so too is the *incitement* to discriminate. Articles 8, 9, and 10 focus on the kind of treatment one should expect under a national legal system so as to ensure a fair, effective hearing. People have the right to be "presumed innocent" and to be treated accordingly, with dignity. Article 11 also states that no one can be held guilty of a crime that had not been codified at the time of the action, and if the crime did exist, "no heavier penalty [may] be imposed than the one that was applicable at the time."

◆ Articles 12–17

Rights related to the family and home in the context of the right to privacy are introduced in Article 12. Note the word *arbitrary* (see Articles 9 and 15). This means that the rights named here are not absolute. Rights to privacy, family, home, and correspondence are protected from "arbi-

View of the assembly hall during the opening of the Human Rights Council's commemorative session marking the sixtieth anniversary of the adoption of the Universal Declaration of Human Rights, at the European headquarters of the United Nations in Geneva (AP/Wide World Photos)

trary interference." If the interference can be justified legally, these rights can be limited.

Articles 13 through 15 discuss the rights to a nationality (including the right to chose a new one) as well as to freedom of movement within and between countries. The word *citizen* does not appear. Whereas the previous articles had assumed that a country would choose to uphold human rights within its constitution and laws, here we discover the rights of citizens whose governments persecute them. The word *enjoy* in Article 14 introduces ambiguity: "Everyone has the right to seek and to enjoy in other countries asylum from persecution." If everyone has the right to "enjoy" asylum, the question arises as to which country has the obligation to grant it.

The family is the focus of Article 16. Marriage, in particular, was the cause of much discussion on the committee, and the delegates worked hard to ensure that different cultural views of this central institution were accommodated. Consent of both spouses is required, they have to be of "full age" (a specific age is not given, however), and the family is entitled to protection by both "society" and "the State." However, this article contains a provision given by Saudi Arabia as a reason for its decision to abstain from the vote, for the Saudis believed it would not be acceptable for a Muslim to marry a person of another religion. Article 16 also raised other concerns among the members of the com-

mission. Many delegates and lobbyists argued that the word *divorce* should not be included in the declaration; here Muslims and Roman Catholics were in perfect agreement. Note that the family is also protected in Articles 12 and 23, which refer to the right to earn a living wage to ensure the "an existence worthy of human dignity." Article 25 protects the rights of children born out of marriage.

Finally, Article 17 states the absolute right to private property, a Western concept. However, the right to hold on to one's property is not absolute: "No one shall be *arbitrarily* deprived of his property."

◆ **Articles 18–21**

These articles focus on two of Franklin Roosevelt's four freedoms: the rights to belief and speech—including the right to change one's belief and even one's religion. This was the second point Saudi Arabia could not accept. Whereas Article 18 focuses on religion, Article 19 is broader in scope, speaking of the right to "freedom of opinion and expression." The next article moves beyond the right to the individual freedom of thought and expression to include the right (but not the obligation) to meet and associate with others, as long as it is done peacefully.

Article 21 shifts to formal political rights: the right to participate in government and to have equal access to public service. This article is important because it permits only one concept of government: "The will of the people shall be the basis of the authority of government." The article goes on to state that regular, public elections incorporating "free voting procedures" should be held and that there should be "universal and equal suffrage"—there shall be no discrimination on the bases outlined in Article 2. The only ambiguity is in the word *equivalent* in reference to methods of voting.

◆ **Articles 22–27**

Article 22 sets out the right to "social security," although this is not specifically defined. Nevertheless, cooperation between nations and the international community is specifically invoked in this article, given limitations on countries' resources. Thus every nation individually and within the international community is obliged to ensure a humane standard of living for all people.

Work issues are the focus of Article 23. These rights have particular challenges, as the burden is placed on the state to protect rights; this assumes that nations have the resources to do so. Freedom to work is spelled out, including the right to choose one's employment. Fair labor conditions and the right to "protection against unemployment" are also noted as human rights. Section 2 states the right to equal pay for equal work for everyone, "without discrimination." Fair pay is another right. The concept of a family wage is implied, with the assumption that each family has one male breadwinner. If the wage is insufficient, there has to be a backup, provided presumably by the state. Finally, the right (but not obligation) to unionize is included.

Article 24 includes what might be considered a surprising right: "the right to rest and leisure"; paid holidays are considered a human right. Leisure could be considered part of a dignified standard of living, the topic of Article 25. In this article, basic needs are spelled out, including food, housing, and medical care, that is, to social security because of "lack of livelihood in circumstances beyond [a person's] control." It then specifies the importance of the needs of mothers and children and calls for the protection of children irrespective of the marital status of their parents.

The right to an education is the core of Article 26. The article says that elementary education should be compulsory and free, but it speaks of the right to other levels of education too. The purpose of education is to support the core values of the UDHR. Finally, parents have a right to choose how their children are educated. It should be clear that many of the rights in the UDHR provide a list of objectives toward which countries should strive. Not every country had, or has, the resources to provide free education, but in the spirit of this declaration, they should work toward this goal.

Article 27 refers to cultural rights specifically: All have the right to participate in the "cultural life of the community" and to "enjoy," "share," and benefit from scientific advances. This article also introduces the right to copyright, to "protection of the moral and material interests" that result from any kind of cultural production in the arts or sciences.

◆ **Articles 28–30**

The final three articles speak of the duties of the international community. Everyone has the right to peace, but duties accompany rights. This was a point made very clearly by many influential thinkers (including the Indian nationalist leader Mohandas Gandhi and the English critic and novelist Aldous Huxley) who were surveyed as the committee began its work. Article 29 specifies this obligation. This article connects individuals to the community, not as bearers of rights but as bearers of duties to others. In order to claim our own human rights, we need to protect the rights of others. This section states that "the free and full development" of human beings is impossible without "the community." The article goes on to acknowledge that rights may be limited, as for example by the need to protect the rights of others, but it also speaks of the "just requirements" of "public order." Section 3 declares that rights and freedoms may be exercised only in line with the goals of the UN. The UDHR closes (Article 30) with a statement that recognizes that interpretations of the various rights and freedoms may vary, but no person, group, or government has the right to interpret the articles in such a way that human rights are violated.

Audience

The intended audience of this document is essentially everyone in the world. The UDHR was written with victims of the World War II Holocaust (systematic elimination of Jews and other "undesirables") in mind, but its more immediate audience was the United Nations, whose members had to approve the declaration. At the same time, each delegate represented a nation and had to be accountable to that particular government.

Finally, the intended audience was the people of the future. Many times during the proceedings, delegates would stop to consider what the future world might be like and how their document might address the needs of future generations. They were acutely aware of the historical burden they carried, although they probably did not realize how their document would retain its moral stature into the next century.

Impact

The declaration provides a yardstick or guidepost for setting goals and measuring progress toward those goals. NGOs and grassroots movements have played a critical role in transforming the words of the UDHR into action and in making governments accountable. Governments have often been quick to pay lip service but slow to protect human rights. The greatest impact globally seems to have been in the inspiration, hope, and empowerment that this document has given to "common people" who do not experience human rights but know that they have a right to seek justice.

However, the declaration has also had significant impact on the constitutions of more than two dozen nations that either became independent from colonial rule

"*All human beings are born free and equal in dignity and rights. They are endowed with reason and conscience and should act towards one another in a spirit of brotherhood.*"

(Article 1)

"*Everyone is entitled to all the rights and freedoms set forth in this Declaration, without distinction of any kind, such as race, colour, sex, language, religion, political or other opinion, national or social origin, property, birth or other status.*"

(Article 2)

"*All are equal before the law and are entitled without any discrimination to equal protection of the law.*"

(Article 7)

"*Everyone has the right to freedom of thought, conscience and religion.*"

(Article 18)

"*Everyone is entitled to a social and international order in which the rights and freedoms set forth in this Declaration can be fully realized.*"

(Article 28)

after 1948 or that have reviewed and rewritten their constitutions. No government is willing to stand in the face of the declaration and deny outright the existence of human rights. Acknowledging the UDHR is an important step toward developing a culture of human rights, but governments must have the political will to implement them within their own national borders as well as internationally, and this has been less forthcoming.

The declaration has been of great importance within the UN system itself. Its moral power has provided the foundation for numerous conventions, treaties, and covenants promoting and protecting human rights. Yet the second half of the twentieth century saw genocide, ethnic cleansing, and continued violence against women and children. However, as former U.S. president Jimmy Carter noted, when countries sign and ratify human rights conventions, at least *some* accountability is required. Political will is also

required of the United Nations itself. The Commission on Human Rights presented two human rights covenants to the General Assembly in 1966, but it took a full ten years for them to be ratified.

Scholars and activists continue to debate whether the UDHR recognizes women's rights. Another key concern is the issue of universality. Many have noted the absence of many African and Asian countries, as well as the dominance of three Western nations, on the core committee. There also appears to be an imbalance within the document itself, with considerable weight given to Western Enlightenment views of individuals' rights. Despite the obstacles and challenges that every person faces in the enjoyment of their basic human rights, the Universal Declaration of Human Rights has no doubt played a critical role in the development of awareness of human rights and the need to promote and protect them.

Further Reading

▪ Articles

Mutua, Makau. "The Ideology of Human Rights." *Virginia Journal of International Law* 36 (1996): 589–657.

▪ Books

Amnesty International. *Human Rights Are Women's Rights*. New York: Amnesty International, 1995.

Ashworth, Georgina. *Of Violence and Violation: Women and Human Rights*. London: CHANGE, 1986.

Bunch, Charlotte, Noeleen Heyzer, Sushma Kapoor, and Joanne Sandler. "Women's Human Rights and Development: A Global Agenda for the 21st Century." In *A Commitment to the World's Women: Perspectives on Development for Beijing and Beyond*, ed. Noeleen Heyzer. New York: UNIFEM, 1995.

Danieli, Yael, Elsa Stamatopoulou, and Clarence J. Dias, eds. *The Universal Declaration of Human Rights: Fifty Years and Beyond*. New York: Baywood, 1998.

Glendon, Mary Ann. *A World Made New: Eleanor Roosevelt and the Universal Declaration of Human Rights*. New York: Random House, 2001.

Hunt, Lynn. *Inventing Human Rights: A History*. New York: W. W. Norton, 2007.

Korey, William. *NGOs and the Universal Declaration of Human Rights: "A Curious Grapevine."* New York: St. Martin's Press, 1998.

Morsink, Johannes. *The Universal Declaration of Human Rights: Origins, Drafting, and Intent*. Philadelphia: University of Pennsylvania Press, 1999.

Pollis, Adamantia, and Peter Schwab, eds. *Human Rights: Cultural and Ideological Perspectives*. New York: Praeger, 1979.

▪ Web Sites

"Ongoing Struggle for Human Rights." Universal Declaration of Human Rights Web site.
    http://www.udhr.org/history/timeline.htm.

Roosevelt, Eleanor. "On the Adoption of the Universal Declaration of Human Rights." American Rhetoric Web site.
    http://www.americanrhetoric.com/speeches/eleanorroosevelt declarationhumanrights.htm.

United Nations. "Human Rights."
    http://www.un.org/en/rights.

—Patricia Van Der Spuy

Questions for Further Study

1. Compare the Universal Declaration of Human Rights with another document that deals with the issue of human rights. Possibilities include Queen Victoria's Proclamation concerning India, Patrice Lumumba's Speech at the Proclamation of Congolese Independence, the Freedom Charter of South Africa, or the Maastricht Treaty. What similar themes and motivations connect the two documents?

2. Based on your reading of the document, what cultural differences could have given rise to differences in what constituted a "human right" in the minds of the document's drafters?

3. Why do you think the drafters of the declaration largely sidestepped the issue of colonies and colonization just at the time when many African and Asian colonies were demanding, or beginning to demand, independence?

4. Many nations continue to be the sites of blatant human rights violations, and in most instances the world is unable to do anything about it. In light of this, do you believe that a document such as the Universal Declaration of Human Rights serves any real purpose?

5. Discuss the complications that arise when issues such as harsh interrogation of terrorist suspects, capital punishment, and strict religious laws (as in some Muslim countries) are examined in the light of the declaration.

UNIVERSAL DECLARATION OF HUMAN RIGHTS

Preamble

Whereas recognition of the inherent dignity and of the equal and inalienable rights of all members of the human family is the foundation of freedom, justice and peace in the world,

Whereas disregard and contempt for human rights have resulted in barbarous acts which have outraged the conscience of mankind, and the advent of a world in which human beings shall enjoy freedom of speech and belief and freedom from fear and want has been proclaimed as the highest aspiration of the common people,

Whereas it is essential, if man is not to be compelled to have recourse, as a last resort, to rebellion against tyranny and oppression, that human rights should be protected by the rule of law,

Whereas it is essential to promote the development of friendly relations between nations,

Whereas the peoples of the United Nations have in the Charter reaffirmed their faith in fundamental human rights, in the dignity and worth of the human person and in the equal rights of men and women and have determined to promote social progress and better standards of life in larger freedom,

Whereas Member States have pledged themselves to achieve, in co-operation with the United Nations, the promotion of universal respect for and observance of human rights and fundamental freedoms,

Whereas a common understanding of these rights and freedoms is of the greatest importance for the full realization of this pledge,

Now, therefore the General Assembly proclaims this universal declaration of human rights as a common standard of achievement for all peoples and all nations, to the end that every individual and every organ of society, keeping this Declaration constantly in mind, shall strive by teaching and education to promote respect for these rights and freedoms and by progressive measures, national and international, to secure their universal and effective recognition and observance, both among the peoples of Member States themselves and among the peoples of territories under their jurisdiction.

◆ **Article 1.**

All human beings are born free and equal in dignity and rights. They are endowed with reason and conscience and should act towards one another in a spirit of brotherhood.

◆ **Article 2.**

Everyone is entitled to all the rights and freedoms set forth in this Declaration, without distinction of any kind, such as race, colour, sex, language, religion, political or other opinion, national or social origin, property, birth or other status. Furthermore, no distinction shall be made on the basis of the political, jurisdictional or international status of the country or territory to which a person belongs, whether it be independent, trust, non-self-governing or under any other limitation of sovereignty.

◆ **Article 3.**

Everyone has the right to life, liberty and security of person.

◆ **Article 4.**

No one shall be held in slavery or servitude; slavery and the slave trade shall be prohibited in all their forms.

◆ **Article 5.**

No one shall be subjected to torture or to cruel, inhuman or degrading treatment or punishment.

◆ **Article 6.**

Everyone has the right to recognition everywhere as a person before the law.

◆ **Article 7.**

All are equal before the law and are entitled without any discrimination to equal protection of the law. All are entitled to equal protection against any discrimination in violation of this Declaration and against any incitement to such discrimination.

◆ **Article 8.**

Everyone has the right to an effective remedy by the competent national tribunals for acts violating the fundamental rights granted him by the constitution or by law.

◆ **Article 9.**

No one shall be subjected to arbitrary arrest, detention or exile.

◆ **Article 10.**

Everyone is entitled in full equality to a fair and public hearing by an independent and impartial tribunal, in the determination of his rights and obligations and of any criminal charge against him.

◆ **Article 11.**

(1) Everyone charged with a penal offence has the right to be presumed innocent until proved guilty according to law in a public trial at which he has had all the guarantees necessary for his defence.

(2) No one shall be held guilty of any penal offence on account of any act or omission which did not constitute a penal offence, under national or international law, at the time when it was committed. Nor shall a heavier penalty be imposed than the one that was applicable at the time the penal offence was committed.

◆ **Article 12.**

No one shall be subjected to arbitrary interference with his privacy, family, home or correspondence, nor to attacks upon his honour and reputation. Everyone has the right to the protection of the law against such interference or attacks.

◆ **Article 13.**

(1) Everyone has the right to freedom of movement and residence within the borders of each state.

(2) Everyone has the right to leave any country, including his own, and to return to his country.

◆ **Article 14.**

(1) Everyone has the right to seek and to enjoy in other countries asylum from persecution.

(2) This right may not be invoked in the case of prosecutions genuinely arising from non-political crimes or from acts contrary to the purposes and principles of the United Nations.

◆ **Article 15.**

(1) Everyone has the right to a nationality.

(2) No one shall be arbitrarily deprived of his nationality nor denied the right to change his nationality.

◆ **Article 16.**

(1) Men and women of full age, without any limitation due to race, nationality or religion, have the right to marry and to found a family. They are entitled to equal rights as to marriage, during marriage and at its dissolution.

(2) Marriage shall be entered into only with the free and full consent of the intending spouses.

(3) The family is the natural and fundamental group unit of society and is entitled to protection by society and the State.

◆ **Article 17.**

(1) Everyone has the right to own property alone as well as in association with others.

(2) No one shall be arbitrarily deprived of his property.

◆ **Article 18.**

Everyone has the right to freedom of thought, conscience and religion; this right includes freedom to change his religion or belief, and freedom, either alone or in community with others and in public or private, to manifest his religion or belief in teaching, practice, worship and observance.

◆ **Article 19.**

Everyone has the right to freedom of opinion and expression; this right includes freedom to hold opinions without interference and to seek, receive and impart information and ideas through any media and regardless of frontiers.

◆ **Article 20.**

(1) Everyone has the right to freedom of peaceful assembly and association.

(2) No one may be compelled to belong to an association.

◆ **Article 21.**

(1) Everyone has the right to take part in the government of his country, directly or through freely chosen representatives.

(2) Everyone has the right of equal access to public service in his country.

(3) The will of the people shall be the basis of the authority of government; this will shall be expressed in periodic and genuine elections which shall be by universal and equal suffrage and shall be held by secret vote or by equivalent free voting procedures.

◆ **Article 22.**

Everyone, as a member of society, has the right to social security and is entitled to realization, through national effort and international co-operation and in accordance with the organization and resources of each State, of the economic, social and cultural rights indispensable for his dignity and the free development of his personality.

◆ **Article 23.**

(1) Everyone has the right to work, to free choice of employment, to just and favourable conditions of work and to protection against unemployment.

(2) Everyone, without any discrimination, has the right to equal pay for equal work.

(3) Everyone who works has the right to just and favourable remuneration ensuring for himself and his family an existence worthy of human dignity, and supplemented, if necessary, by other means of social protection.

(4) Everyone has the right to form and to join trade unions for the protection of his interests.

◆ **Article 24.**

Everyone has the right to rest and leisure, including reasonable limitation of working hours and periodic holidays with pay.

◆ **Article 25.**

(1) Everyone has the right to a standard of living adequate for the health and well-being of himself and of his family, including food, clothing, housing and medical care and necessary social services, and the right to security in the event of unemployment, sickness, disability, widowhood, old age or other lack of livelihood in circumstances beyond his control.

(2) Motherhood and childhood are entitled to special care and assistance. All children, whether born in or out of wedlock, shall enjoy the same social protection.

◆ **Article 26.**

(1) Everyone has the right to education. Education shall be free, at least in the elementary and fundamental stages. Elementary education shall be compulsory. Technical and professional education shall be made generally available and higher education shall be equally accessible to all on the basis of merit.

(2) Education shall be directed to the full development of the human personality and to the strengthening of respect for human rights and fundamental freedoms. It shall promote understanding, tolerance and friendship among all nations, racial or religious groups, and shall further the activities of the United Nations for the maintenance of peace.

(3) Parents have a prior right to choose the kind of education that shall be given to their children.

◆ **Article 27.**

(1) Everyone has the right freely to participate in the cultural life of the community, to enjoy the arts and to share in scientific advancement and its benefits.

(2) Everyone has the right to the protection of the moral and material interests resulting from any scientific, literary or artistic production of which he is the author.

◆ **Article 28.**

Everyone is entitled to a social and international order in which the rights and freedoms set forth in this Declaration can be fully realized.

◆ **Article 29.**

(1) Everyone has duties to the community in which alone the free and full development of his personality is possible.

(2) In the exercise of his rights and freedoms, everyone shall be subject only to such limitations as are determined by law solely for the purpose of securing due recognition and respect for the rights and freedoms of others and of meeting the just requirements of morality, public order and the general welfare in a democratic society.

(3) These rights and freedoms may in no case be exercised contrary to the purposes and principles of the United Nations.

◆ **Article 30.**

Nothing in this Declaration may be interpreted as implying for any State, group or person any right to engage in any activity or to perform any act aimed at the destruction of any of the rights and freedoms set forth herein.

GENEVA CONVENTION RELATIVE TO THE TREATMENT OF PRISONERS OF WAR

"No physical or mental torture ... may be inflicted on prisoners of war to secure from them information of any kind."

Overview

On August 12, 1949, the Geneva Convention Relative to the Treatment of Prisoners of War was signed in Geneva, Switzerland, as the culmination of a diplomatic conference that had begun on April 21 of that year. As its title indicates, the purpose of the convention (an agreement or treaty), was to provide international standards for the humane treatment of prisoners of war (POWs). Signatories to the convention—194 nations as of 2009, although some have agreed to the convention with reservations—agree essentially to treat prisoners of war humanely by, for example, not torturing them and by providing them with basic necessities such as food, water, shelter, and medical care. The convention was an outgrowth of World War II, when large numbers of prisoners were taken by the Allies, Nazi Germany, and the Japanese Empire. In particular, calls for an agreement on the treatment of POWs increased in the wake of the Nuremberg trials in Germany and the Tokyo trials in Japan. In these trials, numerous Nazi and Japanese officials were held accountable for war crimes, many of them involving POWs and civilian populations. Through these trials, the world became more aware of the crimes.

The phrase *Geneva Convention* is popularly used in the singular; when reference is made to the "Geneva Convention," the one pertaining to treatment of POWs is most likely being referred to. Strictly speaking, though, the plural phrase "Geneva Conventions" is more accurate, for in fact there are four such conventions. The First Geneva Convention for the Amelioration of the Condition of the Wounded and Sick in Armed Forces in the Field dates back to August 22, 1864. The Second Geneva Convention for the Amelioration of the Condition of Wounded, Sick and Shipwrecked Members of Armed Forces at Sea extended the First Geneva Convention to navies and warfare at sea on July 6, 1906. The 1949 document, the Third Geneva Convention, was written to replace a convention with the same title that had been signed on July 27, 1929. At the same diplomatic conference that produced the third convention, the Fourth Geneva Convention relative to the Protection of Civilian Persons in Time of War was also negotiated and signed.

In addition to these four conventions are three protocols, or amendments. The first, Protocol I, signed in 1977, is titled Protection of Victims of International Armed Conflicts; Protocol II, also signed in 1977, is titled Protection of Victims of Non-International Armed Conflicts; Protocol III, signed in 2005, is titled Adoption of an Additional Distinctive Emblem and has to do with emblems used to identify wartime medical personnel who object to the use of the Red Cross or Red Crescent emblem, both of which have religious connotations (the cross symbolic of Christianity and the crescent symbolic of Islam). Taken together, these four conventions, plus the three protocols, are the Geneva Conventions.

In the twenty-first century, the Third Geneva Convention has taken on renewed importance as many nations struggle with the issue of detention and interrogation of suspected terrorists, particularly in the wake of the September 11, 2001, terrorist attacks against the United States and later terrorist attacks in other nations such as England and Spain. The fight against terrorism raises complications in the treatment of prisoners who tend to be nonstate actors and whose actions can be regarded as criminal rather than acts of war.

Context

The roots of the Third Geneva Convention extend back to the nineteenth century, specifically to the Battle of Solferino on June 24, 1859. The battle, between the French and the Austrians, was fought during the Second Italian War of Independence, which in turn was part of a larger effort among Italians to unify the various states on the Italian Peninsula as a single nation. The battle is historically significant in part because it was witnessed by a Swiss businessman, Jean-Henri Dunant, who was traveling in Italy in 1859. Dunant, who was also a social activist, was shocked by the bloodiness of the battle and particularly by the fact that some thirty-eight thousand wounded soldiers lay on the field without medical attention. In response, he organized the local civilian population to render aid. Returning to Switzerland, he published a book about the experience, *Un souvenir de Solférino* (*A Memory of Solferino*). More impor-

1859

■ **June 24**
The Battle of Solferino in Italy prompts Jean-Henri Dunant to call for the formation of a neutral relief organization to aid soldiers wounded in battle.

1863

■ **February 17**
The International Committee of the Red Cross is founded in Geneva, Switzerland.

1864

■ **August 22**
The First Geneva Convention for the Amelioration of the Condition of the Wounded and Sick in Armed Forces is signed.

1899

■ **July 29**
The Hague Convention of 1899, dealing with international laws of war, is signed at The Hague, Netherlands.

1906

■ **July 6**
The Second Geneva Convention for the Amelioration of the Condition of Wounded, Sick and Shipwrecked Members of Armed Forces at Sea is signed.

1907

■ **October 18**
The Hague Convention of 1907, modifying the terms of the Hague Convention of 1899, is signed at The Hague, Netherlands.

tant, he developed the idea that there should be a standing, neutral organization committed to the care of those wounded in battle. The result of his efforts was the creation of the International Committee of the Red Cross (ICRC), usually referred to as simply the Red Cross, which was founded on February 17, 1863. (In 1919 the Red Cross would merge with the Red Crescent to form the International Federation of Red Cross and Red Crescent Societies.) Dunant also believed that nations should meet to agree on a set of principles for the care of wounded soldiers. The ICRC backed this effort, leading to the signing of the First Geneva Convention for the Amelioration of the Condition of the Wounded and Sick in Armed Forces in 1864. The convention was initially signed by twelve European nations; the United States signed later, in 1882. For his efforts, Dunant won the first Nobel Peace Prize in 1901.

In the years that followed, modern industrialism was changing the nature of warfare through the development of more powerful, and more lethal, weapons. In response, a peace conference was held at The Hague, Netherlands, in 1899. The outcome of this conference was the Hague Convention of July 29, 1899, which attempted to curb the practice of dropping bombs out of lighter-than-air balloons, the use of projectiles that release "deleterious" gases (that is, poison gases), and the use of hollow-point bullets, which expand after striking the target, increasing their lethality. At a second conference at The Hague in 1907, amendments were made to the 1899 treaty, principally to extend the provisions of the 1899 agreement to include naval warfare and to recognize that airplanes had the potential to replace hot-air balloons in warfare. Meanwhile, the Second Geneva Convention had been signed on July 6, 1906, also with a view to extending to naval warfare the principles applying to land warfare. These agreements were at least in part a response to increased naval activity in the Franco-Prussian War of 1870–1871 and the Spanish American War of 1889. In these wars, steam-powered, iron-hulled vessels capable of launching larger and heavier shells were changing the face of war at sea.

Through these agreements, a body of international law pertaining to warfare was developing; this body of law established precedents that would ultimately lead to the Third Geneva Convention. The horrors of World War I— the world's first "modern," technological war—increased calls for international agreements to mitigate some of those horrors, such as the use of poison gas. Germany first used poison gas in 1915, and the Allies followed suit soon after. It has been estimated that some seventeen thousand combat deaths resulted from gas attacks during 1916–1917 alone. An interesting side note is that in 1918, an Austrian corporal named Adolf Hitler was temporarily blinded by a gas attack, perhaps explaining why, for all his inhumanity as the leader of Nazi Germany during World War II, he never ordered the use of gas in battle. In response to gas warfare in World War I, the Geneva Protocol, containing one section, Protocol for the Prohibition of the Use in War of Asphyxiating, Poisonous or Other Gases, and of Bacteriological Methods of Warfare, was signed in 1925.

As the world still reeled from the effects of World War I, the Swiss Federal Council convened a conference in Geneva in 1929. The purpose of the conference was to revise the 1906 Geneva Convention and the Hague Conventions to establish humanitarian principles for the treatment of prisoners of war. The need to do so seemed pressing in light of the fact that some eight million men were held prisoner during the war and up to 40 percent of the 2.9 million prisoners held in Russia died of starvation and disease. Few individuals surrendered; most prisoners of war were members of entire units that surrendered, in some cases amounting to tens of thousands of troops. These large numbers of POWs prompted calls for standards for their treatment.

The 1929 convention is responsible for the continuing notion that a POW is obligated only to provide "name, rank, and serial number." In its ninety-seven articles, it specified, among other things, that POWs were to be treated humanely; provided with food, shelter, clothing, and medical care; evacuated from combat zones; not required to perform war work such as the manufacture of armaments; paid for work they perform; allowed to communicate with their families; protected from reprisals; allowed access by the Red Cross/Red Crescent; and repatriated at the end of hostilities. This convention applied to POWs during World War II, though apparently with little effect, for historians estimate that between eight and ten million POWs died during the war. Particularly hard hit were Russian POWs held by Germany; estimates are that some 3.3 million Russian POWs, nearly 60 percent of the total, died while in captivity. Conditions in the Pacific were worse. The Japanese explicitly renounced the Hague Conventions in 1937, and over one-third of Western POWs died at Japanese hands (compared with a rate of about 1 to 3 percent of Westerners held by the Nazis).

The treatment of POWs during World War II—and it should be noted that the Allies, too, engaged in the mistreatment of prisoners—prompted the conference at Geneva to address the issue of treatment of POWs and civilians during wartime. The outcome of their deliberations were the Third Geneva Convention Relative to the Treatment of Prisoners of War, as well as the Fourth Geneva Convention Relative to the Protection of Civilian Persons in Time of War.

About the Author

The Third Geneva Convention was produced at the Diplomatic Conference for the Establishment of International Conventions for the Protection of Victims of the War, held in Geneva, Switzerland, from April 21 to August 12, 1949. The actual writing of the document, though, was the work of the Red Cross, specifically the 17th International Conference of the Red Cross. In February 1945 the ICRC announced the goal of revising and expanding the existing Geneva Conventions in light of the destructiveness of World War II. It organized a preliminary conference of Red Cross Societies from around the world, followed by the Conference of Government Experts for the Study of the

Time Line

1919
- **May**
  The International Federation of Red Cross and Red Crescent Societies, headquartered in Geneva, Switzerland, is formed.

1925
- **June 17**
  The Geneva Protocol, containing one section, Protocol for the Prohibition of the Use in War of Asphyxiating, Poisonous or Other Gases, and of Bacteriological Methods of Warfare, is signed.

1929
- **July 27**
  The Convention Relative to the Treatment of Prisoners of War of 1929 is signed.

1939
- **September 1**
  World War II begins in Europe with the invasion of Poland by Nazi Germany.

1941
- **December 7**
  World War II begins in the Pacific with the Japanese bombing of the American naval base at Pearl Harbor, Hawaii.

1945
- **November 21**
  The first of the Nuremberg Trials, officially the Trial of the Major War Criminals, begins, lasting until October 1, 1946; the trials' conclusions would serve as models for the Third Geneva Convention.

1946

■ **May 3**
The International
Military Tribunal for
the Far East (also
known as the Tokyo
Trials or Tokyo War
Crimes Tribunal)
begins, lasting until
November 12, 1948;
Japan is held
accountable for
treatment of prison-
ers of war and
civilians.

1949

■ **August 12**
The Convention
Relative to the
Treatment of Pris-
oners of War, the
Third Geneva Con-
vention, is signed,
replacing the 1929
convention; the
Fourth Geneva
Convention relative
to the Protection
of Civilian Persons
in Time of War
is signed.

1950

■ **October 21**
The Third Geneva
Convention comes
into force.

Conventions for the Protection of War Victims in 1947. The latter conference backed the ICRC's goals. Accordingly, the ICRC worked with Swiss authorities to convene a diplomatic conference; meanwhile, the 17th International Conference of the Red Cross convened in Stockholm, Sweden, to prepare drafts of the third and fourth conventions. Although considerable discussion and debate took place during the four months of the Diplomatic Conference, the documents that were signed were in large part based on drafts the ICRC had prepared. At the time, the ICRC was under the direction of Paul Ruegger (1897–1988), who served as the organization's president from 1948 to 1955.

Explanation and Analysis of the Document

The Third Geneva Convention is a lengthy document, consisting of six parts and 143 articles, making it significantly longer than the 1929 document that it replaced. After Part I outlines general provisions, Part II addresses the general protection of POWs, Part III details conditions

of captivity, Part IV discusses termination of captivity, and Part V touches on information bureaus and relief societies. Finally, Part VI deals with the execution of the convention.

◆ **"Part I: General Provisions"**

Part I comprises the convention's first eleven articles. These articles are essentially administrative in nature and deal with the basic issue of who is covered by the convention and under what circumstances. Article 2 notes that even if one of the parties to an armed conflict is not a signatory to the convention, the other party that is a signatory remains bound by the agreement. Article 3 lays out the essence of the agreement: Combatants who are taken prisoner are not to be subjected to such practices as murder and humiliating or degrading treatment during their captivity. "Hors de combat" is a French expression commonly used in international law to refer to combatants who are "outside the fight": downed pilots, the injured and sick, and prisoners. Article 4 defines who can be considered a prisoner of war. Obviously, captured soldiers can be POWs, but so can members of militias and volunteer corps, crew members, civilians who accompany combat units (for example, journalists and labor contractors), and civilians who spontaneously take up arms against an invading force. This provision requires that soldiers be readily identifiable as such through "a fixed distinctive sign recognizable at a distance."

Subsequent articles summarize legalities pertaining to persons whose status is not known or changes during the course of hostilities. Article 9 requires that humanitarian organizations such as the Red Cross be given access to POWs. Reference is made in this sequence of articles to "protecting powers." This is a phrase used in international diplomacy to refer to one country that either protects or represents the interests of another state. Thus, for example, the United States and Cuba do not have diplomatic relations, but Switzerland functions as Cuba's "protecting power" in the United States and the U.S.'s protecting power in Cuba. Articles 10 and 11 address procedures to be followed in the event of disputes over the application of the convention.

◆ **"Part II: General Protection of Prisoners of War"**

The five articles in this part, as the title suggests, outline in general terms how POWs are to be treated. Article 12 notes that POWs are the prisoners of the nation, not the individuals or units that captured them; accordingly, the nation is responsible for the POWs' welfare. Article 12 also addresses the issue of transfer of POWs to other nations. Article 13 is a core article, stating that "prisoners of war must at all times be humanely treated" and not subject to violence, intimidation, reprisals, or insults. In response to Nazi and Japanese atrocities during World War II, the convention outlaws the use of POWs for medical experimentation. Article 14 requires respect for the "persons and … honour" of POWs and that women be accorded the same respect as men. Article 15 requires that the detaining power provide POWs with medical care, while Article 16 requires that prisoners be treated equally, "without any

Near the end of the Bataan Death March, a thinning line of American and Filipino prisoners of war carry casualties in improvised stretchers as they approach Camp O'Donnell, a new Japanese POW camp, in April 1942. (AP/Wide World Photos)

adverse distinction based on race, nationality, religious belief or political opinions."

◆ "Part III: Captivity"

The third part of the convention goes into detail about the treatment of POWs during the course of their captivity. Section I of Part III, which focuses on the beginning of captivity, limits the amount of information that the captors can demand from prisoners. Captors cannot elicit this information through harsh or degrading treatment. Article 18 requires that prisoners be allowed to keep their personal effects, with the obvious exception of arms and military equipment. Articles 18 and 19 deal with the need to remove prisoners from combat zones and to ensure their safety while they are being moved. It is likely that the framers of the convention had in mind such World War II episodes as the Bataan Death March, when, in April 1942, some seventy-six thousand American and Filipino prisoners held by the Japanese were forced to travel about sixty miles by foot to a POW camp. Thousands died along the way from starvation, beatings, and executions.

Section II of Part III addresses the internment of POWs. Articles 21 through 24 deal with the location of POW camps, requiring captors to provide safe locations away from combat. POW camps are to be on land, and they are to be located in areas that are not unhealthful. POWs may be granted parole, allowing them to be released from camps. It was a common practice in England, for example, to allow German POWs to work on farms, especially given that so many men were away from their farms fighting. A similar practice was followed in the United States. Articles 25 through 28 deal with the specifics of providing POWs with food, water, and clothing. Article 28 calls for the provision of canteens where POWs can purchase necessities. Interestingly, during World War II American prisoners "purchased" items from other prisoners' Red Cross relief packages, as well as services (for example, haircuts), using cigarettes the Red Cross provided as the standard of value and medium of exchange. Prisoners also were able to purchase goods from outside the camps with the collusion of guards, again using cigarettes as currency.

Articles 29 through 32 take up hygiene and medical care. Hygiene encompasses such items as baths and showers, soap, laundry facilities, and toilets. Prisoners are also to be given medical care as needed. Prisoners with medical expertise could be required to provide medical care to fellow prisoners. Articles 33 through 38 deal with similar quality-of-life issues. For example, chaplains are to be provided when possible, and POWs are to be allowed to worship and practice their religious faith. This has become a particular issue in the twenty-first century in connection with the detention of Muslims suspected of terrorist activities. Devout Muslims follow numerous specified religious practices, including prayer and diet, and Western powers have had to accommodate those practices. Additionally, provisions are to be made to provide POWs with opportunities for intellectual and physical exercise.

The issue of discipline is dealt with in Articles 39–42. The chief requirement is that POWs are to be put under the authority of a regular officer from the detaining country's military. Article 39 specifies that POWs are required to salute higher-ranking officers of the detaining country and otherwise show them respect. Prisoners are to be informed of all policies, and weapons are to be used against prisoners only as a last resort. Articles 43–45 address issues of rank, requiring that ranks be recognized and respected. Articles 46–48 concern the matter of transferring prisoners to POW camps, requiring the detaining power "take into account the interests of the prisoners themselves." Prisoners must be transferred safely, and if they are transferred, it must be to a place with climatic conditions to which they are accustomed.

Several articles discuss the issue of labor. The Third Geneva Convention allows the detaining power to compel POWs to perform work. Noncommissioned officers (in the U.S. military, sergeants) can be compelled only to perform supervisory work, and officers cannot be compelled to perform work. Prisoners may not be used to perform work of a military character, and they must be provided with suitable working conditions. They cannot be required to perform excessively dangerous work, and their hours and other working conditions must conform to the standards in place in the detaining power's country. Further, if prisoners perform labor, they must be paid.

Articles 58 through 68, perhaps surprisingly, address issues involving the financial resources of POWs. The detaining power can seize any cash the POW has at the time of his capture, but it must be returned to him on his release. Again, POWs who perform labor must be paid. POWs are allowed to keep cash remittances from home. In all cases, though, the detaining power can determine how much cash the POW can keep in his possession. Perhaps surprisingly, too, POWs must be given an advance on their regular pay in amounts specified in Article 60. In all financial matters, the detaining power is required to keep records and show those records to POWs at the time of their release.

Articles 69 through 77 fall under the heading "Relations of Prisoners of War with the Exterior." The essence of this sequence of articles is that POWs are to be allowed contact with the outside world through, for examples, letters to and from their families; the detaining power is allowed to read and censor mail and can limit the amount of mail only if not enough translators are available to read a greater volume of mail. Additionally, prisoners cannot be held in secret locations; authorities and the prisoner's family must be informed of the prisoner's location, including the new location if the prisoner is transferred. Prisoners are also allowed to receive food, clothing, books, recreational equipment, devotional materials, and the like. Additionally, relief agencies must be allowed to have contact with prisoners and provide for their material needs.

Articles 78–108 specify in detail the relationship between prisoners and the authorities who hold them. In essence, this extensive sequence of chapters establishes the legal principles that govern the detention of POWs. Prisoners have the right to file complaints about their treatment, particularly through representatives chosen from their ranks (either an elected representative or the ranking officer). Detaining powers, on the other hand, have the right to take disciplinary action against prisoners who violate policies. Punishments cannot exceed those that the detaining power would mete out to members of its own forces for the same offense. In general, judicial and disciplinary hearings must be conducted fairly and give the prisoner an opportunity to defend himself. Prisoners who escape or are captured in attempting to escape cannot be subject to anything more than disciplinary punishments; it is assumed that prisoners will try to escape, so the convention does not allow harsh or excessive punishments for doing so, even in the case of repeated attempts. Punishments for offenses can range from two hours of "fatigue duty" to the death penalty for serious offenses.

◆ **"Part IV: Termination of Captivity"**

Articles 109 through 121 deal with the repatriation of POWs. Seriously sick and wounded POWs must be returned to their home countries or transferred to a neutral country. The convention precisely defines those who are eligible for immediate repatriation as a result of illness or injury. This part also addresses issues surrounding repatriation at the end of hostilities. Its key provision is contained in Article 118: "Prisoners of war shall be released and repatriated without delay after the cessation of active hostilities." In the event that a POW has died, he is to be honorably buried and authorities are to be notified of the death. If a POW dies under suspicious circumstances or at the hands of a guard, a full investigation is to be conducted.

◆ **Part V: "Information Bureaux and Relief Societies for Prisoners of War"**

To prevent POWs from being held in secret, Article 122 requires the detaining power to submit information about the identities of POWs to an information bureau. Next of kin are to be notified of the prisoner's status. Additionally, a Central Prisoners of War Information Agency is to be established in a neutral country. The detaining power is required to provide relief and humanitarian organizations access to prisoners.

◆ **"Part VI: Execution of the Convention"**

The final section of the convention touches on procedural issues. It requires the signatories, for example, to disseminate the convention so that its provisions are widely known. Its key provision is contained in Article 129, which requires the signatory nations to search for and bring to

The original document of the First Geneva Convention for the Amelioration of the Condition of the Wounded in Armies in the Field, signed in 1864, is displayed at the International Red Cross and Red Crescent Museum in Geneva, Switzerland. (AP/Wide World Photos)

trial anyone who has been guilty of "grave breaches" of the convention. Thus, the Third Geneva Convention holds nations rather than individuals responsible for adherence to the convention; in turn, nations are obligated to hold individuals responsible for their actions relative to POWs.

Audience

The chief audience for the Third Geneva Convention consists of the signatory nations, which as of 2009 numbered 194. In particular, the convention is addressed to military leaders whose actions and decisions have an impact on POWs, as well as to their governments. Ultimately, governments are held responsible for the treatment of POWs in their care, and the convention requires governments to pass laws criminalizing breaches of the convention. Another audience for the convention has been journalists, commentators, and others who study or comment on conflicts, such as the ongoing conflict in Iraq or that between Israel and the Palestinians. The Third Geneva Convention, in concert with the other three Geneva Conventions, provides watchdogs with a set of guiding principles they can use in commentary about government policies during wartime.

Impact

The impact of the Third Geneva Convention has been widespread. The agreement entered into force on October 21, 1950. During the decade of the 1950s, seventy-four nations ratified the convention. Forty-eight nations followed in the 1960s, and twenty nations ratified the convention in the 1970s, followed by another twenty in the 1980s. After the breakup of the Soviet Union, twenty-six more nations ratified the convention during the 1990s, and seven more did so in the first decade of the 2000s. As of 2009, nearly every nation in the world had ratified the Third Geneva Convention, along with the other three conventions.

The ICRC can provide data about what it has accomplished. For example, during a war between Ethiopia and Eritrea, the Red Cross, in the year 2000, visited one thousand Ethiopian POWs and was able to exchange over sixteen thousand messages between POWs and their families. In Iraq, the ICRC visited more than six thousand POWs in just thirteen months spanning 2003 and 2004, while also passing about sixteen thousand messages from POWs to their families. These kinds of numbers, however, do not tell the entire story. The real story concerns events that might

"Prisoners of war must at all times be humanely treated. Any unlawful act or omission by the Detaining Power causing death or seriously endangering the health of a prisoner of war in its custody is prohibited, and will be regarded as a serious breach of the present Convention."

(Part II, Article 13)

"No physical or mental torture, nor any other form of coercion, may be inflicted on prisoners of war to secure from them information of any kind whatever. Prisoners of war who refuse to answer may not be threatened, insulted, or exposed to unpleasant or disadvantageous treatment of any kind."

(Part III, Article 17)

"Prisoners of war shall enjoy complete latitude in the exercise of their religious duties, including attendance at the service of their faith, on condition that they comply with the disciplinary routine prescribed by the military authorities."

(Part III, Article 34)

"In no circumstances whatever shall a prisoner of war be tried by a court of any kind which does not offer the essential guarantees of independence and impartiality as generally recognized, and, in particular, the procedure of which does not afford the accused the rights and means of defence."

(Part III, Article 84)

"Prisoners of war shall be released and repatriated without delay after the cessation of active hostilities."

(Part IV, Article 118)

"The detaining authorities shall ensure that prisoners of war who have died in captivity are honourably buried, if possible according to the rites of the religion to which they belonged, and that their graves are respected, suitably maintained and marked so as to be found at any time."

(Part IV, Article 120)

have happened but that did not because of the Geneva Conventions. It is highly likely that the existence of the conventions has saved the lives of countless prisoners of war and made the conditions of their captivity at least marginally more tolerable—despite the fact that some nations routinely ignore the provisions of the convention.

The Geneva Conventions, specifically the third convention, entered the public discourse in connection with the war on terrorism. After the terrorist attacks of September 11, 2001, the United States and its allies responded with military campaigns in Afghanistan and Iraq. At the same time, the Western nations conducted internal investigations of suspected terrorists within their borders. The result has been the detention of terrorists and those suspected of plotting terrorism. The question that has arisen is this: How do nations deal with terrorists when there is no declared conflict, terrorists do not fight under the flag of a nation, terrorists target civilian populations, and it is impossible to foresee a specific end to the conflict? A further question involves prying information about future terrorist attacks from prisoners. When is it acceptable, if ever, to use harsh interrogation tactics to learn about upcoming attacks, particularly if that knowledge saves, or may save, civilian lives? Is it acceptable to repatriate terrorist suspects to their countries, knowing that those suspects are likely to be subjected to harsher treatment than they would receive at the hands of the United States? What legal rights to due process do terrorists have under the constitutions of Western nations? These questions confirm that in spite of the best efforts of international organizations, warfare remains a messy business, one that raises moral quandaries. Application of the Third Geneva Convention brings these quandaries into stark relief.

Further Reading

■ Books

Bennett, Angela. *The Geneva Convention: The Hidden Origins of the Red Cross.* Gloucestershire, U.K.: Sutton Publishing, 2005.

Gray, Christine. *International Law and the Use of Force.* 3rd ed. New York: Oxford University Press, 2008.

Jinks, Derek. *The Rules of War: The Geneva Conventions in the Age of Terror.* New York: Oxford University Press, forthcoming.

Schindler, Dietrich, and Jiří Toman, eds. *The Laws of Armed Conflicts: A Collection of Conventions, Resolutions, and Other Documents.* 4th ed. Boston: Martinus Nijhoff Publishers, 2004.

■ Web Sites

"Geneva Conventions: A Reference Guide." Society of Professional Journalists Web site.
http://www.genevaconventions.org.

"Politics and Economy: The Geneva Conventions." PBS "Now" Web site.
http://www.pbs.org/now/politics/geneva.html.

Spoerri, Philip. "The Geneva Conventions of 1949: Origins and Current Significance." International Committee of the Red Cross Web site.
http://www.icrc.org/web/eng/siteeng0.nsf/html/geneva-conventions-statement-120809?opendocument.

—Michael J. O'Neal

Questions for Further Study

1. Imagine that you are at a social gathering and someone mentions the Geneva Convention. How would you respond to the person's puzzled look when you ask, "Which Geneva Convention?"

2. Explain the relationship between the Geneva Conventions and the International Red Cross (or, more accurately, the International Federation of Red Cross and Red Crescent Societies).

3. What complications does the modern fight against terrorism raise in defining who is a prisoner of war and what rights should be extended to suspected terrorists? On what basis would some people argue that suspected terrorists are not protected by the Third Geneva Convention?

4. Do any of the provisions of the Third Geneva Convention come as a surprise to you? That is, do any of the provisions perhaps strike you as requiring nations to be *overly* protective of the welfare of POWs?

5. Given that some, perhaps many, nations ignore agreements such as the Third Geneva Convention, even though they have signed the agreement, do you believe that such agreements have value? Explain.

GENEVA CONVENTION RELATIVE TO THE TREATMENT OF PRISONERS OF WAR

The undersigned Plenipotentiaries of the Governments represented at the Diplomatic Conference held at Geneva from April 21 to August 12, 1949, for the purpose of revising the Convention concluded at Geneva on July 27, 1929 relative to the Treatment of Prisoners of War, have agreed as follows:

Part I. General Provisions

ARTICLE 1
The High Contracting Parties undertake to respect and to ensure respect for the present Convention in all circumstances.

ARTICLE 2
In addition to the provisions which shall be implemented in peace time, the present Convention shall apply to all cases of declared war or of any other armed conflict which may arise between two or more of the High Contracting Parties, even if the state of war is not recognized by one of them.

The Convention shall also apply to all cases of partial or total occupation of the territory of a High Contracting Party, even if the said occupation meets with no armed resistance.

Although one of the Powers in conflict may not be a party to the present Convention, the Powers who are parties thereto shall remain bound by it in their mutual relations. They shall furthermore be bound by the Convention in relation to the said Power, if the latter accepts and applies the provisions thereof.

ARTICLE 3
In the case of armed conflict not of an international character occurring in the territory of one of the High Contracting Parties, each Party to the conflict shall be bound to apply, as a minimum, the following provisions:

(1) Persons taking no active part in the hostilities, including members of armed forces who have laid down their arms and those placed hors de combat by sickness, wounds, detention, or any other cause, shall in all circumstances be treated humanely, without any adverse distinction founded on race, colour, religion or faith, sex, birth or wealth, or any other similar criteria. To this end the following acts are and shall remain prohibited at any time and in any place whatsoever with respect to the above-mentioned persons:

(a) violence to life and person, in particular murder of all kinds, mutilation, cruel treatment and torture; (b) taking of hostages; (c) outrages upon personal dignity, in particular, humiliating and degrading treatment; (d) the passing of sentences and the carrying out of executions without previous judgment pronounced by a regularly constituted court affording all the judicial guarantees which are recognized as indispensable by civilized peoples.

(2) The wounded and sick shall be collected and cared for.

An impartial humanitarian body, such as the International Committee of the Red Cross, may offer its services to the Parties to the conflict.

The Parties to the conflict should further endeavour to bring into force, by means of special agreements, all or part of the other provisions of the present Convention.

The application of the preceding provisions shall not affect the legal status of the Parties to the conflict.

ARTICLE 4
A. Prisoners of war, in the sense of the present Convention, are persons belonging to one of the following categories, who have fallen into the power of the enemy:

(1) Members of the armed forces of a Party to the conflict, as well as members of militias or volunteer corps forming part of such armed forces.

(2) Members of other militias and members of other volunteer corps, including those of organized resistance movements, belonging to a Party to the conflict and operating in or outside their own territory, even if this territory is occupied, provided that such militias or volunteer corps, including such organized resistance movements, fulfil the following conditions: (a) that of being commanded by a person responsible for his subordinates; (b) that of having a fixed distinctive sign recognizable at a distance; (c) that of carrying arms openly; (d) that of conducting their operations in accordance with the laws and customs of war.

(3) Members of regular armed forces who profess allegiance to a government or an authority not recognized by the Detaining Power.

(4) Persons who accompany the armed forces without actually being members thereof, such as civilian members of military aircraft crews, war correspondents, supply contractors, members of labour units or of services responsible for the welfare of the armed forces, provided that they have received authorization, from the armed forces which they accompany, who shall provide them for that purpose with an identity card similar to the annexed model.

(5) Members of crews, including masters, pilots and apprentices, of the merchant marine and the crews of civil aircraft of the Parties to the conflict, who do not benefit by more favourable treatment under any other provisions of international law.

(6) Inhabitants of a non-occupied territory, who on the approach of the enemy spontaneously take up arms to resist the invading forces, without having had time to form themselves into regular armed units, provided they carry arms openly and respect the laws and customs of war.

B. The following shall likewise be treated as prisoners of war under the present Convention:

(1) Persons belonging, or having belonged, to the armed forces of the occupied country, if the occupying Power considers it necessary by reason of such allegiance to intern them, even though it has originally liberated them while hostilities were going on outside the territory it occupies, in particular where such persons have made an unsuccessful attempt to rejoin the armed forces to which they belong and which are engaged in combat, or where they fail to comply with a summons made to them with a view to internment.

(2) The persons belonging to one of the categories enumerated in the present Article, who have been received by neutral or non-belligerent Powers on their territory and whom these Powers are required to intern under international law, without prejudice to any more favourable treatment which these Powers may choose to give and with the exception of Articles 8, 10, 15, 30, fifth paragraph, 58-67, 92, 126 and, where diplomatic relations exist between the Parties to the conflict and the neutral or non-belligerent Power concerned, those Articles concerning the Protecting Power. Where such diplomatic relations exist, the Parties to a conflict on whom these persons depend shall be allowed to perform towards them the functions of a Protecting Power as provided in the present Convention, without prejudice to the functions which these Parties normally exercise in conformity with diplomatic and consular usage and treaties.

C. This Article shall in no way affect the status of medical personnel and chaplains as provided for in Article 33 of the present Convention.

ARTICLE 5

The present Convention shall apply to the persons referred to in Article 4 from the time they fall into the power of the enemy and until their final release and repatriation.

Should any doubt arise as to whether persons, having committed a belligerent act and having fallen into the hands of the enemy, belong to any of the categories enumerated in Article 4, such persons shall enjoy the protection of the present Convention until such time as their status has been determined by a competent tribunal.

ARTICLE 6

In addition to the agreements expressly provided for in Articles 10, 23, 28, 33, 60, 65, 66, 67, 72, 73, 75, 109, 110, 118, 119, 122 and 132, the High Contracting Parties may conclude other special agreements for all matters concerning which they may deem it suitable to make separate provision. No special agreement shall adversely affect the situation of prisoners of war, as defined by the present Convention, nor restrict the rights which it confers upon them.

Prisoners of war shall continue to have the benefit of such agreements as long as the Convention is applicable to them, except where express provisions to the contrary are contained in the aforesaid or in subsequent agreements, or where more favourable measures have been taken with regard to them by one or other of the Parties to the conflict.

ARTICLE 7

Prisoners of war may in no circumstances renounce in part or in entirety the rights secured to them by the present Convention, and by the special agreements referred to in the foregoing Article, if such there be.

ARTICLE 8

The present Convention shall be applied with the cooperation and under the scrutiny of the Protecting Powers whose duty it is to safeguard the interests of the Parties to the conflict. For this purpose, the Protecting Powers may appoint, apart from their diplomatic or consular staff, delegates from amongst their own nationals or the nationals of other neutral Powers. The said delegates shall be subject to the approval of the Power with which they are to carry out their duties.

The Parties to the conflict shall facilitate to the greatest extent possible the task of the representatives or delegates of the Protecting Powers.

The representatives or delegates of the Protecting Powers shall not in any case exceed their mission under the present Convention. They shall, in particular, take account of the imperative necessities of security of the State wherein they carry out their duties.

ARTICLE 9

The provisions of the present Convention constitute no obstacle to the humanitarian activities which the International Committee of the Red Cross or any other impartial humanitarian organization may, subject to the consent of the Parties to the conflict concerned, undertake for the protection of prisoners of war and for their relief.

ARTICLE 10

The High Contracting Parties may at any time agree to entrust to an organization which offers all guarantees of impartiality and efficacy the duties incumbent on the Protecting Powers by virtue of the present Convention.

When prisoners of war do not benefit or cease to benefit, no matter for what reason, by the activities of a Protecting Power or of an organization provided for in the first paragraph above, the Detaining Power shall request a neutral State, or such an organization, to undertake the functions performed under the present Convention by a Protecting Power designated by the Parties to a conflict.

If protection cannot be arranged accordingly, the Detaining Power shall request or shall accept, subject to the provisions of this Article, the offer of the services of a humanitarian organization, such as the International Committee of the Red Cross to assume the humanitarian functions performed by Protecting Powers under the present Convention.

Any neutral Power or any organization invited by the Power concerned or offering itself for these purposes, shall be required to act with a sense of responsibility towards the Party to the conflict on which persons protected by the present Convention depend, and shall be required to furnish sufficient assurances that it is in a position to undertake the appropriate functions and to discharge them impartially.

No derogation from the preceding provisions shall be made by special agreements between Powers one of which is restricted, even temporarily, in its freedom to negotiate with the other Power or its allies by reason of military events, more particularly where the whole, or a substantial part, of the territory of the said Power is occupied.

Whenever in the present Convention mention is made of a Protecting Power, such mention applies to substitute organizations in the sense of the present Article.

ARTICLE 11

In cases where they deem it advisable in the interest of protected persons, particularly in cases of disagreement between the Parties to the conflict as to the application or interpretation of the provisions of the present Convention, the Protecting Powers shall lend their good offices with a view to settling the disagreement.

For this purpose, each of the Protecting Powers may, either at the invitation of one Party or on its own initiative, propose to the Parties to the conflict a meeting of their representatives, and in particular of the authorities responsible for prisoners of war, possibly on neutral territory suitably chosen. The Parties to the conflict shall be bound to give effect to the proposals made to them for this purpose. The Protecting Powers may, if necessary, propose for approval by the Parties to the conflict a person belonging to a neutral Power, or delegated by the International Committee of the Red Cross, who shall be invited to take part in such a meeting.

Part II. General Protection of Prisoners of War

ARTICLE 12

Prisoners of war are in the hands of the enemy Power, but not of the individuals or military units who have captured them. Irrespective of the individual responsibilities that may exist, the Detaining Power is responsible for the treatment given them.

Prisoners of war may only be transferred by the Detaining Power to a Power which is a party to the Convention and after the Detaining Power has satisfied itself of the willingness and ability of such transferee Power to apply the Convention. When prisoners of war are transferred under such circumstances, responsibility for the application of the Convention rests on the Power accepting them while they are in its custody.

Nevertheless, if that Power fails to carry out the provisions of the Convention in any important respect, the Power by whom the prisoners of war were transferred shall, upon being notified by the Protecting Power, take effective measures to correct the situation or shall request the return of the prisoners of war. Such requests must be complied with.

ARTICLE 13

Prisoners of war must at all times be humanely treated. Any unlawful act or omission by the Detaining Power causing death or seriously endangering the health of a prisoner of war in its custody is prohibited, and will be regarded as a serious breach of the present Convention. In particular, no prisoner of war may be subjected to physical mutilation or to medical or scientific experiments of any kind which are not justified by the medical, dental or hospital treatment of the prisoner concerned and carried out in his interest.

Likewise, prisoners of war must at all times be protected, particularly against acts of violence or intimidation and against insults and public curiosity.

Measures of reprisal against prisoners of war are prohibited.

ARTICLE 14

Prisoners of war are entitled in all circumstances to respect for their persons and their honour.

Women shall be treated with all the regard due to their sex and shall in all cases benefit by treatment as favourable as that granted to men.

Prisoners of war shall retain the full civil capacity which they enjoyed at the time of their capture. The Detaining Power may not restrict the exercise, either within or without its own territory, of the rights such capacity confers except in so far as the captivity requires.

ARTICLE 15

The Power detaining prisoners of war shall be bound to provide free of charge for their maintenance and for the medical attention required by their state of health.

ARTICLE 16

Taking into consideration the provisions of the present Convention relating to rank and sex, and subject to any privileged treatment which may be accorded to them by reason of their state of health, age or professional qualifications, all prisoners of war shall be treated alike by the Detaining Power, without any adverse distinction based on race, nationality, religious belief or political opinions, or any other distinction founded on similar criteria.

Part III. Captivity

◆ **Section 1. Beginning of Captivity**

ARTICLE 17

Every prisoner of war, when questioned on the subject, is bound to give only his surname, first names and rank, date of birth, and army, regimental, personal or serial number, or failing this, equivalent information.

If he wilfully infringes this rule, he may render himself liable to a restriction of the privileges accorded to his rank or status.

Each Party to a conflict is required to furnish the persons under its jurisdiction who are liable to become prisoners of war, with an identity card showing the owner's surname, first names, rank, army, regimental, personal or serial number or equivalent information, and date of birth. The identity card may, furthermore, bear the signature or the fingerprints, or both, of the owner, and may bear, as well, any other information the Party to the conflict may wish to add concerning persons belonging to its armed forces. As far as possible the card shall measure 6.5 x 10 cm. and shall be issued in duplicate. The identity card shall be shown by the prisoner of war upon demand, but may in no case be taken away from him.

No physical or mental torture, nor any other form of coercion, may be inflicted on prisoners of war to secure from them information of any kind whatever. Prisoners of war who refuse to answer may not be threatened, insulted, or exposed to unpleasant or disadvantageous treatment of any kind. Prisoners of war who, owing to their physical or mental condition, are unable to state their identity, shall be handed over to the medical service. The identity of such prisoners shall be established by all possible means, subject to the provisions of the preceding paragraph.

The questioning of prisoners of war shall be carried out in a language which they understand.

ARTICLE 18

All effects and articles of personal use, except arms, horses, military equipment and military documents, shall remain in the possession of prisoners of war, likewise their metal helmets and gas masks and like articles issued for personal protection. Effects and articles used for their clothing or feeding shall likewise remain in their possession, even if such effects and articles belong to their regulation military equipment.

At no time should prisoners of war be without identity documents. The Detaining Power shall supply such documents to prisoners of war who possess none.

Badges of rank and nationality, decorations and articles having above all a personal or sentimental value may not be taken from prisoners of war.

Sums of money carried by prisoners of war may not be taken away from them except by order of an officer, and after the amount and particulars of the owner have been recorded in a special register and an itemized receipt has been given, legibly inscribed with the name, rank and unit of the person issuing the said receipt. Sums in the currency of the Detaining Power, or which are changed into such currency at the prisoner's request, shall be placed to the credit of the prisoner's account as provided in Article 64.

The Detaining Power may withdraw articles of value from prisoners of war only for reasons of security; when such articles are withdrawn, the procedure laid down for sums of money impounded shall apply.

Such objects, likewise sums taken away in any currency other than that of the Detaining Power and the conversion of which has not been asked for by the owners, shall be kept in the custody of the Detaining Power and shall be returned in their initial shape to prisoners of war at the end of their captivity.

ARTICLE 19

Prisoners of war shall be evacuated, as soon as possible after their capture, to camps situated in an area far enough from the combat zone for them to be out of danger.

Only those prisoners of war who, owing to wounds or sickness, would run greater risks by being evacuated than by remaining where they are, may be temporarily kept back in a danger zone.

Prisoners of war shall not be unnecessarily exposed to danger while awaiting evacuation from a fighting zone.

ARTICLE 20

The evacuation of prisoners of war shall always be effected humanely and in conditions similar to those for the forces of the Detaining Power in their changes of station.

The Detaining Power shall supply prisoners of war who are being evacuated with sufficient food and potable water, and with the necessary clothing and medical attention. The Detaining Power shall take all suitable precautions to ensure their safety during evacuation, and shall establish as soon as possible a list of the prisoners of war who are evacuated.

If prisoners of war must, during evacuation, pass through transit camps, their stay in such camps shall be as brief as possible.

◆ **Section II. Internment of Prisoners of War**
Chapter 1. General Observations
ARTICLE 21

The Detaining Power may subject prisoners of war to internment. It may impose on them the obligation of not leaving, beyond certain limits, the camp where they are interned, or if the said camp is fenced in, of not going outside its perimeter. Subject to the provisions of the present Convention relative to

penal and disciplinary sanctions, prisoners of war may not be held in close confinement except where necessary to safeguard their health and then only during the continuation of the circumstances which make such confinement necessary.

Prisoners of war may be partially or wholly released on parole or promise, in so far as is allowed by the laws of the Power on which they depend. Such measures shall be taken particularly in cases where this may contribute to the improvement of their state of health. No prisoner of war shall be compelled to accept liberty on parole or promise.

Upon the outbreak of hostilities, each Party to the conflict shall notify the adverse Party of the laws and regulations allowing or forbidding its own nationals to accept liberty on parole or promise. Prisoners of war who are paroled or who have given their promise in conformity with the laws and regulations so notified, are bound on their personal honour scrupulously to fulfil, both towards the Power on which they depend and towards the Power which has captured them, the engagements of their paroles or promises. In such cases, the Power on which they depend is bound neither to require nor to accept from them any service incompatible with the parole or promise given.

ARTICLE 22

Prisoners of war may be interned only in premises located on land and affording every guarantee of hygiene and healthfulness. Except in particular cases which are justified by the interest of the prisoners themselves, they shall not be interned in penitentiaries.

Prisoners of war interned in unhealthy areas, or where the climate is injurious for them, shall be removed as soon as possible to a more favourable climate.

The Detaining Power shall assemble prisoners of war in camps or camp compounds according to their nationality, language and customs, provided that such prisoners shall not be separated from prisoners of war belonging to the armed forces with which they were serving at the time of their capture, except with their consent.

ARTICLE 23

No prisoner of war may at any time be sent to, or detained in areas where he may be exposed to the fire of the combat zone, nor may his presence be used to render certain points or areas immune from military operations.

Prisoners of war shall have shelters against air bombardment and other hazards of war, to the same extent as the local civilian population. With the exception of those engaged in the protection of their quarters against the aforesaid hazards, they may enter such shelters as soon as possible after the giving of the alarm. Any other protective measure taken in favour of the population shall also apply to them.

Detaining Powers shall give the Powers concerned, through the intermediary of the Protecting Powers, all useful information regarding the geographical location of prisoner of war camps.

Whenever military considerations permit, prisoner of war camps shall be indicated in the day-time by the letters PW or PG, placed so as to be clearly visible from the air. The Powers concerned may, however, agree upon any other system of marking. Only prisoner of war camps shall be marked as such.

ARTICLE 24

Transit or screening camps of a permanent kind shall be fitted out under conditions similar to those described in the present Section, and the prisoners therein shall have the same treatment as in other camps.

Chapter II. Quarters, Food and Clothing of Prisoners of War

ARTICLE 25

Prisoners of war shall be quartered under conditions as favourable as those for the forces of the Detaining Power who are billeted in the same area. The said conditions shall make allowance for the habits and customs of the prisoners and shall in no case be prejudicial to their health.

The foregoing provisions shall apply in particular to the dormitories of prisoners of war as regards both total surface and minimum cubic space, and the general installations, bedding and blankets.

The premises provided for the use of prisoners of war individually or collectively, shall be entirely protected from dampness and adequately heated and lighted, in particular between dusk and lights out. All precautions must be taken against the danger of fire.

In any camps in which women prisoners of war, as well as men, are accommodated, separate dormitories shall be provided for them.

ARTICLE 26

The basic daily food rations shall be sufficient in quantity, quality and variety to keep prisoners of war in good health and to prevent loss of weight or the development of nutritional deficiencies. Account shall also be taken of the habitual diet of the prisoners.

The Detaining Power shall supply prisoners of war who work with such additional rations as are necessary for the labour on which they are employed.

Sufficient drinking water shall be supplied to prisoners of war. The use of tobacco shall be permitted.

Prisoners of war shall, as far as possible, be associated with the preparation of their meals; they may be employed for that purpose in the kitchens. Furthermore, they shall be given the means of preparing, themselves, the additional food in their possession.

Adequate premises shall be provided for messing.

Collective disciplinary measures affecting food are prohibited.

ARTICLE 27

Clothing, underwear and footwear shall be supplied to prisoners of war in sufficient quantities by the Detaining Power, which shall make allowance for the climate of the region where the prisoners are detained. Uniforms of enemy armed forces captured by the Detaining Power should, if suitable for the climate, be made available to clothe prisoners of war.

The regular replacement and repair of the above articles shall be assured by the Detaining Power. In addition, prisoners of war who work shall receive appropriate clothing, wherever the nature of the work demands.

ARTICLE 28

Canteens shall be installed in all camps, where prisoners of war may procure foodstuffs, soap and tobacco and ordinary articles in daily use. The tariff shall never be in excess of local market prices.

The profits made by camp canteens shall be used for the benefit of the prisoners; a special fund shall be created for this purpose. The prisoners' representative shall have the right to collaborate in the management of the canteen and of this fund.

When a camp is closed down, the credit balance of the special fund shall be handed to an international welfare organization, to be employed for the benefit of prisoners of war of the same nationality as those who have contributed to the fund. In case of a general repatriation, such profits shall be kept by the Detaining Power, subject to any agreement to the contrary between the Powers concerned.

Chapter III. Hygiene and Medical Attention

ARTICLE 29

The Detaining Power shall be bound to take all sanitary measures necessary to ensure the cleanliness and healthfulness of camps and to prevent epidemics.

Prisoners of war shall have for their use, day and night, conveniences which conform to the rules of hygiene and are maintained in a constant state of cleanliness. In any camps in which women prisoners of war are accommodated, separate conveniences shall be provided for them.

Also, apart from the baths and showers with which the camps shall be furnished prisoners of war shall be provided with sufficient water and soap for their personal toilet and for washing their personal laundry; the necessary installations, facilities and time shall be granted them for that purpose.

ARTICLE 30

Every camp shall have an adequate infirmary where prisoners of war may have the attention they require, as well as appropriate diet. Isolation wards shall, if necessary, be set aside for cases of contagious or mental disease.

Prisoners of war suffering from serious disease, or whose condition necessitates special treatment, a surgical operation or hospital care, must be admitted to any military or civilian medical unit where such treatment can be given, even if their repatriation is contemplated in the near future. Special facilities shall be afforded for the care to be given to the disabled, in particular to the blind, and for their. rehabilitation, pending repatriation.

Prisoners of war shall have the attention, preferably, of medical personnel of the Power on which they depend and, if possible, of their nationality.

Prisoners of war may not be prevented from presenting themselves to the medical authorities for examination. The detaining authorities shall, upon request, issue to every prisoner who has undergone treatment, an official certificate indicating the nature of his illness or injury, and the duration and kind of treatment received. A duplicate of this certificate shall be forwarded to the Central Prisoners of War Agency.

The costs of treatment, including those of any apparatus necessary for the maintenance of prisoners of war in good health, particularly dentures and other artificial appliances, and spectacles, shall be borne by the Detaining Power.

ARTICLE 31

Medical inspections of prisoners of war shall be held at least once a month. They shall include the checking and the recording of the weight of each prisoner of war.

Their purpose shall be, in particular, to supervise the general state of health, nutrition and cleanliness of prisoners and to detect contagious diseases, especially tuberculosis, malaria and venereal disease. For this purpose the most efficient methods available shall be employed, e.g. periodic mass miniature radiography for the early detection of tuberculosis.

ARTICLE 32

Prisoners of war who, though not attached to the medical service of their armed forces, are physicians, surgeons, dentists, nurses or medical orderlies, may be required by the Detaining Power to exercise their medical functions in the interests of prisoners of war dependent on the same Power. In that case they shall continue to be prisoners of war, but shall receive the same treatment as corresponding medical personnel retained by the Detaining Power. They shall be exempted from any other work under Article 49.

Chapter IV. Medical Personnel and Chaplains Retained to Assist Prisoners of War

ARTICLE 33

Members of the medical personnel and chaplains while retained by the Detaining Power with a view to assisting prisoners of war, shall not be considered as prisoners of war. They shall, however, receive as a minimum the benefits and protection of the present Convention, and shall also be granted all facilities necessary to provide for the medical care of, and religious ministration to prisoners of war.

They shall continue to exercise their medical and spiritual functions for the benefit of prisoners of war, preferably those belonging to the armed forces upon which they depend, within the scope of the military laws and regulations of the Detaining Power and under the control of its competent services, in accordance with their professional etiquette. They shall also benefit by the following facilities in the exercise of their medical or spiritual functions:

(a) They shall be authorized to visit periodically prisoners of war situated in working detachments or in hospitals outside the camp. For this purpose, the Detaining Power shall place at their disposal the necessary means of transport.

(b) The senior medical officer in each camp shall be responsible to the camp military authorities for everything connected with the activities of retained medical personnel. For this purpose, Parties to the conflict shall agree at the outbreak of hostilities on the subject of the corresponding ranks of the medical personnel, including that of societies mentioned in Article 26 of the Geneva Convention for the Amelioration of the Condition of the Wounded and Sick in Armed Forces in the Field of August 12, 1949. This senior medical officer, as well as chaplains, shall have the right to deal with the competent authorities of the camp on all questions relating to their duties. Such authorities shall afford them all necessary facilities for correspondence relating to these questions.

(c) Although they shall be subject to the internal discipline of the camp in which they are retained, such personnel may not be compelled to carry out any work other than that concerned with their medical or religious duties.

During hostilities, the Parties to the conflict shall agree concerning the possible relief of retained personnel and shall settle the procedure to be followed.

None of the preceding provisions shall relieve the Detaining Power of its obligations with regard to prisoners of war from the medical or spiritual point of view.

Chapter V. Religious, Intellectual and Physical Activities

ARTICLE 34

Prisoners of war shall enjoy complete latitude in the exercise of their religious duties, including attendance at the service of their faith, on condition that they comply with the disciplinary routine prescribed by the military authorities.

Adequate premises shall be provided where religious services may be held.

ARTICLE 35

Chaplains who fall into the hands of the enemy Power and who remain or are retained with a view to assisting prisoners of war, shall be allowed to minister to them and to exercise freely their ministry amongst prisoners of war of the same religion, in accordance with their religious conscience. They shall be allocated among the various camps and labour detachments containing prisoners of war belonging to the same forces, speaking the same language or practising the same religion. They shall enjoy the necessary facilities, including the means of transport provided for in Article 33, for visiting the prisoners of war outside their camp. They shall be free to correspond, subject to censorship, on matters concerning their religious duties with the ecclesiastical authorities in the country of detention and with international religious organizations. Letters and cards which they may send for this purpose shall be in addition to the quota provided for in Article 71.

ARTICLE 36

Prisoners of war who are ministers of religion, without having officiated as chaplains to their own forces, shall be at liberty, whatever their denomination, to minister freely to the members of their community. For this purpose, they shall receive the same treatment as the chaplains retained by the Detaining Power. They shall not be obliged to do any other work.

ARTICLE 37

When prisoners of war have not the assistance of a retained chaplain or of a prisoner of war minister of their faith, a minister belonging to the prisoners'

or a similar denomination, or in his absence a qualified layman, if such a course is feasible from a confessional point of view, shall be appointed, at the request of the prisoners concerned, to fill this office. This appointment, subject to the approval of the Detaining Power, shall take place with the agreement of the community of prisoners concerned and, wherever necessary, with the approval of the local religious authorities of the same faith. The person thus appointed shall comply with all regulations established by the Detaining Power in the interests of discipline and military security.

ARTICLE 38

While respecting the individual preferences of every prisoner, the Detaining Power shall encourage the practice of intellectual, educational, and recreational pursuits, sports and games amongst prisoners, and shall take the measures necessary to ensure the exercise thereof by providing them with adequate premises and necessary equipment.

Prisoners shall have opportunities for taking physical exercise, including sports and games, and for being out of doors. Sufficient open spaces shall be provided for this purpose in all camps.

Chapter VI. Discipline

ARTICLE 39

Every prisoner of war camp shall be put under the immediate authority of a responsible commissioned officer belonging to the regular armed forces of the Detaining Power. Such officer shall have in his possession a copy of the present Convention; he shall ensure that its provisions are known to the camp staff and the guard and shall be responsible, under the direction of his government, for its application.

Prisoners of war, with the exception of officers, must salute and show to all officers of the Detaining Power the external marks of respect provided for by the regulations applying in their own forces.

Officer prisoners of war are bound to salute only officers of a higher rank of the Detaining Power; they must, however, salute the camp commander regardless of his rank.

ARTICLE 40

The wearing of badges of rank and nationality, as well as of decorations, shall be permitted.

ARTICLE 41

In every camp the text of the present Convention and its Annexes and the contents of any special agreement provided for in Article 6, shall be posted, in the prisoners' own language, in places where all may read them. Copies shall be supplied, on request, to the prisoners who cannot have access to the copy which has been posted.

Regulations, orders, notices and publications of every kind relating to the conduct of prisoners of war shall be issued to them in a language which they understand. Such regulations, orders and publications shall be posted in the manner described above and copies shall be handed to the prisoners' representative. Every order and command addressed to prisoners of war individually must likewise be given in a language which they understand.

ARTICLE 42

The use of weapons against prisoners of war, especially against those who are escaping or attempting to escape, shall constitute an extreme measure, which shall always be preceded by warnings appropriate to the circumstances.

Chapter VII. Rank of Prisoners of War

ARTICLE 43

Upon the outbreak of hostilities, the Parties to the conflict shall communicate to one another the titles and ranks of all the persons mentioned in Article 4 of the present Convention, in order to ensure equality of treatment between prisoners of equivalent rank. Titles and ranks which are subsequently created shall form the subject of similar communications.

The Detaining Power shall recognize promotions in rank which have been accorded to prisoners of war and which have been duly notified by the Power on which these prisoners depend.

ARTICLE 44

Officers and prisoners of equivalent status shall be treated with the regard due to their rank and age.

In order to ensure service in officers' camps, other ranks of the same armed forces who, as far as possible, speak the same language, shall be assigned in sufficient numbers, account being taken of the rank of officers and prisoners of equivalent status. Such orderlies shall not be required to perform any other work.

Supervision of the mess by the officers themselves shall be facilitated in every way.

ARTICLE 45

Prisoners of war other than officers and prisoners of equivalent status shall be treated with the regard due to their rank and age.

Supervision of the mess by the prisoners themselves shall be facilitated in every way.

Chapter VIII. Transfer of Prisoners of War after their Arrival in Camp

ARTICLE 46

The Detaining Power, when deciding upon the transfer of prisoners of war, shall take into account the interests of the prisoners themselves, more especially so as not to increase the difficulty of their repatriation.

The transfer of prisoners of war shall always be effected humanely and in conditions not less favourable than those under which the forces of the Detaining Power are transferred. Account shall always be taken of the climatic conditions to which the prisoners of war are accustomed and the conditions of transfer shall in no case be prejudicial to their health.

The Detaining Power shall supply prisoners of war during transfer with sufficient food and drinking water to keep them in good health, likewise with the necessary clothing, shelter and medical attention. The Detaining Power shall take adequate precautions especially in case of transport by sea or by air, to ensure their safety during transfer, and shall draw up a complete list of all transferred prisoners before their departure.

ARTICLE 47

Sick or wounded prisoners of war shall not be transferred as long as their recovery may be endangered by the journey, unless their safety imperatively demands it.

If the combat zone draws closer to a camp, the prisoners of war in the said camp shall not be transferred unless their transfer can be carried out in adequate conditions of safety, or unless they are exposed to greater risks by remaining on the spot than by being transferred.

ARTICLE 48

In the event of transfer, prisoners of war shall be officially advised of their departure and of their new postal address. Such notifications shall be given in time for them to pack their luggage and inform their next of kin.

They shall be allowed to take with them their personal effects, and the correspondence and parcels which have arrived for them. The weight of such baggage may be limited, if the conditions of transfer so require, to what each prisoner can reasonably carry, which shall in no case be more than twenty-five kilograms per head.

Mail and parcels addressed to their former camp shall be forwarded to them without delay. The camp commander shall take, in agreement with the prisoners' representative, any measures needed to ensure the transport of the prisoners' community property and of the luggage they are unable to take with them in consequence of restrictions imposed by virtue of the second paragraph of this Article.

The costs of transfers shall be borne by the Detaining Power.

◆ Section III. Labour of Prisoners of War

ARTICLE 49

The Detaining Power may utilize the labour of prisoners of war who are physically fit, taking into account their age, sex, rank and physical aptitude, and with a view particularly to maintaining them in a good state of physical and mental health.

Non-commissioned officers who are prisoners of war shall only be required to do supervisory work. Those not so required may ask for other suitable work which shall, so far as possible, be found for them.

If officers or persons of equivalent status ask for suitable work, it shall be found for them, so far as possible, but they may in no circumstances be compelled to work.

ARTICLE 50

Besides work connected with camp administration, installation or maintenance, prisoners of war may be compelled to do only such work as is included in the following classes:

(a) agriculture; (b) industries connected with the production or the extraction of raw materials, and manufacturing industries, with the exception of metallurgical, machinery and chemical industries; public works and building operations which have no military character or purpose; (c) transport and handling of stores which are not military in character or purpose; (d) commercial business, and arts and crafts; (e) domestic service; (f) public utility services having no military character or purpose.

Should the above provisions be infringed, prisoners of war shall be allowed to exercise their right of complaint, in conformity with Article 78.

ARTICLE 51

Prisoners of war must be granted suitable working conditions, especially as regards accommodation, food, clothing and equipment; such conditions shall not be inferior to those enjoyed by nationals of the Detaining Power employed in similar work; account shall also be taken of climatic conditions.

The Detaining Power, in utilizing the labour of prisoners of war, shall ensure that in areas in which such prisoners are employed, the national legislation concerning the protection of labour, and, more particularly, the regulations for the safety of workers, are duly applied.

Prisoners of war shall receive training and be provided with the means of protection suitable to the work they will have to do and similar to those accorded to the nationals of the Detaining Power. Subject to the provisions of Article 52, prisoners may be submitted to the normal risks run by these civilian workers.

Conditions of labour shall in no case be rendered more arduous by disciplinary measures.

ARTICLE 52

Unless he be a volunteer, no prisoner of war may be employed on labour which is of an unhealthy or dangerous nature.

No prisoner of war shall be assigned to labour which would be looked upon as humiliating for a member of the Detaining Power's own forces.

The removal of mines or similar devices shall be considered as dangerous labour.

ARTICLE 53

The duration of the daily labour of prisoners of war, including the time of the journey to and fro, shall not be excessive, and must in no case exceed that permitted for civilian workers in the district, who are nationals of the Detaining Power and employed on the same work.

Prisoners of war must be allowed, in the middle of the day's work, a rest of not less than one hour. This rest will be the same as that to which workers of the Detaining Power are entitled, if the latter is of longer duration. They shall be allowed in addition a rest of twenty-four consecutive hours every week, preferably on Sunday or the day of rest in their country of origin. Furthermore, every prisoner who has worked for one year shall be granted a rest of eight consecutive days, during which his working pay shall be paid him.

If methods of labour such as piece work are employed, the length of the working period shall not be rendered excessive thereby.

ARTICLE 54

The working pay due to prisoners of war shall be fixed in accordance with the provisions of Article 62 of the present Convention.

Prisoners of war who sustain accidents in connection with work, or who contract a disease in the course, or in consequence of their work, shall receive all the care their condition may require. The Detaining Power shall furthermore deliver to such prisoners of war a medical certificate enabling them to submit their claims to the Power on which they depend, and shall send a duplicate to the Central Prisoners of War Agency provided for in Article 123.

ARTICLE 55

The fitness of prisoners of war for work shall be periodically verified by medical examinations at least once a month. The examinations shall have particular regard to the nature of the work which prisoners of war are required to do.

If any prisoner of war considers himself incapable of working, he shall be permitted to appear before the medical authorities of his camp. Physicians or surgeons may recommend that the prisoners who are, in their opinion, unfit for work, be exempted therefrom.

ARTICLE 56

The organization and administration of labour detachments shall be similar to those of prisoner of war camps.

Every labour detachment shall remain under the control of and administratively part of a prisoner of war camp. The military authorities and the commander of the said camp shall be responsible, under the direction of their government, for the observance of the provisions of the present Convention in labour detachments.

The camp commander shall keep an up-to-date record of the labour detachments dependent on his camp, and shall communicate it to the delegates of the Protecting Power, of the International Committee of the Red Cross, or of other agencies giving relief to prisoners of war, who may visit the camp.

ARTICLE 57

The treatment of prisoners of war who work for private persons, even if the latter are responsible for guarding and protecting them, shall not be inferior to that which is provided for by the present Convention. The Detaining Power, the military authorities and the commander of the camp to which such prisoners belong shall be entirely responsible for the maintenance, care, treatment, and payment of the working pay of such prisoners of war.

Such prisoners of war shall have the right to remain in communication with the prisoners' representatives in the camps on which they depend.

◆ **Section IV. Financial Resource of Prisoners of War**

ARTICLE 58

Upon the outbreak of hostilities, and pending an arrangement on this matter with the Protecting Power, the Detaining Power may determine the maximum amount of money in cash or in any similar form, that prisoners may have in their possession. Any amount in excess, which was properly in their possession and which has been taken or withheld from them, shall be placed to their account, together with any monies deposited by them, and shall not be converted into any other currency without their consent.

If prisoners of war are permitted to purchase services or commodities outside the camp against payment in cash, such payments shall be made by the prisoner himself or by the camp administration who will charge them to the accounts of the prisoners concerned. The Detaining Power will establish the necessary rules in this respect.

ARTICLE 59

Cash which was taken from prisoners of war, in accordance with Article 18, at the time of their capture, and which is in the currency of the Detaining Power, shall be placed to their separate accounts, in accordance with the provisions of Article 64 of the present Section.

The amounts, in the currency of the Detaining Power, due to the conversion of sums in other currencies that are taken from the prisoners of war at the same time, shall also be credited to their separate accounts.

ARTICLE 60

The Detaining Power shall grant all prisoners of war a monthly advance of pay, the amount of which shall be fixed by conversion, into the currency of the said Power, of the following amounts:

Category I: Prisoners ranking below sergeants: eight Swiss francs.

Category II: Sergeants and other non-commissioned officers, or prisoners of equivalent rank: twelve Swiss francs.

Category II: Warrant officers and commissioned officers below the rank of major or prisoners of equivalent rank: fifty Swiss francs.

Category IV: Majors, lieutenant-colonels, colonels or prisoners of equivalent rank: sixty Swiss francs.

Category V: General officers or prisoners of war of equivalent rank: seventy-five Swiss francs.

However, the Parties to the conflict concerned may by special agreement modify the amount of advances of pay due to prisoners of the preceding categories.

Furthermore, if the amounts indicated in the first paragraph above would be unduly high compared with the pay of the Detaining Power's armed forces or would, for any reason, seriously embarrass the Detaining Power, then, pending the conclusion of a special agreement with the Power on which the prisoners depend to vary the amounts indicated above, the Detaining Power:

(a) shall continue to credit the accounts of the prisoners with the amounts indicated in the first paragraph above; (b) may temporarily limit the amount made available from these advances of pay to prisoners of war for their own use, to sums which are reasonable, but which, for Category I, shall never be inferior to the amount that the Detaining Power gives to the members of its own armed forces.

The reasons for any limitations will be given without delay to the Protecting Power.

ARTICLE 61

The Detaining Power shall accept for distribution as supplementary pay to prisoners of war sums which the Power on which the prisoners depend may forward to them, on condition that the sums to be paid shall be the same for each prisoner of the same category, shall be payable to all prisoners of that category depending on that Power, and shall be placed in their separate accounts, at the earliest opportunity, in accordance with the provisions of Article 64. Such supplementary pay shall not relieve the Detaining Power of any obligation under this Convention.

ARTICLE 62

Prisoners of war shall be paid a fair working rate of pay by the detaining authorities direct. The rate shall be fixed by the said authorities, but shall at no time be less than one-fourth of one Swiss franc for a full working day. The Detaining Power shall inform prisoners of war, as well as the Power on which they depend, through the intermediary of the Protecting Power, of the rate of daily working pay that it has fixed.

Working pay shall likewise be paid by the detaining authorities to prisoners of war permanently detailed to duties or to a skilled or semi-skilled occupation in connection with the administration, installation or maintenance of camps, and to the prisoners who are required to carry out spiritual or medical duties on behalf of their comrades.

The working pay of the prisoners' representative, of his advisers, if any, and of his assistants, shall be paid out of the fund maintained by canteen profits. The scale of this working pay shall be fixed by the prisoners' representative and approved by the camp commander. If there is no such fund, the detaining authorities shall pay these prisoners a fair working rate of pay.

ARTICLE 63

Prisoners of war shall be permitted to receive remittances of money addressed to them individually or collectively.

Every prisoner of war shall have at his disposal the credit balance of his account as provided for in the following Article, within the limits fixed by the Detaining Power, which shall make such payments as are requested. Subject to financial or monetary restrictions which the Detaining Power regards as essential, prisoners of war may also have payments made abroad. In this case payments addressed by prisoners of war to dependents shall be given priority.

In any event, and subject to the consent of the Power on which they depend, prisoners may have payments made in their own country, as follows: the Detaining Power shall send to the aforesaid Power through the Protecting Power, a notification giving all the necessary particulars concerning the prisoners of war, the beneficiaries of the payments, and the amount of the sums to be paid, expressed in the Detaining Power's currency. The said notification shall be signed by the prisoners and countersigned by the camp commander. The Detaining Power shall debit the prisoners' account by a corresponding amount; the sums thus debited shall be placed by it to the credit of the Power on which the prisoners depend.

To apply the foregoing provisions, the Detaining Power may usefully consult the Model Regulations in Annex V of the present Convention.

ARTICLE 64

The Detaining Power shall hold an account for each prisoner of war, showing at least the following:

(1) The amounts due to the prisoner or received by him as advances of pay, as working pay or derived from any other source; the sums in the currency of the Detaining Power which were taken from him; the sums taken from him and converted at his request into the currency of the said Power.

(2) The payments made to the prisoner in cash, or in any other similar form; the payments made on his behalf and at his request; the sums transferred under Article 63, third paragraph.

ARTICLE 65

Every item entered in the account of a prisoner of war shall be countersigned or initialled by him, or by the prisoners' representative acting on his behalf.

Prisoners of war shall at all times be afforded reasonable facilities for consulting and obtaining copies of their accounts, which may likewise be inspected by the representatives of the Protecting Powers at the time of visits to the camp.

When prisoners of war are transferred from one camp to another, their personal accounts will follow them. In case of transfer from one Detaining Power to another, the monies which are their property and are not in the currency of the Detaining Power will follow them. They shall be given certificates for any other monies standing to the credit of their accounts.

The Parties to the conflict concerned may agree to notify to each other at specific intervals through the Protecting Power, the amount of the accounts of the prisoners of war.

ARTICLE 66

On the termination of captivity, through the release of a prisoner of war or his repatriation, the Detaining Power shall give him a statement, signed by an authorized officer of that Power, showing the credit balance then due to him. The Detaining Power shall also send through the Protecting Power to the government upon which the prisoner of war depends, lists giving all appropriate particulars of all prisoners of war whose captivity has been terminated by repatriation, release, escape, death or any other means, and showing the amount of their credit balances. Such lists shall be certified on each sheet by an authorized representative of the Detaining Power.

Any of the above provisions of this Article may be varied by mutual agreement between any two Parties to the conflict.

The Power on which the prisoner of war depends shall be responsible for settling with him any credit balance due to him from the Detaining Power on the termination of his captivity.

ARTICLE 67

Advances of pay, issued to prisoners of war in conformity with Article 60, shall be considered as made on behalf of the Power on which they depend. Such advances of pay, as well as all payments made by the said Power under Article 63, third paragraph, and Article 68, shall form the subject of arrangements between the Powers concerned, at the close of hostilities.

ARTICLE 68

Any claim by a prisoner of war for compensation in respect of any injury or other disability arising out of work shall be referred to the Power on which he depends, through the Protecting Power. In accordance with Article 54, the Detaining Power will, in all cases, provide the prisoner of war concerned with a statement showing the nature of the injury or disability, the circumstances in which it arose and particulars of medical or hospital treatment given for it. This statement will be signed by a responsible officer of the Detaining Power and the medical particulars certified by a medical officer.

Any claim by a prisoner of war for compensation in respect of personal effects monies or valuables impounded by the Detaining Power under Article 18 and not forthcoming on his repatriation, or in respect of loss alleged to be due to the fault of the Detaining Power or any of its servants, shall likewise be referred to the Power on which he depends. Nevertheless, any such personal effects required for use by the prisoners of war whilst in captivity shall be replaced at the expense of the Detaining Power. The Detaining Power will, in all cases, provide the prisoner of war with a statement, signed by a responsible officer, showing all available information regarding the reasons why such effects, monies or valuables have not been restored to him. A copy of this statement will be forwarded to the Power on which he depends through the Central Prisoners of War Agency provided for in Article 123.

◆ **Section V. Relations of Prisoners of War with the Exterior**

ARTICLE 69

Immediately upon prisoners of war falling into its power, the Detaining Power shall inform them and the Powers on which they depend, through the Protecting Power, of the measures taken to carry out the provisions of the present Section. They shall likewise inform the parties concerned of any subsequent modifications of such measures.

ARTICLE 70

Immediately upon capture, or not more than one week after arrival at a camp, even if it is a transit camp, likewise in case of sickness or transfer to hospital or to another camp, every prisoner of war shall be enabled to write direct to his family, on the one hand, and to the Central Prisoners of War Agency provided for in Article 123, on the other hand, a card similar, if possible, to the model annexed to the present Convention, informing his relatives of his capture, address and state of health. The said cards shall be forwarded as rapidly as possible and may not be delayed in any manner.

ARTICLE 71

Prisoners of war shall be allowed to send and receive letters and cards. If the Detaining Power deems it necessary to limit the number of letters and cards sent by each prisoner of war, the said number shall not be less than two letters and four cards monthly, exclusive of the capture cards provided for in Article 70, and conforming as closely as possible to the models annexed to the present Convention. Further limitations may be imposed only if the Protecting Power is satisfied that it would be in the interests of the prisoners of war concerned to do so owing to difficulties of translation caused by the Detaining Power's inability to find sufficient qualified linguists to carry out the necessary censorship. If limitations must be placed on the correspondence addressed to prisoners of war, they may be ordered only by the

Power on which the prisoners depend, possibly at the request of the Detaining Power. Such letters and cards must be conveyed by the most rapid method at the disposal of the Detaining Power; they may not be delayed or retained for disciplinary reasons.

Prisoners of war who have been without news for a long period, or who are unable to receive news from their next of kin or to give them news by the ordinary postal route, as well as those who are at a great distance from their homes, shall be permitted to send telegrams, the fees being charged against the prisoners of war's accounts with the Detaining Power or paid in the currency at their disposal. They shall likewise benefit by this measure in cases of urgency.

As a general rule, the correspondence of prisoners of war shall be written in their native language. The Parties to the conflict may allow correspondence in other languages.

Sacks containing prisoner of war mail must be securely sealed and labelled so as clearly to indicate their contents, and must be addressed to offices of destination.

ARTICLE 72

Prisoners of war shall be allowed to receive by post or by any other means individual parcels or collective shipments containing, in particular, foodstuffs, clothing, medical supplies and articles of a religious, educational or recreational character which may meet their needs, including books, devotional articles, scientific equipment, examination papers, musical instruments, sports outfits and materials allowing prisoners of war to pursue their studies or their cultural activities.

Such shipments shall in no way free the Detaining Power from the obligations imposed upon it by virtue of the present Convention.

The only limits which may be placed on these shipments shall be those proposed by the Protecting Power in the interest of the prisoners themselves, or by the International Committee of the Red Cross or any other organization giving assistance to the prisoners, in respect of their own shipments only, on account of exceptional strain on transport or communications.

The conditions for the sending of individual parcels and collective relief shall, if necessary, be the subject of special agreements between the Powers concerned, which may in no case delay the receipt by the prisoners of relief supplies. Books may not be included in parcels of clothing and foodstuffs. Medical supplies shall, as a rule, be sent in collective parcels.

ARTICLE 73

In the absence of special agreements between the Powers concerned on the conditions for the receipt and distribution of collective relief shipments, the rules and regulations concerning collective shipments, which are annexed to the present Convention, shall be applied.

The special agreements referred to above shall in no case restrict the right of prisoners' representatives to take possession of collective relief shipments intended for prisoners of war, to proceed to their distribution or to dispose of them in the interest of the prisoners.

Nor shall such agreements restrict the right of representatives of the Protecting Power, the International Committee of the Red Cross or any other organization giving assistance to prisoners of war and responsible for the forwarding of collective shipments, to supervise their distribution to the recipients.

ARTICLE 74

All relief shipments for prisoners of war shall be exempt from import, customs and other dues.

Correspondence, relief shipments and authorized remittances of money addressed to prisoners of war or despatched by them through the post office, either direct or through the Information Bureaux provided for in Article 122 and the Central Prisoners of War Agency provided for in Article 123, shall be exempt from any postal dues, both in the countries of origin and destination, and in intermediate countries.

If relief shipments intended for prisoners of war cannot be sent through the post office by reason of weight or for any other cause, the cost of transportation shall be borne by the Detaining Power in all the territories under its control. The other Powers party to the Convention shall bear the cost of transport in their respective territories. In the absence of special agreements between the Parties concerned, the costs connected with transport of such shipments, other than costs covered by the above exemption, shall be charged to the senders.

The High Contracting Parties shall endeavour to reduce, so far as possible, the rates charged for telegrams sent by prisoners of war, or addressed to them.

ARTICLE 75

Should military operations prevent the Powers concerned from fulfilling their obligation to assure the transport of the shipments referred to in Articles 70, 71, 72 and 77, the Protecting Powers concerned, the International Committee of the Red Cross or any other organization duly approved by the Parties to the conflict may undertake to ensure the conveyance of such shipments by suitable means (railway wagons, motor vehicles, vessels or aircraft, etc.). For this purpose, the High Contracting Parties shall endeavour to supply them with such transport and to allow its circulation, especially by granting the necessary safe-conducts.

Such transport may also be used to convey:

(a) correspondence, lists and reports exchanged between the Central Information Agency referred to in Article 123 and the National Bureaux referred to in Article 122;

(b) correspondence and reports relating to prisoners of war which the Protecting Powers, the International Committee of the Red Cross or any other body assisting the prisoners, exchange either with their own delegates or with the Parties to the conflict.

These provisions in no way detract from the right of any Party to the conflict to arrange other means of transport, if it should so prefer, nor preclude the granting of safe-conducts, under mutually agreed conditions, to such means of transport.

In the absence of special agreements, the costs occasioned by the use of such means of transport shall be borne proportionally by the Parties to the conflict whose nationals are benefited thereby.

ARTICLE 76

The censoring of correspondence addressed to prisoners of war or despatched by them shall be done as quickly as possible. Mail shall be censored only by the despatching State and the receiving State, and once only by each.

The examination of consignments intended for prisoners of war shall not be carried out under conditions that will expose the goods contained in them to deterioration; except in the case of written or printed matter, it shall be done in the presence of the addressee, or of a fellow-prisoner duly delegated by him. The delivery to prisoners of individual or collective consignments shall not be delayed under the pretext of difficulties of censorship.

Any prohibition of correspondence ordered by Parties to the conflict, either for military or political reasons, shall be only temporary and its duration shall be as short as possible.

ARTICLE 77

The Detaining Powers shall provide all facilities for the transmission, through the Protecting Power or the Central Prisoners of War Agency provided for in Article 123 of instruments, papers or documents intended for prisoners of war or despatched by them, especially powers of attorney and wills.

In all cases they shall facilitate the preparation and execution of such documents on behalf of prisoners of war; in particular, they shall allow them to consult a lawyer and shall take what measures are necessary for the authentication of their signatures.

◆ **Section VI. Relations between Prisoners of War and the Authorities**

Chapter I. Complaints of Prisoners of War respecting the Conditions of Captivity

ARTICLE 78

Prisoners of war shall have the right to make known to the military authorities in whose power they are, their requests regarding the conditions of captivity to which they are subjected.

They shall also have the unrestricted right to apply to the representatives of the Protecting Powers either through their prisoners' representative or, if they consider it necessary, direct, in order to draw their attention to any points on which they may have complaints to make regarding their conditions of captivity.

These requests and complaints shall not be limited nor considered to be a part of the correspondence quota referred to in Article 71. They must be transmitted immediately. Even if they are recognized to be unfounded, they may not give rise to any punishment.

Prisoners' representatives may send periodic reports on the situation in the camps and the needs of the prisoners of war to the representatives of the Protecting Powers.

Chapter II. Prisoner of War Representatives

ARTICLE 79

In all places where there are prisoners of war, except in those where there are officers, the prisoners shall freely elect by secret ballot, every six months, and also in case of vacancies, prisoners' representatives entrusted with representing them before the military authorities, the Protecting Powers, the International Committee of the Red Cross and any other organization which may assist them. These prisoners' representatives shall be eligible for re-election.

In camps for officers and persons of equivalent status or in mixed camps, the senior officer among the prisoners of war shall be recognized as the camp prisoners' representative. In camps for officers, he shall be assisted by one or more advisers chosen by the officers; in mixed camps, his assistants shall be chosen from among the prisoners of war who are not officers and shall be elected by them.

Officer prisoners of war of the same nationality shall be stationed in labour camps for prisoners of war, for the purpose of carrying out the camp administration duties for which the prisoners of war are responsible. These officers may be elected as prisoners' representatives under the first paragraph of this Article. In such a case the assistants to the prisoners' representatives shall be chosen from among those prisoners of war who are not officers.

Every representative elected must be approved by the Detaining Power before he has the right to commence his duties. Where the Detaining Power refuses to approve a prisoner of war elected by his fellow prisoners of war, it must inform the Protecting Power of the reason for such refusal.

In all cases the prisoners' representative must have the same nationality, language and customs as the prisoners of war whom he represents. Thus, prisoners of war distributed in different sections of a camp, according to their nationality, language or customs, shall have for each section their own prisoners' representative, in accordance with the foregoing paragraphs.

ARTICLE 80

Prisoners' representatives shall further the physical, spiritual and intellectual well-being of prisoners of war.

In particular, where the prisoners decide to organize amongst themselves a system of mutual assistance, this organization will be within the province of the prisoners' representative, in addition to the special duties entrusted to him by other provisions of the present Convention.

Prisoners' representatives shall not be held responsible, simply by reason of their duties, for any offences committed by prisoners of war.

ARTICLE 81

Prisoners' representatives shall not be required to perform any other work, if the accomplishment of their duties is thereby made more difficult.

Prisoners' representatives may appoint from amongst the prisoners such assistants as they may require. All material facilities shall be granted them, particularly a certain freedom of movement necessary for the accomplishment of their duties (inspection of labour detachments, receipt of supplies, etc.).

Prisoners' representatives shall be permitted to visit premises where prisoners of war are detained, and every prisoner of war shall have the right to consult freely his prisoners' representative.

All facilities shall likewise be accorded to the prisoners' representatives for communication by post and telegraph with the detaining authorities, the Protecting Powers, the International Committee of the Red Cross and their delegates, the Mixed Medical Commissions and the bodies which give assistance to prisoners of war. Prisoners' representatives

of labour detachments shall enjoy the same facilities for communication with the prisoners' representatives of the principal camp. Such communications shall not be restricted, nor considered as forming a part of the quota mentioned in Article 71.

Prisoners' representatives who are transferred shall be allowed a reasonable time to acquaint their successors with current affairs.

In case of dismissal, the reasons therefor shall be communicated to the Protecting Power.

Chapter III. Penal and Disciplinary Sanctions

I. General Provisions

ARTICLE 82

A prisoner of war shall be subject to the laws, regulations and orders in force in the armed forces of the Detaining Power; the Detaining Power shall be justified in taking judicial or disciplinary measures in respect of any offence committed by a prisoner of war against such laws, regulations or orders. However, no proceedings or punishments contrary to the provisions of this Chapter shall be allowed.

If any law, regulation or order of the Detaining Power shall declare acts committed by a prisoner of war to be punishable, whereas the same acts would not be punishable if committed by a member of the forces of the Detaining Power, such acts shall entail disciplinary punishments only.

ARTICLE 83

In deciding whether proceedings in respect of an offence alleged to have been committed by a prisoner of war shall be judicial or disciplinary, the Detaining Power shall ensure that the competent authorities exercise the greatest leniency and adopt, wherever possible, disciplinary rather than judicial measures.

ARTICLE 84

A prisoner of war shall be tried only by a military court, unless the existing laws of the Detaining Power expressly permit the civil courts to try a member of the armed forces of the Detaining Power in respect of the particular offence alleged to have been committed by the prisoner of war.

In no circumstances whatever shall a prisoner of war be tried by a court of any kind which does not offer the essential guarantees of independence and impartiality as generally recognized, and, in particular, the procedure of which does not afford the accused the rights and means of defence provided for in Article 105.

ARTICLE 85

Prisoners of war prosecuted under the laws of the Detaining Power for acts committed prior to capture shall retain, even if convicted, the benefits of the present Convention.

ARTICLE 86

No prisoner of war may be punished more than once for the same act or on the same charge.

ARTICLE 87

Prisoners of war may not be sentenced by the military authorities and courts of the Detaining Power to any penalties except those provided for in respect of members of the armed forces of the said Power who have committed the same acts.

When fixing the penalty, the courts or authorities of the Detaining Power shall take into consideration, to the widest extent possible, the fact that the accused, not being a national of the Detaining Power, is not bound to it by any duty of allegiance, and that he is in its power as the result of circumstances independent of his own will. The said courts or authorities shall be at liberty to reduce the penalty provided for the violation of which the prisoner of war is accused, and shall therefore not be bound to apply the minimum penalty prescribed.

Collective punishment for individual acts, corporal punishment, imprisonment in premises without daylight and, in general, any form of torture or cruelty, are forbidden.

No prisoner of war may be deprived of his rank by the Detaining Power, or prevented from wearing his badges.

ARTICLE 88

Officers, non-commissioned officers and men who are prisoners of war undergoing a disciplinary or judicial punishment, shall not be subjected to more severe treatment than that applied in respect of the same punishment to members of the armed forces of the Detaining Power of equivalent rank.

A woman prisoner of war shall not be awarded or sentenced to a punishment more severe, or treated whilst undergoing punishment more severely, than a woman member of the armed forces of the Detaining Power dealt with for a similar offence.

In no case may a woman prisoner of war be awarded or sentenced to a punishment more severe, or treated whilst undergoing punishment more severely, than a male member of the armed forces of the Detaining Power dealt with for a similar offence.

Prisoners of war who have served disciplinary or judicial sentences may not be treated differently from other prisoners of war.

II. Disciplinary Sanctions

ARTICLE 89

The disciplinary punishments applicable to prisoners of war are the following:

(1) A fine which shall not exceed 50 per cent of the advances of pay and working pay which the prisoner of war would otherwise receive under the provisions of Articles 60 and 62 during a period of not more than thirty days.

(2) Discontinuance of privileges granted over and above the treatment provided for by the present Convention.

(3) Fatigue duties not exceeding two hours daily.

(4) Confinement.

The punishment referred to under (3) shall not be applied to officers.

In no case shall disciplinary punishments be inhuman, brutal or dangerous to the health of prisoners of war.

ARTICLE 90

The duration of any single punishment shall in no case exceed thirty days. Any period of confinement awaiting the hearing of a disciplinary offence or the award of disciplinary punishment shall be deducted from an award pronounced against a prisoner of war.

The maximum of thirty days provided above may not be exceeded, even if the prisoner of war is answerable for several acts at the same time when he is awarded punishment, whether such acts are related or not.

The period between the pronouncing of an award of disciplinary punishment and its execution shall not exceed one month.

When a prisoner of war is awarded a further disciplinary punishment, a period of at least three days shall elapse between the execution of any two of the punishments, if the duration of one of these is ten days or more.

ARTICLE 91

The escape of a prisoner of war shall be deemed to have succeeded when:

(1) he has joined the armed forces of the Power on which he depends, or those of an allied Power;

(2) he has left the territory under the control of the Detaining Power, or of an ally of the said Power;

(3) he has joined a ship flying the flag of the Power on which he depends, or of an allied Power, in the territorial waters of the Detaining Power, the said ship not being under the control of the last named Power.

Prisoners of war who have made good their escape in the sense of this Article and who are recaptured, shall not be liable to any punishment in respect of their previous escape.

ARTICLE 92

A prisoner of war who attempts to escape and is recaptured before having made good his escape in the sense of Article 91 shall be liable only to a disciplinary punishment in respect of this act, even if it is a repeated offence.

A prisoner of war who is recaptured shall be handed over without delay to the competent military authority.

Article 88, fourth paragraph, notwithstanding, prisoners of war punished as a result of an unsuccessful escape may be subjected to special surveillance. Such surveillance must not affect the state of their health, must be undergone in a prisoner of war camp, and must not entail the suppression of any of the safeguards granted them by the present Convention.

ARTICLE 93

Escape or attempt to escape, even if it is a repeated offence, shall not be deemed an aggravating circumstance if the prisoner of war is subjected to trial by judicial proceedings in respect of an offence committed during his escape or attempt to escape.

In conformity with the principle stated in Article 83, offences committed by prisoners of war with the sole intention of facilitating their escape and which do not entail any violence against life or limb, such as offences against public property, theft without intention of self-enrichment, the drawing up or use of false papers, or the wearing of civilian clothing, shall occasion disciplinary punishment only.

Prisoners of war who aid or abet an escape or an attempt to escape shall be liable on this count to disciplinary punishment only.

ARTICLE 94

If an escaped prisoner of war is recaptured, the Power on which he depends shall be notified thereof in the manner defined in Article 122, provided notification of his escape has been made.

ARTICLE 95

A prisoner of war accused of an offence against discipline shall not be kept in confinement pending the hearing unless a member of the armed forces of the Detaining Power would be so kept if he were accused of a similar offence, or if it is essential in the interests of camp order and discipline.

Any period spent by a prisoner of war in confinement awaiting the disposal of an offence against discipline shall be reduced to an absolute minimum and shall not exceed fourteen days.

The provisions of Articles 97 and 98 of this Chapter shall apply to prisoners of war who are in confinement awaiting the disposal of offences against discipline.

ARTICLE 96

Acts which constitute offences against discipline shall be investigated immediately.

Without prejudice to the competence of courts and superior military authorities, disciplinary punishment may be ordered only by an officer having disciplinary powers in his capacity as camp commander, or by a responsible officer who replaces him or to whom he has delegated his disciplinary powers.

In no case may such powers be delegated to a prisoner of war or be exercised by a prisoner of war.

Before any disciplinary award is pronounced, the accused shall be given precise information regarding the offences of which he is accused, and given an opportunity of explaining his conduct and of defending himself. He shall be permitted, in particular, to call witnesses and to have recourse, if necessary, to the services of a qualified interpreter. The decision shall be announced to the accused prisoner of war and to the prisoners' representative.

A record of disciplinary punishments shall be maintained by the camp commander and shall be open to inspection by representatives of the Protecting Power.

ARTICLE 97

Prisoners of war shall not in any case be transferred to penitentiary establishments (prisons, penitentiaries, convict prisons, etc.) to undergo disciplinary punishment therein.

All premises in which disciplinary punishments are undergone shall conform to the sanitary requirements set forth in Article 25. A prisoner of war undergoing punishment shall be enabled to keep himself in a state of cleanliness, in conformity with Article 29.

Officers and persons of equivalent status shall not be lodged in the same quarters as non-commissioned officers or men.

Women prisoners of war undergoing disciplinary punishment shall be confined in separate quarters from male prisoners of war and shall be under the immediate supervision of women.

ARTICLE 98

A prisoner of war undergoing confinement as a disciplinary punishment shall continue to enjoy the benefits of the provisions of this Convention except in so far as these are necessarily rendered inapplicable by the mere fact that he is confined. In no case may he be deprived of the benefits of the provisions of Articles 78 and 126.

A prisoner of war awarded disciplinary punishment may not be deprived of the prerogatives attached to his rank.

Prisoners of war awarded disciplinary punishment shall be allowed to exercise and to stay in the open air at least two hours daily.

They shall be allowed, on their request, to be present at the daily medical inspections. They shall receive the attention which their state of health requires and, if necessary, shall be removed to the camp infirmary or to a hospital.

They shall have permission to read and write, likewise to send and receive letters. Parcels and remittances of money however, may be withheld from them until the completion of the punishment; they shall meanwhile be entrusted to the prisoners' representative, who will hand over to the infirmary the perishable goods contained in such parcels.

III. Judicial Proceedings

ARTICLE 99

No prisoner of war may be tried or sentenced for an act which is not forbidden by the law of the Detaining Power or by international law, in force at the time the said act was committed.

No moral or physical coercion may be exerted on a prisoner of war in order to induce him to admit himself guilty of the act of which he is accused.

No prisoner of war may be convicted without having had an opportunity to present his defence and the assistance of a qualified advocate or counsel.

ARTICLE 100

Prisoners of war and the Protecting Powers shall be informed as soon as possible of the offences which are punishable by the death sentence under the laws of the Detaining Power.

Other offences shall not thereafter be made punishable by the death penalty without the concurrence of the Power on which the prisoners of war depend.

The death sentence cannot be pronounced on a prisoner of war unless the attention of the court has, in accordance with Article 87, second paragraph, been particularly called to the fact that since the accused is not a national of the Detaining Power, he is not bound to it by any duty of allegiance, and that he is in its power as the result of circumstances independent of his own will.

ARTICLE 101

If the death penalty is pronounced on a prisoner of war, the sentence shall not be executed before the expiration of a period of at least six months from the date when the Protecting Power receives, at an indicated address, the detailed communication provided for in Article 107.

ARTICLE 102

A prisoner of war can be validly sentenced only if the sentence has been pronounced by the same courts according to the same procedure as in the case of members of the armed forces of the Detaining Power, and if, furthermore, the provisions of the present Chapter have been observed.

ARTICLE 103

Judicial investigations relating to a prisoner of war shall be conducted as rapidly as circumstances permit and so that his trial shall take place as soon as possible. A prisoner of war shall not be confined while awaiting trial unless a member of the armed forces of the Detaining Power would be so confined if he were accused of a similar offence, or if it is essential to do so in the interests of national security. In no circumstances shall this confinement exceed three months.

Any period spent by a prisoner of war in confinement awaiting trial shall be deducted from any sentence of imprisonment passed upon him and taken into account in fixing any penalty.

The provisions of Articles 97 and 98 of this Chapter shall apply to a prisoner of war whilst in confinement awaiting trial.

ARTICLE 104

In any case in which the Detaining Power has decided to institute judicial proceedings against a prisoner of war, it shall notify the Protecting Power as soon as possible and at least three weeks before the opening of the trial. This period of three weeks shall run as from the day on which such notification reaches the Protecting Power at the address previously indicated by the latter to the Detaining Power.

The said notification shall contain the following information:

(1) Surname and first names of the prisoner of war, his rank, his army, regimental, personal or serial number, his date of birth, and his profession or trade, if any;

(2) Place of internment or confinement;

(3) Specification of the charge or charges on which the prisoner of war is to be arraigned, giving the legal provisions applicable;

(4) Designation of the court which will try the case, likewise the date and place fixed for the opening of the trial.

The same communication shall be made by the Detaining Power to the prisoners' representative.

If no evidence is submitted, at the opening of a trial, that the notification referred to above was received by the Protecting Power, by the prisoner of war and by the prisoners' representative concerned, at least three weeks before the opening of the trial, then the latter cannot take place and must be adjourned.

ARTICLE 105

The prisoner of war shall be entitled to assistance by one of his prisoner comrades, to defence by a qualified advocate or counsel of his own choice, to the calling of witnesses and, if he deems necessary, to the services of a competent interpreter. He shall be advised of these rights by the Detaining Power in due time before the trial.

Failing a choice by the prisoner of war, the Protecting Power shall find him an advocate or counsel, and shall have at least one week at its disposal for the purpose. The Detaining Power shall deliver to the said Power, on request, a list of persons qualified to present the defence. Failing a choice of an advocate or counsel by the prisoner of war or the Protecting Power, the Detaining Power shall appoint a competent advocate or counsel to conduct the defence.

The advocate or counsel conducting the defence on behalf of the prisoner of war shall have at his disposal a period of two weeks at least before the opening of the trial, as well as the necessary facilities to prepare the defence of the accused. He may, in particular, freely visit the accused and interview him in private. He may also confer with any witnesses for the defence, including prisoners of war. He shall have the benefit of these facilities until the term of appeal or petition has expired.

Particulars of the charge or charges on which the prisoner of war is to be arraigned, as well as the documents which are generally communicated to the accused by virtue of the laws in force in the armed forces of the Detaining Power, shall be communicated to the accused prisoner of war in a language which he understands, and in good time before the opening of the trial. The same communication in the same circumstances shall be made to the advocate or counsel conducting the defence on behalf of the prisoner of war.

The representatives of the Protecting Power shall be entitled to attend the trial of the case, unless, exceptionally, this is held in camera in the interest of State security. In such a case the Detaining Power shall advise the Protecting Power accordingly.

ARTICLE 106

Every prisoner of war shall have, in the same manner as the members of the armed forces of the Detaining Power, the right of appeal or petition from any sentence pronounced upon him, with a view to the quashing or revising of the sentence or the reopening of the trial. He shall be fully informed of his right to appeal or petition and of the time limit within which he may do so.

ARTICLE 107

Any judgment and sentence pronounced upon a prisoner of war shall be immediately reported to the Protecting Power in the form of a summary communication, which shall also indicate whether he has the right of appeal with a view to the quashing of the sentence or the reopening of the trial. This communication shall likewise be sent to the prisoners' representative concerned. It shall also be sent to the accused prisoner of war in a language he understands, if the sentence was not pronounced in his presence. The Detaining Power shall also immediately communicate to the Protecting Power the decision of the prisoner of war to use or to waive his right of appeal.

Furthermore, if a prisoner of war is finally convicted or if a sentence pronounced on a prisoner of war in the first instance is a death sentence, the Detaining Power shall as soon as possible address to the Protecting Power a detailed communication containing:

(1) the precise wording of the finding and sentence;

(2) a summarized report of any preliminary investigation and of the trial, emphasizing in particular the elements of the prosecution and the defence;

(3) notification, where applicable, of the establishment where the sentence will be served.

The communications provided for in the foregoing sub-paragraphs shall be sent to the Protecting Power at the address previously made known to the Detaining Power.

ARTICLE 108

Sentences pronounced on prisoners of war after a conviction has become duly enforceable, shall be served in the same establishments and under the same conditions as in the case of members of the armed forces of the Detaining Power. These conditions shall in all cases conform to the requirements of health and humanity.

A woman prisoner of war on whom such a sentence has been pronounced shall be confined in separate quarters and shall be under the supervision of women.

In any case, prisoners of war sentenced to a penalty depriving them of their liberty shall retain the benefit of the provisions of Articles 78 and 126 of the present Convention. Furthermore, they shall be entitled to receive and despatch correspondence, to receive at least one relief parcel monthly, to take regular exercise in the open air, to have the medical care required by their state of health, and the spiritual assistance they may desire. Penalties to which they may be subjected shall be in accordance with the provisions of Article 87, third paragraph.

Part IV. Termination of Captivity

◆ Section I. Direct Repatriation and Accommodation in Neutral Countries

ARTICLE 109

Subject to the provisions of the third paragraph of this Article, Parties to the conflict are bound to send back to their own country, regardless of number or rank, seriously wounded and seriously sick prisoners of war, after having cared for them until they are fit to travel, in accordance with the first paragraph of the following Article.

Throughout the duration of hostilities, Parties to the conflict shall endeavour, with the cooperation of the neutral Powers concerned, to make arrangements for the accommodation in neutral countries of the sick and wounded prisoners of war referred to in the second paragraph of the following Article. They may, in addition, conclude agreements with a view to the direct repatriation or internment in a neutral country of able-bodied prisoners of war who have undergone a long period of captivity.

No sick or injured prisoner of war who is eligible for repatriation under the first paragraph of this Article, may be repatriated against his will during hostilities.

ARTICLE 110

The following shall be repatriated direct:

(1) Incurably wounded and sick whose mental or physical fitness seems to have been gravely diminished.

(2) Wounded and sick who, according to medical opinion, are not likely to recover within one year, whose condition requires treatment and whose mental or physical fitness seems to have been gravely diminished.

(3) Wounded and sick who have recovered, but whose mental or physical fitness seems to have been gravely and permanently diminished.

The following may be accommodated in a neutral country:

(1) Wounded and sick whose recovery may be expected within one year of the date of the wound or the beginning of the illness, if treatment in a neutral country might increase the prospects of a more certain and speedy recovery.

(2) Prisoners of war whose mental or physical health, according to medical opinion, is seriously threatened by continued captivity, but whose accommodation in a neutral country might remove such a threat.

The conditions which prisoners of war accommodated in a neutral country must fulfil in order to permit their repatriation shall be fixed, as shall likewise their status, by agreement between the Powers concerned. In general, prisoners of war who have been accommodated in a neutral country, and who belong to the following categories, should be repatriated:

(1) Those whose state of health has deteriorated so as to fulfil the condition laid down for direct repatriation;

(2) Those whose mental or physical powers remain, even after treatment, considerably impaired.

If no special agreements are concluded between the Parties to the conflict concerned, to determine the cases of disablement or sickness entailing direct repatriation or accommodation in a neutral country, such cases shall be settled in accordance with the principles laid down in the Model Agreement concerning direct repatriation and accommodation in neutral countries of wounded and sick prisoners of war and in the Regulations concerning Mixed Medical Commissions annexed to the present Convention.

ARTICLE 111

The Detaining Power, the Power on which the prisoners of war depend, and a neutral Power agreed upon by these two Powers, shall endeavour to conclude agreements which will enable prisoners of war to be interned in the territory of the said neutral Power until the close of hostilities.

ARTICLE 112

Upon the outbreak of hostilities, Mixed Medical Commissions shall be appointed to examine sick and wounded prisoners of war, and to make all appropriate decisions regarding them. The appointment, duties and functioning of these Commissions shall be in conformity with the provisions of the Regulations annexed to the present Convention.

However, prisoners of war who, in the opinion of the medical authorities of the Detaining Power, are manifestly seriously injured or seriously sick, may be repatriated without having to be examined by a Mixed Medical Commission.

ARTICLE 113

Besides those who are designated by the medical authorities of the Detaining Power, wounded or sick prisoners of war belonging to the categories listed below shall be entitled to present themselves for examination by the Mixed Medical Commissions provided for in the foregoing Article:

(1) Wounded and sick proposed by a physician or surgeon who is of the same nationality, or a national of a Party to the conflict allied with the Power on which the said prisoners depend, and who exercises his functions in the camp.

(2) Wounded and sick proposed by their prisoners' representative.

(3) Wounded and sick proposed by the Power on which they depend, or by an organization duly recognized by the said Power and giving assistance to the prisoners.

Prisoners of war who do not belong to one of the three foregoing categories may nevertheless present themselves for examination by Mixed Medical Commissions, but shall be examined only after those belonging to the said categories.

The physician or surgeon of the same nationality as the prisoners who present themselves for examination by the Mixed Medical Commission, likewise the prisoners' representative of the said prisoners, shall have permission to be present at the examination.

ARTICLE 114

Prisoners of war who meet with accidents shall, unless the injury is self-inflicted, have the benefit of the provisions of this Convention as regards repatriation or accommodation in a neutral country.

ARTICLE 115

No prisoner of war on whom a disciplinary punishment has been imposed and who is eligible for repatriation or for accommodation in a neutral country, may be kept back on the plea that he has not undergone his punishment.

Prisoners of war detained in connection with a judicial prosecution or conviction, and who are designated for repatriation or accommodation in a neutral country, may benefit by such measures before the end of the proceedings or the completion of the punishment, if the Detaining Power consents.

Parties to the conflict shall communicate to each other the names of those who will be detained until the end of the proceedings or the completion of the punishment.

ARTICLE 116

The cost of repatriating prisoners of war or of transporting them to a neutral country shall be borne, from the frontiers of the Detaining Power, by the Power on which the said prisoners depend.

ARTICLE 117

No repatriated person may be employed on active military service.

◆ **Section II. Release and Repatriation of Prisoners of War at the Close of Hostilities**

ARTICLE 118

Prisoners of war shall be released and repatriated without delay after the cessation of active hostilities.

In the absence of stipulations to the above effect in any agreement concluded between the Parties to the conflict with a view to the cessation of hostilities, or failing any such agreement, each of the Detaining Powers shall itself establish and execute without delay a plan of repatriation in conformity with the principle laid down in the foregoing paragraph.

In either case, the measures adopted shall be brought to the knowledge of the prisoners of war.

The costs of repatriation of prisoners of war shall in all cases be equitably apportioned between the Detaining Power and the Power on which the prisoners depend. This apportionment shall be carried out on the following basis:

(a) If the two Powers are contiguous, the Power on which the prisoners of war depend shall bear the costs of repatriation from the frontiers of the Detaining Power. (b) If the two Powers are not contiguous, the Detaining Power shall bear the costs of transport of prisoners of war over its own territory as far as its frontier or its port of embarkation nearest to the territory of the Power on which the prisoners of war depend. The Parties concerned shall agree between themselves as to the equitable apportionment of the remaining costs of the repatriation. The conclusion of this agreement shall in no circumstances justify any delay in the repatriation of the prisoners of war.

ARTICLE 119

Repatriation shall be effected in conditions similar to those laid down in Articles 46 to 48 inclusive of the present Convention for the transfer of prisoners of war, having regard to the provisions of Article 118 and to those of the following paragraphs.

On repatriation, any articles of value impounded from prisoners of war under Article 18, and any foreign currency which has not been converted into the currency of the Detaining Power, shall be restored to them. Articles of value and foreign currency which, for any reason whatever, are not restored to prisoners of war on repatriation, shall be despatched to the Information Bureau set up under Article 122.

Prisoners of war shall be allowed to take with them their personal effects, and any correspondence and parcels which have arrived for them. The weight of such baggage may be limited, if the conditions of repatriation so require, to what each prisoner can reasonably carry. Each prisoner shall in all cases be authorized to carry at least twenty-five kilograms.

The other personal effects of the repatriated prisoner shall be left in the charge of the Detaining Power which shall have them forwarded to him as soon as it has concluded an agreement to this effect, regulating the conditions of transport and the payment of the costs involved, with the Power on which the prisoner depends.

Prisoners of war against whom criminal proceedings for an indictable offence are pending may be detained until the end of such proceedings, and, if necessary, until the completion of the punishment. The same shall apply to prisoners of war already convicted for an indictable offence.

Parties to the conflict shall communicate to each other the names of any prisoners of war who are detained until the end of the proceedings or until punishment has been completed.

By agreement between the Parties to the conflict, commissions shall be established for the purpose of searching for dispersed prisoners of war and of assuring their repatriation with the least possible delay.

◆ Section III. Death of Prisoners of War
ARTICLE 120

Wills of prisoners of war shall be drawn up so as to satisfy the conditions of validity required by the legislation of their country of origin, which will take steps to inform the Detaining Power of its requirements in this respect. At the request of the prisoner of war and, in all cases, after death, the will shall be transmitted without delay to the Protecting Power; a certified copy shall be sent to the Central Agency.

Death certificates, in the form annexed to the present Convention, or lists certified by a responsible officer, of all persons who die as prisoners of war shall be forwarded as rapidly as possible to the Prisoner of War Information Bureau established in accordance with Article 122. The death certificates or certified lists shall show particulars of identity as set out in the third paragraph of Article 17, and also the date and place of death, the cause of death, the date and place of burial and all particulars necessary to identify the graves.

The burial or cremation of a prisoner of war shall be preceded by a medical examination of the body with a view to confirming death and enabling a report to be made and, where necessary, establishing identity.

The detaining authorities shall ensure that prisoners of war who have died in captivity are honourably buried, if possible according to the rites of the religion to which they belonged, and that their graves are respected, suitably maintained and marked so as to be found at any time. Wherever possible, deceased prisoners of war who depended on the same Power shall be interred in the same place.

Deceased prisoners of war shall be buried in individual graves unless unavoidable circumstances require the use of collective graves. Bodies may be cremated only for imperative reasons of hygiene, on account of the religion of the deceased or in accordance with his express wish to this effect. In case of cremation, the fact shall be stated and the reasons given in the death certificate of the deceased.

In order that graves may always be found, all particulars of burials and graves shall be recorded with a Graves Registration Service established by the Detaining Power. Lists of graves and particulars of the prisoners of war interred in cemeteries and elsewhere shall be transmitted to the Power on which such prisoners of war depended. Responsibility for the care of these graves and for records of any subsequent moves of the bodies shall rest on the Power controlling the territory, if a Party to the present Convention. These provisions shall also apply to the ashes, which shall be kept by the Graves Registration Service until proper disposal thereof in accordance with the wishes of the home country.

ARTICLE 121

Every death or serious injury of a prisoner of war caused or suspected to have been caused by a sentry, another prisoner of war, or any other person, as well as any death the cause of which is unknown, shall be immediately followed by an official enquiry by the Detaining Power.

A communication on this subject shall be sent immediately to the Protecting Power. Statements shall be taken from witnesses, especially from those who are prisoners of war, and a report including such statements shall be forwarded to the Protecting Power.

If the enquiry indicates the guilt of one or more persons, the Detaining Power shall take all measures for the prosecution of the person or persons responsible.

Part V. Information Bureaux and Relief Societies for Prisoners of War

ARTICLE 122

Upon the outbreak of a conflict and in all cases of occupation, each of the Parties to the conflict shall institute an official Information Bureau for prisoners of war who are in its power. Neutral or non-belligerent Powers who may have received within their territory persons belonging to one of the categories referred to in Article 4, shall take the same action with respect to such persons. The Power concerned shall ensure that the Prisoners of War Information

Bureau is provided with the necessary accommodation, equipment and staff to ensure its efficient working. It shall be at liberty to employ prisoners of war in such a Bureau under the conditions laid down in the Section of the present Convention dealing with work by prisoners of war.

Within the shortest possible period, each of the Parties to the conflict shall give its Bureau the information referred to in the fourth, fifth and sixth paragraphs of this Article regarding any enemy person belonging to one of the categories referred to in Article 4, who has fallen into its power. Neutral or non-belligerent Powers shall take the same action with regard to persons belonging to such categories whom they have received within their territory.

The Bureau shall immediately forward such information by the most rapid means to the Powers concerned, through the intermediary of the Protecting Powers and likewise of the Central Agency provided for in Article 123.

This information shall make it possible quickly to advise the next of kin concerned. Subject to the provisions of Article 17, the information shall include, in so far as available to the Information Bureau, in respect of each prisoner of war, his surname, first names, rank, army, regimental, personal or serial number, place and full date of birth, indication of the Power on which he depends, first name of the father and maiden name of the mother, name and address of the person to be informed and the address to which correspondence for the prisoner may be sent.

The Information Bureau shall receive from the various departments concerned information regarding transfers, releases, repatriations, escapes, admissions to hospital, and deaths, and shall transmit such information in the manner described in the third paragraph above.

Likewise, information regarding the state of health of prisoners of war who are seriously ill or seriously wounded shall be supplied regularly, every week if possible.

The Information Bureau shall also be responsible for replying to all enquiries sent to it concerning prisoners of war, including those who have died in captivity; it will make any enquiries necessary to obtain the information which is asked for if this is not in its possession.

All written communications made by the Bureau shall be authenticated by a signature or a seal.

The Information Bureau shall furthermore be charged with collecting all personal valuables, including sums in currencies other than that of the Detaining Power and documents of importance to the next of kin, left by prisoners of war who have been repatriated or released, or who have escaped or died, and shall forward the said valuables to the Powers concerned. Such articles shall be sent by the Bureau in sealed packets which shall be accompanied by statements giving clear and full particulars of the identity of the person to whom the articles belonged, and by a complete list of the contents of the parcel. Other personal effects of such prisoners of war shall be transmitted under arrangements agreed upon between the Parties to the conflict concerned.

ARTICLE 123

A Central Prisoners of War Information Agency shall be created in a neutral country. The International Committee of the Red Cross shall, if it deems necessary, propose to the Powers concerned the organization of such an Agency.

The function of the Agency shall be to collect all the information it may obtain through official or private channels respecting prisoners of war, and to transmit it as rapidly as possible to the country of origin of the prisoners of war or to the Power on which they depend. It shall receive from the Parties to the conflict all facilities for effecting such transmissions.

The High Contracting Parties, and in particular those whose nationals benefit by the services of the Central Agency, are requested to give the said Agency the financial aid it may require.

The foregoing provisions shall in no way be interpreted as restricting the humanitarian activities of the International Committee of the Red Cross, or of the relief societies provided for in Article 125.

ARTICLE 124

The national Information Bureaux and the Central Information Agency shall enjoy free postage for mail, likewise all the exemptions provided for in Article 74, and further, so far as possible, exemption from telegraphic charges or, at least, greatly reduced rates.

ARTICLE 125

Subject to the measures which the Detaining Powers may consider essential to ensure their security or to meet any other reasonable need, the representatives of religious organizations, relief societies, or any other organization assisting prisoners of war, shall receive from the said Powers, for themselves and their duly accredited agents, all necessary facilities for visiting the prisoners, for distributing relief supplies and material, from any source, intended for religious, educational or recreative purposes, and for assisting them in organizing their leisure time within the camps. Such societies or organizations may be constituted in the territory of the Detaining Power or in any other country, or they may have an international character.

The Detaining Power may limit the number of societies and organizations whose delegates are allowed to carry out their activities in its territory and under its supervision, on condition, however, that such limitation shall not hinder the effective operation of adequate relief to all prisoners of war.

The special position of the International Committee of the Red Cross in this field shall be recognized and respected at all times.

As soon as relief supplies or material intended for the above-mentioned purposes are handed over to prisoners of war, or very shortly afterwards, receipts for each consignment, signed by the prisoners' representative, shall be forwarded to the relief society or organization making the shipment. At the same time, receipts for these consignments shall be supplied by the administrative authorities responsible for guarding the prisoners.

Part VI. Execution of the Convention

◆ **Section I. General Provisions**

ARTICLE 126

Representatives or delegates of the Protecting Powers shall have permission to go to all places where prisoners of war may be, particularly to places of internment, imprisonment and labour, and shall have access to all premises occupied by prisoners of war; they shall also be allowed to go to the places of departure, passage and arrival of prisoners who are being transferred. They shall be able to interview the prisoners, and in particular the prisoners' representatives, without witnesses, either personally or through an interpreter.

Representatives and delegates of the Protecting Powers shall have full liberty to select the places they wish to visit. The duration and frequency of these visits shall not be restricted. Visits may not be prohibited except for reasons of imperative military necessity, and then only as an exceptional and temporary measure.

The Detaining Power and the Power on which the said prisoners of war depend may agree, if necessary, that compatriots of these prisoners of war be permitted to participate in the visits.

The delegates of the International Committee of the Red Cross shall enjoy the same prerogatives. The appointment of such delegates shall be submitted to the approval of the Power detaining the prisoners of war to be visited.

ARTICLE 127

The High Contracting Parties undertake, in time of peace as in time of war, to disseminate the text of the present Convention as widely as possible in their respective countries, and, in particular, to include the study thereof in their programmes of military and, if possible, civil instruction, so that the principles thereof may become known to all their armed forces and to the entire population.

Any military or other authorities, who in time of war assume responsibilities in respect of prisoners of war, must possess the text of the Convention and be specially instructed as to its provisions.

ARTICLE 128

The High Contracting Parties shall communicate to one another through the Swiss Federal Council and, during hostilities, through the Protecting Powers, the official translations of the present Convention, as well as the laws and regulations which they may adopt to ensure the application thereof.

ARTICLE 129

The High Contracting Parties undertake to enact any legislation necessary to provide effective penal sanctions for persons committing, or ordering to be committed, any of the grave breaches of the present Convention defined in the following Article.

Each High Contracting Party shall be under the obligation to search for persons alleged to have committed, or to have ordered to be committed, such grave breaches, and shall bring such persons, regardless of their nationality, before its own courts. It may also, if it prefers, and in accordance with the provisions of its own legislation, hand such persons over for trial to another High Contracting Party concerned, provided such High Contracting Party has made out a prima facie case.

Each High Contracting Party shall take measures necessary for the suppression of all acts contrary to the provisions of the present Convention other than the grave breaches defined in the following Article.

In all circumstances, the accused persons shall benefit by safeguards of proper trial and defence, which shall not be less favourable than those provided by Article 105 and those following of the present Convention.

ARTICLE 130

Grave breaches to which the preceding Article relates shall be those involving any of the following acts, if committed against persons or property protected by the Convention: wilful killing, torture or inhuman treatment, including biological experiments, wilfully causing great suffering or serious injury to body or health, compelling a prisoner of war to serve in the forces of the hostile Power, or wilfully depriving a prisoner of war of the rights of fair and regular trial prescribed in this Convention.

ARTICLE 131

No High Contracting Party shall be allowed to absolve itself or any other High Contracting Party of any liability incurred by itself or by another High Contracting Party in respect of breaches referred to in the preceding Article.

ARTICLE 132

At the request of a Party to the conflict, an enquiry shall be instituted, in a manner to be decided between the interested Parties, concerning any alleged violation of the Convention.

If agreement has not been reached concerning the procedure for the enquiry, the Parties should agree on the choice of an umpire who will decide upon the procedure to be followed.

Once the violation has been established, the Parties to the conflict shall put an end to it and shall repress it with the least possible delay.

◆ **Section II. Final Provisions**

ARTICLE 133

The present Convention is established in English and in French. Both texts are equally authentic.

The Swiss Federal Council shall arrange for official translations of the Convention to be made in the Russian and Spanish languages.

ARTICLE 134

The present Convention replaces the Convention of July 27, 1929, in relations between the High Contracting Parties.

ARTICLE 135

In the relations between the Powers which are bound by the Hague Convention respecting the Laws and Customs of War on Land, whether that of July 29, 1899, or that of October 18, 1907, and which are parties to the present Convention, this last Convention shall be complementary to Chapter II of the Regulations annexed to the above-mentioned Conventions of the Hague.

ARTICLE 136

The present Convention, which bears the date of this day, is open to signature until February 12, 1950, in the name of the Powers represented at the Conference which opened at Geneva on April 21, 1949; furthermore, by Powers not represented at that Conference, but which are parties to the Convention of July 27, 1929.

ARTICLE 137

The present Convention shall be ratified as soon as possible and the ratifications shall be deposited at Berne.

A record shall be drawn up of the deposit of each instrument of ratification and certified copies of this record shall be transmitted by the Swiss Federal Council to all the Powers in whose name the Convention has been signed, or whose accession has been notified.

ARTICLE 138

The present Convention shall come into force six months after not less than two instruments of ratification have been deposited.

Thereafter, it shall come into force for each High Contracting Party six months after the deposit of the instrument of ratification.

ARTICLE 139

From the date of its coming into force, it shall be open to any Power in whose name the present Convention has not been signed, to accede to this Convention.

ARTICLE 140

Accessions shall be notified in writing to the Swiss Federal Council, and shall take effect six months after the date on which they are received.

The Swiss Federal Council shall communicate the accessions to all the Powers in whose name the Convention has been signed, or whose accession has been notified.

ARTICLE 141

The situations provided for in Articles 2 and 3 shall give immediate effect to ratifications deposited and accessions notified by the Parties to the conflict before or after the beginning of hostilities or occupation. The Swiss Federal Council shall communicate by the quickest method any ratifications or accessions received from Parties to the conflict.

ARTICLE 142

Each of the High Contracting Parties shall be at liberty to denounce the present Convention.

The denunciation shall be notified in writing to the Swiss Federal Council, which shall transmit it to the Governments of all the High Contracting Parties.

The denunciation shall take effect one year after the notification thereof has been made to the Swiss Federal Council. However, a denunciation of which notification has been made at a time when the denouncing Power is involved in a conflict shall not take effect until peace has been concluded, and until after operations connected with release and repatriation of the persons protected by the present Convention have been terminated.

The denunciation shall have effect only in respect of the denouncing Power. It shall in no way impair the obligations which the Parties to the conflict shall remain bound to fulfil by virtue of the principles of the law of nations, as they result from the usages established among civilized peoples, from the laws of humanity and the dictates of the public conscience.

ARTICLE 143

The Swiss Federal Council shall register the present Convention with the Secretariat of the United Nations. The Swiss Federal Council shall also inform the Secretariat of the United Nations of all ratifications, accessions and denunciations received by it with respect to the present Convention.

In Witness Whereof the undersigned, having deposited their respective full powers, have signed the present Convention.

DONE at Geneva this twelfth day of August 1949, in the English and French languages. The original shall be deposited in the Archives of the Swiss Confederation. The Swiss Federal Council shall transmit certified copies thereof to each of the signatory and acceding States.

"The State shall not deny to any person equality before the law."

Overview

The Constitution of India is the fundamental and supreme law that provides the framework for all of the individual laws of the country. It was adopted by the Constituent Assembly of India on November 26, 1949, and came into effect on January 26, 1950, marking the twentieth anniversary of Purna Swaraj (complete self-rule) as adopted by the Indian National Congress (the dominant political party) in Lahore in 1930. The day is celebrated as Republic Day in India. An embodiment of the ideals and aspirations of the people of the nation, the constitution is continuously growing, responding to the needs and requirements of a changing society. In the excerpted document, the bracketed portions are changes in the constitution that have been enacted in intervening years; the unbracketed portions represent the original 1949 text. Most of the changes are relatively minor and intended to clarify or amplify language from the original constitution or to deleted passages that are no longer applicable. In some instances, new provisions have been added to the constitution to reflect social, economic, or other changes in India.

The constitution draws on various sources, among them existing constitutions, the Government of India Act of 1935, and the Objectives Resolution drafted by Jawaharlal Nehru and adopted by the Constituent Assembly on January 22, 1947. In forming its diverse aspects, the constitution's makers relied upon and borrowed heavily from concepts in the constitutions of Ireland (directive principles), Great Britain (the parliamentary system), the United States (fundamental rights), Canada (federal structure and provisions regarding union-state relations), and Australia (trade and commerce).

The document lays down detailed administrative provisions that are based primarily on its preceding document, the Government of India Act of 1935. That act provided the foundation for the current constitution, as it established a parliamentary system, framed a federal system, and made provisions for provincial legislatures on the basis of elections. While the constitution retained the structure of the 1935 act, it fundamentally differed in its aims and objectives. The 1935 act was designed to give ultimate authority to the British, whereas the Constitution of India draws its legitimacy from the people of India.

This basic distinction between the two documents derives from the Objectives Resolution drafted by Nehru and adopted on January 22, 1947 by the Constituent Assembly. This document resolved to proclaim India as an "Independent Sovereign Republic and to draw up for her future governance a Constitution" wherein all power and authority were to derive from the people. The spirit of this resolution continued to shape the core principles of the constitution and is reflected in the Preamble, which since the adoption of the Forty-second Amendment (passed in 1976) declares India as a "sovereign socialist secular democratic republic" (http://parliamentofindia.nic.in/ls/debates/vol1p5.htm).

Context

The history of the constitution is directly rooted in the processes, demands, and aspirations that developed during the Indian independence movement. The constitution reflects the evolution of a responsible government and a continuous process of negotiations and struggle by the Indian people to achieve it. This historical dynamic goes back to the aftermath of the Indian Rebellion of 1857 (also referred to as the Great Rebellion), when the Government of India Act of 1858 placed India under the direct rule of Great Britain with the British Crown assuming sovereignty over India. Over the next one hundred years imperial control gradually relaxed, and a responsible government evolved.

The first substantial attempt to form a representative government came in the first decade of the twentieth century with the Government of India Act of 1909, also known as the Indian Councils Act of 1909 and commonly called the Morley-Minto Reforms after John Morley, secretary of state for India, and Gilbert Elliot-Murray-Kynynmound, 4th Earl of Minto, the viceroy of India. These reforms were meant to control growing patriotic militancy and political unrest, particularly in Bengal, where various groups were agitating to remove the British from power and improve economic conditions in India and to unite the administrative districts that had been partitioned by the British. The

1946

■ **December 9**
The Constituent
Assembly meets
for the first time.

■ **December 13**
The Objectives
Resolution is
drafted and moved
by Jawaharlal
Nehru in the
Constituent
Assembly.

1947

■ **January 22**
The Objectives
Resolution is
adopted by the
Constituent
Assembly.

■ **June 3**
The Mountbatten
Plan, for the
partition of the
British-ruled India
into the separate
nations of India and
Pakistan, is
announced.

■ **July 26**
The governor-
general announces
the establishment
of a separate
constituent
assembly for
Pakistan under the
Mountbatten Plan.

■ **August 29**
A draft committee
on the constitution,
under the
chairmanship of
Bhimrao Ramji
Ambedkar with six
other members, is
appointed.

1949

■ **November 26**
The constitution
receives the signa-
ture of the presi-
dent of the assem-
bly and is declared
as passed.

1950

■ **January 26**
The constitution
takes effect.

reforms also were meant to address the demands of the moderate wing of the Indian National Congress leadership for better representation of Indians in the government. The outcome of this joint venture was the Indian Councils Act, whereby the provincial legislative councils were enlarged, elected nonofficial members were incorporated into these councils, and elections were introduced in the Legislative Council at the center. Except for specified subjects, such as the armed forces and foreign affairs, elected Indian members were allowed to move resolutions. An important aspect of the 1909 act was its provision for separate representation of the Muslim community, inaugurating a new phase of the officially sanctioned politics of separatism that was to culminate in the partition of the entire Indian Subcontinent in 1947.

The next phase of constitutional reforms began with the Montagu-Chelmsford Report of 1918, leading to the enactment of the Government of India Act of 1919. The report outlined the Montagu-Chelmsford Reforms, named after Edwin Samuel Montagu, secretary of state for India, and Frederic John Thesiger, 1st Viscount Chelmsford, viceroy of India, and aimed at increased "association of Indians in every branch of the administration and the gradual development of self-governing institutions with a view to the progressive realization of responsible government in India as an integral part of the British Empire" (Basu, p. 6). The act established the model of dual government known as diarchy, dividing the administration into central and provincial subjects. Central subjects were kept under direct control of the central government, and provincial subjects were further split into "transferred" subjects (administered by the governors with the help of ministers, both elected and nonelected, who were accountable to the Legislative Council) and "reserved" subjects (directly under the governor and his executive council without any interference from the legislature).

Provincial legislatures were empowered to present their own budgets and to impose taxes related to their respective provincial sources of revenue. Except in increasing the percentage of elected Indian representatives in the Council of States (composed of sixty members, thirty-four of whom were elected) and in the Legislative Assembly (composed of 144 members, 104 of whom were elected), the 1919 act failed to make substantial advancement toward self-rule. The governor-general remained an all-powerful authority, with overriding power over almost all significant matters in the center and in the provinces, thus hampering any move toward a federal government.

Disappointment with the much-awaited act led to a nationwide noncooperation movement (September 1920–February 1922) led by Mohandas Gandhi. The movement came to an abrupt end with Gandhi's withdrawal from it following the news of a violent incident in which a group of peasants burned policemen in the remote village of Chauri Chaura in 1922. However, Gandhi put forward the demand for self-determination as an ultimate goal of swaraj (self-rule) when in 1922 he claimed that "*swaraj* will not be a free gift of the British Parliament; it will be a declaration of India's full self-expression ... expressed through an act of Parliament" (Kashyap, p. 2). The Indian National Congress officially made the demand for a constituent assembly for the first time in 1934 and in following years reiterated the demand for a constitution drawn from the people and framed without outside interference. This demand was directly linked with the desire for dominion status for India.

The Indian Statutory Commission, commonly known as the Simon Commission, came to India in 1927 to look after constitutional affairs and to review the 1919 act. The commission did not include a single Indian member and hence was boycotted by Indian nationalists. In 1929 the commission announced that dominion status was the goal of Indian political development, but the promise remained unfulfilled even in the Government of India Act of 1935, which is otherwise recognized as the cornerstone of the Constitution of India.

The 1935 act divided subjects into three categories—federal, provincial, and concurrent. Provinces were given autonomy from the central legislatures. The executive authority of a province was also made autonomous, and the governors were no longer subservient to the governor-general. The governor of a province was to act with the advice of elected ministers. The act widened the electoral base from seven million to nearly thirty-five million. A large measure of self-government was provided to provinces, and some decision-making power was given to Indians in various departments. However, sections 93 and 102 severely tamed this autonomy and ministerial input by inserting "safeguards" allowing governors to act at their discretion or to implement "individual judgment," enabling the British government to intervene and seize administrative control through the provincial governors and the viceroy. The much-promised dominion status for India was not mentioned. The act also imposed a very difficult hurdle for the creation of an all-India federation. Provinces were to gain autonomy after the election, but federation was to come into effect only after one-half of the Indian states, on the basis of population, agreed to accede.

The denial of dominion status and the provision of safeguards for British authorities infuriated Indian leaders across party lines. In 1938 Nehru gave voice to this anger, stating that "the National Congress stands for independence and a democratic state" (Basu, p. 14). He followed up by insisting that a constitution had to be devised by Indians themselves, through a freely elected constituent assembly. The Lahore Resolution of March 1940, a formal political statement adopted by the Muslim League and calling for greater Muslim autonomy, crucially altered the aspiration for a single constitution. Essentially, the Muslim League demanded a reconsideration of the whole constitutional plan, only after due consultation with the Muslim community.

The constitution-making process took shape with the establishment of the Constituent Assembly in the final phase of the Indian freedom struggle against foreign rule. The growing pressure of nationalist forces, followed by the widespread Quit India movement (a mass civil protest against British rule launched by the Indian National Congress under the leadership of Gandhi) in the environment of World War II, necessitated the transfer of power in India from the British government to representatives of the Indian people. In September 1945 the Labour Party came to power in Britain under Clement Attlee, and three British cabinet members—Frederick Pethick-Lawrence (secretary of state), Sir Stafford Cripps, and A. V. Alexander—were sent to India to speed up the transfer of power. They, along with the viceroy of India, Lord Archibald Wavell, were given the task of initiating dialogue with Indian representatives on the issues of an interim government, a new constitution, and a constitution-making body. The Cabinet Mission, however, failed to bring together the two major parties—the Indian National Congress and the Muslim League—on a common scheme for the transfer of power. Despite larger disagreements, the Indian National Congress agreed to be part of the constitution-making process. The Cabinet Mission recommended the formation of a constituent assembly by utilizing the recently elected Provincial Legislative Assemblies as representatives of the native people. They also suggested a basic framework for the future constitution and charted out the procedures to be followed by the constitution-making body. With the Indian Independence Act of 1947, the Constituent Assembly became a fully sovereign body in effect from August 15, 1947, and having "unlimited power to frame and adopt any constitution and to repeal any act of the British Parliament, including the Indian Independence Act" (Basu, p. 17).

About the Author

The Constituent Assembly, which came into being through the efforts of the Cabinet Mission, spent nearly three years completing the draft of the constitution and held eleven sessions for this task. The membership of the Constituent Assembly was based on indirect election by the elected members of the Provincial Legislative Assemblies. The provinces were given representation in the assembly in the ratio of one to one million of their population. The members of three communities (Muslims, Sikhs, and general—a category that included Hindus and all other communities) were given the option to elect their delegations separately according to their percentage of population in the provinces. "Princely states"—units directly governed by native rulers who had accepted the sovereignty of the British Crown—were given ninety-three seats, but the selection was left to consultation between the assembly and the rulers of the states. After Indian independence in 1949 these states were annexed by the Indian government.

The total number of members was to be 389, with 292 elected members of the Provincial Legislative Assemblies, ninety-three representatives of Indian princely states, and four members from chief commissioners' provinces. However, with enactment of the Mountbatten Plan (named for Louis Mountbatten, 1st Viscount Mountbatten of Burma, the last viceroy of India) of June 3, 1947, Pakistan was

Archibald Wavell (left), viceroy of India (AP/Wide World Photos)

declared a separate, sovereign country. This event reduced the total strength of the Constituent Assembly of India to 299, in effect making it a one-party assembly in the hands of the Indian National Congress. Nevertheless, because of active participation from the provincial wings of the Indian National Congress and the wisdom of the party leadership, the internal decision-making processes were quite democratic. While the Cabinet Mission plan guaranteed seats only for Muslims and Sikhs, the Indian National Congress enlarged the scope by bringing in Parsis, Anglo-Indians, Indian Christians, scheduled castes and tribes (the "untouchables"), and women, assuring their representation in the highest decision-making process.

Dr. B. R. Ambedkar (1891–1956) was the chairman of the Draft Committee of the Constitution and is widely regarded as the chief architect of the constitution. A lawyer by profession, throughout his life he advocated for the fight against "untouchability," a discriminatory Indian social structure based on the caste system in which the social standing of a person is determined not by merit but by the birth.

Explanation and Analysis of the Document

The Constitution of India is a comprehensive document, and its uniqueness lies in the manner in which it seeks a balance between a rigid constitution and a flexible code with enough scope to respond to the changing needs of the world's largest democracy. In fact, the Constitution of India is the lengthiest and most detailed constitution in the world. The Preamble, though not enforceable in a court of law, states both the source of the constitution's authority and the objectives that it seeks to establish and promote. In this way, the Preamble remains the guiding spirit for legal interpretations wherever the language of the constitution appears ambiguous. In all other contexts, the constitution has to be interpreted liberally (that is, the wording is construed to imply its usual or common-sense meaning), and normal rules used for the interpretation of any statutes apply to constitutional provisions. In its original form, the constitution had twenty-two parts, 395 articles, and nine schedules. Since 1950 there have been ninety-four amendments, and in its present form it contains 448 articles. From the standpoint of world history, the most significant parts of the constitution are the first three, the Preamble and the sections on citizenship issues and fundamental rights.

The framers of the constitution wanted to derive positive qualities and provisions from of all the leading constitutions of the world but were also conscious of their limitations. Hence proper safeguards were necessary in incorporating elements of other constitutions. For example, while the Constitution of India drew on the structure of the parliamentary democracy of the United Kingdom, it was also informed by representative democracies, which adopted a different standard in colonial situations and denied colonies the same rights that were the building blocks for such democracy in the mother country. Similarly, the constitution took fundamental rights from the United States but also tied these rights to the need for the security of the state itself. The goal was not merely political and legal equality for citizens but also social equality.

The constitution relied heavily on the 1935 Government of India Act for administrative provisions, as the act was a familiar structure for the people of India and also because the nascent democracy needed a robust and detailed administrative framework. Unlike the United States, India has a single constitution for both the union and the states. Only the state of Jammu and Kashmir was given special status and allowed to have its own constitution. Nevertheless, the framers were sensitive to the vastness and diversity of the nation; for this reason, specific provisions were adopted to protect regional characteristics and to address their specific requirements.

The constitution is also a growing document, contributing to its mammoth size. Unlike the U.S. Constitution, for which a constitutional amendment is quite difficult to achieve, in India a majority of constitutional provisions can be amended by a simple two-thirds majority of the members of Parliament. Since India adopted its constitution, amendments have substantially changed the nature of various features as conceived in the original document of 1949. These amendments have widened the scope and meanings of democracy and deepened the spirit of the original constitution rather than diluting it.

◆ **Preamble**

The heterogeneity of the composition and the ideological moorings of the members of the Constituent Assembly shaped the philosophy and character of the constitution and are reflected in the Preamble. The Preamble clearly mentions that sovereignty resides in the people of India. In the very beginning, the Preamble defines the objective of the constitution—to constitute the country as a "sovereign socialist secular democratic republic." The terms *socialist* and *secular*, though present in their essence, were not overtly mentioned in the original text of the constitution and were included only after the passage of the Forty-second Amendment.

The democracy envisioned in the Preamble was not merely political but also was related to a democratic social order. Thus, the constitution formulated a framework of representative democracy based on universal adult franchise and combined it with the principles of justice, liberty, equality, and fraternity. The concept of justice here implies "harmonious reconcilement of individual conduct with the general welfare of the society" (Paylee, p. 48).

◆ **Parts I and II**

Parts I and II of the constitution deal, respectively, with the union and its territory (Articles 1–4) and issues pertaining to citizenship (Articles 5–11). Part I clearly establishes that the Indian federation is not an outcome of any agreement by its constituting units and that these units do not have the power to secede from it. One of the unique features of the constitution is that it conceptualized future needs; hence on various issues the original constitution only lays down basic premises and authorizes Parliament to make laws accordingly. Citizenship is one such area where the makers were deeply aware of the changing historical context, and detailed provisions in this regard were provided by the Citizenship Act of 1955. In particular, the constitution takes up the issue of the movement of people across the Indian-Pakistani border in the wake of the partition of India after the British withdrawal. The constitution clarifies, then, who is to be regarded as "Indian," both in the case of people who have migrated into India from Pakistan and those of Indian birth who have migrated to Pakistan.

◆ **Part III**

The values and concepts listed in the Preamble are explained and made legally executable under the fundamental rights outlined in Part III of the constitution (Articles 12–35). Fundamental rights constitute one organic whole and proclaim the fundamental values and principles of the constitution. Most important, the constitution guaranteed equality before the law and equal protection of law and justice to all citizens. The concepts of equality and liberty were further tied to the idea of fraternity to ensure the growth not merely of an individual but indeed of an entire country, as both were considered to be interdependent. The idea of fraternity was directly influenced by the ideals of the French Revolution as well as the United Nations Charter (1948), which talks of universal brotherhood. For

Ambedkar, the chairman of the draft committee, to divorce one (equality, liberty, and fraternity) from the others was to defeat the very purpose of democracy. The concept of liberty as incorporated in the constitution is not merely the absence of arbitrary restraints on the freedom of an individual but is also a positive attribute, facilitating and creating an environment in which an individual can develop his or her personality in the fullest manner. To make this ideal possible, the constitution guaranteed equal opportunity for all its citizens, irrespective of social or economic status, and made illegal all discrimination on the grounds of religion, race, caste, sex, or place of birth (Article 15). By Article 17, untouchability—social caste discrimination based on one's birth—was abolished.

These rights guarantee certain basic provisions for an individual against any arbitrary action of the state (executive or legislative). They are set forth under six broad categories, addressing the right to equality (Articles 14–18), the right to freedom (Articles 19–22), protection against exploitation (Articles 23–24), the right to freedom of conscience, profession, and religion (Articles 25–28), and the rights of minorities (Articles 29–30, with Article 31 addressing issues surrounding the state's acquisition of property), and protection of these fundamental rights through constitutional remedies (Article 32–35). In the words of Ambedkar, while nonfundamental rights are created by agreement between parties, "fundamental Rights are the gift of Law" (Kashyap, p. 87). Article 13(2) guarantees fundamental rights by making any other laws and orders that are not consistent with the fundamental rights void. The Supreme Court is given the power of judicial review over any such law made by the government, Parliament, state legislatures, local authorities, or any "other authorities" created by the constitution.

Thus, Part III is the core of the constitution, at least from the perspective of individual Indians and their rights. Part III makes clear, for example, that all people are to have access to public facilities (Article 15), all people are to have equal opportunity in employment (Article 16), people are to have the right of free expression and assembly (Article 19), no person can be deprived of life or liberty without due process of law (Articles 21 and 22), and children under the age of fourteen cannot be compelled to work in hazardous occupations (Article 24). These and similar rights reflect the influence of the United Nations Declaration of Human Rights and the provisions protecting individual rights contained in the constitutions of other democratic nations.

Audience

With perhaps the exception of the Preamble, the Constitution of India is not inspirational reading. The constitution is a highly detailed compendium of the rules according to which the nation of India operates. The audience of the Constitution of India at the time of its adoption in 1950 consisted of the members of the Constituent Assembly. However, the constitution was made by and for the

Governor-general Lord Mountbatten salutes India's national flag as Edwina Mountbatten (second right) and Prime Minister Jawaharlal Nehru (right) look on during India's first Independence Day celebrations in New Delhi in August 1947. (AP/Wide World Photos)

people of India. It was drafted keeping in mind the welfare of four hundred million Indians (now nearly 1.2 billion Indians). With regard to the nation's government, there are three custodians of the constitution to implement its provisions: the state (legislature), the executive branch, and the judiciary. In this sense, the constitution is directly addressed to these three bodies. In particular, it provides a framework for the nation's judiciary to ensure that the nation's democratic institutions are preserved and that the people's fundamental rights are recognized. For example, in a landmark decision in *Keshavnanda Bharti v. State of Kerala*, the Supreme Court ruled in 1973 that all provisions, including fundamental rights, could be amended, but Parliament could not alter the basic structure of the constitution as outlined in the Preamble.

Impact

With the adoption of the constitution, India ceased to be a colony of Great Britain and declared its sovereignty. The Constitution of India was framed with the ideals of a social revolution, and its impact can be gauged from the fact that it has enabled the nation to come out of the shadow of imperial and other premodern models of governance that fostered unequal social relationships. Simultaneously, it has functioned as a guardian of democratic principles, contributing to the nation-making process in India. Since its adoption it has provided a basis for the articulation and assertion of rights by the marginalized and the downtrodden sections of Indian society and as an inclusive doctrine has helped to empower hitherto unheard voices and unrepresented sections of the society.

As noted, the constitution is regularly amended, for the process of doing so in India is relatively easy. Thus, for example, in 2002, the Eighty-sixth Amendment added Article 21A, which provides for free and compulsory education for children between the ages of six and fourteen. In portions of the constitution not reproduced here, equal pay for men and women has been guaranteed by the constitution. These kinds of changes, brought about by evolving social, political, economic, and other needs, indicate that the Constitution of India is a living, breathing document, one that is constantly examined and reexamined with a view to maintaining democratic institutions in a highly complex, diverse nation.

"WE, THE PEOPLE OF INDIA, *having solemnly resolved to constitute India into a [SOVEREIGN SOCIALIST SECULAR DEMOCRATIC REPUBLIC] and to secure to all its citizens: JUSTICE, social, economic and political; LIBERTY of thought, expression, belief, faith and worship; EQUALITY of status and of opportunity; and to promote among them all FRATERNITY assuring the dignity of the individual and the [unity and integrity of the Nation]."*

(Preamble)

"At the commencement of this Constitution, every person who has his domicile in the territory of India and—(a) who was born in the territory of India; or (b) either of whose parents was born in the territory of India; or (c) who has been ordinarily resident in the territory of India for not less than five years immediately preceding such commencement, shall be a citizen of India."

(Part II)

"All laws in force in the territory of India immediately before the commencement of this Constitution, in so far as they are inconsistent with the provisions of this Part, shall, to the extent of such inconsistency, be void."

(Part III)

"The State shall not deny to any person equality before the law or the equal protection of the laws within the territory of India."

(Part III)

"All citizens shall have the right—(a) to freedom of speech and expression; (b) to assemble peaceably and without arms; (c) to form associations or unions; (d) to move freely throughout the territory of India; (e) to reside and settle in any part of the territory of India ... [and] (g) to practise any profession, or to carry on any occupation, trade or business."

(Part III)

"No person shall be deprived of his life or personal liberty except according to procedure established by law."

(Part III)

Further Reading

■ Articles

Nigam, Aditya. "A Text without Author: Locating the Constituent Assembly as Event." *Economic and Political Weekly,* May 22, 2004: 2107–2113.

Singh, Mahendra Pal, and Surya Deva. "The Constitution of India: Symbol of Unity in Diversity." *Jahrbuch des öffentlichen Rechts der Gegenwart* 53 (2005): 649–686.

■ Books

Austin, Granville. *Working a Democratic Constitution: The Indian Experience.* New Delhi, India: Oxford University Press, 1999.

———. *The Indian Constitution: Cornerstone of a Nation.* New Delhi, India: Oxford University Press, 2007.

Basu, Durga Das. *Introduction to the Constitution of India*, 20th ed. New Delhi, India: Lexis Nexis Butterworths Wadhwa Nagpur, 2008.

Bhargava, Rajeev, ed., *Politics and Ethics of the Indian Constitution.* New Delhi, India: Oxford University Press, 2008.

Kashyap, Subhash C. *Our Constitution: An Introduction to India's Constitution and Constitutional Law.* New Delhi, India: National Book Trust, India, 1994.

Paylee M. V. *An Introduction to the Constitution of India.* Delhi, India: Vikash Publishing House, 1995.

■ Web Sites

"Constituent Assembly of India—Volume I." Parliament of India Web site.
    http://parliamentofindia.nic.in/ls/debates/vol1p5.htm.

"Constitution of India: An Insight on Constitution of India." Legal Service India Web site.
    http://www.legalserviceindia.com/constitution/const_home.htm.

"Constitution of India (Updated up to 94th Amendment Act)." National Informatics Centre, Ministry of Communications and Information Technology Web site.
    http://indiacode.nic.in/coiweb/welcome.html.

—Sadan Jha

Questions for Further Study

1. India and the People's Republic of China both that have modern constitutions—one in a democracy (India) and the other in a Communist state (China). Compare the Constitution of India with the Constitution of the People's Republic of China. What provisions do they have in common? How do they differ? What do the similarities and differences tell you about the nature of government in the two countries?

2. What influence did British colonial administration and institutions have on the Constitution of India? Do you think that those institutions have had a beneficial effect in an independent India?

3. In India, more than four hundred languages are spoken—twenty-nine by a million or more people and 122 spoken by ten thousand or more people. What effect, if any, do you think this kind of linguistic complexity might have on the emergence and maintenance of democratic institutions in India?

4. In contrast to the Constitution of the United States, that of India can be amended relatively easily. Do you think this ability to amend the constitution is a positive or a negative attribute of Indian democracy? Explain.

5. India historically had a caste system, assigning people to social strata based on their birth. The lowest class consisted of the "untouchables," but "untouchability" was outlawed by the Indian constitution. Why do you think the Indian government wanted to do away with untouchability? Do you think that a constitutional provision to that end has any effect on the attitudes of Indians? In that regard, compare India's abolition of untouchability with laws in the United States banning discrimination against racial groups.

CONSTITUTION OF INDIA

Preamble

WE, THE PEOPLE OF INDIA, having solemnly resolved to constitute India into a [Sovereign Socialist Secular Democratic Republic] and to secure to all its citizens: JUSTICE, social, economic and political; LIBERTY of thought, expression, belief, faith and worship; EQUALITY of status and of opportunity; and to promote among them all FRATERNITY assuring the dignity of the individual and the [unity and integrity of the Nation]; In Our Constituent Assembly this twenty-sixth day of November, 1949, do HEREBY ADOPT, ENACT AND GIVE TO OURSELVES THIS CONSTITUTION.

Part I. The Union and Its Territory

NAME AND TERRITORY OF THE UNION.

1. (1) India, that is Bharat, shall be a Union of States.

[(2) The States and the territories thereof shall be as specified in the First Schedule.]

(3) The territory of India shall comprise—

(a) the territories of the States;

[(b) the Union territories specified in the First Schedule; and]

(c) such other territories as may be acquired.

ADMISSION OR ESTABLISHMENT OF NEW STATES.

2. Parliament may by law admit into the Union, or establish, new States on such terms and conditions as it thinks fit....

FORMATION OF NEW STATES AND ALTERATION OF AREAS, BOUNDARIES OR NAMES OF EXISTING STATES.

3. Parliament may by law—

(a) form a new State by separation of territory from any State or by uniting two or more States or parts of States or by uniting any territory to a part of any State;

(b) increase the area of any State;

(c) diminish the area of any State;

(d) alter the boundaries of any State;

(e) alter the name of any State:

[Provided that no Bill for the purpose shall be introduced in either House of Parliament except on the recommendation of the President and unless, where the proposal contained in the Bill affects the area, boundaries or name of any of the States, the Bill has been referred by the President to the Legislature of that State for expressing its views thereon within such period as may be specified in the reference or within such further period as the President may allow and the period so specified or allowed has expired.]

[*Explanation I.*—In this article, in clauses (a) to (e), "State" includes a Union territory, but in the proviso, "State" does not include a Union territory.

Explanation II.—The power conferred on Parliament by clause (a) includes the power to form a new State or Union territory by uniting a part of any State or Union territory to any other State or Union territory.]

LAWS MADE UNDER ARTICLES 2 AND 3 TO PROVIDE FOR THE AMENDMENT OF THE FIRST AND THE FOURTH SCHEDULES AND SUPPLEMENTAL, INCIDENTAL AND CONSEQUENTIAL MATTERS.

4. (1) Any law referred to in article 2 or article 3 shall contain such provisions for the amendment of the First Schedule and the Fourth Schedule as may be necessary to give effect to the provisions of the law and may also contain such supplemental, incidental and consequential provisions (including provisions as to representation in Parliament and in the Legislature or Legislatures of the State or States affected by such law) as Parliament may deem necessary.

(2) No such law as aforesaid shall be deemed to be an amendment of this Constitution for the purposes of article 368.

Part II. Citizenship

CITIZENSHIP AT THE COMMENCEMENT OF THE CONSTITUTION.

5. At the commencement of this Constitution, every person who has his domicile in the territory of India and—

(a) who was born in the territory of India; or

(b) either of whose parents was born in the territory of India; or

(c) who has been ordinarily resident in the territory of India for not less than five years immediately preceding such commencement, shall be a citizen of India.

RIGHTS OF CITIZENSHIP OF CERTAIN PERSONS WHO HAVE MIGRATED TO INDIA FROM PAKISTAN.

6. Notwithstanding anything in article 5, a person who has migrated to the territory of India from the territory now included in Pakistan shall be deemed to be a citizen of India at the commencement of this Constitution if—

(a) he or either of his parents or any of his grandparents was born in India as defined in the Government of India Act, 1935 (as originally enacted); and

(b) (i) in the case where such person has so migrated before the nineteenth day of July, 1948, he has been ordinarily resident in the territory of India since the date of his migration, or

(ii) in the case where such person has so migrated on or after the nineteenth day of July, 1948, he has been registered as a citizen of India by an officer appointed in that behalf by the Government of the Dominion of India on an application made by him therefor to such officer before the commencement of this Constitution in the form and manner prescribed by that Government:

Provided that no person shall be so registered unless he has been resident in the territory of India for at least six months immediately preceding the date of his application.

RIGHTS OF CITIZENSHIP OF CERTAIN MIGRANTS TO PAKISTAN.

7. Notwithstanding anything in articles 5 and 6, a person who has after the first day of March, 1947, migrated from the territory of India to the territory now included in Pakistan shall not be deemed to be a citizen of India:

Provided that nothing in this article shall apply to a person who, after having so migrated to the territory now included in Pakistan, has returned to the territory of India under a permit for resettlement or permanent return issued by or under the authority of any law and every such person shall for the purposes of clause (b) of article 6 be deemed to have migrated to the territory of India after the nineteenth day of July, 1948.

RIGHTS OF CITIZENSHIP OF CERTAIN PERSONS OF INDIAN ORIGIN RESIDING OUTSIDE INDIA.

8. Notwithstanding anything in article 5, any person who or either of whose parents or any of whose grandparents was born in India as defined in the Government of India Act, 1935 (as originally enacted), and who is ordinarily residing in any country outside India as so defined shall be deemed to be a citizen of India if he has been registered as a citizen

of India by the diplomatic or consular representative of India in the country where he is for the time being residing on an application made by him therefor to such diplomatic or consular representative, whether before or after the commencement of this Constitution, in the form and manner prescribed by the Government of the Dominion of India or the Government of India.

PERSONS VOLUNTARILY ACQUIRING CITIZENSHIP OF A FOREIGN STATE NOT TO BE CITIZENS.

9. No person shall be a citizen of India by virtue of article 5, or be deemed to be a citizen of India by virtue of article 6 or article 8, if he has voluntarily acquired the citizenship of any foreign State.

CONTINUANCE OF THE RIGHTS OF CITIZENSHIP.

10. Every person who is or is deemed to be a citizen of India under any of the foregoing provisions of this Part shall, subject to the provisions of any law that may be made by Parliament, continue to be such citizen.

PARLIAMENT TO REGULATE THE RIGHT OF CITIZENSHIP BY LAW.

11. Nothing in the foregoing provisions of this Part shall derogate from the power of Parliament to make any provision with respect to the acquisition and termination of citizenship and all other matters relating to citizenship.

Part III. Fundamental Rights

◆ General

DEFINITION.

12. In this Part, unless the context otherwise requires, "the State" includes the Government and Parliament of India and the Government and the Legislature of each of the States and all local or other authorities within the territory of India or under the control of the Government of India.

LAWS INCONSISTENT WITH OR IN DEROGATION OF THE FUNDAMENTAL RIGHTS.

13. (1) All laws in force in the territory of India immediately before the commencement of this Constitution, in so far as they are inconsistent with the provisions of this Part, shall, to the extent of such inconsistency, be void.

(2) The State shall not make any law which takes away or abridges the rights conferred by this Part and any law made in contravention of this clause shall, to the extent of the contravention, be void.

(3) In this article, unless the context otherwise requires,—

(a) "law" includes any Ordinance, order, bye-law, rule, regulation, notification, custom or usage having in the territory of India the force of law;

(b) "laws in force" includes laws passed or made by a Legislature or other competent authority in the territory of India before the commencement of this Constitution and not previously repealed, notwithstanding that any such law or any part thereof may not be then in operation either at all or in particular areas.

[(4) Nothing in this article shall apply to any amendment of this Constitution made under article 368.]

◆ Right to Equality

EQUALITY BEFORE LAW.

14. The State shall not deny to any person equality before the law or the equal protection of the laws within the territory of India.

PROHIBITION OF DISCRIMINATION ON GROUNDS OF RELIGION, RACE, CASTE, SEX OR PLACE OF BIRTH.

15. (1) The State shall not discriminate against any citizen on grounds only of religion, race, caste, sex, place of birth or any of them.

(2) No citizen shall, on grounds only of religion, race, caste, sex, place of birth or any of them, be subject to any disability, liability, restriction or condition with regard to—

(a) access to shops, public restaurants, hotels and places of public entertainment; or

(b) the use of wells, tanks, bathing ghats, roads and places of public resort maintained wholly or partly out of State funds or dedicated to the use of the general public.

(3) Nothing in this article shall prevent the State from making any special provision for women and children.

[(4) Nothing in this article or in clause (2) of article 29 shall prevent the State from making any special provision for the advancement of any socially and educationally backward classes of citizens or for the Scheduled Castes and the Scheduled Tribes.]

(5) Nothing in this article or in sub-clause (g) of clause (1) of article 19 shall prevent the State from making any special provision, by law, for the advancement of any socially and educationally backward classes of citizens or for the Scheduled Castes or the Scheduled Tribes in so far as such special provisions relate to their admission to educational institutions including private educational institutions, whether aided or unaided by the State, other than the minority educational institutions referred to in clause (1) of article 30.]

EQUALITY OF OPPORTUNITY IN MATTERS OF PUBLIC EMPLOYMENT.

16. (1) There shall be equality of opportunity for all citizens in matters relating to employment or appointment to any office under the State.

(2) No citizen shall, on grounds only of religion, race, caste, sex, descent, place of birth, residence or any of them, be ineligible for, or discriminated against in respect of, any employment or office under the State.

(3) Nothing in this article shall prevent Parliament from making any law prescribing, in regard to a class or classes of employment or appointment to an office [under the Government of, or any local or other authority within, a State or Union territory, any requirement as to residence within that State or Union territory] prior to such employment or appointment.

(4) Nothing in this article shall prevent the State from making any provision for the reservation of appointments or posts in favour of any backward class of citizens which, in the opinion of the State, is not adequately represented in the services under the State.

[(4A) Nothing in this article shall prevent the State from making any provision for reservation [in matters of promotion, with consequential seniority, to any class] or classes of posts in the services under the State in favour of the Scheduled Castes and the Scheduled Tribes which, in the opinion of the State, are not adequately represented in the services under the State.]

[(4B) Nothing in this article shall prevent the State from considering any unfilled vacancies of a year which are reserved for being filled up in that year in accordance with any provision for reservation made under clause (4) or clause (4A) as a separate class of vacancies to be filled up in any succeeding year or years and such class of vacancies shall not be considered together with the vacancies of the year in which they are being filled up for determining the ceiling of fifty per cent. reservation on total number of vacancies of that year.]

(5) Nothing in this article shall affect the operation of any law which provides that the incumbent of an office in connection with the affairs of any religious or denominational institution or any member of the governing body thereof shall be a person professing a particular religion or belonging to a particular denomination.

ABOLITION OF UNTOUCHABILITY.

17. "Untouchability" is abolished and its practice in any form is forbidden. The enforcement of any

disability arising out of "Untouchability" shall be an offence punishable in accordance with law.

Abolition of titles.

18. (1) No title, not being a military or academic distinction, shall be conferred by the State.

(2) No citizen of India shall accept any title from any foreign State.

(3) No person who is not a citizen of India shall, while he holds any office of profit or trust under the State, accept without the consent of the President any title from any foreign State.

(4) No person holding any office of profit or trust under the State shall, without the consent of the President, accept any present, emolument, or office of any kind from or under any foreign State.

◆ **Right to Freedom**

Protection of certain rights regarding freedom of speech, etc.

19. (1) All citizens shall have the right—

(a) to freedom of speech and expression;

(b) to assemble peaceably and without arms;

(c) to form associations or unions;

(d) to move freely throughout the territory of India;

(e) to reside and settle in any part of the territory of India;

(f) [abrogated]

(g) to practise any profession, or to carry on any occupation, trade or business.

[(2) Nothing in sub-clause (a) of clause (1) shall affect the operation of any existing law, or prevent the State from making any law, in so far as such law imposes reasonable restrictions on the exercise of the right conferred by the said sub-clause in the interests of [the sovereignty and integrity of India,] the security of the State, friendly relations with foreign States, public order, decency or morality, or in relation to contempt of court, defamation or incitement to an offence.]

(3) Nothing in sub-clause (b) of the said clause shall affect the operation of any existing law in so far as it imposes, or prevent the State from making any law imposing, in the interests of [the sovereignty and integrity of India or] public order, reasonable restrictions on the exercise of the right conferred by the said sub-clause.

(4) Nothing in sub-clause (c) of the said clause shall affect the operation of any existing law in so far as it imposes, or prevent the State from making any law imposing, in the interests of [the sovereignty and integrity of India or] public order or morality, reason-

able restrictions on the exercise of the right conferred by the said sub-clause.

(5) Nothing in [sub-clauses (d) and (e)] of the said clause shall affect the operation of any existing law in so far as it imposes, or prevent the State from making any law imposing, reasonable restrictions on the exercise of any of the rights conferred by the said sub-clauses either in the interests of the general public or for the protection of the interests of any Scheduled Tribe.

(6) Nothing in sub-clause (g) of the said clause shall affect the operation of any existing law in so far as it imposes, or prevent the State from making any law imposing, in the interests of the general public, reasonable restrictions on the exercise of the right conferred by the said sub-clause, and, in particular, [nothing in the said sub-clause shall affect the operation of any existing law in so far as it relates to, or prevent the State from making any law relating to,—

(i) the professional or technical qualifications necessary for practising any profession or carrying on any occupation, trade or business, or

(ii) the carrying on by the State, or by a corporation owned or controlled by the State, of any trade, business, industry or service, whether to the exclusion, complete or partial, of citizens or otherwise].

Protection in respect of conviction for offences.

20. (1) No person shall be convicted of any offence except for violation of a law in force at the time of the commission of the Act charged as an offence, nor be subjected to a penalty greater than that which might have been inflicted under the law in force at the time of the commission of the offence.

(2) No person shall be prosecuted and punished for the same offence more than once.

(3) No person accused of any offence shall be compelled to be a witness against himself.

Protection of life and personal liberty.

21. No person shall be deprived of his life or personal liberty except according to procedure established by law.

Right to education.

[21A. The State shall provide free and compulsory education to all children of the age of six to fourteen years in such manner as the State may, by law, determine.]

Protection against arrest and detention in certain cases.

22. (1) No person who is arrested shall be detained in custody without being informed, as soon as may be, of the grounds for such arrest nor shall he

be denied the right to consult, and to be defended by, a legal practitioner of his choice.

(2) Every person who is arrested and detained in custody shall be produced before the nearest magistrate within a period of twenty-four hours of such arrest excluding the time necessary for the journey from the place of arrest to the court of the magistrate and no such person shall be detained in custody beyond the saidperiod without the authority of a magistrate.

(3) Nothing in clauses (1) and (2) shall apply—

(a) to any person who for the time being is an enemy alien; or

(b) to any person who is arrested or detained under any law providing for preventive detention.

(4) No law providing for preventive detention shall authorise the detention of a person for a longer period than three months unless—

(a) an Advisory Board consisting of persons who are, or have been, or are qualified to be appointed as, Judges of a High Court has reported before the expiration of the said period of three months that there is in its opinion sufficient cause for such detention:

Provided that nothing in this sub-clause shall authorise the detention of any person beyond the maximum period prescribed by any law made by Parliament under sub-clause (b) of clause (7); or

(b) such person is detained in accordance with the provisions of any law made by Parliament under subclauses (a) and (b) of clause (7).

(5) When any person is detained in pursuance of an order made under any law providing for preventive detention, the authority making the order shall, as soon as may be, communicate to such person the grounds on which the order has been made and shall afford him the earliest opportunity of making a representation against the order.

(6) Nothing in clause (5) shall require the authority making any such order as is referred to in that clause to disclose facts which such authority considers to be against the public interest to disclose.

(7) Parliament may by law prescribe—

(a) the circumstances under which, and the class or classes of cases in which, a person may be detained for a period longer than three months under any law providing for preventive detention without obtaining the opinion of an Advisory Board in accordance with the provisions of sub-clause (a) of clause (4);

(b) the maximum period for which any person may in any class or classes of cases be detained under any law providing for preventive detention; and

(c) the procedure to be followed by an Advisory Board in an inquiry under [sub-clause (a) of clause (4)].

◆ Right against Exploitation

PROHIBITION OF TRAFFIC IN HUMAN BEINGS AND FORCED LABOUR.

23. (1) Traffic in human beings and begar and other similar forms of forced labour are prohibited and any contravention of this provision shall be an offence punishable in accordance with law.

(2) Nothing in this article shall prevent the State from imposing compulsory service for public purposes, and in imposing such service the State shall not make any discrimination on grounds only of religion, race, caste or class or any of them.

PROHIBITION OF EMPLOYMENT OF CHILDREN IN FACTORIES, ETC.

24. No child below the age of fourteen years shall be employed to work in any factory or mine or engaged in any other hazardous employment.

◆ Right to Freedom of Religion

FREEDOM OF CONSCIENCE AND FREE PROFESSION, PRACTICE AND PROPAGATION OF RELIGION.

25. (1) Subject to public order, morality and health and to the other provisions of this Part, all persons are equally entitled to freedom of conscience and the right freely to profess, practise and propagate religion.

(2) Nothing in this article shall affect the operation of any existing law or prevent the State from making any law—

(a) regulating or restricting any economic, financial, political or other secular activity which may be associated with religious practice;

(b) providing for social welfare and reform or the throwing open of Hindu religious institutions of a public character to all classes and sections of Hindus.

Explanation I.—The wearing and carrying of kirpans shall be deemed to be included in the profession of the Sikh religion.

Explanation II.—In sub-clause (b) of clause (2), the reference to Hindus shall be construed as including a reference to persons professing the Sikh, Jaina or Buddhist religion, and the reference to Hindu religious institutions shall be construed accordingly.

FREEDOM TO MANAGE RELIGIOUS AFFAIRS.

26. Subject to public order, morality and health, every religious denomination or any section thereof shall have the right—

(a) to establish and maintain institutions for religious and charitable purposes;

(b) to manage its own affairs in matters of religion;

(c) to own and acquire movable and immovable property; and

(d) to administer such property in accordance with law.

FREEDOM AS TO PAYMENT OF TAXES FOR PROMOTION OF ANY PARTICULAR RELIGION.

27. No person shall be compelled to pay any taxes, the proceeds of which are specifically appropriated in payment of expenses for the promotion or maintenance of any particular religion or religious denomination.

FREEDOM AS TO ATTENDANCE AT RELIGIOUS INSTRUCTION OR RELIGIOUS WORSHIP IN CERTAIN EDUCATIONAL INSTITUTIONS.

28. (1) No religious instruction shall be provided in any educational institution wholly maintained out of State funds.

(2) Nothing in clause (1) shall apply to an educational institution which is administered by the State but has been established under any endowment or trust which requires that religious instruction shall be imparted in such institution.

(3) No person attending any educational institution recognised by the State or receiving aid out of State funds shall be required to take part in any religious instruction that may be imparted in such institution or to attend any religious worship that may be conducted in such institution or in any premises attached thereto unless such person or, if such person is a minor, his guardian has given his consent thereto.

◆ Cultural and Educational Rights
PROTECTION OF INTERESTS OF MINORITIES.

29. (1) Any section of the citizens residing in the territory of India or any part thereof having a distinct language, script or culture of its own shall have the right to conserve the same.

(2) No citizen shall be denied admission into any educational institution maintained by the State or receiving aid out of State funds on grounds only of religion, race, caste, language or any of them.

RIGHT OF MINORITIES TO ESTABLISH AND ADMINISTER EDUCATIONAL INSTITUTIONS.

30. (1) All minorities, whether based on religion or language, shall have the right to establish and administer educational institutions of their choice.

[(1A) In making any law providing for the compulsory acquisition of any property of an educational institution established and administered by a minority, referred to in clause (1), the State shall ensure that the amount fixed by or determined under such law for the acquisition of such property is such as would not restrict or abrogate the right guaranteed under that clause.]

(2) The State shall not, in granting aid to educational institutions, discriminate against any educational institution on the ground that it is under the management of a minority, whether based on religion or language.

31. *[Compulsory acquisition of property.] Rep. by the Constitution (Forty-fourth Amendment) Act, 1978, s. 6 (w.e.f. 20-6-1979).*

◆ Saving of Certain Laws
SAVING OF LAWS PROVIDING FOR ACQUISITION OF ESTATES, ETC.

[31A. [(1) Notwithstanding anything contained in article 13, no law providing for—

(a) the acquisition by the State of any estate or of any rights therein or the extinguishment or modification of any such rights, or

(b) the taking over of the management of any property by the State for a limited period either in the public interest or in order to secure the proper management of the property, or

(c) the amalgamation of two or more corporations either in the public interest or in order to secure the proper management of any of the corporations, or

(d) the extinguishment or modification of any rights of managing agents, secretaries and treasurers, managing directors, directors or managers of corporations, or of any voting rights of shareholders thereof, or

(e) the extinguishment or modification of any rights accruing by virtue of any agreement, lease or licence for the purpose of searching for, or winning, any mineral or mineral oil, or the premature termination or cancellation of any such agreement, lease or licence, shall be deemed to be void on the ground that it is inconsistent with, or takes away or abridges any of the rights conferred by [article 14 or article 19]:

Provided that where such law is a law made by the Legislature of a State, the provisions of this article shall not apply thereto unless such law, having been reserved for the consideration of the President, has received his assent:]

[Provided further that where any law makes any provision for the acquisition by the State of any estate and where any land comprised therein is held by a person under his personal cultivation, it shall not be lawful for the State to acquire any portion of such land as is within the ceiling limit applicable to him under any law for the time being in force or any building or structure standing thereon or appurtenant thereto, unless the law relating to the acquisition of such land, building or structure, provides for payment of compensation at a rate which shall not be less than the market value thereof.]

(2) In this article,—

3 [(a) the expression "estate" shall, in relation to any local area, have the same meaning as that expression or its local equivalent has in the existing law relating to land tenures in force in that area and shall also include—

(i) any *jagir*, *inam* or *muafi* or other similar grant and in the States of [Tamil Nadu] and Kerala, any *janmam* right;

(ii) any land held under *ryotwari* settlement;

(iii) any land held or let for purposes of agriculture or for purposes ancillary thereto, including waste land, forest land, land for pasture or sites of buildings and other structures occupied by cultivators of land, agricultural labourers and village artisans;]

(b) the expression "rights", in relation to an estate, shall include any rights vesting in a proprietor, subproprietor, under-proprietor, tenure-holder, [raiyat, under-raiyat] or other intermediary and any rights or privileges in respect of land revenue.]

VALIDATION OF CERTAIN ACTS AND REGULATIONS.

[31B. Without prejudice to the generality of the provisions contained in article 31A, none of the Acts and Regulations specified in the Ninth Schedule nor any of the provisions thereof shall be deemed to be void, or ever to have become void, on the ground that such Act, Regulation or provision is inconsistent with, or takes away or abridges any of the rights conferred by, any provisions of this Part, and notwithstanding any judgment, decree or order of any court or Tribunal to the contrary, each of the said Acts and Regulations shall, subject to the power of any competent Legislature to repeal or amend it, continue in force.]

SAVING OF LAWS GIVING EFFECT TO CERTAIN DIRECTIVE PRINCIPLES.

[31C. Notwithstanding anything contained in article 13, no law giving effect to the policy of the State towards securing [all or any of the principles laid down in Part IV] shall be deemed to be void on the ground that it is inconsistent with, or takes away or abridges any of the rights conferred by [article 14 or article 19]; *and no law containing a declaration that it is for giving effect to such policy shall be called in question in any court on the ground that it does not give effect to such policy:*

Provided that where such law is made by the Legislature of a State, the provisions of this article shall not apply thereto unless such law, having been reserved for the consideration of the President, has received his assent.

31D. *[Saving of laws in respect of anti-national activities.] Rep. by the Constitution (Forty-third Amendment) Act,* 1977, s. 2 (w.e.f. 13-4-1978).

◆ **Right to Constitutional Remedies**

REMEDIES FOR ENFORCEMENT OF RIGHTS CONFERRED BY THIS PART.

32. (1) The right to move the Supreme Court by appropriate proceedings for the enforcement of the rights conferred by this Part is guaranteed.

(2) The Supreme Court shall have power to issue directions or orders or writs, including writs in the nature of *habeas corpus, mandamus, prohibition, quo warranto* and *certiorari*, whichever may be appropriate, for the enforcement of any of the rights conferred by this Part.

(3) Without prejudice to the powers conferred on the Supreme Court by clauses (1) and (2), Parliament may by law empower any other court to exercise within the local limits of its jurisdiction all or any of the powers exercisable by the Supreme Court under clause (2).

(4) The right guaranteed by this article shall not be suspended except as otherwise provided for by this Constitution.

32A. *[Constitutional validity of State laws not to be considered in proceedings under article 32.] Rep. by the Constitution (Forty-third Amendment) Act,* 1977, s. 3 (w.e.f. 13-4-1978).

POWER OF PARLIAMENT TO MODIFY THE RIGHTS CONFERRED BY THIS PART IN THEIR APPLICATION TO FORCES, ETC.

[33. Parliament may, by law, determine to what extent any of the rights conferred by this Part shall, in their application to,—

(a) the members of the Armed Forces; or

(b) the members of the Forces charged with the maintenance of public order; or

(c) persons employed in any bureau or other organisation established by the State for purposes of intelligence or counter intelligence; or

(d) person employed in, or in connection with, the telecommunication systems set up for the purposes of any Force, bureau or organization referred to in clauses (a) to (c), be restricted or abrogated so as to ensure the proper discharge of their duties and the maintenance of discipline among them.]

RESTRICTION ON RIGHTS CONFERRED BY THIS PART WHILE MARTIAL LAW IS IN FORCE IN ANY AREA.

34. Notwithstanding anything in the foregoing provisions of this Part, Parliament may by law indemnify any person in the service of the Union or of a State or any other person in respect of any act done by him in connection with the maintenance or restoration of order in any area within the territory of India where martial law was in force or validate any sentence passed, punishment inflicted, forfeiture ordered or other act done under martial law in such area.

LEGISLATION TO GIVE EFFECT TO THE PROVISIONS OF THIS PART.

35. Notwithstanding anything in this Constitution,—

(a) Parliament shall have, and the Legislature of a State shall not have, power to make laws—

(i) with respect to any of the matters which under clause (3) of article 16, clause (3) of article 32, article 33 and article 34 may be provided for by law made by Parliament; and

(ii) for prescribing punishment for those acts which are declared to be offences under this Part; and Parliament shall, as soon as may be after the commencement of this Constitution, make laws for prescribing punishment for the acts referred to in sub-clause (ii);

(b) any law in force immediately before the commencement of this Constitution in the territory of India with respect to any of the matters referred to in sub-clause (i) of clause (a) or providing for punishment for any act referred to in sub-clause (ii) of that clause shall, subject to the terms thereof and to any adaptations and modifications that may be made therein under article 372, continue in force until altered or repealed or amended by Parliament.

Explanation.—In this article, the expression "law in force" has the same meaning as in article 372.

Glossary

bathing ghats	areas in which river waters are accessible by steps
jagir*, *inam* or *muafi	different forms of territorial grants
janmam	rights; certain rights held by an original landowner over land that has been sold to someone else
kirpans	ceremonial swords or daggers, to be worn by all baptized Sikhs
ryotwari	in British India, a system for collecting revenue from farmers
w.e.f	with effect from

Juan Perón (AP/Wide World Photos)

"We want a socially just, economically free, and politically sovereign Argentina."

Overview

On October 17, 1950, the Argentine president Juan Domingo Perón gave his "Twenty Fundamental Truths of Justicialism" speech to a crowd of supporters. He was elected president of Argentina for two consecutive terms, serving from 1946 until 1955, and then took office again in 1973. Perón's political party went through several name changes during his presidency, transforming in December 1947 from the Sole Party of the National Revolution to the Peronist Party, which emphasized his personal power. In 1948 Perón began using the term *Justicialism* to refer to his political beliefs. He was the central figure of Justicialism, and he strategically portrayed himself as the leader of a social movement rather than of a political party.

Perón's governing tactics were both populist and authoritarian. His power base came from the working class, unions, and industrialists. None of the major political parties in Argentina up until Perón's entrance into politics had assisted workers or improved their rights and working conditions. Perón's connection to the workers thus became critical in his consolidation of power. "Twenty Truths of Justicialism," according to Perón, formed the heart of the movement, which was intended to transform Argentina socially, politically, and economically.

Context

On June 4, 1943, the soldiers at the Campo de Mayo, an army training camp just outside Buenos Aires, the capital of Argentina, rose up against and deposed the conservative president Ramón Castillo. The Group of United Officers, composed of officers who wanted a strong nationalist government, was one of the key organizations within the army that had advocated for an end to Castillo's civilian rule. Juan Perón was a colonel in the army and a member of the Group of United Officers. The coup was not well led and did not have a manifesto or clear goals for the governance of Argentina. This disorganization led to a series of changes in command in which the coup leader, General

Arturo Rawson, was soon replaced by Pedro Pablo Ramírez, a minister in the former Castillo government. The army quickly deposed Ramírez and supplanted him with the war minister, General Edelmiro J. Farrell. Wanting to quiet social protest and political rallies, the military outlawed the Communist Party, persecuted the unions, and intervened in Argentina's General Labor Confederation (known in Spanish as Confederación General del Trabajo, or CGT).

Five months after the coup, in November 1943, Perón was serving in the Department of Labor under the military government. He worked with the trade unions, associations of workers in particular trades that use collective bargaining in order to secure fair pay, benefits, and working conditions. The CGT was divided into two factions. Perón allied himself with one camp and displaced the opposing side; he also opposed the Socialist and Communist leaders in the CGT. While in office at the Department of Labor, Perón established new unions at a time when many workers in Argentina were unaware of what a union was. Indeed, among Perón's most decisive actions at the Department of Labor were his efforts to organize workers whose trades previously were not unionized. Perón helped them draft rules for their unions, organized meetings, established union headquarters, and advocated for the union movement. He also augmented workers' wages and implemented plans on behalf of workers' rights, including a welfare program that established paid holidays; the *aguinaldo*, or yearly bonus; severance pay; controls on female and child labor; subsidized housing; legal services; vacation resorts; legal status for trade unions; and employment agencies. As a result of these initiatives, the depressed sections of the agricultural and industrial working class became Perón's main supporters. In 1944 he became minister of war and then vice president while remaining head of the Department of Labor.

By 1945 dissatisfaction among the Argentine populace against the military government had grown. Demonstrations in favor of a constitutional government were carried out; in Buenos Aires on September 19, 1945, the March for the Constitution and Freedom called for an end to the military de facto government. Under these pressures, a divide grew in the military leadership, and on October 8 the Campo de Mayo garrison (the same garrison that was

1943

- **June 4**
  General Arturo Rawson leads a military coup to depose President Ramón Castillo.

1945

- **October 9**
  The military forces Juan Domingo Perón to resign from the vice presidency.

- **October 13**
  Perón is arrested and detained at Martin García Island.

- **October 17**
  Popular protests by workers and union leaders call for Perón's release; the Peronist movement begins.

1946

- **February 24**
  Perón wins the presidential election.

- **June 4**
  Perón begins his first term as president of Argentina.

1950

- **October 17**
  Perón announces the "Twenty Fundamental Truths of Justicialism" at the Plaza de Mayo.

1951

- **November 11**
  Women vote in Argentina for the first time.

1952

- **June 4**
  Reelected, Perón begins his second presidential term.

---

instrumental in the 1943 military coup), headed by General Eduardo Avalos, responded to pressure from the public, the opposition, and the U.S. embassy by asking President Farrell to demand Perón's resignation because Perón was becoming too powerful and controversial. On October 9, 1945, the military leadership of the Campo de Mayo forced Perón to resign from the vice presidency and his other government positions. Afterward, the military decided that even removed from his posts, Perón was still dangerous; the military arrested him on October 13 and sent him to prison on Martin García Island in the Río de la Plata and then held him in the military hospital in Buenos Aires. Perón's advocates attempted to get the CGT and other unions to support Perón and rise up against the government. Cipriano Reyes, a meatpacking workers' leader; Colonel Domingo Mercante, an associate from the Department of Labor; and Eva Duarte, an actress who was soon to be Perón's wife, canvassed working-class neighborhoods to rally support for Perón.

The CGT held a general strike on October 17, 1945. Thousands of workers marched at the Plaza de Mayo, the main square in Buenos Aires, where the Casa Rosada, the presidential headquarters, is located. The armed forces did not attempt to stop the marchers and through their inaction showed their support for the protestors and for Perón. This date thus marks the beginning of the rise of Peronism, which at its core was a union movement backed by the military. Under pressure from the striking masses of workers, the military leaders released Perón, who appeared that same night on the balcony of the Casa Rosada and addressed the protestors. Lacking support, Perón's government opponents, including General Eduardo Avalos, soon resigned. Farrell announced that presidential elections would be held in February 1946, and Perón publicized his presidential candidacy, with Juan Hortensio Quijano as his running mate. Although José P. Tamborini and Enrique Mosca, the candidates of the opposition Radical Civic Union, accused him of being a Nazi sympathizer, Perón won the election of February 24, 1946, with 53 percent of the vote. He took office on June 4, 1946. In January 1949, Perón proposed to create a Justicialist constitution to replace the Constitution of 1853. The Constitution of 1949 allowed the incumbent president to seek reelection for an unlimited number of six-year terms, which permitted Perón to be reelected in 1952.

About the Author

"Twenty Fundamental Truths of Justicialism" was authored by Juan Domingo Perón, who was president of Argentina from 1946 to 1955 and then again in 1973. He was born on October 8, 1895, into a middle-class immigrant family. Entering the Argentine military academy in 1911, Perón made a career as a military officer; he became an instructor at the War Academy in 1931. Beginning in 1939 he spent three years in Italy, where he observed firsthand Benito Mussolini's Fascist government. Back in Argentina

---

in 1943, he took part in the coup against President Ramón Castillo, then becoming secretary in the Department of Labor. In 1944 he gained the posts of secretary of war and vice president. Because of a split among the military coup leaders, Perón was arrested, but he soon was released owing to mass protests in October 1945. That month he married Eva Duarte, an actress who quickly became a popular figure in the Justicialist movement. In 1952 Perón won the presidential election for a second time, but a military coup removed him from power on September 19, 1955. He was exiled to Spain for eighteen years, returning to Argentina in 1973. After the resignation of his political ally Héctor J. Cámpora, Perón was reelected to the Argentine presidency in September 1973. He was unable to see the end of his term, however, as he died on July 1, 1974.

Explanation and Analysis of the Document

Perón enumerated his "Twenty Fundamental Truths of Justicialism" in a speech given on October 17, 1950, from a balcony in the Casa Rosada, the Argentine presidential headquarters, facing the Plaza de Mayo. The crowd was gathered there to celebrate the fifth anniversary of Perón's release from military prison, which Perón deemed a national holiday called Loyalty Day. Underprivileged workers and the poor, known as the *masas descamisadas* ("shirtless masses"), were Perón's main supporters, and they had replaced the wealthy landowning elite as the most influential voting bloc in politics. To identify himself with the workers, Perón removed his blazer and rolled up his shirtsleeves when he spoke in public.

In the speech, Perón outlines in plain but nonspecific language the goals of Justicialism, using vocabulary that is accessible to the working class. While it was his workers' rights movement that swept him into office, Perón did not clarify and define Justicialism until he was already in power and was able to reflect on the rationalization for an alliance of forces among the workers, the military, and the church. He originally referred to his political movement as Peronism; in an attempt to change the movement's creed from that of one man to an ideology for the citizens and state agencies, he began instead to call the doctrine "Justicialism" and strived to root it in universal values. The term *Justicialism* was used because its principles are supposed to be fundamentally founded in justice and in the understanding that each person should get what he or she deserves and needs from society. The tenets of Justicialism were incorporated into the Argentine Constitution of 1949. Perón's "Twenty Fundamental Truths of Justicialism" constitute a distilled version of the Justicialist doctrine.

Peronism/Justicialism is often compared to Fascism, though it is a distinct political creation. Fascism's characteristics include militaristic nationalism, contempt for electoral democracy, and political and cultural liberalism. Fascists believe in a natural social hierarchy and rule by the privileged, allowing for the creation of a state in which individual interests are subordinated for the good of the nation. Perón, in fact, admired the Italian Fascist leader

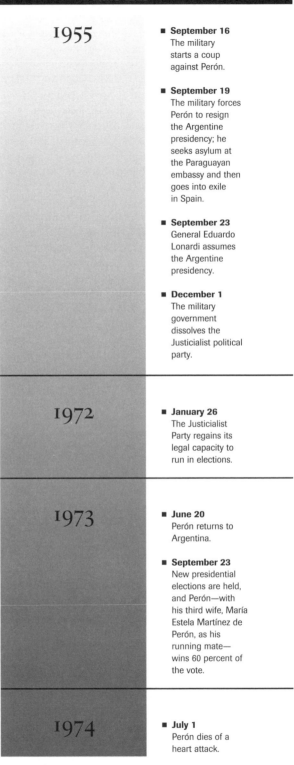

Time Line

1955

- **September 16**
  The military starts a coup against Perón.

- **September 19**
  The military forces Perón to resign the Argentine presidency; he seeks asylum at the Paraguayan embassy and then goes into exile in Spain.

- **September 23**
  General Eduardo Lonardi assumes the Argentine presidency.

- **December 1**
  The military government dissolves the Justicialist political party.

1972

- **January 26**
  The Justicialist Party regains its legal capacity to run in elections.

1973

- **June 20**
  Perón returns to Argentina.

- **September 23**
  New presidential elections are held, and Perón—with his third wife, María Estela Martínez de Perón, as his running mate—wins 60 percent of the vote.

1974

- **July 1**
  Perón dies of a heart attack.

Benito Mussolini, and many individuals with Fascist inclinations supported Perón. However, Justicialism was not an Argentine version of Italian Fascism. Mussolini disbanded the working class; Perón, on the other hand, politicized the working class. He also identified Justicialism with humanism by placing a central emphasis on humankind. In addition, the Peronist model sought the support of the whole society, not just its elite sectors.

Justicialism was more than a political movement; it was an ideological belief that attracted many devout followers and many fierce detractors. Perón himself conceived of the Justicialist doctrine. He determined its contents, defined its general principles, and analyzed and developed its different aspects in articles, public speeches, and declarations as president of Argentina. The Justicialist doctrine has three fundamental principles: social justice, economic independence, and Argentine sovereignty. These three principles are vaguely outlined in Perón's "Twenty Truths of Justicialism."

◆ Truths 1–3

Perón begins his "Twenty Fundamental Truths of Justicialism" by establishing the doctrine's populist core. Populism is the political representation of the common person and the working class. Adherence to populism is why Perón asserts in the first truth that the only interest of Justicialism is the people—that Justicialism *is* the will of the people. Yet he declines to indicate how a government should establish what exactly the populace's will is. Truth 2 also emphasizes Justicialism's grounding in populism, as Perón contrasts Justicialism with other political parties by declaring that all other political circles are anti-Peronist and antipopulist. In his third truth Perón states that a *caudillo*—a head of state, especially a military dictator, in a Spanish-speaking country—is one only in name. Here Perón accentuates that Peronists work together for a movement and not for specific interests or for the gain of one leader.

◆ Truths 4 and 5

In the fourth truth, Perón states that the only class in Justicialism is the working class. Common laborers were his main source of support, and Perón was the first Argentine president to bolster the working class. Truth 4 and some of Perón's other proposals are incongruous. In his fourth truth Perón implies that he is against unearned wealth and power based on inheritance, while in Truth 11 he declares that Justicialism seeks national unity. A movement that fights for the cause of the working class cannot at the same time foster an alliance of all classes intended to achieve national unity. Perón returns to highlighting the Justicialist identification with the working class in Truth 5, stressing the people's right to work as well as their obligation to be productive members of society.

◆ Truths 6–9

In Truths 6 through 9, Perón enunciates the moral beliefs that a good Justicialist should uphold and follow. He speaks of Peronism in quasi-religious terms and also makes several ambiguous statements. He states in Truth 6 that "for a good Peronist there can be nothing better than another Peronist." This statement does not hold much meaning and has historically been viewed as a weak declaration. In Truth 7, he seeks to maintain the idea of equality among the Peronist following. He asserts that if a Peronist begins to gain too much power, that Peronist will convert into an oligarch, a leader in a government in which only a few people wield power. In Truths 8 and 9, to clarify the priorities of Justicialism, Perón declares that the nation is the dominant concern for Peronists. The Justicialist movement follows the nation but precedes the individual in terms of importance in the Peronist political hierarchy.

◆ Truths 10–12

In Truths 10 to 12, Perón abstractly lays out the political aspects of the populist and nationalistic Peronist doctrine. In Truth 10 he pronounces that the two main branches of Peronism are social justice and social assistance. The Justicialist doctrine asserts that the just distribution of the country's wealth among the masses can alleviate social injustice. Toward this goal, Justicialism sought political balance between the social classes and special-interest groups. Under the arm of social assistance, Perón and his influential wife opened the Eva Perón Foundation in 1948 to obtain a base of support from previously ignored social sectors. Through social help, Justicialism incorporated the weakest members of society, including the poor, women, children, adolescents, and the unemployed and underemployed, into the Peronist movement and thereby created a strong populist voting bloc.

In Truth 11, Perón expresses his doctrine's goal of implementing national unity instead of provoking national struggle. Yet Peronism leans toward a single-party system in which political opposition is not tolerated. Perón's Justicialist movement did not permit the expression of points of view that opposed the party ideology, and Perón uses strong-arm techniques that purportedly diminish any possibility of resistance that could lead to national disunity. In Truth 12, Perón asserts that "children are the only privileged ones," thereby rendering false the earlier pronouncement that no one sector of society or social class should be favored over others.

◆ Truths 13 and 14

Truths 13 and 14 communicate Perón's creed that Justicialism extends beyond the bounds of political party. Rather, Justicialism is an ideology based in a socially conscious Christian philosophy with Catholic roots. Perón originally allied himself with the Catholic Church, and early in his first term he established Christian religious instruction in schools. However, despite his emphasis on Justicialism's connection to Christianity, he eventually turned against the Catholic Church. During his second term in office, he saw the Church as a competitive power and wanted to eliminate its political influence in Argentina.

◆ Truths 15–18

The core political, economic, and social tenets of the Justicialist doctrine are not explicitly laid out in the "Twenty Truths," but Perón does touch on them briefly. For example, Truth 15 iterates the social balance that Justicialism seeks between the individual and the community. He calls for political equilibrium between individualism and collectivism; in other words, he did not follow either Communism or capitalism, the two dominant political ideologies of the time. Truth 16 explains the economic doctrine of Justicialism, which entailed commercial nationalization, or the transfer of economic activities formerly owned and run by foreign companies into the hands of the Argentine state. For example, in 1946, under Perón's leadership, the state took over the nation's railways and gas and electric companies from foreign (mostly British-run) companies. Economic independence for Perón translated into autonomy in national development, which was an especially crucial issue because Argentina experienced industrial economic development later than Europe and the United States.

In Truth 17 he declares that social justice under Justicialism entails the just distribution of the country's wealth to alleviate social inequality. In 1950 the average worker was earning a 20 percent higher salary than he had earned in 1943. Truth 18 reiterates the third main tenet of Justicialism, which is national political sovereignty. This tenet provided an alternative to the alliances motivated by the cold war between the United States and the Soviet Union, known as the "third position." Rather than adhering to capitalism or Communism, Perón advocated international nonalignment so that Argentina could remain free of foreign influence and maintain national control in its economic and political affairs.

◆ Truths 19 and 20

In Truths 19 and 20, Perón returns to his populist rhetoric. He emphasizes that Justicialists have a centralized government, or a government in which power is concentrated in a central authority to which local governments are subject. In this truth he also states that people are free under Peronism. This assertion is often contested because Perón resorted to authoritarian tactics. Perón's twentieth and closing truth ends much like his introductory truth by praising the people and firmly underscoring Justicialism's populist underpinning.

Audience

Perón's initial audience for the "Twenty Fundamental Truths of Justicialism" was the crowd of Justicialist supporters who gathered in the Plaza de Mayo on October 17, 1950, to celebrate Loyalty Day and to hear Perón speak. Perón conceived the "Twenty Truths" for the unions and workers who were his main voting bloc. The twenty principles that he iterated became the official beliefs of the Justicialist movement, which developed into a national doctrine. The doctrine became a compulsory part of Argentine children's education while Perón was in power, so the second audience became the Argentine schoolchildren of the early 1950s. Perón also indirectly addressed the "Twenty Fundamental Truths of Justicialism" to the United States, the Soviet Union, and other foreign countries in his assertion that the "third position" offered an alternative stance to Soviet Communism and U.S. capitalism.

A former employee of the newspaper La Prensa *warns spectators that he is about to throw a huge portrait of the deposed Argentine president Juan Perón from the balcony of the newspaper's building in Buenos Aires on September 22, 1955.* (AP/Wide World Photos)

Impact

Perón's creation of the Peronist movement and Justicialist Party had long-term effects on Argentine politics through the second half of the twentieth century, and the party came to dominate Argentine politics in the first decade of the twenty-first century. Yet historians writing about Perón have both positive and negative views of his government and legacy, and Justicialism has historically been viewed from two different perspectives. On the one side, the original Peronist government was a dictatorship that doled out subsidies to favored trade unionists and practiced idolatrous devotion to Eva Perón. On the other side, Justicialism has been seen as populist, nationalistic, and committed to social justice. From this second camp, Peronist believers have treated the "Twenty Fundamental Truths of Justicialism" as dogma of divine inspiration.

Historians in the opposing camp point out that although he was voted in under a democracy, Perón resorted to dictatorial repression in attempts to unite a profoundly divided society. He also restricted civil liberties, and his government control extended to press censorship. He bought all the private radio stations in Argentina and established a chain of government newspapers and magazines. He

"These are the twenty fundamental truths of Justicialism. I wanted to bring them together here so that every one of you engrave it in your hearts and minds; so that you spread them everywhere as a message of love and justice; so that you live happily in accordance with them; and also so that you die happily in their defense if it were necessary."

(Introduction)

"The two arms of Peronism are Social Justice and Social Assistance. With them we embrace the people in Justice and Love."

(Truth 10)

"A government without a doctrine is a body without a soul."

(Truth 13)

"As a political doctrine Justicialism realizes the equilibrium between the rights of the individual and those of the community."

(Truth 15)

"We want a socially just, economically free, and politically sovereign Argentina."

(Truth 18)

purged universities of those who were against him and dismissed all of the Argentine Supreme Court judges opposed to him. Perón retained his hold on power during his 1951 reelection bid by breaking up opposition meetings and arresting those who did not favor him politically.

One of Juan Perón's original supporters was the Catholic Church. However, the Church soon turned against him, as it was opposed to the idea of Justicialism as a doctrine and disagreed with the practice of calling proponents of Justicialism "followers." The Church asserted instead that the only doctrine that people should follow was the Christian doctrine. The Catholic Church was able to shelter opposition to the Peronist party, and it became a critical organization in the demise of Perón's power.

Owing to the church's opposition and other factors, Perón never completed his second term in office. Argenti-

na's economic and social situation began to falter beginning in 1949. Out of fear of civil war, the Argentine military removed Perón from power on September 19, 1955. He fled to Paraguay first and then went into exile in Spain. On December 1, 1955, the military officially dissolved the Peronist political party. While in Spain, Perón continued to experience strong support among Justicialist followers for eighteen years.

From 1965 to 1973 Argentina once again experienced civil and economic volatility, and in March 1973 Argentina held general elections for the first time in ten years. In an effort to restore Argentina's stability, the military reinstituted Peronism as a legal party, but followers had divided into extreme and conflicting left- and right-wing factions. Perón was prevented from running, but voters elected the Justicialist candidate, Héctor Cámpora, as president. In July 1973, Cámpora resigned in order to clear the way for

Perón's candidacy; new elections were held on October 10, 1973, and Perón won the Argentine presidential election for a third time and was sworn in. He was able to serve his term only for a few months, however, before passing away. His third wife, María Estela Martínez de Perón, known as Isabel Perón, who was the vice president, became president on the day of his death, July 1, 1974.

Isabel Perón was removed from office by a military coup on March 24, 1976, and the Peronists did not hold power from 1976 to 1989. In 1989, under Carlos Saúl Menem, the Justicialist Party won the elections in Argentina for the first time without Perón as its leader. Another Justicialist, Néstor Kirchner, captured the presidency in May 2003, and in December 2007, Cristina Fernández de Kirchner, Néstor Kirchner's wife, became the latest Justicialist president of Argentina. Many Argentineans support the Justicialist Party, and the Peronist doctrine of the 1940s and 1950s continues its influential and controversial legacy in Argentine politics.

Further Reading

■ Articles

Berhó, Deborah L. "Working Politics: Juan Domingo Perón's Creation of Positive Social Identity." *Rocky Mountain Review of Language and Literature* 54, no. 2 (Fall 2000): 65–76.

McLynn, F. J. "Perón's Ideology and Its Relation to Political Thought and Action." *Review of International Studies* 9 (1983): 1–15.

Sebastiani, M. G. "The Other Side of Peronist Argentina: Radicals and Socialists in the Political Opposition to Perón (1946–1955)." *Journal of Latin American Studies* 35, no. 2 (2003): 311–340.

■ Books

Brennan, James P., ed. *Peronism and Argentina*. Wilmington, Del.: SR Books, 1998.

Horvath, Laszlo, ed. *A Half Century of Peronism, 1943–1993: An International Bibliography*. Stanford, Calif.: Hoover Institution, Stanford University, 1993.

Levitsky, Steven. *Transforming Labor-Based Parties in Latin America: Argentine Peronism in Comparative Perspective*. Cambridge, U.K.: Cambridge University Press, 2003.

Page, Joseph A. *Perón: A Biography*. New York: Random House, 1983.

Rock, David. *Argentina, 1516–1987: From Spanish Colonization to Alfonsín*. Berkeley: University of California Press, 2000.

■ Web Sites

"Argentine History Source Book." Thomas M. Edsall Web site.

Questions for Further Study

1. To what extent did distinctions in social class in Argentina lead to Perón's rise to power and his development of the principles of Justicialism?

2. How would you respond to the following statement: Justicialism was a thinly disguised version of Peronism, which was nothing more than Argentina's version of the Fascism practiced in Italy under Benito Mussolini and in Nazi Germany under Adolf Hitler in the 1930s and 1940s.

3. Perón said that he wanted to replace the strong-arm tactics of the past and rule by oligarchy (that is, rule by the elite few) with a new form of governance that created national unity. At the same time, he concentrated considerable power in his own hands and was intolerant of political opposition. How do you think Perón and his followers reconciled these apparently contradictory views?

4. What role did the Catholic Church play in Perón's rise to power and in his fall? Why did the Church oppose the doctrine of Justicialism? Why did Perón come to regard the Church as a threat to his power?

5. Many historians—and Argentines—regard Peronism as a dictatorship, with power concentrated in the hands of one person. Yet after Perón's exile to Spain, he was reelected as president, and in the 1980s and beyond members of the Justicialist Party have been elected to the nation's presidency. Why did Perón's doctrines and his approach to governance hold such appeal, and continue to do so, among large segments of the Argentine population?

http://web.archive.org/web/20030611195130/edsall-history-
    page.org/html/argentine_sourcebook.html.

"Juan Domingo Peron Argentine Presidential Messages." Latin
Americanist Research Resources Project Web site.
    http://lanic.utexas.edu/project/arl/pm/sample2/argentin/peron/.

—Marisa Lerer

JUAN PERÓN'S "TWENTY FUNDAMENTAL TRUTHS OF JUSTICIALISM"

These are the twenty fundamental truths of Justicialism. I wanted to bring them together here so that every one of you engrave it in your hearts and minds; so that you spread them everywhere as a message of love and justice; so that you live happily in accordance with them; and also so that you die happily in their defense if it were necessary.

—Juan Perón, October 17, 1950

1. True democracy is one where the government does what the people want and defends only one interest: The People.

2. Peronism is popular in its essence. All political circles are anti-popular and for this reason are not Peronist.

3. The Peronist works for the Movement. Whoever in its name serves a circle or a *caudillo* is one only in name.

4. For Peronism there exists only one class of men: workers.

5. In the new Argentina work is a right that creates human dignity and is a duty, for it is right that everyone produce at least what he consumes.

6. For a good Peronist there can be nothing better than another Peronist.

7. No Peronist should feel himself to be more than he is, or less than he should be. When a Peronist begins to feel himself to be more than he is he begins to convert himself into an oligarch.

8. In political action the scale of values of every Peronist is the following: first the Fatherland, then the Movement, and then Men.

9. For us politics are not an end, rather only a means for the good of the Fatherland, which is the happiness of its children and national greatness.

10. The two arms of Peronism are Social Justice and Social Assistance. With them we embrace the people in Justice and Love.

11. Peronism wants national unity and not struggle. It wants heroes and not martyrs.

12. In the new Argentina children are the only privileged ones.

13. A government without a doctrine is a body without a soul. For this reason Peronism has its own political, economic, and social doctrine, which is Justicialism.

14. Justicialism is a new philosophy of life that is simple, practical, popular, profoundly Christian, and profoundly popular.

15. As a political doctrine Justicialism realizes the equilibrium between the rights of the individual and those of the community.

16. As economic doctrine Justicialism realizes the social economy, placing capital at the service of the economy and the latter at the service of social well-being.

17. As a social doctrine Justicialism realizes social justice, which gives every person their right to a social function.

18. We want a socially just, economically free, and politically sovereign Argentina.

19. We constitute a centralized government, an organized state, and a free people.

20. The best we have on this earth is the People.

Glossary

caudillo	a head of state, especially a military dictator, in a Spanish-speaking country
oligarch	a leader in a government in which only a few people wield power

Fidel Castro (Library of Congress)

*"Cuban policy in the Americas [is] one of close solidarity
with the democratic peoples of this continent."*

Overview

On July 26, 1953, Fidel Castro led 113 Cuban revolutionaries in an attack on the Moncada military barracks in Santiago de Cuba, the headquarters of the Cuban dictator Fulgencio Batista's military in the southern region of Cuba and therefore one of the most important military posts in the country. Castro and his men were fighting to overturn the rule of Batista, who had seized power on March 10, 1952, in a coup d'état. Castro's plan failed, and he and many of his troops were captured by Batista's army and put on trial. Castro had been educated as a lawyer, and on October 16, 1953, acting as his own attorney, he delivered his now-famous speech, *History Will Absolve Me*, which was later published in full. Over two hours long, the speech outlined the five laws that encompassed the socioeconomic agrarian reform that Castro's movement wished to implement. His discourse was less a legal defense than a denunciation of the Batista regime and a proposal for a new government. Although the Moncada Barracks attack failed, it signaled the beginning of the revolutionary movement against Batista and brought Castro into the international spotlight.

Context

The major event leading up to Castro's speech was the attack on the Moncada Barracks, located on the southern part of the island in Santiago de Cuba, and the simultaneous attack on Carlos Manuel de Céspedes Barracks in the city of Bayamo. The Moncada Barracks were the second-largest military base in Cuba at the time, and Castro's failed attack on it was the first attempt at armed struggle against the Batista regime and the first battle in the Cuban revolutionary war. Although it was unsuccessful, the assault put Castro on the national stage as the main revolutionary leader against Fulgencio Batista. Batista ruled Cuba twice. His first presidency was from 1933 to 1944. The second time Batista came to power was through a coup on March 10, 1952, and he then ruled until December 31, 1958. Batista's government became widely unpopular among Cuban citizens because of the regime's corruption, repression, and censorship.

Castro's organization was one of many that sought to oust Batista. In Havana in 1952, soon after Batista's coup, Castro began organizing with student leaders to overthrow the regime. For one year he gathered supplies and weapons and worked with two hundred other members of the Orthodox Party. The Orthodox Party's political platform encompassed the reformation of political corruption, nationalism, social reform, and economic independence. Included in this group were Fidel Castro's brother, Raúl, who was second in command; Abel Santamaría, one of the commanders who had served under Fidel Castro during the Moncada Barracks attack; and Santamaría's sister, Haydée. Their objective was to take over the Moncada Barracks and to occupy the Palace of Justice, the Joaquín Castillo Duany Military Hospital, and a radio station. The attack began in the morning on July 26, 1953. One hundred and eleven men and two women fought against seven hundred troops from the Batista military. Castro hoped that the Cuban people would rally in support of his plan and that Batista's army would break ranks and join his forces. However, neither of these plans came to fruition. Castro and his troops were severely outnumbered. Eight of Castro's people were killed during combat, and Batista's troops captured sixty-one others. Francisco Tabernilla, Batista's chief of staff, ordered the torture and execution of the detainees.

Fidel Castro escaped and hid on a farm in the Sierra Maestra range in Santiago Province. One week later Castro turned himself in, after being assured by the Batista government that he would not be tortured or killed. He was held in Boniato, a large prison near Santiago. On August 1, 1953, Castro was imprisoned in the Provincial de Oriente prison, and it was while awaiting trial there that he wrote *History Will Absolve Me*. With help from the imprisoned Castro fighters, other inmates, and the custodian and prison employees, the prisoners were able to maintain an open flow of information to prepare for their defense. Castro and thirty of his men were put on trial between September 21 and October 16, 1953. In the course of his trial, Castro delivered a speech defending his rebellion and asserting his political position.

1952

- **March 10**
  Fulgencio Batista instigates a coup against the Cuban president, Carlos Prío Socarrás.

1953

- **July 26**
  Fidel Castro and more than one hundred Cuban revolutionaries attack the Moncada Barracks in Santiago de Cuba.

- **October 16**
  Castro makes his *History Will Absolve Me* speech during his trial for the Moncada Barracks attack and is soon sentenced to fifteen years in prison.

1955

- **May 15**
  Batista grants amnesty to Castro and the other fighters from the Moncada Barracks attack, and Castro plans to leave for Mexico.

1956

- **December 2**
  Castro, along with the Argentine revolutionary Ernesto "Che" Guevara and eighty other men, return to Cuba from Mexico aboard the yacht *Granma* for the purpose of waging a guerrilla war to overthrow the Batista government.

1959

- **January 1**
  Castro's forces enter Havana, and Batista, his family, and associates flee Cuba for the Dominican Republic.

About the Author

Fidel Alejandro Castro Ruz was born on August 13, 1926, in Cuba's Oriente Province to a wealthy sugar plantation owner of Spanish descent. Educated at a Jesuit institution, he began studying law at the University of Havana in 1945. In July 1947 Castro traveled to the Dominican Republic with a group of Cuban students with the aim of starting a coup against the Dominican dictator Rafael Trujillo, who had been in power since 1930. The coup failed, and Castro returned to his studies at the university. It was at this time that he joined the Orthodox Party. In 1948 he was elected president of the Law Students Association, which he represented at a Latin American university students' congress in Colombia. The congress coincided with a civil war breaking out in Colombia, and Castro participated in skirmishes there before returning to Cuba. Castro earned his law degree in October 1950, but he soon abandoned his law practice to engage in revolutionary activities against the dictatorship of Batista.

At the end of his trial for his part in the Moncada Barracks attack, Castro was sentenced to fifteen years in prison. While he was being held at the prison on Isla de Pinos, he continued to plot Batista's overthrow. After having served less than two years, Castro was released in May of 1955 under a general amnesty granted by Batista. He went to Mexico to reorganize his revolutionary movement, which took the name 26th of July Movement. In December 1956 Castro and his followers returned to Cuba and were met by Batista's forces. Only about twenty escaped death or capture, Castro among them. Castro and his followers continued to wage a guerrilla war against the Batista government until January 1, 1959, when Castro claimed victory and Batista fled Cuba for the Dominican Republic. Castro became Cuba's prime minister on February 16, 1959, and eventually turned from his ideals of a democratic government to a dictatorship. When, on April 16, 1961, he declared the Cuban Revolution to be Marxist-Leninist, he turned Cuba into the first Socialist state in the Western Hemisphere. Cuba became a close ally of the Soviet Union, thus creating hostile relations with the United States. This conflict led the United States to declare an embargo against Cuba on February 17, 1962. Castro remained in power in Cuba until February 19, 2008, at which time flagging health forced him to formally relinquish the presidency.

Explanation and Analysis of the Document

On October 16, 1953, Fidel Castro made his more than two-hour-long *History Will Absolve Me* speech in his own defense in court in Cuba. Castro begins with an outline of the events leading up to the attack on the Moncada Barracks. He denounces the authorities for attempting to pretend that he was too sick to appear in court. In his speech, Castro analyzes the factors that led to the failure of the Moncada Barracks attack. Although he accepts full responsibility for his acts and admits that the attack was a military failure, he proclaims the attack to be a political victory for the Cuban people. He announces that there is a new popular armed struggle for Cuban independence against Fulgencio Batista's dictatorship. Castro maintains an anti-imperialist tone throughout his argument and outlines how he plans to transform Cuban society.

◆ **Cuba's Economic and Social State**

In his speech Castro describes the difficult social and economic climate created by the Batista regime in Cuba. Unemployment was the most pressing social problem in Cuba at this time. In 1953 the number of out-of-work Cubans reached six hundred thousand, and only 51.5 percent of the working-age population was employed. The government under Batista embezzled the retirement funds of the elderly and used the money for the regime's own gain. In addition, many Cuban farmers did not own the land that they worked and therefore were also impoverished. Speaking of these farmers, Castro refers to the tyranny of the Rural Guard, which the Cuban government had established in 1902 to protect the countryside; the Rural Guard soon became an arm of the large plantations primarily owned by U.S. citizens, and it repressed the rural population in an effort to keep Cuban citizens from owning their own land. Along with land distribution issues, the quality and accessibility of education were major concerns of the day. Hundreds of thousands of Cuban citizens in 1953 were illiterate, and six hundred thousand children did not attend school. There were ten thousand out-of-work teachers, and many recent Cuban college graduates were forced to take jobs that had nothing to do with their degrees.

◆ **The Five Revolutionary Laws**

The five revolutionary laws sought to solve Cuba's economic and social crisis. Castro wrote them before the Moncada Barracks attack. Had the attack been successful and had Castro's forces taken over the radio station, the laws would have been broadcast for the Cuban public to hear. Castro suggests that Colonel Alberto R. del Río Chaviano, the officer who arrested him and his companions, destroyed the papers that had the five revolutionary laws written on them. Some of these laws were put into effect when the revolutionary government gained power in 1959.

The first revolutionary law proposed to return power to the people and to reinstitute the 1940 Cuban Constitution that Batista had revoked in 1952. Castro claims that the revolutionary movement is the only source of legitimate power and that it would take over the legislative, executive, and judicial branches of the Cuban government. For Castro, a reformation of the judicial branches was imperative, because most of the judges and magistrates had pledged their allegiance to Batista after the coup. The second revolutionary law calls for the redistribution of land to small farmers in order to solve the problem of rural poverty. Castro describes redistributing the land according to *caballerías*, a measurement of land that is often used in Cuba and which is equivalent to 13.43 hectares.

The third revolutionary law would grant laborers the right to a share in the profits of the industrial, mercantile,

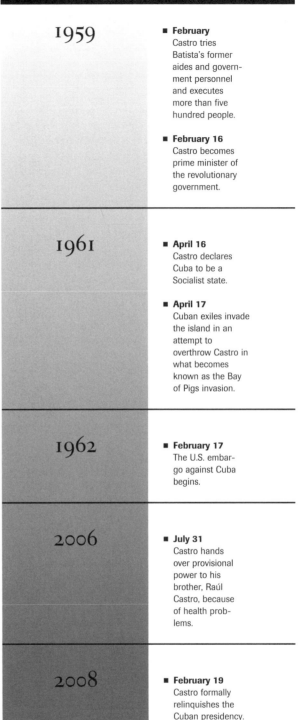

Time Line

1959

■ **February**
Castro tries Batista's former aides and government personnel and executes more than five hundred people.

■ **February 16**
Castro becomes prime minister of the revolutionary government.

1961

■ **April 16**
Castro declares Cuba to be a Socialist state.

■ **April 17**
Cuban exiles invade the island in an attempt to overthrow Castro in what becomes known as the Bay of Pigs invasion.

1962

■ **February 17**
The U.S. embargo against Cuba begins.

2006

■ **July 31**
Castro hands over provisional power to his brother, Raúl Castro, because of health problems.

2008

■ **February 19**
Castro formally relinquishes the Cuban presidency.

and mining companies. Castro exempts agriculture because it is covered by the agrarian reform law. The fourth revolutionary law grants all sugar planters the right to share 55 percent of the sugar production in Cuba and establishes a minimum allocation of profits for each sugarcane crop farmer. Castro describes the allotted sugar production in *arrobas*, a weight measurement used for cane sugar in

Cuba. One *arroba* is equivalent to twenty-five pounds, and forty thousand *arrobas* is equivalent to 460 metric tons. Finally, the fifth revolutionary law lays out Castro's plan and terms for recuperating funds that were misappropriated under the Batista government. He proposes to apply these reclaimed finances to workers' retirement and the construction and betterment of social service institutions such as hospitals.

Castro also takes the opportunity to outline aspects of Cuba's foreign policy under a revolutionary government. He would unify Cuba with the rest of the Americas just as the Cuban independence leader José Martí had hoped to do after gaining Cuban independence from Spain in 1898. Castro claims that this policy, along with the aforementioned laws, would have been put immediately into place had his forces been successful. Castro also emphasizes that the five revolutionary laws are based on the articles of the 1940 Cuban Constitution. For example, Article 90 outlaws large estates, and Article 60 requires that the government provide employment for its citizens.

Castro's economic goals were to convert Cuba from a supplier of raw materials—such as sugarcane and tobacco—to a producer of industrial goods and to return Cuba's land to Cuban ownership. He explains that because of this unequal land distribution, the breadwinner in the Cuban family could work only four months a year during the sugarcane harvest season. Multinational corporations such as the United Fruit Company and the West Indian Company owned 25 percent of all Cuban land, much of which they had appropriated through fraud and force.

Castro peppers his speech with literary and biblical references. He alludes to a character in the nineteenth-century French writer Honoréde Balzac's short story "The Fatal Skin" to emphasize the assumption of Batista and his followers that wealth and power places them above constitutional law. Castro quotes the character Taillefer, who says, "Let us drink to the power of gold! Mr. Valentine, a millionaire six times over, has just ascended the throne. He is king, … is above everyone, as all the rich are." And he goes on to say, "The country cannot continue begging on its knees for miracles from a few golden calves, like the Biblical one destroyed by the prophet's fury." Castro also condemns Carlos Saladrigas, a conservative politician and adviser to Batista. Castro claims that Saladrigas's capitalist economic model is nonfunctioning and asserts that none of Cuba's ruling elite who live on Fifth Avenue, the wealthiest street in Havana, have remedied any of Cuba's social and economic problems.

◆ The Moncada Program: Fixing Cuba's Six Socioeconomic Problems

The next part of Castro's argument outlines the principal methods of the Moncada program. Castro offers solutions for the six socioeconomic problems that he identifies as the most pressing: land distribution, the need for industrialization, the housing problem, unemployment, access to education, and health care reform. Castro states that the solution to the problem of land redistribution begins with

economists' and other experts' reevaluation of Cuba's industrial complex and the prompt removal of corrupt officials from office. He wants to provide housing for both rural and urban Cuban citizens and to implement infrastructure development throughout the island. He also plans to redistribute land to one hundred thousand small tenant farmers. His plan includes draining the swamps, replanting the forest, creating agricultural cooperatives, lowering rent prices, constructing new apartment buildings, and using atomic power to bring electricity to the most remote parts of the island. All of this, he asserts, would be accomplished if Cuba would stop investing in the military to defend the island, which Castro is quick to point out does not have any land borders. Castro again refers to the Cuban independence hero Martí, whom he calls the "apostle," in order to bolster support for an education reform plan that encompasses urban and rural education.

◆ Justification of the Moncada Barracks Defeat

Next, Castro justifies the rebels' loss at the Moncada Barracks. He uses their defeat to disprove the accusation that Carlos Prío Socarrás, president of the Republic of Cuba from 1948 until Batista seized power in 1952, supplied Castro and his movement with a million pesos. Castro wanted to be sure to publicly denounce any affiliation that his movement was rumored to have with Prío, whose government was characterized as overly interested in North American economic and political interests as well as being corrupt and anti-Communist. Castro refutes accusations of an affiliation on the ground that, had his forces been given that much money, they would have had enough supplies and combatants to prevail at Moncada. Castro also brings up the testimony of the ballistic technicians, lieutenants Eusebio Berrio and Heriberto Amador Cruz. Contrary to what Batista had claimed, on October 5, 1953, the lieutenants testified that the weapons used at the Moncada Barracks attacks were not bought by the rebels from foreign countries.

Castro then refers to the Batista regime's crime against those of Castro's fellow combatants who were captured at the Moncada Barracks. He once again quotes Martí in order to associate his revolutionary cause with the hero of Cuba's independence movement. Martí's poem "To My Dead Brothers on November 27th" pays homage to eight Cuban medical students whom the Spanish courts accused of desecrating the tomb of the Spanish journalist Gonzalo de Castañón (d. 1871). They were found guilty after a hurried trial and executed by firing squad on November 27, 1871. This event took place during the Ten Years' War (1868–1878), the first of Cuba's three wars of independence against Spain. Castro declares that the crimes of 1871 (the shooting of the eight medical students) are multiplied by ten on July 26–29, 1953, thus denouncing the murder of his men by Batista's troops.

Castro goes on to counter Batista's assertion that his coup on March 10, 1952, had the aim of stopping a planned coup by President Prío. Batista maintained that Prío was planning his own coup in April 1952 in order to thwart a

Following an unsuccessful uprising against Fulgencio Batista,
the dead bodies of shot insurgents lie on the grounds of the Moncada Barracks. (AP/Wide World Photos)

win by the Orthodox Party in the general elections sched-uled to take place in June of that year. There is no histori-cal evidence to back up Batista's declaration. Castro goes on to counter the false accusations that Batista made against Castro's troops who participated in the Moncada Barracks attacks. Batista claimed that Castro's men had killed sick patients in the hospital that they took over. Colonel Alberto del Río Chaviano also stated that Castro's people had stabbed three patients in the hospital. However, Edmundo Tamayo Silveiro, the director of the Joaquín Castillo Duany Military Hospital, swore in court that no military personnel were killed by knives or any other sharp weapons during the assault. Castro tries to demonstrate that the soldiers serving under Batista sympathize with the revolutionary cause. He states that the soldiers are also indignant and shamed by the murder of Castro's comrades. Castro ends his speech with the now famous line that is the title of this text, "I do not fear prison, as I do not fear the fury of the miserable tyrant who took the lives of 70 of my comrades. Condemn me. It does not matter. History will absolve me."

Audience

Castro initially addressed his speech to the court that was prosecuting him for his role in the Moncada Barracks attacks. Those who were present during Castro's trial

included the three presiding judges—Adolfo Nieto Piñeiro-Osoria, Juan Francisco Mejías Valdivieso, and Ricardo Díaz Olivera—and the secretary of the tribunal, Raúl Fernán-dez-Mascaró Arini. Although Cuba's courts at the time were supposed to be open, the public was nevertheless banned from attending the trial. However, several attorneys were present, as were a number of guards and soldiers. Six journalists, including Marta Rojas, were in court and in this instance represented the public.

After his trial, Castro transcribed the speech from mem-ory while he served his prison sentence on the Isla de Pinos off the coast of Cuba. Although Marta Rojas authenticated the version presented here, historians are certain that Cas-tro added some ideas and polished others for publication. The composition of *History Will Absolve Me* was a tedious process. Castro wrote fragments of the speech with lemon juice between the lines of letters to his friends and family. When these letters were heated with a clothing iron, the words written in lemon juice would appear. In 1954 the pieces of the speech were compiled, and in the spring of that year, twenty thousand copies were published for distri-bution. The last words of his speech, "History will absolve me," were transformed into the title of the "little book" of the revolution. It was reprinted in 1958 by the 26th of July Movement, which had based its principles on this text. Today *History Will Absolve Me* is mandatory reading for Cuban students. It is the most cited work in Cuba, and

> "A government acclaimed by the mass of rebel people would be vested with every power, everything necessary in order to proceed with the effective implementation of popular will and real justice."
>
> (Paragraph 4)

> "Furthermore, it was declared that the Cuban policy in the Americas would be one of close solidarity with the democratic peoples of this continent, and that all those politically persecuted by bloody tyrannies oppressing our sister nations would find generous asylum, brotherhood and bread in the land of Martí; not the persecution, hunger and treason they find today."
>
> (Paragraph 9)

> "When you try a defendant for robbery, Honorable Judges, do you ask him how long he has been unemployed? Do you ask him how many children he has, which days of the week he ate and which he didn't, do you investigate his social context at all?"
>
> (Paragraph 20)

> "I know that many of the soldiers are indignant at the barbaric assassinations perpetrated. I know that they feel repugnance and shame at the smell of homicidal blood that impregnates every stone of Moncada Barracks."
>
> (Paragraph 39)

scholars consider it to be one of the principal revolutionary texts of Cuba and Latin America.

Impact

Castro's speech did not lead to his release. Despite his defense of his actions at the Moncada Barracks and his condemnation of the Batista regime, the judges sentenced him to fifteen years in prison. In the end, he only served one year and seven months. On May 15, 1955, Archbishop Pérez Serrantes secured Castro's release, assuring Batista that Castro was no longer a public threat. Batista granted amnesty to Castro and his colleagues. Castro went into exile in Mexico, where he continued to build support for

his revolutionary movement. The date of the Moncada Barracks attack became the name of the revolutionary movement: the 26th of July Movement. In 1956 the 26th of July Movement—which included Fidel and Raúl Castro, Ruz Camilo Cienfuegos, José A. Echeverria, Ernesto "Che" Guevara, Frank País, Abel Santamaria, and Hubér Matos—launched a full-scale guerilla war against Batista and his supporters, and *History Will Absolve Me* was their manifesto. Castro finally received the support of the people that he had sought during the attack on the Moncada Barracks and led a successful guerilla war against the dictatorship. On January 1, 1959, Castro's forces entered Havana and defeated Batista.

The full impact of *History Will Absolve Me* and the revolutionary laws that were iterated in it were felt in 1959.

Castro became prime minister on February 16, 1959. On May 17, 1959, the Cuban revolutionary government instituted the agrarian reform law to appropriate property owned by foreigners and limit property owners from holding more than thirty *caballerías*. The law eradicated the plantations and did away with North American control and exploitation of Cuban land. The fifth revolutionary law was realized in 1959 when the revolutionary government created the Ministry of the Recuperation of Financial Embezzlement. The Cuban state was then able to recuperate more than four hundred million pesos in embezzled funds as well as properties that were owned by people linked to the Batista regime who had become rich through illegal revenues. In August and October 1960, Castro's revolutionary government nationalized both foreign and Cuban private enterprises. Castro also succeeded in implementing universal health care in Cuba as well as free college education.

Although Castro's government was able to institute some of the social, economic, and political measures outlined in *History Will Absolve Me*, many of his original proposals were never executed. For example, Castro was never able to turn Cuba into an industrialized nation and therefore never broke Cuba's economic dependence on sugar and tobacco crops. Another idiosyncrasy appears in his solution for the six problems facing Cuba. Castro states

that Cuba should invest in its people instead of in weapons. As historians are quick to point out, Castro did not comply with his own economic plan; the Soviet Union during the cold war continually supplied Cuba with military weapons in order to maintain a strategic military location close to the United States. Another discrepancy between Castro's plan and his implementation is found in the first revolutionary law, which people initially understood as a reinstatement of the articles of the 1940 constitution mandating regular elections and alternating political parties. However, Castro never set a time frame for the revolutionary forces to relinquish power, and he never restored Cuba to democracy after defeating Batista. Castro held power for forty-nine years.

Further Reading

■ Articles

Farber, Samuel. "The Cuban Communists in the Early Stages of the Cuban Revolution: Revolutionaries or Reformists?" *Latin American Research Review* 18, no. 1 (1983): 59–83.

Miller, Nicola. "The Absolution of History: Uses of the Past in Castro's Cuba." *Journal of Contemporary History* 38, no. 1 (2003): 147–162.

Questions for Further Study

1. The events of Castro's life suggest that in the years following World War II a great deal of political turmoil existed not just in Cuba but, indeed, throughout Central and South America. What economic and political factors likely contributed to this unrest?

2. What conditions in Cuba accounted for having turned Castro and his followers into revolutionaries?

3. Castro places considerable emphasis on land reform and land ownership. Why would these matters have been of great concern to Cubans during this time period?

4. In the decades since Castro's seizure of power in Cuba, the nation has had a troubled relationship with the United States, which has regarded Castro as a rogue dictator. Given that Castro's campaign was against the corruption of the Batista government, why were American political leaders uncomfortable with Castro and his views of government?

5. What role did Communism (and anti-Communism) play in the events that led to Castro's assumption of power and his position as dictator of Cuba?

6. Revolutionary figures like Castro often spend some portion of their lives in prison and frequently use their time to write documents outlining their views. Locate such a document from a person who was sentenced to prison for challenging the established order and compare that person's views with Castro's. Example might include Martin Luther King's "Letter from a Birmingham Jail"; Adolf Hitler's *Mein Kampf* ("My Struggle"); or Nelson Mandela's autobiography, *Long Walk to Freedom*, which he began writing while in a South African prison.

Smith. Wayne S. "Cuba's Long Reform." *Foreign Affairs* 75, no. 2 (March–April, 1996): 99–112.

■ Books

Castro, Fidel, Ann Louise Bardach, and Luis Conte Agüero. *The Prison Letters of Fidel Castro*. New York: Nation Books, 2007.

De la Cova, Antonio Rafael. *The Moncada Attack: Birth of the Cuban Revolution*. Columbia: University of South Carolina Press, 2007.

Martí, José, Deborah Shnookal, and Mirta Muñiz. *José Martí Reader: Writings on the Americas*. New York: Ocean Press, 2007.

Sweig, Julia. *Inside the Cuban Revolution: Fidel Castro and the Urban Underground*. Cambridge, Mass.: Harvard University Press, 2002.

Szulc, Tad. *Fidel: A Critical Portrait*. New York: Morrow, 1986.

■ Web Sites

"Castro Speech Data Base." Latin American Network Information Center Web site.
http://lanic.utexas.edu/la/cb/cuba/castro.html.

"The Cuban Revolution (1952–1958)." Latin American Studies Web site.
http://www.latinamericanstudies.org/cuban-revolution.htm.

"Fidel Castro History Archive." Marxists Internet Archive Web site.
http://www.marxists.org/history/cuba/archive/castro/.

—Marisa Lerer

FIDEL CASTRO'S *HISTORY WILL ABSOLVE ME* SPEECH

In terms of struggle, when we talk about people we're talking about the six hundred thousand Cubans without work, who want to earn their daily bread honestly without having to emigrate from their homeland in search of a livelihood; the five hundred thousand farm laborers who live in miserable shacks, who work four months of the year and starve the rest, sharing their misery with their children, who don't have an inch of land to till and whose existence would move any heart not made of stone; the four hundred thousand industrial workers and laborers whose retirement funds have been embezzled, whose benefits are being taken away, whose homes are wretched quarters, whose salaries pass from the hands of the boss to those of the moneylender, whose future is a pay reduction and dismissal, whose life is endless work and whose only rest is the tomb; the one hundred thousand small farmers who live and die working land that is not theirs, looking at it with the sadness of Moses gazing at the promised land, to die without ever owning it, who like feudal serfs have to pay for the use of their parcel of land by giving up a portion of its produce, who cannot love it, improve it, beautify it nor plant a cedar or an orange tree on it because they never know when a sheriff will come with the rural guard to evict them from it; the thirty thousand teachers and professors who are so devoted, dedicated and so necessary to the better destiny of future generations and who are so badly treated and paid; the twenty thousand small business men weighed down by debts, ruined by the crisis and harangued by a plague of grafting and venal officials; the ten thousand young professional people: doctors, engineers, lawyers, veterinarians, school teachers, dentists, pharmacists, newspapermen, painters, sculptors, etc., who finish school with their degrees anxious to work and full of hope, only to find themselves at a dead end, all doors closed to them, and where no ears hear their clamor or supplication. These are the people, the ones who know misfortune and, therefore, are capable of fighting with limitless courage! To these people whose desperate roads through life have been paved with the bricks of betrayal and false promises, we were not going to say: "We will give you … " but rather: "Here it is, now fight for it with everything you have, so that liberty and happiness may be yours!"

The five revolutionary laws that would have been proclaimed immediately after the capture of the Moncada Barracks and would have been broadcast to the nation by radio must be included in the indictment. It is possible that Colonel Chaviano may deliberately have destroyed these documents, but even if he has I remember them.

The first revolutionary law would have returned power to the people and proclaimed the 1940 Constitution the Supreme Law of the State until such time as the people should decide to modify or change it. And in order to effect its implementation and punish those who violated it—there being no electoral organization to carry this out—the revolutionary movement, as the circumstantial incarnation of this sovereignty, the only source of legitimate power, would have assumed all the faculties inherent therein, except that of modifying the Constitution itself: in other words, it would have assumed the legislative, executive and judicial powers.

This attitude could not be clearer nor more free of vacillation and sterile charlatanry. A government acclaimed by the mass of rebel people would be vested with every power, everything necessary in order to proceed with the effective implementation of popular will and real justice. From that moment, the Judicial Power—which since March 10th had placed itself against and outside the Constitution—would cease to exist and we would proceed to its immediate and total reform before it would once again assume the power granted it by the Supreme Law of the Republic. Without these previous measures, a return to legality by putting its custody back into the hands that have crippled the system so dishonorably would constitute a fraud, a deceit, one more betrayal.

The second revolutionary law would give nonmortgageable and non-transferable ownership of the land to all tenant and subtenant farmers, lessees, share croppers and squatters who hold parcels of five caballerías of land or less, and the State would indemnify the former owners on the basis of the rental which they would have received for these parcels over a period of ten years.

The third revolutionary law would have granted workers and employees the right to share 30% of the profits of all the large industrial, mercantile and mining enterprises, including the sugar mills. The strictly agricultural enterprises would be exempt in consideration of other agrarian laws which would be put into effect.

The fourth revolutionary law would have granted all sugar planters the right to share 55% of sugar production and a minimum quota of forty thousand arrobas for all small tenant farmers who have been established for three years or more.

The fifth revolutionary law would have ordered the confiscation of all holdings and ill-gotten gains of those who had committed frauds during previous regimes, as well as the holdings and ill-gotten gains of all their legates and heirs. To implement this, special courts with full powers would gain access to all records of all corporations registered or operating in this country, in order to investigate concealed funds of illegal origin, and to request that foreign governments extradite persons and attach holdings rightfully belonging to the Cuban people. Half of the property recovered would be used to subsidize retirement funds for workers and the other half would be used for hospitals, asylums and charitable organizations.

Furthermore, it was declared that the Cuban policy in the Americas would be one of close solidarity with the democratic peoples of this continent, and that all those politically persecuted by bloody tyrannies oppressing our sister nations would find generous asylum, brotherhood and bread in the land of Martí; not the persecution, hunger and treason they find today. Cuba should be the bulwark of liberty and not a shameful link in the chain of despotism.

These laws would have been proclaimed immediately. As soon as the upheaval ended and prior to a detailed and far reaching study, they would have been followed by another series of laws and fundamental measures, such as the Agrarian Reform, the Integral Educational Reform, nationalization of the electric power trust and the telephone trust, refund to the people of the illegal and repressive rates these companies have charged, and payment to the treasury of all taxes brazenly evaded in the past.

All these laws and others would be based on the exact compliance of two essential articles of our Constitution: one of them orders the outlawing of large estates, indicating the maximum area of land any one person or entity may own for each type of agricultural enterprise, by adopting measures which would tend to revert the land to the Cubans. The other categorically orders the State to use all means at its disposal to provide employment to all those who lack it and to ensure a decent livelihood to each manual or intellectual laborer. None of these laws can be called unconstitutional. The first popularly elected government would have to respect them, not only because of moral obligations to the nation, but because when people achieve something they have yearned for throughout generations, no force in the world is capable of taking it away again.

The problem of the land, the problem of industrialization, the problem of housing, the problem of unemployment, the problem of education and the problem of the people's health: these are the six problems we would take immediate steps to solve, along with restoration of civil liberties and political democracy.

This exposition may seem cold and theoretical if one does not know the shocking and tragic conditions of the country with regard to these six problems, along with the most humiliating political oppression.

Eighty-five per cent of the small farmers in Cuba pay rent and live under constant threat of being evicted from the land they till. More than half of our most productive land is in the hands of foreigners. In Oriente, the largest province, the lands of the United Fruit Company and the West Indian Company link the northern and southern coasts. There are two hundred thousand peasant families who do not have a single acre of land to till to provide food for their starving children. On the other hand, nearly three hundred thousand caballerías of cultivable land owned by powerful interests remain uncultivated. If Cuba is above all an agricultural State, if its population is largely rural, if the city depends on these rural areas, if the people from our countryside won our war of independence, if our nation's greatness and prosperity depend on a healthy and vigorous rural population that loves the land and knows how to work it, if this population depends on a State that protects and guides it, then how can the present state of affairs be allowed to continue?

Except for a few food, lumber and textile industries, Cuba continues to be primarily a producer of raw materials. We export sugar to import candy, we export hides to import shoes, we export iron to import plows.... Everyone agrees with the urgent need to industrialize the nation, that we need steel industries, paper and chemical industries, that we must improve our cattle and grain production, the technology and processing in our food industry in order to defend ourselves against the ruinous competition from Europe in cheese products, condensed milk, liquors and edible oils, and the United States in canned goods; that we need cargo ships; that tourism should be an enormous source of revenue. But the capitalists insist that the workers remain under the yoke. The State sits back with its arms crossed and industrialization can wait forever.

Just as serious or even worse is the housing problem. There are two hundred thousand huts and hovels in Cuba; four hundred thousand families in the countryside and in the cities live cramped in huts and tenements without even the minimum sanitary requirements; two million two hundred thousand of our urban population pay rents which absorb between one fifth and one third of their incomes; and two million eight hundred thousand of our rural and suburban population lack electricity. We have the same situation here: if the State proposes the lowering of rents, landlords threaten to freeze all construction; if the State does not interfere, construction goes on so long as landlords get high rents; otherwise they would not lay a single brick even though the rest of the population had to live totally exposed to the elements. The utilities monopoly is no better; they extend lines as far as it is profitable and beyond that point they don't care if people have to live in darkness for the rest of their lives. The State sits back with its arms crossed and the people have neither homes nor electricity.

Our educational system is perfectly compatible with everything I've just mentioned. Where the peasant doesn't own the land, what need is there for agricultural schools? Where there is no industry, what need is there for technical or vocational schools? Everything follows the same absurd logic; if we don't have one thing we can't have the other. In any small European country there are more than 200 technological and vocational schools; in Cuba only six such schools exist, and their graduates have no jobs for their skills. The little rural schoolhouses are attended by a mere half of the school age children—barefooted, half-naked and undernourished—and frequently the teacher must buy necessary school materials from his own salary. Is this the way to make a nation great?

Only death can liberate one from so much misery. In this respect, however, the State is most helpful—in providing early death for the people. Ninety per cent of the children in the countryside are consumed by parasites which filter through their bare feet from the ground they walk on. Society is moved to compassion when it hears of the kidnapping or murder of one child, but it is indifferent to the mass murder of so many thousands of children who die every year from lack of facilities, agonizing with pain. Their innocent eyes, death already shining in them, seem to look into some vague infinity as if entreating forgiveness for human selfishness, as if asking God to stay His wrath. And when the head of a family works only four months a year, with what can he purchase clothing and medicine for his children? They will grow up with rickets, with not a single good tooth in their mouths by the time they reach thirty; they will have heard ten million speeches and will finally die of misery and deception. Public hospitals, which are always full, accept only patients recommended by some powerful politician who, in return, demands the votes of the unfortunate one and his family so that Cuba may continue forever in the same or worse condition.

With this background, is it not understandable that from May to December over a million persons are jobless and that Cuba, with a population of five and a half million, has a greater number of unemployed than France or Italy with a population of forty million each?

When you try a defendant for robbery, Honorable Judges, do you ask him how long he has been unemployed? Do you ask him how many children he has, which days of the week he ate and which he didn't, do you investigate his social context at all? You just send him to jail without further thought. But those who burn warehouses and stores to collect insurance do not go to jail, even though a few human beings may have gone up in flames. The insured have money to hire lawyers and bribe judges. You imprison the poor wretch who steals because he is hungry; but none of the hundreds who steal millions from the Government has ever spent a night in jail. You dine with them at the end of the year in some elegant club and they enjoy your respect. In Cuba, when a government official becomes a millionaire overnight and enters the fraternity of the rich, he could very well be greeted with the words of that opulent character out of Balzac—Taillefer—who in his toast to the young heir to an enormous fortune, said: "Gentlemen, let us drink to the power of gold! Mr. Valentine, a millionaire six times over, has just ascended the throne. He is king, can do everything, is above everyone, as all the rich are. Henceforth, equality before the law, established by the Constitution, will be a myth for him; for he will not be subject to laws: the laws will be subject to him. There are no courts nor are there sentences for millionaires."

The nation's future, the solutions to its problems, cannot continue to depend on the selfish interests of a dozen big businessmen nor on the cold calculations of profits that ten or twelve magnates draw up in their air-conditioned offices. The country cannot continue begging on its knees for miracles from a few golden calves, like the Biblical one destroyed by the prophet's fury. Golden calves cannot perform miracles of any kind. The problems of the Republic can be solved only if we dedicate ourselves to fight for it with the same energy, honesty and patriotism our liberators had when they founded it. Statesmen like Carlos Saladrigas, whose statesmanship consists of preserving the status quo and mouthing phrases like "absolute freedom of enterprise," "guarantees to investment capital" and "law of supply and demand," will not solve these problems. Those ministers can chat away in a Fifth Avenue mansion until not even the dust of the bones of those whose problems require immediate solution remains. In this present-day world, social problems are not solved by spontaneous generation.

A revolutionary government backed by the people and with the respect of the nation, after cleansing the different institutions of all venal and corrupt officials, would proceed immediately to the country's industrialization, mobilizing all inactive capital, currently estimated at about 1.5 billion pesos, through the National Bank and the Agricultural and Industrial Development Bank, and submitting this mammoth task to experts and men of absolute competence totally removed from all political machines for study, direction, planning and realization.

After settling the one hundred thousand small farmers as owners on the land which they previously rented, a revolutionary government would immediately proceed to settle the land problem. First, as set forth in the Constitution, it would establish the maximum amount of land to be held by each type of agricultural enterprise and would acquire the excess acreage by expropriation, recovery of swampland, planting of large nurseries, and reserving of zones for reforestation. Secondly, it would distribute the remaining land among peasant families with priority given to the larger ones, and would promote agricultural cooperatives for communal use of expensive equipment, freezing plants and unified professional technical management of farming and cattle raising. Finally, it would provide resources, equipment, protection and useful guidance to the peasants.

A revolutionary government would solve the housing problem by cutting all rents in half, by providing tax exemptions on homes inhabited by the owners; by tripling taxes on rented homes; by tearing down hovels and replacing them with modern apartment buildings; and by financing housing all over the island on a scale heretofore unheard of, with the criterion that, just as each rural family should possess its own tract of land, each city family should own its own house or apartment. There is plenty of building material and more than enough manpower to make a decent home for every Cuban. But if we continue to wait for the golden calf, a thousand years will have gone by and the problem will remain the same. On the other hand, today possibilities of taking electricity to the most isolated areas on the island are greater than ever. The use of nuclear energy in this field is now a reality and will greatly reduce the cost of producing electricity.

With these three projects and reforms, the problem of unemployment would automatically disappear and the task of improving public health and fighting against disease would become much less difficult.

Finally, a revolutionary government would undertake the integral reform of the educational system, bringing it into line with the projects just mentioned with the idea of educating those generations which will have the privilege of living in a happier land. Do not forget the words of the Apostle: "A grave mistake is being made in Latin America: in countries that live almost completely from the produce of the land, men are being educated exclusively for urban life and are not trained for farm life." "The happiest country is the one which has best educated its sons, both in the instruction of thought and the direction of their feelings." "An educated country will always be strong and free."

The soul of education, however, is the teacher, and in Cuba the teaching profession is miserably underpaid. Despite this, no one is more dedicated than the Cuban teacher. Who among us has not learned his three Rs in the little public schoolhouse? It is time we stopped paying pittances to these young men and women who are entrusted with the sacred task of teaching our youth. No teacher should earn less than 200 pesos, no secondary teacher should make less than 350 pesos, if they are to devote themselves exclusively to their high calling without suffering want. What is more, all rural teachers should have free use of the various systems of transportation; and, at least once every five years, all teachers should enjoy a sabbatical leave of six months with pay so they may attend special refresher courses at home or abroad to keep abreast of the latest developments in their field. In this way, the curriculum and the teaching system can be easily improved. Where will the money be found for all this? When there is an end to the embezzlement of government funds, when public officials stop taking graft from the large companies that owe taxes to the State, when the enormous resources of the country are brought into full use, when we no longer buy tanks, bombers and guns for this country (which has no frontiers to defend and where these instruments of war, now being purchased, are used against the people), when there is more interest in educating the people than in killing them there will be more than enough money.

Cuba could easily provide for a population three times as great as it has now, so there is no excuse for the abject poverty of a single one of its present inhabitants. The markets should be overflowing with produce, pantries should be full, all hands should be working. This is not an inconceivable thought. What is inconceivable is that anyone should go to bed hungry while there is a single inch of unproductive land; that children should die for lack of medical attention; what is inconceivable is that 30% of our farm people cannot write their names and that 99% of them know nothing of Cuba's history. What is inconceivable is that the majority of our rural people are now living in worse circumstances than the Indians Columbus discovered in the fairest land that human eyes had ever seen.

To those who would call me a dreamer, I quote the words of Martí: "A true man does not seek the path where advantage lies, but rather the path where duty lies, and this is the only practical man, whose dream of today will be the law of tomorrow, because he who has looked back on the essential course of history and has seen flaming and bleeding peoples seethe in the cauldron of the ages knows that, without a single exception, the future lies on the side of duty."

Only when we understand that such a high ideal inspired them can we conceive of the heroism of the young men who fell in Santiago. The meager material means at our disposal was all that prevented sure success. When the soldiers were told that Prío had given us a million pesos, they were told this in the regime's attempt to distort the most important fact: the fact that our Movement had no link with past politicians: that this Movement is a new Cuban generation with its own ideas, rising up against tyranny; that this Movement is made up of young people who were barely seven years old when Batista perpetrated the first of his crimes in 1934. The lie about the million pesos could not have been more absurd. If, with less than 20,000 pesos, we armed 165 men and attacked a regiment and a squadron, then with a million pesos we could have armed 8,000 men, to attack 50 regiments and 50 squadrons—and Ugalde Carrillo still would not have found out until Sunday, July

26th, at 5:15 a.m. I assure you that for every man who fought, twenty well trained men were unable to fight for lack of weapons. When these young men marched along the streets of Havana in the student demonstration of the Martí Centennial, they solidly packed six blocks. If even 200 more men had been able to fight, or we had possessed 20 more hand grenades, perhaps this Honorable Court would have been spared all this inconvenience.

The politicians spend millions buying off consciences, whereas a handful of Cubans who wanted to save their country's honor had to face death barehanded for lack of funds. This shows how the country, to this very day, has been governed not by generous and dedicated men, but by political racketeers, the scum of our public life.

With the greatest pride I tell you that in accordance with our principles we have never asked a politician, past or present, for a penny. Our means were assembled with incomparable sacrifice. For example, Elpidio Sosa, who sold his job and came to me one day with 300 pesos "for the cause"; Fernando Chenard, who sold the photographic equipment with which he earned his living; Pedro Marrero, who contributed several months' salary and who had to be stopped from actually selling the very furniture in his house; Oscar Alcalde, who sold his pharmaceutical laboratory; Jesús Montané, who gave his five years' savings, and so on with many others, each giving the little he had.

One must have great faith in one's country to do such a thing. The memory of these acts of idealism bring me straight to the most bitter chapter of this defense—the price the tyranny made them pay for wanting to free Cuba from oppression and injustice.

Beloved corpses, you that once
Were the hope of my Homeland,
Cast upon my forehead
The dust of your decaying bones!
Touch my heart with your cold hands!
Groan at my ears!
Each of my moans will
Turn into the tears of one more tyrant!
Gather around me! Roam about,
That my soul may receive your spirits
And give me the horror of the tombs
For tears are not enough
When one lives in infamous bondage!

Multiply the crimes of November 27th, 1871 by ten and you will have the monstrous and repulsive crimes of July 26th, 27th, 28th and 29th, 1953, in the province of Oriente. These are still fresh in our memory, but someday when years have passed, when the skies of the nation have cleared once more, when tempers have calmed and fear no longer torments our spirits, then we will begin to see the magnitude of this massacre in all its shocking dimension, and future generations will be struck with horror when they look back on these acts of barbarity unprecedented in our history. But I do not want to become enraged. I need clearness of mind and peace in my heavy heart in order to relate the facts as simply as possible, in no sense dramatizing them, but just as they took place. As a Cuban I am ashamed that heartless men should have perpetrated such unthinkable crimes, dishonoring our nation before the rest of the world.

The tyrant Batista was never a man of scruples. He has never hesitated to tell his people the most outrageous lies. To justify his treacherous coup of March 10th, he concocted stories about a fictitious uprising in the Army, supposedly scheduled to take place in April, and which he "wanted to avert so that the Republic might not be drenched in blood." A ridiculous little tale nobody ever believed! And when he himself did want to drench the Republic in blood, when he wanted to smother in terror and torture the just rebellion of Cuba's youth, who were not willing to be his slaves, then he contrived still more fantastic lies. How little respect one must have for a people when one tries to deceive them so miserably! On the very day of my arrest I publicly assumed the

responsibility for our armed movement of July 26th. If there had been an iota of truth in even one of the many statements the Dictator made against our fighters in his speech of July 27th, it would have been enough to undermine the moral impact of my case. Why, then, was I not brought to trial? Why were medical certificates forged? Why did they violate all procedural laws and ignore so scandalously the rulings of the Court? Why were so many things done, things never before seen in a Court of Law, in order to prevent my appearance at all costs? In contrast, I could not begin to tell you all I went through in order to appear. I asked the Court to bring me to trial in accordance with all established principles, and I denounced the underhanded schemes that were afoot to prevent it. I wanted to argue with them face to face. But they did not wish to face me. Who was afraid of the truth, and who was not?

The statements made by the Dictator at Camp Columbia might be considered amusing if they were not so drenched in blood. He claimed we were a group of hirelings and that there were many foreigners among us. He said that the central part of our plan was an attempt to kill him—him, always him. As if the men who attacked the Moncada Barracks could not have killed him and twenty like him if they had approved of such methods. He stated that our attack had been planned by ex-President Prío, and that it had been financed with Prío's money. It has been irrefutably proven that no link whatsoever existed between our Movement and the last regime. He claimed that we had machine guns and hand-

Glossary

Apostle	a reference to José Martí, known as the "apostle of independence"
arrobas	measures of weight (1 arroba = 11.3 kilograms, or about 25 pounds)
caballería	measure of land used in Spanish-speaking countries; in Cuba, 33.2 acres
ex-president Prío	Carlos Prío Socarrás, who in 1952 was deposed as president of Cuba by Fulgencio Batista in a military coup
land of Martí	Cuba; that is, the homeland of the Cuban poet and revolutionary José Martí
rickets	a nutritional deficiency disease that results in bone deformations in children
Ugalde Carrillo	colonel in Batista's Military Intelligence Service who nearly uncovered Castro's plans to storm the Moncada Barracks
... who fell in Santiago	a reference to Castro's men who died at Moncada

grenades. Yet the military technicians have stated right here in this Court that we only had one machine gun and not a single hand-grenade. He said that we had beheaded the sentries. Yet death certificates and medical reports of all the Army's casualties show not one death caused by the blade. But above all and most important, he said that we stabbed patients at the Military Hospital. Yet the doctors from that hospital—Army doctors—have testified that we never even occupied the building, that no patient was either wounded or killed by us, and that the hospital lost only one employee, a janitor, who imprudently stuck his head out of an open window.

Whenever a Chief of State, or anyone pretending to be one, makes declarations to the nation, he speaks not just to hear the sound of his own voice. He always has some specific purpose and expects some specific reaction, or has a given intention. Since our military defeat had already taken place, insofar as we no longer represented any actual threat to the dictatorship, why did they slander us like that? If it is still not clear that this was a blood-drenched speech, that it was simply an attempt to justify the crimes that they had been perpetrating since the night before and that they were going to continue to

perpetrate, then, let figures speak for me: On July 27th, in his speech from the military headquarters, Batista said that the assailants suffered 32 dead. By the end of the week the number of dead had risen to more than 80 men. In what battles, where, in what clashes, did these young men die? Before Batista spoke, more than 25 prisoners had been murdered. After Batista spoke fifty more were massacred.

What a great sense of honor those modest Army technicians and professionals had, who did not distort the facts before the Court, but gave their reports adhering to the strictest truth! These surely are soldiers who honor their uniform; these, surely, are men! Neither a real soldier nor a true man can degrade his code of honor with lies and crime. I know that many of the soldiers are indignant at the barbaric assassinations perpetrated. I know that they feel repugnance and shame at the smell of homicidal blood that impregnates every stone of Moncada Barracks....

I know that imprisonment will be harder for me than it has ever been for anyone, filled with cowardly threats and hideous cruelty. But I do not fear prison, as I do not fear the fury of the miserable tyrant who took the lives of 70 of my comrades. Condemn me. It does not matter. History will absolve me.

Ben Bella (AP/Wide World Photos)

PROCLAMATION OF THE ALGERIAN NATIONAL LIBERATION FRONT

"The struggle will be long, but the outcome is certain."

Overview

On November 1, 1954, the National Liberation Front (Front de libération nationale, or FLN) issued a proclamation declaring Algeria's separation from France, the result of decades of resistance to French rule. The proclamation sparked a brutal eight-year war of independence.

The proclamation marked the coalescence of Algeria's move to sever itself from French rule, a process that had begun decades earlier. That process crescendoed in 1951, when several smaller groups joined to create the Algerian Front (Front algerien). However, the coalition fell apart in 1954, and a small militant group calling for armed rebellion formed the Revolutionary Committee for Unity and Action (Comité révolutionnaire d'unité et d'action) with headquarters in Cairo, Egypt. Between March and October 1954 the group divided Algeria into six military districts and selected commanders to launch direct action against France. On November 1, the Revolutionary Committee for Unity and Action changed its name to the National Liberation Front, and its military wing was the National Liberation Army. The FLN claimed authority and responsibility for leading the Algerian people to freedom and creating a viable state. This goal attracted all of the factions to one purpose. On the day of its name change, November 1, 1954, the FLN agitated for direct action against the French, airing its final challenge by calling upon all Muslims in Algeria to join the struggle for independence. The goal was to restore the pre-existing Algerian state based on Islamic principles and law. These aspirations were expressed in the Proclamation of the Algerian National Liberation Front.

Context

Prior to the French invasion and conquest of 1830, the people of the Maghreb (a word that means "place of sunset" and refers to the region of North Africa that comprises Morocco, Tunisia, and Algeria) had lived together for centuries as residents of various empires that controlled the Mediterranean Basin. The last great invasion brought Islam to North Africa, and Arab and Berber speakers learned to live together under Islam. They continued their lives as an autonomous province of the Muslim Ottoman Empire for three hundred years until the arrival of the French. The French government viewed the conquest of this territory across the Mediterranean as a way to strengthen its internal government and to expand its control over the western Mediterranean Basin by establishing colonies in Morocco, Algeria, and Tunisia.

Unlike other Francophone colonies in Africa, Algeria became a settler colony to which French and other European settlers, or *colons* (colonials), emigrated to begin new lives—and to exploit Algeria's agricultural resources for France's benefit. Algeria had been a breadbasket for earlier empires centered in the Mediterranean Basin, and France became interested in its agricultural resources and minerals, especially after the discovery of oil. The *colons* consisted of farmers from rural southern France and from other areas such as Corsica and the eastern Pyrenees and Alps. Later, many settlers arrived from Alsace and Lorraine, two provinces that were ripped from France by the victorious Prussians in the war of 1870. The *colons* were joined by various other European groups escaping unrest at home, including people from Spain, Italy, and Malta. At first the French government ruled the colony through its military. Having secured the land from the indigenous people in 1830, many soldiers immigrated to the new colony. They were followed by French workers, peasants who had escaped the Industrial Revolution, exiled political dissidents, and political prisoners.

The French and other Europeans who moved to Algeria brought with them new European ideas and laws, resulting, essentially, in the dismantling of the Algerian ways of life. Prior to the arrival of the French, for example, Algerians were not acquainted with the concept of private property (land). The idea of land usage for the indigenous Algerians, as for many people throughout Africa, was that of stewardship of the land through a hierarchy of rights of use. Land was not owned but instead was cared for and managed. Under the Ottoman government, there were two categories of rights to land: the rights of the governor, called the *dey*, and the rights of the indigenous people in their local clan-based groups. When the French imposed rights of private property, the French state took the land that had belonged

1926

- Ahmed Messali Hadj forms the Star of North Africa movement in Paris, the first organization to call for Algerian independence.

1937

- Hadj founds the Algerian People's Party.

1944

- Algeria experiences a poor wheat harvest, which continues into the following year.

1945

- **May 1**
  The Friends of the Manifesto and Liberty organize demonstrations in twenty-one towns across the country demanding independence for Algeria.

- **May 8**
  Algerians protest for self-determination.

1947

- The French National Assembly approves democratic representation at the local level.

1954

- **March**
  Nine exiled Algerian revolutionaries create the Revolutionary Council for Unity and Action, headquartered in Cairo.

to the previous governor and divided it among the *colons*. From 1847 to 1863 more land was made available "to own" to attract would-be settlers from France and other European nations.

The consequences of these actions were the destruction of a system of land usage by making land a commodity and the opening up of all Muslim lands for sale. Thus, the *colons* tried to buy the land; if that did not work, many seized it. The government also seized the lands of Islamic religious institutions such as mosques and schools to be divided and offered for sale in the marketplace. Europeans were able to increase their landholdings to millions of acres from various sources. In addition to the laws governing private-property ownership, the government devised a program by which it destroyed the power of the indigenous leaders and thus broke down the clan-based society. These measures removed the safety net used during times of crisis. For example, during lean years, when harvests had been poor, the people would receive free grain that had been collected by their leaders as taxes. The religious institutions, too, had been rendered impotent and were unable to come to society's aid with food in times of crisis.

Muslims suffered under French rule because, by supposed right of conquest, European settlers usurped all the best land for their farms. As Christians, the Europeans saw Muslims as the enemy, and Muslim resistance incurred more loss of their fertile land. During the forty years prior to the Franco-Prussian War, the French government dismantled Muslim economic and political practices and indoctrinated Algerian Muslims into what the French considered to be the modern world, with European-style culture, infrastructure, economics, education, and government institutions. Consequently, the Muslim Algerian world became unrecognizable as Algerians lost rights and their ability to provide for themselves in times of crisis. Eventually, Algeria became a sharply divided colony of rural versus urban, Muslim versus Christian, citizens versus subjects, and pro-French versus anti-French. What the French government began as a shift of cultural allegiance the *colons* used to rend the fabric of Muslim society.

One plan of the French government was to assimilate the indigenous people of the region by making them equal to the *colons* and giving them the hope of French citizenship But the *colons* resisted the government's attempt at assimilation of the indigenous people. They lobbied the government, only to win their point, if only by default, when the French lost to Prussia in 1870. Since the French government was now preoccupied with the terms of its loss to Prussia, *colons* were in charge of the colony, and they intended to make as much profit as they could by subjugating the indigenous population to France's economic needs. The Europeans had no respect for the Muslim indigenous people because they did not understand their lifestyle and because, as Christians, they believed that Muslims were infidels. While the *colons* enjoyed full rights as citizens, the indigenous people were "subjects" for whom the *colons* invented various forms of servitude. Muslims could be detained without due process, were charged a land-use tax, and were selected to perform forced labor (the *corvé*). In 1881 the French government enacted the Native Code (Code de l'indigénat) legalizing these oppressive measures. But the French government became concerned about the political loyalties of the large number of non-French residents. In 1889 it passed a law allowing the mass naturalization of all those who had not been born in France and thus conferred on them French citizenship. By 1900 Algeria changed from a French province to three departments (administrative subdivisions, somewhat analogous to U.S. states), with *colons* electing representatives to the French National Assembly. Algeria was France; France was Algeria.

Because French policies and programs divested the individual Muslim Algerian of land and social commitment, it was not difficult for Algerians to leave. As Muslim Algerians were forced from their lands, they became destitute and looked for jobs in France. When a 1908 law drafted Muslims into the army, many left Algeria for the lands of the Muslim Ottoman Empire, such as Turkey, Tripolitania, and Syria. After World War I, Muslim men left Algeria for France to fill the labor demands of various metropolitan centers. The French government became the state placement agency acting as recruiter and importer of Algerian labor in post–World War I France. This was a problem for the *colons* because they saw their pool of free labor exit the country.

Algerian nationalism began as early as 1926 in France when educated Muslims and Muslim workers organized to begin their quest for autonomy from French rule. In the wake of World War I, some moderate organizations fought for equal rights within the French Empire, while others had members who adapted and assimilated and who hoped to become more than second-class citizens. Algerians studying and working in France followed Ahmed Messali Hadj, who in 1926 organized the first group to protest for Algerian autonomy, the Star of North Africa (Étoile Nord-Africain). The Star of North Africa advocated for freedom of the press, freedom of association, and a parliament elected by universal suffrage. In 1937 Hadj founded the Algerian People's Party (Parti de peuple algérien) to organize Algerians in France and Algeria to orchestrate better political positions for Algerian independence. This party was banned by the government in 1939, although it went underground with the support of students and workers.

During World War II, under Vichy rule—referring to the rule of the French district unoccupied by the Nazis during World War II, the seat of the French collaborationist government—Algerian Muslims in France, supported by students and workers, continued to agitate for independence. In 1944 a moderate named Ferhat Abbas, who had appealed for equal rights for Algerian Muslims, joined Ahmed Messali Hadj to form the Friends of the Manifesto and of Liberty (Amis du manifeste et de la liberté, or AML), an organization that called for Algeria to be a republic federated with France. Social unrest in Algeria grew because a failed wheat harvest (1944–1945) and shortages of other staples caused by the war created desperation among the indigenous people. On May 1, 1945, the AML organized demonstrations in twenty-one towns across the country

1954

■ **November 1**
The Proclamation of the Algerian National Liberation Front is delivered on Cairo radio.

1958

■ **September**
A provisional Algerian government is established with Ferhat Abbas as president and headquarters in Cairo and Tunis.

1962

■ **March 18**
The Évian Accords between French president Charles de Gaulle and the National Liberation Front are signed.

■ **July 1**
A referendum is held on Algerian independence.

■ **July 3**
Algerian independence is proclaimed by French president Charles de Gaulle; Algerians select July 5 as their independence day.

demanding independence for Algeria. Then on May 8, 1945—V-E Day (also known as Victory in Europe Day, the day when the Allies formally accepted the surrender of Nazi Germany)—nationalist leaders led a nonviolent demonstration that the *colons* turned into violent reprisals, and violence became the direct action to wrest independence from France. In 1946 the Friends of the Manifesto and of Liberty became the Democratic Union of the Algerian Manifesto (Union démocratique du manifeste algérien), which advocated for a fully autonomous Algeria. This group became a political party, the Movement for the Triumph of Democratic Liberties (mouvement pour le triomphe des libertés démocratique, or MTLD), which had a platform of Algerian autonomy; it won five of fifteen seats in the 1946 parliamentary elections for the French National Assembly.

In 1947 the French National Assembly appeared to side with the Muslim constituency over the *colons* in Algeria by approving more democratic representation at the local level, Arabic as an official language with French, and an Algerian assembly whose elections would be in 1948. The *colons* were unnerved by the increasing possibility of future power sharing with the Muslims and by the MTLD success at the polls in the 1947 Algerian municipal election. Thus the *colons* conspired to make sure they would be successful in the 1948 Algerian assembly elections by initiating a more intense program of Muslim political repression. These experiences in 1947 spawned the creation of an underground guerrilla movement, the Special Organization (Organisation spéciale, or OS) by Hocine Aït Ahmed, who conducted terrorist acts against government facilities. In the 1948 elections for the French National Assembly, the MTLD lost all of the five seats it had previously won to election-rigging tactics by the *colons*; after 1948 all elections were deemed to have been "rigged." By 1950 the MTLD suffered from police repression.

Years of a separate-but-not-equal Algeria, international promises of self-determination after both World War I and World War II, and failed attempts at using nonviolent tactics to work within the system spawned a desire for more direct action. On November 1, 1954, the Algerian government in exile and the FLN issued a proclamation declaring Algeria's separation from France. Later, in September 1958, exiled indigenous Algerian leaders met in Cairo and created the Provisional Government of Algeria, claiming to speak for the Algerian people as their government in exile.

About the Author

The proclamation reflected the spirit of nine Algerians considered the leaders of the Algerian War of Independence: Hocine Aït Ahmed, Ahmed Ben Bella, Mohamed Khider, Rabah Bitat, Moustafa Ben Boulaid, Mourad Didouche, Larbi Ben M'hidi, Belkacem Krim, and Mohamed Boudiaf. The first three, who were in self-imposed exile in Cairo (the "externals"), gave the document its final form. The rest were in Algeria (the "internals") acting as commanders of the army and liaisons to all factions involved in the rebellion. This group of men had several things in common, such as being in the same socioeconomic class and generation and having some form of military experience.

Of the externals, Aït Ahmed, a founding member of the OS, had collected arms and munitions, set up OS cells throughout Algeria, and forged strategies to take back the land. Ben Bella, a founding member of the OS, had successfully robbed a post office for funds to finance the war but was eventually caught and imprisoned, escaped, and exiled himself. Khider, who had been a past member of Messali Hadj's Star of North Africa, was from the working class and had served as a deputy to the French Assembly. He, too, exiled himself because he had been implicated in the same robbery as Ben Bella.

The internals were the commanders of the six regions: Moustafa Ben Boulaid commanded Aures, Rabah Bitat commanded Constantine, Mourad Didouche commanded coastal Algiers, Larbi Ben M'hidi commanded Oran, and Belkacem Krim was responsible for Kabylia. Mohamed Boudiaf was the liaison officer who kept the lines of communication open with the externals by conducting meetings in Switzerland and calling the meeting of the commanders to set in motion the simultaneous revolt across Algeria at midnight on November 1, 1954.

The one person who stands out from among these important leaders is Ahmed Ben Bella, who came from Maghnia, Algeria. He was French educated, a decorated soldier from World War II, and a member of Hadj's 1940s underground movement. In response to the rigged election of 1946, he was a founding member of the OS, created to set the rebellion in motion. He was imprisoned after he was caught in a bank robbery in 1950 but escaped and exiled himself to Cairo. In 1954 he and eight other leaders joined to create the FLN and deliver the proclamation of independence. Acting as a peace negotiator in Algiers in 1956, he was arrested and imprisoned from 1956 to 1962. He was released after the Évian Accords were signed with France in 1962 and moved from the jailhouse to the statehouse as the president of Algeria charged with the task of rebuilding the new Algerian state.

Explanation and Analysis of the Document

The Proclamation of the Algerian National Liberation Front is a call to all Muslim Algerians for "direct action"—armed rebellion—and open resistance to the French colonizers. The FLN took upon itself the responsibility of leading the liberation movement and creating a provisional government that would provide direction after gaining independence. The document is addressed to the militants of the national cause. It challenges those who judge the actions of the FLN to understand that the purpose of distributing the proclamation is to help those less militant to understand the profound reasons that have forced the militants to call for direct action. The goal, of course, was independence. The document's drafters wanted to clarify their position to avoid the confusion promulgated by corrupt imperialist politicians and administrators.

The document opens by emphasizing that the independence movement struggled for decades against the French colonizers and has now reached its final stage. A goal of the movement, it states, has been to create conditions favorable to a liberation movement. Its first point is that the Algerian people are united behind the goal of independence and direct action. Its second point is that the Arab and Muslim communities across the region support the final step toward independence. The document makes reference to events in Morocco and Tunisia, which were embroiled in their own independence movements. During the early 1950s, Moroccans turned on the French after the French government exiled the country's sultan and replaced him with a puppet; the result was outbreaks of violence. At the same time, Tunisians clashed violently with

A jeep of the Algerian Liberation Front is surrounded by an enthusiastic crowd in Algiers in July 1962, when Algeria gained its independence from France. (AP/Wide World Photos)

the French government largely because of the imprisonment of Habib Bourguiba, the leader of the Tunisian independence movement (and, later, the country's first president), who was imprisoned by the French. The proclamation suggests that it is unfortunate that there had never been unity of action among the three countries. The three North African Muslim countries were all French colonies; however, Algeria was engaged in a furious independence war with France, while Morocco and Tunisia would negotiate their independence in 1956.

On the day the proclamation was read, the FLN resolutely stood on the direct path to independence, leaving behind all the years of internal conflict that had stalled the movement and had diminished its effectiveness. The proclamation notes that the movement had slowly begun to disintegrate while the *colons*, thinking that they had silenced the Algerian militants, increased their hold on the colony. But the hour had come, because a group of young leaders and activists had reinvigorated the national liberation movement by returning to the important cause and overcoming internal conflict. They put the movement back on the path to direct action. The FLN identifies itself as independent of any other factions vying for power and announces that it places national interest above all else. Its actions, it is said,

are directed against colonialism in general and France in particular, which had always refused to grant Algeria freedom by peaceful means. The FLN opens up the possibility that all Algerian patriots of all social classes and all the purely Algerian parties and movements can integrate themselves into the current struggle for liberation.

The FLN then "spells out … the major elements of [its] political program": The goal of the program was national independence. As the provisional government, the FLN proposes restoring the Algerian state to its former sovereignty within the principles of Islam. Because of its experience with discrimination at the hands of the French, it vows to preserve fundamental freedoms and disavows discrimination based on race or religion. The internal objective for the rebellion is to remove all political and governmental corruption that kept Algeria underdeveloped and to gather and organize the Algerian people to remove the last vestiges of the colonial system, thus returning to indigenous Muslim customs, traditions, and values. The external objectives included bringing Algerian complaints to the world, exposing the damage caused by colonialism, proposing North African unity within an Arab-Islamic framework, and seeking from the United Nations recognition of Algerian nationhood, separate from France.

"*Our National Movement, prostrated by years of immobility and routine, badly directed was disintegrating little by little. Faced with this situation, a youthful group … judged that the moment had come to take the National Movement out of the impasse into which it had been forced by the conflicts of persons and of influence and to launch it into the true revolutionary struggle.*"

"*The struggle will be long, but the outcome is certain. To limit the bloodshed, we propose an honourable platform for discussion with the French authorities: The opening of negotiations with the authorized spokesmen of the Algerian people on the basis of recognition of Algerian sovereignty, one and indivisible.*"

"*Algerians: The F.L.N. is your front; its victory is your victory. For our part, strong in your support, we shall give the best of ourselves to the Fatherland.*"

The FLN specifies that the "Means of Struggle" would be to conform to revolutionary principles by any methods possible until the goal of independence was achieved. The FLN notes that the task ahead would necessitate the mobilization of all resources and manpower; it would be a long struggle, but the results were certain.

To prove a real desire for peace and limit the number of lives lost, the FLN proposes to French authorities a way to open negotiations. Negotiations would be with an authorized spokesperson of the Algerian people, based on recognition of sovereignty through Algerian liberation. A climate of confidence would be created through the liberation of all political prisoners, the lifting of all measures of exception to Algerian emigration to France, the end of all pursuit of fighting forces, and the recognition of Algerian nationality by an official declaration abrogating the edicts, decrees, and laws making Algeria "French soil."

In return, the FLN pledges that "French cultural and economic interests, honestly acquired, will be respected, as will persons and families." French people who want to remain in Algeria would choose between their nationality of origin, in which case they would be considered foreign-

ers, or Algerian nationality, in which case they would be granted the rights of Algerians. The bonds between France and Algeria would be defined and would be the object of an agreement between the two powers on the basis of equality and mutual respect.

In the penultimate paragraph, the FLN invites all Algerians to join with the militants to save their country and restore it to freedom. The proclamation states that the National Liberation Front is their front, and victory is theirs. The FLN is resolved to pursue the struggle and give themselves to their homeland.

Audience

Delivered as a radio address, the proclamation was intended to reach both Algerian and international audiences. It notified the Algerian audience that the direct action of the conflict had begun and encouraged others to join the fight. At the same time, it put the French government on notice that Algeria was serious about securing its independence. It also proclaimed to the world that Algeria was seeking its independence. That world audience included the neighboring countries of Morocco and Tunisia, the Muslim world, other international countries who might aid the Algerians, and other African colonies that were interested in their own independence.

Impact

While the words of the proclamation rang out a challenge, the Algerian National Liberation Army initiated simultaneous attacks against government military installations, police stations, and infrastructure across Algeria. The immediate response of the French government was to declare war. While the French had lost in Indochina (its colonial empire in Southeast Asia, comprising mainly Cambodia, Laos, and Vietnam), the situation in Algeria was different; there could be no secession of the Algerian departments because they were one with the French Republic.

Atrocities were committed by both sides. The FLN used terrorist tactics to challenge France's greater military force. It drew on the heroic and historic past when Abd al-Kader (also spelled Abd al-Qadir) fought a thirteen-year guerrilla war against the initial French invasion. The French proceeded with a scorched-earth policy by erecting electrified fences along Algeria's borders to stop FLN attacks from outside and by interring Algerians in concentration camps so they could not help the FLN inside the country. The French tortured and massacred entire villages. Yet the *colons* thought the French were not doing enough to destroy the Muslims and created their own terrorist group,

the Secret Army (Organisation de l'armèe secréte), which worked in France and Algeria. World opinion turned against France because of these events and France's inability to put an end to the war.

In 1959 Charles de Gaulle was inaugurated as president of France's Fifth Republic. He attempted to resolve the Algerian crisis but came to understand that this was a war that could not be won. His attitude was seen as a betrayal of the *colons*. In 1962 a cease-fire was called, and the FLN and the French government agreed to the Évian Accords, which would allow Muslim Algerians parity with the European *colons* over a three-year period. After the accords were approved by 91 percent of the French electorate, there was a mass exodus of European *colons*, the Jewish community, and some pro-French Muslims. On July 1, 1962, the Algerian people voted nearly unanimously for independence. On July 3, De Gaulle proclaimed Algerian independence. However, the Algerians decided that their independence day would be symbolic, so they chose July 5, 1962, the 132nd anniversary of the French invasion.

Further Reading

■ Books

Alexander, Martin S., Martin Evans, and J. F. V. Keiger, eds. *The Algerian War and the French Army, 1954–62: Experiences, Images, Testimonies*. New York: Palgrave MacMillan, 2002.

Andrews, William G. *French Politics and Algeria: The Process of Policy Formation 1954–1962*. New York: Appleton-Century Crofts, 1962.

Questions for Further Study

1. What cultural differences led to intense friction between the French and the Algerians, particularly in the nineteenth century?

2. Why would some Algerians want their country to remain part of the French Empire, while others wanted complete independence?

3. Compare the proclamation with the events surrounding the Proclamation of the Provisional Government of the Irish Republic. Comment on the similarities—or differences—in Algeria's quest for independence from France and Ireland's troubled relationship with England.

4. What are the common themes in the Proclamation of the Algerian National Liberation Front and the Arusha Declaration of 1967? How do the two documents, read side by side, help modern readers form a picture of colonialism in twentieth-century Africa?

5. In the twenty-first century, France is regarded as a peaceful nation, one very reluctant to go to war or to commit its troops in foreign nations. Yet in the mid-1900s, it fought hard to hold on to its colony in Algeria. Why did France stoutly resist Algerian independence?

Horne, Alistair. *A Savage War of Peace: Algeria 1954–1962.* New York: New York Review of Books, 2006.

Hrbek, Ivan. "North Africa and the Horn." In *UNESCO General History of Africa.* Vol. 8: *Africa since 1935,* ed. Ali A. Mazuri. Berkeley: University of California Press, 1993.

Kraft, Joseph. *The Struggle for Algeria.* Garden City, N.Y.: Doubleday, 1961.

Martinez, Luis, and John Entelis. *The Algerian Civil War.* New York: Columbia University Press, 2000.

Matthews, Tanya. *War in Algeria: Background for Crisis.* New York: Fordham University Press, 1961. Available online. Internet Archive Web site. http://www.archive.org/stream/warinalgeriaback 011376mbp/warinalgeriaback011376mbp_djvu.txt.

Moore, Clement Henry. *Politics in North Africa: Algeria, Morocco, and Tunisia.* Boston: Little, Brown, 1970.

Stora, Benjamin. *Algeria 1830–2000: A Short History,* trans. Jane Marie Todd. Ithaca, N.Y.: Cornell University Press, 2004.

■ Web Sites

"Algerian National Liberation (1954–1962)." GlobalSecurity.org Web site.
   http://www.globalsecurity.org/military/world/war/algeria.htm.

Cooper, Tom. "Algerian War 1954–1962." Air Combat Information Group Web site.
   http://www.acig.org/artman/publish/article_354.shtml.

"WWW-VL History: Algeria." World Wide Web Virtual Library Web site.
   http://vlib.iue.it/history/africa/algeria.html#History.

—Dianne White Oyler

PROCLAMATION OF THE ALGERIAN NATIONAL LIBERATION FRONT

Milestone Documents

To the Algerian people

To the Militants of the National Cause

To you who are called upon to judge us, the Algerian people in a general way, the militants more particularly, our purpose in distributing this proclamation is to enlighten you concerning the profound reasons which have impelled us to act by revealing to you our program, the meaning of our action, and the cogency of our views the, goal of which remains National Independence within the North African framework. Our wish as well is to help you avoid the confusion maintained by imperialism and its corrupt political and administrative agents.

Before all else, we consider that after decades of struggle the National Movement has reached its final stage of realization. In fact, as the goal of the revolutionary movement is to create all the favorable conditions needed for the launching of operations for liberation, we believe that internally the people are united behind the sign of independence and action; and externally the climate of détente is favorable for the settling of minor problems (among them ours) with the support of our Arab and Muslim brothers above all. The events in Morocco and Tunisia are significant in this regard, and profoundly mark the process of the liberation struggle in North Africa. It is worth noting that for quite some time we have been, in this regard, precursors in the unity of action, unfortunately never realized among the three countries.

Today, many are resolutely engaged on this path and we, relegated to the rear, suffer the fate of those who events have passed by. It is thus that our national movement, overwhelmed by years of immobilisme and routine, poorly oriented, deprived of the indispensable support of public opinion, and overtaken by events, has progressively disintegrated, to the great satisfaction of colonialism, which thinks it has carried off its greatest victory in its struggle against the Algerian vanguard. The hour is serious.

Facing this situation, which risks becoming irreparable, a group of young leaders and conscious activists, rallying around it the majority of the healthy and decisive elements, has judged that the moment has arrived to move the National Movement out of the impasse into which it was backed by personal struggles and fights over influence, in order to launch it, at the side of the Moroccan and Tunisian brothers, into the true revolutionary struggle.

To this end, we insist on specifying that we are independent of the two clans that are fighting over power. Placing national interest above all petty and erroneous considerations of personality and prestige, in conformity with revolutionary principles, our action is directly solely against colonialism, our only blind and obstinate enemy, which has always refused to grant the least freedom by peaceful means.

These are, we think, sufficient, reasons for a movement of renewal to present itself under the name of National Liberation Front, releasing itself in this way from all possible compromises, and offering the possibility to all Algerian patriots of all social classes, of all the purely Algerian parties and movements, to integrate themselves into the struggle for liberation, without any other consideration.

In summary, we spell out below the major elements of our political program:

Goal: National Independence by:

The restoration of the sovereign, democratic and social Algerian state, within the framework of Islamic principles.

The respect of all fundamental liberties without distinction of race or religion.

Internal Objectives:

Political reform by the returning of the National Revolutionary Movement to its true path and by the wiping-out of the vestiges of corruption and reformism, the causes of our current regression.

The gathering together and organization of all the healthy energies of the Algerian people for the liquidation of the colonial system.

External Objectives:

The internalization of the Algerian problem.

The realization of North African unity within its natural Arabo-Islamic framework.

Within the framework of the UN Charter, the affirmation of our active sympathy with regard to all nations who support our operations for liberation.

Means of Struggle: In conformity with revolutionary principles, and taking into account the internal and external situations, the continuation of the struggle by all possible means until the realization of our goal.

In order to reach these objectives, the National Liberation front will have two essential tasks to carry out simultaneously: an internal action, on the fronts of politics and action, and an external action, with the goal of the making of the Algerian problem a reality for the entire world, with the support of all our natural allies.

This is a heavy task which necessitates the mobilization of all national energy and resources. It is true that the struggle will be long, but the result is certain.

In the last place, in order to avoid all false interpretations and subterfuges, in order to prove our real desire for peace, to limit the number of human lives lost and the amount of blood spilled, we propose to French authorities an honorable platform of discussion, if these latter are animated by good faith and recognize once and for all in the people they subjugate the right to dispose of themselves:

The opening of negotiations with the authorized spokesmen of the Algerian people on the basis of the recognition of sovereignty through Algerian liberation, one and indivisible.

The creation of a climate of confidence through the liberation of all political prisoners, the lifting of all measures of exception, and the ceasing of all pursuit of the fighting forces.

The recognition of Algerian nationality by an official declaration abrogating the edicts, decrees and laws making Algeria a "French land," which is a denial of the History, the geography, the language, the religion, and the mores of the Algerian people.

In return:

French cultural and economic interests, honestly acquired, will be respected, as will persons and families.

All Frenchmen wishing to remain in Algeria will have the choice between their nationality of origin, in which case they will be considered foreigners vis à vis the laws in place, or they will opt for Algerian nationality, in which case they will be considered such in rights and obligations.

The bonds between France and Algeria will be defined and will be the object of an agreement between the two powers on the basis of equality and mutual respect.

Algerians! We invite you to think over our above Charter. Your obligation is to join with it in order to save our country and restore to it its freedom. The National Liberation Front is your front. Its victory is yours.

As for us, resolved to pursue the struggle, sure of your anti-imperialist sentiments, we give the best of ourselves to the Fatherland.

The Secretariat

Glossary

Algerian problem	how the French saw the increasingly insistent demands for independence on the part of non-European Algerians
events in Morocco and Tunisia	anticolonialist actions on the part of radical groups in the Maghreb
immobilisme	inability to make decisions because of instability in government
National Revolutionary Movement	not the name of an organization; simply the various groups that had worked for independence from France

FREEDOM CHARTER OF SOUTH AFRICA

"South Africa belongs to all who live in it, black and white."

Overview

The Freedom Charter is the key document in the struggle against apartheid in the Republic of South Africa. Drafted by a small committee, on the basis of a vast number of submissions, and adopted at the Congress of the People, held at Kliptown outside Johannesburg on June 25–26, 1955, it acquired enormous symbolic importance as a visionary statement setting out what a future democratic South Africa—not centered on distinctions of race—should look like. It became especially significant in the 1980s, when those whose philosophy was based on the charter, known as "charterists," dominated the antiapartheid resistance in the country. The Freedom Charter embodied the ideals for which the liberation struggle was being fought. After apartheid had come to an end, the new constitution of 1996 was to some extent based on ideas in the Freedom Charter, but many in the struggle thought that the new South Africa did not live up to the aspirations of the charter.

Context

The road to the passage of the Freedom Charter in 1955 may be said to have begun with the establishment of the South African Native National Congress in 1912, after decades of oppression of blacks by white South Africans. In 1910 whites had formed the Union of South Africa—an entity made up of Cape Colony, Natal, Transvaal, and the Orange Free State under primarily British dominion. Blacks had no voice in the making of laws and no part in administration. In 1923 the congress changed its name to the African National Congress (ANC) and, in the 1940s, emerged as the leading organization opposing the policies of the racist state. After the formal introduction of apartheid—legal segregation of the races—in 1948, the ANC moved toward more direct forms of nonviolent protest.

In 1952, together with the South African Indian Congress, the ANC embarked on the Campaign of Defiance against Unjust Laws. In this passive resistance protest, begun on June 26, more than eight thousand people,

including some whites, defied key racial laws, and many were imprisoned. Among the imprisoned was Nelson Mandela, later to be president of South Africa. The campaign petered out as the government issued a proclamation banning all meetings of more than ten Africans anywhere in the country. Soon thereafter the government enacted two laws, the Public Safety Act and the Criminal Law Amendment Act—the first to suppress future campaigns by allowing the government to declare a state of emergency when public peace was threatened and the second to impose severe penalties, including imprisonment, fines, and whipping, for publicly protesting a law. During the campaign, membership of the ANC grew to more than one hundred thousand. For the leaders of the organization, the question was how to maintain the momentum of protest action.

At the annual conference of the Cape region of the ANC in August 1953, one of the organization's leading members, Z. K. Matthews, suggested convening a congress of people from all over the country to draw up a charter for a future South African democracy. The proposal was approved by the national conference of the ANC in December 1953. At the invitation of the ANC, a number of other antiapartheid organizations—the South African Indian Congress, the Coloured People's Organisation, and the white Congress of Democrats—agreed to enter an alliance with the ANC, to be called the Congress Alliance, which then co-sponsored the Congress of the People. The Congress Alliance set up a joint action committee to plan the event, a call went out for fifty thousand "freedom volunteers" to attend, and committees were established to collect funds that would enable as many as possible to travel to Kliptown for the meeting, set to take place on June 25–26, 1955.

In a memorandum setting out his ideas for the Congress of the People, Matthews expressed the hope that the Freedom Charter to be drawn up would inspire people with fresh hope and turn their minds from negative struggles to a positive program for the future. For the first time in South African history, ordinary people were asked to take part in forming their future. A multiracial initiative, the Freedom Charter was to embody the demands and aspirations of South Africa's people as a whole, and it was hoped that those who attended the congress would in some sense represent people all across the country.

1912

■ **January**
The South African
Native National
Congress is
founded.

1923

■ The South
African Native
National Con-
gress changes
its name to the
African National
Congress.

1948

■ **May**
The white National
Party comes to
power and begins
to introduce
apartheid.

1949

■ **December 17**
The ANC con-
ference adopts
a program call-
ing for direct
action against
apartheid.

1952

■ **June 26**
The Campaign
of Defiance
against Unjust
Laws begins.

1953

■ Z. K. Matthews
proposes a Con-
gress of the
People.

1954–1955

■ Preparations are
made for the
Congress of the
People.

1955

■ **June 25–26**
The Congress of
the People con-
venes and adopts
the Freedom
Charter.

In the months before the congress convened, people were asked to put forward their wishes on pieces of paper that were then sent to the small committee that drafted the Freedom Charter. Members of this committee had in mind the People's Charter of 1838, which had called for franchise and parliamentary reform in Britain, and the Universal Declaration of Human Rights adopted by the United Nations in 1948, but this was to be a charter specific to South Africa and a statement that presented an alternative to the apartheid order of the day. Those who drafted the Freedom Charter were inspired by the fact that representatives from the ANC and the South African Indian Congress had attended the pioneering Asian-African conference held in Bandung, Indonesia, two months before the Congress of the People was to be held. The Bandung meeting was the first to bring together those who had obtained independence from colonial rule and those still fighting for such independence. At Bandung, the representatives received encouragement from others in the third world who shared similar anticolonial views.

All who opposed apartheid were invited to attend the Congress of the People. The Liberal Party (a party without racial distinctions), anticipating that Communists, in close alliance with the ANC, would be actively involved, decided not to participate. This was a decision that many liberals later regretted, for they might have been able to influence the formers of the Freedom Charter to steer away from its more Socialist aspects.

Although the police prevented some who set out for Kliptown from attending by stopping buses heading there and claiming that the passengers did not have the necessary permits, some 2,844 delegates gathered in a dusty field close to a squatter settlement in what is now Soweto on June 25 and began to consider the Freedom Charter clause by clause, under the watching eyes of the police. Soon after the start of the afternoon session on June 26, it was announced that armed police were to search the delegates. As this process began, the rest of the charter was adopted by acclamation, and the delegates sang the ANC anthem "Nkosi Sikelele Afrika." The police then took down the names and addresses of all the delegates.

About the Author

The Freedom Charter was to embody the ideas sent from all over the country, but the actual drafting was the work of a small committee. Precisely how that committee worked is still unclear. What is known is that the committee included leading white members of the underground Communist Party. Decades later Rusty Bernstein and Ben Turok, who in the 1950s worked closely with the ANC and were presumably appointed to the committee because they were known to be skilled writers, wrote memoirs in which they recounted how they had helped draft key clauses of the charter, but others who were involved have not been identified. Turok and Bernstein both went into exile in the 1960s. Turok, who drafted the controversial economic clause of the charter, returned to the country in the 1990s and became an ANC member of parliament. Those who opposed what the Freedom Charter said stressed the fact that it was largely the work of white Communists and used that as an argument against accepting it, but the fact that white Communists were important in its drafting did not make it a Communist document.

Explanation and Analysis of the Document

Much of the Freedom Charter sets out a vision of South Africa opposite to the apartheid order of the day, which divided people by race and treated them differently, in practice subordinating blacks to whites. The Freedom Charter begins by saying that "South Africa belongs to all who live in it, black and white" and that government must rest on the will of the people. This set the charter against the government of the day, which was based on the will of the white electorate only and which believed in separating black from white wherever possible. The charter goes on to refer to "our people" having been robbed of their birthright to land, liberty, and peace. Colonial rule had dispossessed the indigenous majority of much of the land of the country, and apartheid meant the country was in effect a police state for blacks in which they had virtually no rights. It therefore meant conflict and instability. The Freedom Charter states that the country will never be prosperous or free until all enjoy equal rights. That statement proved to be accurate. Although there was prosperity for some under apartheid, it was only when equal rights were enshrined in the new constitution that there was both wider prosperity and freedom.

The Freedom Charter calls for every man and woman to have the right to vote and to stand as a candidate for all bodies that make laws. This directly challenged the existing order, in which only white men and women had the vote and could enter parliament. The charter goes on to demand that rights should be the same for all, regardless of race, color, or sex. This had been a demand of the ANC since its formation; instead, discrimination had progressively increased. The charter calls for a democratic state, in which all should have equal status and equal freedoms protected by law. It explicitly states that all apartheid laws should be set aside. But it should be noted that it also calls for all "national groups" to have equal rights, which suggests that the drafters did not see South Africa as one nation but rather as a nation made up of distinct cultural and linguistic groups. This reflects the fact that the Congress Alliance was multiracial (that is, it was made up of racially defined groups working together), accepting the racial categories of the apartheid state. Although the Freedom Charter did not speak of racial groups, some critics claimed that it did not sufficiently get away from the idea of such groups.

One of the most controversial sections of the Freedom Charter deals with economic issues. This section begins by saying that "The People Shall Share in the Country's Wealth" and states that the wealth of the country is to be restored to the people, implying that the process of colonial

Time Line

1956
- The ANC adopts the Freedom Charter.
- **December**
  Some 156 of those who attended the Congress of the People are arrested and charged with treason.
- **December 19**
  A trial on treason charges begins, ending in March of 1961 with the acquittal of those still on trial.

1958
- The Africanists break away from the ANC.

1959
- **April**
  The Africanists form the Pan Africanist Congress.

1983
- **August**
  The United Democratic Front is formed. It later adopts the Freedom Charter.

1996
- The final constitution for a democratic South Africa is approved by the Constitutional Assembly and the Constitutional Court.

dispossession of the indigenous people would be reversed, though how this would take place is not outlined. One clause, which was much debated later, reads: "The mineral wealth beneath the soil, the Banks and monopoly industry shall be transferred to the ownership of the people as a whole." Some saw this as implying a Socialist state. But another clause in the same section reads: "All people shall

A public beach for whites only in 1960s South Africa (Corbis)

have equal rights to trade where they choose, to manufacture and to enter all trades, crafts and professions," suggesting that only certain sections of the economy would be nationalized. ANC leaders were later to deny that the organization was Socialist or that the Freedom Charter aimed at a Socialist state.

The Freedom Charter asks that the land of the country be "re-divided amongst those who work it" in order "to banish famine and land hunger." It goes on to set out basic liberal freedoms, for example, that no one should be imprisoned except for a serious crime and after a fair trial. All have the right "to speak, to organise, to meet together, to publish, to preach, to worship" and to travel freely anywhere. There is specific mention of the abolition of the hated pass laws, which restricted the movement of black African people and decreed that passes had to be produced on demand. The Freedom Charter speaks of various worker demands, such as a forty-hour workweek, a national minimum wage, and paid leave. There should be no forced labor, child labor, or compound labor, all of which were common features of the apartheid state. "Compound labor" refers to the practice of requiring black Africans to live in certain areas while they engaged in contracted work. Thus,

Africans laboring in diamond mines, for example, might be forbidden to leave their "compounds" for as long as three months— purportedly on the theory that it would prevent theft—and would be cut off from their families and the outside world.

In another idealistic clause, education was to "be free, compulsory, universal and equal for all children." The charter states that "higher education and technical training shall be opened to all by means of state allowances and scholarships awarded on the basis of merit." This was written at a time when the apartheid state was shutting down access to higher education for blacks, who were soon to be barred from attending the leading universities and forced to study at separate tribal colleges. Adult illiteracy, which was widespread, should, the Freedom Charter continues, "be ended by a mass state education plan." All should have the right to live where they chose, and there should be a health scheme run by the state to provide free medical care for all. Although a national health system had been proposed in the 1940s, nothing had come of the idea. In 1955 there were relatively good health facilities only for the white minority. Most black South Africans had no ready access to such facilities.

Newly appointed South African Deputy President Phumzile Mlambo-Ngcuka dances during the fiftieth anniversary celebration of the Freedom Charter at Kliptown, South Africa, on June 26, 2005. (AP/Wide World Photos)

The Freedom Charter declares that slums should be demolished and new suburbs built "where all have transport, roads, lighting, playing fields, créches and social centres." This sets out a vision of a world totally different from that of South Africa in 1955, where, because of the apartheid policy, black people were being forcibly removed from urban areas and dumped in remote townships with virtually no facilities of any kind. The Freedom Charter recognizes this when it says that "fenced locations and ghettoes shall be abolished." Most black people then lived and would remain in rural areas far from the cities, without easy access to transport or any social or medical facilities and certainly not day care centers. They could not readily move from place to place without official permission that was often difficult to obtain. Men who went to the cities to work could not take their families with them, and millions employed as migrant workers in the mines or towns had to return to the rural areas to see their wives and children. The Freedom Charter makes explicit reference to this when it says "laws which break up families shall be repealed."

At a time when the apartheid government was calling for Britain to allow South Africa to incorporate the so-called High Commission Territories, the Freedom Charter says that "the people of the protectorates Basutoland, Bechuanaland and Swaziland shall be free to decide for themselves their own future" (which they did in the 1960s when they moved to independence). The Freedom Charter ends with a pledge to continue the struggle "side by side" until its aims are achieved.

The Freedom Charter consists of visionary goals for the future, statements about what could be achieved when apartheid was abolished. When South Africans drew up a new constitution in the early 1990s, the question was raised concerning which elements from the charter could be incorporated in the constitution. Many of them were set out in the final constitution of 1996, especially in the bill of rights.

Audience

The Freedom Charter begins with the words: "We, the people of South Africa, declare for all our country and the world to know." It therefore claims to represent the views of the people of the country and to be addressed to all the people of South Africa and to the wider world, for those who drew it up recognized that in the struggle against

"*South Africa belongs to all who live in it, black and white, and ... no government can justly claim authority unless it is based on the will of all the people.*"

(Paragraph 2)

"*Our people have been robbed of their birthright to land, liberty and peace by a form of government founded on injustice and inequality.*"

(Paragraph 3)

"*Our country will never be prosperous or free until all our people live in brotherhood, enjoying equal rights and opportunities.*"

(Paragraph 4)

"*Only a democratic state, based on the will of all the people, can secure to all their birthright without distinction of colour, race, sex or belief.*"

(Paragraph 5)

"*We pledge ourselves to strive together, sparing neither strength nor courage, until the democratic changes here set out have been won.*"

(Paragraph 7)

"*These freedoms we will fight for, side by side, throughout our lives, until we have won our liberty.*"

(Paragraph 74)

apartheid it would be vital to win support from the outside world. Such support could be won, they thought, because of the recognition of no racial distinctions that lay at the heart of the charter and because it appealed to universal values. Those who drew up the Freedom Charter intended it to circulate widely in South Africa and to serve as a rallying cry for people struggling against apartheid and working for a different society. One can understand the appeal of the Freedom Charter to those who enjoyed none of the rights and freedoms it proclaimed. That its goals are expressed in simple and direct language made it accessible to almost all and increased its appeal. Its drafters hoped that it would be the central document around which differ-

ent antiapartheid organizations would be able to unite. The Freedom Charter includes a pledge "to strive together, sparing neither strength nor courage, until the democratic changes here set out have been won."

Impact

After the Freedom Charter was adopted, it was taken to the various Congress Alliance organizations to be approved. In the ANC there was fierce objection to it by those who called themselves Africanists. They disliked the clause that said the country belonged to all who lived in it. They did not think that white settlers had a right to the country that was equal to the right of its indigenous inhabitants. Because of these concerns, they decided to break away from the ANC in 1958, and in April the following year they launched the Pan Africanist Congress. Members of the Pan Africanist Congress considered the Freedom Charter to be the work of white Communists and others in a multiracial alliance of which they did not approve.

Of those who attended the Congress of the People, 156 were arrested and charged with treason. In the treason trial, which ran from 1956 to 1961, a key part of the case made by the state was that the Freedom Charter presented a view of a Socialist society. The state's lawyers argued that the charter was therefore a revolutionary document and implied that revolutionary means would be used to achieve its goals. In response to such arguments, the defense argued successfully that the Freedom Charter was not Socialist and that the ANC and the other organizations in the Congress Alliance had not abandoned nonviolent forms of resistance. Nelson Mandela, one of the leading figures on trial, made it clear in his evidence that he did not see the charter as a Socialist document, though it has to be remembered that he was on trial for treason. When he was released from jail in 1990, he continued to argue the case for nationalization, based on his interpretation of the Freedom Charter.

After the last people put on trial for treason were acquitted in 1961, the year after the ANC and the Pan Africanist Congress were declared unlawful organizations and forced to go underground, the Freedom Charter was relatively little referred to for many years. Although June 26 continued to be observed internationally as South African Freedom Day, mainly because it was the day on which the Freedom Charter had been adopted, it was only in the 1980s that the charter took on new significance. The United Nation's Centre against Apartheid published the charter in a brochure in June 1979 for distribution in connection with the twenty-fifth anniversary of its adoption. On January 8, 1980, in celebration of that anniversary, the ANC president Oliver Tambo characterized the charter as being a fundamental rallying cry for the liberation sought by the people of South Africa. He called it the people's charter, the essential statement of their political goals.

Long regarded as a banned document in South Africa, the Freedom Charter began to circulate widely within the country in the 1980s, and it came into prominence as a statement to which the United Democratic Front, formed in 1983, and other antiapartheid organizations committed themselves. As the country moved toward a democratic system, people looked to the Freedom Charter for inspiration and a vision of the kind of state that should be brought into being. The struggle was not only about ending apartheid but also about forging a new society based on equality, justice, and liberty. Not surprisingly, there was to be much disillusionment as it became clear that many of the ideals set out in the charter were unattainable, at least in the short run. Apartheid laws were repealed, but providing such things as free education and housing and health care for all was quite another matter. Although some slums were demolished, the number of squatter settlements and the percentage of poverty grew in the new South Africa. In 2009 there continued to be debate in South Africa over how and to what extent the ideals of the Freedom Charter could be realized.

Questions for Further Study

1. Read the Freedom Charter in conjunction with Nelson Mandela's Inaugural Address of 1994. To what extent do the two documents embody the same aspirations and goals? Do they differ in any important ways?

2. Some efforts were made to discredit the Freedom Charter because "it was drafted by white Communists." What role did Communism and Socialism play in the development of the document? More important, do you believe that any influence of Communism was relevant to the document's authority?

3. Read the Freedom Charter in conjunction with the UN Universal Declaration of Human Rights. What principles and specific proposals do the two documents have in common?

4. Why did the Africanists and the Pan African Congress break away from the African National Congress? Do you believe this rupture helped or impeded the work of the ANC?

5. Racism was always a factor in the colonization of Africa, the Middle East, and Asia, but world opinion held the racism of South Africa to be particularly repugnant, leading to concerted worldwide efforts to end it. What aspects of racial division in South Africa might have led to this ire?

Further Reading

■ **Books**

African National Congress. *Selected Writings on the Freedom Charter: 1955–1985*. London: African National Congress, 1985.

Bernstein, Rusty. *Memory against Forgetting: Memoirs of a Life in South African Politics*. London: Viking, 1999.

Dubow, Saul. *The African National Congress*. Johannesburg, South Africa: Jonathan Ball, 2000.

Joseph, Helen. *Side by Side: The Autobiography of Helen Joseph*. Parklands, South Africa: Ad Donker, 1993.

Karis, Thomas, and Gwendolen Carter, eds. *From Protest to Challenge: A Documentary History of African Politics in South Africa, 1882–1964*. Vol. 3: *Challenge and Violence, 1953–1964*. Stanford, Calif.: Hoover Institution, 1977.

Lodge, Tom. *Black Politics in South Africa since 1945*. Johannesburg, South Africa: Ravan, 1983.

Luthuli, Albert. *Let My People Go*. London: Fontana Books, 1963.

Mandela, Nelson. *Long Walk to Freedom: The Autobiography of Nelson Mandela*. London: Abacus, 1995.

Meli, Francis. *South Africa Belongs to Us: A History of the ANC*. London: James Currey, 1989.

Suttner, Raymond, and Jeremy Cronin. *50 Years of the Freedom Charter*. Pretoria, South Africa: Unisa Press, 2006.

Turok, Ben. *Nothing but the Truth: Behind the ANC's Struggle Politics*. Johannesburg, South Africa: Jonathan Ball, 2003.

Vadi, Ismail. *The Congress of the People and the Freedom Charter Campaign*. New Delhi, India: Sterling, 1995.

■ **Web Sites**

Reddy, E. S. "The Freedom Charter and the United Nations." African National Congress Web site.
http://www.anc.org.za/un/reddy/fc-un.html.

—Christopher Saunders

FREEDOM CHARTER OF SOUTH AFRICA

We, the People of South Africa, declare for all our country and the world to know:

that South Africa belongs to all who live in it, black and white, and that no government can justly claim authority unless it is based on the will of all the people;

that our people have been robbed of their birthright to land, liberty and peace by a form of government founded on injustice and inequality;

that our country will never be prosperous or free until all our people live in brotherhood, enjoying equal rights and opportunities;

that only a democratic state, based on the will of all the people, can secure to all their birthright without distinction of colour, race, sex or belief;

and therefore, we, the people of South Africa, black and white together equals, countrymen and brothers adopt this Freedom Charter;

and we pledge ourselves to strive together, sparing neither strength nor courage, until the democratic changes here set out have been won.

◆ The People Shall Govern!

Every man and woman shall have the right to vote for and to stand as a candidate for all bodies which make laws;

All people shall be entitled to take part in the administration of the country;

The rights of the people shall be the same, regardless of race, colour or sex;

All bodies of minority rule, advisory boards, councils and authorities shall be replaced by democratic organs of self-government.

◆ All National Groups Shall Have Equal Rights!

There shall be equal status in the bodies of state, in the courts and in the schools for all national groups and races;

All people shall have [the] equal right to use their own languages, and to develop their own folk culture and customs;

All national groups shall be protected by law against insults to their race and national pride;

The preaching and practice of national, race or colour discrimination and contempt shall be a punishable crime;

All apartheid laws and practices shall be set aside.

◆ The People Shall Share in the Country's Wealth!

The national wealth of our country, the heritage of South Africans, shall be restored to the people;

The mineral wealth beneath the soil, the Banks and monopoly industry shall be transferred to the ownership of the people as a whole;

All other industry and trade shall be controlled to assist the wellbeing of the people;

All people shall have equal rights to trade where they choose, to manufacture and to enter all trades, crafts and professions.

◆ The Land Shall Be Shared among Those Who Work It!

Restrictions of land ownership on a racial basis shall be ended, and all the land re-divided amongst those who work it to banish famine and land hunger;

The state shall help the peasants with implements, seed, tractors and dams to save the soil and assist the tillers;

Freedom of movement shall be guaranteed to all who work on the land;

All shall have the right to occupy land wherever they choose;

People shall not be robbed of their cattle, and forced labour and farm prisons shall be abolished.

◆ All Shall Be Equal before the Law!

No-one shall be imprisoned, deported or restricted without a fair trial; No-one shall be condemned by the order of any Government official;

The courts shall be representative of all the people;

Imprisonment shall be only for serious crimes against the people, and shall aim at re-education, not vengeance;

The police force and army shall be open to all on an equal basis and shall be the helpers and protectors of the people;

All laws which discriminate on grounds of race, colour or belief shall be repealed.

◆ All Shall Enjoy Equal Human Rights!

The law shall guarantee to all their right to speak, to organise, to meet together, to publish, to preach, to worship and to educate their children;

The privacy of the house from police raids shall be protected by law;

All shall be free to travel without restriction from countryside to town, from province to province, and from South Africa abroad;

Pass Laws, permits and all other laws restricting these freedoms shall be abolished.

◆ There Shall Be Work and Security!

All who work shall be free to form trade unions, to elect their officers and to make wage agreements with their employers;

The state shall recognise the right and duty of all to work, and to draw full unemployment benefits;

Men and women of all races shall receive equal pay for equal work;

There shall be a forty-hour working week, a national minimum wage, paid annual leave, and sick leave for all workers, and maternity leave on full pay for all working mothers;

Miners, domestic workers, farm workers and civil servants shall have the same rights as all others who work;

Child labour, compound labour, the tot system and contract labour shall be abolished.

◆ The Doors of Learning and Culture Shall Be Opened!

The government shall discover, develop and encourage national talent for the enhancement of our cultural life;

All the cultural treasures of mankind shall be open to all, by free exchange of books, ideas and contact with other lands;

The aim of education shall be to teach the youth to love their people and their culture, to honour human brotherhood, liberty and peace;

Education shall be free, compulsory, universal and equal for all children; Higher education and technical training shall be opened to all by means of state allowances and scholarships awarded on the basis of merit;

Adult illiteracy shall be ended by a mass state education plan;

Teachers shall have all the rights of other citizens;

The colour bar in cultural life, in sport and in education shall be abolished.

◆ There Shall Be Houses, Security and Comfort!

All people shall have the right to live where they choose, be decently housed, and to bring up their families in comfort and security;

Unused housing space [is] to be made available to the people;

Rent and prices shall be lowered, food plentiful and no-one shall go hungry;

A preventive health scheme shall be run by the state;

Free medical care and hospitalisation shall be provided for all, with special care for mothers and young children;

Slums shall be demolished, and new suburbs built where all have transport, roads, lighting, playing fields, créches and social centres;

The aged, the orphans, the disabled and the sick shall be cared for by the state;

Rest, leisure and recreation shall be the right of all:

Fenced locations and ghettoes shall be abolished, and laws which break up families shall be repealed.

◆ There Shall Be Peace and Friendship!

South Africa shall be a fully independent state which respects the rights and sovereignty of all nations;

South Africa shall strive to maintain world peace and the settlement of all international disputes by negotiation—not war;

Glossary

colour bar	barrier preventing blacks from equal participation with whites in activities
compound labour	the practice of requiring blacks to live in certain restricted areas when engaged in contracted work
créches	day care centers
pass laws	laws that restricted blacks from free movement within South Africa
tot system	a system of paying blacks for their labor in part with alcohol

Peace and friendship amongst all our people shall be secured by upholding the equal rights, opportunities and status of all;

The people of the protectorates Basutoland, Bechuanaland and Swaziland shall be free to decide for themselves their own future;

The right of all peoples of Africa to independence and self-government shall be recognised, and shall be the basis of close co-operation.

Let all people who love their people and their country now say, as we say here:

These Freedoms We Will Fight For, Side By Side, Throughout Our Lives, Until We Have Won Our Liberty.

Gamel Abdel Nasser (AP/Wide World Photos)

"The assets and rights of the nationalized company in the Republic of Egypt and abroad are hereby frozen."

Overview

On July 26, 1956, President Gamal Abdel Nasser of Egypt issued the President of the Republic Order concerning the Issuance of Law No. 285 of 1956 on the Nationalization of the Universal Company of the Suez Maritime Canal. Under this law, Egypt nationalized the Suez Canal—that is, took over its ownership and operation, thus removing the canal from British (and to a lesser extent French) control. The Suez Canal links the Mediterranean Sea and the Red Sea, the latter of which provides access to the Indian Ocean. The area surrounding the Suez Canal is the only land bridge connecting Africa and Asia. For nearly a century prior to nationalization, the canal had played a vital role in world commerce and in Britain's ability to communicate with and defend its colonies in Asia. More recently, the canal has functioned as a pipeline for oil and other commodities.

Nasser's decision to nationalize the canal was a critical move in the geopolitics of the 1950s, when European colonial empires were crumbling and the world was growing more dependent on oil. During this period the Arab states stood in opposition to the nascent state of Israel, tensions were increasing between Communist China and the Nationalist government of Taiwan, and the United States and its allies viewed the Soviet Union and the Eastern bloc across an ideological divide. The nationalization of the canal sparked the Suez Crisis of 1956 and threatened peace throughout the world. In the years that followed, the nationalization of the Suez Canal would bolster Nasser's position as leader of a pan-Arabist movement. It would also lay the foundation for his remilitarization of the Sinai Peninsula, which led to the Six-Day War with Israel in June 1967.

Context

The nationalization of the Suez Canal was one move in a complex geopolitical chess match. The canal, which had opened in 1869, was originally financed by the governments of France and Egypt. It was placed under the control of an enterprise chartered by the Egyptians called the Universal Company of the Suez Maritime Canal. In 1875 the Egyptian viceroy, Isma'il Pasha, was forced to sell his shares in the company because of a financial crisis. The British government bought the shares, which gave it a 44 percent interest in the canal company. British influence in the region increased as a result of the Anglo-Egyptian War of 1882. In response to a revolt by the Egyptian army, Britain invaded, defeated the Egyptians, and occupied the country in an effort to protect the canal and British financial interests in the region. The key battle in the conflict was the Battle of Tel el Kebir, near the Canal Zone, on September 13, 1882.

Britain had physical control of the canal and its operations, but France still held the majority of the company's shares. France hoped to weaken Britain's control of the canal by persuading other European powers to support internationalization of the canal. As a compromise, Britain, France, Russia, Austria-Hungary, and other European nations as well as the Ottoman Empire signed the Convention of Constantinople on October 29, 1888. The purpose of this treaty was to declare the canal and the Canal Zone neutral territory that would be open to all nations during peacetime and wartime. Britain and France, though, had strong reservations about the treaty; Britain expressed its reservations in the tortuous language of international diplomacy:

> The delegates of Great Britain, in offering this text as the definitive rule to secure the free use of the Suez Canal, believe it is their duty to announce a general reservation as to the applicability of its provisions in so far as they are incompatible with the transitory and exceptional state in which Egypt is actually found and so far as they might fetter the liberty of action of the government during the occupation of Egypt by the British forces. (Allain, p. 53)

Because of these reservations, the treaty did not come into effect until 1904 with the signing of the Entente cordiale (usually translated as "cordial agreement"), which ended nearly a thousand years of intermittent conflict between Britain and France and formed the alignment of European powers that would later prevail at the end of World War I.

1859

- Construction of the Suez Canal begins under the supervision of Ferdinand de Lesseps.

1869

- **November 17**
  The Suez Canal opens.

1882

- British forces defeat the Egyptian army and begin an occupation of Egypt.

1888

- **October 29**
  Britain, France, and other European nations together with the Ottoman Empire sign the Convention of Constantinople, making the canal neutral territory.

1904

- **April 8**
  Britain and France sign the Entente cordiale, formally becoming allies; the provisions of the Convention of Constantinople go into effect.

1936

- **August 26**
  The Anglo-Egyptian Treaty, giving Britain a twenty-year lease on the Suez Canal, is signed.

1948

- **May 14**
  The state of Israel declares its independence.

In the early years of the twentieth century, the strategic importance of the canal had become apparent. For example, during the Russo-Japanese War of 1904–1905, Britain refused to allow Russian ships to pass through the canal because of an agreement that Britain had with Japan. This gave Japan a strategic advantage, since Russian ships based on the Baltic Sea were forced to sail all the way around the southern tip of Africa in order to reach East Asia. During World War I, Britain refused to allow non-Allied shipping to pass through the canal. In 1936 England and Egypt signed the Anglo-Egyptian Treaty, by which Britain agreed to reduce its troop levels in Egypt and to defend Egypt in case of war. The Egyptian government wanted the treaty because it feared invasion by Italian forces under the direction of the dictator Benito Mussolini, who had recently invaded Ethiopia. But in the decades after World War II, the role of the canal began to change. As the world was becoming more dependent on Middle Eastern oil, roughly half of the traffic through the canal consisted of oil tankers.

In the years following World War II, tensions between Britain and Egypt began to mount. England was the dominant power in the Middle East, with interests not only in Egypt but also in Iran, Iraq, and other Middle Eastern countries. It maintained a large military force—some eighty thousand troops—at a garrison in the Canal Zone, at the time one of the largest military forces stationed in a foreign nation. Predictably, opposition to the British presence in Egypt began to grow. Egypt was experiencing economic distress, with inflation and high unemployment. Various radical political groups emerged, including the Communist Party, the Arab Socialist Party, and the Muslim Brotherhood. Founded in 1928, the Muslim Brotherhood was one of the first Islamist groups that called for a pan-Islamist, anti-Western imposition of Islamic law throughout the Middle East and North Africa. These radical groups opposed the British presence in Egypt and had been particularly bitter about the Anglo-Egyptian Treaty. Opposition to the British spread throughout the Egyptian population; Egyptians who worked for the canal company went on strike, and those who were thought to be collaborators with the British were attacked. In light of this opposition to Britain, the Egyptian government under the leadership of King Farouk I abrogated the treaty in 1951. Three years earlier, Israel had declared its independence as a nation on May 14, 1948. Egypt, opposing this "Zionist" takeover of Palestine, led the coalition of Arab nations that attacked Israel—unsuccessfully—the following day, launching the Arab-Israeli War. The Egyptians closed the canal to Israeli shipping, though in 1951 the UN Security Council passed a resolution calling on Egypt to discontinue this practice.

Tensions grew in 1952. In January, conflict broke out between British troops and the police force in Ismailia, a city on the west bank of the Suez Canal and the canal's administrative center. After some forty Egyptians died in the clash, rioting broke out in Egypt's capital, Cairo, resulting in the death of eleven British citizens. In the turmoil, an organization called the Free Officers Movement made its move to unseat King Farouk, drive out the British, and establish a republic. The Free Officers Movement consisted entirely of young military officers, many of them from humble backgrounds, who felt humiliated and betrayed because of Egypt's defeat in the Arab-Israeli War. On July 23, 1952, the officers staged a coup d'état that overthrew the king. The organization was led by Nasser, then a colonel in the Egyptian army, and Muhammad Neguib, who would serve as Egypt's first president.

Britain tried to mend fences with Egypt, but to no avail. The nations agreed to a phased withdrawal of British troops, but many Egyptians objected to the continued British presence in their country. Although Nasser did not assume the presidency of Egypt until June 23, 1956, he held most of the power in Egypt, largely as a result of disputes with Neguib, whom Nasser would later imprison. In the years after the 1952 revolt, Nasser took steps to frustrate the British. He positioned himself as the leader of a Pan-Arabist movement—in effect, the leader of the Islamic world. He believed that Britain was attempting to form a bloc of nations to the east that would neutralize Egypt. He was particularly disturbed by the signing of the Middle East Treaty Organization in 1955. This agreement, referred to informally as the Baghdad Pact, was a military and economic pact signed by Britain, Iran, Iraq, Turkey, and Pakistan. In response, Nasser formed an alliance with Saudi Arabia in an effort to check Britain's growing influence in not only the nations that had signed the Baghdad Pact but also in Syria and Lebanon. By allying with Saudi Arabia, Nasser played on the traditional animosity between the Saudi royal family and the Hashemite Dynasty that ruled Iraq until 1958. Nasser also successfully fomented opposition to the British in Lebanon.

The scope of the developing crisis widened when Nasser signed an arms deal with Czechoslovakia, then a member of the Soviet bloc in Eastern Europe, effectively ending Egyptian reliance on Western arms. This gave the Soviets and the Warsaw Pact (the name given to the Eastern European Communist bloc) a presence in the Middle East. In response, Britain tried to enlist the support of the United States. However, the strongest U.S. ally in the region was Saudi Arabia; therefore, the U.S. government under President Dwight Eisenhower refused to support the Baghdad Pact and chose instead to appease Nasser. Then, in May 1956, Egypt formally recognized the Communist People's Republic of China. This move troubled the U.S. government, particularly Secretary of State John Foster Dulles, who strongly supported the Nationalist government that the Chinese Communists had driven off the mainland to Taiwan; Taiwan was a major point of contention between the United States and Communist China. In response to Egypt's diplomatic recognition of China, Eisenhower withdrew American financial support for the construction the Aswan Dam, a massive project undertaken to control flooding of the Nile River and provide hydroelectric power. The dam was eventually completed in 1970 with the assistance of the Soviet Union.

For Nasser, the withdrawal of American financial support was the last straw. On July 26 he gave a speech in

Time Line

1951

- **September 1**
  The UN Security Council passes a resolution calling on Egypt to discontinue the practice of denying Israel use of the Suez Canal.

- **October**
  Egypt abrogates the Anglo-Egyptian Treaty of 1936.

1952

- **July 23**
  King Farouk I of Egypt is overthrown in a coup d'état; Muhammad Neguib is proclaimed president five days later.

1955

- The Baghdad Pact is signed by the United Kingdom, Iran, Iraq, Pakistan, and Turkey.

1956

- **May 16**
  Egypt formally recognizes the People's Republic of China; diplomatic relations between the two nations are established on May 30.

- **June 23**
  Gamal Abdel Nasser becomes president of Egypt.

- **July 19**
  The United States withdraws its financial support for the construction of the Aswan Dam in Egypt.

- **July 26**
  President Nasser of Egypt issues the Order concerning the Issuance of Law No. 285 of 1956 on the Nationalization of the Universal Company of the Suez Maritime Canal.

1956

■ **October 24**
Britain, France, and Israel sign the Protocol of Sèvres, an agreement that would allow Britain to regain control of the Suez Canal.

1958

■ **February 1**
The United Arab Republic, linking Egypt and Syria, is created, with Nasser as president. Syria will withdraw in 1961, although Egypt will retain the name United Arab Republic for another decade.

1964

■ **May 28**
The Palestinian National Charter, creating the Palestine Liberation Organization, is adopted.

1967

■ **June 5**
Start of the Six-Day War between Israel and the combined forces of Egypt, Syria, and Jordan, lasting until a cease-fire is called on June 10.

1970

■ **September 28**
Nasser dies of a heart attack in Cairo, Egypt (at the time the United Arab Republic).

Alexandria, Egypt, during which he repeatedly mentioned the name of the canal's French builder, Ferdinand de Lesseps. Nasser's use of this name was a code that instructed Egyptian forces to seize the canal. In that speech Nasser announced that the canal had been nationalized under the terms of the Order concerning the Issuance of Law No. 285 of 1956 on the Nationalization of the Universal Company of the Suez Maritime Canal.

About the Author

Gamal Abdel Nasser was born in Alexandria, Egypt, on January 15, 1918. As a child, he moved frequently because of his father's employment with the postal service. As a high school student, he was politically active and was already asserting the anti-British, pro-nationalist viewpoints that would define his career. He began his career as a military officer; his first battlefield service was during the Arab-Israeli War in 1948. In 1949 he was part of the delegation that negotiated the cease-fire agreement with Israel, but he regarded the terms of the agreement as a humiliation for Egypt. After the war, he was deeply involved in the Free Officers Movement, a small group consisting of just fourteen military officers whose ultimate aim was to overthrow Egypt's monarchy and establish a republic. The Free Officers Movement accomplished its goal in 1952 with the removal of King Farouk I, Egypt's ruler. Nasser's colleague Muhammad Neguib was named president of new Egyptian republic. Nasser, however, disagreed with Neguib on several important points of policy and was able to neutralize his influence. Nasser himself became president on June 23, 1956, a position he held until his death on September 28, 1970. In July 1956 he nationalized the Suez Canal.

Nasser was a cautious but forceful leader. In October 1954 he was the target of an assassination attempt. In response, he ordered a crackdown against a wide range of politically disaffected groups, including the Muslim Brotherhood, Communists, and members of dissident political parties. Some twenty thousand people were arrested. Yet in 1955, when Israel attacked the Gaza Strip, territory held by the Egyptians, Nasser responded with extreme caution, believing that the Egyptian military was not strong enough to repel the assault. He was frequently the target of criticism, but he was a skillful politician who was able to win the support of the Egyptian people. In the years following the nationalization of the canal, he jockeyed himself into the position of leader of a pan-Arabist movement—a movement to unite Arab countries into a single political entity. He started to achieve this goal when the United Arab Republic, a union of Egypt and Syria, was formed on February 1, 1958, with himself as president. Syria withdrew in 1961, but Egypt retained the name United Arab Republic until 1971.

Throughout the 1950s and 1960s, Nasser strengthened the Egyptian military and presided over a period of rapid industrialization, including the Aswan Dam project. Pan-Arabists and pan-Islamists throughout the Middle East

---

looked to him for leadership. Nasser was also a key leader in opposition to Israel and was instrumental in the formation of the Palestine Liberation Organization in 1964. In 1967 he received a false warning from the Soviets that the Israelis were planning a surprise attack. Accordingly, he massed troops near the Israeli border, but before he could strike, the Israelis launched a preemptive attack, starting the Six-Day War on June 5. In the wake of Egypt's defeat in the Six-Day War, Nasser announced his resignation as president, but he rescinded his resignation after an outpouring of support from Egyptians. He then launched a campaign of harassment of Israel in the Sinai Peninsula, the so-called War of Attrition, which included skirmishes, air strikes, and missile attacks. He continued this strategy until his death. Nasser's successor was his former military aide who had become Egypt's vice-president, Anwar Sadat.

Explanation and Analysis of the Document

The Order concerning the Issuance of Law No. 285 of 1956 on the Nationalization of the Universal Company of the Suez Maritime Canal is a brief document that announces that "in the name of the nation" the president (Nasser) is seizing control of the ownership and operation of the Suez Canal. The document begins with a preamble that makes reference to various laws over the years that had vested control of the canal in the hands of private stockholders. The document uses the word *firmans*, which means "royal decrees" and refers to laws that were promulgated when Egypt was a monarchy. At the time construction of the canal began in 1859, the Egyptian viceroy was Sa'id Pasha, who ruled from 1854 to 1863; his successor, Ismail Pasha, presided over the opening of the canal, and it was his policy of westernizing Egypt that nearly bankrupted the nation, forcing him to sell his shares to the British. The preamble also makes reference to later laws having to do with the ownership of the canal company. It refers to three types of ownership: joint-stock companies, limited partnerships, and limited-liability companies. Joint-stock companies issue transferable shares, much like a corporation, but owners of these shares face personal liability for the company's obligations. Limited partnerships are similar in that share owners retain personal liability for the company's obligations; however, their shares are not freely transferable. A limited-liability company issues transferable shares, and its shareholders have no personal liability for the company's obligations.

Article I is the core of the document. It states simply that the Universal Company of the Suez Maritime Canal has been nationalized, meaning that the state of Egypt has seized control of the canal's ownership and operation. The assets, rights, and obligations of the previous company have been dissolved. Article I also stipulates that shareholders would be reimbursed based on the value of their shares on the Paris Stock Exchange the previous day and that payment would be made once the assets of the company had been transferred to Egypt.

Article II turns to the new administration of the canal. It states that a new organization "endowed with juristic personality" was to take over operation of the canal. "Juristic personality," or "juristic person," is a term used in law to refer to a "legal person"—that is, an entity (such as a corporation or government agency) that has status as a separate person for certain defined legal purposes. This organization was to be under the authority of the Ministry of Commerce. The Suez Canal Transit Service, which had been operating the canal, would continue to operate as an independent agency not subject to any rules and regulations imposed by the Egyptian government. Article II also gave the transit service broad authority to appoint officials and conduct research studies.

Article III announces that the assets of the canal company had been frozen. This meant that banks, organizations, and individuals could not sell their assets or engage in any financial transactions that involved the assets or shares of the company. The freezing of assets can be a source of great stress to owners of overseas enterprises. According to Article I, holders of shares in the Suez Canal were to be reimbursed eventually, but in the meantime those shares could not be liquidated or transferred.

The remainder of the document consists of legalities. According to Article IV, employees of the canal company were required to continue at their jobs; this article thus ensured the smooth operation of the canal during the transition to national ownership. Article V imposed penalties for violations of Articles III and IV. Finally, Article VI states that the act will be published in "the Official Gazette." The *Egyptian Official Gazette* (*Al-waqa'ie al-misriyya*) is the oldest newspaper in Egypt; its first issue was published in 1828. It has since been considered the newspaper of record in Egypt, in which laws, legal judgments, and presidential decrees have been published. The date of the proclamation is cited as "1375 A.H." A.H. is an abbreviation meaning *Anno Hegirae*, which is the Latinized form of *H*, or *Hijri*, both of which refer to the Islamic prophet Muhammad's emigration from Mecca to Medina in Saudi Arabia in the year 622. In the Islamic calendar, dates are computed using this year as a base; A.H. is thus similar to the notation of AD or CE in Western dates. "*Zull Heggah*," usually spelled *Dhul-Hijjah* or *Thul-Hijjah*, is a reference to the twelfth month in the Islamic lunar year.

Audience

The audience for the act nationalizing the Suez Canal was first the stockholders of the Universal Company of the Suez Maritime Canal, that is, the owners of the canal. The act simply and directly informed them that Egypt was taking over control of the canal and that they would be reimbursed for their shares. A second audience was the Egyptian people. This act was a bold move that buttressed Nasser's support among Egyptians, many of whom had been resisting European influence in their country for years. A third audience was the Israelis. In the wake of the Arab-Israeli War of 1948, tensions with Israel had remained

Scuttled ships block the entrance to the Suez Canal at Port Said. (AP/Wide World Photos)

high. The Arab nations, including Egypt, questioned the right of Israel even to exist in Palestine. By nationalizing the canal, Nasser was sending a message to the Israelis that their shipping through the canal was at the sufferance of Egypt. A fourth audience consisted of other Arab states in the region. Nationalizing the canal was a key step in Nasser's vision of uniting the Arab states into a single polity; it was also a subtle warning to those states in the region that were forming or continued to maintain close ties with the West. Finally, the audience for the act was the world community. By nationalizing the canal, Nasser declared to the world—especially Europe and the United States—that Egypt would be asserting itself on the world stage and was no longer to be regarded as any nation's colony.

Impact

The nationalization of the Suez Canal struck a serious blow to British economic interests in the Middle East. Some members of Parliament believed that the only appro-

priate response was military action. Britain, however, lacked support from the United States and did not want to further damage its relationship with the Arab nations. Accordingly, it conducted secret talks with Israel and France to decide on a course of action. Diplomatic representatives from Britain, the United States, and France held meetings in London. Meanwhile, the United States discreetly sought a way to resolve the crisis peacefully, but these efforts proved to be unavailing.

In October 1956 representatives from Britain, France, and Israel (including Israel's prime minister, David Ben-Gurion) met in the French town of Sèvres. After two days of discussion, the parties agreed to the Protocol of Sèvres, which was signed on October 24. Under the terms of this agreement, Israeli forces would invade and occupy the Sinai Peninsula. British and French forces would use the Israeli occupation as a pretense to intervene, restore peace, and act as a buffer separating the warring parties. Britain would then use the event to argue that Egypt was not capable of defending the canal. After the protocol had been signed, diplomacy became a bit of a cloak-and-dagger

"*The Universal Company of the Suez Maritime Canal (Egyptian joint-stock company) is hereby nationalized. All its assets, rights and obligations are transferred to the Nation and all the organizations and committees that now operate its management are hereby dissolved.*"

(Article I)

"*An independent organization endowed with juristic personality and annexed to the Ministry of Commerce, shall take over the management of the Suez Canal Transit Service.*"

(Article II)

"*The assets and rights of the nationalized company in the Republic of Egypt and abroad are hereby frozen.*"

(Article III)

affair. Britain denied the existence of such an agreement. Efforts were made to collect all copies to eliminate the paper trail, but the French refused to relinquish their copy; so did the Israelis, who did not trust Britain and did not want to be left stranded by their allies in the middle of an armed conflict. Israel did, in fact, invade the Sinai Peninsula (Operation Kadesh) beginning on October 29, and British and French forces intervened (Operation Musketeer and Operation Telescope) beginning on October 31. Hostilities continued into early November.

At this point, the Canadians became involved in the Suez Crisis. Lester B. Pearson, who would later become Canada's prime minister, suggested that a neutral UN peacekeeping force be dispatched to the region. Britain and France rejected the idea in the UN Security Council, but with the support of the United States, Pearson's suggestion prevailed in the UN General Assembly. Canadian troops and troops from neutral nations not aligned with either the Western powers or the Warsaw Pact were sent as part of the United Nations Emergency Force. In effect, this was the first UN peacekeeping force. Pearson has been credited with creating the modern principle of UN peacekeeping, and for his efforts he won the Nobel Peace Prize in 1957.

Britain and France were under enormous pressure to withdraw and were accused of naked aggression. The Saudis imposed an oil embargo against both countries, and other members of the North Atlantic Treaty Organization (NATO), the major Western defense pact, refused to fill the gap by selling their oil to the two nations. Some members of NATO

proposed that Britain and France be ejected from the organization. The Soviets threatened to attack Paris, London, and Tel Aviv. The United States threatened to sell off its holdings of British government bonds, which would have had a devastating effect on the value of the British pound and Britain's ability to pay for imported goods, including food. In the face of this pressure, the British prime minister, Anthony Eden, called a cease-fire on November 6, 1956. British and French forces were withdrawn before Christmas, and the Israelis withdrew from the Sinai in March 1957. Because of the crisis, Eden suffered a severe mental breakdown and retired. The canal, which Nasser had blocked by sinking old ships, was reopened for traffic in 1957.

The nationalization of the Suez Canal and the ensuing Suez Crisis had profound and far-reaching effects. The events of 1956 and 1957 marked the beginning of the decline of Britain and France as major world powers. The Suez Crisis was the last time that Britain acted militarily in its crumbling empire without the backing of the United States. From this point forward, Britain behaved less like the imperial power it had been for more than a century and focused more on European cooperation. The crisis exposed the inability of NATO to act outside its immediate sphere of influence. France, in response, withdrew its military from NATO, pursued its development of nuclear weapons, and may have sold nuclear weapons technology to Israel. Furthermore, relations between France and Canada became strained. Because of the crisis, Canada changed the design of its national flag to the simple maple leaf in order to eliminate images that suggested its former status as a colony of France and England. It is thought that in retaliation for Canada's role in resolving the Suez Crisis, French president Charles de Gaulle fomented separatist sentiment in French-speaking Quebec. Many historians mark the Suez Crisis as the beginning of an era in which the United States and the Soviet Union became the world's two sole "superpowers." Meanwhile, Nasser enjoyed a boost to his reputation in the Arab world. His vision of pan-Arabism was adopted by many people in the Middle East and North Africa, and at least partly under his leadership the Palestine Liberation Organization was formed in opposition to Israel in 1964.

The United Nations Emergency Force remained on the Sinai Peninsula and was able to keep the peace. However, by 1967 the size of the force had shrunk to just over three thousand troops, and its hold over the peninsula and the canal was tenuous at best. The Soviets interfered in 1967 by passing along to Egypt a false report that the Israelis were planning a surprise attack. In response, Nasser, in concert with other Arab nations, massed troops along the border with Israel. Alarmed, Israel launched a preemptive attack, which began the Six-Day War of June 1967. Israel delivered a stunning defeat of the Arab forces arrayed to attack, consolidating its hold on additional portions of Palestine. During the war, Israel occupied the Gaza Strip, the Golan Heights, the West Bank, and the Sinai Peninsula. Israel's occupation of this territory remains a source of hostility in the region, even though it returned the Sinai Peninsula to Egypt in 1982 and withdrew from the Gaza Strip in 2005.

In the twenty-first century, the Suez Canal remains under the authority of the Suez Canal Authority, a government-owned agency that was established by the act that nationalized the canal in 1956. About twenty thousand ships pass through the canal each year.

Further Reading

■ Books

Allain, Jean. *International Law in the Middle East: Closer to Power than Justice*. Burlington, Vt.: Ashgate Publishing, 2004.

Arnstein, Walter L. *Britain Yesterday and Today: 1830 to the Present*, 8th ed. Boston: Houghton Mifflin, 2001.

Barnett, Michael N. *Confronting the Costs of War: Military Power, State, and Society in Egypt and Israel*. Princeton, N.J.: Princeton University Press, 1992.

Bregman, Ahron. *Israel's Wars: A History since 1947*. New York: Routledge, 2002.

Butler, L. J. *Britain and Empire: Adjusting to a Post-Imperial World*. London: I. B. Tauris, 2002.

Cash, Damien. "Suez Crisis." In *The Oxford Companion to Australian History*, ed. Graeme Davison, et al. New York: Oxford University Press, 2001.

Questions for Further Study

1. Nasser's nationalization of the Suez Canal was part of a series of international developments with which the nations involved had to contend. Summarize these developments and indicate the role that each played in the deepening crisis.

2. What role did the United States play in the events surrounding the nationalization of the Suez Canal? Why was the United States reluctant to become involved in the matter?

3. In your judgment, who was most at fault in fomenting the Suez Canal Crisis: Egypt, for closing the canal in the first place, or Britain and France, for their secret diplomacy and military response?

4. It seems as though the Suez Canal Crisis would have been the sort of matter that the United Nations could have and should have resolved. Eventually the United Nations sent a peacekeeping force, but that did not happen until after hostilities erupted. Why do you think this was so?

5. Nasser objected to the presence of the British and French in Egypt, regarding their presence as indicative of the Western colonial presence in the Middle East. Yet at the same time Nasser was willing to accept American financial support for construction of the Aswan Dam, and it was the withdrawal of that support that for him was "the straw that broke the camel's back" as tensions gathered. Do you see any inconsistency in Nasser's attitudes? Why or why not?

Childers, Erskine B. *The Road to Suez: A Study of Western-Arab Relations.* London: MacGibbon & Kee, 1962.

Darwin, John. *Britain and Decolonisation: The Retreat from Empire in the Post-War World.* New York: St Martin's Press, 1988.

Haykal, Muhammad Hasanayn. *The Cairo Documents: The Inside Story of Nasser and His Relationship with World Leaders, Rebels, and Statesmen.* New York: Doubleday, 1973.

Hendershot, Robert M. *Family Spats: Perception, Illusion, and Sentimentality in the Anglo-American Special Relationship. 1950–1976.* Saarbrücken, Germany: VDM Verlag, 2008.

Hyam, Ronald. *Britain's Declining Empire: The Road to Decolonisation 1918–1968.* New York: Cambridge University Press, 2006.

Kunz, Diane B. *The Economic Diplomacy of the Suez Crisis.* Chapel Hill: University of North Carolina Press, 1991.

Kyle, Keith. *Suez: Britain's End of Empire in the Middle East.* 1991. Reprint. London: I. B. Tauris, 2003.

Love, Kennett. *Suez: The Twice-Fought War: A History.* New York: McGraw-Hill, 1969.

McLean, Iain, and Alistair McMillan, eds. "Suez Crisis." In *The Concise Oxford Dictionary of Politics*, 2nd ed. New York: Oxford University Press, 2003.

Owen, Roger. "Suez Crisis." In *The Oxford Companion to the Politics of the World*, 2nd ed., ed. Joel Krieger. New York: Oxford University Press, 2001.

Reynolds, David. *Britannia Overruled: British Policy and World Power in the Twentieth Century*, 2nd ed. London: Longman, 2000.

Tal, David, ed. *The 1956 War: Collusion and Rivalry in the Middle East.* Portland, Ore.: Frank Cass Publishers, 2001.

Turner, Barry. *Suez 1956: The Inside Story of the First Oil War.* London: Hodder & Stoughton, 2007.

Verbeek, Bertjan. *Decision-Making in Great Britain during the Suez Crisis: Small Groups and a Persistent Leader.* Burlington, Vt.: Ashgate Publishing, 2003.

Yaqub, Salim. *Containing Arab Nationalism: The Eisenhower Doctrine and the Middle East.* Chapel Hill: University of North Carolina Press, 2004.

Yergin, Daniel. *The Prize: The Epic Quest for Oil, Money, and Power.* New York: Simon & Schuster, 1991.

■ Web Sites

Neely, Matthew. "The Suez Crisis." University of Oxford Bodleian Library Web site.
  http://www.bodley.ox.ac.uk/dept/scwmss/projects/suez/suez.html.

"On This Day—1956: Egypt Seizes Suez Canal." BBC Web site.
  http://news.bbc.co.uk/onthisday/hi/dates/stories/july/26/newsid _2701000/2701603.stm.

Reynolds, Paul. "Suez: End of Empire." BBC Web site.
  http://news.bbc.co.uk/2/hi/middle_east/5199392.stm.

—Michael J. O'Neal

GAMAL ABDEL NASSER ON THE NATIONALIZATION OF THE SUEZ CANAL

In the Name of the Nation

The President of the Republic,

Considering the two firmans issued on November 30, 1854 and January 5, 1856 (respectively) concerning the preferential rights relating to the administration of the Suez Canal Transit Service and the establishment of an Egyptian joint-stock company to operate it; and Law No. 129 of 1947 concerning public utility concessions; and Law No. 317 of 1952 concerning individual labor contracts; and Law No. 26 of 1954 concerning joint-stock companies, limited partnerships by shares and limited liability companies; with the advice of the State Council; has issued the following law;

◆ Article I

The Universal Company of the Suez Maritime Canal (Egyptian joint-stock company) is hereby nationalized. All its assets, rights and obligations are transferred to the Nation and all the organizations and committees that now operate its management are hereby dissolved.

Stockholders and holders of founders shares shall be compensated for the ordinary or founders shares they own in accordance with the value of the shares shown in the closing quotations of the Paris Stock Exchange on the day preceding the effective date of the present law.

The payment of said indemnity shall be effected after the Nation has taken delivery of all the assets and properties of the nationalized company.

◆ Article II

An independent organization endowed with juristic personality and annexed to the Ministry of Commerce, shall take over the management of the Suez Canal Transit Service. The composition of the organization and the remuneration of its members shall be fixed in an order of the President of the Republic. In so far as managing the Transit Service is concerned the organization shall have all the necessary powers required for the purpose without being restricted by Government regulations and procedures.

Without prejudice to the auditing of its final accounts by the State Audit Department, the organization shall have an independent budget prepared in accordance with the rules in force for commercial concerns. Its financial year shall begin on July 1 and end on June 30 each year. The budget and final accounts shall be approved by an order of the President of the Republic. The first financial year shall begin on the effective date of the present law and end with June 30, 1957.

The organization may delegate one or several of its members to implement its decisions or to discharge any duty assigned to these members.

It may also set up from among its own members or from among other people, a technical committee to assist it in its own research work and studies.

The chairman of the organization shall represent it before the courts, government agencies, and other places, and in its dealings with third parties.

◆ Article III

The assets and rights of the nationalized company in the Republic of Egypt and abroad are hereby frozen. Without specific permission obtained in advance from the organization provided for in Article II above, banks, organizations and private persons are hereby prohibited from disposing of those assets or making any payment requested them or due by them.

◆ Article IV

The organization shall retain all the present officials, employees and laborers of the nationalized company at their posts; they shall have to continue with the discharge of their duties; no one will be allowed to leave his work or vacate his post in any manner and for any reason whatsoever except with the permission of the organization provided for in Article II above.

◆ Article V

All violations of the provisions of Article III above shall be punished by imprisonment and a fine equal to three times the value of the amount involved in the offense. All violations of the provisions of Article IV shall be punished by imprisonment in addition to the forfeiture by the offender of all rights to compensation, pension or indemnity.

◆ Article VI

The present order shall be published in the Official Gazette and shall have the force of law. It shall come into force on the date of its publication. The Minister of Commerce shall issue the necessary administrative orders for its implementation.

It shall bear the Seal of the State and be implemented as one of the State laws.

Given this 18th day of Zull Heggah, 1375 A.H. [July 26, 1956]

Gamal Abdel Nasser

Hands tied behind his back, the deposed Congolese premier Patrice Lumumba leaves a plane in Léopoldville in December 1960, under guard. (AP/Wide World Photos)

PATRICE LUMUMBA'S SPEECH AT THE PROCLAMATION OF CONGOLESE INDEPENDENCE

"No Congolese worthy of the name can ever forget that we fought to win [independence]."

Overview

Patrice Lumumba, the first prime minister of the former Belgian Congo, led his country to independence. In a speech on Independence Day (June 30, 1960), Lumumba denounced the oppression and humiliation of colonial rule in the presence of Belgium's King Baudouin. The king, scandalized, nearly left Léopoldville (modern-day Kinshasa), but he was persuaded to stay for the lunch that followed the ceremony. Lumumba, for his part, was persuaded to give a second speech at the lunch, in which he attempted to make amends, crediting Belgium and its monarchy for its positive contributions to Congo. However, the damage had been done.

Lumumba's speech had not been included in the program for the day's events, a program negotiated by representatives of Congo and Belgium. The heads of state, King Baudouin of Belgium and President Joseph Kasavubu of Congo, were to exchange speeches. In Lumumba's view, Kasavubu was a figurehead chief of state who owed his post to support from Lumumba and his coalition. Kasavubu, he believed, should have cleared his speech with the prime minister. Moreover, Lumumba apparently feared that Kasavubu would fail to say some things that needed to be said.

Lumumba's fiery speech was prepared beforehand, so it was not a reaction or reply to what the previous speakers had said. However, he must have known what to expect from the Belgian ruler and from his political rival Kasavubu. It is too simple to suggest that without Lumumba's speech, Congo's decolonization might have been more successful. The speech certainly seemed to have provided ammunition for those who opposed Lumumba and his vision of a strong, independent Congo.

Context

The Congo crisis of 1960 and thereafter was a consequence of failed decolonization. The Belgian Congo came into existence in 1908 in response to the international scandal provoked by the massive violence of the Congo Free State (1885–1908). Under Belgian rule, considerable economic development had taken place, but within a highly paternalistic framework. Africans were confined to the lowest ranks of the administration and the economy. Opposition to Belgian rule simmered throughout the colonial era and took a variety of forms, including armed resistance to the imposition of colonial rule, rural revolts, and urban strikes. Religious movements, notably the church created by Simon Kimbangu, provided an alternative channel for resistance to colonialism.

Belgium ruled according to an unofficial policy of "no elites, no problems." Political parties were slow to emerge. Not until rioting occurred in Léopoldville in January 1959 did Belgium decide to undertake what was called *le pari congolais* ("the Congo gamble"). An agreement was reached under which the colony gained independence the following year. The Congo was given a provisional constitution, the Loi fondamentale, or "fundamental law." Approved by the Belgian parliament in May 1960, the Loi fondamentale was a virtual copy of the Belgian constitution, with none of the implicit understandings that had grown up over the years in Belgium. In particular, the Belgian monarch is a constitutional monarch who reigns but does not rule. The Congolese president was not considered a monarch, and his relationship with the prime minister was sketchily defined. A power struggle soon broke out between President Joseph Kasavubu, leader of the ethnoregional party Alliance des Bakongo (Alliance of Bakongo, or ABAKO), and the prime minister, Patrice Lumumba, leader of the faction of the Mouvement national congolais (Congolese National Movement) that bore his name (MNC-Lumumba). The battle to deliver Congo's response to King Baudouin was an early expression of this struggle.

In the elections to the 137-member national assembly, MNC-Lumumba had won thirty-three seats, far from a majority but far more than the next most successful party, the pro-Belgian Parti national du progrès (National Progress Party), which won twenty-two. MNC-Lumumba and Parti national du progrès were the only parties to propose candidates in all six provinces. Lumumba was able to form a government only by offering ministerial seats to opposing parties, notably Kasavubu's ABAKO and Moise Tshombe's Tribales confédération des associations du Katanga (Confederation of Tribal Associations of Katanga).

1878

■ **November**
King Leopold II
forms the Comité
d'études du Haut
Congo (Committee
for Studies of the
Upper Congo), later
renamed the Asso-
ciation interna-
tionale du Congo
(International Asso-
ciation of the
Congo—the prede-
cessor to the
Congo Free State).

1881

■ Henry M. Stan-
ley, hired by
King Leopold,
sets out to
establish trading
posts and make
treaties with
local chiefs.

1885

■ **February 5**
At the Berlin Con-
ference, European
powers applaud the
announcement of
Leopold's founding
of the Congo
Free State.

1908

■ **November 15**
In response to
growing criticism of
the treatment of the
African population,
the Belgian parlia-
ment annexes the
Congo Free State,
which becomes the
Belgian Congo.

1921

■ **April**
Simon Kimbangu
begins preaching to
the Kongo people
and founds the
movement that
becomes the Kim-
banguist Church,
more formally, the
Church of Christ on
Earth by His Special
Envoy Simon
Kimbangu.

The ceremony recognizing Congo's independence began with Baudouin praising his ancestor, King Leopold II, who allegedly had saved the Congolese from the horrors of the slave trade and had built the colony to which Belgium was now giving its independence. He then went on to state that it was up to Congo's leaders to prove themselves worthy of Belgium's confidence. President Kasavubu, representing the newly independent state, spoke next. He invoked the "gratitude we feel towards all those who have worked, whether privately or publicly, for our national emancipation, and all those who, throughout our vast land, have been unsparing in giving of their strength, their sufferings, and even their lives, in order to realize their bold dream of a free and independent Congo" (Kanza, p. 157). In line with his party's ethnic and federalist orientation, he noted the cultural diversity that had to be overcome in order to develop a true national consciousness. He praised Belgium for having had the wisdom not to oppose the current of history and to lead the colony directly from foreign domination to independence.

About the Author

Patrice Lumumba was born in Onalua, a village in Katako-Kombe territory, in the northeastern corner of the province of Kasai. He was a member of the Tetela ethnic group, which forms the majority in Katako-Kombe territory and in Sankuru district but is outnumbered within Kasai by the Luba-Kasai ethnic community. After attending Protestant and Catholic mission schools in his home area, Lumumba went to work in Maniema and then to Stanleyville (now Kisangani), where he found a job in the post office. He was sent to Léopoldville to the postal school, from which he obtained a diploma. With that certificate, he at last had the right to claim the status of *évolué*, someone who has "evolved" to the point of being able to live and work in the new world created by colonialism. Lumumba returned to Stanleyville, where he became an accountant in the post office. There he continued to contribute to the Congolese press.

At Stanleyville, Lumumba was recruited to work as a research assistant on a UN educational, scientific and cultural organization project studying the urbanization of Stanleyville. He became a leader of the *évolués* of Stanleyville. At one point, in 1953, he occupied seven posts in ethnic, professional, and other associations. Under his leadership, the Association of Évolués of Stanleyville became a political movement, defending the interests of its members, notably with respect to housing. As president of the association in 1954, he was able to meet the minister of colonies, Auguste Buisseret, who was promoting lay schools (not run by missions). Two years later, he met King Baudouin, who was visiting the capital of the province of Orientale.

Lumumba was invited with others to make a study tour of Belgium under the auspices of Buisseret. On his return he was arrested on a charge of embezzlement from the post office. He was convicted one year later, and after various reductions of sentence, he was sentenced to twelve months' imprisonment and a fine. When Lumumba was freed from prison, he moved to Léopoldville, the capital, and joined the MNC, the first nationwide Congolese political party. He then became president of the MNC, which soon split. His faction, the MNC-Lumumba, was centralist in orientation. The other faction, the MNC-Kalonji, was federalist and became a de facto ethnic party of the Luba-Kasai. (Centralists favored a strong central government, while federalists favored granting important powers to the provincial governments.) In December 1958 Lumumba attended the First All-African People's Conference in Accra, Ghana, where he met nationalists from across the African continent and was made a member of the permanent organization set up by the conference. From this point on, his outlook and vocabulary were colored by Pan-Africanist goals.

Lumumba's second experience of colonial justice came at the end of 1959. A rally of the MNC-Lumumba in Stanleyville led to rioting and a number of deaths. Lumumba was briefly imprisoned on charges of inciting the riot but was set free in time to attend a roundtable of Congolese leaders held in Brussels in January of 1960. Reportedly, the other political leaders insisted on his release. Lumumba's party received more votes than any other in the elections of May 1960. The Belgians tried to find an alternative but failed, and they were obliged to invite Lumumba to form a government.

Five days after independence, the army mutinied against its European officers. In response, the Lumumba government was obliged to Africanize the officer corps. From July 6 to July 9, the mutiny spread to Equateur and Katanga provinces, and Belgium sent in paratroopers, allegedly to protect its citizens. Moise Tshombe declared Katanga independent, whereupon Lumumba and Kasavubu requested UN military assistance in the face of Belgian aggression and Katanga secession. On July 12 the UN Security Council called for Belgian withdrawal and authorized UN intervention.

In August, Albert Kalonji led South Kasai into secession. Lumumba sent the national army into the breakaway province, where it carried out massacres of civilians. Concerned that the UN force sent to help restore order was not helping to crush the secessionists, Lumumba turned to the Soviet Union for assistance. The U.S. government saw the Soviet activity as a maneuver to spread Communist influence in central Africa. Kasavubu, upset by the Soviet arrival, dismissed Lumumba. Lumumba declared Kasavubu deposed. Both Lumumba and Kasavubu then ordered Joseph Mobutu, army chief of staff, to arrest the other. On September 14, 1960, Mobutu took control in a coup sponsored by the Central Intelligence Agency. The new regime placed Lumumba under house arrest for the second time and kept Kasavubu as president. In November 1960 Deputy Prime Minister Antoine Gizenga went to Stanleyville to establish a rival national government. Lumumba, under house arrest, left to join Gizenga but was arrested and imprisoned. In January 1961 Lumumba was

Time Line

1921

- **September**
  Kimbangu is arrested and sentenced to life in prison.

1956

- **August 23**
  ABAKO publishes a manifesto calling for immediate independence.

1958

- **October 10**
  The Congolese National Movement is founded.

1959

- **January**
  Belgium recognizes total independence as the goal for Belgian Congo.

1960

- **January**
  The Round Table Conference is held in Brussels to discuss independence.

- **May**
  MNC-Lumumba wins the largest number of seats in the national legislature; after attempts to find an alternative, Belgium invites Lumumba to form a government.

- **June 24**
  The ABAKO leader Kasavubu is elected president by the parliament; the Lumumba government receives a vote of confidence.

- **June 30**
  Lumumba addresses the Congolese people at a ceremony to celebrate their independence from Belgium.

1961

■ **January 17**
Lumumba is executed in Katanga.

1966

■ As president, Joseph Mobutu proclaims Lumumba a "National Hero."

transferred to Katanga, where, on January 17, he was executed by firing squad.

Explanation and Analysis of the Document

Lumumba's speech at the ceremony celebrating Congolese independence contrasted sharply with the contributions of King Baudouin and President Kasavubu. It was reported that Lumumba was writing while the king and the president were speaking, giving the impression that he composed his speech on the spot. In fact, the speech was written several days before and was made available in mimeographed form by the prime minister's office. In delivering the speech, Lumumba made several changes from the prepared text. The speech as delivered was recorded, broadcast, and subsequently transcribed. Three versions of the speech survive.

The Independence Day ceremony was held in the Palais de la nation (Palace of the Nation), built as the residence of the governor-general of the Belgian Congo. Following the speeches of Belgium's King Baudouin and Congo's president, Joseph Kasavubu, Lumumba took the microphone after he was introduced by the president of the lower house of parliament, Joseph Kasongo of the MNC-Lumumba. Lumumba spoke as prime minister, head of the Council of Ministers. He did not address himself to King Baudouin or to the president of the republic, Kasavubu. Instead, he addressed the Congolese population. He saluted them because this day marked their triumph. They had struggled for independence and now they had achieved it, he said.

There is a slight shift in the third paragraph, in that Lumumba addresses his "friends"—perhaps not all the Congolese but all of those who "have fought unceasingly at our side"—and gives them the task of passing on to their children and grandchildren the true meaning of this date of independence, a meaning that he then defines. The day does not mark merely a transfer of sovereignty but, in fact, the culmination of the people's struggle for independence.

In the fourth paragraph Belgium is mentioned, although King Baudouin still is not. Belgium is Congo's equal, a friendly country but not the one that has given Congo its independence. Rather, the Congolese have taken it. The

tears, fire, and blood of the independence struggle were necessary if the Congolese were to put an end to "humiliating slavery." Colonialism, according to the new prime minister, was not merely oppression and not merely exploitation, but a form of slavery, which wounded the slaves. Congo had suffered eighty years of colonialism, according to Lumumba, who lumps together the Congo Free State and the Belgian Congo that followed it. He argues that the main characteristic of colonial rule had been forced labor, for which the monetary return was very low. In the sixth paragraph, Lumumba addresses more specifically the humiliation of daily life under colonial rule. He refers to the fact that whites typically addressed Congolese in the second person singular (*tu, toi*), used for friends and loved ones, children, and servants. It is the equivalent of calling an adult black man "boy" in the Jim Crow American South.

When the Europeans arrived, they declared their sovereignty within boundaries negotiated with other Europeans. They took from the Congolese control over their land. So-called vacant land—a meaningless concept in a country of shifting cultivation and of hunting rights over vast forests—was declared to belong to the colonial state. Large tracts of land were given as "concessions" to mining companies, ranches, and religious missions. By 1960 a substantial number of Congolese lived in cities and towns, but the loss of control over land was still a burning issue to them, as it was to the rural majority.

As Lumumba notes in the seventh paragraph, "The law was quite different for whites and blacks." It is a point that would have been recognized as valid by all the Congolese hearing him. Colonial rule in Congo was rather like the apartheid regime in South Africa. The colonial administration told the Congolese where they could live. They had to carry a card identifying them by their parentage and their ethnic origin. They had to obtain permission to move or to travel from one place to another. Their court cases were tried in a separate set of tribunals.

So-called relegation (alluded to in the ninth paragraph) was a fairly common practice under Belgian rule. The most famous case was that of the prophet Simon Kimbangu, founder of what became a church of millions of members. Kimbangu was arrested, found guilty of sedition (a capital offense), and condemned to die. Belgium's King Albert commuted his sentence, and instead he was relegated to Elisabethville (now Lubumbashi), where he died in 1951. Thousands of followers of Kimbangu and members of other religious movements were "banished," based on the naive belief that they would be harmless far from their home areas. In fact, many soon learned the local languages and recruited local people to their beliefs. Segregation in housing and in public facilities existed for all Congolese but was particularly resented by those (the so-called *évolués*) who had obtained some Western education, had learned French, and had worked in public sector or private sector jobs without receiving equal pay for equal work. Segregation was very strict in the Belgian Congo.

The eleventh paragraph, which concludes the section on grievances, dwells on prison. Of course, Lumumba himself had been sentenced to prison twice. He asks, "Who can forget, finally, the burst of rifle fire in which so many of our brothers perished, the cells into which the authorities threw those who no longer were willing to submit to a rule where justice meant oppression and exploitation?" As strong as this statement is in the form read at the ceremony, it could have been stronger still. According to Jean Van Lierde, the mimeographed text of Lumumba's speech read, "the cells into which the authorities brutally threw those who had escaped the bullets of the soldiers whom the colonialists had made the tool of their domination" (p. 222). The words are true enough but unwise, since the soldiers in question were going to constitute the army of the newly independent Congo Republic. Presumably he thought better of it or was persuaded by trusted advisers not to read the sentence as written. At any rate, the soldiers were suspicious of Lumumba and would mutiny against his government a few days later.

At the beginning of the next section, Lumumba insists that his government is doubly legitimate: It is made up of children of the country (not foreigners from Europe) and was voted into office by deputies elected by the country's voters. The struggle for independence is over, he tells the Congolese, but the struggle to achieve their goals is just beginning. He begins with vague goals, which become slightly more specific in the following passages. "We are going to institute social justice together," he says. Among other goals he names ending "suppression of free thought," doing away with "every sort of discrimination," and bringing "peace to the country … the peace that comes from men's hearts."

In paragraph 22, Lumumba refers to Congo's immense riches—and they are immense—with no suggestion that those riches could pose any problem. In the event, mineral-rich Katanga would attempt to secede a week later. If that secession had been allowed to succeed, it would have carried with it half of the revenues of the Congolese state. Lumumba also hints at a policy of nonalignment—the Congo would rely on the assistance of many countries as long as they did not try to impose any policy. This was said at the time of the cold war—the nearly fifty-year-long state of tension and rivalry between the Soviet Union and the United States in the aftermath of World War II. The U.S. administration of President Dwight Eisenhower considered "nonalignment"—the political attitude of one country's refusing to align itself or abide by the political policies of another country—to be immoral.

Van Lierde notes that the first sentence in paragraph 23 in the mimeographed text read: "Belgium herself has finally realized what direction history was moving in and no longer attempted" to oppose Congo's independence (p. 223). Lumumba dilutes it slightly in his oral version when he says, "Belgium has finally realized what direction history was moving in and has not attempted to oppose our independence." Although he suggests that he is optimistic ("I am certain that this cooperation will be beneficial to both countries"), the phrase "though we shall continue to be vigilant" conveys wariness regarding Belgian intentions.

In paragraph 24 the new prime minister asks for the help of all the legislators and the citizens in the task of

Armed with an automatic weapon, a Congolese soldier stands guard at a window of the town hall in Matadi, Congo, where a lorry loads supposedly looted Belgian property, taken after the owners fled the country.
(AP/Wide World Photos)

state building that he will lead. It is questionable whether all of the quarrels they are asked to set aside were "trivial." The questions of federalism versus a strong unitary state, of close cooperation with Belgium versus a radical break, to mention only two, were not trivial.

Paragraph 28, more than most of the speech, raises the question of Lumumba's foresight. Some bad behavior on the part of foreigners in Congo and on the part of Congolese toward the foreigners had already taken place. Did he fear (with reason) that both were about to get much worse? He would not have long to wait, in that the mutiny of the army was only a few days away.

"The independence of the Congo represents a decisive step toward the liberation of the entire African continent," does not appear in the mimeographed text. It reflects the influence of Kwame Nkrumah and other Pan-African activists, whom Lumumba had met at the First All-African People's Conference in Accra, Ghana, in December 1958. The sentence is prophetic, in that the Congo crisis of 1960 was indeed a turning point in the struggle for African liberation. The position of various governments—pro- or anti-Lumumba—led to the split between the Casablanca group of radicals and the Monrovia group of moderates, a split that was papered over when the Organization of African Unity was created in 1963.

Winding up his speech, Lumumba begins paragraph 30 with the words "Your Majesty, Your Excellencies, Ladies and Gentlemen," which do not appear in the mimeographed text. Lumumba apparently added this reference to the presence of the Belgian king as he delivered

"*I ask all my friends, all of you who have fought unceasingly at our side, to make this thirtieth of June, 1960, an illustrious date that will be indelibly engraved upon your hearts, a date whose meaning you will teach your children with pride, so that they in turn will tell their children and their children's children the glorious story of our struggle for independence.*"

(Paragraph 3)

"*For though this independence of the Congo is today being proclaimed in a spirit of accord with Belgium, a friendly country with whom we are dealing as one equal with another, no Congolese worthy of the name can ever forget that we fought to win it.... It was a noble and just struggle, an indispensable struggle if we were to put an end to the humiliating slavery that had been forced upon us.*"

(Paragraph 4)

"*We have been the victims of ironic taunts, of insults, of blows that we were forced to endure morning, noon, and night because we were blacks. Who can forget that a black was addressed in the familiar form, not because he was a friend, certainly, but because the polite form of address was to be used only for whites?*"

(Paragraph 6)

"*Who can forget, finally, the burst of rifle fire in which so many of our brothers perished, the cells into which the authorities threw those who no longer were willing to submit to a rule where justice meant oppression and exploitation?*"

(Paragraph 11)

his message. In a rousing climax, he also extemporaneously added, "Long live independence and African unity!" before closing with "Long live the independent and sovereign Congo!"

Audience

Lumumba was addressing those present in the Palace of the Nation in Kinshasa, on Independence Day. The audience included the new political class of the Republic of Congo (deputies, senators, and ministers) but also key representatives of the former colonial power, including King Baudouin. Lumumba's speech is sometimes interpreted as a response to the paternalistic speech of King Baudouin. This cannot be literally true, since Lumumba prepared his speech and had it duplicated beforehand, when he had not yet heard what the king had to say. Clearly however, he could anticipate a paternalistic speech that glossed over the suffering of the Congolese.

Lumumba was also speaking to his rival, Joseph Kasavubu, elected president of Congo with the support of the deputies of the MNC-Lumumba. Lumumba considered Kasavubu to be a figurehead like a European constitutional monarch, and according to his adviser, Thomas Kanza, he was furious that the president had not consulted with the prime minister or even shared his text before delivering it.

Lumumba likewise was addressing the citizens of the vast former colony. His speech was recorded and broadcast over the radio. Finally, Lumumba clearly was speaking to future generations of Congolese. As he declared, June 30, 1960, must be "a date whose meaning you will teach your children with pride, so that they in turn will tell their children and their children's children the glorious story of our struggle for independence."

Impact

Lumumba's speech, however "shocking," was not the sole or even the principal cause of the Congo crisis of 1960. The principal cause was Belgian policy, which remained "no elites, no problems" until very late in the day. Once Belgian officials had decided that independence was inevitable, they opted for a neocolonial policy that would have permitted the Belgian companies and the Catholic Church (two of the three pillars of the colonial regime) to continue to operate as before. Nationalization of the economy and indigenization of the Church continued to be issues into the 1960s and 1970s.

The army mutinied largely because Belgium had refused to Africanize the officer corps. In response to the mutiny, Belgium sent in troops, ostensibly to protect Belgian lives. Many Congolese saw this action as aggression and perhaps even an attempt by Belgium to reoccupy its former colony. The United States soon became involved, seeing in Lumumba an African Fidel Castro (the Communist leader of Cuba) to be eliminated. The newly independent African countries divided over the Congo question and the person of Lumumba. The friends of Lumumba, led by Nkrumah of Ghana, Sékou Touré of Guinea, and others, formed the so-called Casablanca Group, whereas the "moderates" of the Monrovia Group supported Kasavubu and Tshombe. The split persisted for many years. Lumumba's speech had an enormous impact within Congo and beyond. Congolese tell of memorizing the speech and reciting it among friends. It is considered a founding text of Pan-Africanism.

Further Reading

■ Articles

Lemarchand, René. The C.I.A. in Africa: How Central? How Intelligent? *Journal of Modern African Studies* 14, no. 3 (September 1976): 401–426.

■ Books

Devlin, Larry. *Chief of Station, Congo: Fighting the Cold War in a Hot Zone.* New York: PublicAffairs, 2007.

Questions for Further Study

1. What role did ethnic differences play in the turmoil that surrounded Congolese independence? Why do you think these ethnic differences were so deeply rooted?

2. One of the chief issues surrounding Congolese independence was whether the nation should be organized and governed in a "centralist" or "federalist" fashion. What is the distinction between the two forms of government? In this regard, do you see any parallels between the Congo in the 1960s and the United States in the twenty-first century?

3. In the 1960s the cold war between the United States and its allies (the West) and the Soviet Union and its allies (the East) was at its height. Throughout this era, many wars, rebellions, and independence movements became proxy disputes between East and West. To what extent could the situation in the Congo be regarded as such a dispute? Why were the United States and the Soviets interested in the outcome of the dispute?

4. What is "Pan-Africanism"? In what way does Lumumba's speech reflect the principles of Pan-Africanism? With regard to this issue, why was Lumumba's speech considered divisive?

5. Imagine that you are Belgian King Baudouin and that you are seated behind Lumumba, listening to his speech. How do you think you would have reacted? If you had the opportunity, what response do you think you would make to Lumumba's speech?

De Witte, Ludo. *The Assassination of Lumumba*, trans. Ann Wright and Renée Fenby. New York: Verso, 2001.

Kalb, Madeleine G. *The Congo Cables: The Cold War in Africa—From Eisenhower to Kennedy*. New York: Macmillan, 1982.

Kanza, Thomas R. *The Rise and Fall of Patrice Lumumba: Conflict in the Congo*. Boston: G. K. Hall, 1979.

Nkrumah, Kwame. *Challenge of the Congo*. New York: International Publishers, 1967.

Nzongola-Ntalaja, Georges. *The Congo from Leopold to Kabila: A People's History*. London: Zed Books, 2002.

Turner, Thomas. "Crimes of the West in Democratic Congo: Reflections on Belgian Acceptance of 'Moral Responsibility' for the Death of Lumumba." In *Genocide, War Crimes and the West: History and Complicity*, ed. Adam Jones. London: Zed Books, 2004.

———. "The Congolese Revolution." In *Revolutionary Movements in World History: From 1750 to the Present*, Vol. 1, ed. James DeFronzo. Santa Barbara, Calif.: ABC-CLIO, 2006.

Van Lierde, Jean, ed. *Lumumba Speaks: The Speeches and Writings of Patrice Lumumba, 1958–1961*, trans. Helen R. Lane. Boston: Little, Brown, 1972.

Weissman, Stephen R. *American Foreign Policy in the Congo, 1960–1964*. Ithaca, N.Y.: Cornell University Press, 1974.

Young, Crawford. *The African Colonial State in Comparative Perspective*. New Haven, Conn.: Yale University Press, 1997.

—Thomas Turner

PATRICE LUMUMBA'S SPEECH AT THE PROCLAMATION OF CONGOLESE INDEPENDENCE

Congolese men and women:

As combatants for independence who today are victorious, I salute you in the name of the Congolese government.

I ask all my friends, all of you who have fought unceasingly at our side, to make this thirtieth of June, 1960, an illustrious date that will be indelibly engraved upon your hearts, a date whose meaning you will teach your children with pride, so that they in turn will tell their children and their children's children the glorious story of our struggle for freedom.

For though this independence of the Congo is today being proclaimed in a spirit of accord with Belgium, a friendly country with which we are dealing as one equal with another, no Congolese worthy of the name can ever forget that we fought to win it a fight waged each and every day, a passionate and idealistic fight, a fight in which there was not one effort, not one privation, not one suffering, not one drop of blood that we ever spared ourselves. We are proud of this struggle amid tears, fire, and blood, down to our very heart of hearts, for it was a noble and just struggle, an indispensable struggle if we were to put an end to the humiliating slavery that had been forced upon us.

The wounds that are the evidence of the fate we endured for eighty years under a colonialist regime are still too fresh and painful for us to be able to erase them from our memory. Back-breaking work has been exacted from us, in return for wages that did not allow us to satisfy our hunger, or to decently clothe or house ourselves, or to raise our children as creatures very dear to us.

We have been the victims of ironic taunts, of insults, of blows that we were forced to endure morning, noon, and night because we were blacks. Who can forget that a black was addressed in the familiar form, not because he was a friend, certainly, but because the polite form of address was to be used only for whites?

We have had our lands despoiled under the terms of what was supposedly the law of the land but was only a recognition of the right of the strongest.

We have known that the law was quite different for whites and blacks; it was most accommodating for the former, and cruel and inhuman for the latter.

We have known the atrocious sufferings of those banished to remote regions because of their political opinions or religious beliefs; exiles in their own country, their fate was truly worse than death.

We have known that there were magnificent mansions for whites in the cities and ramshackle straw hovels for blacks, that a black was never allowed into the so-called European movie theaters or restaurants or stores; that a black traveled in the hold of boats below the feet of the white in his deluxe cabin.

Who can forget, finally, the burst of rifle fire in which so many of our brothers perished, the cells into which the authorities threw those who no longer were willing to submit to a rule where justice meant oppression and exploitation?

We have grievously suffered all this, my brothers.

But we who have been chosen to govern our beloved country by the vote of your elected representatives, we whose bodies and souls have suffered from colonialist oppression, loudly proclaim: all this is over and done with now.

The Republic of the Congo has been proclaimed and our country is now in the hands of its own children.

We are going to begin another struggle together, my brothers, my sisters, a sublime struggle that will bring our country peace, prosperity, and grandeur.

We are going to institute social justice together and ensure everyone just remuneration for his labor.

We are going to show the world what the black man can do when, he works in freedom, and we are going to make the Congo the focal point for the development of all of Africa.

We are going to see to it that the soil of our country really benefits its children. We are going to review all the old laws and make new ones that will be just and noble.

We are going to put an end to the suppression of free thought and see to it that all citizens enjoy to the fullest all the fundamental freedoms laid down in the Declaration of the Rights of Man.

We are going to do away with any and every sort of discrimination and give each one the rightful place that his human dignity, his labor, and his devotion to the country will have earned him.

We are going to bring peace to the country, not the peace of rifles and bayonets, but the peace that comes from men's hearts and their good will.

And in order to achieve all this, dear compatriots, rest assured that we will be able to count not only on our tremendous strength and our immense riches, but also on the assistance of many foreign countries, whose collaboration we will always accept if it is sincere and does not seek to force any policy of any sort whatsoever on us.

In this regard, Belgium has finally realized what direction history was moving in and has not attempted to oppose our independence. She is ready to grant us her aid and her friendship, and a treaty to this effect has just been signed between our two equal and independent countries. I am certain that this cooperation will be beneficial to both countries. We for our part, though we shall continue to be vigilant, will respect all commitments freely made.

Thus the new Congo, our beloved republic that my government is going to create, will be a rich, free, and prosperous country, with regard to both its domestic relations and its foreign relations. But in order for us to reach this goal without delay, I ask all of you, Congolese legislators and citizens alike, to aid me with all the strength at your command.

I ask all of you to forget the trivial quarrels that are draining our strength and threaten to earn us the contempt of those in other countries.

I ask the parliamentary minority to aid my government by constructive opposition and to stay strictly within legal and democratic paths.

I ask all of you not to shrink from making any sacrifice necessary to ensure the success of our great undertaking.

I ask you, finally, to respect unconditionally the life and property of your fellow citizens and foreigners who have settled in our country. If the behavior of these foreigners leaves something to be desired, our justice will be swift and they will be expelled from the territory of the republic; if, on the other hand, they conduct themselves properly, they must be left in peace, for they too will be working for the prosperity of our country.

The independence of the Congo represents a decisive step toward the liberation of the entire African continent.

Your Majesty, Your Excellencies, Ladies and Gentlemen, my dear compatriots, my black brothers, my brothers in the struggle, that is what I wanted to say to you in the name of the government on this magnificent day of our complete and sovereign independence.

Our strong, national, popular government will be the salvation of this country.

I invite all Congolese citizens, men, women, and children, to set to work to create a prosperous national economy that will be the crowning proof of our economic independence.

Honor to those who fought for national freedom!
Long live independence and African unity!
Long live the independent and sovereign Congo!

Glossary

Declaration of the Rights of Man [and Citizen]	document drafted during the French Revolution, adopted as the preamble to the constitution in 1791 and setting forth the beliefs animating the new government: that all men were equal; that the people should rule; and that the rights to life, liberty, and security were inalienable
Your Majesty	King Baudouin of Belgium

"MAO TSE-TUNG'S THOUGHT IS THE TELESCOPE AND MICROSCOPE OF OUR REVOLUTIONARY CAUSE"

"The class enemy won't fall down, if you don't hit him."

Overview

The Great Proletarian Cultural Revolution (1966–1976), often referred to simply as the Cultural Revolution, was one of the most chaotic and tragic events in the history of modern China. Devised by the chairman of the Chinese Communist Party, Mao Zedong (also spelled Mao Tse-tung), the Cultural Revolution was ostensibly a campaign to rid the country of "capitalist roaders" who had used culture to promote bourgeois ideas. A capitalist roader in this context refers to those people who were supposedly harboring capitalist sentiments. In reality, the movement also became a means for Mao to remove his enemies from power.

Executing the Cultural Revolution consumed nearly all of China's resources. At first, Mao turned to powerful allies within the party for support. One such ally was Lin Biao, who was the head of the People's Liberation Army. Beginning in the 1960s, Lin emphasized the study of Mao Zedong Thought among China's soldiers. "Mao Zedong Thought" refers to the theoretical work of Mao Zedong. Mao had positioned himself as one of the foremost Marxist theoreticians of the twentieth century. The key ideas that he espoused were that the revolutionary potential of the peasant was equal to that of the factory worker and that "permanent revolution" (that is, the need to engage in class struggle even after a Communist revolution had taken place) was essential to protecting Communist governments against counterrevolution. During the 1950s, the relationship between China and the Soviet Union gradually worsened, and the two countries diverged in their Communist ideology. Mao then began to write about the danger of revisionist leaders in the Soviet Union and the threat that these leaders posed to China. Another important ally was Mao's wife, Jiang Qing, who was in charge of overseeing Chinese culture. Despite the support of Lin and Jiang, Mao soon realized that he needed to rally the Chinese masses.

In order to foster broad support, Mao and his allies used every possible resource, including the press, to promote a cultish allegiance to him and the Cultural Revolution. In the spring and summer of 1966, countless editorials extolling the Cultural Revolution appeared in some of China's most important newspapers. One such editorial, titled "Mao Tse-tung's Thought Is the Telescope and Microscope of Our Revolutionary Cause," was published on June 7, 1966, in *People's Liberation Army Daily* (*Jiefangjun Bao*) and captured the essence of the early days of the Cultural Revolution. This editorial and others like it were significant for three reasons. First, they helped whip up the public, especially Chinese students, into revolutionary frenzy. Beginning in 1966, students quit school and voluntarily formed Red Guard units. They began to gather in Beijing's Tiananmen Square, clamoring to catch a glimpse of Chairman Mao. Second, these editorials laid out the goals of the Cultural Revolution and helped set the tone for the movement. This article and others like it also justified the students' turn toward violence. Finally, the string of editorials published in 1966 represented a major victory for Mao and his allies over the Chinese bureaucracy. For nearly six months, the party bureaucracy had largely stifled any discussion of the Cultural Revolution. The publication of these editorials, however, thrust the Cultural Revolution into the public spotlight and made the public fully aware of this new revolutionary movement.

Context

The Chinese civil war began at the conclusion of World War II and ended in 1949. During World War II the Communists temporarily allied themselves with the ruling Nationalist government in order to fight the Japanese (who had invaded China in 1937). However, at the end of World War II, fighting between the Nationalists and the Communists began almost immediately. After a protracted war, the Communists captured Beijing and established the People's Republic of China, while the Nationalist government fled to Taiwan. Despite being outmanned and facing a major tactical disadvantage, the Communists were victorious in the civil war owing to a combination of the Nationalist government's extreme corruption and their inability to stabilize the economy after World War II, as well as the Communist Party's ability to appeal to the countryside and to recruit the peasantry to their cause.

1960

- After several years of increased tension between China and the Soviet Union, China declares that it will no longer consult the Soviet Union on international affairs, effectively signifying the end of the relationship between the two Communist countries.

- The Great Leap Forward comes to a tragic end. Liu Shaoqi and Deng Xiaoping are given the task of fixing China's decimated economy.

1962

- Mao initiates the Socialist Education Movement. The campaign, intended to eliminate revisionists and prevent the Communist Party's complete bureaucratization, is largely muted by Communist officials.

1965

- **November 10** Yao Wenyuan publishes "On the New Historical Play *Hai Rui Dismissed from Office*" in Shanghai. The editorial heavily criticizes Wu Han and deems his play a veiled attack on Mao Zedong.

By the early 1960s the Communist Party had been in control of China for more than a decade. These initial years of Communist rule produced mixed results. Since seizing control of the country in 1949, the Communist Party had curbed the rampant inflation that had plagued the economy for many years and had increased industrialization. But repressive movements like the Anti-Rightist Campaign had suppressed many of the party's alleged critics. Of these repressive and brutal movements, the so-called Great Leap Forward proved to be the most disastrous. One of the leading advocates of the Great Leap Forward was Mao Zedong. Mao believed that the Great Leap, implemented in 1958, would vastly increase industrial production and thus stimulate the Chinese economy. However, poor harvests due to bad weather, obfuscation of statistics to support false claims of record-setting harvests, and general neglect from the central government soon resulted in catastrophe. Not wanting to face the wrath of the Communist Party, many officials had simply lied about how much was being produced in the countryside. As a result, the central government collected taxes based on inflated statistics, thereby taking more crops from the countryside and leaving the peasants with very little to eat. The central government, and especially Mao, refused to recognize the extent of the famine or the disaster of the Great Leap Forward, even when warned by colleagues. It is estimated that between 1959 and 1961 more than 20 million people died of famine as a result of the overall policies of the Great Leap Forward.

Mao's prestige was greatly diminished because of the failure of the Great Leap Forward. In 1959 he decided to step away from the day-to-day operations of the government, in favor of Liu Shaoqi, who had been chairman of the standing committee of the People's National Congress. After the Great Leap Forward ended, Liu and his colleague Deng Xiaoping were made responsible for restoring the damage that had been done to the Chinese economy. New policies that included incentives to individual farmers proved successful, and the economy began to recover. In encouraging recovery, however, Liu and Deng had to abandon some of Mao's preferred economic programs.

Mao was greatly alarmed by Liu and Deng's actions. He feared that these two men would destroy the revolution and the Communist Party that he had worked his entire life to build. China's increasingly tenuous relationship with the Soviet Union heightened this concern. Despite being China's primary ally, the two countries had clashed in the late 1950s over ideological differences. One of the many reasons for this clash centered on the policies of Nikita Khrushchev, who had become the first secretary of the Soviet Communist Party after Joseph Stalin's death in 1953 and premier of the Soviet Union in 1958. Mao's relationship with Khrushchev began to sour in 1956, when Khrushchev gave a speech condemning some Stalinist policies. Mao greatly admired Stalin and was outraged that Khrushchev had launched such an attack. Relations worsened when Khrushchev harshly criticized the Great Leap Forward and declared that the Communist and capitalist worlds could peacefully coexist. For Mao, Khrushchev had hijacked the Communist Party in the Soviet Union, and he thus represented the worst kind of revisionist leader. Mao believed that if revisionists could gain control in the Soviet Union, they could also make significant inroads in China. One of the main goals of the Cultural Revolution was to expose all revisionists in the Chinese government who, like Khrushchev, had betrayed the Communist cause.

After observing developments in the Soviet Union, Mao attempted to reassert his power at home. He launched the Socialist Education Movement in 1962, hoping that it would reinvigorate the masses and return to him the prestige that he had lost during the Great Leap Forward. The campaign, however, produced mixed results, frustrating Mao. Mao's cult of personality had grown in appeal during the Socialist Education Movement, though an apathetic party apparatus had kept the movement largely in check. By 1965 Mao realized that if he wanted to reassert his power over the party and the country, he would need to circumvent the bureaucracy and take his appeal directly to the people.

This appeal to the masses manifested itself as the Cultural Revolution. Mao's primary goals for launching the Cultural Revolution were straightforward: He meant to regain his control over Chinese politics by promoting his thought while simultaneously urging the masses to expose all those enemies who had supposedly adopted a capitalist and revisionist mindset. The opening salvos of the Cultural Revolution were fired in 1965. Mao and Jiang Qing both felt that hidden enemies in China were furtively using culture to attack him and restore capitalism. Jiang instructed Yao Wenyuan, a writer in Shanghai, to draft an editorial condemning the play by Wu Han titled *Hai Rui Dismissed from Office*, which she believed was especially critical of Mao. Wu Han's historical play centered on an official who had criticized the emperor during a brutal famine; although it was set in ancient China, the plot appeared to make reference to Mao's policies during the Great Leap Forward.

To Mao's chagrin, the party barely reacted to Yao's editorial, which sharply critiqued the play. Many Communist officials considered discussion of Wu Han's play to be an academic topic rather than a matter for political debate. In the spring of 1966, however, the discourse surrounding the Cultural Revolution began to change. The army became more involved, and media attacks on Wu Han grew increasingly antagonistic and political. In April, Peng Zhen, the mayor of Beijing, and four other prominent officials were accused of having suppressed the Cultural Revolution and were replaced with officials who strongly supported Mao's policies. With Mao's supporters now in several top positions in the government and the media, a plethora of editorials were published in promotion of the Cultural Revolution and the supremacy of Mao Zedong Thought. These editorials were a direct appeal by Mao and his allies to the masses, urging them to take up the cause of the Cultural Revolution.

Editorials like "Mao Tse-tung's Thought Is the Telescope and Microscope of Our Revolutionary Cause," published in the *People's Liberation Army Daily* on June 7, 1966, not only set the tone for the movement but also represented the beginning of mass participation in the Cultur-

Time Line

1966

- **April**
  Five high-ranking Communist officials, including Peng Zhen, the mayor of Beijing, are criticized and purged from the party; their removal paves the way for a rash of editorials praising Mao Zedong Thought and the Cultural Revolution.

- **May 25**
  Nie Yuanzi and seven classmates at Beijing University hang the Cultural Revolution's first big-character poster, which claims that university officials secretly harbor bourgeois tendencies and have suppressed the students.

- **June 7**
  "Mao Tse-tung's Thought Is the Telescope and Microscope of Our Revolutionary Cause" appears in the *People's Liberation Army Daily*.

- **August 10–20**
  Liu Shaoqi is publicly criticized for having suppressed the student movement and the Cultural Revolution and is stripped of most of his power. Lin Biao, who has promoted Mao's cult since the beginning of the Cultural Revolution, is chosen as Mao's successor.

1971

- **September 13**
  In the wake of the deterioration of his relationship with Mao and accusations of having conspired to take over the government, Lin Biao attempts to flee China; his plane crashes in Mongolia, and he is killed.

1976

- **September 9**
  Mao Zedong dies. Before his death, he appoints Hua Guofeng as his successor.

- **October 6**
  The "Gang of Four," which includes Jiang Qing and Yao Wenyuan, is arrested and subsequently accused of having tried to usurp power. Their arrest signals an unofficial end to the Cultural Revolution.

1981

- **June**
  At the Sixth Plenum of the Chinese Communist Party, party members issue an official assessment of the Mao Zedong era. Although Mao is widely praised for his accomplishments, he is also criticized for several mistakes, including the Cultural Revolution.

power. Lin Biao, who had promoted Mao's cult since the beginning of the Cultural Revolution, was chosen as the future successor to Mao.

About the Author

Articles and editorials published in China's major newspapers during the Cultural Revolution were usually of murky authorship. In 1966 Xiao Hua was the chief of the political department at the *People's Liberation Army Daily*. Although Xiao exerted control over the newspaper, he also followed directives from above, most originating from the Cultural Revolution Small Group (CRSG). At the beginning of the Cultural Revolution, Mao had been extremely frustrated with the Propaganda Department and its failure to spread the ideology of the Cultural Revolution. He eventually removed nine top members of the department but spared his trusted ally, Chen Boda, who was also in charge of the CRSG. Chen's survival meant that the CRSG and the Propaganda Department were permanently fused. The unadulterated word of the CRSG found its way into every Chinese newspaper. Because of its connection to the military and its prominence in Chinese society, the *People's Liberation Army Daily* in particular played a central role in spreading the ideas of the Cultural Revolution. It was one of the first newspapers to use some of the vocabulary that would dominate the movement. Because of the connection between Chen Boda, the CRSG, and the country's newspapers, propagandist editorials thrived during the Cultural Revolution and brought Mao Zedong Thought and the ideology of the movement to the masses.

Explanation and Analysis of the Document

Perhaps the most shocking aspect of the Cultural Revolution was the ferocity with which China's students worshipped Mao Zedong. Editorials such as "Mao Tse-tung's Thought Is the Telescope and Microscope of Our Revolutionary Cause" were filled with the highest praise of Mao, promoting a quasi-religious worship of him and ensuring that his words and ideas would guide the Cultural Revolution. The document's title and the language used throughout suggest just how important Mao's words were to the participants of the Cultural Revolution. Notice how the editorial describes Mao Zedong Thought as the "telescope and microscope" of the revolution, suggesting that Maoism could resolve both major and minor problems. Since this editorial was written at the beginning of the Cultural Revolution, it established the movement's nearly limitless boundaries; participants were to not only confront China's major problems (use the telescope, figuratively speaking) but also examine the microscopic details of their lives to make sure that they were living in conformity with Maoist ideals. Mao Zedong Thought was to be used to scrutinize top party leaders as well as teachers, parents, classmates, and even oneself.

al Revolution. Such editorials ensured that China's bureaucrats and allegedly revisionist leaders would not stifle the Cultural Revolution, as they had the Socialist Education Movement. These editorials also made it abundantly clear what was required of participants in the Cultural Revolution: Only by studying and applying Mao Zedong Thought could the new revolutionary cause succeed. Students, in particular, took notice of this message and responded with at times brutal ferocity. In May of 1966, Nie Yuanzi and seven classmates at Beijing University hung the Cultural Revolution's first big-character poster, which claimed that university officials secretly harbored bourgeois tendencies and suppressed the students. Such posters in public settings were used to voice a person's or group's opinion about a certain issue, criticizing a particular target or showing their support for Mao Zedong or the Cultural Revolution. Throughout Beijing, students soon followed Nie's example and hung their own posters in public. These large, handwritten posters quickly became a staple of the Cultural Revolution. In August of 1966, Liu Shaoqi was publicly criticized for having suppressed the student movement and the Cultural Revolution and was stripped of most of his

Mao Zedong, standing in the lead car, reviews the Red Guards in Beijing, October 19, 1966. (AP/Wide World Photos)

◆ **Paragraphs 1–3**

The editorial begins by clarifying exactly how the Cultural Revolution was to be carried out. The message is unequivocal: Participants in the revolution should follow Mao Zedong Thought. The stated revolutionary goal, "to sweep away all monsters," was a phrase commonly used during the movement, though it is somewhat ambiguous in meaning. Mao did not always identify exactly who those monsters were. This gave revolutionary students some autonomy, but it also led to the persecution of many innocent people during the Cultural Revolution. The second paragraph continues the theme that Mao Zedong Thought is the only true weapon of the Cultural Revolution. The language becomes slightly more aggressive here, urging readers to "attack boldly and seize victory," which suggests that daring actions would be necessary in the Cultural Revolution. More often than not, such language justified the use of violence.

The maxim of Mao quoted at the beginning of the third paragraph epitomizes the Cultural Revolution, playing further on the theme of those who opposed the government. It begins: "After the enemies with guns have been wiped out, there will still be enemies without guns." Although Mao and the Communist Party had taken control of the country almost twenty years prior to the Cultural Revolution, China's domestic enemies still abounded. These "enemies" were often poorly defined. From Mao's perspective, enemies ranged from capitalist roaders—those who secret-

ly harbored capitalist tendencies—to revisionists who no longer supported Mao's radical brand of Communism. The sentence would perhaps better read that "Mao believed that China's domestic enemies abounded." Mao thought that his enemies and the enemies of the Communist Party had not yet been eliminated and were poised for counterrevolution. For students, however, identifying enemies was a much more nebulous process. Ostensibly, "enemies" referred to all those in Chinese society who opposed Mao Zedong and who had undermined the Communist Party. However, in the chaos of the Cultural Revolution, students often sought revenge against those who had wronged them in the past and named these people as the "enemies" of the Cultural Revolution.

The editorial instructs participants in the revolution to expose enemies, some of whom may have been hiding within the ranks of the Chinese Communist Party. These enemies, while seeming to serve the Communist cause, supposedly harbored capitalist, revisionist sentiments and subscribed to the so-called black line. The "black line," another phrase frequently used during the Cultural Revolution, describes those who harbored secret anti-party, anti–Mao Zedong ideas. These alleged foes of the Cultural Revolution are also characterized as opposing "the red flag by hoisting the red flag," referring to the flag of China. Once again, the editorial emphasizes that enemies of the Cultural Revolution could be anywhere and that participants in the movement should be suspicious even of seeming supporters of the party and Mao's policies.

◆ **Paragraphs 4 and 5**

Paragraph 4 reinforces the assertion that China's enemies could be hidden among the Communist Party's supporters. Such stark and distinct language suggests that participants in the revolution should not be afraid to criticize high officials, something that was not often done in Communist China. In many ways this paragraph laid the groundwork for the attacks on figures such as Liu Shaoqi and Deng Xiaoping. Before the Cultural Revolution, it had been unimaginable that these highly credentialed Communists, two of China's most powerful leaders, could come under such intense scrutiny. Nevertheless, soon after the Cultural Revolution began, Liu and Deng were accused of being revisionists and secret enemies of the party.

The enemies of the state are said to be "wolves in sheep's clothing and man-eating tigers with smiling faces." *Tigers* and *wolves* are commonly used expressions in Chinese and reflect a linguistic characteristic rather than imagery that was distinct to the Cultural Revolution. These animals were used to describe any person or country that was particularly aggressive or cunning. In this case, the "tigers" and "wolves" probably refer to capitalist roaders in China and to revisionists in the Soviet Union. They also refer to officials in China who claimed to believe in Communism but had largely abandoned the ideas of Mao Zedong Thought.

The document's fifth paragraph attempts to resolve an important question: How will participants in the Cultural Revolution distinguish between the party's real allies and enemies who pose as friends? The answer is for participants to be grounded in Mao Zedong Thought. The editorial declares that Mao's "methodology of dialectical materialism and historical materialism" offers the ideological tools necessary to conduct the Cultural Revolution. In hindsight, the ideas expressed in this paragraph (and, indeed, throughout the essay) would prove disastrous and incite a great deal of violence. Despite making the statement that Mao Zedong Thought should guide the Cultural Revolution, the editorial fails to address the breadth and range of Mao's work or the possibility that participants could interpret it in different ways. During the revolution, when two student groups with opposing ideas about Mao Zedong Thought confronted each other, they rarely hesitated to use violence to resolve their differences. Student factionalism was one of the main sources of violence during the Cultural Revolution.

◆ **Paragraph 6**

This paragraph makes direct reference to Chinese culture, asserting that the resurgent bourgeoisie have used the theater, film, radio, academic publications, and a host of other media to infiltrate Communist China. An underlying theme is the need to reinvigorate a new generation of revolutionaries in China. In the 1960s many high officials had become concerned that the generation of workers, soldiers, and students born after the Communist Revolution in 1949 did not have the revolutionary acumen to continue what Mao and others had started. Here the editorial reminds this new generation that the Communist state and its citizens always need to be vigilant and that capitalists within the government could take over at any time. China's youth, the editorial exhorts, must recommit themselves to studying Mao Zedong Thought and to Mao's revolutionary cause by participating in the Cultural Revolution.

◆ **Paragraph 7**

The seventh paragraph alludes to the bitter struggle that had erupted in the early 1960s between China and the Soviet Union. The editorial here condemns revisionism. Revisionists were those within the Communist Party who had lost their revolutionary zeal and were no longer committed to the revolutionary cause. This fear of revisionism came primarily from events that had occurred within the Soviet Union in the 1950s and early 1960s. Mao thought that Nikita Khrushchev, the premier of the Soviet Union, was the worst kind of revisionist and that he was leading his country away from Communism toward capitalism. Mao's fear that this could happen in China infused the Cultural Revolution. This paragraph also lifts up Mao as the true inheritor of the legacy of Karl Marx and Vladimir Lenin, two of the world's leading Communist theoreticians. During the Cultural Revolution, Mao wanted not only to reassert his control of the Communist Party in China but also to establish himself as the world's premier Communist leader. To accomplish these goals, however, he had to eliminate revisionists and demonstrate China's superiority over the Soviet Union. Perhaps no other factors better explained the "why" of the Cultural Revolution than the Sino-Soviet split and Mao's fear of revisionism.

◆ **Paragraphs 8 and 9**

The editorial goes on to encourage revolutionaries to destroy the "four olds"—old ideas, customs, culture, and habits. During the Cultural Revolution, officials like Lin Biao continually urged students to destroy cultural artifacts that in some way embodied the "four olds." This campaign originated in the belief that the Chinese people needed to abandon "ancient superstitions" like Buddhism and Confucianism so that China could progress and Communism as espoused by Mao could succeed. As a consequence, the Red Guards tore down, burned, or destroyed some of China's most treasured religious sites and cultural objects.

Paragraph 9 demonstrates the Manichaean nature of the Cultural Revolution. Mao and his allies viewed the Cultural Revolution in black-and-white terms. Either you were an ally of the party and a true revolutionary, or you were an enemy and therefore should be criticized and attacked. Once the Red Guards had been unleashed on the Chinese population, they adopted this same attitude. Many Red Guard contingents did not abide explanation or nuance. Whenever they determined someone to be an enemy of Mao

Teachers and students march in support of the Cultural Revolution. (AP/Wide World Photos)

Zedong Thought, he or she was ruthlessly persecuted, often with tragic results. The editorial unequivocally states that the true revolutionary will follow Mao Zedong Thought and that anyone who slanders or even questions the wisdom of Mao is to be considered an enemy of the party.

◆ Paragraph 10

The last paragraph reasserts the editorial's main themes. It plainly states that the task of the true revolutionary remained unfinished. Although the Communists had been victorious in the civil war in 1949, enemies of the party had managed to infiltrate every level of Chinese society, the article claims. Therefore, the people were urged to arm themselves with Mao Zedong Thought and confront these enemies. The editorial insinuates that the people's search for enemies should be relentless and the methods used to root them out draconian. The Cultural Revolution was to be a battle for the survival of the People's Republic of China; only by arming themselves with Mao Zedong Thought and recommitting themselves to the revolution could the people hope for victory.

In this paragraph, too, mention is made of "the preparations to smash aggressive war by U.S. imperialism." Smash-

ing U.S. imperialism was a phrase evoked constantly by the Communist government, particularly after the Korean War (1950–1953). The Chinese government resented America's presence in East Asia as well as the U.S. commitment to protect Taiwan should the Communist Party make good on their threat to invade the island.

The editorial concludes by stating that "Chairman Mao is the radiant sun lighting our minds. Mao Tse-tung's thought is our lifeline." Mao was referred to as the "radiant sun" throughout the Cultural Revolution. In many ways, the Cultural Revolution was an attempt to reestablish Mao's predominance in Chinese society, which had declined since the Great Leap Forward. In so doing, the Communist government fostered the "cult of Mao." The Cultural Revolution was therefore filled with language that was meant to evoke Mao's power and prestige in Chinese society. Mao was often presented as infallible and the guiding light in China's struggle to establish a Communist utopia. Mao worship was one of the primary reasons for the violence of the Cultural Revolution. Students so believed in the truth of Mao Zedong Thought that they were willing to abuse and even murder anyone whom they thought opposed his ideas.

> "Mao Tse-tung's thought is our political orientation, the highest instruction for our actions; it is our ideological and political telescope and microscope for observing and analysing all things. In this unprecedented great cultural revolution, we should apply Mao Tse-tung's thought to observe, analyse and transform everything."
>
> (Paragraph 2)

> "Tigers with smiling faces are ten times more ferocious than tigers with their fangs bared and their claws sticking out. Sugar-coated bullets are ten times more destructive than real bullets. A fortress is most vulnerable when attacked from within."
>
> (Paragraph 4)

> "The representatives of the bourgeoisie, by using their position and power, usurped and controlled the leadership of a number of departments, did all they could to spread bourgeois and revisionist poison through the media of literature, the theatre, films, music, the arts, the press, periodicals, the radio, publications and academic research and in schools."
>
> (Paragraph 6)

> "The class enemy won't fall down, if you don't hit him. He still tries to rise to his feet after he has fallen. When one black line is eliminated, another appears."
>
> (Paragraph 10)

Audience

Despite publication in the *People's Liberation Army Daily*, the editorial was directed at a wider audience than the army; a broad cross-section of the Chinese population read it. The editorial specifically made reference to workers, peasants, and soldiers, and it urged them to take up the cause of the Cultural Revolution. Generally, however, Mao and his allies wanted to spur the entire population to action. Interestingly, the editorial does not specifically mention students, likely because the party had not yet officially sanctioned the students' actions in Beijing. Nie Yuanzi's first big-character poster had appeared only two weeks before the publication of this

article, and work teams were still in control of many college campuses. However, once students had received Mao's endorsement, they became the ones to put the editorial's words into action.

Student fervor during the Cultural Revolution was overwhelming. Because of editorials such as this one, Mao became a quasi-religious figure. The chant "Long live Chairman Mao!" echoed throughout much of the Cultural Revolution, and most students were never without their personal copies of *The Quotations of Chairman Mao Zedong*. That many students treated Mao like a deity also may help to explain some of the violence of the movement. As this editorial prescribed, Mao's words and his revolutionary thought were to guide the Cultural Revolution participants. In the end, the cult of Mao made Red Guard fanaticism all the more acute.

Impact

There is no other way to begin a discussion of the Cultural Revolution's impact than by focusing on the many victims of the movement. It has been estimated that nearly two million people died in the ten years of the Cultural Revolution. Much of this was the result of the philosophy epitomized in this editorial and its adoption by a generation of students. Soon after this article appeared, Mao endorsed the students as the main purveyors of the Cultural Revolution and allowed them a great deal of autonomy. The Red Guards roamed the country, criticizing, attacking, and humiliating their enemies. Many officials turned a blind eye when these types of attacks became violent, fearing that they would become the Red Guards' next target. Mao himself was eager to expunge his enemies from the party, and if the Red Guards used violence in the process he seemed willing to accept their excesses. The result was that countless people faced physical and psychological abuse at the hands of the Red Guards.

The Cultural Revolution also had a tremendous political impact on China. Zhou Enlai's death in 1976 and the subsequent outpouring of emotion indicated that many Chinese had been greatly disheartened by the extreme policies of the Cultural Revolution. Zhou, who had served as Mao's prime minister and foreign minister, had always been perceived as a moderate during the Cultural Revolution, and

his death was used as an opportunity for the masses to express their frustration with the extremist policies of the past decade. When Hua Guofeng succeeded Mao, he attempted to curb some of these radical policies. In the fall of 1976, only weeks after Mao's death, he ordered the arrest of the "Gang of Four"—Jiang Qing and Yao Wenyuan having been two of the four—who had been the most vocal proponents of the Cultural Revolution. All four were found guilty of numerous crimes committed during the Cultural Revolution. The arrest of the Gang of Four, however, was not enough to ensure Hua's political survival. Officials grew weary of Hua's claim that more cultural revolutions would be needed in the future. Fearing that Hua would continue Mao's extreme policies, many in the party turned to Deng Xiaoping, who himself had been criticized and suffered greatly during the Cultural Revolution. Because he was a victim of the movement, he seemed the perfect fit to lead China away from the policies of the Cultural Revolution and to ensure that such an event would never occur again.

The long-term consequences of the Cultural Revolution are still being felt today. Upon coming to power, Deng Xiaoping abandoned some of Mao's most extreme policies. The party, too, was transformed. Fearing that another campaign akin to the Cultural Revolution would permanently destroy the party, many officials began to advocate for a change of direction. This included a move toward a more capitalist economy. Such a transformation allowed China's economy to grow at an astonishing rate. Although there are many reasons for this economic growth, there is little doubt that China's capitalist transformation was partially precipitated by the memories of the Cultural Revolution,

Questions for Further Study

1. This document was written in 1966. The year 1927 saw the publication of Mao Zedong's "Report on an Investigation of the Peasant Movement in Hunan." What differences do you see in these two documents?

2. To what extent, if any, does the Constitution of the People's Republic of China, written in 1982, reject (or accept) any of the principles articulated in "Mao Tse-tung's Thought"?

3. Examine the document as a piece of propaganda. What rhetorical devices does the author use to foster sentiment for "Mao Tse-tung's Thought"? Why do you think the Chinese people were so enthusiastic about the message contained in the document?

4. How were Mao and his associates able to use the press to advance their goals? Why was it important for them to do so? To what extent do contemporary American politicians similarly enlist the support of the press in the furtherance of their agendas?

5. After the Communists took power in China, Western politicians and military planners feared a "monolithic" Communist movement whereby the Soviet bloc and China would become allies and overwhelm the West. The alliance never really happened. Why?

which represented the worst of Mao's extreme brand of Communism. In 1981, at the Sixth Plenum of the Chinese Communist Party, party members issued an official assessment of the Mao Zedong era. Although he was widely praised for his accomplishments, he was also criticized for several mistakes, including the Cultural Revolution. Today, the Cultural Revolution is often referred to as the "ten years of madness" or the "forgotten years." Such sentiments suggest that many in China are determined never again to return to the chaos of that terrible decade.

Further Reading

■ Articles
Lee, Hong Yung. "The Radical Students in Kwangtung during the Cultural Revolution." *China Quarterly* 64 (December 1975): 645–683.

Walder, Andrew "Beijing Red Guard Factionalism: Social Interpretations Reconsidered." *Journal of Asian Studies* 61, no. 2 (May 2002): 437–471.

■ Books
Clark, Paul. *The Chinese Cultural Revolution: A History.* New York: Cambridge University Press, 2008.

Hinton, William. *Hundred Day War: The Cultural Revolution at Tsinghua University.* New York: Monthly Review Press, 1972.

MacFarquhar, Roderick, and Michael Schoenhals. *Mao's Last Revolution.* Cambridge, Mass.: Belknap Press of Harvard University Press, 2006.

Perry, Elizabeth, and Li Xun. *Proletarian Power: Shanghai in the Cultural Revolution.* Boulder, Colo.: Westview Press, 1997.

———. "Revolutionary Rudeness: The Language of Red Guards and Rebel Workers in China's Cultural Revolution." In *Twentieth-century China: New Approaches*, ed. Jeffrey N. Wasserstrom. New York: Routledge, 2003.

White, Lynn T. *Policies of Chaos: The Organizational Causes of Violence in China's Cultural Revolution.* Princeton, N.J.: Princeton University Press, 1986.

Yang, Rae. *Spider Eaters: A Memoir.* Berkeley: University of California Press, 1997.

—Zachary A. Scarlett

"MAO TSE-TUNG'S THOUGHT IS THE TELESCOPE AND MICROSCOPE OF OUR REVOLUTIONARY CAUSE"

The current great socialist cultural revolution is a great revolution to sweep away all monsters and a great revolution that remoulds the ideology of people and touches their souls. What weapon should be used to sweep away all monsters? What ideology should be applied to arm people's minds and remould their souls? The most powerful ideological weapon, the only one, is the great Mao Tse-tung's thought.

Mao Tse-tung's thought is our political orientation, the highest instruction for our actions; it is our ideological and political telescope and microscope for observing and analysing all things. In this unprecedented great cultural revolution, we should apply Mao Tse-tung's thought to observe, analyse and transform everything, and, in a word, put it in command of everything. We should apply Mao Tse-tung's thought to attack boldly and seize victory.

Chairman Mao teaches us: "After the enemies with guns have been wiped out, there will still be enemies without guns; they are bound to struggle desperately against us; we must never regard these enemies lightly." Our struggle against the anti-Party, anti-socialist black line and gangsters is a mighty, life-and-death class struggle. The enemies without guns are more hidden, cunning, sinister and vicious than the enemies with guns. The representatives of the bourgeoisie and all monsters, including the modern revisionists, often oppose the red flag by hoisting a red flag and oppose Marxism-Leninism and Mao Tse-tung's thought under the cloak of Marxism-Leninism and Mao Tse-tung's thought when they attack the Party and socialism, because Marxism-Leninism and Mao Tse-tung's thought are becoming more popular day by day, the prestige of our Party and Chairman Mao are incomparably high and the dictatorship of the proletariat of our country is becoming more consolidated. These are the tactics that the revisionists always use in opposing Marxism-Leninism. This is a new characteristic of the class struggle under the conditions of the dictatorship of the proletariat.

The many facts exposed during the great cultural revolution show us more clearly that the anti-Party and anti-socialist elements are all careerists, schemers and hypocrites of the exploiting classes. They are double-dealing. They feign compliance while acting in opposition. They appear to be men but are demons at heart. They speak human language to your face, but talk devil's language behind your back. They are wolves in sheep's clothing and man-eating tigers with smiling faces. They often use the phrases of Marxism-Leninism and Mao Tse-tung's thought as a cover while greatly publicizing diametrically opposed views behind the word "but" and smuggling in bourgeois and revisionist stuff. The enemies holding a false red banner are ten times more vicious than enemies holding a white banner. Wolves in sheep's clothing are ten times more sinister than ordinary wolves. Tigers with smiling faces are ten times more ferocious than tigers with their fangs bared and their claws sticking out. Sugar-coated bullets are ten times more destructive than real bullets. A fortress is most vulnerable when attacked from within. Enemies who have wormed their way into our ranks are far more dangerous than enemies operating in the open. We must give this serious attention and be highly vigilant.

In such a very complicated and acute class struggle, how are we to draw a clear-cut line between the enemy and ourselves and maintain a firm stand? How are we to distinguish between revolutionaries and counter-revolutionaries, genuine revolutionaries and sham revolutionaries, and Marxism-Leninism and revisionism? We must master Mao Tse-tung's thought, the powerful ideological weapon, and use it as a telescope and a microscope to observe all matters. With the invincible Mao Tse-tung's thought, with the scientific world outlook and methodology of dialectical materialism and historical materialism which have been developed by Chairman Mao, and with the sharp weapon of Chairman Mao's theory of classes and class struggle, we have the highest criterion for judging right and wrong. We are able to penetrate deeply into all things and to recognize the whole through observation of the part. We can see the essence behind outward appearance, and clear away the miasma to achieve profound insight into things and thus monsters of all sorts will be unable to hide themselves. We can stand on an eminence, become far-sighted and view the whole situation, the future and the great significance and far-reaching influence of the great socialist cultural revolution. We can advance without the slightest fear and stand in the forefront of the great socialist cultural revolution.

Chairman Mao teaches us: "The proletariat seeks to transform the world according to its own world outlook, so does the bourgeoisie." In the sharp clash between the two world outlooks, either you crush me, or I crush you. It will not do to sit on the fence; there is no middle road. The overthrown bourgeoisie, in their plots for restoration and subversion, always give first place to ideology, take hold of ideology and the superstructure. The representatives of the bourgeoisie, by using their position and power, usurped and controlled the leadership of a number of departments, did all they could to spread bourgeois and revisionist poison through the media of literature, the theatre, films, music, the arts, the press, periodicals, the radio, publications and academic research and in schools, etc., in an attempt to corrupt people's minds and perpetrate "peaceful evolution" as ideological preparation and preparation of public opinion for capitalist restoration. If our proletarian ideology does not take over the position, then the bourgeois ideology will have free rein; it will gradually nibble away and chew you up bit by bit. Once proletarian ideology gives way, so will the superstructure and the economic base and this means the restoration of capitalism. Therefore, we must arm our minds with Mao Tse-tung's thought and establish a firm proletarian world outlook. We must use the great Mao Tse-tung's thought to fight and completely destroy the bourgeois ideological and cultural positions.

Mao Tse-tung's thought is the acme of Marxism-Leninism in the present era. It is living Marxism-Leninism at its highest. It is the powerful, invincible weapon of the Chinese people, and it is also a powerful invincible weapon of the revolutionary people the world over. Mao Tse-tung's thought has proved to be invincible truth through the practice of China's democratic revolution, socialist revolution and socialist construction, and through the struggle in the international sphere against U.S. imperialism and its lackeys and against Khrushchev revisionism. Chairman Mao has, with the gifts of genius, creatively and comprehensively developed Marxism-Leninism. Basing himself on the fundamental theses of Marxism-Leninism, Chairman Mao has summed up the experience of the practice of the Chinese revolution and the world revolution, and the painful lesson of the usurpation of the leadership of the Party and the state of the Soviet Union by the modern revisionist clique, systematically put forward the theory concerning classes, class contradictions and class struggle that exist in socialist society, greatly enriched and developed the Marxist-Leninist theory on the dictatorship of the proletariat, and put forward a series of wise policies aimed at opposing and preventing revisionism and the restoration of capitalism. All this ensures that our country will always maintain its revolutionary spirit and never change its colour, and it is of extremely great theoretical and practical significance to the revolutionary cause of the international proletariat. Every sentence by Chairman Mao is truth, and carries more weight than ten thousand ordinary sentences. As the Chinese people master Mao Tse-tung's thought, China will be prosperous and ever-victorious. Once the world's people master Mao Tse-tung's thought which is living Marxism-Leninism, they are sure to win their emancipation, bury imperialism, modern revisionism and all reactionaries lock, stock and barrel, and realize communism throughout the world step by step.

The most fundamental task in the great socialist cultural revolution in our country is to eliminate thoroughly the old ideology and culture, the old customs and habits which were fostered by all the exploiting classes for thousands of years to poison the minds of the people, and to create and form an entirely new, proletarian ideology and culture, new customs and habits among the masses of the people. This is to creatively study and apply Mao Tse-tung's thought in tempestuous class struggle, popularize it and let it become closely integrated with the masses of workers, peasants and soldiers. Once the masses grasp it, Mao Tse-tung's thought will be transformed into a mighty material force. Facts show that those armed with Mao Tse-tung's thought are the bravest, wisest, most united, most steadfast in class stand and have the sharpest sight. In this great, stormy cultural revolution, the masses of workers, peasants and soldiers are the main force—this is the result of their efforts in creatively studying and applying Mao Tse-tung's thought and arming their ideology with it. This is another eloquent proof of the fact that when the masses of workers, peasants and soldiers master the political telescope and microscope of Mao Tse-tung's thought, they are invincible and ever-triumphant. None of the monsters can escape their sharp sight, no matter what the tricks used or what the clever camouflage employed, "36 stratagems" or "72 metamorphoses." Not a single bourgeois stronghold can escape thorough destruction.

The attitude towards Mao Tse-tung's thought, whether to accept it or resist it, to support it or oppose it, to love it warmly or be hostile to it, this is the touchstone to test and the watershed between true revolution and sham revolution, between revolution and counter-revolution, between Marxism-Leninism and revisionism. He who wants to make revolution must accept Mao Tse-tung's thought and act in accordance with it. A counter-revolutionary will inevitably disparage, distort, resist, attack and oppose Mao Tse-tung's thought. The "authorities" of the bourgeoisie and all monsters, including the modern revisionists, use every means to slander Mao Tse-tung's thought, and they are extremely hostile to the creative study and application of Mao Tse-tung's works by the masses of workers, peasants and soldiers. They wildly attack the creative study and application of Mao Tse-tung's works by workers, peasants and soldiers as "philistinism," "over-simplification" and "pragmatism." The only explanation is that this flows from their exploiting class instinct. They fear Mao Tse-tung's thought, the revolutionary truth of the proletariat, and particularly the integration of Mao Tse-tung's thought with the worker, peasant and soldier masses. Once the workers, peasants and soldiers master the sharp weapon of Mao Tse-tung's thought, all monsters have no ground left to stand on. All their intrigues and plots will be thoroughly exposed, their ugly features will be brought into the broad light of day and their dream to restore capitalism will be utterly shattered.

The class enemy won't fall down, if you don't hit him. He still tries to rise to his feet after he has fallen. When one black line is eliminated, another appears. When one gang of representatives of the bourgeoisie has been laid low, a new one takes the stage. We must follow the instructions of the Central Committee of the Communist Party of China and never forget the class struggle, never forget the dictatorship of the proletariat, never forget to put politics first, never forget to hold aloft the great red banner of Mao Tse-tung's thought. We must firmly put politics first. We must creatively study and apply still better Chairman Mao Tse-tung's works, putting stress on the importance of application. We must consider Chairman Mao's works the supreme directive for all our work. We must master Mao Tse-tung's thought and pass it on from generation to generation. This is dictated by the needs of the revolution, the situation, the struggle against the enemy, the preparations to smash aggressive war by U.S. imperialism, of opposing and preventing revisionism, preventing the restoration of capitalism, of building socialism with greater, faster, better and more economical results and of ensuring the gradual transition from socialism to communism in China. Chairman Mao is the radiant sun lighting our minds. Mao Tse-tung's thought is our lifeline. Those who oppose Mao Tse-tung's thought, at any time and no matter what kind of "authorities" they are, will be denounced by the entire Party and the whole nation.

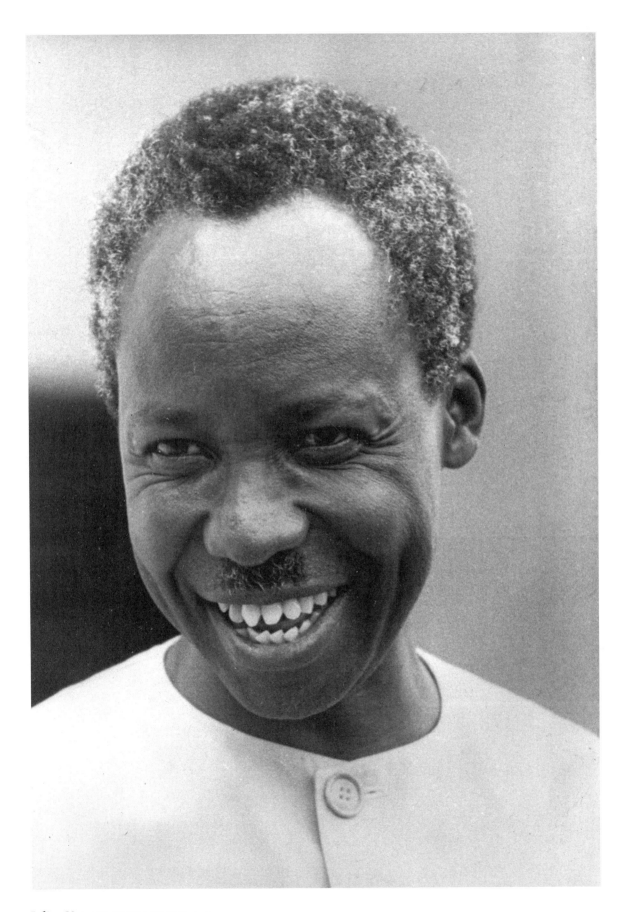

Julius Nyerere (AP/Wide World Photos)

ARUSHA DECLARATION

"The development of a country is brought about by people, not by money."

Overview

The Arusha Declaration of 1967 was written principally by Julius Nyerere, the first president of Tanzania, and approved by an executive committee of the Tanganyika African National Union (TANU), the new nation's governing party. The declaration was published just over five years after Tanganyika gained independence from Great Britain, who had governed the territory since 1920 under mandates from the League of Nations and then the United Nations. Tanganyika and Zanzibar united to form Tanzania in 1964. The Arusha Declaration represents the philosophy developed by Nyerere and TANU as they worked to bring economic and social development to their impoverished country and navigate the complex global economic and political arena. The declaration outlines policies that together constituted "Ujamaa," Tanzania's unique version of African Socialism, and explains in accessible regional idioms how the citizenry and state policies should work to address the challenges of development and modernization.

Tanzania's Socialism served to unite a diverse population, build a national identity through the Swahili language, provide political stability, and guarantee people's access to basic necessities. Critics of Ujamaa lamented the centralization of economic and political power by the state, which they predicted would facilitate the creation of a new class of elites. The declaration uses plain language to describe the risks involved with various possible solutions to the economic problems facing newly independent Tanzania. Many of these descriptions seem applicable to problems the country faces today, more than two decades after the end of Tanzania's Socialist experiment; beginning in the 1980s, Tanzania privatized resources, property, and services and liberalized economic policies instituted by the state after the Arusha Declaration. Accompanying these changes were increases in national debt—somewhat addressed by international debt-relief schemes—and decreases in government accountability, which critics have linked to greater reliance on international aid and investment. In addition, since the 1980s Tanzania has seen reductions in literacy rates, average life-expectancy rates,

and standards of living among rural households. The Arusha Declaration remains a significant document for historians and also for Tanzanians who debate the direction of their country. It is also important to others internationally who are concerned with global economic challenges.

Context

The Arusha Declaration was prepared in the context of economic crises in newly independent Tanzania in the mid-1960s. The country faced struggles with foreign donors over the control of financial resources. Members of TANU, the ruling party, saw less industrial investment than anticipated, reminding them of agriculture's centrality to their country. Rural development schemes had failed to produce strong results, pointing to a need for more involvement of rural people in such efforts. Moreover, the growing disparities between urban growth and rural poverty, a legacy of postwar colonial rule, were being continued by postindependence policies.

As in other African colonies, Tanganyika's colonial rulers sought to control most aspects of people's civic lives; such top-down models of governance remained common in newly independent African countries. Britain devoted less attention to Tanganyika's economic and infrastructural development than it did to some other colonies, leaving the newly independent country poor and without clear direction for economic growth. The widespread use of the Swahili language in the nineteenth- and twentieth-century long-distance trade and the work of TANU since the 1950s created possibilities for national unity and development.

Mainland Tanzania has an area of roughly 364,000 square miles, slightly more than twice the size of California, in which people belonging to approximately 125 ethnic groups speak languages that belong to four different language families. At the time of the declaration, the country's population was roughly twelve million (compared with about forty-four million by 2010). Tanzania's ethnic diversity is considered a source of pride, especially because the country has maintained a stable government since gaining independence more than forty years ago. Stability across such diversity is in part attributable to the use of Swahili as a national language. The choice of an African language for this role dif-

1920
- The League of Nations designates Tanganyika a mandate trust under the administration of Great Britain.

1946
- Tanganyika becomes a trustee territory of the United Nations, administered by Britain.

1954
- **July 7**
  The Tanganyika African National Union (TANU) is formed as the first political party in Tanganyika.

1960
- **August**
  TANU dominates the legislative election, and Julius Nyerere is subsequently appointed chief minister.

1961
- **December 9**
  Tanganyika is granted independence; Nyerere becomes prime minister.

1962
- **January 22**
  Nyerere resigns as prime minister to focus on political work and party organizing.

- **December 9**
  Following November elections, Nyerere is sworn in to the new office of president of the Republic of Tanganyika.

ferentiates Tanzania from some neighboring countries, such as Malawi, that have emphasized the use of their colonizers' languages in official realms, even though those languages are less accessible to the majority populations.

Internationally, Tanzania is often associated with African Socialism, or Ujamaa, because of the policies of TANU and the political philosophy of Nyerere. The Tanganyika African Association, which preceded TANU, was an organization of African clerks and civil servants that Nyerere joined in the 1940s and helped move toward more nationalist leanings. In the 1950s, Nyerere helped found TANU, a broader and more inclusive nationalist political party, in which he was elected to leadership positions. After independence was gained in 1961, Nyerere played an instrumental role in the unification of Tanganyika and Zanzibar to form the United Republic of Tanzania in 1964. The union led to the creation in 1977 of Chama Cha Mapinduzi, the Party of the Revolution, which remains the dominant political party in Tanzania. Some in Tanzania continue to criticize the unions of Tanganyika and Zanzibar and of their political parties as well as the power yet wielded by Chama Cha Mapinduzi.

Produced in 1967, the Arusha Declaration outlined the basis for Socialism by bringing together many elements that had been put in place since independence. Nyerere had introduced the concept of Ujamaa into political discussions in a 1962 essay, using a Swahili word (of distant Arabic origin) for "family" to characterize a kind of Socialism that differed substantially from that which people in Europe sought to institute. Rather than something imposed or created, Nyerere viewed Ujamaa as the political implementation of forms of social cooperation already present in African societies. Striving to please Europeans by using their models would be futile, Nyerere contended, and Africans needed to recognize their own practices and institutions as valuable models for national political organization.

About the Author

Julius Kambarage Nyerere was born in 1922 into a family of the small Zanaki ethnic group in a village east of Lake Victoria. Educated in Catholic schools in Musoma and Tabora, Tanganyika, he attended Makerere University in Uganda in the 1940s. At Makerere, the only East African university at the time, Nyerere pursued studies in history and philosophy with an eye toward becoming a teacher, *mwalimu* in Swahili. After teaching at a Catholic secondary school in Tabora for several years, he traveled in 1949 to study at the University of Edinburgh, in Scotland, returning in 1952 with a master's degree. While teaching in his next position at St. Francis College, near Dar es Salaam, he became an officer in the Tanganyika African Association, and he was elected its president in 1953. The growing emphasis on nationalism in the association led to political conflicts with Tanganyika's British governor, and on July 7, 1954, Nyerere and others created TANU as a political party.

Nyerere was a leader in negotiating independence from Britain, and he devoted considerable effort to political organizing and philosophical grounding of the party. An accomplished intellectual, he translated Shakespeare's *Julius Caesar* and *The Merchant of Venice* into Swahili in the 1960s in part to show the versatility of the African language in presenting such complex and respected British literature. He became the first president of the United Republic of Tanzania following Zanzibar's independence and subsequent unification with Tanganyika. Nyerere is recalled in Tanzania, both officially and commonly, as the "father of the nation." Feelings about him remain strong, connected to both historical memories and concern for the country's current state of affairs. Most Tanzanians continue to respect him, but some loathe him; his most bitter critics are those who were directly affected by his harshest policies, including the forced relocations during villagization in the 1970s, as well as members of the political opposition in Zanzibar, who blame Nyerere's influence in the governing party for their oppression. Indeed, attention to Nyerere's humble origins and practical wisdom as a leader can obscure his skills in bare-knuckled politics, through which he and other TANU activists transformed an impoverished former British colony into an independent country known globally for its unique Socialist system and international influence.

Explanation and Analysis of the Document

The Arusha Declaration was the result of efforts by Nyerere and other leaders of TANU to develop a governing philosophy to address the problems faced by newly independent Tanzania, which were similar to problems faced by neighboring countries. Tanzania's population was predominantly rural and poor in 1967, and it appeared that most paths to "development" and "modernization"—important political and economic goals at the time—would further bind the country into the global economic system, perpetuating dependence on foreign capital and knowledge while sacrificing the interests of rural farmers. The declaration is Nyerere and TANU's outline of how Tanzania would attain essential economic and social goals without jeopardizing its independence.

◆ Part One: "The TANU Creed"

Part One of the document explains that TANU's policy is "to build a socialist state," which the official Swahili-language version consistently refers to as a "country of *Ujamaa*." Nyerere intended the term *Ujamaa* to convey notions of mutual respect, self-reliance, and equitable work toward shared ends, which he argued were already practiced in Tanzanian and African communities and should be the basis for their development and governance. Part One lays out nine principle beliefs of TANU relating to Ujamaa, followed by twelve aims. The first seven beliefs concern the rights of individual Tanzanians, while the final two explain the role of the state (which the Swahili version notes is the people themselves) in controlling the means of production and preventing the accumulation of wealth and the exploitation (*unyonyaji*) of citizens. Critics of the declaration immediately viewed these last two beliefs as contra-

Time Line

1963

- **December 10**
  Zanzibar is granted independence.

1964

- **April 26**
  Tanganyika unites with Zanzibar; the country is renamed the United Republic of Tanzania on October 29.

1967

- **February 5**
  Having been approved by the National Executive Committee of TANU in January, the Arusha Declaration is published.

1973

- Villagization policies become forced; in all, some thirteen million people would be relocated to organized Ujamaa villages.

1977

- **February 5**
  Chama Cha Mapinduzi is formed by the merger of TANU and the Afro-Shirazi Party of Zanzibar, to become the ruling party.

1985

- **November 6**
  Nyerere retires as president of Tanzania while remaining in control of Chama Cha Mapinduzi.

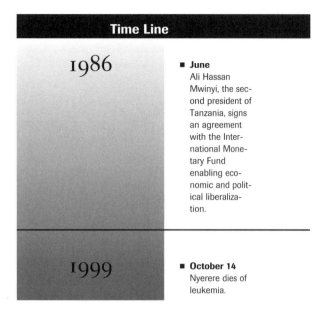

■ **June**
Ali Hassan Mwinyi, the second president of Tanzania, signs an agreement with the International Monetary Fund enabling economic and political liberalization.

■ **October 14**
Nyerere dies of leukemia.

dicting the commitment to democratic Socialism spelled out in the earlier points by facilitating the creation of a new dominant class of political elites.

The aims of TANU included safeguarding the rights of the Tanzanian people, and the declaration explains how the government would act as the nation's controlling force. Items (d) and (k) refer to "the liberation of all Africa" and "African unity," phrasing that constituted not only rhetoric about shared histories, interests, and vulnerabilities in newly independent Africa but also motivation for political action, such as Tanzania's support for peoples fighting against apartheid and colonial rule in southern Africa. The stated commitment to working with other countries through the United Nations for peace and security was primarily realized in Nyerere and Tanzania's roles in the Non-Aligned Movement during the cold war and in the Organization for African Unity. Nyerere was involved with both organizations from the outset, and Tanzania's participation in each was critically important.

◆ **Part Two: "The Policy of Socialism"**

The second part of the document explains the policy of Ujamaa, stating that in a Socialist country broad income equality is required, and all people work according to their abilities. Tanzania is said to be "a nation of peasants" that struggles against elements of capitalism and feudalism (*ukabaila*, also indicating hierarchy). The government—or, rather, "the peasants through the machinery of their Government"—should control the means of production. However, in contrast to the control of resources and production maintained by the white minority governments of Rhodesia and South Africa, the declaration asserts that Ujamaa in Tanzania would involve both the ideals and the practice of democracy. The declaration asserts that the principles of Socialism and human rights are international and that these principles must characterize the lives and beliefs of TANU leaders if they are to succeed.

◆ **Part Three: "The Policy of Self-Reliance"**

The longest part of the document, Part Three explains that TANU is fighting to lift the Tanzanian people from a state of poverty and oppression into a communal position of strength and well-being. Many important keywords of Tanzanian Socialism are deployed and explained in this section. Tanzania in the 1960s needed schools, roads, health care, efficient food production and distribution, clean water sources, and many other basic elements of life in modern society. The declaration explains that these needs are often equated with money, which the government must raise either through taxation or from outside sources in the form of gifts, loans, and investment. Rural Tanzanians negatively associated taxation with colonial rule; to counter this, the declaration explains that money from other countries would arrive with terms of use, conditions of repayment, and the need for profits and interest, all of which would sacrifice Tanzania's independence and commitment to the betterment of its citizens. Thus, expecting money from abroad to result in effective Tanzanian development would be "stupid," the declaration asserts. Recognizing the rural basis of Tanzania's economy, Part Three contends that an emphasis on industrial development would require foreign capital and experts, which would threaten Ujamaa. Industrialization also overemphasizes urban development, which villagers and farmers would ultimately have to pay for, either through taxation or production, thereby creating urban exploitation (*unyonyaji*) of rural people, labor, and resources. Development comes from people, not money, the declaration contends, and Tanzania already possesses the prerequisites of development in people, land, good policies, and good leadership.

The section "Conditions of Development" cites first and foremost "hard work" (*juhudi*, or "effort" in Swahili), through which rural people can produce crops that can be converted into money and economic betterment. Self-reliance (*kujitegemea*) is collectively defined as the contribution of one's own efforts, to the best of one's abilities, to the national community, thus allowing the country to rely on its productive citizens rather than external dependence. The declaration explains that TANU leadership must be trained in these policies if Ujamaa is to be understood and implemented successfully.

◆ **Part Four: "TANU Membership"**

In the 1950s, TANU found it necessary to increase party membership by including people of diverse interests—members of trades and cooperative unions, rural farmers, educated bureaucrats, and civil servants alike. In 1967, beyond mass membership, adherence to party philosophy was seen as especially important for the independent country. The declaration makes linked assertions that TANU is the party of the farmers and workers and that a member should accept the faith and directions of the party, assertions that serve to codify political ambiguity. On one hand, party elites are to remember that they are fed by and serve the farmers and workers; on the other hand, farmers and workers are obliged to belong to the party and accept

TANU youth league members march past Tanzanian president Julius Nyerere during a celebration parade in Dar es Salaam on the first anniversary of the Arusha Declaration. (AP/Wide World Photos)

the positions mandated by the party elite—failure to do so, according to Part Three, should cause shame.

◆ Part Five: "The Arusha Resolution"

Part Five provides the resolutions of the TANU National Executive Committee concerning the responsibilities of leadership (at practically all levels and on the part of spouses as well) to personally follow the principles of Ujamaa, including being a farmer or worker and not a capitalist, not having shares in or directorship of a company, not receiving two or more salaries, and not owning rental properties. It calls upon the government to implement Ujamaa without further delay—to bring existing plans into accord with the principles of self-reliance, to ensure pay equity between public and private sector workers, and to improve the rural standard of living.

Audience

There were many audiences for the Arusha Declaration, and they populated a broad international arena. The TANU

executive committee was Nyerere's immediate audience with his draft of the declaration, which they approved in Arusha on January 29, 1967. Here he had to convince both those who were skeptical of a Socialist path and those who urged a more rapid effort toward Socialist reform. A second audience consisted of rural farmers—the majority of Tanzania's population—as well as rural and urban workers, to whom Nyerere had to explain the declaration and its implications. The document uses common language and metaphors that refer to the perspectives and experiences of Tanzania's rural people, and it outlines a response to the nation's economic challenges based on idioms of family and overall social responsibility. One such idiom is Ujamaa itself, with its implications of family and the linked assumptions of obligations and responsibilities. The actual Swahili-language idioms of the declaration and of Tanzania's Socialist experiment subsequently spread globally, as the declaration offered a response to global capitalism and imperialism from the perspective of the impoverished and with an emphasis on the rural basis for development.

TANU leaders were concerned about international trade with other African governments, who made up a third audience for the document, and they also wanted to influence the people of other African countries, who can be viewed as a fourth audience. TANU sought to inspire progressive development in Africa without creating hostility among potential allies—where other nations' leaders could be protective of existing political establishments—or isolating Tanzania. At the same time, TANU wished to notify the remaining colonial rulers in southern Africa and the apartheid regime in South Africa that Tanzania had a fundamental concern with change in those countries. A fifth audience for the document consisted of the economically dominant countries of Europe and North America, to whom TANU needed to explain that Tanzania intended to build its own economy but would also be open to trade and investment.

Impact

The Arusha Declaration was initially very popular in Tanzania. Nyerere received praise in the public realm, where he was already highly regarded following the successful path to independence. One widespread complaint at the time concerned the loss of the country's wealth and resources to economic and political elites in Tanzania and abroad. Since colonial times, people often spoke of elites' exploiting their positions at the expense of the majority. The actions of those who drained the wealth of the people came to be referred to by a vivid popular idiom describing colonial relationships as literally draining the blood of the people. The declaration was intended to speak directly to these fears. Still, many people were concerned about the disparities between the ideals of Socialism and democracy as explained in the document and the implications of absolute state control—and some would experience the realities of alienation in the course of the nationalization campaign.

Within days of publishing the declaration, Nyerere and TANU began nationalizing privately held businesses, whether domestic or foreign owned. The government took control of banks and financial institutions as well as grain-milling companies that were important to rural production, and it sought majority control in manufacturing companies. In 1970 the government nationalized import and export operations; in 1971 it nationalized housing, taking control of property in which owners did not reside; and by 1976 it had nationalized the cooperative unions, a difficult undertaking because the unions tended to be popular among farmers and had been of major importance during the movement against colonialism. Nationalization was effectively complete by 1977.

Socialism was generally successful before the early to mid-1970s: The country witnessed economic growth, broad improvements in health care, and successful efforts toward universal literacy through primary education in Swahili. The emphasis on rural development had led TANU to design a voluntary program of Socialist villages, with about a thousand created between 1960 and 1963, which in theory would be rationally organized and provide residents with access to such things as water, education, and health facilities. Ideally, villages would be linked to the national political network through representatives of nested units, including house groups, wards, villages, and districts. Villagization was formally initiated in September 1967, putting into practice the philosophy that Nyerere had sketched out earlier in the 1960s. Voluntary Ujamaa villages, however, were not very popular, and the lack of success along with new economic challenges led to a campaign of forced villagization after 1973. Some thirteen million people were ultimately resettled into Ujamaa villages.

By the late 1970s, Tanzania was facing a deep political and economic crisis. The global oil shocks since 1973 had increased the costs of imports and decreased the relative value of Tanzania's exports, which exacerbated the country's debt. War with Idi Amin's Uganda in 1978–1979 was also costly, as was Tanzania's stance against colonial and white minority governments in southern Africa. Meanwhile, political elites found ways to make state control work for their own benefit, becoming personally wealthy and building patronage networks through their government positions and the wealth of the country while still using the language of antiexploitation. Opponents of these excesses and state policies came to refer to Ujamaa as "Socialism from the top down." They found creative ways to evade state controls and mocked the Swahili idioms that had been used to define Ujamaa policies. In his last years in office, Nyerere began new discussions with international economic forces such as the World Bank and the International Monetary Fund, paving the way for the economic liberalization that was officially implemented in the mid-1980s by his successor, Ali Hassan Mwinyi, the second president of Tanzania.

Following the end of the cold war and the move away from Socialism in Tanzania, people continued to use the common Swahili-language idioms of Ujamaa, reworking them in debating and discussing current challenges. People today use the notion of "self-reliance" (*kujitegemea*) to mean that they must depend on themselves to get by economically—or to create whatever benefit for themselves they can, by almost any means, because the government no longer provides substantial entitlements or a public safety net, nor does it set commonly applied restrictions on economic activities. Similarly, many people today have taken the emphasis on "hard work" in the declaration and in practice in Tanzanian development to be a description of a requirement for survival rather than a condition for development.

Many people in other African countries came to view the Arusha Declaration as a model for possible actions in their own countries or as a means to measure the policies and practices of their own governments. In the United States, people involved in progressive or left-wing political movements adopted principles from the declaration. Some Swahili words and idioms from the declaration became widely used and recognized in the United States. "Ujamaa" is commonly understood as a form of African Socialism, even aside from the Tanzanian specifics. By the 1980s, for example, an African American theater company in New York used the name, which the *New York Times* glossed as "the Swahili word for working together" (Frasier, p. C14). That influence is also seen in the Kwanzaa holiday. One of Kwan-

"A truly socialist state is one in which all people are workers and in which neither capitalism nor feudalism exists."

(Part Two: "The Policy of Socialism")

"To build and maintain socialism it is essential that all the major means of production and exchange in the nation are controlled and owned by the peasants through the machinery of their Government and their co-operatives. Further, it is essential that the ruling Party should be a Party of peasants and workers."

(Part Two: "The Policy of Socialism")

"Socialism is a way of life, and a socialist society cannot simply come into existence. A socialist society can only be built by those who believe in, and who themselves practice, the principles of socialism."

(Part Two: "The Policy of Socialism")

"Although when we talk of exploitation we usually think of capitalists, we should not forget that there are many fish in the sea. They eat each other. The large ones eat the small ones, and small ones eat those who are even smaller."

(Part Three: "The Policy of Self-Reliance")

"The development of a country is brought about by people, not by money. Money, and the wealth it represents, is the result and not the basis of development."

(Part Three: "The Policy of Self-Reliance")

"If every individual is self-reliant [the] ten-house cell will be self-reliant; if all the cells are self-reliant the whole ward will be self-reliant; and if the wards are self-reliant the District will be self-reliant. If the Districts are self-reliant, then the Region is self-reliant, and if the Regions are self-reliant, then the whole nation is self-reliant and this is our aim."

(Part Three: "The Policy of Self-Reliance")

zaa's seven principles ("*nguzo saba*" in Swahili) is Ujamaa, which the holiday's founder, Maulana Karenga, characterized as a communal building and maintaining of businesses to gain a collective profit. This use of Ujamaa as a kind of cultural economics derives from Nyerere's development of the concept of "familyhood" to refer to African Socialism.

The declaration was a political and societal landmark with such wide-reaching effects in Tanzania that it would be hard to write a history of almost anything in the country without some accounting for it. The declaration was so widely discussed in Tanzania that some oral historians have even used it as a time datum by which to ascertain the relative ages of events people speak about in oral histories. The document's effects extended well beyond Tanzania, as for many people since the 1960s African Socialism and Ujamaa have become synonymous.

Further Reading

■ Articles

Askew, Kelly M. "Sung and Unsung: Musical Reflections on Tanzanian Postsocialisms." *Africa* 76, no. 1 (2006): 15–43.

Brennan, James. "Blood Enemies: Exploitation and Urban Citizenship in the Nationalist Political Thought of Tanzania, 1958–75." *Journal of African History* 47, no. 3 (2006): 389–413.

Frasier, C. Gerald. "Stage: Show by Ujamaa on the Blues." *New York Times*. August 15, 1983.

Stöger-Eising, Viktoria. "Ujamaa Revisited: Indigenous and European Influences in Nyerere's Social and Political Thought." *Africa* 70, no. 1 (2000): 118–143.

■ Books

Coulson, Andrew. *Tanzania: A Political Economy*. New York: Oxford University Press, 1982.

Geiger, Susan. *TANU Women: Gender and Culture in the Making of Tanganyikan Nationalism, 1955–1965*. Portsmouth, N.H.: Heinemann, 1996.

Hartmann, Jeannette, ed. *Re-thinking the Arusha Declaration*. Copenhagen: Centre for Development Research, 1991.

Iliffe, John. *A Modern History of Tanganyika*. Cambridge, U.K.: Cambridge University Press, 1978.

Jennings, Michael. *Surrogates of the State: NGOs, Development, and Ujamaa in Tanzania*. Bloomfield, Conn.: Kumarian Press, 2008.

Nyerere, Julius K. *Freedom and Unity/Uhuru na Umoja: A Selection from Writings and Speeches, 1952–65*. Dar es Salaam: Oxford University Press, 1968.

—James Ellison

Questions for Further Study

1. The Arusha Declaration was one of many key documents created as the nations of Africa emerged from colonialism. Compare this document with the Freedom Charter of South Africa, Patrice Lumumba's Speech at the Proclamation of Congolese Independence, or the Proclamation of the Algerian National Liberation Front. How do the documents express similar—or differing—goals and aspirations?

2. What is African Socialism? Put differently, how did Socialism in Africa reflect the unique needs of a country such as Tanzania?

3. In a country such as Tanzania, why were "growing disparities between urban growth and rural poverty," as the entry states, a "legacy of postwar colonial rule"? Why would these disparities not have been the result equally of the attitudes and behaviors of the nation's elites?

4. Why do the Arusha Declaration and its concept of Ujamaa continue to be regarded as influential, given that Tanzania continues to have severe economic problems?

5. The Arusha Declaration states: "The development of a country is brought about by people, not by money. Money, and the wealth it represents, is the result and not the basis of development." If this is true, then why is it necessary for a country such as Tanzania to attract foreign investment and to have its debts relieved by other nations?

ARUSHA DECLARATION

Part One. The TANU Creed

The policy of TANU is to build a socialist state. The principles of socialism are laid down in the TANU Constitution and they are as follows:

WHEREAS TANU believes:

(a) That all human beings are equal;

(b) That every individual has a right to dignity and respect;

(c) That every citizen is an integral part of the nation and has the right to take an equal part in Government at local, regional and national level;

(d) That every citizen has the right to freedom of expression, of movement, of religious belief and of association within the context of the law;

(e) That every individual has the right to receive from society protection of his life and of property held according to law;

(f) That every individual has the right to receive a just return for his labour;

(g) That all citizens together possess all the natural resources of the country in trust for their descendants;

(h) That in order to ensure economic justice the state must have effective control over the principal means of production; and

(i) That it is the responsibility of the state to intervene actively in the economic life of the nation so as to ensure the well-being of all citizens, and so as to prevent the exploitation of one person by another or one group by another, and so as to prevent the accumulation of wealth to an extent which is inconsistent with the existence of a classless society.

Now, therefore, the principal aims and objects of TANU shall be as follows:

(a) To consolidate and maintain the independence of this country and the freedom of its people;

(b) To safeguard the inherent dignity of the individual in accordance with the Universal Declaration of Human Rights;

(c) To ensure that this country shall be governed by a democratic socialist government of the people;

(d) To co-operate with all political parties in Africa engaged in the liberation of all Africa;

(e) To see that the Government mobilizes all the resources of this country towards the elimination of poverty, ignorance and disease;

(f) To see that the Government actively assists in the formation and maintenance of co-operative organizations;

(g) to see that wherever possible the Government itself directly participates in the economic development of this country;

(h) To see that the Government gives equal opportunity to all men and women irrespective of race, religion or status;

(i) To see that the Government eradicates all types of exploitation, intimidation, discrimination, bribery and corruption;

(j) To see that the Government exercises effective control over the principal means of production and pursues policies which facilitate the way to collective ownership of the resources of this country;

(k) To see that the Government co-operates with other states in Africa in bringing about African unity;

(l) To see that Government works tirelessly towards world peace and security through the United Nations Organization.

Part Two. The Policy of Socialism

(a) Absence of Exploitation

A truly socialist state is one in which all people are workers and in which neither capitalism nor feudalism exists. It does not have two classes of people, a lower class composed of people who work for their living and an upper class of people who live on the work of others. In a really socialist country no person exploits another; everyone who is physically able to work does so; every worker obtains a just return for the labour he performs; and the incomes derived from different types of work are not grossly divergent. In a socialist country, the only people who live on the work of others, and who have the right to be dependent upon their fellows, are small children, people who are too old to support themselves, the crippled, and those whom the state at any one time cannot provide with an opportunity to work for their living.

Tanzania is a nation of peasants but is not yet a socialist society. It still contains elements of feudalism and capitalism—with their temptations. These feudalistic and capitalistic features of our society could spread and entrench themselves.

(b) The Major Means of Production and Exchange Are under the Control of the Peasants and Workers

To build and maintain socialism it is essential that all the major means of production and exchange in the nation are controlled and owned by the peasants through the machinery of their Government and their co-operatives. Further, it is essential that the ruling Party should be a Party of peasants and workers.

The major means of production and exchange are such things as: land; forests; minerals; water; oil and electricity; news media; communications; banks; insurance; import and export trade; wholesale trade; iron and steel, machine tool, arms, motor-car, cement, fertilizer, and textile industries; and any big factory on which a large section of the people depend for their living, or which provides essential components of other industries; large plantations, and especially those which provide raw materials essential to important industries.

Some of the instruments of production and exchange which have been listed here are already owned or controlled by the people's Government of Tanzania.

(c) The Existence of Democracy

A state is not socialist simply because its means of production and exchange are controlled or owned by the government, either wholly or in large part. If a country [is] to be socialist, it is essential that its government is chosen and led by the peasants and workers themselves. If the minority governments of Rhodesia or South Africa controlled or owned the entire economies of these respective countries, the result would be a strengthening of oppression, not the building of socialism. True socialism cannot exist without democracy also existing in the society.

(d) Socialism Is a Belief

Socialism is a way of life, and a socialist society cannot simply come into existence. A socialist society can only be built by those who believe in, and who themselves practice, the principles of socialism. A committed member of TANU will be a socialist, and his fellow socialist – that is, his fellow believers in this political and economic system – are all those in Africa or elsewhere in the world who fight for the rights of peasants and workers. The first duty of a TANU member, and especially of a TANU leader, is to accept these socialist principles, and to live his own life in accordance with them. In particular, a genuine TANU leader will not live off the sweat of another man, nor commit any feudalistic or capitalistic actions.

The successful implementation of socialist objectives depends very much upon the leaders, because socialism is a belief in a particular system of living, and it is difficult for leaders to promote its growth if they do not themselves accept it.

Part Three. The Policy of Self-Reliance

We Are at War

TANU is involved in a war against poverty and oppression in our country; the struggle is aimed at moving the people of Tanzania (and the people of Africa as a whole) from a state of poverty to a State of prosperity.

We have been oppressed a great deal, we have been exploited a great deal and we have been disregarded a great deal. It is our weakness that has led to our being oppressed, exploited and disregarded. Now we want a revolution – a revolution which brings an end to our weakness, so that we are never again exploited, oppressed, or humiliated.

A Poor Man Does Not Use Money as a Weapon

But it is obvious that in the past we have chosen the wrong weapon for our struggle, because we chose money as our weapon. We are trying to overcome our economic weakness by using the weapons of the economically strong—weapons which in fact we do not possess. By our thoughts, words and actions it appears as if we have come to the conclusion that without money we cannot bring about the revolution we are aiming at. It is as if we have said, "Money is the basis of development. Without money there can be no development."

That is what we believe at present. TANU leaders, and Government leaders and officials, all put great emphasis and dependence on money. The people's leaders, and the people themselves, in TANU, NUTA, Parliament, UWT, the co-operatives, TAPA, and in other national institutions think, hope and pray for Money. It is as if we had all agreed to speak with one voice, saying, "If we get money we shall develop, without money we cannot develop."

In brief, our Five-Year Development Plan aims at more food, more education, and better health; but the weapon we have put emphasis upon is money. It is as if we said, "In the next five years we want to have more food, more education, and better health, and in order to achieve these things we shall spend £250,000,000." We think and speak as if the most important thing to depend upon is Money and anything else we intend to use in our struggle is of minor importance.

When a member of Parliament says that there is a shortage of water in his constituency; and he asks the Government how it intends to deal with the problem, he expects the Government to reply that it is planning to remove the shortage of water in his constituency—with Money.

When another Member of Parliament asks what the Government is doing about the shortage of roads, schools or hospitals in his constituency, he also expects the Government to tell him that it has specific plans to build roads, schools and hospitals in his constituency—with Money.

When a NUTA official asks the Government about its plans to deal with the low wages and poor housing of the workers, he expects the Government to inform him that the minimum wage will be increased and that better houses will be provided for the workers—With Money.

When a TAPA official asks the Government what plans it has to give assistance to the many TAPA schools which do not get Government aid, he expects the Government to state that it is ready the following morning to give the required assistance—With Money.

When an official of the co-operative movement mentions any problem facing the farmer, he expects to hear that the Government will solve the farmer's problems—With Money. In short, for every problem facing our nation, the solution that is in everybody's mind is Money.

Each year, each Ministry of Government makes its estimates of expenditure, i.e. the amount of money it will require in the coming year to meet recurrent and development expenses. Only one Minister and his Ministry make estimates of revenue. This is the Minister for Finance.

Every Ministry puts forward very good development plans. When the Ministry presents its estimates, it believes that the money is there for the asking but that the Minister for Finance and his Ministry are being obstructive. And regularly each year the Minister of Finance has to tell his fellow Ministers that there is no money. And each year the Ministers complain about the Ministry of Finance when it trims down their estimates.

Similarly, when Members of Parliament and other leaders demand that the Government should carry out a certain development, they believe that there is a lot of money to spend on such projects, but that the Government is the stumbling block. Yet such belief on the part of Ministries, Members of Parliament and other leaders does not alter the stark truth, which is that Government has no money.

When it is said that Government has no money, what does this mean? It means that the people of Tanzania have insufficient money. The people pay taxes out of the very little wealth they have; it is from these taxes that the Government meets its recurrent and development expenditure. When we call on the Government to spend more money on development projects, we are asking the Government to use more money. And if the Government does not have any more, the only way it can do this is to increase its revenue through extra taxation.

If one calls on the Government to spend more, one is in effect calling on the Government to increase taxes. Calling on the Government to spend more without raising taxes is like demanding that the Government should perform miracles; it is equivalent to asking for more milk from a cow while insisting that the cow should not be milked again. But our refusal to admit that calling on the Government to spend more is the same as calling on the Government to raise taxes shows that we fully realize the difficulties of increasing taxes. We realize that the cow has no more milk—that is, that the people find it difficult to pay more taxes. We know that the cow would like to have more milk herself, so that her calves could drink it, or that she would like more milk which could be sold to provide more comfort for herself or her calves. But knowing all the things which could be done with more milk does not alter the fact that the cow has no more milk!

◆ **What of External Aid?**

One method we use to try and avoid a recognition of the need to increase taxes if we want to have more money for development, is to think in terms of getting the extra money from outside Tanzania. Such external finance falls into three main categories.

(a) Gifts: This means that another government gives our Government a sum of money as a free gift for a particular development scheme. Sometimes it may be that an institution in another country gives our Government, or an institution in our country, financial help for development programmes.

(b) Loans: The greater portion of financial help we expect to get from outside is not in the form of gifts or charity, but in the form of loans. A foreign government or a foreign institution, such as a bank, lends our Government money for the purposes of development. Such a loan has repayment conditions attached to it, covering such factors as the time period for which it is available and the rate of interest.

(c) Private Investment: The third category of financial help is also greater than the first. This takes the form of investment in our country by individuals or companies from outside. The important condition which such private investors have in mind is that the enterprise into which they put their money should bring them profit and that our Government should permit them to repatriate these profits. They also prefer to invest in a country whose policies they agree with and which will safeguard their economic interests.

These three are the main categories of external finance. And there is in Tanzania a fantastic amount of talk about getting money from outside. Our Government, and different groups of our leaders, never stop thinking about methods of getting finance from abroad. And if we get some money or even if we just get a promise of it, our newspapers, our radio, and our leaders, all advertise the fact in order that every person shall know that salvation is coming, or is on the way. If we receive a gift we announce it, if we receive a loan we announce it, if we get a new factory we announce it—and always loudly. In the same way, when we get a promise of a gift, a loan, or a new industry, we make an announcement of the promise. Even when we have merely started discussions with a foreign government or institution for a gift, a loan, or a new industry, we make an announcement—even though we do not know the outcome of the discussions. Why do we do all this? Because we want people to know that we have started discussions which will bring prosperity.

◆ **Do Not Let Us Depend upon Money for Development**

It is stupid to rely on money as the major instrument of development when we know only too well that our country is poor. It is equally stupid, indeed it is even more stupid, for us to imagine that we shall rid ourselves of our poverty through foreign financial assistance rather than our own financial resources. It is stupid for two reasons.

Firstly, we shall not get the money. It is true that there are countries which can, and which would like to, help us. But there is no country in the world which is prepared to give us gifts or loans, or establish industries, to the extent that we would be able to achieve all our development targets. There are many needy countries in the world. And even if all the prosperous nations were willing to help the needy countries, the assistance would still not suffice. But in any case the prosperous nations have not accepted a responsibility to fight world poverty. Even within their own borders poverty still exists, and the rich individuals do not willingly give money to the government to help their poor fellow citizens.

It is only through taxation, which people have to pay whether they want to or not, that money can be extracted from the rich in order to help the masses. Even then there would not be enough money. However heavily we taxed the citizens of Tanzania and the aliens living here, the resulting revenue would not be enough to meet the costs of the development we want. And there is no World Government which can tax the prosperous nations in order to help the poor nations; nor if one did exist could it raise enough revenue to do all that is needed in the world. But in fact, such a World Government does not exist. Such money as the rich nations offer to the poor nations is given voluntarily, either through their own goodness, or for their own benefit. All this means that it is impossible for Tanzania to obtain from overseas enough money to develop our economy.

◆ **Gifts and Loans Will Endanger Our Independence**

Secondly, even if it were possible for us to get enough money for our needs from external sources, is this what we really want? Independence means self-reliance. Independence cannot be real if a nation depends upon gifts and loans from another for its development. Even if there was a nation, or nations, prepared to give us all the money we need for our development, it would be improper for us to accept such assistance without asking ourselves how this would affect our independence and our very survival as a nation. Gifts which increase, or act as a catalyst, to our own efforts are valuable. Gifts which could have the effect of weakening or distorting our own efforts should not be accepted until we have asked ourselves a number of questions.

The same applies to loans. It is true that loans are better than "free" gifts. A loan is intended to increase our efforts or make those fruitful. One condition of a loan is that you show how you are going to repay it. This means you have to show that you intend to use the loan profitably and will therefore be able to repay it.

But even loans have their limitations. You have to give consideration to the ability to repay. When we borrow money from other countries it is the Tanzanian who pays it back. And as we have already stated, Tanzanians are poor people. To burden the people with big loans, the repayment of which will be beyond their means, is not to help them but to make them suffer. It is even worse when the loans they are asked to repay have not benefited the majority of the people but have only benefited a small minority.

How about the enterprises of foreign investors? It is true we need these enterprises. We have even passed an Act of Parliament protecting foreign investments in this country. Our aim is to make foreign investors feel that Tanzania is a good place in which to invest because investments would be safe and profitable, and the profits can be taken out of the country without difficulty. We expect to get money through this method. But we cannot get enough. And even if we were able to convince foreign investors and foreign firms to undertake all the projects and programmes of economic development that we need, is that what we actually want to happen?

Had we been able to attract investors from America and Europe to come and start all the industries and all the projects of economic development that we need in this country, could we do so without questioning ourselves?

Could we agree to leave the economy of our country in the hands of foreigners who would take the profits back to their countries? Or supposing they did not insist upon taking their profits away, but decided to reinvest them in Tanzania; could we really accept this situation without asking ourselves what disadvantages our nation would suffer? Would this allow the socialism we have said it is our objective to build?

How can we depend upon gifts, loans, and investments from foreign countries and foreign companies without endangering our independence? The English people have a proverb which says, "He who pays the piper calls the tune." How can we depend upon foreign governments and companies for the major part of our development without giving to those governments and companies a great part of our freedom to act as we please? The truth is that we cannot.

Let us repeat. We made a mistake in choosing money—something we do not have—to be the big instrument of our development. We are making a mistake to think that we shall get the money from other countries; first, because in fact we shall not be able to get sufficient money for our economic development; and secondly, because even if we could get all that we need, such dependence upon others would endanger our independence and our ability to choose our own political policies.

◆ We Have Put Too Much Emphasis on Industries

Because of our emphasis on money, we have made another big mistake. We have put too much emphasis on industries. Just as we have said, "Without money there can be no development," we also seem to say, "Industries are the basis of development, without industries there is no development." This is true. The day when we have lots of money we shall be able to say we are a developed country. We shall be able to say, "When we began our development plans we did not have enough money and this situation made it difficult for us to develop as fast as we wanted. Today we are developed and we have enough money." That is to say, our money has been brought by development. Similarly, the day we become industrialized we shall be able to say we are developed. Development would have us to have industries. The mistake we are making is to think that development begins with industries. It is a mistake because we do not have the means to establish many modern industries in our country. We do not have either the necessary finances or the technical know-how. It is not enough to say that we shall borrow the finances and the technicians from other countries to come and start the industries. The answer to this is the same one we gave earlier, that we cannot get enough money and borrow enough technicians to start all the industries we need. And even if we could get the necessary assistance, dependence on it could interfere with our policy on socialism. The policy of inviting a chain of capitalists to come and establish industries in our country might succeed in giving us all the industries we need but it would also succeed in preventing the establishment of socialism unless we believe that without first building capitalism, we cannot build socialism.

◆ Let Us Pray and Heed to the Peasant

Our emphasis on money and industries has made us concentrate on urban development. We recognize that we do not have enough money to bring the kind of development to each village which would benefit everybody. We also know that we cannot establish an industry in each village and through this means erect a rise in the real incomes of the people. For these reasons we spend most of our money in the urban areas and our industries are established in the towns.

Yet the greater part of this money that we spend in the towns comes from loans. Whether it is used to build schools, hospitals, houses or factories, etc., it still has to be repaid. But it is obvious that it cannot be repaid just out of money obtained from urban and industrial development. To repay the loans we have to use foreign currency which is obtained from the sale of our exports. But we do not now sell our industrial products in foreign markets, and indeed it is likely to be a long time before our industries produce for export. The main aim of our new industries is "import substitution"—that is, to produce things which up to now we have had to import from foreign countries.

It is therefore obvious that the foreign currency we shall use to pay back the loans used in the development of the urban areas will not come from the towns or the industries. Where, then, shall we get it from? We shall get it from the villages and from agriculture. What does this mean? It means that the people who benefit directly from development which is brought about by borrowed money are not the ones who will repay the loans. The largest proportion of the loans will be spent in, or for, the urban areas, but the largest proportion of the repayment will be made through the efforts of the farmers.

This fact should always be borne in mind, for there are various forms of exploitation. We must not forget that people who live in towns can possibly become the exploiters of those who live in the rural areas. All our big hospitals are in towns and they benefit only a small section of the people of Tanzania. Yet if we had built them with loans from outside Tanzania, it is the overseas sale of the peasants' produce which provides the foreign exchanges for repayment. Those who do not get the benefit of the hospital thus carry the major responsibility for paying for them. Tarmac roads, too, are mostly found in towns and are of especial value to the motor-car owners. Yet if we have built those roads with loans, it is again the farmer who produces the goods which will pay for them. What is more, the foreign exchange with which the car was bought also came from the sale of the farmers' produce. Again, electric lights, water pipes, hotels and other aspects of modern development are mostly found in towns. Most of them have been built with loans, and most of them do not benefit the farmer directly, although they will be paid for by the foreign exchange earned by the sale of his produce. We should always bear this in mind.

Although when we talk of exploitation we usually think of capitalists, we should not forget that there are many fish in the sea. They eat each other. The large ones eat the small ones, and small ones eat those who are even smaller. There are two possible ways of dividing the people in our country. We can put the capitalists and feudalists on one side, and the farmers and workers on the other. But we can also divide the people into urban dwellers on one side and those who live in the rural areas on the other. If we are not careful we might get to the position where the real exploitation in Tanzania is that of the town dwellers exploiting the peasants.

◆ The People and Agriculture

The development of a country is brought about by people, not by money. Money, and the wealth it represents, is the result and not the basis of development. The four prerequisites of development are different; they are (i) People; (ii) Land; (iii) Good Policies; (iv) Good Leadership. Our country has more than ten million people and its area is more than 362,000 square miles.

◆ Agriculture Is the Basis of Development

A great part of Tanzania's land is fertile and gets sufficient rain. Our country can produce various crops for home consumption and for export.

We can produce food crops (which can be exported if we produce in large quantities) such as maize, rice, wheat, beans, groundnuts, etc. And we can produce such cash crops as sisal, cotton, coffee, tobacco, pyrethrum, tea, etc. Our land is also good for grazing cattle, goats, sheep, and for raising chickens, etc.; we can get plenty of fish from our rivers, lakes, and from the sea. All of our farmers are in areas which can produce two or three or even more of the food and cash crops enumerated above, and each farmer could increase his production so as to get more food or more money. And because the main aim of development is to get more food and more money for our other needs, our purpose must be to increase production of these agricultural crops. This is in fact the only road through which we can develop our country—in other words, only by increasing our production of these things can we get more food and more money for every Tanzanian.

◆ The Conditions of Development

(a) Hard Work

Everybody wants development; but not everybody understands and accepts the basic requirements for development. The biggest requirement is hard work. Let us go to the villages and talk to our people and see whether or not it is possible for them to work harder.

In towns, for example, wage-earners normally work for seven and a half or eight hours a day, and for six or six and a half days a week. This is about 45 hours a week for the whole year, except for two or three weeks leave. In other words, a wage-earner works for 45 hours a week for 48 or 50 weeks of the year.

In a country like ours these are really quite short working hours. In other countries, even those which are more developed than we are, people work for more than 45 hours a week. It is not normal for a young country to start with such a short working week. The normal thing is to begin with long working hours and decrease them as the country becomes more and more prosperous. By starting with such short working hours and asking for even shorter hours, we are in fact imitating the more developed countries. And we shall regret this imitation. Nevertheless, wage earners do work for 45 hours per week and their annual vacation does not exceed four weeks.

It would be appropriate to ask our farmers, especially the men, how many hours a week and how many weeks a year they work. Many do not even work for half as many hours as the wage-earner does. The truth is that in the villages the women work very hard. At times they work for 12 or 14 hours a day. They even work on Sundays and public holidays. Women who live in the villages work harder than anybody else in Tanzania. But the men who live in villages (and some of the women in towns) are on leave for half of their life. The energies of the millions of men in the villages and thousands of women in the towns which are at present wasted in gossip, dancing and drinking, are a great treasure which could contribute more towards the development of our country than anything we could get from rich nations.

We would be doing something very beneficial to our country if we went to the villages and told our people that they hold this treasure and that it is up to them to use it for their own benefit and the benefit of our whole nation.

(b) Intelligence

The second condition of development is the use of intelligence. Unintelligent hard work would not bring the same good results as the two combined. Using a big hoe instead of a small one; using a plow pulled by oxen instead of an ordinary hoe; the use of fertilizers; the use of insecticides; knowing the right crop for a particular season or soil; choosing good seeds for planting; knowing the right time for planting, weeding, etc.; all these things show the use of knowledge and intelligence. And all of them combine with hard work to produce more and better results.

The money and time we spend on passing this knowledge to the peasants are better spent and bring more benefits to our country than the money and great amount of time we spend on other things which we call development.

These facts are well known to all of us. The parts of our Five-Year Development Plan which are on target, or where the target has been exceeded, are those parts which depend solely upon the people's own hard work. The production of cotton, coffee, cashew nuts, tobacco and pyrethrum has increased enormously for the past three years. But these are things which are produced by hard work and the good leadership of the people, not by the use of great amounts of money.

Furthermore the people, through their own hard work and with a little help and leadership, have finished many development projects in the villages. They have built schools, dispensaries, community centers, and roads; they have dug wells, water channels, animal dips, small dams, and completed various other development projects. Had they waited for money, they would not now have the use of these things.

◆ **Hard Work Is the Root of Development**

Some Plan projects which depend on money are going on well, but there are many which have stopped and others which might never be fulfilled because of lack of money. Yet still we talk about money and our search for money increases and takes nearly all our energies. We should not lessen our efforts to get the money we really need, but it would be more appropriate for us to spend time in the villages showing the people how to bring about development through their own efforts rather than going on so many long and expensive journeys abroad in search of development money. This is the real way to bring development to everybody in the country.

None of this means that from now on we will not need money or that we will not start industries or embark upon development projects which require money. Furthermore, we are not saying that we will not accept, or even that we shall not look for, money from other countries for our development. This is not what we are saying. We will continue to use money; and each year we will use more money for the various development projects than we used the previous year because this will be one of the signs of our development.

What we are saying, however, is that from now on we shall know what is the foundation and what is the fruit of development. Between money and people it is obvious that the people and their hard work are the foundation of development, and money is one of the fruits of that hard work.

From now on we shall stand upright and walk forward on our feet rather than look at this problem upside down. Industries will come and money will come but their foundation is the people and their hard work, especially in agriculture. This is the meaning of self-reliance.

Our emphasis should therefore be on: (a) The Land and Agriculture, (b) The People, (c) The Policy of Socialism and Self-Reliance, and (d) Good Leadership.

(a) The Land

Because the economy of Tanzania depends and will continue to depend on agriculture and animal husbandry, Tanzanians can live well without depending on help from outside if they use their land properly. Land is the basis of human life and all Tanzanians should use it as a valuable investment for future development. Because the land belongs to the nation, the Government has to see to it that it is being used for the benefit of the whole nation and not for the benefit of one individual or just a few people.

It is the responsibility of TANU to see that the country produces enough food and enough cash crops for export. It is the responsibility of the Government and the co-operative societies to see to it that our people get the necessary tools, training and leadership in modern methods of agriculture.

(b) The People

In order properly to implement the policy of self-reliance, the people have to be taught the meaning of self-reliance and its practice. They must become self-sufficient in food, serviceable clothes and good housing.

In our country work should be something to be proud of, and laziness, drunkenness and idleness should be things to be ashamed of. And for the defense of our nation, it is necessary for us to be on guard against internal stooges who could be used by external enemies who aim to destroy us. The people should always be ready to defend their nation when they are called upon to do so.

(c) Good Policies

The principles of our policy of self-reliance go hand in hand with our policy of socialism. In order to prevent exploitation it is necessary for everybody to work and to live on his own labour. And in order to distribute the national wealth fairly, it is necessary for everybody to work to the maximum of his ability. Nobody should go and stay for a long time with his relative, doing no work, because in doing so he will be exploiting his relative. Likewise, nobody should be allowed to loiter in towns or villages without doing work which would enable him to be self-reliant without exploiting his relatives.

TANU believes that everybody who loves his nation has a duty to serve it by co-operating with his fellows in building the country for the benefit of all the people of Tanzania. In order to maintain our independence and our people's freedom we ought to be self-reliant in every possible way and avoid depending upon other countries for assistance. If every individual is self-reliant [the] ten-house cell will be self-reliant; if all the cells are self-reliant the whole ward will be self-reliant; and if the wards are self-reliant the District will be self-reliant. If the Districts are self-reliant, then the Region is self-reliant, and if the Regions are self-reliant, then the whole nation is self-reliant and this is our aim.

(d) Good Leadership

TANU recognizes the urgency and importance of good leadership. But we have not yet produced systematic training for our leaders; it is necessary that TANU Headquarters should now prepare a programme of training for all leaders—from the national level to the ten-house cell level—so that every one of them understands our political and economic policies. Leaders must set a good example to the rest of the people in their lives and in all their activities.

Part Four. TANU Membership

Since the Party was founded we have put great emphasis on getting as many members as possible. This was the right policy during the independence struggle. But now the National Executive feels that the time has come when we should put more emphasis on the beliefs of our Party and its policies of socialism.

That part of the TANU Constitution which relates to the admission of a member should be adhered to, and if it is discovered that a man does not appear to accept the faith, the objects, and the rules and regulations of the Party, then he should not be accepted as a member. In particular, it should not be forgotten that TANU is a party of peasants and workers.

Part Five. The Arusha Resolution

Therefore, the National Executive Committee, meeting in the Community Centre at Arusha from 26.1.67 to 29.1.67 resolves:

(a) The Leadership

1. Every TANU and Government leader must be either a peasant or a worker, and should in no way be associated with the practices of capitalism or feudalism.

2. No TANU or Government leader should hold shares in any company.

3. No TANU or Government leader should hold directorships in any privately owned enterprise.

4. No TANU or Government leader should receive two or more salaries.

5. No TANU or Government leader should own houses which he rents to others.

6. For the purposes of this Resolution the term "leader" should comprise the following:

Members of the TANU National Executive Committee; Ministers; Members of Parliament; senior officials of organizations affiliated to TANU; senior officers of parastatal organizations; all those appointed or elected under any clause of the TANU Constitution; councilors; and civil servants in the high and middle cadres. (In this context "leader" means a man or a man and his wife; a woman or a woman and her husband.)

(b) The Government and other Institutions

1. Congratulates the Government for the steps it has taken so far in the implementation of the policy of socialism.

2. Calls upon the Government to take further steps in the implementation of our policy of socialism as described in Part Two of this document without waiting for a Commission on Socialism.

3. Calls upon the Government to put emphasis, when preparing its development plans, on the ability of this country to implement the plans rather than depending on foreign loans and grants as has been done in the current Five-Year Development Plan. The National Executive Committee also resolves that the Plan should be amended so as to make it fit in with the policy of self-reliance.

4. Calls upon the Government to take action designed to ensure that the incomes of workers in the private sector are not very different from the incomes of workers in the public sector.

5. Calls upon the Government to put great emphasis on actions which will raise the standard of living of the peasants, and the rural community.

6. Calls upon NUTA, the co-operatives, TAPA, UWT, TYL, and other Government institutions to take steps to implement the policy of socialism and self-reliance.

(c) Membership

Members should get thorough teaching on Party ideology so that they may understand it, and they should always be reminded of the importance of living up to its principles.

Glossary

NUTA	the National Union of Tanganyika Workers; the only trade union in the country before 1962
parastatal organizations	entities wholly or partly owned or controlled by government
TAPA	the Tanganyika African Parents Association
TYL	the Tanganyika Youth League
UWT	the Tanganyika National Women's Organization (in Swahili: *Umoja wa Wanawake wa Tanganyika*)

UN SECURITY COUNCIL RESOLUTION 242

"The Security Council [calls for the] withdrawal of Israeli armed forces from territories occupied in the recent conflict."

Overview

On November 22, 1967, the United Nations Security Council passed Resolution 242 in response to the Six-Day War. This war, which began on June 5 of that year and continued until a cease-fire was called on June 10, pitted Israel against the combined forces of Egypt, Jordan, and Syria, with lesser involvement by other Arab states. The conflict was the latest in a series of conflicts between the Jewish state of Israel and its Arab neighbors since the founding of Israel in 1948. The purpose of the resolution was to outline a process for achieving peace in the Middle East by reducing the belligerency of the combatants and establishing secure territorial boundaries. The resolution served as a blueprint for Middle East peace efforts throughout the decades that followed.

Resolution 242 was not the first effort to resolve the Six-Day War. Immediately after the war, the UN Security Council tried to pass a resolution but failed. The matter was taken up by the UN General Assembly, but it, too, failed to pass a resolution. Finally, in November, the U.S. ambassador to the United Nations, Arthur Goldberg, made a proposal for a permanent peace agreement to the Security Council. The Arab states, with the backing of the Soviet Union, resisted Goldberg's proposal. Much of Goldberg's language, though, was used in Resolution 242, which was submitted to the Security Council for a vote by the British ambassador Hugh Foot, Lord Caradon. Although the Soviets, who blamed Israel for the war, were not entirely satisfied with the resolution, they concluded that it was the best outcome they could achieve. Accordingly, the Security Council vote on the resolution was unanimous.

Context

The roots of modern hostility between Arab Muslims and Israeli Jews, the Six-Day War, and Resolution 242 extend back to the late nineteenth and early twentieth centuries. In 1896 Theodor Herzl, an Austro-Hungarian journalist, published *Der Judenstaat*, or *The Jewish State*. This influential book marked the beginning of Zionism, a move-

ment calling for Jews to return to their biblical homeland and establish a Jewish state in Palestine, territory that Muslim Arabs claimed as their own. During World War I, Palestine came under occupation by the British, and in 1917 the British foreign secretary, Arthur James Balfour, pledged in the Balfour Declaration that the British were committed to the establishment of a safe homeland for Jews in Palestine. In 1922 the newly formed League of Nations (predecessor to the United Nations) officially designated Palestine a British mandate, or territory under British administration. Britain's responsibilities under the mandate were to secure a Jewish national homeland and to protect the religious and civil rights of all inhabitants of Palestine.

In August 1929 the status quo changed dramatically when rioting broke out over disputes about access to the Wailing Wall, a holy site in Jerusalem. Charges, counter-charges, and rumors led to outbreaks of violence, particularly in the city of Hebron. A British investigative team laid the blame for the unrest primarily on the Arab community, which felt that its agricultural land was being taken over by Jewish immigrants. In 1936 Britain recommended that Palestine be divided into Jewish and Arab areas, but militancy among Arabs and Jews had increased, both sides rejected the proposal, and Palestinian Arabs launched three years of terrorist activities against Jews. Acting on the recommendations of a report called the White Paper of 1939, which suggested that the source of the tension was Jewish immigration, Britain limited Jewish immigration into Palestine for a period of five years, thus ensuring an Arab majority in Palestine. A practical effect of this restriction was that many Jews were trapped in Europe during World War II and the Nazi-perpetrated Holocaust.

After the horrors of World War II, which left many of Europe's Jews homeless and displaced, calls increased for the establishment of a Jewish homeland, particularly after the British mandate in Palestine ended in 1948. Anticipating Britain's withdrawal, in November 1947 the United Nations adopted Resolution 181, which partitioned Palestine into a Jewish zone and an Arab zone. Jews accepted the plan, but the Arabs rejected it.

On May 14, 1948, Israel declared its existence as an independent state, but the following day, Egypt, Syria, Iraq, Lebanon, and Jordan (then called Transjordan) attacked

1947

- **November 29**
  With UN General Assembly Resolution 181, the United Nations votes to partition Palestine into Arab and Jewish sectors.

1948

- **May 14**
  Israel declares its independence.

- **May 15**
  Arab states attack Israel, launching the Arab-Israeli War.

1956

- **May 22**
  Egypt closes the Straits of Tiran to Israeli shipping.

- **July 26**
  The Egyptian president Gamal Abdel Nasser nationalizes the Suez Canal, leading to eruption of hostilities with Israel, Britain, and France on October 29.

1964

- **May 28**
  The Palestinian National Charter, creating the Palestinian Liberation Organization (PLO), is adopted.

1967

- **May 22**
  Egypt blockades the Straits of Tiran, interrupting Israeli shipping.

- **June 5**
  The Six-Day War, between Israel and the combined forces of Egypt, Syria, and Jordan, begins.

Israel, beginning the 1948 Arab-Israeli War, which lasted until March 1949. Indeed, Israel was in a vulnerable position from its inception. The nation occupied just a tenth of 1 percent of the Middle Eastern landmass and had less than 2 percent of the Middle Eastern population, making it a very small nation (about the size of the U.S. state of New Jersey) surrounded by much larger and more populous nations. The armistice lines established after the 1948 war were precarious. Syria overlooked northern Israel and the Sea of Galilee, Israel's major water source, from the Golan Heights; Jordan dominated the coastal plain from the West Bank of the Jordan River; and the southern suburbs of the major Israeli city of Tel Aviv were just thirty miles from Egypt along the Gaza Strip. Israelis thus lived in fear of a surprise attack.

From one point of view, the Six-Day War of 1967 was simply a third phase of the 1948 war, for the Arab states continued to call for the destruction of Israel in the two decades between the wars. A second phase of the conflict took place in 1956, after Egypt closed the Suez Canal and the Straits of Tiran to Israeli shipping. The result was armed conflict between Egypt and a coalition of Israel, France, and Great Britain. In the late 1950s and early 1960s, the Egyptian president Gamal Abdel Nasser, having lost stature when he backed down during the Suez crisis of 1956, spearheaded a pan-Arabist movement. This was an effort to unite Arab states of the Middle East and North Africa into a single political entity—and the effort entailed continued calls for the destruction of Israel. Influenced by the pan-Arabist movement, the Palestine Liberation Organization (PLO), whose charter calls for the destruction of Israel, was formed in 1964.

The situation in the Middle East grew increasingly tense yet again in 1967. Border skirmishes between Israel and Syria were frequent. The PLO, which represented the interests of the Arab Palestinians in the region, made frequent terrorist attacks against Israel, often backed by Syria, Jordan, and Egypt. Egypt moved troops into the Sinai Peninsula and Gaza Strip, and other Arab nations mobilized their militaries. The Soviet Union fueled tension by claiming falsely that Israel planned to attack Syria in May. On May 22, Egypt blockaded the Straits of Tiran, a violation of maritime law and an act of war. Nasser also demanded that UN troops, placed on the frontier between Israel and Egypt after the 1956 crisis, be withdrawn. Later that month, Egypt and Jordan signed a mutual defense pact. Troops from several Arab Muslim nations poured into the Sinai Peninsula.

With the Arab coalition poised to attack, the Israeli cabinet decided to make a preemptive attack on June 5, 1967. Israeli forces moved swiftly and with overwhelming success. They crippled the Egyptian air force and routed Egyptian ground troops from Sinai and the Gaza Strip, drove Jordanian forces out of the West Bank, and crushed Syrian forces in the Golan Heights. The UN Security Council called a cease-fire, which went into effect on June 10, leaving Israel with the West Bank, the Gaza Strip, and the Golan Heights in its hands. Additionally, Israel was in control of the entire city of Jerusalem, which had been divided after the 1948 war.

Between the cease-fire and the passage of Resolution 242 in November 1967, considerable diplomatic wrangling occurred. At a summit in Khartoum, Sudan, held from August 29 to September 1, the Arab nations rejected peace proposals and continued to call for the destruction of Israel. The U.S. president Lyndon Johnson, in a speech on June 19, outlined a set of five principles that he believed could lead to peace in the region: respect for the right of the nations in the region to exist, justice for war refugees, respect for maritime rights, reduction of arms buildups in the Middle East, and respect for territorial integrity. Israel accepted these five principles, but the Arab nations, still with the backing of the Soviet Union, rejected them. Efforts were made on each side to court nonaligned nations—that is, nations not allied with either the United States or the Soviet Union. Despite the cease-fire, the situation remained incendiary, with frequent violations of the terms of the cease-fire on both sides.

About the Author

The UN Security Council has five permanent members: the United States, the Russian Federation (in 1967, the Soviet Union), the United Kingdom, France, and China. Ten other nations have seats on the Security Council for two-year terms. In 1967 those nations were Argentina, Brazil, Bulgaria, Canada, Denmark, Ethiopia, India, Japan, Mali, and Nigeria. Security Council resolutions on substantive matters require unanimous votes by the permanent members; Resolution 242 was affirmed unanimously by the entire Security Council.

The chief drafter of Resolution 242 was Hugh M. Foot, Lord Caradon. Foot, born in 1907, enjoyed a long and distinguished career as a British ambassador to several nations and oversaw the independence of numerous former British colonies. In 1964, during the administration of the British prime minister Harold Wilson, he was appointed minister of state for foreign affairs and the United Kingdom's ambassador to the United Nations, where he served until 1970. He died in 1990.

Three other individuals played a significant role in drafting the resolution. George A. Brown, born in 1914, began his career as a trade-union organizer and then served the British government as foreign minister, secretary of state for economic affairs, and first secretary of state. He was also a major leader of Britain's Labour Party. He was made a peer in 1970, taking as his peerage name Lord George-Brown. He died in 1985.

Arthur Goldberg, born in 1908, was a distinguished American statesman. During World War II he served as a spy for the Office of Strategic Services, the precursor to the Central Intelligence Agency. He was secretary of labor in the cabinet of President John F. Kennedy until Kennedy appointed him as an associate justice of the U.S. Supreme Court. Under President Lyndon B. Johnson he served as the U.S. ambassador to the United Nations. He died in 1990.

Finally, Eugene Rostow, born in 1913, was a legal scholar and dean of the law school at Yale University. During

Time Line

1967

- **June 10**
  A cease-fire is called in the Six-Day War.

- **September 1**
  Concluding a summit in Sudan, the Arab states reject proposals for a negotiated peace with Israel in the Khartoum Resolution.

- **November 22**
  The UN Security Council adopts Resolution 242, which outlines a blueprint for peace in the Middle East.

1968

- **July 17**
  An amended Palestinian National Charter, calling for the destruction of Israel, is adopted by the PLO.

1970

- **June 19**
  The U.S. secretary of state William P. Rogers announces the Rogers Plan for the implementation of UN Resolution 242.

1973

- **October 6**
  Egypt and Syria attack Israel, launching the Yom Kippur War, called the Ramadan War or October War in the Arab countries.

- **October 26**
  A cease-fire in the Yom Kippur War is called.

Time Line

1978

■ **September 17**
The Camp David
Accords, nor-
malizing rela-
tions between
Egypt and Israel,
are signed fol-
lowing negotia-
tions at the U.S.
president's
country retreat
in Maryland.

World War II he served in the U.S. State Department, where he was a vocal opponent of the wartime internment of Japanese American and Japanese civilians in the United States in the wake of Japan's attack on Pearl Harbor, Hawaii, in December 1941. From 1966 to 1969 he was the U.S. undersecretary of state for political affairs. He returned to teach at Yale Law School and died in 2002.

Explanation and Analysis of the Document

Resolution 242 is a relatively brief and simple document. The preamble acknowledges the "grave situation in the Middle East." It goes on to note the "inadmissibility" of seizing territory by war—an allusion to Israel's occupation of the West Bank, the Golan Heights, and the Gaza Strip as a result of the war—and the need for all nations in the region to live in security. The preamble concludes by stating that all member states of the United Nations are obligated to act in accordance with Article 2 of the UN Charter. This article states, among other provisions, that the United Nations "is based on the principle of the sovereign equality of all its Members" and that all members "shall fulfill in good faith the obligations assumed by them in accordance with the present Charter"; "shall settle their international disputes by peaceful means in such a manner that international peace and security, and justice, are not endangered"; and "shall refrain in their international relations from the threat or use of force against the territorial integrity or political independence of any state" (http://www.un.org/en/documents/charter/chapter1.shtml).

The core of the resolution is contained in clause 1, which states that a "just and lasting peace" in the region is predicated on withdrawal of Israeli military forces from areas occupied during the war. This provision was the subject of intense negotiation and the need for later clarification. It was pointed out that the resolution does not specifically call for Israel to withdraw to the armistice lines established after the 1948 conflict. And much was made of the fact that it asks for Israeli withdrawal "from territories" recently occupied—not "the territories" or "all the territories" in the English version, although the French version does contain the definite article. (English and French were

the two working languages of the United Nations at the time, and it was the English version on which the Security Council voted.) When questioned about this parsing of the grammar of the statement in an interview for the *Journal of Palestine Studies*, Lord Caradon, the resolution's principal drafter, responded,

> We could have said: well, you go back to the 1967 line. But I know the 1967 line, and it's a rotten line. You couldn't have a worse line for a permanent international boundary. It's where the troops happened to be on a certain night in 1948. It's got no relation to the needs of the situation. (qtd. at http://www.sixday war.org/content/242drafters.asp)

In defending the wording of subclause 1(i), the drafters of the resolution pointed to subclause 1(ii), which calls for "respect for and acknowledgement of the sovereignty, territorial integrity and political independence" of all nations in the region. The key phrase from the drafters' point of view is the reference to "secure and recognized boundaries." In interpreting that phrase, the drafters appealed to the armistice agreement that followed the 1948 Arab-Israeli War. Article V, clause 2, of that agreement states, "The Armistice Demarcation Line is not to be construed in any sense as a political or territorial boundary, and is delineated without prejudice to rights, claims and positions of either Party to the Armistice as regards ultimate settlement of the Palestine question" (http://avalon.law.yale.edu/20th_century/arm01.asp). In other words, Resolution 242 does not insist that Israel withdraw to the position it held as of June 4, 1967, nor does it suggest that the armistice lines from the 1948 war constituted permanent national boundaries. In effect, the resolution neglects to address the extent to which Israel should withdraw, as the drafters believed that negotiations would later determine precisely where the boundaries of Israel should lie.

Clause 2 of the resolution takes up ancillary matters. The first subclause relates to maritime law and calls for freedom of navigation in the region's waters. This is a clear reference to Egypt's blockade of Israeli shipping through the Straits of Tiran, both in 1956 and in 1967. The straits are a narrow sea passage between the Sinai and Arabian peninsulas, connecting the Gulf of Aqaba and the Red Sea. They were important to Israel because they provided access to shipping from the Indian Ocean through the Israeli port of Eilat. Reference is made in subclause 2(b) to the problem of refugees. In 1948 some seven hundred thousand Arabs fled Palestine to in effect give Arab forces a free-fire zone. Large numbers of those Palestinian Arabs did not return, and the number of refugees increased by about a quarter million as a result of the 1967 war. Virtually all of the refugees wound up in refugee camps in the Gaza Strip, on the West Bank, and in Syria, Lebanon, and Jordan; ironically, Egypt, which provoked the 1948 war, refused to accept refugees. These refugees and their descendants now number about 4.25 million of about 10.6 million Palestinian Arabs, a state of affairs that continues to fuel tensions

*Hugh Foot (**center**)* (AP/Wide World Photos)

between Israel and the Arab world. Finally, subclause 2(c) calls for "territorial inviolability and political independence" through the creation of demilitarized zones. Chief among these zones have been various areas of the Sinai Peninsula.

Clauses 3 and 4 are more administrative in nature. Clause 3 instructs the UN secretary general, who at the time was U Thant, to send a special representative to the region to find ways to enforce the resolution. The following day, the secretary general appointed Gunnar Jarring, the Swedish ambassador to the Soviet Union, to the post. The so-called Jarring Mission, marked by shuttle diplomacy among the parties to the war, lasted until 1971, when it was clear that no permanent peace agreement would be reached.

Audience

The audience for Resolution 242 was principally the warring parties, including Israel, under the leadership of Prime Minister Levi Eshkol and Defense Minister Moshe Dayan; Egypt, under the leadership of President Gamal Abdel Nasser; Syria, ruled by President Noureddin Mustafa al-Atassi (although al-Atassi was largely a figurehead, with real power in the hands of Deputy Secretary General Salah Jadid and Defense Minister Hafez al-Assad); and Jordan, ruled by King Hussein bin Talal.

When the UN Security Council acts, however, all the world's nations form the audience. At the time of the Six-Day War and the passage of Resolution 242, the cold war was at its height. The Western powers, principally the United States and its allies, backed Israel, although none of the Western nations provided direct military aid during the conflict. The Arab states, in turn, were backed by the Soviet Union, which sent ten warships to the eastern Mediterranean as the prewar situation grew more tense, and most Arab warplanes were MiGs provided by the Soviets. Thus, in certain respects, the Six-Day War was one of the era's many proxy wars with broader cold war implications; and many observers feared that the conflict could escalate into a broader war, engulfing not only the Middle East but also the United States and the Soviet Union. Accordingly, the world took considerable interest in the

Israeli troops enter Gaza City in the Gaza Strip on June 7, 1967. (AP/Wide World Photos)

question of what steps the United Nations would take in response to the war.

A further audience was future negotiators. Throughout the last half of the twentieth century and into the twenty-first, numerous parties have attempted to broker an elusive peace in the Middle East. Resolution 242 has provided a framework for such peace initiatives as the 1978 Camp David Accords between Egypt and Israel, the 1993 Oslo Accords, and President George W. Bush's 2002 "road map for peace."

Impact

Israel and Jordan immediately accepted the terms of Resolution 242. Egypt also stated that it did, but President Nasser then refused to negotiate with the Israelis. In July 1968 he declared openly that there would be no negotiations with Israel, no peace with Israel, and no recognition by Egypt of Israel's right to exist. Syria took a particularly hard-line position, openly rejecting Resolution 242, refusing to engage in talks with Gunnar Jarring, and denying Israel's right to exist. The Palestinians, too, flatly rejected the resolution. In 1968, largely in response to the Six-Day War, the PLO amended its

1964 charter, clearly denying Israel's right to exist. Article 15 of the amended charter states, "The liberation of Palestine ... is a national duty and it attempts to repel the Zionist and imperialist aggression against the Arab homeland, and aims at the elimination of Zionism in Palestine"; Article 19 states, "The partition of Palestine in 1947 and the establishment of the state of Israel are entirely illegal" (http://avalon.law.yale .edu/20th_ century/plocov.asp). In general, the Arab nations reiterated the position they had taken in the Khartoum Resolution of September 1, 1967. Meanwhile, the cease-fire was repeatedly broken. The Soviet Union rearmed Egypt with MiG fighter jets, artillery, and surface-to-air missiles, and Egypt launched numerous artillery attacks against Israel from across the border.

The diplomatic Jarring Mission, which began in 1968, proved a failure. Despite Jarring's best efforts to bring the parties to the negotiating table, the question of the occupied territories seemed intractable. In a report to the United Nations, U Thant wrote,

When the Special Representative first met with the parties in December 1967, he found that the Israeli Government was of the firm view that a settlement of

> "*Emphasizing the inadmissibility of the acquisition of territory by war and the need to work for a just and lasting peace in which every State in the area can live in security.*"
>
> (Preamble)

> "*Withdrawal of Israeli armed forces from territories occupied in the recent conflict.*"
>
> (Clause 1[i])

> "*Termination of all claims or states of belligerency and respect for and acknowledgement of the sovereignty, territorial integrity and political independence of every State in the area and their right to live in peace within secure and recognized boundaries free from threats or acts of force.*"
>
> (Clause 1[ii])

the Middle East question could be reached only through direct negotiations between the parties culminating in a peace treaty and that there could be no question of withdrawal of their forces prior to such a settlement.

U Thant noted that the Arab nations were equally insistent on their position "that there could be no question of discussions between the parties until the Israeli forces had been withdrawn to the positions occupied by them prior to 5 June 1967" (http://www.jewishvirtuallibrary.org/jsource/History/jarring.html). Negotiations were at an impasse.

Accordingly, the United States attempted its own diplomatic initiative for implementing Resolution 242. Secretary of State William P. Rogers formally announced the "Rogers Plan" on June 19, 1970. The essence of the Rogers Plan was the following provisions: Negotiations would continue under Jarring's leadership, Israel would withdraw from the Egyptian territory it had occupied since the war, the two sides would sign a peace accord officially ending the war, demilitarized zones would be established, Israel would be guaranteed free passage into the Gulf of Aqaba, and the refugee problem would be settled fairly. The Israelis, however, rejected the Rogers Plan, largely because of the Egyptian military buildup, which included three Soviet brigades.

Peace thus remained elusive. War broke out again on October 6, 1973, when combined Arab forces led by Egypt and Syria crossed the cease-fire lines from the Six-Day War

and invaded Israel. The first forty-eight hours of the war saw Arab successes, for they surprised Israel by launching the assault on Yom Kippur, the Jewish Day of Atonement, giving the war its name, the Yom Kippur War. Israeli forces quickly regrouped. They drove the Syrians out of the Golan Heights, and they met Egyptian forces on the Sinai Peninsula and cut off their supply lines just as the United Nations announced a cease-fire on October 26. This cease-fire was supported by the Arab nations' Soviet backers, who feared a total defeat, and so the war ended in a stalemate.

The Arab nations had felt humiliated by their defeat in the Six-Day War, but Arab successes in the early days of the Yom Kippur War emboldened them. In the middle of the war, Middle Eastern members of the Organization of the Petroleum Exporting Countries imposed an oil embargo against the United States. Yet after the cease-fire, Israel and the U.S. secretary of state, Henry Kissinger, were stunned by a message received from Egypt: Egypt would be willing to enter into peace talks with Israel provided that Israel honor the cease-fire and allow nonmilitary supplies to be delivered to its encircled army on the Sinai Peninsula. Consequently, for the first time since 1948, Egyptian and Israeli officials met face-to-face, and in early 1974 an armistice was hammered out. The Egyptian president Anwar as-Sadat meanwhile began introducing economic liberalization policies in Egypt and, inexplicably, expressed impatience with the slow pace of the peace process. In the years that followed, Egypt took part in diplomatic initiatives, and as-Sadat expelled the Soviets from Egypt and removed the nation from the Soviets' sphere of influence. His efforts, as well as those of the U.S. president Jimmy Carter and the Israeli prime minister Menachem Begin, led to the signing of the Camp David Accords—named for the presidential retreat in Maryland—on September 17, 1978. The accords normalized relations between Egypt and Israel.

Further Reading

▪ Books

Bowen, Jeremy. *Six Days: How the 1967 War Shaped the Middle East*. New York: Thomas Dunne Books, 2005.

Herzog, Chaim. *The Arab-Israeli Wars: War and Peace in the Middle East*. New York: Vintage, 1982.

Hirst, David. *The Gun and the Olive Branch: The Roots of Violence in the Middle East*, 3rd ed. New York: Thunder's Mouth Press/Nation Books, 2003.

Korn, David A. *The Making of United Nations Security Council Resolution 242: Centerpiece of Arab-Israeli Negotiations*. Washington, D.C.: Georgetown University, Institute for the Study of Diplomacy, 1992.

Oren, Michael B. *Six Days of War: June 1967 and the Making of the Modern Middle East*. New York: Ballantine Books, Presidio Press, 2002.

▪ Web Sites

"Chapter 1: Purposes and Principles." Charter of the United Nations, United Nations Web site.
    http://www.un.org/en/documents/charter/chapter1.shtml.

"Egyptian-Israeli General Armistice Agreement, February 24, 1949." Yale Law School Avalon Project Web site.
    http://avalon.law.yale.edu/20th_century/arm01.asp.

"The Jarring Mission (January 4, 1971)." Jewish Virtual Library Web site.
    http://www.jewishvirtuallibrary.org/jsource/History/jarring.html.

"The Palestinian National Charter: Resolutions of the Palestine National Council, July 1–17, 1968." Yale Law School Avalon Project Web site.
    http://avalon.law.yale.edu/20th_century/plocov.asp.

Questions for Further Study

1. UN Security Council Resolution 242 is one of a cluster of documents that chart the history of Judaism, the state of Israel, and Israel's relations with the Arab states and the Palestinians. Among them are Theodor Herzl's essay "A Solution to the Jewish Question," the Declaration of Independence of the State of Israel, the Gamal Abdel Nasser order on the Nationalization of the Suez Canal, and the Palestinian National Charter. Using these documents, prepare a consolidated time line of key events in this troubled region of the world and be prepared to justify the inclusion of each item.

2. Why were the Arab states and the Palestinians so adamantly opposed to the existence of a Jewish state in Palestine, particularly from the 1940s through the 1960s?

3. How do you think the history of events in the Middle East might have evolved differently if Palestine had not been declared a British mandate and if Britain had played no role in the politics of the region during the 1920s into the 1940s?

4. Documents such as a UN Security Council resolution attempting to establish peace after an armed conflict are the result, generally, of intensive negotiations and are potentially fraught with problems involving language: what the document actually says and means. What problems of this nature did the United Nations face in drafting Resolution 242?

5. The conflict between the Arab nations and the Palestinians on the one hand and Israel on the other has been long and complex, with other nations often feeling forced to choose a side. Based on your reading of this document and others associated with the conflict, prepare an outline for a debate in which each side in the conflict would present its case as to why its actions have been justified.

"Resolution 242: The Drafters Clarify Its Meaning." Committee for Accuracy in Middle East Reporting in America "Six-Day War" Web site.
http://www.sixdaywar.org/content/242drafters.asp.

"The Six-Day War: Causes and Consequences." Committee for Accuracy in Middle East Reporting in America "Six-Day War" Web site.
http://www.sixdaywar.org/index.asp.

—Michael J. O'Neal

UN SECURITY COUNCIL RESOLUTION 242

The Security Council,

Expressing its continuing concern with the grave situation in the Middle East,

Emphasizing the inadmissibility of the acquisition of territory by war and the need to work for a just and lasting peace in which every State in the area can live in security,

Emphasizing further that all Member States in their acceptance of the Charter of the United Nations have undertaken a commitment to act in accordance with Article 2 of the Charter,

1. Affirms that the fulfillment of Charter principles requires the establishment of a just and lasting peace in the Middle East which should include the application of both the following principles:

(i) Withdrawal of Israeli armed forces from territories occupied in the recent conflict;

(ii) Termination of all claims or states of belligerency and respect for and acknowledgement of the sovereignty, territorial integrity and political independence of every State in the area and their right to live in peace within secure and recognized boundaries free from threats or acts of force;

2. Affirms further the necessity

(a) For guaranteeing freedom of navigation through international waterways in the area;

(b) For achieving a just settlement of the refugee problem;

(c) For guaranteeing the territorial inviolability and political independence of every State in the area, through measures including the establishment of demilitarized zones;

3. Requests the Secretary General to designate a Special Representative to proceed to the Middle East to establish and maintain contacts with the States concerned in order to promote agreement and assist efforts to achieve a peaceful and accepted settlement in accordance with the provisions and principles in this resolution;

4. Requests the Secretary-General to report to the Security Council on the progress of the efforts of the Special Representative as soon as possible.

Yasser Arafat (AP/Wide World Photos)

PALESTINIAN NATIONAL CHARTER

"Armed struggle is the only way to liberate Palestine."

Overview

The Palestinian National Charter, sometimes called the Palestinian National Covenant and transliterated from Arabic script as al-Mithaq al-Watani al-Filastini, states the aims of the Palestine Liberation Organization (PLO). The PLO claims to represent the interests of the Palestinian people in and around Israel, a claim that the United Nations recognizes. The charter is part constitution, part "declaration of independence," and part political manifesto.

An earlier charter, which formed the PLO, was adopted on May 28, 1964. Attached to that document was another referred to variously as the Basic Constitution, Basic Law, or Fundamental Law, which outlined the structure of the PLO. On July 17, 1968, however, the charter was extensively amended as a result of the Six-Day War (June 5–10, 1967) between Israel and the combined forces of Egypt, Syria, and Jordan. As a consequence of this war, in which Israel prevailed by launching preemptive surprise attacks against massed Arab forces, Israel made several territorial gains, including the Gaza Strip and Sinai Peninsula from Egypt, the Golan Heights from Syria, and the West Bank, including East Jerusalem, from Jordan. The revised charter's emphasis is on the "liberation" of the Palestinian people and the assertion that the Jewish state of Israel is illegitimate, a declaration that many observers interpret to mean that the PLO was calling for the destruction of Israel.

Context

The roots of the Palestinian National Charter and the formation of the PLO can be traced to hostility between Muslims and Jews that extends back hundreds of years. Beginning in the late nineteenth century and throughout much of the twentieth century, however, a number of significant events took place that laid the foundation for the charter and modern manifestations of that hostility. In 1896 an Austro-Hungarian journalist, Theodor Herzl, published *Der Judenstaat* (*The Jewish State*). The publication of this book marked the beginning of the movement called

Zionism, which called for the establishment of a Jewish state in Palestine. The core concept of Zionism was that Jews should return to their biblical homeland in and around the city of Jerusalem—territory that Muslim Arabs claimed as their own. The Zionist movement began a process of Jewish immigration to Palestine. During World War I, the British occupied Palestine, and on November 17, 1917, the British foreign secretary Arthur James Balfour, in the Balfour Declaration, pledged to an organization called the Zionist Federation that the British would ensure a safe homeland for Jews in Palestine. After the war, the newly formed League of Nations (the predecessor to today's United Nations) designated Palestine as a British mandate, or territory that would fall under British administration. In a resolution dated July 24, 1922, establishing the British Mandate for Palestine, the League of Nations specified Britain's responsibilities in Palestine: to "secure the establishment of the Jewish national home" but also to protect "the civil and religious rights of all the inhabitants of Palestine," including those of Muslims (http://www.mfa .gov.il/MFA/Peace+Process/Guide+to+the+Peace+Process/ The+Mandate+for+Palestine.htm).

Jews and Muslims lived side by side in relative peace throughout most of the 1920s, but that changed in August 1929 when rioting broke out over disputes about access to the Wailing Wall, a holy site in Jerusalem. Charges and countercharges, all fueled by rumor, led to outbreaks of violence, particularly in the city of Hebron, resulting in a death toll of 133 Jews and 116 Arab Palestinians. The Shaw Commission, led by Sir Walter Shaw, arrived in Palestine from England to report on the causes of the unrest. The commission's March 1930 account, "Report of the Commission on the Palestine Disturbances of August, 1929," laid the blame for the unrest primarily on the Arab community. The report did, however, note that Jewish immigration to Palestine was increasing tensions between Arabs and Jews. Accordingly, on October 1, 1930, a document called the "Report on Immigration, Land Settlement and Development," referred to informally as the Hope-Simpson Report, recommended that Jewish immigration to Palestine be halted. At the same time, a 1930 document called the Passfield White Paper reinforced the policy that the rights of Arabs in Palestine were coequal with those of

1917

■ **November 2**
The British gov-
ernment issues
the Balfour Dec-
laration.

1922

■ **July 24**
The British
Mandate for
Palestine is
enacted by the
League of
Nations.

1930

■ **March**
The Shaw Com-
mission issues
the "Report of
the Commission
on the Palestine
Disturbances of
August, 1929,"
blaming the
unrest primarily
on the Arab
community.

■ **October 1**
"Report on
Immigration, Land
Settlement and
Development," also
called the Hope-
Simpson Report,
recommends that
Jewish immigration
to Palestine be
halted; the report is
released on
October 21.

■ **October 1**
The Passfield White
Paper reinforces
the policy that the
rights of Arabs in
Palestine are
coequal with those
of the Zionists.

1936

■ Britain recommends
that Palestine be
divided into Jewish
and Arab areas;
Palestinian Arabs
launch the three-
year Great Uprising
against Jews in
Palestine.

---

the Zionists. In 1936, Britain recommended that Palestine be divided into Jewish and Arab areas, but by this time militancy among Arabs and Jews had increased. Both sides rejected the proposal, and the Palestinian Arabs launched three years of terrorist activities against Jews, known as the Great Uprising (1936–1939). In response, Britain, acting on the recommendations of a report called the White Paper, issued on May 17, 1939, limited Jewish immigration to Palestine for a period of five years. This restriction ensured an Arab majority in Palestine, and some observers regarded it as an act of appeasement. The effect of this restriction was to trap many Jews in Europe during World War II and the Nazi-perpetrated Holocaust.

World War II muted tensions between Muslims and Jews (and between Jews and the British, who the Jews believed were selling them out). After the war and the Holocaust, which left many European Jews homeless and displaced, calls for the establishment of a Jewish homeland grew louder, particularly after the British Mandate for Palestine ended in 1948. In anticipation of British withdrawal, the United Nations adopted Resolution 181 on November 29, 1947. The resolution, relying on a report by the United Nation's Special Committee on Palestine, called for partitioning Palestine into a Jewish zone and an Arab zone, with Jerusalem as a *corpus separatum*, or "separate body." In effect, Jerusalem was internationalized. Jews accepted the plan, but the Arabs rejected it. On May 14, 1948, Israel declared its existence as an independent state.

The next day, Egypt, Syria, Jordan, Iraq, and Lebanon attacked Israel, beginning the Arab-Israeli War of 1948. To give Arab forces a free-fire zone, some seven hundred thousand Palestinian Arabs fled, but the Arab states' failure to defeat the Israelis left these refugees trapped, unable to return to their homes in Israel. Today's Palestinian refugees, numbering some 4.25 million (of a total Palestinian population of about 10.6 million), include these refugees as well as their descendants and refugees from the 1967 Six-Day War. While these refugees, many of whom live in refugee camps, are scattered across the Middle East, the bulk live in Jordan (1.8 million), Gaza (nearly one million), and the West Bank (nearly seven hundred thousand); ironically, Egypt, which led the fight against Israel in the 1940s and 1950s, is home to only about seventy thousand Palestinian refugees. Meanwhile, from 1948 to 1952 roughly seven hundred thousand Jews immigrated to Israel, many of them from other Arab countries, and by 1970 the number of Jewish immigrants to Israel had increased to some 850,000.

Throughout the 1950s and into the 1960s, the Arab world continued its resistance to Israel. Jews were expelled from Arab countries. Egypt closed the Suez Canal to Israeli shipping in 1956. Egyptian president Gamal Abdel Nasser spearheaded a pan-Arabist movement, which was an effort to unite Arab states into a single political entity that would encompass the Middle East and North Africa—and that called for the destruction of Israel. It was this movement that provided the immediate spark for the original Palestinian National Charter in 1964. The charter was amended in 1968 as a result of the 1967 Six-Day War. Israel delivered a stunning defeat of the Arab forces arrayed to attack, consolidating its hold on additional portions of Palestine. The Six-Day War and its aftermath, with Israeli occupation of the Gaza Strip, the Golan Heights, the West Bank, and the Sinai Peninsula, continue to shape Palestinian-Israeli relations in the region.

About the Author

The author of the 1964 Palestinian National Charter was Ahmed Shukeiri, the first chairman of the PLO. He was born on January 1, 1908, in Lebanon. He studied law in Jerusalem and then became a member of the Syrian delegation to the United Nations (1949–1951). He served as the assistant secretary general of the Arab League (1950–1956), followed by a position as Saudi ambassador to the United Nations (1957–1962). He was appointed chairman of the PLO when the organization was formed in 1964. In 1967 he was forced to resign because it was believed that his fiery anti-Zionist rhetoric had helped foment the Six-Day War. He was succeeded as PLO chairman by Yahya Hammuda and died on February 26, 1980. The authorship of the 1968 revision is less clear cut. The Fourth Palestine National Assembly, the executive and legislative body of the PLO, convened in Cairo, Egypt, on July 10, 1968. The assembly appointed a committee to amend the charter.

Explanation and Analysis of the Document

The amended Palestinian National Charter of 1968 consists of thirty-three articles. It differs from the earlier 1964 charter by striking a more militant tone against Israel, largely because it was written in the aftermath of the Arab states' humiliating defeat in the 1967 Six-Day War. The charter serves a number of purposes. It represents an effort to rally the Palestinian people scattered across the Middle East by giving them a sense of national unity. It also represents a kind of declaration of independence from the state of Israel. Most important, it declares the state of Israel illegitimate.

Articles 1 through 3 define Palestine as the homeland of the Palestinian people. Reflecting the pan-Arabism of the Egyptian president Gamal Abdel Nasser in the 1950s and early 1960s, the charter asserts that Palestine is an indivisible part of a larger Arab nation. In this sense, the charter is a subtle appeal to the surrounding Arab nations for support in the Palestinians' struggle against Israel. The charter asserts that the Palestinians have a legal right to their homeland in Palestine and to self-determination. Articles 4 through 6 then specify who a Palestinian is. After declaring that the Palestinians have a genuine identity as a people—an important point, given that the Palestinians were dispersed throughout the Middle East—the charter defines a Palestinian as any Arab who lived in Palestine prior to the "Zionist occupation," or the creation of the state of Israel. Palestinians also included anyone born to a Palestinian father, whether in Palestine or elsewhere. The charter also notes

Time Line

1939

- **May 17**
  The British White Paper of 1939 is issued, severely restricting Jewish immigration to Palestine.

1947

- **February 7**
  The British government announces its intention to withdraw from Palestine.

- **August 31**
  The UN Special Committee on Palestine recommends the partition of the British Mandate.

- **November 29**
  The United Nations votes to partition Palestine into Arab and Jewish sectors and internationalizes Jerusalem.

1948

- **May 14**
  Israel declares its independence.

- **May 15**
  Arab states attack Israel, launching the Arab-Israeli War.

1964

- **May 28**
  The Palestinian National Charter, creating the Palestinian Liberation Organization, is adopted.

1967

- **June 5**
  The Six-Day War between Israel and the combined forces of Egypt, Syria, and Jordan begins.

Milestone Documents

1967

- **June 10**
  A cease-fire to
  the Six-Day War
  is called.

1968

- **July 17**
  The amended
  Palestinian
  National Charter
  is adopted.

1974

- The Arab states
  recognize the
  Palestine Liber-
  ation Organiza-
  tion as the sole
  legitimate repre-
  sentative of the
  Palestinian
  people.

- **June 8**
  The Palestinian
  Liberation
  Organization issues
  its Ten Point
  Program.

1978

- **September 17**
  The Camp David
  Accords
  between Egypt
  and Israel are
  signed at the
  U.S. president's
  country retreat
  in Maryland.

1987

- **December**
  Palestinians
  launch the First
  Intifada, or
  uprising, against
  Israeli occupa-
  tion; the intifada
  lasts until 1993.

1993

- **September 13**
  The Oslo
  Accords are
  signed in Wash-
  ington, D.C.

that Jews who lived in Palestine before the "Zionist invasion" are likewise considered Palestinians. Thus, the charter defines Palestine and Palestinians in secular rather than religious terms. A Palestinian is a citizen of a state rather than a member of an ethnic or religious group. This issue is taken up later, in Article 20, which states that Judaism is a religion, not a nationality, and that Jews are citizens of whatever state they live in—and thus have no historical claim to Palestine. In general, the Palestinians would claim that they are not opposed to Judaism. Rather, they oppose Zionism, which in their view has led to the usurpation of their homeland.

Articles 7 through 10 take up the issue of armed struggle against Zionism. The charter asserts the Palestinians' "historical connection" to Palestine—an issue that forms the core of the dispute between the Arab Palestinians and the Jews, for Jewish analysts deny any such historical connection on the part of Arab Palestinians and point to Old Testament history to document their claim to Palestine. The charter then asserts that it is the duty of every Palestinian parent to bring up children to sacrifice their possessions and their lives, if necessary, to bring about the liberation of Palestine. The charter notes that there is dissension among Palestinian factions but urges Palestinians to put aside those dissensions to achieve a larger goal, the defeat of "the forces of Zionism and colonialism." The only way that goal can be achieved is through "armed struggle." That struggle would be conducted by fedayeen (rendered as "Feday'ee" in the document), an Arabic word that means "ones who sacrifice." The word refers to commandoes who volunteer to give up their lives for the state. From the viewpoint of the West, the fedayeen are terrorists and suicide bombers. The fedayeen, according to the charter, "constitute the nucleus of the Palestinian popular liberation war." Again the charter calls on the Arab and Palestinian people to put aside their differences so that the war can be prosecuted.

Articles 11 through 14 stress the theme of unity. The charter announces three mottoes: "national unity, national mobilization, and liberation." The charter affirms that the Palestinians are part of a larger Arab identity but also states that during the present phase of their existence Palestinians have to assert a uniquely Palestinian national identity. Nevertheless, the destiny of Palestine and that of the Arab world are intertwined. The "interdependence" of Palestinians and the larger Arab community means that only with Arab support could Palestine be liberated.

Articles 15 through 18 enumerate the advantages of a liberated Palestine from a number of viewpoints. From an Arab stance, it would "repel the Zionist and imperialist aggression against the Arab homeland" and lead to "the elimination of Zionism in Palestine." For decades, this and similar assertions in the charter have been a key sticking point. From the standpoint of Israel and its allies, chiefly the United States, the goal of the Palestinians is the eradication of Israel. In the face of this kind of threat, the Israelis have argued that their nation has to take whatever steps are necessary to prevent its own destruction, including force of arms. The result is a massive public relations problem for Israel. Many observers worldwide regard the Palestinians as the weaker party in the dispute, able to fight only with the primitive tools at its disposal; the modern phrase is *asymmetrical warfare*, referring to a war between an armed power and a much weaker opponent. The Israelis, on the other hand, can employ the apparatus of a modern state—sophisticated weaponry, an organized and highly trained military, security services—in reprisals against Palestinian aggression. In this environment, many intellectuals, especially in Europe, see Israel as the aggressor nation; Israel would respond that it is protecting itself against aggression, particularly aggression directed at civilians in terrorist attacks, and that in contrast to the more fanatical Palestinians, Israel makes every effort to avoid civilian casualties in its military operations.

The charter goes on to say that from a spiritual point of view, the liberation of Palestine would protect the Holy Land and make it a place of "safety and tranquillity" for all, regardless of "race, color, language, or religion." It would restore to Palestinians their "dignity, pride, and freedom." From an international point of view, Palestinian liberation is part of an ongoing worldwide struggle by oppressed peoples for liberation and self-determination.

Article 19 through 23 return to the issue of Zionism. The charter asserts that the 1947 partition of Palestine into Arab and Jewish zones is "illegal" because it was done contrary to the will of the Palestinian people and in opposition to their right of self-determination. The charter also claims that the Balfour Declaration and the Mandate for Palestine are "null and void." The charter goes on to openly challenge Zionism, saying that it is "associated with international imperialism" and that it is "racist and fanatic in its nature, aggressive, expansionist and colonial in its aims, and fascist in its methods." Article 23 urges the international community to "consider Zionism an illegitimate movement, to outlaw its existence, and to ban its operations."

Articles 24 through 27 turn to the Palestinian Liberation Organization, which was formed by the 1964 charter and Basic Law. The 1968 charter affirms the role of the PLO as the representative of the Palestinian people. Articles 28 through 33 represent a summing up. Again the charter asserts the right of Palestinians to liberation and control over their homeland, a process that would be accomplished through "fighters and carriers of arms." In the future, the Palestinians were to have a flag, a national anthem, and an oath of allegiance. The Basic Statute of the Palestine Liberation Organization would be attached to the charter and would constitute the framework for the PLO's procedures and organization. The charter concludes by specifying procedures for amending the charter.

Audience

The Palestinian National Charter is from one perspective a manifesto, and as such it had a number of audiences. The first was the Palestinian people. At the time it was issued and in the decades that followed, no "Palestine" existed as a separate, independent nation. The Palestinians are an Arab people, but they lacked a national identity, and

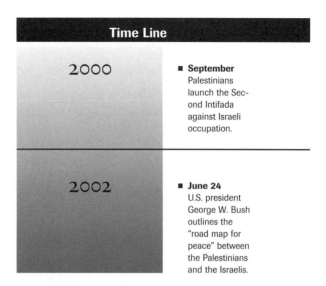

they were scattered about the Middle East. Those who continued to live in Israel believed that they lived under an occupying force—that Israel was an illegitimate state that had seized land from the Palestinians illegally. Thus, the purpose of the charter was to reinforce a sense of a national identity among the Palestinians—to foster among them the belief that Palestine was a nation with its own history, culture, aspirations, and future. It was a rallying cry.

Another audience, of course, was the state of Israel. The charter was in effect a "declaration of independence" from the Israelis. It sent the message that the Palestinian people regarded the state of Israel as illegitimate and the Israeli regime as brutal, Fascist, and imperialistic. It sent the further message that the Palestinians were prepared to fight for what they regarded as their homeland and that they would take whatever steps necessary to defeat the Israeli regime—in effect, to eliminate the state of Israel as a political entity. In this sense, the audience for the charter was the world. As a declaration of independence, it informed the world of the Palestinians' goals and appealed to "progressive movements in the world" to support its struggle for "liberation" from Israel.

Impact

The impact of the Palestinian National Charter and the formation of the PLO—and the reassertion of the PLO's role as representative of the Palestinians in the 1968 charter—would have profound effects in the decades that followed. The Six-Day War of 1967 took the military option for the liberation of Palestine off the table; the Arab countries' humiliating defeat made it clear that they could not defeat a heavily armed and determined Israel on the battlefield. This defeat cleared the way for the ascension of Yasser Arafat as chairman of the PLO, which became an umbrella organization for a number of political parties and factions, including Fatah, the Popular Front for the Liberation of Palestine, the Democratic Front for the Liberation of Palestine, and the Palestine Liberation Front. Arafat was an advocate of guerrilla warfare

The principals in the Middle East Summit meet for the first time at Camp David, Maryland, on September 6, 1978. From left are Egyptian president Anwar as-Sadat, U.S. president Jimmy Carter, and Israeli prime minister Menachem Begin. (AP/Wide World Photos)

against the Israelis, and in 1969–1970 he launched cross-border artillery attacks on Israel and terrorist attacks against Israeli citizens. But the PLO did not enjoy the support of other Arab Muslim nations, which saw the organization as too militant and too secular in its aims. The PLO was headquartered in Jordan, but the Jordanians expelled the PLO and took military action against its armed factions in an event known as Black September (1970). (This event is not to be confused with the armed faction of the Fatah Party called Black September, infamous for its slaughter of Israeli Olympic athletes in 1972.) The PLO relocated to Damascus, Syria, and then to Beirut, Lebanon, where it continued to sponsor attacks on Israel and Israeli civilians.

A breakthrough of sorts came in June 9, 1974, when the PLO approved the Ten Point Program, which appeared to call for a binational state occupied by Palestinians and Israelis. The program was rejected by the PLO's more militant factions, and Israel regarded the program with hostility, believing that it was a Trojan horse to gain Israeli concessions that would improve the Palestinians' ability to attack—a not unreasonable view given that point 2 of the ten points stated: "The Palestine Liberation Organization will employ all means, and first and foremost armed struggle, to liberate Palestinian territory and to establish the independent combatant national authority for the people over every part of

Palestinian territory that is liberated" (http://www.jewish virtuallibrary.org/jsource/Terrorism/PNC Program1974.html). The division between Palestinian moderates and the PLO's more hard-line factions marked the beginning of a tumultuous period for the PLO as it attempted to achieve the goals of its charter. The so-called Rejectionist Front opposed negotiations with Israel and rejected a 1976 UN resolution calling for a two-state solution. Many Palestinians regarded the Camp David Accords, a peace agreement signed between Israel and Egypt on September 17, 1978, as a setback, for it appeared to them that Egypt was abandoning the Palestinians. Then the Palestinians became embroiled in civil war in Lebanon, the result of which was the death of thousands of Palestinians in that country's refugee camps. The Israeli government refused to negotiate with the PLO, regarding it as a terrorist organization bent on Israel's destruction. The PLO was exiled in Tunis from 1982 to 1991, Israel responded to Palestinian attacks with military force, the Arab community offered little support to the Palestinians, and many Palestinians saw little hope for liberation. The consequence was the First Intifada from 1987 to 1993, a period of resistance on the West Bank and Gaza marked by strikes, boycotts, demonstrations, civil disobedience, and violence.

Another breakthrough of sorts came in 1993 when the PLO negotiated the Oslo Accords with Israel, which led to

❝ *"Palestine is the homeland of the Arab Palestinian people."*

(Article 1)

"The Palestinian Arab people possess the legal right to their homeland and to self-determination after the completion of the liberation of their country."

(Article 3)

"Armed struggle is the only way to liberate Palestine."

(Article 9)

"The liberation of Palestine ... is a national duty and it attempts to repel the Zionist and imperialist aggression against the Arab homeland, and aims at the elimination of Zionism in Palestine."

(Article 15)

"The partition of Palestine in 1947, and the establishment of the state of Israel are entirely illegal."

(Article 19)

"Zionism is a political movement organically associated with international imperialism and antagonistic to all action for liberation and to progressive movements in the world. It is racist and fanatic in its nature, aggressive, expansionist and colonial in its aims, and fascist in its methods. Israel is the instrument of the Zionist movement." ❞

(Article 22)

the formation of the Palestinian Authority as the official representative of the Palestinians. The most noteworthy feature of the Oslo Accords was that the PLO recognized the right of the state of Israel to exist—a clear departure from the aims announced in the Palestinian National Charter. Questions arose as to whether those portions of the charter that call for the elimination of Israel were still operative. In 1998, Palestinian Authority chairman Yasser Arafat sent letters to U.S. president Bill Clinton and British prime minister Tony Blair in which he suggested that those portions of the charter bearing on Israel had been amended and were no longer in force. Yet in 1999 a Palestinian

report on the charter's status made no mention of any changes to the charter. In 2001 the PLO Central Committee, the PLO's governing body, issued a draft of a new constitution that toned down the rhetoric of the 1968 charter. To this day there is debate about whether the Palestinians have revoked or annulled the provisions of the charter calling for the destruction of Israel.

Again, however, hard-liners rejected any proposal that recognized Israel's right to exist, so terrorist attacks and guerrilla warfare resumed in 2000, the start of the Second Intifada. Diplomatic efforts to secure a peaceful solution continued, with the United States, the European Union,

Russia, and the United Nations formulating the "road map for peace" in 2003. The core of the road map was that the Palestinians had to renounce terrorism in exchange for a Palestinian state, another version of the "two-state" solution. As of 2009, however, hostilities continued, and the two-state solution had not taken effect.

In the four decades that followed the issuance of the charter, the issue of relations between the Israelis and the Palestinians has dominated newspaper headlines and foreign affairs discussions. Although numerous attempts have been made to resolve the conflict, notably through the creation of two separate states, no proposed solution has achieved peace. Israelis and Palestinians continue to live in mutual distrust and hostility, with intermittent terrorist acts by Palestinians and armed reprisals by Israel a fact of life in that troubled region of the world.

Further Reading

■ Books

Amos, John W., II. *Palestinian Resistance: Organization of a National Movement*. New York: Pergamon, 1980.

Bernards, Neal. *The Palestinian Conflict: Identifying Propaganda Techniques*. San Diego, Calif.: Greenhaven Press, 1990.

Cobban, Helena. *The Palestinian Liberation Organisation: People, Power, and Politics*. New York: Cambridge University Press, 1984.

Gerner, Deborah J. *One Land, Two Peoples: The Conflict over Palestine*, 2nd ed. Denver, Colo.: Westview Press, 1994.

Hirst, David. *The Gun and the Olive Branch: The Roots of Violence in the Middle East*, 3rd ed. New York: Nation Books, 2003.

La Guardia, Anton. *War without End: Israelis, Palestinians, and the Struggle for a Promised Land*. New York: Thomas Dunne Books, 2002.

Lukacs, Yehuda. *The Israeli-Palestinian Conflict: A Documentary Record*. New York: Cambridge University Press, 1992.

Morris, Benny. *1948 and After: Israel and the Palestinians*. Oxford, U.K.: Clarendon Press, 1990.

Nassar, Jamal R. *The Palestine Liberation Organization: From Armed Struggle to the Declaration of Independence*. New York: Praeger, 1991.

■ Web Sites

"The Mandate for Palestine, July 24, 1922." Israeli Ministry for Foreign Affairs Web site.
    http://www.mfa.gov.il/MFA/Peace+Process/Guide+to+the+ Peace+Process/The+Mandate+for+Palestine.htm.

"The Oslo Accords, 1993." U.S. Department of State Web site.
    http://www.state.gov/r/pa/ho/time/pcw/97181.htm.

"The PLO's Ten Point Plan." The Jewish Virtual Library Web site.
http://www.jewishvirtuallibrary.org/jsource/Terrorism/PNCPro gram1974.html.

—Michael J. O'Neal

Questions for Further Study

1. Using this document, in conjunction with the Declaration of Independence of the State of Israel and the document Nationalization of the Suez Canal, trace the history of the events that led to the writing of the Palestinian National Charter.

2. Imagine that a friend tells you, in effect, that the entire Israel-Palestine conflict is confusing and that he or she does not understand what all the hostility and fighting is about. In three or four succinct sentences, explain to your friend the roots of the hostility and why it is ongoing.

3. Why did the Palestinians revise their national charter in light of the outcome of the Six-Day War of 1967?

4. The Palestinians regard themselves as an Arab people. What do you sense to be the attitude of other Arab states in the region to the PLO and its aims?

5. The assertion is frequently made that displaced Palestinians live in "refugee camps," a term that creates a picture of poverty and despair. Yet official data show that both the life expectancy and incomes of Palestinians are greater than those of people in most other Arab nations. How would you resolve this apparent inconsistency?

PALESTINIAN NATIONAL CHARTER

Article 1. Palestine is the homeland of the Arab Palestinian people; it is an indivisible part of the greater Arab homeland, and the Palestinian people are an integral part of the Arab nation.

Article 2: Palestine, with the boundaries it had during the British Mandate, is an indivisible territorial unit.

Article 3: The Palestinian Arab people possess the legal right to their homeland and to self-determination after the completion of the liberation of their country in accordance with their wishes and entirely of their own accord and will.

Article 4: The Palestinian identity is a genuine, essential, and inherent characteristic; it is transmitted from fathers to children. The Zionist occupation and the dispersal of the Palestinian Arab people, through the disasters which befell them, do not make them lose their Palestinian identity and their membership in the Palestinian community, nor do they negate them.

Article 5: The Palestinians are those Arab nationals who, until 1947, normally resided in Palestine regardless of whether they were evicted from it or stayed there. Anyone born, after that date, of a Palestinian father—whether in Palestine or outside it—is also a Palestinian.

Article 6: The Jews who had normally resided in Palestine until the beginning of the Zionist invasion are considered Palestinians.

Article 7: There is a Palestinian community and that it has material, spiritual, and historical connection with Palestine are indisputable facts. It is a national duty to bring up individual Palestinians in an Arab revolutionary manner. All means of information and education must be adopted in order to acquaint the Palestinian with his country in the most profound manner, both spiritual and material, that is possible. He must be prepared for the armed struggle and ready to sacrifice his wealth and his life in order to win back his homeland and bring about its liberation.

Article 8: The phase in their history, through which the Palestinian people are now living, is that of national (watani) struggle for the liberation of Palestine. Thus the conflicts among the Palestinian national forces are secondary, and should be ended for the sake of the basic conflict that exists between the forces of Zionism and of colonialism on the one hand, and the Palestinian Arab people on the other. On this basis the Palestinian masses, regardless of whether they are residing in the national homeland or in Diaspora (mahajir) constitute—both their organizations and the individuals—one national front working for the retrieval of Palestine and its liberation through armed struggle.

Article 9: Armed struggle is the only way to liberate Palestine. This is the overall strategy, not merely a tactical phase. The Palestinian Arab people assert their absolute determination and firm resolution to continue their armed struggle and to work for an armed popular revolution for the liberation of their country and their return to it. They also assert their right to normal life in Palestine and to exercise their right to self-determination and sovereignty over it.

Article 10: Commando (Feday'ee) action constitutes the nucleus of the Palestinian popular liberation war. This requires its escalation, comprehensiveness, and the mobilization of all the Palestinian popular and educational efforts and their organization and involvement in the armed Palestinian revolution. It also requires the achieving of unity for the national (watani) struggle among the different groupings of the Palestinian people, and between the Palestinian people and the Arab masses, so as to secure the continuation of the revolution, its escalation, and victory.

Article 11: Palestinians have three mottoes: national unity, national (al-qawmiyya) mobilization, and liberation.

Article 12: The Palestinian Arab people believe in Arab unity. In order to contribute their share toward the attainment of that objective, however, they must, at the present stage of their struggle, safeguard their Palestinian identity and develop their consciousness of that identity, oppose any plan that may dissolve or impair it.

Article 13: Arab unity and the liberation of Palestine are two complementary goals, the attainment of either of which facilitates the attainment of the other. Thus, Arab unity leads to the liberation of Palestine, the liberation of Palestine leads to Arab unity; and the work toward the realization of one objective proceeds side by side with work toward the realization of the other.

Article 14: The destiny of the Arab Nation, and indeed Arab existence itself, depend upon the destiny of the Palestinian cause. From this interdependence springs the Arab nation's pursuit of, and striving for, the liberation of Palestine. The people of Palestine play the role of the vanguard in the realization of this sacred (qawmi) goal.

Article 15: The liberation of Palestine, from an Arab viewpoint, is a national (qawmi) duty and it attempts to repel the Zionist and imperialist aggression against the Arab homeland, and aims at the elimination of Zionism in Palestine. Absolute responsibility for this falls upon the Arab nation—peoples and governments—with the Arab people of Palestine in the vanguard. Accordingly, the Arab nation must mobilize all its military, human, moral, and spiritual capabilities to participate actively with the Palestinian people in the liberation of Palestine. It must, particularly, in the phase of the armed Palestinian revolution, offer and furnish the Palestinian people with all possible help, and material and human support, and make available to them the means and opportunities that will enable them to continue to carry out their leading role in the armed revolution, until they liberate their homeland.

Article 16: The liberation of Palestine, from a spiritual viewpoint, will provide the Holy Land with an atmosphere of safety and tranquillity, which in turn will safeguard the country's religious sanctuaries and guarantee freedom of worship and of visit to all, without discrimination of race, color, language, or religion. Accordingly, the Palestinian people look to all spiritual forces in the world for support.

Article 17: The liberation of Palestine, from a human point of view, will restore to the Palestinian individual his dignity, pride, and freedom. Accordingly, the Palestinian Arab people look forward to the support of all those who believe in the dignity of man and his freedom in the world.

Article 18: The liberation of Palestine, from an international point of view, is a defensive action necessitated by the demands of self-defense. Accordingly, the Palestinian people, desirous as they are of the friendship of all people, look to freedom-loving and peace-loving states for support in order to restore their legitimate rights in Palestine, to re-establish peace and security in the country, and to enable its people to exercise national sovereignty and freedom.

Article 19: The partition of Palestine in 1947, and the establishment of the state of Israel are entirely illegal, regardless of the passage of time, because they were contrary to the will of the Palestinian peo-ple and its natural right in their homeland, and were inconsistent with the principles embodied in the Charter of the United Nations, particularly the right to self-determination.

Article 20: The Balfour Declaration, the Palestine Mandate, and everything that has been based on them, are deemed null and void. Claims of historical or religious ties of Jews with Palestine are incompatible with the facts of history and the conception of what constitutes statehood. Judaism, being a religion, is not an independent nationality. Nor do Jews constitute a single nation with an identity of their own; they are citizens of the states to which they belong.

Article 21: The Arab Palestinian people, expressing themselves by armed Palestinian revolution, reject all solutions which are substitutes for the total liberation of Palestine and reject all proposals aimed at the liquidation of the Palestinian cause, or at its internationalization.

Article 22: Zionism is a political movement organically associated with international imperialism and antagonistic to all action for liberation and to progressive movements in the world. It is racist and fanatic in its nature, aggressive, expansionist and colonial in its aims, and fascist in its methods. Israel is the instrument of the Zionist movement, and the geographical base for world imperialism placed strategically in the midst of the Arab homeland to combat the hopes of the Arab nation for liberation, unity, and progress. Israel is a constant source of threat vis-à-vis peace in the Middle East and the whole world. Since liberation of Palestine will destroy the Zionist and imperialist presence and will contribute to the establishment of peace in the Middle East. That is why the Palestinian people look to the progressive and peaceful forces and urge them all, irrespective of their affiliations and beliefs, to offer the Palestinian people all aid and support in their just struggle for the liberation of their homeland.

Article 23: The demand of security and peace, as well as the demand of right and justice, require all states to consider Zionism an illegitimate movement, to outlaw its existence, and to ban its operations, in order that friendly relations among peoples may be preserved, and the loyalty of citizens to their respective homelands safeguarded.

Article 24: The Palestinian people believe in the principles of justice, freedom, sovereignty, self-determination, human dignity, and the right of peoples to exercise them.

Article 25: For the realization of the goals of this Charter and its principles, the Palestine Liberation

Organization will perform its role in the liberation of Palestine.

Article 26: The Palestine Liberation Organization, the representative of the Palestinian revolutionary forces, is responsible for the Palestinian Arab peoples movement in its struggle—to retrieve its homeland, liberate and return to it and exercise the right to self-determination in it—in all military, political, and financial fields and also for whatever may be required by the Palestinian cause on the inter-Arab and international levels.

Article 27: The Palestine Liberation Organization shall cooperate with all Arab states, each according to its potentialities; and will adopt a neutral policy among them in light of the requirements of the battle of liberation; and on this basis does not interfere in the internal affairs of any Arab state.

Article 28: The Palestinian Arab people assert the genuineness and independence of their national revolution and reject all forms of intervention, trusteeship, and subordination.

Article 29: The Palestinian people possess the fundamental and genuine legal right to liberate and retrieve their homeland. The Palestinian people determine their attitude toward all states and forces on the basis of the stands they adopt vis-à-vis the Palestinian revolution to fulfill the aims of the Palestinian people.

Article 30: Fighters and carriers of arms in the war of liberation are the nucleus of the popular army which will be the protective force for the gains of the Palestinian Arab people.

Article 31: This Organization shall have a flag, an oath of allegiance, and an anthem. All this shall be decided upon in accordance with a special law.

Article 32: A law, known as the Basic Statute of the Palestine Liberation Organization, shall be annexed to this Covenant. It will lay down the manner in which the Organization, and its organs and institutions, shall be constituted; the respective competence of each; and the requirements of its obligation under the Charter.

Article 33: This Charter shall not be amended save by [vote of] a majority of two-thirds of the total membership of the National Council of the Palestine Liberation Organization [taken] at a special session convened for that purpose.

Ayatollah Khomeini (AP/Wide World Photos)

"It is your oil they are after—why should they worry about your prayers?"

Overview

Ayatollah Ruhollah Musawi Khomeini's *Islamic Government: Governance of the Jurist* (in Persian, *Hokumat-e Islami: Velayat-e faqih*, which is sometimes translated as "Islamic Government: Guardianship of the Jurist") is an argument for the establishment of Islamic law in the ayatollah's native Iran and elsewhere. The essence of Khomeini's belief is that because the laws of God govern society, all government leaders should be knowledgeable in Islamic law. And since Islamic jurists, called *faqih* (or *faqīh* in the document), have studied Islamic law, any ruler should also be a *faqih* and thus able to counter anti-Islamic influences emanating from non-Muslim sources, a role that Khomeini calls "guardianship."

The book had its origins in a series of speeches given by Khomeini in January and February 1970 to students in An Najaf, Iraq. An Najaf remains an important center of Islamic scholarship and the spiritual center of Shia Islam, the second-largest branch of the religion, behind Sunni Islam. The city is the location of a shrine to Imam 'Alī, the first Shia leader and a son-in-law of the Prophet Muhammad, the founder of Islam. It was also where the ayatollah (a title meaning "signs of God," given to high-ranking Shia clerics) spent thirteen years as a teacher at the Shaykh Murtazǎ Ansǎrǐ madrassa, a religious school. Later that year, the speeches, which had been recorded and transcribed by a student, were collected and published in Beirut, Lebanon.

In the 1970s the book had to be smuggled into Iran under different titles, including *Authority of the Jurist* and *A Letter from Imam Musavi Kashef al-Qita*, the latter using a fake name to deceive government censors. At that time, Iran was under the control of a secular regime headed by a shah (or king), Mohammad Reza Pahlavi, who enforced his rule through his notorious and feared secret police, the SAVAK, short for Sazeman-e Ettela'at va Amniyat-e Keshvar, or National Intelligence and Security Organization. In the face of growing revolutionary activity, the shah instituted repressive measures again militant Muslims, including Khomeini. In 1964 Khomeini was exiled from Iran in an effort to lessen his domestic influence. In 1977 Khomeini's son died under mysterious circumstances; many Iranians believed that his death was the work of SAVAK. Despite the shah's efforts to retain power, his regime was overthrown in the 1979 Islamic Revolution.

Islamic Government: Governance of the Jurist became an important text in the establishment of the Islamic Republic of Iran, when Khomeini was proclaimed the nation's supreme leader. Khomeini was a revered figure in Iran, acquiring the title imam, which means "guide" or "one who walks in front"; the title had previously been reserved for Shia Islam's original twelve infallible leaders, the rightful successors to the prophet Muhammad. During the revolution, Khomeini's name and face became familiar to westerners primarily for his support of the seizure of fifty-three Americans who were held hostage at the American embassy in Tehran, Iran, from November 4, 1979, to January 20, 1981.

Context

The context for Khomeini's militancy and for *Islamic Government* extends back at least to World War II, when Iran's oil and strategic geographical position were vital to Allied interests in the fight against Nazi Germany. In 1941 the Allies installed Mohammad Reza Pahlavi as shah, correctly believing that he would support the Allies against Germany, unlike his father, who had declared neutrality in the war. After the war, Mohammad Mosaddeq was democratically elected as Iran's prime minister, but the U.S. government believed that Mosaddeq's sympathies were increasingly leaning toward the Communist Soviet Union. Accordingly, the U.S. Central Intelligence Agency, in concert with its British counterpart, engineered a 1953 coup d'état that deposed Mosaddeq. The United States and Great Britain supported the shah because of his secularism and pro-West stance, seen as crucial at a time when the West feared the expansion of Iran's northern neighbor, the Soviet Union. These events set the stage for ongoing clashes between Iran's secular government and Muslims, who believed that the monarchal government was corrupt, extravagant, repressive, godless, and a puppet of the United States.

Khomeini rose to prominence in the 1960s during the so-called White Revolution—an effort on the part of Shah Pahlavi to promote Western values, break up the landhold-

1902

- **ca. September 24**
Ruhollah Musawi (Khomeini) is born in Khomein, Iran.

1941

- **September 16**
Mohammad Reza Pahlavi replaces his father as shah of Iran.

1951

- **April 28**
Mohammad Mosaddeq is elected Iranian prime minister, thenceforth competing with the shah for power.

1953

- **August 19**
An American-sponsored coup d'état removes Mosaddeq from office; Shah Pahlavi returns from temporary exile to resume full power three days later.

1957

- The Sazeman-e Ettela'at va Amniyat-e Keshvar (SAVAK), Iran's feared secret police, is formed.

1963

- **January 9**
The Iranian shah announces the White Revolution, a series of reforms perceived by Muslim clerics as pro-Western.

ings of religious institutions, give women the right to vote, increase literacy in state-run schools, and allow non-Muslims to hold political office, among other measures. Khomeini strongly denounced the shah and his pro-Western plans in a statement released on January 22, 1963. Then, on June 3 of that year, he delivered a speech further denouncing the shah. Two days later he was arrested, sparking three days of mass protests called the Movement of 15 Khordad, the date on the Persian calendar corresponding to June 5 on the Western calendar. Khomeini was held under house arrest until April 1964. After his release, he continued his antigovernment agitation, singling out the government's cooperation with Israel and its "capitulations" giving diplomatic immunity to Western military personnel in Iran. He was arrested again in November 1964 and went into exile, eventually settling in An Najaf, Iraq.

During these years Khomeini and others developed the ideology that would lead to the Islamic Revolution in Iran. Jalal Al-e-Ahmad, a political activist and writer, coined the term *gharbzadegi*, translated variously as "westoxification," "weststruckness," or "occidentosis"; the present document refers to those afflicted with this condition as "xenomaniacs." *Gharbzadegi* refers to Muslims who have become intoxicated or seduced by Western cultural models, which Al-e-Ahmad believed constituted a plague that had to be done away with; he used the word as the title of his most influential book, published in 1952. Ali Shariati, a sociologist regarded as the intellectual father of the Islamic Revolution, taught that Islam was uniquely able to liberate the Third World from repressive colonialism and capitalism. Khomeini began to formulate the views that would become the basis of *Islamic Government*, particularly what he called *vilāyat-i faqīh*, meaning "guardianship of the jurist." This is the belief that Muslims require the guardianship of Islamic jurists, whose knowledge of sharia, or Islamic law, can protect Muslims from plundering by foreign, non-Muslim influences. As his views spread through Iran, often in the form of speeches and sermons recorded on smuggled cassette tapes, revolutionary fervor began to grow. In response, the shah's regime became more oppressive. The fuse was lit for the 1979 Islamic Revolution, which drove the shah into exile, established the Islamic Republic of Iran, and created the post of supreme leader based on principles outlined in *Islamic Government*.

About the Author

Ruhollah Musawi was born in Khomein, Iran, the source of "Khomeini," a later addition to his name. Regarding the date of his birth, some contend that he was born in 1900, but many others cite his birth date as September 24 or 25, 1902. The early decades of his life were spent in study, teaching, and writing. He was particularly interested in philosophy, ethics, and Islamic law, and he also wrote a considerable amount of poetry. He rose to political power in 1963, when he gained the title ayatollah and led Muslim clerics in their opposition to Shah Pahlavi's White Revolution, for which he was placed under house arrest from June 5, 1963, until April the following year. After his release he continued to oppose the shah, and he was forced into exile in November 1964, first in Turkey and then in An Najaf, Iraq, where he delivered the speeches that would form *Islamic Government*. In 1978 he was forced out of Iraq by the future dictator Saddam Hussein, and he spent the last few months of his exile just outside Paris, France.

Throughout the 1970s, while he was living in Iraq, Khomeini consolidated his position as Iran's immensely popular spiritual leader. When he believed that he had the backing of Iran's important clerics and of the Iranian people, he ordered the revolution against the shah to begin. In the face of widespread protest in 1978, the government broke down. The shah fled Iran on January 16, 1979, and Khomeini returned in triumph on February 1, to denounce the provisional government and call for a referendum on replacing the monarchy with an Islamic republic. The referendum was held on March 30 and 31, 1979, and passed with an overwhelming majority of the vote. In the months that followed, Khomeini and his supporters accomplished the prompt passage of a constitution that would place the spiritual and governmental leadership of the country under a supreme religious leader. Khomeini himself took the oath of office as supreme leader on December 3, 1979. Despite his popularity, numerous political organizations throughout the country opposed the type of theocracy Khomeini envisioned. The supreme leader banned these organizations and proceeded to rule Iran with an iron fist.

Throughout the 1980s Khomeini was the face of Islam, particularly radical Islam, to the West. He supported the seizure of hostages at the American embassy in Iran, setting off a 444-day crisis that dominated headlines in the United States; ironically, the precipitating invasion of the embassy by students was intended merely to be symbolic. Khomeini led the nation through the Iran-Iraq War of the 1980s, and he was back in the headlines in 1989 when he issued a fatwa, or theocratic ruling, that called for the assassination of the British author Salman Rushdie, whose novel *The Satanic Verses* was perceived to be offensive to Islam. Khomeini died on June 3, 1989, of a heart attack suffered while recovering from surgery.

Explanation and Analysis of the Document

The present excerpt from *Islamic Government* is the book's introduction. The introduction does not lay down a thorough plan for an Islamist government. Rather, it expounds a number of ideas that form the historical justification for such a government. The core of Khomeini's argument is that the Qur'an and sharia law provide humans with all the guidance they need; accordingly, a secular government is not necessary. The favorable alternative is a government under the leadership of Muslim jurists, or clerics who are knowledgeable about Islamic law.

Time Line

1963

- **January 22**
  Ayatollah Khomeini denounces the White Revolution.

- **June 5**
  Khomeini is placed under house arrest for ten months for opposition to the shah, sparking the Movement of 15 Khordad.

1964

- **November**
  Khomeini is again arrested and is driven into exile.

1970

- **January 21**
  In the city of An Najaf, Iraq, Khomeini gives the first of a series of lectures that would form the basis of *Islamic Government*; the final lecture is given on February 8.

1978

- The Iranian government under Shah Pahlavi begins to break down in the face of widespread protests.

1979

- **January 16**
  Shah Pahlavi leaves Iran and goes into exile.

- **February 1**
  Khomeini returns to Iran and denounces the provisional government.

1979

- **February 11**
  The Islamic Revolution in Iran is completed when the nation's Supreme Military Council declares itself neutral in the political disputes, allowing Muslim revolutionaries to overrun the provisional government.

- **November 4**
  Iranian revolutionaries take fifty-three Americans hostage in Tehran.

- **December 3**
  Khomeini takes the oath as Iran's supreme leader.

1981

- **January 20**
  The American hostages in Tehran are released.

1989

- **June 3**
  Khomeini dies of a heart attack.

◆ **Paragraphs 1–3**

The opening paragraphs of the introduction set the tone for Khomeini's exposition. He argues that the principles of governance of the jurist are "self-evident" but that they have been neglected because of historical circumstances. He refers to "anti-Islamic propaganda" from Jews and other groups; although he does not refer by name to the United States, it is likely that the United States and its allies, particularly Great Britain, are the groups he had in mind. He states that the goal of these outside influences has been "imperialist penetration of the Muslim countries," a process that began at least three hundred years before but which could be traced back to the Crusades, the two-hundred-year-long series of wars between Christian Europe and Muslim Arabs for the control of Palestine in the twelfth and thirteenth centuries. He argues that it was not the purpose of these groups to eliminate Islam and replace it with Christianity, for "the imperialists really have no reli-

gious belief." He goes on to say that the imperialists instead planted agents in the government, publishing, and education to "distort the principles of Islam," as the religion was considered an obstacle to political power and materialism.

◆ **Paragraphs 4–7**

Khomeini next draws a distinction between true Islam and Islam as it has been depicted by its adversaries. He states that "Islam is the religion of militant individuals who are committed to truth and justice" and that it is only by fulfilling the ordinances of Islam that Muslims can live full lives. He also emphasizes the revolutionary aspect of Islam in opposing imperialism. He then proceeds to develop a core argument. Countering the belief that Islam "is not a comprehensive religion" and "has nothing to say about human life in general and the ordering of society," he argues that, on the contrary, Islam is about much more than ritual observances. He refers to the Qur'an, Islam's sacred scripture. Muslims believe that the Qur'an, from an Arabic word meaning "the recitation," is the literal word of Allah, revealed to the prophet Muhammad by the archangel Jibra'il (Gabriel) beginning in 610 until his death. Reference is also made to the hadiths, or compilations of the Prophet's sayings during his lifetime; some twenty-six hundred hadiths, out of six hundred thousand that were gathered, are regarded as authentic, and they provide guidance in matters ranging from law to personal behavior. Khomeini notes that large portions of both the Qur'an and the hadiths deal with "social, economic, legal, and political questions—in short, the gestation of society." His point is that the sacred writings of Islam provide people with all the guidance they need, not just in private matters but in public, social matters as well.

◆ **Paragraphs 8–11**

After urging young people to be of service to Islam, Khomeini sketches in the historical background of his views. He notes that in Muhammad's time, the West was in a state of "darkness and obscurity," while nations such as Iran were under tyrannical rule. In this context the Prophet emerged and, from God, "sent laws that astound people with their magnitude." He continues by saying that God "instituted laws and practices for all human affairs and laid injunctions for man extending from even before the embryo is formed until after he is placed in the tomb." This key point reinforces Khomeini's view that Islam is sufficient for governing all human affairs. He concludes by saying that "there is not a single topic in human life for which Islam has not provided instructions and established a norm." He dismisses the views of ākhūnds—a word that literally means "Muslim clerics" but that has become a derogatory term for misguided and hypocritical clerics—and argues that they have been in part responsible for the view that Islam concerns itself only with rituals. He even concedes that some of the 'ulamā, or Islamic scholars, have been guilty.

◆ **Paragraphs 12–19**

Khomeini turns next to some specific matters of law. He begins by noting that the nation's constitution, as implemented under the monarchy, is essentially a Western document, borrowing heavily from the constitutions of Britain, Belgium, and France; the few Islamic ordinances contained in the constitution were inserted as a way of deceiving Muslims into believing that the constitution reflected Islamic law. He continues by insisting that while the Iranian constitution thus embodies a monarchal form of government, Islam "proclaims monarchy and hereditary succession wrong and invalid." He reviews historical circumstances, recalling how Muhammad enjoined the rulers of the Byzantine Empire and Iran to abandon monarchy, as had been done in Islamic countries such as Egypt. Arguing that God is the only true monarch, he calls monarchy a "sinister, evil system of government." Its influence was what caused Imam Husayn ibn 'Alī, Muhammad's grandson, to refuse to pledge his allegiance to Yazīd I, head of the Umayyad Caliphate, in the seventh century. Husayn became the "Doyen of the Martyrs" when he was killed during the Battle of Karbala in 680, a major historical event in the development of the Shia movement.

Khomeini addresses the fact that Islam has no specific laws against such behaviors as usury, the consumption of alcohol, and sexual vice. For Khomeini, the fact that Islamic countries have not had to enact laws forbidding these practices is a sign of the religion's "perfection." He goes on to say that this legal system was "worked out by the imperialist government of Britain" to render Islam impotent. Khomeini then outlines some of the inadequacies of the Western legal system imposed on Iran, suggesting that it has been a source of delayed justice owing to endless litigation. Legal matters are not resolved swiftly, and people have to waste their time trying to enforce their rights. In earlier times, sharia (spelled *sharī'ah* in the document) law could quickly settle matters. Western law, in contrast, is a source of "frustration and perplexity" as well as corruption and bribery.

◆ Paragraphs 20–23

Khomeini takes up the issue of whether Islamic law is "too harsh," a view he says is widely prevalent in the West because of the work of "agents of imperialism." He notes that in the West a person can be executed for the possession of ten grams of heroin and asks whether this is not a harsh punishment, one that is disproportionate to the crime. He acknowledges that a person living under Islamic rule can receive eighty lashes for the consumption of alcohol, but he is indignant at the notion that this punishment is "too harsh" in light of Western laws governing drug possession. This leads to a discussion of alcohol. Khomeini argues that "many forms of corruption that have appeared in society derive from alcohol," including road accidents, murders, and suicides, and that alcohol addiction can lead to heroin addiction. Yet in the West alcohol can be bought and sold freely. He defends the practice of whipping fornicators and stoning adulterers by saying that "these penal provisions of Islam are intended to keep great nations from being destroyed by corruption." He concludes by asking, "Why should it be regarded as harsh if Islam stipulates that an offender must be publicly flogged in order to protect the younger generation from corruption?"

◆ Paragraphs 24–31

Khomeini next returns to a discussion of history. He begins by observing that Western powers can wage war in Vietnam but that wars waged by Islam to stamp out corruption are considered questionable. He asserts that everything he has discussed so far represents "plans drawn up several centuries ago that are now being implemented and bearing fruit." He objects to the establishment of schools that turn people into "Christians or unbelievers." He says that the Western plan has been to keep Muslims "backward" and to exploit the resources of Muslim lands. In preaching Islam, clerics have to practice *taqiyyah*, or circumspection in the face of danger, a practice sanctioned in the Qur'an. He defends the wearing of military apparel, pointing out that the early leaders of Islam, including the "Commander of the Faithful," 'Alī ibn Abī Tālib, who was the Prophet's cousin and son-in-law and the first of the Twelve Imams, proudly wore military attire. All of the anti-Islamic developments he discusses are considered the result of a "wave of propaganda."

◆ Paragraphs 32–35

Khomeini turns from the external factors that have corrupted and diminished Islam to internal factors, in particular, "the dazzling effect that the material progress of the imperialist countries has had on some members of our society." He argues that morality and happiness derive not from technical and scientific progress, such as going to the moon (accomplished by the Americans in the summer of 1969) but from "the faith, the conviction, and the morality of Islam," which "serve humanity instead of endangering it." Meanwhile, some Muslims have been seduced by the Western idea that Islam has no "specific form of government or governmental institutions." Khomeini sees this as part of the propaganda campaign designed to prevent the creation of an Islamic society.

Examining government from a historical perspective, Khomeini says that the Prophet established a system for determining his successors. The purpose of those successors, though, was not simply to expound law, for the law had already been expounded in the Qur'an and other documents. Rather, the successors' purpose was to execute the laws, for laws are of no avail unless they are carried out. Islamic law, then, was part of the prophetic mission of God, carried out by Muhammad. It was this argument that led to the creation of the position of supreme leader after the Islamic Revolution in Iran.

◆ Paragraphs 36–41

In the final paragraphs, Khomeini addresses his audience directly. He urges Muslims to fulfill the prophetic mission: "*Know that it is your duty to establish an Islamic government.*" He tells them to present Islam in its true form and to make clear to others that Islam is not a religion of forms and observances but a vital part of the political structure of Islamic nations. He says that Muslims must engage not only in prayer and study but also in political agitation. Otherwise, the imperialists will maintain control of Islam-

One of sixty U.S. hostages, blindfolded and with his hands bound, is displayed to the crowd outside the U.S. Embassy in Tehran, November 9, 1979. (AP/Wide World Photos)

ic countries through industrialization and the exploitation of oil, not caring about Islam if it restricts itself to *azān*, or the call to prayer. He concludes by warning that the imperialists want to "prevent you from intervening in the affairs of society and struggling against treacherous governments and their anti-national and anti-Islamic politics."

Audience

The original audience for the ideas of *Islamic Government: Governance of the Jurist* consisted of students at An Najaf, Iraq. Khomeini's series of speeches was recorded and transcribed to form the basis of the book, which was published in Lebanon. In time it was smuggled into Iran under various titles and was circulated among the ayatollah's core supporters. It is uncertain whether and to what extent Khomeini intended the book to have wider circulation. Some observers have maintained that he deliberately restricted circulation of the book because he did not want to alienate Iranian moderates, who likely would have opposed the establishment of a theocracy and would there-

fore have impeded progress toward the revolution. It was only after Khomeini's supporters had consolidated their own positions of power that the book was given wider circulation. After the success of the revolution, the book was disseminated to the wider public, and many of the views expressed therein became part of the new constitution passed by the Islamic Republic of Iran.

Impact

Islamic Government: Governance of the Jurist was Khomeini's most influential text. It established the principles of guardianship by jurists, meaning that governance in Islamic countries (and ideally all countries) is to be placed under the authority of Islamic clerics and Islamic sharia law. To the extent that Iran became an Islamic republic, Khomeini succeeded in his principal objectives. Iran, which was an ally of the United States and the West during the cold war (the state of tension and hostility between the West and the Communist Soviet bloc), became in the late twentieth century a firm adversary.

"Islam is the religion of militant individuals who are committed to truth and justice. It is the religion of those who desire freedom and independence. It is the school of those who struggle against imperialism."

(Paragraph 4)

"God, Exalted and Almighty ... instituted laws and practices for all human affairs and laid injunctions for man extending from even before the embryo is formed until after he is placed in the tomb. In just the same way that there are laws setting forth the duties of worship for man, so too there are laws, practices, and norms for the affairs of society and government."

(Paragraph 9)

"Their plan is to keep us backward, to keep us in our present miserable state so they can exploit our riches, our underground wealth, our lands, and our human resources. They want us to remain afflicted and wretched, and our poor to be trapped in their misery. Instead of surrendering to the injunctions of Islam ... they and their agents wish to ... enjoy lives of abominable luxury."

(Paragraph 27)

"The necessity for the implementation of divine law, the need for an executive power, and the importance of that power in fulfilling the goals of the prophetic mission and establishing a just order that would result in the happiness of mankind—all of this made the appointment of a successor synonymous with the completion of the prophetic mission."

(Paragraph 35)

"If you pay no attention to the policies of the imperialists, and consider Islam to be simply the few topics you are always studying and never go beyond them, then the imperialists will leave you alone. Pray as much as you like; it is your oil they are after—why should they worry about your prayers? They are after our minerals, and want to turn our country into a market for their goods."

(Paragraph 40)

The question of whether "governance of the jurist" has been successful in Iran remains an open one. Many conservative Muslims in that nation would argue that it has, for, they would say, Iran was purged of Western influences and came under the control of Islamist leaders committed to enforcing Islamic law. Nominally democratic, Iran has an elected president, a 290-member elected Majlis (the parliament), and an elected eighty-six-member Assembly of Experts, who appoint the supreme leader. Real power in Iran, however, is held by unelected officials, in particular, the supreme leader—Khomeini's successor since 1989 has been Ayatollah Ali Khamenei—and the twelve-member Guardian Council. Although members of the latter group have to be approved by the parliament, they are appointed or screened by the supreme leader, they have veto power over any measures passed by parliament that they deem to be inconsistent with Islamic law, and they control the military and the media. The council can also bar candidates from standing for election to parliament or the presidency. Effectively, then, the government in Iran is answerable to clerics.

Thus, in the short term, Khomeini achieved the objectives he articulated in *Islamic Government: Governance of the Jurist*—though many observers would argue that he did so at a terrible price, for he silenced criticism, and thousands were put to death for opposition to his theocratic rule. In the longer term, though, there has been growing resistance to Iran's theocratic government. As of 2010, Iran is a young country, with large numbers of voters under the age of thirty. Many are coming to resent the influence of the Basij, or morality police, and would like to live in an Iran that is more liberal and less repressive. Reformers in Iran want the nation to continue to be an Islamic republic but would also like the government to respect the democratic institutions enshrined in the nation's constitution. They believe that the legacy left by Ayatollah Khomeini is inconsistent with the democratic freedoms written into the constitution that he and his backers produced.

Further Reading

■ Books

Arjomand, Said Amir. *Turban for the Crown: The Islamic Revolution in Iran.* New York: Oxford University Press, 1988.

Bakhash, Shaul. *The Reign of the Ayatollahs: Iran and the Islamic Revolution.* New York: Basic Books, 1984.

Brumberg, Daniel. *Reinventing Khomeini: The Struggle for Reform in Iran.* Chicago: University of Chicago Press, 2001.

Coughlin, Con. *Khomeini's Ghost: The Iranian Revolution and the Rise of Militant Islam.* New York: Ecco, 2009.

Dabashi, Hamid. *Theology of Discontent: The Ideological Foundations of the Islamic Revolution in Iran.* New York: New York University Press, 1993.

Hoveyda, Fereydoun. *The Shah and the Ayatollah: Iranian Mythology and Islamic Revolution.* Westport, Conn.: Greenwood, 2003.

Keddie, Nikki. *Roots of Revolution: An Interpretive History of Modern Iran.* New Haven, Conn.: Yale University Press, 1981.

Wright, Robin. *In the Name of God: The Khomeini Decade.* New York: Simon and Schuster, 1989.

■ Web Sites

Fukuyama, Francis. "Authoritarian Iran, Islam and the Rule of Law." Livemint.com Web site.
   http://www.livemint.com/2009/07/28204901/Authoritarian-Iran-Islam-and.html.

—Michael J. O'Neal

Questions for Further Study

1. Explain what Khomeini means by the concept of "guardianship."

2. What historical circumstances enabled Khomeini to rise to a position of power and influence in Iran?

3. Compare this selection with Al-Māwardī's "On Qāīs," particularly as the latter pertains to Islamic jurisprudence. What do you think Al-Māwardī's reaction to Khomeini's text might have been?

4. What does Khomeini regard as the weakness of the Western legal system? Why did he believe that concepts of Western law are inapplicable in Islamic countries?

5. Ayatollah Khomeini became a figure who was feared, perhaps even hated, among many people in the West. At the very least, he was looked on with suspicion. Why do you think this was so?

AYATOLLAH KHOMEINI'S *ISLAMIC GOVERNMENT:* *GOVERNANCE OF THE JURIST*

Introduction

The subject of the governance of the jurist (*vilāyat-i faqīh*) provides us with the opportunity to discuss certain related matters and questions. The governance of the *faqīh* is a subject that in itself elicits immediate assent and has little need of demonstration, for anyone who has some general awareness of the beliefs and ordinances of Islam will unhesitatingly give his assent to the principle of the governance of the *faqīh* as soon as he encounters it; he will recognize it as necessary and self-evident. If little attention is paid to this principle today, so that it has come to require demonstration, it is because of the social circumstances prevailing among the Muslims in general and the teaching institution in particular. These circumstances, in turn, have certain historical roots to which I will now briefly refer.

From the very beginning, the historical movement of Islam has had to contend with the Jews, for it was they who first established anti-Islamic propaganda and engaged in various stratagems, and as you can see, this activity continues down to the present. Later they were joined by other groups, who were in certain respects, more satanic than they. These new groups began their imperialist penetration of the Muslim countries about three hundred years ago, and they regarded it as necessary to work for the extirpation of Islam in order to attain their ultimate goals. It was not their aim to alienate the people from Islam in order to promote Christianity among them, for the imperialists really have no religious belief, Christian or Islamic. Rather, throughout this long historical period, and going back to the Crusades, they felt that the major obstacle in the path of their materialistic ambitions and the chief threat to their political power was nothing but Islam and its ordinances, and the belief of the people in Islam. They therefore plotted and campaigned against Islam by various means.

The preachers they planted in the religious teaching institution, the agents they employed in the universities, government educational institutions, and publishing houses, and the orientalists who work in the service of the imperialistic states—all these people have pooled their energies in an effort to distort the principles of Islam. As a result, many persons, particularly the educated, have formed misguided and incorrect notions of Islam.

Islam is the religion of militant individuals who are committed to truth and justice. It is the religion of those who desire freedom and independence. It is the school of those who struggle against imperialism. But the servants of imperialism have presented Islam in a totally different light. They have created in men's minds a false notion of Islam. The defective version of Islam, which they have presented in the religious teaching institution, is intended to deprive Islam of its vital, revolutionary aspect and to prevent Muslims from arousing themselves in order to gain their freedom, fulfill the ordinances of Islam, and create a government that will assure their happiness and allow them to live lives worthy of human beings.

For example, the servants of imperialism declared that Islam is not a comprehensive religion providing for every aspect of human life and has no laws or ordinances pertaining to society. It has no particular form of government. Islam concerns itself only with rules of ritual purity after menstruation and parturition. It may have a few ethical principles, but it certainly has nothing to say about human life in general and the ordering of society.

This kind of evil propaganda has unfortunately had an effect. Quite apart from the masses, the educated class—university students and also many students at the religious teaching institutions—have failed to understand Islam correctly and have erroneous notions. Just as people may, in general, be unacquainted with a stranger, so too they are unacquainted with Islam. Islam lives among the people of this world as if it were a stranger. If somebody were to present Islam as it truly is, he would find it difficult to make people believe him. In fact, the agents of imperialism in the religious teaching institutions would raise a hue and cry against him.

In order to demonstrate to some extent, the difference between Islam and what is presented as Islam, I would like to draw your attention to the difference between the Holy Qur'an and the books of *hadīth*, on the one hand, and the practical treatises of jurisprudence, on the other. The Holy Qur'an and the books of *hadīth*, which represent the sources for the commands and ordinances of Islam, are completely different from the treatises written by the *mujtahīds* of the present age both in breadth of scope and in the effects they are capable of exerting on the life of society. The ratio of Qur'anic verses concerned with the affairs of society to those concerned with ritual worship is greater than a hundred to one. Of the approximately fifty sections of the corpus of *hadīth* containing all the ordinances of Islam, not more than three or four sections relate to matters of ritual worship and the duties of man toward his Creator and Sustainer. A few more are concerned with questions of ethics, and all the rest are concerned with social, economic, legal, and political questions—in short, the gestation of society.

You who represent the younger generation and who, God willing, will be of service to Islam in the future must strive diligently all your lives to pursue the aims I will now set forth and to impart the laws and ordinances of Islam. In whatever way you deem most beneficial, in writing or in speech, instruct the people about the problems Islam has had to contend with since its inception and about the enemies and afflictions that now threaten it. Do not allow the true nature of Islam to remain hidden, or people will imagine that Islam is like Christianity (nominal, not true Christianity), a collection of injunctions pertaining to man's relation to God, and the mosques will be equated with the church.

At a time when the West was a realm of darkness and obscurity—with its inhabitants living in a state of barbarism, and America still peopled by half-savaged redskins—and the two vast empires of Iran and Byzantium were under the rule of tyranny, class privilege, and discrimination, and the powerful dominated all without any trace of law or popular government, God, Exalted and Almighty, by means of the Most Noble Messenger(s), sent laws that astound people with their magnitude. He instituted laws and practices for all human affairs and laid injunctions for man extending from even before the embryo is formed until after he is placed in the tomb. In just the same way that there are laws setting forth the duties of worship for man, so too there are laws, practices, and norms for the affairs of society and government. Islamic law is a progressive, evolving, and comprehensive system. All the voluminous books that have been compiled from the earliest times on different areas of law, such as judicial procedure, social transactions, penal law, retribution, international relations, regulations pertaining to peace and war, private and public law—taken together, these contain a mere sample of the laws and injunctions of Islam. There is not a single topic in human life for which Islam has not provided instructions and established a norm.

In order to make the Muslims, especially the intellectuals, and the younger generation, deviate from the path of Islam, foreign agents have constantly insinuated that Islam has nothing to offer, that Islam consists of a few ordinances concerning menstruation and parturition, and that this is the proper field of study for the *ākhūnds*.

There is something of truth here, for it is fitting that those *ākhūnds* who have no intention of expounding the theories, injunctions and worldview of Islam and who spend most of their time on precisely such matters, forgetting all the other topics of Islamic law, be attacked and accused in this manner. They too are at fault; foreigners are not the only ones to be blamed. For several centuries, as might be expected, the foreigners laid certain plans to realize their political and economic ambitions, and the neglect that has overtaken the religious teaching institution has made it possible for them to succeed. There have been individuals among us, the *'ulamā*, who have unwittingly contributed to the fulfillment of those aims, with the result that you now see.

It is sometimes insinuated that the injunctions of Islam are defective, and said that the laws of judicial procedure, for example, are not all that they should be. In keeping with this insinuation and propaganda, agents of Britain were instructed by their masters to take advantage of the idea of constitutionalism in order to deceive the people and conceal the true nature of their political crimes (the pertinent proofs and documents are now available). At the beginning of the constitutional movement, when people wanted to write laws and draw up a constitution, a copy of the Belgian legal code was borrowed from the Belgian embassy and a handful of individuals (whose names I do not wish to mention here) used it as the basis for the constitution they then wrote, supplementing its deficiencies with borrowings from the French and British legal codes. True, they added some of the ordinances of Islam in order to deceive the people, but the basis of the laws that were now thrust upon the people was alien and borrowed.

What connections do all the various articles of the Constitution as well as the body of Supplementary Law concerning the monarchy, the succession, and so forth, have with Islam? They are all opposed to Islam; they violate the system of government and the laws of Islam.

Islam proclaims monarchy and hereditary succession wrong and invalid. When Islam first appeared in Iran, the Byzantine Empire, Egypt, and the Yemen, the entire institution of monarchy was abolished. In the blessed letters that the Most Noble Messenger wrote to the Byzantine Emperor Heraclius and the Shāhanshāh of Iran, he called upon them to abandon the monarchical and imperial form of government, to cease compelling the servants of God to worship them with absolute obedience, and to permit men to worship God, Who has no partner and is the True Monarch. Monarchy and hereditary succession represent the same sinister, evil system of government that prompted the Doyen of the Martyrs to rise up in revolt and seek martyrdom in an effort to prevent its establishment. He revolted in repudiation of the hereditary succession of Yazīd, to refuse it his recognition.

Islam, then, does not recognize monarchy and hereditary succession; they have no place in Islam. If that is what is meant by the so-called deficiency of Islam, then Islam is indeed deficient. Islam has laid down no laws for the practice of usury, for banking on the basis of usury, for the consumption of alcohol, or for the cultivation of sexual vice, having radically prohibited all of these. The ruling cliques, therefore, who are the puppets of imperialism and wish to promote these vices in the Islamic world, will naturally regard Islam as defective. They must import the appropriate laws from Britain, France, Belgium, and most recently, America. The fact that Islam makes no provision for the orderly pursuit of these illicit activities, far from being a deficiency, is a sign of perfection and a source of pride.

The conspiracy worked out by the imperialist government of Britain at the beginning of the constitutional movement had two purposes. The first, which was already known at that time, was to eliminate the influence of Tsarist Russia in Iran, and the second was to take the laws of Islam out of force and operation by introducing Western laws.

The imposition of foreign laws on our Islamic society has been the source of numerous problems and difficulties. Knowledgeable people working in our judicial system have many complaints concerning the existing laws and their mode of operation. If a person becomes caught up in the judicial system of Iran or that of analogous countries, he may have to spend a whole lifetime trying to prove his case. In my youth I once encountered a learned lawyer who said, "I can spend my whole life following a litigation back and forth through the judicial machinery, and then

bequeath it to my son for him to do the same thing!" That is the situation that now prevails, except, of course, when one of the parties has influence, in which case the matter is examined and settled swiftly, albeit unjustly.

Our present judicial laws have brought our people nothing but trouble, causing them to neglect their daily tasks and providing the occasion for all kinds of misuse. Very few people are able to obtain their legitimate rights. In the adjudication of cases, it is necessary not only that everyone should obtain his rights, but also that correct procedure be followed. People's time must be considered, as well as the way of life and profession of both parties, so that matters are resolved as swiftly and simply as possible.

A case that a *sharī'ah* judge in earlier times settled in one or two days cannot be settled now in twenty years. The needy, young, and old alike, must spend the entire day at the Ministry of Justice, from morning to evening, wasting their time in corridors or standing in front of some official's desk, and in the end they will still not know what has transpired. Anyone who is more cunning, and more willing and able to give bribes, has his case settled expeditiously, but at the cost of justice. Otherwise, they must wait in frustration and perplexity until their entire lives are gone.

The agents of imperialism sometimes write in their books and their newspapers that the legal provisions of Islam are too harsh. One person was even so impudent as to write that the laws of Islam are harsh because they have originated with the Arabs, so that the "harshness" of the Arabs is reflected in the harshness of Islamic law!

I am amazed at the way these people think. They kill people for possessing ten grams of heroin and say, "That is the law" (I have been informed that ten people were put to death some time ago, and another person more recently, for possession of ten grams of heroin). Inhuman laws like this are concocted in the name of a campaign against corruption, and they are not to be regarded as harsh. (I am not saying it is permissible to sell heroin, but this is not the appropriate punishment. The sale of heroin must indeed be prohibited but the punishment must be in proportion to the crime.) When Islam, however, stipulates that the drinker of alcohol should receive eighty lashes, they consider it "too harsh." They can *execute* someone for possessing ten grams of heroin and the question of harshness does not even arise!

Many forms of corruption that have appeared in society derive from alcohol. The collisions that take place on our roads, and the murders and suicides are very often caused by the consumption of alcohol. Indeed, even the use of heroin is said to derive from addiction to alcohol. But still, some say, it is quite unobjectionable for someone to drink alcohol (after all, they do it in the West); so let alcohol be bought and sold freely.

But when Islam wishes to prevent the consumption of alcohol—one of the major evils—stipulating that the drinker should receive eighty lashes, or sexual vice, decreeing that the fornicator be given one hundred lashes (and the married man or woman be stoned), then they start wailing and lamenting: "What a harsh law that is, reflecting the harshness of the Arabs!" They are not aware that these penal provisions of Islam are intended to keep great nations from being destroyed by corruption. Sexual vice has now reached such proportions that it is destroying entire generations, corrupting our youth, and causing them to neglect all forms of work. They are all rushing to enjoy the various forms of vice that have become so freely available and so enthusiastically promoted. Why should it be regarded as harsh if Islam stipulates that an offender must be publicly flogged in order to protect the younger generation from corruption?

At the same time, we see the masters of this ruling class of ours enacting slaughters in Vietnam over fifteen years, devoting enormous budgets to this business of bloodshed, and no one has the right to object! But if Islam commands its followers to engage in warfare or defense in order to make men submit to laws that are beneficial for them, and kill a few corrupt people or instigators of corruption, then they ask: "What's the purpose for that war?"

All of the foregoing represent plans drawn up several centuries ago that are now being implemented and bearing fruit.

First, they opened a school in a certain place and we overlooked the matter and said nothing. Our colleagues also were negligent in the matter and failed to prevent it from being established so that now, as you can observe, these schools have multiplied, and their missionaries have gone out into the provinces and villages, turning our children into Christians or unbelievers.

Their plan is to keep us backward, to keep us in our present miserable state so they can exploit our riches, our underground wealth, our lands, and our human resources. They want us to remain afflicted and wretched, and our poor to be trapped in their misery. Instead of surrendering to the injunctions of Islam, which provide a solution for the problem of poverty, they and their agents wish to go on living in huge places and enjoy lives of abominable luxury.

These plans of theirs are so broad in scope that they have even touched the institutions of religious learning. If someone wishes to speak about an Islamic government and the establishment of Islamic government, he must observe the principle of *taqiyyah* and count upon the opposition of those who have sold themselves to imperialism. When this book was first printed, the agents of the embassy undertook certain desperate measures to prevent its dissemination, which succeeded only in disgracing themselves more than before.

Matters have now come to the point where some people consider the apparel of a soldier incompatible with true manliness and justice, even though the leaders of our religion were all soldiers, commanders, and warriors. They put on military dress and went into battle in the wars that are described for us in our history; they killed and they were killed. The Commander of the Faithful himself would place a helmet on his blessed head, don his coat of chain mail, and gird on a sword. Imām Hasan and the Doyen of the Martyrs acted likewise. The later Imāms did not have the opportunity to go into battle, even though Imām Bāqir was also a warrior by nature. But now the wearing of military apparel is thought to detract from a man's quality of justice, and it is said that one should not wear military dress. If we want to form an Islamic government, then we must do it in our cloaks and turbans; otherwise, we commit an offense against decency and justice!

This is all the result of the wave of propaganda that has now reached the religious institution and imposed on us the duty of proving that Islam also possesses rules of government.

That is our situation then—created for us by the foreigners through their propaganda and their agents. They have removed from operation all the judicial processes and political laws of Islam and replaced them with European importations, thus diminishing the scope of Islam and ousting it from Islamic society. For the sake of exploitation they have installed their agents in power.

So far, we have sketched the subversive and corrupting plan of imperialism. We must now take into consideration as well certain internal factors notably the dazzling effect that the material progress of the imperialist countries has had on some members of our society. As the imperialist countries attained a high degree of wealth and affluence—the result both of scientific and technical progress and of their plunder of the nations of Asia and Africa—these individuals lost all their self-confidence and imagined that the only way to achieve technical progress was to abandon their own laws and beliefs. When the moon landings took place, for instance, they concluded that Muslims should jettison their laws! But what is the connection between going to the moon and the laws of Islam? Do they not see that countries having opposing laws and social systems compete with each other in technical and scientific progress and the conquest of space? Let them go all the way to Mars or beyond the Milky Way; they will still be deprived of true happiness, moral virtues and spiritual advancement and be unable to solve their own social problems. For the solution of social problems and the relief of human misery require foundations in faith and moral; merely acquiring material power and wealth, conquering nature and space, have no effect in this regard. They must be supplemented by, and balanced with, the faith, the conviction, and the morality of Islam in order truly to serve humanity instead of endangering it. This conviction, this morality, and these laws that are needed, we already possess. So, as soon as someone goes somewhere or invents something, we should not hurry to abandon our religion and its laws, which regulate the life of man and provide for his well being in this world and hereafter.

The same applies to the propaganda of the imperialists. Unfortunately some members of our society have been influenced by their hostile propaganda, although they should not have been. The imperialists have propagated among us the view that Islam does not have a specific form of government or governmental institutions. They say further that even if Islam does have certain laws, it has no method for enforcing them, so that its function is purely legislative. This kind of propaganda forms part of the overall plan of the imperialists to prevent the Muslims from becoming involved in political activity and establishing an Islamic government. It is in total contradiction with our fundamental beliefs.

We believe in government and believe that the Prophet was bound to appoint a successor, as he indeed did. Was a successor designated purely for the sake of expounding law? The expounding of law did not require a successor to the Prophet. He himself, after all, had expounded the laws; it would have been enough for the laws to be written down in a book and put into people's hands to guide them in their actions. It was logically necessary for a successor to be appointed for the sake of exercising government. Law requires a person to execute it. The same holds true

in all countries of the world, for the establishment of a law is of little benefit in itself and cannot secure the happiness of man. After a law is established, it is necessary also to create an executive power. If a system of law or government lacks an executive power, it is clearly deficient. Thus Islam, just as it established laws, also brought into being an executive power.

There was still a further question: who was to hold the executive power? If the Prophet had not appointed a successor to assume the executive power, he would have failed to complete his mission, as the Qur'an testifies. The necessity for the implementation of divine law, the need for an executive power, and the importance of that power in fulfilling the goals of the prophetic mission and establishing a just order that would result in the happiness of mankind—all of this made the appointment of a successor synonymous with the completion of the prophetic mission. In the time of the Prophet, laws were not merely expounded and promulgated; they were also implemented. The Messenger of God was an executor of the law. For example, he implemented the penal provisions of Islam: he cut off the hand of the thief and administered lashings and stonings. The successor to the Prophet must do the same; his task is not legislation, but the implementation of the divine laws that the Prophet has promulgated. It is for this reason that the formation of a government and the establishment of executive organs are necessary. Belief in the necessity for these is part of the general belief in the Imamate, as are, too, exertion and struggle for the sake of establishing them.

Pay close attention. Whereas hostility toward you has led them to misrepresent Islam, it is necessary for you to present Islam and the doctrine of the Imamate correctly. You must tell people: "We believe in the Imamate; we believe that the Prophet, appointed a successor to assume responsibility for the affairs of the Muslims, and that he did so in conformity with the divine will. Therefore, we must also believe in the necessity for the establishment of government, and we must strive to establish organs for the execution of law and the administration of affairs." Write and publish books concerning the laws of Islam and their beneficial effects on society. Improve your style and method of preaching and related activity. *Know that it is your duty to establish an Islamic government.* Have confidence in yourselves and know that you are capable of fulfilling this task. The imperialists began laying their plans three or four centuries ago; they started out with nothing, but see where they are now! We too will begin with nothing, and we will pay no attention to the uproar created by a few "xenomaniacs" and devoted servants of imperialism.

Present Islam to the people in its true form, so that our youth do not picture the *ākhūnds* as sitting in some corner in Najaf or Qum, studying the questions of menstruation and parturition instead of concerning themselves with politics, and draw the conclusion that religion must be separate from politics. This slogan of the separation of religion from politics and the demand that Islamic scholars should not intervene in social and political affairs have been formulated and propagated by the imperialists; it is only the irreligious who repeat them. Were religion and politics separate in the time of the Prophet? Did there exist, on one side, a group of clerics, and opposite it, a group of politicians and leaders? Were religion and politics separate in the time of the caliphs—even if they were not legitimate—or in the time of the Commander of the Faithful? Did two separate authorities exist? These slogans and claims have been advanced by the imperialists and their political agents in order to prevent religion from ordering the affairs of this world and shaping Muslim society, and at the same time to create a rift between the scholars of Islam, on the one hand, and the masses and those struggling for freedom and independence, on the other. They will thus been able to gain dominance over our people and plunder our resources, for such has always been their ultimate goal.

If we Muslims do nothing but engage in the canonical prayer, petition God, and invoke His name, the imperialists and the oppressive governments allied with them will leave us alone. If we were to say "Let us concentrate on calling the *azān* and saying our prayers. Let them come and rob us of everything we own—God will take care of them! There is no power or recourse except in Him, and God willing, we will be rewarded in the hereafter!"—if this were our logic, they would not disturb us.

Once during the occupation of Iraq, a certain British officer asked, "Is the *azān* I hear being called now on the minaret harmful to British policy?" When he was told that it was harmless, he said: "Then let him call for prayers as much as he wants!"

If you pay no attention to the policies of the imperialists, and consider Islam to be simply the few topics you are always studying and never go beyond them, then the imperialists will leave you alone. Pray as much as you like; it is your oil they are after—why should they worry about your prayers? They are after

Glossary

a school in a certain place	elsewhere in the document source, it is acknowledged that no particular school among the various foreign-run schools in Iran can be identified.
… as the Qur'an testifies	at 4:67
Commander of the Faithful	leader of the Muslims
desperate measures	attempts by the Iranian embassy in Baghdad to prevent the dissemination of earlier versions of this document
Imāam Hasan and … Imāam Bāqir	respectively, the second and fifth imams
Most Noble Messenger	the Prophet Muhammad
mujtahīds	an Islamic legal authority whose opinions on a law's specific provisions are based on deductions from Muslim principles and ordinances
These new groups	European countries, beginning with the Portuguese in the mid-1500s, that colonized Muslim countries
"xenomaniacs"	English rendition of a Persian term designating persons excessively partial to the culture of foreign, especially Western, nations

our minerals, and want to turn our country into a market for their goods. That is the reason the puppet governments they have installed prevent us from industrializing, and instead, establish only assembly plants and industry that is dependent on the outside world.

They do not want us to be true human beings, for they are afraid of true human beings. Even if only one true human being appears, they fear him, because others will follow him and he will have an impact that can destroy the whole foundation of tyranny, imperialism, and government by puppets.

So, whenever some true human being has appeared they have either killed or imprisoned and exiled him, and tried to defame him by saying: "This is a political *ākhūnd*!" Now the Prophet was also a political person. This evil propaganda is undertaken by the political agents of imperialism only to make you shun politics, to prevent you from intervening in the affairs of society and struggling against treacherous governments and their anti-national and anti-Islamic politics. They want to work their will as they please, with no one to bar their way.

"[Every participating nation] affirms the recognized objective of effective prohibition of chemical weapons."

Overview

The Convention on the Prohibition of the Development, Production and Stockpiling of Bacteriological (Biological) and Toxin Weapons and on Their Destruction was opened for signature by the world's nations on April 10, 1972. The goal of the convention was, and remains, to rid the world of biological weapons, primarily viruses, bacteria, fungi, rickettsias, and protozoa that are designed to kill or incapacitate people or, in some instances, to infect crops or livestock. The convention also targets toxins, meaning any harmful substances produced from living organisms. The document went into effect on March 26, 1975, after the first twenty-two signatories to the agreement had submitted their legislatures' ratifications. Over the ensuing years additional nations signed the convention, such that the number of signatories reached 163 by the end of the year 2009.

The Biological Weapons Convention, as it is commonly known, is an important part of a concerted effort launched in the nineteenth century and continued in the twentieth century to create a body of international law regulating the methods and conditions of warfare. Among the earliest such broad measures were the Hague conventions of 1899 and 1907. As weaponry became more sophisticated and as the massive scope of wars such as World War I and World War II wreaked havoc on civilian populations, the nations of the world entered into further agreements to define the rules of war, limit the use of weapons of mass destruction (that is, weapons that produce widespread and indiscriminate destruction and death), minimize civilian casualties, ensure humane treatment of prisoners of war, and the like. The landmark Geneva Conventions, which address a variety of humanitarian wartime concerns, were concluded in 1949, incorporating and modifying prior agreements dating as far back as 1864. The Biological Weapons Convention and the 1993 Chemical Weapons Convention represent the latest efforts to achieve the humanitarian restriction of wartime activity.

The issue of biological and chemical weapons has taken on new urgency in the twenty-first century. Many nations have gained or have historically possessed stock-piles of biological and chemical weapons, and the fear that these weapons, or the expertise to produce them, could fall into the hands of terrorists, who could use them to decimate a civilian population, has increased in light of recent global terrorist activity. The U.S.-led invasion of Iraq in 2003 was based in part on the suspicion that Iraq's leader, Saddam Hussein, had weapons of mass destruction, including biological weapons, and the intent to use them.

Context

The history of biological and chemical warfare is nearly as old as the history of warfare itself. In the ancient world, the Hittites, according to texts dating to 1500 BCE, forced plague victims into enemy territory in the hope of spreading the disease. The ancient Greeks and Romans would poison the water wells of besieged enemy towns and fortresses, while the Carthaginians threw pots filled with poisonous snakes onto the decks of enemy ships. Although it does not pertain to warfare, one ghastly method of executing convicted criminals in the ancient world was to tie a corpse to the criminal, forcing him to carry it around and grow sick as the corpse decomposed. These kinds of practices continued during the medieval period. Common conflict strategies included poisoning enemy water wells and using catapults to hurl cadavers, rotting animal corpses, clothing from diseased people, and human or animal feces over enemy walls with the intention of producing disease. It is speculated that these practices may have been responsible for outbreaks of bubonic plague—the so-called black death—that devastated European populations in the Middle Ages.

Crude forms of biological and chemical warfare continued into the eighteenth and nineteenth centuries, with bubonic plague and smallpox often the weapons of choice. Blankets infected with smallpox were allegedly given to American Indian tribes by the U.S. military (though some historians dispute this, arguing that plans to do so were never implemented and that outbreaks of smallpox among Indians would have occurred anyway). During the U.S. Civil War, Confederate troops threw animal corpses into

1899

■ **July 29**
The Hague Convention of 1899, dealing with international laws of war and attempting to outlaw the use of poison gas in warfare, is signed at The Hague, Netherlands.

1907

■ **October 18**
The Hague Convention of 1907, modifying the terms of the Hague Convention of 1899, is signed.

1925

■ **June 17**
The Geneva Protocol, prohibiting the use of lethal and poisonous gases and bacteriological weaponry, is signed.

1943

■ **June**
During World War II, President Franklin Roosevelt renounces the initiating use of chemical weapons by the United States.

1949

■ **August 12**
The Geneva Conventions, regulating the conduct of land and sea warfare and the treatment of prisoners of war and civilian populations, are signed.

ponds and other sources of water that Union troops would have used.

In the twentieth century biological warfare became more sophisticated, as scientists developed the ability to culture and mass-produce pathogens in laboratories and military planners developed sophisticated methods of delivery. During World War I the Germans were at the forefront of the production of bioweapons, including anthrax, a highly lethal spore that can infect livestock and humans, and glanders, a pathogen that primarily infects equines but can be transferred to humans. The Germans distributed ampoules of anthrax to saboteurs in several enemy nations and similarly distributed glanders to be used against livestock belonging to the Allies. One German saboteur living in Maryland produced glanders in his basement and succeeded in infecting livestock along the East Coast of the United States. Prior to World War II, the Japanese established what was called Unit 731, a laboratory in China that developed biological and chemical weapons. It has been estimated that the number of people killed by Japanese germ warfare and bioweapons experimentation—often through the dropping of infected fleas over cities—during the Second Sino-Japanese War (1937–1945) and World War II was nearly six hundred thousand, with most of the victims being Chinese and Koreans.

Meanwhile, in response to the horrors of World War I, the Geneva Protocol, officially titled the Protocol for the Prohibition of the Use in War of Asphyxiating, Poisonous or Other Gases, and of Bacteriological Methods of Warfare, was signed in 1925. Although this protocol attempted to prohibit bacteriological warfare methods, it was developed primarily in response to the use of poison gases, such as mustard gas and chlorine gas, during the Great War. Germany first used poison gas in 1915, and the Allies followed suit soon after. An estimated hundred thousand deaths resulted from gas attacks over the course of the war, while many soldiers who survived gas attacks were blinded or horribly disfigured. In this context, biological and chemical weapons were often discussed in tandem. During the Conference for the Reduction and Limitation of Armaments of 1932 to 1934, held in Geneva, Switzerland, efforts were made to outlaw biological and chemical weapons, but the efforts proved unsuccessful.

During World War II, both the Allies and the Axis powers developed new, more sophisticated chemical and biological weapons, but neither side deployed them. In June 1943 U.S. president Franklin Roosevelt declared, principally with regard to chemical weapons,

> Use of such weapons has been outlawed by the general opinion of civilized mankind. This country has not used them, and I hope we never will be compelled to use them. I state categorically that we shall under no circumstances resort to the use of such weapons unless they are first used by our enemies. (http://www.americanheritage.com/articles/magazine /ah/1985/5/1985_5_40.shtml)

The issue was taken up once again during the 1962 sessions of the Eighteen-Nation Committee on Disarmament, held in Geneva. During these negotiations, the Soviet Union argued that biological and chemical weapons should be considered together; the elimination of only one class of weapons could potentially spark a race to develop the other class. The United States and Great Britain, however, took the position that the two forms of weapons should be considered separately, and the British were highly instrumental in promoting a biological weapons agreement first. Their argument was that outlawing biological weapons would be easier than outlawing chemical weapons, and the one step should not be held up because of complex and protracted negotiations about the other. The basis of this position was likely that the chemicals used in chemical weapons often have legitimate peacetime uses, making the identification of a "chemical weapon" more difficult, while the pathogens used in biological weapons have fewer such uses and so can be more easily identified and restricted.

After President Richard Nixon took office in 1969, he ordered a review of all U.S. practices with regard to biological and chemical weapons. On November 25, 1969, he declared that the United States renounced any initiating usage of chemical weapons in warfare and renounced unconditionally any usage of biological weapons. This declaration marked a significant step toward a multilateral agreement and was internationally celebrated. The Soviets continued to argue that both biological and chemical weapons had to be included together in any agreement, but pressure was building on them to soften their position and agree to a separate agreement on biological weapons. The UN General Assembly and the Conference of the Committee on Disarmament continued to debate the issue through 1970; a breakthrough occurred on March 30, 1971, when the Soviets agreed in principle to an agreement on biological weapons alone. On August 5 of that year, the U.S. and Soviet representatives to the disarmament committee, who were its cochairs, submitted a joint draft of an agreement to the United Nations.

On December 16, 1971, the UN General Assembly voted unanimously, with one abstention (France, which believed that the Geneva Protocol of 1925 would thus be weakened), to approve the Biological Weapons Convention. On April 10, 1972, the agreement was opened for signatures in Moscow, London, and Washington, D.C. On August 10, 1972, Nixon submitted the convention to the U.S. Senate (which is constitutionally required to approve treaties), calling it "the first international agreement since World War II to provide for the actual elimination of an entire class of weapons from the arsenals of nations" (http://www.state.gov/www/global/arms/treaties/bwc1.html). The Senate delayed consideration of the agreement until 1974. Finally, on December 16, 1974, the Senate unanimously approved the convention, and President Gerald Ford signed the ratification agreement on January 22, 1975. Consistent with the convention, on May 22, 1990, the U.S. Biological Weapons Anti-Terrorism Act of 1989

Time Line

1969

- **November 25**
  President Richard Nixon announces that the United States unconditionally renounces the use of biological weapons and renounces the initiating use of chemical weapons.

1971

- **August 5**
  The U.S. and Soviet cochairmen of the Conference of the Committee on Disarmament submit to the United Nations a joint draft agreement for a biological weapons convention.

- **December 16**
  The UN General Assembly votes unanimously to approve the Biological Weapons Convention.

1972

- **April 10**
  The Biological Weapons Convention is opened for signatures.

1974

- **December 16**
  The U.S. Senate unanimously approves the convention.

1975

- **January 22**
  President Gerald Ford signs the ratification agreement for the convention.

- **March 26**
  The Biological Weapons Convention goes into effect.

1990

- **May 22**
  The U.S. Biological Weapons Anti-Terrorism Act of 1989 goes into effect, implementing the provisions of the Biological Weapons Convention and establishing criminal penalties for its violation.

2004

- **April 28**
  The UN Security Council adopts Resolution 1540 to inhibit the spread of weapons of mass destruction, including biological weapons, to nonstate actors.

went into effect to implement the convention's provisions and establish criminal penalties for its violation.

About the Author

It is impossible to specify a particular author or group of authors who wrote the text for the Biological Weapons Convention. Much of the text was developed in individual nations by foreign affairs or state departments and by civilian and military defense planners. Throughout the debate over the convention, various nations proposed passages that found their way into the final document.

Much of the work on the text was accomplished by the Conference of the Committee on Disarmament, which acted in an advisory capacity to the United Nations. The U.S. representative to the committee was James Fulton Leonard, Jr. Born in 1920 in Pennsylvania, Leonard earned a bachelor's degree from Princeton University in 1942, to then serve in the U.S. Army Corps of Engineers through World War II. Over the next twenty years, he held various positions with the U.S. State Department and also attended Harvard University and Columbia University. Under President Richard Nixon, Leonard served as assistant director of the U.S. Arms Control and Disarmament Agency from 1969 to 1973; in this capacity, he was the chief U.S. negotiator for the Biological Weapons Convention. He retired from government service in 1973, but he returned to serve as ambassador to the United Nations from 1977 to 1979. Throughout the 1980s and beyond he offered his expertise to a variety of nongovernmental organ-

izations, and in 1989 he cofounded the Scientists Working Group on Biological and Chemical Weapons.

Explanation and Analysis of the Document

The Convention on the Prohibition of the Development, Production and Stockpiling of Bacteriological (Biological) and Toxin Weapons and on Their Destruction consists of a preamble and fifteen articles. It undertakes to prohibit the signatory nations from developing biological weapons. It was the product of years of negotiation that finally bore fruit in 1972, when the talks were concluded. The convention took effect on March 26, 1975.

◆ Preamble

The preamble, like the preambles to most such documents, outlines the broad goals of the convention and the rationale behind it. The document opens by stating that the parties to the convention are committed to the goal of total disarmament and that prohibiting the development, production, and stockpiling of biological weapons "will facilitate the achievement of general and complete disarmament under strict and effective control." The concept of "strict and effective control," however, turned out to be elusive; many observers have noted that the document is weak on the issue of verification and that some signatories to the convention have violated its terms. The preamble next makes reference to the 1925 Geneva Protocol, which outlawed biological weapons, and affirms its goals. The preamble also ties the issue of biological weapons to that of chemical weapons. As noted, differences among the parties emerged as to whether an agreement pertaining to biological weapons could be effective in the absence of a similar agreement pertaining to chemical weapons. Only when the Soviet Union backed down from its insistence that the two forms of weaponry be addressed in tandem were negotiations leading to an agreement able to proceed. The preamble concludes by stating that the use of biological weapons is "repugnant to the conscience of mankind."

◆ Articles I and II

The first two articles are the core of the convention. Article I states that the parties to the agreement agree "never in any circumstance to develop, produce, stockpile," or otherwise possess biological weapons. It has often been noted that the convention does not specifically prohibit the *use* of biological weapons, retaining for the signatories the possibility of using such weapons in retaliation for their use by other nations. The article specifically prohibits "microbial or other biological agents," as well as toxins (substances derived from living organisms) that do not serve legitimate peaceful, medical purposes. The first article further prohibits the development of weapons that would be used for the delivery of bioweapons. Most bioweapons would be most effectively spread throughout a large population by missiles that would deliver them to targets. Generally, bioweapons need to be dispersed in aerosol form to have maximum effect. One of the concerns about the regime of Saddam Hussein in Iraq was that it might have been developing and testing missiles to be used to launch chemical and biological attacks. Many nations, including the United States, came to believe that Iraq had biological weapons capability, leading to the U.S.-led invasion of Iraq in 2003 and the toppling of Hussein's government.

Article II requires the parties to the agreement to either destroy or convert to peaceful uses any of the materials mentioned in Article I. Nations are given nine months to do so. Destruction of these materials is to be accomplished in a way that protects civilian populations.

◆ Articles III and IV

Article III turns to the issue of exchanges of biological weapons, specifically prohibiting the transfer of such weapons to other states or organizations. It also prohibits nations from helping, encouraging, or inducing any nation or group to acquire biological weapons or their means of delivery. This would become an issue in ensuing years, when fears grew that with the breakup of the Soviet Union and the Eastern bloc in the early 1990s, biological weapons and technology might be sold to the highest bidders on the international market. Further, fear grew that rogue nations such as North Korea could sell bioweapons to terrorist organizations or other rogue states. Article IV calls on the agreement's signatories to take legal steps to ensure that no one within their borders develop, produce, or stockpile biological weapons. In the United States, this provision of the convention was fulfilled in 1990 when the U.S. Biological Weapons Anti-Terrorism Act of 1989 went into effect. Later, in 2004, UN Security Council Resolution 1540 attempted to strengthen this provision, particularly with regard to nonstate actors—that is, terrorists and black market organizations.

◆ Articles V–IX

Articles V through IX deal generally with the relationship among the parties to the convention. Article V, for example, calls on the parties to consult and cooperate with one another in matters pertaining to the convention and ways of implementing it. Cooperation can be facilitated through the offices of the United Nations. Article VI deals with breaches of the convention and allows parties to call the attention of the United Nations to such breaches. It also urges nations to cooperate in investigations of nations suspected of having breached the convention. Article VII states that the parties to the convention are obligated to provide support and assistance to any nation that, in the view of the UN Security Council, faces danger as a result of breaches of the convention. Article VIII again alludes to the 1925 Geneva Protocol and indicates that the current convention does not change any nation's obligations under the earlier agreement. Article IX calls on the signatories to continue to negotiate in good faith to develop a parallel convention that would deal with chemical weapons. That goal would be reached in 1993 when the Convention on the Prohibition of the Development, Production, Stockpil-

German schoolchildren learn to don gas masks on the eve of World War II. (AP/Wide World Photos)

ing and Use of Chemical Weapons and on Their Destruction was signed; the agreement went into effect in 1997.

◆ Article X

Article X is a key provision, and one that unwittingly gave rise to problems in future years. The purpose of the article was to acknowledge that nations carry on biological research for numerous legitimate purposes. Clause 1 of the article states that nations "have the right to participate in, the fullest possible exchange of equipment, materials and scientific and technological information for the use of bacteriological (biological) agents and toxins for peaceful purposes." Clause 2 states that the convention "shall be implemented in a manner designed to avoid hampering the economic or technological development of States Parties to the Convention." These provisions, allowing the pursuit of biological research, left the door open for dual-use research, or research that could be conducted for peaceful purposes but could also be applied to biological weapons. Dual-use technology has made verification of compliance with the convention an ongoing challenge.

◆ Articles XI–XV

The remaining articles deal with legalities. Article XI touches on procedures for amending the convention. Arti-

Under the supervision of UN inspectors, workers in Iraq destroy growth media that could be used to produce biological weapons. (AP/Wide World Photos)

cle XII calls for a conference in five years to determine what progress had been made on implementing the convention. Such follow-up conferences have been ongoing, and numerous governmental and nongovernmental organizations assist in monitoring compliance with the convention. Article XIII states that the agreement will have "unlimited duration" but allows any signatory to withdraw from the convention in the face of "extraordinary events" that threaten the nation's "supreme interests." Article XIV outlines procedures associated with the signing and ratification of the convention, and the final article lists the languages in which the convention will be promulgated.

Audience

The chief audience of the Biological Weapons Convention comprised the nations that signed it, presumably because they wanted to see biological weapons eradicated. National governments were called on to pass laws making the production of bioweapons illegal and providing for the punishment of those who violate the laws. Military planners, in turn, were informed that bioweapons were no longer part of their nation's arsenal. Most of the signatories to the convention

were unlikely to have ever had the desire to produce such weapons or even the technical and financial wherewithal to do so. The real fear was that major powers such as the United States and the Soviet Union, along with their allies, could resort to the use of bioweapons. In this sense, the convention amounted to a kind of treaty, with each major nation's adversaries and potential adversaries as its respective audience. The convention's broader audience also included all people of the world. The convention alleviated at least one source of anxiety among people who might be caught in a war zone, and it announced that the world's powers were at least attempting to reduce tensions and find sources of agreement. The Biological Weaons Convention was agreed to at roughly the same time that the Soviets and the United States were making efforts to reduce their stockpiles of nuclear weapons. It thus was part of a larger movement to mitigate some of the horrors of war, particularly for wars yet to be fought.

Impact

It is difficult to assess the impact of the Biological Weapons Convention. On the one hand, no major biological attack has been launched against a large population. In

1984 a dissident political group infected salad bars in The Dalles, Oregon, with salmonella, infecting over seven hundred people. Then, in the wake of the terrorist attacks on the United States of September 11, 2001, letters tainted with anthrax were sent to U.S. politicians and media officials, killing five people; the Federal Bureau of Investigation later concluded that the anthrax attacks were the work of a biodefense researcher named Bruce Ivins, who committed suicide in 2008. Otherwise, calamitous bioweapon-attack scenarios have largely gone unrealized.

The chief problem with combating biological weapons is the issue of dual use. Virtually any type of scientific research can be used for the benefit of humankind or in the development of a weapon. As scientists continue to use emerging technologies to unlock the secrets of life, the danger remains that knowledge could be hijacked to develop biological weapons. In fact, not a great deal of technology or scientific expertise is needed to produce certain biological agents. In 2002, for example, authorities arrested six people in Manchester, England, after they found an apartment-based laboratory being used for the production of ricin, a toxin derived from castor beans. Making ricin a more feared weapon is the circumstance that over a million tons of castor beans are processed worldwide each year in the production of castor oil, a product with numerous legitimate uses in medicine and industry.

Beyond dual use, many observers have noted that the Biological Weapons Convention is weak on the issue of enforcement. Evidence strongly suggests that the former Soviet Union violated the terms of the convention, and suspicions remain that Egypt, Israel, Russia, North Korea, Syria, Iran, and China have retained offensive biological weapons capabilities. During the 1990s, efforts were made to negotiate a protocol for verification of compliance with the bioweapons convention. Those efforts collapsed in 2001 when the United States withdrew from the negotiations, arguing that the suggested protocol would be ineffective and would hamper the work of U.S. biodefense, biotechnology, and pharmaceutical industries. Meantime, nations such as the United States have continued to conduct research in biological weapons, largely for defensive purposes. The U.S. government annually spends some $3 billion researching these weapons with a view to developing vaccines against them—a figure that represents a massive increase in the budget in the wake of the 2001 terrorist attacks.

Many scientists have argued that another fundamental weakness of the bioweapons convention is that it does not effectively deal with concerns related to biodefense. At issue is the concern that a "biodefense arms race" has developed, with numerous nations around the world conducting research in biological weapons, which they profess not to intend to stockpile, in the interest of defending against them. Large numbers of scientists, technicians, and others can thus gain access to biological materials that could be used to do harm or sold to those who wish to do harm. There are also concerns about the accidental release of pathogens into the general population, which could create an epidemic that authorities would not be equipped to handle. A final concern is that any country that has biological weapons could elect to use them as a source of revenue by selling them to terrorist groups or other rogue nations.

To address some of these matters, the UN Security Council adopted Resolution 1540 in April 2004. The resolution imposed binding obligations on UN member states to take steps to prevent the spread of weapons of mass destruction, including biological weapons. It prohibits member states from supporting nonstate actors, such as terrorists, who are trying to acquire such weapons; while it obligates member states to pass laws that prohibit the proliferation of such weapons to nonstate actors and to take effective measures to ensure that such nonstate actors are cut off from financial support. The belief is that successful implementation of the resolution will bolster international standards having to do with the export of biological materials and keep them out of the hands of terrorists and black market organizations.

In sum, some observers believe that the Biological Weapons Convention was and is a noble failure. Its goal of banning biological weapons is laudatory, but the convention failed to take into account the complexities of modern biological sciences and, in particular, the thorny issue of verification. One scholar, Jez Littlewood, assesses that the convention "has failed to achieve complete biological disarmament among its states parties"; he notes that "by the early 1990s, it was clear that certain states parties had failed to comply with their obligations not to develop, produce or stockpile biological or toxin weapons." He concludes that "amiable people had in fact deceived themselves that they were safe from the use of disease as a weapon" (p. 9). Scientists and others continue to fear what is referred to as a "maximum credible event"—a worst-case scenario, such as a biological attack capable of killing and injuring thousands, overwhelming medical facilities, and inducing widespread panic.

Further Reading

■ Articles

Appel, Jacob M. "Is All Fair in Biological Warfare? The Controversy over Genetically Engineered Biological Weapons." *Journal of Medical Ethics* 35, no. 7 (2009): 429–432.

Bernstein, Barton J. "Why We Didn't Use Poison Gas in World War II." *American Heritage* 36, no. 5 (August–September 1985). Available online. AmericanHeritage.com Web site.
   http://www.americanheritage.com/articles/magazine/ah/1985/5/1985_5_40.shtml.

Rózsa, Lajos. "The Motivation for Biological Aggression Is an Inherent and Common Aspect of the Human Behavioural Repertoire." *Medical Hypotheses* 72, no. 2 (2009): 217–219.

■ Books

Barenblatt, Daniel. *A Plague upon Humanity: The Secret Genocide of Axis Japan's Germ Warfare Operation*. New York: HarperCollins, 2004.

"Each State Party to this Convention undertakes never in any circumstance to develop, produce, stockpile or otherwise acquire or retain: (1) Microbial or other biological agents, or toxins whatever their origin or method of production, of types and in quantities that have no justification for prophylactic, protective or other peaceful purposes; (2) Weapons, equipment or means of delivery designed to use such agents or toxins for hostile purposes or in armed conflict."

(Article I)

"Each State Party to this Convention undertakes to destroy, or to divert to peaceful purposes, as soon as possible … all agents, toxins, weapons, equipment and means of delivery specified in Article I of the Convention."

(Article II)

"Each State Party to this Convention undertakes not to transfer to any recipient whatsoever, directly or indirectly, and not in any way to assist, encourage, or induce any State, group of States or international organizations to manufacture or otherwise acquire any of the agents, toxins, weapons, equipment or means of delivery."

(Article III)

"Each State Party to this Convention affirms the recognized objective of effective prohibition of chemical weapons and, to this end, undertakes to continue negotiations in good faith with a view to reaching early agreement on effective measures for the prohibition of their development, production and stockpiling and for their destruction."

(Article IX)

"The States Parties to this Convention undertake to facilitate, and have the right to participate in, the fullest possible exchange of equipment, materials and scientific and technological information for the use of bacteriological (biological) agents and toxins for peaceful purposes."

(Article X)

Croddy, Eric A., and James J. Wirtz, eds. *Weapons of Mass Destruction: An Encyclopedia of Worldwide Policy, Technology, and History*. Santa Barbara, Calif.: ABC-CLIO, 2004.

Endicott, Stephen, and Edward Hagerman. *The United States and Biological Warfare: Secrets from the Early Cold War and Korea*. Bloomington: Indiana University Press, 1998.

Harris, Robert, and Jeremy Paxman. *A Higher Form of Killing: The Secret History of Chemical and Biological Warfare*. New York: Random House, 2002.

Littlewood, Jez. *The Biological Weapons Convention: A Failed Revolution*. Aldershot, U.K.: Ashgate Publishing, 2005.

Mangold, Tom, and Jeff Goldberg. *Plague Wars: A True Story of Biological Warfare*. London: Macmillan, 1999.

Mayor, Adrienne. *Greek Fire, Poison Arrows and Scorpion Bombs: Biological and Chemical Warfare in the Ancient World*. Rev. ed. New York: Overlook, 2009.

Orent, Wendy. *Plague: The Mysterious Past and Terrifying Future of the World's Most Dangerous Disease*. New York: Simon & Schuster, 2004.

Sims, Nicholas. *The Diplomacy of Biological Disarmament: Vicissitudes of a Treaty in Force, 1975–85*. New York: St. Martin's Press, 1988.

Wheelis, Mark, Lajos Rózsa, and Malcolm Dando, eds. *Deadly Cultures: Biological Weapons since 1945*. Cambridge, Mass.: Harvard University Press, 2006.

Wright, Susan, ed. *Preventing a Biological Arms Race*. Cambridge, Mass.: MIT Press, 1990.

———, ed. *Biological Warfare and Disarmament: New Problems/New Perspectives*. Lanham, Md.: Rowan & Littlefield, 2002.

■ **Web Sites**

"Biological and Chemical Weapons." Center for Arms Control and Non-Proliferation Web site.
   http://www.armscontrolcenter.org/policy/biochem.

Katzman, Kenneth. *Iraq: Weapons Threat, Compliance, Sanctions, and U.S. Policy*. U.S. State Department Web site.
   http://fpc.state.gov/documents/organization/18224.pdf.

—Michael J. O'Neal

Questions for Further Study

1. Why are biological weapons considered so heinous? Is there a moral difference between launching a biological attack against an enemy and conducting a bombing operation that might kill and injure large numbers of enemy combatants and civilians? Is there a moral difference between a bullet and bacteria?

2. Many nations, including the United States, conduct research in biological weapons for the avowed purpose of producing vaccines that can be used to protect their citizens. In the process, they have to produce quantities of the biological agent itself. Do you think this is a fundamental weakness that threatens to undermine the Biological Weapons Convention?

3. A biological "attack" can be readily carried out by nonstate actors, including terrorists, within a civilian population. Do you believe that this fact would justify a nation in launching a preemptive attack against another nation with biological weapons capability as a means of negating that capability?

4. Explain the concept of "dual use" and why dual use complicates the issue of biological (and chemical) weapons control.

5. Evidence suggests that some nations that have signed the Biological Weapons Convention have violated its terms. Do you think that these violations suggest that the convention has been a failure?

BIOLOGICAL WEAPONS CONVENTION

The States Parties to this Convention,

Determine to act with a view to achieving effective progress toward general and complete disarmament, including the prohibition and elimination of all types of weapons of mass destruction, and convinced that the prohibition of the development, production and stockpiling of chemical and bacteriological (biological) weapons and their elimination, through effective measures, will facilitate the achievement of general and complete disarmament under strict and effective control,

Recognizing the important significance of the Protocol for the Prohibition of the Use in War of Asphyxiating, Poisonous or Other Gases, and of Bacteriological Methods of Warfare, signed at Geneva on June 17, 1925, and conscious also of the contribution which the said Protocol has already made and continues to make, to mitigating the horrors of war,

Reaffirming their adherence to the principles and objectives of that Protocol and calling upon all States to comply strictly with them,

Recalling that the General Assembly of the United Nations has repeatedly condemned all actions contrary to the principles and objectives of the Geneva Protocol of June 17, 1925,

Desiring to contribute to the strengthening of confidence between peoples and the general improvement of the international atmosphere,

Desiring also to contribute to the realization of the purposes and principles of the Charter of the United Nations,

Convinced of the importance and urgency of eliminating from the arsenals of States, through effective measures, such dangerous weapons of mass destruction as those using chemical or bacteriological (biological) agents,

Recognizing that an agreement on the prohibition of bacteriological (biological) and toxin weapons represents a first possible step towards the achievement of agreement on effective measures also for the prohibition of the development, production and stockpiling of chemical weapons, and determined to continue negotiations to that end,

Determined, for the sake of all mankind, to exclude completely the possibility of bacteriological (biological) agents and toxins being used as weapons,

Convinced that such use would be repugnant to the conscience of mankind and that no effort should be spared to minimize this risk,

Have agreed as follows:

◆ Article I

Each State Party to this Convention undertakes never in any circumstance to develop, produce, stockpile or otherwise acquire or retain:

(1) Microbial or other biological agents, or toxins whatever their origin or method of production, of types and in quantities that have no justification for prophylactic, protective or other peaceful purposes;

(2) Weapons, equipment or means of delivery designed to use such agents or toxins for hostile purposes or in armed conflict.

◆ Article II

Each State Party to this Convention undertakes to destroy, or to divert to peaceful purposes, as soon as possible but not later than nine months after the entry into force of the Convention, all agents, toxins, weapons, equipment and means of delivery specified in Article I of the Convention, which are in its possession or under its jurisdiction or control. In implementing the provisions of this Article all necessary safety precautions shall be observed to protect populations and the environment.

◆ Article III

Each State Party to this Convention undertakes not to transfer to any recipient whatsoever, directly or indirectly, and not in any way to assist, encourage, or induce any State, group of States or international organizations to manufacture or otherwise acquire any of the agents, toxins, weapons, equipment or means of delivery specified in Article I of the Convention.

◆ Article IV

Each State Party to this Convention shall, in accordance with its constitutional processes, takes any necessary measures to prohibit and prevent the development, production, stockpiling, acquisition or retention of the agents, toxins, weapons, equipment and means of delivery specified in Article I of the

Convention, within the territory of such State, under its jurisdiction or under its control anywhere.

◆ Article V

The States Parties to this Convention undertake to consult one another and to cooperate in solving any problems which may arise in relation to the objective of, or in the application of the provisions of, the Convention. Consultation and cooperation pursuant to this Article may also be undertaken through appropriate international procedures within the framework of the United Nations and in accordance with its Charter.

◆ Article VI

(1) Any State Party to this Convention which finds that any other State Party is acting in breach of obligations deriving from the provisions of the Convention may lodge a complaint with the Security Council of the United Nations. Such a complaint should include all possible evidence confirming its validity, as well as a request for its consideration by the Security Council.

(2) Each State Party to this Convention undertakes to cooperate in carrying out any investigation which the Security Council may initiate, in accordance with the provisions of the Charter of the United Nations, on the basis of the complaint received by the Council. The Security Council shall inform the States Parties to the Convention of the results of the investigation.

◆ Article VII

Each State Party to this Convention undertakes to provide or support assistance, in accordance with the United Nations Charter, to any Party to the Convention which so requests, if the Security Council decides that such Party has been exposed to danger as a result of violation of the Convention.

◆ Article VIII

Nothing in this Convention shall be interpreted as in any way limiting or detracting from the obligations assumed by any State under the Protocol for the Prohibition of the Use in War of Asphyxiating, Poisonous or Other Gases, and of Bacteriological Methods of Warfare, signed at Geneva on June 17, 1925.

◆ Article IX

Each State Party to this Convention affirms the recognized objective of effective prohibition of chemical weapons and, to this end, undertakes to continue negotiations in good faith with a view to reaching early agreement on effective measures for the prohibition of their development, production and stockpiling and for their destruction, and on appropriate measures concerning equipment and means of delivery specifically designed for the production or use of chemical agents for weapons purposes.

◆ Article X

(1) The States Parties to this Convention undertake to facilitate, and have the right to participate in, the fullest possible exchange of equipment, materials and scientific and technological information for the use of bacteriological (biological) agents and toxins for peaceful purposes. Parties to the Convention in a position to do so shall also cooperate in contributing individually or together with other States or international organizations to the further development and application of scientific discoveries in the field of bacteriology (biology) for prevention of disease, or for other peaceful purposes.

(2) This Convention shall be implemented in a manner designed to avoid hampering the economic or technological development of States Parties to the Convention or international cooperation in the field of peaceful bacteriological (biological) activities, including the international exchange of bacteriological (biological) agents and toxins and equipment for the processing, use or production of bacteriological (biological) agents and toxins for peaceful purposes in accordance with the provisions of the Convention.

◆ Article XI

Any State Party may propose amendments to this Convention. Amendments shall enter into force for each State Party accepting the amendments upon their acceptance by a majority of the States Parties to the Convention and thereafter for each remaining State Party on the date of acceptance by it.

◆ Article XII

Five years after the entry into force of this Convention, or earlier if it is requested by a majority of the Parties to the Convention by submitting a proposal to this effect to the Depositary Governments, a conference of States Parties to the Convention shall be held at Geneva, Switzerland, to review the operation of the Convention, with a view to assuring that the purposes of the preamble and the provisions of the Convention, including the provisions concerning negotiations on chemical weapons, are being realized. Such review shall take into account any new scientific and technological developments relevant to the Convention.

◆ Article XIII

(1) This Convention shall be of unlimited duration.

(2) Each State Party to this Convention shall in exercising its natural sovereignty have the right to withdraw from the Convention if it decides that extraordinary events, related to the subject matter of the Convention, have jeopardized the supreme interests of its country. It shall give notice of such withdrawal to all other States Parties to the Convention and to the United Nations Security Council three months in advance. Such notice shall include a statement of the extraordinary events it regards as having jeopardized its supreme interests.

◆ Article XIV

(1) This Convention shall be open to all States for signature. Any State which does not sign the Convention before its entry into force in accordance with paragraph (3) of this Article may accede to it at any time.

(2) This Convention shall be subject to ratification by signatory States. Instruments of ratification and instruments of accession shall be deposited with the Governments of the United States of America, the United Kingdom of Great Britain and Northern Ireland and the Union of Soviet Socialist Republics, which are hereby designated the Depositary Governments.

(3) This Convention shall enter into force after the deposit of instruments of ratification by twenty-two Governments, including the Governments designated as Depositaries of the Convention.

(4) For States whose instruments of ratification or accession are deposited subsequent to the entry into force of this Convention, it shall enter into force on the date of the deposit of their instrument of ratification or accession.

(5) The Depositary Governments shall promptly inform all signatory and acceding States of the date of each signature, the date of deposit of each instrument of ratification or of accession and the date of the entry into force of this Convention, and of the receipt of other notices.

(6) This Convention shall be registered by the Depositary Governments pursuant to Article 102 of the Charter of the United Nations.

◆ Article XV

This Convention, the English, Russian, French, Spanish and Chinese texts of which are equally authentic, shall be deposited in the archives of the Depositary Governments. Duly certified copies of the Convention shall be transmitted by the Depositary Governments of the signatory and acceding States.

"The participating States will respect human rights and fundamental freedoms."

Overview

The Helsinki Final Act, the Helsinki Accords, and the Helsinki Declaration are all common names for the Final Act of the Conference on Security and Co-operation in Europe, signed at Helsinki, Finland, on August 1, 1975. It was signed by nearly all the states of Europe (including the Holy See—the Vatican—but excluding Albania and Andorra) as well as by Canada, the United States (under Gerald Ford), and the Soviet Union (under Leonid Brezhnev)—a total of thirty-five countries. A lengthy document, spanning fifty-eight pages in the official English-language copy, it covers a wide array of major political, economic, and social topics, being designed overall to secure peace and stability within and beyond Europe in the context of the cold war. Negotiations began in 1972 and were continued for two years during the Conference on Security and Co-operation in Europe, which opened in Helsinki in July 1973 and shifted to Geneva, Switzerland, in September 1973. The North Atlantic Treaty Organization, the Warsaw Pact, and non-aligned states were all represented, giving the act great international weight and significance. The interests of a group of nonparticipating Mediterranean states—Algeria, Egypt, Israel, Morocco, Syria, and Tunisia—are also recognized in the act, accompanied by statements on the importance of the Mediterranean region in general to the overarching goals of peace and security.

The act is usually seen as important in two ways: first, for recognizing Soviet control over the Eastern European satellite nations (the so-called Eastern bloc, comprising Bulgaria, Czechoslovakia, East Germany, Hungary, Poland, and Romania) and, second, for promoting international standards for human rights and freedoms that eventually helped undermine the repressive Soviet system in general. In fact, the document does not so much explicitly recognize Soviet rights in Eastern Europe as merely imply them—allowing historians to offer varying interpretations of the authors' intent and the dynamics of the relevant negotiations. The language on human rights, on the other hand, is unambiguous, and efforts to publicize and enforce these rights did indeed contribute significantly to the demise of the Soviet Union.

Context

The Helsinki Final Act was the culmination of decades of on-again, off-again international diplomacy with roots in the postwar realities of a divided Europe and the overarching confrontation between the United States and Soviet Union. Since immediately after World War II, through which the Red Army liberated Eastern Europe from Nazism, the Soviet Union had sought formal recognition of existing political boundaries between Eastern and Western Europe—and thus uncontested control over its recently acquired satellites. An important step was made toward this Soviet goal when in 1972 the international community recognized the German Democratic Republic (Soviet-dominated East Germany). These negotiations had been conducted primarily among the Europeans, with the United States playing only a minor role; from the Soviet viewpoint, any further progress would almost certainly be impossible without full U.S. participation. Yet the U.S. administration, then under President Richard Nixon, was reluctant to give up Eastern Europe officially to Soviet control, even if there was little hope of changing the actual political circumstances. The Soviets were also drawn to the negotiating table by their desires for access to more advanced technologies, for increased trade, and for reduced arms spending; they also sought to lessen the threat of major war. All but the first of these considerations likewise motivated the United States and the Western European nations. Nonetheless, the two sides remained highly suspicious of each other.

More broadly, the Helsinki Final Act was both a symptom and major achievement of détente—a warming of relations between Communist and democratic nations that began in the late 1960s, accelerated during Nixon's presidency, and continued intermittently through the 1970s (until it was derailed by the Soviet invasion of Afghanistan in 1979 and the election the following year of Ronald Reagan as U.S. president). Détente resulted from a wide array of emerging new realities that pushed the two sides closer together, if reluctantly. The overarching concern was to avoid allowing cold war tensions to escalate into outright conflict and a possible third world war in Europe. Since the end of World War II, there had been numerous confrontations between the cold war adver-

1945

■ In the aftermath of World War II, Moscow begins to engineer the creation of puppet regimes in Bulgaria, Czechoslovakia, East Germany, Hungary, Poland, and Romania, a process that continues until 1949. These countries will become known collectively as the Eastern (or Soviet) bloc.

1948

■ **June 24**
The Berlin blockade begins in an effort by the Soviets to isolate West Berlin and bring it under their influence.

■ **June 26**
The United Kingdom and United States lead the response to the blockade by initiating the delivery of supplies to West Berlin through a successful daily airlift.

1949

■ **May 11**
The Soviets call off the Berlin blockade.

1961

■ **August 13**
East Germany begins construction of the Berlin Wall.

1962

■ **October**
The Cuban missile crisis brings the world close to nuclear conflict, raising interest in the limitation of nuclear weapons and improvement of U.S.-Soviet relations.

saries. Berlin, in particular, had been simmering. Although it was located deep in Soviet-controlled East Germany, West Berlin was under Western jurisdiction, while East Berlin was held by the Soviets. The Soviet Union blocked railway and road access to the sectors of Berlin under Western control, with the aim of forcing the West to allow the Soviets to start supplying West Berlin with food and fuel, thereby essentially giving them control over the entire city. The United States and its allies responded with the successful "Berlin airlift"—two hundred thousand flights over the course of about one year, during which thousands of tons of food and supplies were delivered daily, rendering the Soviet blockade useless and further humiliating Moscow. Thereafter, the existence of West Berlin provided an escape route for those wishing to flee Soviet control and reach the West. To plug this gap, in 1961 the Soviets erected the Berlin Wall.

Even more ominously, the Cuban missile crisis of October 1962 brought the world to the brink of nuclear war. Thereafter, a variety of treaties were negotiated—primarily between the United States and Soviet Union—as designed to slow the arms race and reduce international tensions. The first such accord was the Partial Test Ban Treaty of 1963. This was followed by a series of agreements that, taken together, marked the early history of cold war détente and helped set the scene for the Helsinki negotiations. These included the Outer Space Treaty (1967), the Nuclear Non-Proliferation Treaty (1968), the first Strategic Arms Limitation Treaty (1972), the Anti-Ballistic Missile Treaty (1972), and the Biological Weapons Convention (1972). Negotiations for the second Strategic Arms Limitation Treaty, which would be signed in 1979, also began in 1972.

Financial and economic concerns also drove détente. The arms race had become almost ruinously expensive for both sides. The Soviet-planned economy was proving inefficient, making ever-ballooning military budgets increasingly unsustainable. Although at other points in history the U.S. economy—much larger and more dynamic than the Soviet one—might have been able to shoulder the burden better, by the end of the 1960s the United States was bogged down with the costs of the Vietnam War and the major expansions of the welfare state conducted under the administrations of Lyndon Johnson and then Richard Nixon. Thus, the United States was also interested in controlling military spending. The oil shock of 1973, when dollar-denominated prices tripled, and huge declines in the stock market during 1973 and 1974 provided further motivation. As an exporter of oil and gas, the Soviet Union in some ways benefited from the rise of oil prices, but not sufficiently to offset the general inefficiencies of its planned economy, especially in agriculture. (In fact, during the 1960s the Soviet Union became increasingly dependent on U.S. grain imports.) In any case, the arms race had reached a stalemate. Both sides had similar quantities of weapons, little real tactical advantage, and firepower enough to destroy each other completely. Stepping back from the brink made abundant sense.

Finally, the drive toward the Helsinki negotiations was also helped by shifting diplomatic winds fanned by events in Europe and China. Beginning in 1969 a new West German government, under Chancellor Willy Brandt, switched course and sought closer ties with East Germany and the Soviet Union. This so-called *Ostpolitik* (German for "Eastern policy") reduced tensions in Europe more generally. Meanwhile, Soviet relations with Maoist China were cooling, raising fears in Moscow that China and the United States might come to terms and isolate the Soviet Union. President Nixon's groundbreaking visit to China in 1972 only raised these fears, prompting the USSR to redouble efforts to improve its own relations with America. It was in this environment that the Conference on Security and Cooperation in Europe began, as initiated by the Soviet leadership under Leonid Brezhnev.

About the Author

The Helsinki Final Act was negotiated and written by diplomatic teams responsible to the foreign affairs offices of their respective governments. The U.S. team was headed by Secretary of State Henry Kissinger and the Soviet team by Minister for Foreign Affairs Andrei Gromyko. The final signing, attended by the heads of thirty-five states, was the largest gathering of European leaders in the twentieth century up to that point.

Henry A. W. Kissinger was born to Jewish parents in Bavaria, Germany, in 1923. In 1938 he and his family fled Nazi Germany and settled in New York City. Beginning at New York's City College he studied politics, eventually earning a PhD from Harvard, where he later taught. During the later stages of World War II he served in the U.S. military, primarily as an interpreter. Kissinger was U.S. national security adviser (1968–1975) and served as secretary of state (1973–1977) to presidents Richard Nixon and Gerald Ford. He is generally regarded as a pragmatist, having typically preferred practical approaches and solutions that accept the world and its actors as they really are, rather than trying significantly to change them. This is sometimes termed *realpolitik*. Kissinger played only a supervisory role in the long negotiations toward the Helsinki Final Act, leaving the majority of the work to subordinates.

Andrei Andreyevich Gromyko was born in 1909 in Belarus (then part of the Russian Empire and subsequently a Soviet republic). His parents were peasants. Educated in agriculture and economics, he rose rapidly through the Communist hierarchy during the 1930s. Helped by his legendary tough negotiating skills and a reputation for never giving in to others' demands, he quickly carved out a successful career in foreign relations. For more than a decade, beginning in 1943, he served as a foreign ambassador, posted variously to the United States, the United Nations, and the United Kingdom. From 1957 to 1985 he was Soviet Minister of Foreign Affairs; it was from this post that he inherited oversight of the Helsinki negotiations. He died in 1989.

Time Line	
1963	■ **August 5** The Partial Test Ban Treaty, forbidding aboveground nuclear testing, is signed by the U.S., Soviet, and British governments.
1967	■ **January 27** The Outer Space Treaty, banning the placement of nuclear weapons in space, is signed by the United States, USSR, and United Kingdom.
1968	■ **July 1** The Nuclear Non-Proliferation Treaty is concluded, placing further limits on the spread of nuclear weapons internationally.
1969	■ The newly elected West German chancellor Willy Brandt pursues a new *Ostpolitik* ("Eastern policy"), aimed at improving relations with Moscow and the Eastern bloc nations.
1972	■ **April 10** The Biological Weapons Convention is signed, outlawing production of this entire class of weapons.

1972

- **May 26**
  The Strategic Arms Limitation Treaty and Anti-Ballistic Missile Treaty are signed, disallowing any increases in strategic missile launchers and the combined number of submarine-launched ballistic missiles and intercontinental ballistic missiles.

- **November**
  At the suggestion of the Soviets, whose goal is formal recognition of their control over the Eastern bloc states, preliminary international talks begin in Helsinki.

1973

- **July 3**
  In Helsinki, the Conference on Security and Co-operation in Europe officially opens.

1975

- **August 1**
  The Helsinki Final Act is signed.

1976

- **May 12**
  The Public Group for Assistance in Fulfilling the Helsinki Agreements in the USSR—better known as the Moscow Helsinki Group—is founded by a small group of prominent scientists, intellectuals, and activists.

Explanation and Analysis of the Document

The Helsinki Final Act was written on the understanding that European and global security could best be achieved by attention to a wide array of interrelated issues. These were conceptualized in three general domains, or "baskets": political and military (Basket I), economic and environmental (Basket II), and human rights and freedoms (Basket III). All of these topics are treated in the first part of the act, "Questions Relating to Security in Europe," in subsection 1(a), which is reproduced in full here. Also presented are excerpts from the second part, "Co-operation in the Field of Economics, of Science and Technology and of the Environment"; excerpts from the fourth part, "Co-operation in Humanitarian and Other Fields"; and the short fifth part at the back of the act, "Follow-up to the Conference," which calls for participants to continue and build upon the work done at Geneva and Helsinki.

◆ "Questions Relating to Security in Europe"

The signatories begin with a general assertion of their common interests in peace and cooperation and their mutual desire to continue and expand the process of détente. World War II—though it was by then three decades in the past—provides an important part of the agreement's framework. Neither the cold war nor World War II is cited explicitly here, but both are intended in references to "confrontation" and "past relations." In general, however, both the introductory statement and the overall document focus as much as possible on the signatories' common history, traditions, and values as well as on their common interests in peace and security now and in the future.

Subsection 1(a), "Declaration on Principles Guiding Relations between Participating States," establishes and outlines the main principles of the whole document. As preceded by a short introductory statement—the main point of which is to assert the preeminence of the United Nations and its charter as well as the conformity of the Helsinki Final Act thereto—these principles are treated under ten headings, each of which is considered equally important. Taken together, and at first glance, they may appear simply to be general and rather generic statements of goodwill and mutual respect. In fact, they reflect long and careful negotiations aimed at balancing the different concerns of the various signatories, especially those of the United States and Soviet Union. Primary among these concerns was the status of Eastern European nations then under Soviet control. As noted, the Soviets' main goal was to secure formal recognition of the status quo and thus acceptance of their hegemony in the region. It is commonly stated that the Soviets succeeded; in many ways this is correct, as can be gleaned from the titles of the first six principles, which support "sovereign equality," reject the use of force, and guarantee the "inviolability of frontiers," "territorial integrity of states," "peaceful settlement of disputes," and "non-intervention in internal affairs." These principles were generally understood by the Soviets and were indeed largely intended to indicate that the Western

European and North American allies would never invade or seek to "liberate" the Eastern bloc from Soviet domination. (Principle IV, for example, requires signatories to "refrain from making each other's territory the object of military occupation or other direct or indirect measures of force … or the object of acquisition by means of such measures or the threat of them.") For these reasons, the Helsinki Final Act has sometimes been criticized as a sellout of the Eastern bloc states to Soviet control.

At least two counterarguments have been made, however. First, while principles I–VI do rule out military action in the Eastern bloc nations (and generally), they also establish responsibilities that technically could be interpreted as hostile to Soviet interests in the region. In principle I, for example, the signatories agree to "respect each other's right freely to choose and develop its political, social, economic and cultural systems" and to "define and conduct as it wishes its relations with other States in accordance with international law." Applied to the Eastern bloc nations, this could certainly be interpreted as arguing against Soviet interference and control—perhaps even as promoting independence for Eastern European states. The same is true for the following sentences, which assert states' rights "to belong or not to belong to international organizations" or treaties, including "treaties of alliance," and also recognize the right to neutrality. In reality, however, so long as the Eastern bloc nations remained under the control of governments sponsored by and publicly friendly to Moscow, these general principles were far more readily interpreted as protecting Soviet interests. This is true as well for the emphasis on "self-determination of peoples" in principle VIII, given that the primary authority representing each "people" would have been the Soviet-dominated political machine in their respective state.

Second, it has also been pointed out that any concessions given to the Soviet Union on its territorial claims in Eastern Europe should be balanced against the positive results achieved by the West from inclusion of Principle VII. This principle required signatories to "respect human rights and fundamental freedoms, including the freedom of thought, conscience, religion or belief." The North American and Western European allies pushed for this principle in the face of Soviet reluctance. In the end, it was the price the Soviets agreed to pay for the guarantees of security and noninterference they won elsewhere. But in agreeing, they accepted that human rights were uniform across states—that is, that there existed one international standard to which all could, and would, be held; that standard was and remains the 1948 UN Universal Declaration of Human Rights. It is clear that the Soviet leadership underestimated the degree to which they would be held accountable to that declaration. Certainly, they were signing on to notions that in many ways ran directly counter to the whole thrust of the Soviet system, its historical precedents and traditions, and its political culture. How, for example, could a one-party state accommodate a requirement to allow political freedom? What could economic freedom mean in a state that condemned the exchange of goods or services for private

Time Line

1989

■ Nonviolent revolutions sweep away Communist regimes in Poland, Czechoslovakia, Hungary, East Germany, and Bulgaria. A more bloody revolution achieves the same result in Romania.

1991

■ **December 26** Amid political and economic turmoil, and following the failure in August 1991 of a coup designed to restore hard-line Communist rule, the Soviet Union is officially dissolved.

profit as a criminal act? How might an officially atheist state with a history of suppressing religion react to the requirement to allow freedom of religion? In the end, the Soviet Union had put itself into the untenable position of having to choose either to ignore these questions—which risked negative international and domestic reaction—or to address them—which implied significant and difficult reforms. Successive Soviet regimes tried first one course and then the other—both with profound consequences for the ultimate demise of the entire Soviet system.

◆ **"Co-operation in the Field of Economics, of Science and Technology and of the Environment"**

This second part of the treaty builds largely on the general point made in principle IX of the first part, calling for signatories to promote and share the benefits of progress in all fields, including economic development, scientific research, education, and culture. This reflects a core value of the document: the belief that greater cooperation and interdependence among states—particularly more and freer trade—tend to lessen the chance of conflict and war and lead to everyone's general benefit and enrichment. More prosaically, principle IX and its expansion in the third part ("Questions Relating to Security and Co-operation in the Mediterranean") also reflect the various parties' interests in specific trade and technology goals at the time. Among them were Soviet desires to access technology and North American grain. All signatories were also interested in expanding markets for their own goods and services.

Soviet general secretary Leonid Brezhnev shakes hands with President Gerald Ford after their first round of talks in Helsinki, July 30, 1975. (AP/Wide World Photos)

This part's section 1, "Commercial Exchanges," emphasizes the importance of increasing trade among all the signatories, placing this goal above other desired forms of interaction (such as tourism and shared research). Indeed, the importance of many of these other forms is partly construed, in the sections that follow, in terms of their role in further promoting this one overarching economic goal. Current levels of international trade are recognized as inadequate. Specific measures are recommended to improve the situation, including the use of "most favoured nation" trade status and the reduction and elimination of trade barriers. The Helsinki Final Act is thus one of a number of postwar statements and initiatives designed to promote peace and security through increased trade. The act can be linked in this regard, at least conceptually, to the development of the European Union and of international free-trade agreements more generally.

At the same time, however, this section of the act also records concern about possible negative consequences of freer and greater international trade, including "abrupt fluctuations" and "market disruption." These terms refer to a wide array of possible scenarios. One example might be a rapid collapse of jobs in a given industry—such as the case of a country whose established producers suddenly find themselves unable to compete with cheaper imports that have begun to appear in response to the abolition of tariffs or other trade barriers. In general, the act's authors strove in this section to achieve a balance between free trade and protectionism. The ultimate goal, however, was not a static middle ground but a steady and stable long-term transition away from protections and toward freer international trade.

◆ "Co-operation in Humanitarian and Other Fields"

This fourth part of the treaty reaffirms the act's primary goal of peace among nations while also emphasizing an important additional (and less tangible) goal: "spiritual enrichment of the human personality." Together, these are understood to be best served by attention to various issues, including "cultural and educational exchanges," as in travel and contact among peoples and across borders. Humanitarian problems must be treated and addressed seriously.

The issues addressed in section 1 here, "Human Contacts," proved particularly nettlesome for the Soviet and Eastern bloc governments. Freedom of movement and travel, improved access to exit visas, greater levels of contact and openness across borders—all these goals were relatively easy to accommodate within and among the democratic nations but ran counter to practice in the more repressive

A U.S. Air Force C-54 Skymaster comes in for a landing at Templehoff Air Base during the Berlin airlift.
(AP/Wide World Photos)

Soviet bloc. For example, throughout the Communist nations, foreign travel was very restricted. Even simply declaring a desire to leave the USSR often exposed the applicant to significant risk—including loss of employment and housing—since the authorities often saw it as prima facie evidence of a lack of patriotism or worse. Acknowledging the existence of relatives abroad sometimes carried similar risks. These circumstances are reflected in the final sentence under subheading (a), which requires that the simple act of applying for permission to travel abroad must not "modify the rights" of the person applying or of his/her family. As already noted, the Soviets signed on to requirements of this sort in order to win concessions in other areas. Their concerns about being held accountable to what they were signing might have been assuaged slightly by language in this section and elsewhere acknowledging the right of each government not to relinquish control over the pace and methods by which it would move toward compliance. Of course, all signatory states shared some interest in retaining controls of this sort over implementation.

After supporting travel for purposes of family reunification and marriage, the section goes on to promote travel for a wide variety of other reasons, including business, education, cultural exchange and enrichment, tourism, sports, and more. Considerable emphasis is placed on promoting exchanges and interactions among young people and on opening broader dialogues about numerous issues of glob-

al significance, among them, religion, environment, and women's issues.

◆ "Follow-up to the Conference"

The Helsinki Final Act is a particularly important document in that it was significantly implemented and thus had real effects. This fifth and final part lays the groundwork for positive practical outcomes. It expresses the resolve of all signatories to "pay due regard to and implement" what they have signed on to; it establishes that the act would be a stepping-stone to further such agreements; and it puts forward a specific time and place for a follow-up meeting at which to begin the next steps.

Audience

The signatory governments provided the primary audience for the Helsinki Final Act. It was also intended for consumption by the countries' own citizens; however, not all signatories had the same aims or interests in this regard. The leadership of the USSR, including Leonid Brezhnev personally, hoped to gain an important propaganda victory by emphasizing domestically the act's recognition of Soviet control over the Eastern bloc. Much attention was given in the Soviet press to the act's contributions to détente, which was represented as a highly worthy process of great impor-

"The States participating in the Conference on Security and Co-operation in Europe [reaffirm] their objective of promoting better relations among themselves and ensuring conditions in which their people can live in true and lasting peace free from any threat to or attempt against their security."

("Questions Relating to Security in Europe")

"The participating States regard as inviolable all one another's frontiers as well as the frontiers of all States in Europe and therefore they will refrain now and in the future from assaulting these frontiers."

("Questions Relating to Security in Europe")

"The participating States will likewise refrain from making each other's territory the object of military occupation or other direct or indirect measures of force in contravention of international law, or the object of acquisition by means of such measures or the threat of them. No such occupation or acquisition will be recognized as legal."

("Questions Relating to Security in Europe")

"The participating States will respect human rights and fundamental freedoms, including the freedom of thought, conscience, religion or belief, for all without distinction as to race, sex, language or religion."

("Questions Relating to Security in Europe")

"They will promote and encourage the effective exercise of civil, political, economic, social, cultural and other rights and freedoms all of which derive from the inherent dignity of the human person and are essential for his free and full development."

("Questions Relating to Security in Europe")

tance to the Soviet Union. The clauses on human rights, on the other hand, were glossed over. The Soviet leadership was thus caught off guard when precisely this part of the act began to garner significant and sustained attention both at home and abroad, in conjunction with the quick rise and relentless activism of domestic monitoring groups aiming to hold the USSR accountable to the act's terms. These groups were persecuted vigorously by the Soviet leadership, which made every effort to minimize domestic publicity of its responsibilities under Basket III, particularly principle VII. In turn, international efforts to monitor Soviet compliance on human rights issues were sometimes denounced by Moscow as foreign meddling in Soviet internal affairs.

In North America and Western Europe, the accords were intended from the start for wide audiences. Although there was criticism of the supposed capitulation to Soviet territorial interests in Eastern Europe, an array of politicians, activists, nongovernmental organizations, and others embraced the act's articles on human rights and made great efforts to hold the USSR, in particular, accountable. Thus, the Soviets faced growing and continual criticisms at Helsinki follow-up meetings in Madrid, Ottawa, and elsewhere as well as in other forums.

Impact

The portions of the act constituting Basket I asserted that the borders of Eastern Europe could not be changed by force. This did not turn out to be the Soviet victory it at first seemed. Simply recognizing the status quo did not grant the Soviets anything they did not already have, beyond an undoubtedly important sense of security. Moreover, President Gerald Ford made clear around the time of signing that the United States would still not recognize the Soviet annexation of Estonia, Lithuania, and Latvia—formerly independent states that had been forcibly made Soviet republics (as opposed to Soviet satellites) during World War II.

In the long run, Basket III proved much more significant than Basket I. In signing principle VII, the Soviet leadership had agreed to show "respect for human rights and fundamental freedoms, including the freedom of thought, conscience, religion or belief." Despite wishing largely to ignore these commitments, the Soviets found themselves confronted with the formation in 1976 of the Moscow Helsinki Group. Comprising a small core of courageous and committed Soviet dissidents—including Yelena Bonner, Alexander Ginzburg, and Natan Sharansky—the group actively and publicly sought to hold their government to the terms of the accord. The Soviets responded with harsh and continued repression, including beatings, imprisonment (even in psychiatric institutions), internal exile, deportation, and other measures. The Moscow Helsinki Group's efforts quickly gained attention and momentum, however. Soviet citizens demonstrated to show their support; foreign journalists gave the efforts huge exposure; and Jimmy Carter, speaking initially as a candidate in the 1976 U.S. presidential election, offered explicit support and called on the Soviet government to release jailed dissidents. Once elected, he made human rights an important emphasis of his presidency.

Soon, Helsinki monitoring groups were established in other Soviet republics, in the Eastern bloc, and internationally. The Conference for Security and Co-operation in Europe itself oversaw efforts to monitor implementation of the act and was the sponsor of follow-up meetings held in Belgrade (then in Yugoslavia) in 1977–1978, Madrid in 1980–1983, Ottawa in 1985, Vienna in 1986–1989, and Paris in 1990. These various activities gave rise also to the International Helsinki Federation for Human Rights and to Human Rights Watch. After 1975, American Jewish, Armenian, and German groups used the Helsinki Final Act in their lobbying efforts on behalf of the rights of their peoples to emigrate from the Soviet Union, with much success. The passage in the United States earlier that year of the Trade Act and its Jackson-Vanik amendment—which tied the granting of most-favored-nation trade status to a

Questions for Further Study

1. Examine the Helsinki Final Act alongside the Biological Weapons Convention, signed just three years earlier. How would you characterize the relationship between the West and the Soviet bloc in the mid-1970s?

2. British prime minister Winston Churchill, the author of "The Sinews of Peace" speech warning the West about the "iron curtain," died ten years before the Helsinki Final Act was signed. Had he lived, how do you think he would have reacted to the agreement?

3. Compare this document with the United Nations Universal Declaration of Human Rights, signed in 1948. Explain why the more recent document was necessary—if it was—in light of the human rights guarantees provided by the UN document.

4. What motivated the Soviet Union—which U.S. president Ronald Reagan would later call the "evil empire"—to engage in negotiations with the West and sign the accord? What motivated the United States and its allies?

5. Evidence suggests that the Soviets violated the human rights terms of the Helsinki agreement. Does this mean that the agreement was a failure? On what grounds could it be argued that despite violations and the inability to enforce such an agreement, the agreement ultimately served a purpose?

country's record on human rights, especially emigration—also had an important impact in this respect.

Thus, the momentum gained by Western Europe and its allies in the original agreement continued to grow until the end of the cold war itself. In addition to the political repercussions, the act led to increased contacts between the Communist and democratic nations in the areas of culture, science and technology, education, and even tourism. This helped Soviet and Eastern bloc citizens become ever-more familiar with the higher standards of living and greater freedoms to the west, which in turn further contributed to the decline and ultimate collapse of the Soviet Communist system. Indeed, the Helsinki Final Act, by virtue of the seriousness with which its implementation was pursued by Helsinki monitoring groups and others, led in large part to the end of the cold war, the collapse of Communist regimes in Eastern Europe in 1989, and the demise of the Soviet Union itself two years later.

Further Reading

■ Articles

Davy, Richard. "Helsinki Myths: Setting the Record Straight on the Final Act of the CSCE, 1975." *Cold War History* 9, no. 1 (February 2009): 1–22.

■ Books

Bange, Oliver, and Gottfried Niedhart, eds. *Helsinki 1975 and the Transformation of Europe*. New York: Berghahn Books, 2008.

Gaddis, John Lewis. *The Cold War: A New History*. New York: Penguin Press, 2005.

Nelson, Anna Kasten, ed. *The Policy Makers: Shaping American Foreign Policy from 1947 to the Present*. Lanham, Md.: Rowman & Littlefield, 2009.

Van Oudenaren, John. *Détente in Europe: The Soviet Union and the West since 1953*. Durham, N.C.: Duke University Press, 1991.

Wenger, Andreas, Vojtech Mastny, and Christian Nuenlist, eds. *Origins of the European Security System: The Helsinki Process Revisited, 1965–75*. London: Routledge, 2008.

■ Web Sites

"OSCE Magazine October 2005." Organization for Security and Co-operation in Europe Web site.
   http://www.osce.org/item/16724.html.

—Brian Bonhomme

HELSINKI FINAL ACT

Questions Relating to Security in Europe

The States participating in the Conference on Security and Co-operation in Europe,

Reaffirming their objective of promoting better relations among themselves and ensuring conditions in which their people can live in true and lasting peace free from any threat to or attempt against their security;

Convinced of the need to exert efforts to make détente both a continuing and an increasingly viable and comprehensive process, universal in scope, and that the implementation of the results of the Conference on Security and Cooperation in Europe will be a major contribution to this process;

Considering that solidarity among peoples, as well as the common purpose of the participating States in achieving the aims as set forth by the Conference on Security and Cooperation in Europe, should lead to the development of better and closer relations among them in all fields and thus to overcoming the confrontation stemming from the character of their past relations, and to better mutual understanding;

Mindful of their common history and recognizing that the existence of elements common to their traditions and values can assist them in developing their relations, and desiring to search, fully taking into account the individuality and diversity of their positions and views, for possibilities of joining their efforts with a view to overcoming distrust and increasing confidence, solving the problems that separate them and cooperating in the interest of mankind;

Recognizing the indivisibility of security in Europe as well as their common interest in the development of cooperation throughout Europe and among selves and expressing their intention to pursue efforts accordingly;

Recognizing the close link between peace and security in Europe and in the world as a whole and conscious of the need for each of them to make its contribution to the strengthening of world peace and security and to the promotion of fundamental rights, economic and social progress and well-being for all peoples;

Have adopted the following:

(a) Declaration on Principles Guiding Relations between Participating States

The participating States,

Reaffirming their commitment to peace, security and justice and the continuing development of friendly relations and co-operation;

Recognizing that this commitment, which reflects the interest and aspirations of peoples, constitutes for each participating State a present and future responsibility, heightened by experience of the past;

Reaffirming, in conformity with their membership in the United Nations and in accordance with the purposes and principles of the United Nations, their full and active support for the United Nations and for the enhancement of its role and effectiveness in strengthening international peace, security and justice, and in promoting the solution of international problems, as well as the development of friendly relations and cooperation among States;

Expressing their common adherence to the principles which are set forth below and are in conformity with the Charter of the United Nations, as well as their common will to act, in the application of these principles, in conformity with the purposes and principles of the Charter of the United Nations;

Declare their determination to respect and put into practice, each of them in its relations with all other participating States, irrespective of their political, economic or social systems as well as of their size, geographical location or level of economic development, the following principles, which all are of primary significance, guiding their mutual relations:

◆ **I. Sovereign equality, respect for the rights inherent in sovereignty**

The participating States will respect each other's sovereign equality and individuality as well as all the rights inherent in and encompassed by its sovereignty, including in particular the right of every State to juridical equality, to territorial integrity and to freedom and political independence. They will also respect each other's right freely to choose and develop its political, social, economic and cultural systems as well as its right to determine its laws and regulations.

Within the framework of international law, all the participating States have equal rights and duties. They will respect each other's right to define and conduct as it wishes its relations with other States in accordance with international law and in the spirit of the present Declaration. They consider that their frontiers can be changed, in accordance with international law, by peaceful means and by agreement. They also have the right to belong or not to belong to international organizations, to be or not to be a party to bilateral or multilateral treaties including the right to be or not to be a party to treaties of alliance; they also have the right to neutrality.

◆ II. Refraining from the threat or use of force

The participating States will refrain in their mutual relations, as well as in their international relations in general, from the threat or use of force against the territorial integrity or political independence of any State, or in any other manner inconsistent with the purposes of the United Nations and with the present Declaration. No consideration may be invoked to serve to warrant resort to the threat or use of force in contravention of this principle.

Accordingly, the participating States will refrain from any acts constituting a threat of force or direct or indirect use of force against another participating State. Likewise they will refrain from any manifestation of force for the purpose of inducing another participating State to renounce the full exercise of its sovereign rights.

Likewise they will also refrain in their mutual relations from any act of reprisal by force.

No such threat or use of force will be employed as a means of settling disputes, or questions likely to give rise to disputes, between them.

◆ III. Inviolability of frontiers

The participating States regard as inviolable all one another's frontiers as well as the frontiers of all States in Europe and therefore they will refrain now and in the future from assaulting these frontiers.

Accordingly, they will also refrain from any demand for, or act of, seizure and usurpation of part or all of the territory of any participating State.

◆ IV. Territorial integrity of States

The participating States will respect the territorial integrity of each of the participating States.

Accordingly, they will refrain from any action inconsistent with the purposes and principles of the Charter of the United Nations against the territorial integrity, political independence or the unity of any participating State, and in particular from any such action constituting a threat or use of force.

The participating States will likewise refrain from making each other's territory the object of military occupation or other direct or indirect measures of force in contravention of international law, or the object of acquisition by means of such measures or the threat of them. No such occupation or acquisition will be recognized as legal.

◆ V. Peaceful settlement of disputes

The participating States will settle disputes among them by peaceful means in such a manner as not to endanger international peace and security, and justice.

They will endeavour in good faith and a spirit of cooperation to reach a rapid and equitable solution on the basis of international law.

For this purpose they will use such means as negotiation, enquiry, mediation, conciliation, arbitration, judicial settlement or other peaceful means of their own choice including any settlement procedure agreed to in advance of disputes to which they are parties.

In the event of failure to reach a solution by any of the above peaceful means, the parties to a dispute will continue to seek a mutually agreed way to settle the dispute peacefully.

Participating States, parties to a dispute among them, as well as other participating States, will refrain from any action which might aggravate the situation to such a degree as to endanger the maintenance of international peace and security and thereby make a peaceful settlement of the dispute more difficult.

◆ VI. Non-intervention in internal affairs

The participating States will refrain from any intervention, direct or indirect, individual or collective, in the internal or external affairs falling within the domestic jurisdiction of another participating State, regardless of their mutual relations.

They will accordingly refrain from any form of armed intervention or threat of such intervention against another participating State.

They will likewise in all circumstances refrain from any other act of military, or of political, economic or other coercion designed to subordinate to their own interest the exercise by another participating State of the rights inherent in its sovereignty and thus to secure advantages of any kind.

Accordingly, they will, inter alia, refrain from direct or indirect assistance to terrorist activities, or to subversive or other activities directed towards the violent overthrow of the regime of another participating State.

◆ VII. Respect for human rights and fundamental freedoms, including the freedom of thought, conscience, religion or belief

The participating States will respect human rights and fundamental freedoms, including the freedom of thought, conscience, religion or belief, for all without distinction as to race, sex, language or religion.

They will promote and encourage the effective exercise of civil, political, economic, social, cultural and other rights and freedoms all of which derive from the inherent dignity of the human person and are essential for his free and full development.

Within this framework the participating States will recognize and respect the freedom of the individual to profess and practice, alone or in community with others, religion or belief acting in accordance with the dictates of his own conscience.

The participating States on whose territory national minorities exist will respect the right of persons belonging to such minorities to equality before the law, will afford them the full opportunity for the actual enjoyment of human rights and fundamental freedoms and will, in this manner, protect their legitimate interests in this sphere.

The participating States recognize the universal significance of human rights and fundamental freedoms, respect for which is an essential factor for the peace, justice and well-being necessary to ensure the development of friendly relations and co-operation among themselves as among all States.

They will constantly respect these rights and freedoms in their mutual relations and will endeavour jointly and separately, including in co-operation with the United Nations, to promote universal and effective respect for them.

They confirm the right of the individual to know and act upon his rights and duties in this field.

In the field of human rights and fundamental freedoms, the participating States will act in conformity with the purposes and principles of the Charter of the United Nations and with the Universal Declaration of Human Rights. They will also fulfil their obligations as set forth in the international declarations and agreements in this field, including inter alia the International Covenants on Human Rights, by which they may be bound.

◆ VIII. Equal rights and self-determination of peoples

The participating States will respect the equal rights of peoples and their right to self-determination, acting at all times in conformity with the purposes and principles of the Charter of the United Nations and with the relevant norms of international law, including those relating to territorial integrity of States.

By virtue of the principle of equal rights and self-determination of peoples, all peoples always have the right, in full freedom, to determine, when and as they wish, their internal and external political status, without external interference, and to pursue as they wish their political, economic, social and cultural development.

The participating States reaffirm the universal significance of respect for and effective exercise of equal rights and self-determination of peoples for the development of friendly relations among themselves as among all States; they also recall the importance of the elimination of any form of violation of this principle.

◆ IX. Cooperation among States

The participating States will develop their co-operation with one another and with all States in all fields in accordance with the purposes and principles of the Charter of the United Nations. In developing their co-operation the participating States will place special emphasis on the fields as set forth within the framework of the Conference on Security and Cooperation in Europe, with each of them making its contribution in conditions of full equality.

They will endeavour, in developing their co-operation as equals, to promote mutual understanding and confidence, friendly and good-neighbourly relations among themselves, international peace, security and justice. They will equally endeavour, in developing their cooperation, to improve the well-being of peoples and contribute to the fulfilment of their aspirations through, inter alia, the benefits resulting from increased mutual knowledge and from progress and achievement in the economic, scientific, technological, social, cultural and humanitarian fields. They will take steps to promote conditions favourable to making these benefits available to all; they will take into account the interest of all in the narrowing of differences in the levels of economic development, and in particular the interest of developing countries throughout the world.

They confirm that governments, institutions, organizations and persons have a relevant and positive role to play in contributing toward the achievement of these aims of their cooperation.

They will strive, in increasing their cooperation as set forth above, to develop closer relations among themselves on an improved and more enduring basis for the benefit of peoples.

◆ X. Fulfilment in good faith of obligations under international law

The participating States will fulfil in good faith their obligations under international law, both those obligations arising from the generally recognized principles and rules of international law and those obligations arising from treaties or other agreements, in conformity with international law, to which they are parties.

In exercising their sovereign rights, including the right to determine their laws and regulations, they will conform with their legal obligations under international law; they will furthermore pay due regard to and implement the provisions in the Final Act of the Conference on Security and Cooperation in Europe.

The participating States confirm that in the event of a conflict between the obligations of the members of the United Nations under the Charter of the United Nations and their obligations under any treaty or other international agreement, their obligations under the Charter will prevail, in accordance with Article 103 of the Charter of the United Nations.

All the principles set forth above are of primary significance and, accordingly, they will be equally and unreservedly applied, each of them being interpreted taking into account the others.

The participating States express their determination fully to respect and apply these principles, as set forth in the present Declaration, in all aspects, to their mutual relations and cooperation in order to ensure to each participating State the benefits resulting from the respect and application of these principles by all.

The participating States, paying due regard to the principles above and, in particular, to the first sentence of the tenth principle, "Fulfilment in good faith of obligations under international law", note that the present Declaration does not affect their rights and obligations, nor the corresponding treaties and other agreements and arrangements.

The participating States express the conviction that respect for these principles will encourage the development of normal and friendly relations and the progress of co-operation among them in all fields. They also express the conviction that respect for these principles will encourage the development of political contacts among them which in time would contribute to better mutual understanding of their positions and views.

The participating States declare their intention to conduct their relations with all other States in the spirit of the principles contained in the present Declaration....

Co-operation in the Field of Economics, of Science and Technology and of the Environment

The participating States,

Convinced that their efforts to develop cooperation in the fields of trade, industry, science and technology, the environment and other areas of economic activity contribute to the reinforcement of peace and security in Europe and in the world as a whole,

Recognizing that cooperation in these fields would promote economic and social progress and the improvement of the conditions of life,

Aware of the diversity of their economic and social systems,

Reaffirming their will to intensify such cooperation between one another, irrespective of their systems,

Recognizing that such cooperation, with due regard for the different levels of economic development, can be developed, on the basis of equality and mutual satisfaction of the partners, and of reciprocity permitting, as a whole, an equitable distribution of advantages and obligations of comparable scale, with respect for bilateral and multilateral agreements,

Taking into account the interests of the developing countries throughout the world, including those among the participating countries as long as they are developing from the economic point of view; reaffirming their will to co-operate for the achievement of the aims and objectives established by the appropriate bodies of the United Nations in the pertinent documents concerning development, it being understood that each participating State maintains the positions it has taken on them; giving special attention to the least developed countries,

Convinced that the growing world-wide economic interdependence calls for increasing common and effective efforts towards the solution of major world economic problems such as food, energy, commodities, monetary and financial problems, and therefore emphasizes the need for promoting stable and equitable international economic relations, thus contributing to the continuous and diversified economic development of all countries,

Having taken into account the work already undertaken by relevant international organizations and wishing to take advantage of the possibilities offered by these organizations, in particular by the United Nations Economic Commission for Europe, for giving effect to the provisions of the final documents of the Conference,

Considering that the guidelines and concrete recommendations contained in the following texts are aimed at promoting further development of their mutual economic relations, and convinced that their cooperation in this field should take place in full respect for the principles guiding relations among participating States as set forth in the relevant document,

Have adopted the following:

◆ **1. Commercial Exchanges**

General provisions

The participating States,

Conscious of the growing role of international trade as one of the most important factors in economic growth and social progress,

Recognizing that trade represents an essential sector of their co-operation …,

Considering that the volume and structure of trade among the participating States do not in all cases correspond to the possibilities created by the current level of their economic, scientific and technological development,

are resolved to promote, on the basis of the modalities of their economic cooperation, the expansion of their mutual trade in goods and services, and to ensure conditions favourable to such development;

recognize the beneficial effects which can result for the development of trade from the application of most favoured nation treatment;

will encourage the expansion of trade on as broad a multilateral basis as possible, thereby endeavouring to utilize the various economic and commercial possibilities;

recognize the importance of bilateral and multilateral intergovernmental and other agreements for the long-term development of trade;

note the importance of monetary and financial questions for the development of international trade, and will endeavour to deal with them with a view to contributing to the continuous expansion of trade;

will endeavour to reduce or progressively eliminate all kinds of obstacles to the development of trade;

will foster a steady growth of trade while avoiding as far as possible abrupt fluctuations in their trade;

consider that their trade in various products should be conducted in such a way as not to cause or threaten to cause serious injury—and should the situation arise, market disruption—in domestic markets for these products and in particular to the detriment of domestic producers of like or directly competitive products; as regards the concept of market disruption, it is understood that it should not be invoked in a way inconsistent with the relevant provisions of their international agreements; if they resort to safeguard measures, they will do so in conformity with their commitments in this field arising from international agreements to which they are parties and will take account of the interests of the parties directly concerned;

will give due attention to measures for the promotion of trade and the diversification of its structure;

note that the growth and diversification of trade would contribute to widening the possibilities of choice of products;

consider it appropriate to create favourable conditions for the participation of firms, organizations and enterprises in the development of trade…

Co-operation in Humanitarian and Other Fields

The participating States,

Desiring to contribute to the strengthening of peace and understanding among peoples and to the spiritual enrichment of the human personality without distinction as to race, sex, language or religion,

Conscious that increased cultural and educational exchanges, broader dissemination of information, contacts between people, and the solution of humanitarian problems will contribute to the attainment of these aims,

Determined therefore to cooperate among themselves, irrespective of their political, economic and social systems, in order to create better conditions in the above fields, to develop and strengthen existing forms of co-operation and to work out new ways and means appropriate to these aims,

Convinced that this co-operation should take place in full respect for the principles guiding relations among participating States as set forth in the relevant document,

Have adopted the following:

◆ **1. Human Contacts**

The participating States,

Considering the development of contacts to be an important element in the strengthening of friendly relations and trust among peoples,

Affirming, in relation to their present effort to improve conditions in this area, the importance they attach to humanitarian considerations,

Desiring in this spirit to develop, with the continuance of détente, further efforts to achieve continuing progress in this field

And conscious that the questions relevant hereto must be settled by the States concerned under mutually acceptable conditions,

Make it their aim to facilitate freer movement and contacts, individually and collectively, whether privately or officially, among persons, institutions and organizations of the participating States, and to contribute to the solution of the humanitarian problems that arise in that connexion,

Declare their readiness to these ends to take measures which they consider appropriate and to conclude agreements or arrangements among themselves, as may be needed, and

Express their intention now to proceed to the implementation of the following:

(a) Contacts and Regular Meetings on the Basis of Family Ties

In order to promote further development of contacts on the basis of family ties the participating States will favourably consider applications for travel with the purpose of allowing persons to enter or leave their territory temporarily, and on a regular basis if desired, in order to visit members of their families.

Applications for temporary visits to meet members of their families will be dealt with without distinction as to the country of origin or destination: existing requirements for travel documents and visas will be applied in this spirit. The preparation and issue of such documents and visas will be effected within reasonable time limits, cases of urgent necessity—such as serious illness or death—will be given priority treatment. They will take such steps as may be necessary to ensure that the fees for official travel documents and visas are acceptable.

They confirm that the presentation of an application concerning contacts on the basis of family ties will not modify the rights and obligations of the applicant or of members of his family.

(b) Reunification of Families

The participating States will deal in a positive and humanitarian spirit with the applications of persons who wish to be reunited with members of their family, with special attention being given to requests of an urgent character—such as requests submitted by persons who are ill or old.

They will deal with applications in this field as expeditiously as possible.

They will lower where necessary the fees charged in connexion with these applications to ensure that they are at a moderate level.

Applications for the purpose of family reunification which are not granted may be renewed at the appropriate level and will be reconsidered at reasonably short intervals by the authorities of the country of residence or destination, whichever is concerned—under such circumstances fees will be charged only when applications are granted.

Persons whose applications for family reunification are granted may bring with them or ship their household and personal effects; to this end the participating States will use all possibilities provided by existing regulations.

Until members of the same family are reunited meetings and contacts between them may take place in accordance with the modalities for contacts on the basis of family ties.

The participating States will support the efforts of Red Cross and Red Crescent Societies concerned with the problems of family reunification.

They confirm that the presentation of an application concerning family reunification will not modify the rights and obligations of the applicant or of members of his family.

The receiving participating State will take appropriate care with regard to employment for persons from other participating States who take up permanent residence in that State in connexion with family reunification with its citizens and see that they are afforded opportunities equal to those enjoyed by its own citizens for education, medical assistance and social security.

(c) Marriage between Citizens of Different States

The participating States will examine favourably and on the basis of humanitarian considerations requests for exit or entry permits from persons who have decided to marry a citizen from another participating State.

The processing and issuing of the documents required for the above purposes and for the marriage will be in accordance with the provisions accepted for family reunification.

In dealing with requests from couples from different participating States, once married, to enable them and the minor children of their marriage to transfer their permanent residence to a State in which either one is normally a resident, the participating States will also apply the provisions accepted for family reunification.

(d) Travel for Personal or Professional Reasons

The participating States intend to facilitate wider travel by their citizens for personal or professional reasons and to this end they intend in particular:

—gradually to simplify and to administer flexibly the procedures for exit and entry;

—to ease regulations concerning movement of citizens from the other participating States in their territory, with due regard to security requirements.

They will endeavour gradually to lower, where necessary, the fees for visas and official travel documents.

They intend to consider, as necessary, means—including, in so far as appropriate, the conclusion of multilateral or bilateral consular conventions or other relevant agreements or understandings—for the improvement of arrangements to provide consular services, including legal and consular assistance.

They confirm that religious faiths, institutions and organizations, practising within the constitutional framework of the participating States, and their representatives can, in the field of their activities, have contacts and meetings among themselves and exchange information.

(e) Improvement of Conditions for Tourism on an Individual or Collective Basis

The participating States consider that tourism contributes to a fuller knowledge of the life, culture and history of other countries, to the growth of understanding among peoples, to the improvement of contacts and to the broader use of leisure. They intend to promote the development of tourism, on an individual or collective basis, and, in particular, they intend:

—to promote visits to their respective countries by encouraging the provision of appropriate facilities and the simplification and expediting of necessary formalities relating to such visits;

—to increase, on the basis of appropriate agreements or arrangements where necessary, co-operation in the development of tourism, in particular by considering bilaterally possible ways to increase information relating to travel to other countries and to the reception and service of tourists, and other related questions of mutual interest.

(f) Meetings among Young People

The participating States intend to further the development of contacts and exchanges among young people by encouraging:

—increased exchanges and contacts on a short or long term basis among young people working, training or undergoing education through bilateral or multilateral agreements or regular programmes in all cases where it is possible;

—study by their youth organizations of the question of possible agreements relating to frameworks of multilateral youth co-operation;

—agreements or regular programmes relating to the organization of exchanges of students, of international youth seminars, of courses of professional training and foreign language study;

—the further development of youth tourism and the provision to this end of appropriate facilities;

—the development, where possible, of exchanges, contacts and co-operation on a bilateral or multilateral basis between their organizations which represent wide circles of young people working, training or undergoing education;

—awareness among youth of the importance of developing mutual understanding and of strengthening friendly relations and confidence among peoples.

(g) Sport

In order to expand existing links and co-operation in the field of sport the participating States will encourage contacts and exchanges of this kind, including sports meetings and competitions of all sorts, on the basis of the established international rules, regulations and practice.

(h) Expansion of Contacts

By way of further developing contacts among governmental institutions and non-governmental organizations and associations, including women's organizations, the participating States will facilitate the convening of meetings as well as travel by delegations, groups and individuals…

Follow-up to the Conference

The participating States,

Having considered and evaluated the progress made at the Conference on Security and Co-operation in Europe,

Considering further that, within the broader context of the world, the Conference is an important part of the process of improving security and developing co-operation in Europe and that its results will contribute significantly to this process,

Intending to implement the provisions of the Final Act of the Conference in order to give full effect to its results and thus to further the process of improving security and developing co-operation in Europe,

Convinced that, in order to achieve the aims sought by the Conference, they should make further unilateral, bilateral and multilateral efforts and continue, in the appropriate forms set forth below, the multilateral process initiated by the Conference,

1. *Declare their resolve*, in the period following the Conference, to pay due regard to and implement the provisions of the Final Act of the Conference:

(a) unilaterally, in all cases which lend themselves to such action;

(b) bilaterally, by negotiations with other participating States;

(c) multilaterally, by meetings of experts of the participating States, and also within the framework of existing international organizations, such as the United Nations Economic Commission for Europe and UNESCO, with regard to educational, scientific and cultural cooperation;

2. *Declare furthermore their resolve* to continue the multilateral process initiated by the Conference:

(a) by proceeding to a thorough exchange of views both on the implementation of the provisions of the Final Act and of the tasks defined by the Conference, as well as, in the context of the questions dealt with by the latter, on the deepening of their mutual relations, the improvement of security and the development of co-operation in Europe, and the development of the process of détente in the future;

(b) by organizing to these ends meetings among their representatives, beginning with a meeting at the level of representatives appointed by the Ministers of Foreign Affairs. This meeting will define the appropriate modalities for the holding of other meetings which could include further similar meetings and the possibility of a new Conference;

3. The first of the meetings indicated above will be held at Belgrade in 1977. A preparatory meeting to organize this meeting will be held at Belgrade on 15 June 1977. The preparatory meeting will decide on the date, duration, agenda and other modalities of the meeting of representatives appointed by the Ministers of Foreign Affairs;

4. The rules of procedure, the working methods and the scale of distribution for the expenses of the Conference will, *mutatis mutandis*, be applied to the meetings envisaged in paragraphs 1 (c), 2 and 3 above. All the above-mentioned meetings will be held in the participating States in rotation. The services of a technical secretariat will be provided by the host country.

Glossary

Red Cross and Red Crescent Societies	the International Federation of Red Cross and Red Crescent Societies; the humanitarian organization consisting of 186 member societies, which are identified as Red Crescent Societies in many Islamic countries

Deng Xiaoping (AP/Wide World Photos)

CONSTITUTION OF THE PEOPLE'S REPUBLIC OF CHINA

"[Citizens] have the right to criticize and make suggestions to any state organ or functionary."

Overview

The Constitution of the People's Republic of China (PRC) was composed in 1981 and adopted by the Fifth National People's Congress (NPC) on December 4, 1982. This was a new constitution for a new era. Mao Zedong, the leader of Communist China, had died in 1976. His successors in the NPC and the Chinese Communist Party (CCP) wanted to rebuild China as a Socialist and economic powerhouse. Thus, a modern constitution that rallied the people, addressed economic policies, and announced China's place in world politics was needed. The constitution would also take on legal significance. Like its predecessors, the 1982 constitution emphasized the role of Socialism in the creation of the modern Chinese state and placed the power of the country in the hands of its people. Unlike its predecessors, however, it detailed fundamental changes in law that affected the previously untouchable CCP. It also addressed the role China would play in the world and the place of Socialism in the new money economy, where communal farms were becoming multimillion-dollar enterprises.

Context

The first modern constitutions in China were written at the end of the Qing Dynasty and the beginning of control by the Nationalist Party in 1912. The Nationalist constitution was based on a democratic model but was largely ignored as power shifted to warlords in the 1920s. Further constitutional development was halted when Japan invaded China in the 1930s and by World War II in the 1940s. The Communist Party then gained control over China in 1949 by defeating the Nationalists in a civil war. The new centralized government under Mao Zedong created a provisional constitution called the Common Program of the Chinese People's Political Consultative Conference. In 1954 the governing body of the party's Central Committee ratified the constitution.

Under the 1954 constitution, the Communist Party had encouraged people to express their political views openly in what was called the "One-hundred Flowers" campaign. The government asked for an evaluation of all government agencies in order to improve them and continue on the Socialist path outlined in the constitution. Intellectuals who felt that the government was not heading in the right direction, especially with its economic plans, spoke up. However, the reaction by Mao and his government to the criticism was to persecute intellectuals, officials, students, artists, and anyone who was considered a "rightist," meaning that they supported capitalism and were against collectivism. This persecution was called the Anti-Rightist Movement.

The 1954 constitution, however, was provisional. While it created the structure of the government, a permanent constitution was needed in order to map out the future of the PRC. The first full PRC constitution was written during the Great Leap Forward (1958–1961), a government-initiated social and economic program to move China from an agrarian to an industrialized economy so that it could compete with industrialized countries such as the United States and the Soviet Union. While many politicians called for gradual reform, Mao and his supporters wanted sweeping and immediate changes. China's farms and industry were collectivized, meaning that they belonged to the state, which represented the people, and personal ownership of land and businesses no longer existed. Workers' communes were created, and labor was diverted into steel production. Initially these changes improved the economy, but the peasant farmers began to suffer. Locusts and drought destroyed crops, but grain yield reports were exaggerated. The result was insufficient crops to feed everyone moving into the cities. Mass starvation set in. It has been estimated that fourteen to twenty million people died in the famine of 1960–1961. Mao took full responsibility for the outcome and stepped down as chairman of the PRC, though he remained de facto leader of the country until his death in 1976.

The Anti-Rightist Movement set the stage for yet another social development in China, the Great Proletarian Cultural Revolution, which began in 1966. The Cultural Revolution was a mass national movement focused on doing away with traditional culture in order to modernize the country—and it ignored the 1954 constitution. It began as a movement among students and young people

1949

- **September**
  Civil war in China ends with the defeat of the Nationalist army and the victory of the Communists; a new government, the Chinese People's Political Consultative Conference, is formed in Beijing.

- **October 1**
  The People's Republic of China is proclaimed.

1953

- **January**
  The Central People's Government calls for a new constitution.

1954

- **September 20**
  The new constitution is approved at the first meeting of the National People's Congress; the constitution sets up how the Communist government will work.

1957

- The Anti-Rightist Movement, the first political movement calling for the removal of pro-capitalist, pro-Western people from the government, begins; this movement is a forerunner to the Cultural Revolution.

1966

- The Cultural Revolution begins; many leaders, including Deng Xiaoping, are denounced and arrested.

called the Red Guards, demanding reforms and the abolition of the "four olds": old customs, old culture, old habits, and old ideas. Mao supported this new Socialist revolution. Friends and families turned on each other, informing officials about anything that could be viewed as pro-capitalist action. Many youths were sent to the countryside for reeducation, and universities were closed. Anyone opposed to the revolution, such as educated elites and others deemed to be "capitalist roaders"—that is, people who were believed to support capitalism and oppose Socialism—were arrested on no legal grounds and sent to be reeducated in work prisons. Whether or not the accusations were true, many intellectuals were saddled with this label and were the victims of open hostility. Fueling the oppression of the arts and culture was Mao's wife, Jiang Qing, and her three supporters, commonly known as the Gang of Four.

In the hope of reducing the excessive violence and persecution of the people, a 1970 provisional draft constitution was created by Lin Biao, then defense minister and vice-chairman of the NPC. He was also named by Mao as his successor. However, his constitution was never put into practice because Lin suddenly died in 1971 in a plane crash. His political opponents believed that he was planning a coup against Mao, but when the plan was leaked, he tried to flee to the Soviet Union. At the same time, as Mao became ill and slowly went senile, internal power struggles worsened. A 1975 draft constitution, also called the Gang of Four constitution, was ignored. When Mao died in 1976, the Gang of Four was removed from power and imprisoned, and the country still had no constitution. The new government under Premier Hua Guofeng wanted to end the madness of the Cultural Revolution. His 1978 constitution was the forerunner to the 1982 constitution in its call for Socialism and the continuation of Mao Zedong's ideology. This constitution was short-lived, as Hua was defeated in the NPC and forced to retire.

The new political leader, Deng Xiaoping, and his government sought to reverse almost all of Mao's policies. A pragmatist, Deng was a long-time Communist, having fought against the Japanese and the Nationalists. However, Deng's focus as leader was not to renew revolution or to launch campaigns against capitalism with slogans but to end the economic poverty of China. He also hoped to reverse the damage created during the Cultural Revolution. China was poor, with little technology, so Deng believed that foreign technology and investment with an increase in local production were needed to modernize the country. Agriculture communes were dismantled, and peasants were free to sell their crops in the free market after paying taxes to the government. Large-scale and urban industrial production was doubled. In the cities, people were given bonuses for doing good work and encouraged to own their own apartments. This was a popular move: People wanted to forget the lean years and enjoy new economic growth and the personal rewards that came with it. These policies and other changes were part of the 1982 constitution.

Deng Xiaoping (1904–1997) was head of the CCP and a powerful political leader despite never being premier or president of the PRC. He was also chairman of the Central Military Commission, a position that put him in change of foreign affairs and the military. Educated in France, he was a long-time backer of Mao Zedong but was labeled an antirevolutionary in internal struggles. Despite being in and out of political favor, he had enough support to be named chairman of the CCP in 1979. His policies were to bring a Socialist government into the world economy by adopting capitalist approaches to industry and agricultural production. He headed the committee that wrote the constitution. Deng is also known as being instrumental in supporting continued ties with the West. In 1984 he negotiated the return of Hong Kong to China. He died on February 19, 1997, a few months before the official handover of Hong Kong.

Hua Guofeng (1921–2008; birth name Su Zhu), was instrumental in creating the constitution of 1979, upon which the 1982 constitution heavily relied. He joined the Communist Party during World War II and rose slowly to power as a staunch supporter of Mao Zedong. When Zhou Enlai died suddenly in a plane crash in 1976, Hua was named acting premier. Two political factions then emerged in the PRC: One consisted of Hua Guofeng and his supporters, who followed the teachings of Mao; the other consisted of Deng Xiaoping's moderates. After Mao died in 1976, Hua announced the end of the Cultural Revolution and arrested the Gang of Four, which made him a popular leader. He also headed the committee to write a new constitution. His constitution made it clear that China would uphold Mao's policies and restore the government bureaucracy, which had been in chaos since the Cultural Revolution. However, Deng began to gain control of the CCP as Hua made various political mistakes. He was demoted to being an ordinary member of the Central Committee until his retirement in 1991.

Explanation and Analysis of the Document

The 1982 constitution was created over a four-year period of reviews and reforms by the NPC and the Central Committee. Deng Xiaoping and his supporters in the CCP and the Central Committee were by then the majority and were able to make significant reforms in China's governmental, political, and economic operations. The constitution was viewed as the document that marked these changes. Unlike the older constitutions, the 1982 one was written with the understanding that it could be amended rather than having to be completely rewritten.

◆ "Preamble"

The preamble sets the positive tone of the whole document. It addresses the nation's past, present, and future. The first paragraph paints the past as a struggle against imperialism, feudalism, and bureaucratic capitalism by all

Time Line

1975
- A new draft of the constitution is created by the Gang of Four with Mao's blessing; Mao is named chairman of the Communist Party, and the position of president is abolished.

1976
- **September 9** Mao Zedong dies; that year, the Gang of Four is tried and imprisoned for "crimes against the people."

1978
- Chairman Hua Guofeng and his supporters rewrite the constitution, which emphasizes that the state still follows Marxism-Leninism and Mao Zedong's thinking.
- **December** The Communist Party Central Committee meets to reform the constitution under the new leader, Deng Xiaoping.

1982
- **December 4** The fourth constitution of the People's Republic of China is announced and ratified by the Central Committee.

the peoples of China, including minority groups. The second paragraph discusses the years between 1949 and 1982. The transformation of the state was completed, and communes were created. Success is attributed to the Communist principles that the means of production should be in the hands of the working class and that the peasants were the dictatorship of the proletariat.

The third paragraph focuses on the future plans and direction of China as a modern Socialist nation. Socialist modernization was an idea put forth by the leaders of the

CCP and Deng Xiaoping, who called for improvement in several economic areas that had been neglected during the Cultural Revolution. The constitution stresses that despite this modernization, the country would still "follow the socialist road," a saying used since the inception of Communism in China. The teachings of Mao Zedong, based on Marxist-Leninist ideology but infused with Chinese properties, would not be disregarded. It asserts that a class struggle continues within certain limits and that the Socialist revolution must continue within and outside the CCP. Maintaining the path of Socialism would affect the way in which China would deal with other nations. The constitution states the five principles of "mutual respect for sovereignty and territorial integrity, mutual non-aggression, non-interference in each other's internal affairs, equality and mutual benefit, and peaceful coexistence in developing diplomatic relations and economic and cultural exchanges with other countries." Taiwan, however, was not seen as a sovereign state. The defeated Nationals had fled to the island of Taiwan and set up their own government, calling that country the Republic of China. The PRC considered Taiwan a rogue state; indeed, it was thought to be "part of the sacred territory" of the PRC, and the constitution declared it to be "the lofty duty of the entire Chinese people … to accomplish the great task of reunifying the motherland."

◆ **Chapter I: "General Principles"**

This section deals with the primary issues of personal freedom, the power of the people, and the rights and responsibilities of the state. Article 1 sets the tone: China is a "socialist state under the people's democratic dictatorship." The idea of a Socialist state varies and is dependent on each country's application of Socialist principles. In the 1982 constitution, Socialism refers to an ideal of economic organization in which the government controls most of the production and distribution of goods and advocates public or cooperative worker ownership of the means of production. Moreover, the Socialist state promotes equal access to resources for all people. "Democratic dictatorship" refers to the country being under the control of one party, the Chinese Communist Party, which is supported by the people. The term *democracy* also refers to the election of local representatives by the people, further detailed in Chapter III.

Another issue of importance is the treatment of ethnic minorities (Article 4). The country is dominated by the Han majority, but there are over forty other ethnic groups that make up 9 percent of the population. One such group, the Muslim Hui people, have been integrated into Han society, while others, such as the Muslim Uygur, have decided to push for their own autonomy. For centuries, however, many of these groups have been subjugated and marginalized by the dominant Han ethnic majority. In an effort to unify all groups, this article supports these minorities economically and their right to maintain traditional ways and customs.

Articles 6–18 address the Socialist state economy and government's managerial role. Since the inception of the PRC in 1949, the cornerstone of the economy had been

public ownership. One example was agriculture, where no one person owned the land. Rather, land was owned by a cooperative made up of many farmers. The 1982 constitution allows farmers to own private plots of land and sell their wares on the open market (Article 8). Land in the cities would continue to be owned by the state, as would the natural resources on the land, such as minerals (Articles 9 and 10). However, Article 11 clearly states that the state protects the individual's right of access to the economy, meaning that the state was not to punish people who grew rich or owned businesses. This shift to a personal economy is also seen in Article 13, which allows citizens to earn an income, have savings, and own property that does not belong to the state.

How the Socialist economy has to function in the world is addressed in Articles 16 to 18. Collectivization and state planning, not personal companies or individuals, would dominate economic decisions. For example, capitalist economies function with large privately owned businesses that dominate the market. In the PRC, the state is still the largest owner of business. Foreign industry is permitted to work with Chinese companies in joint-ownership projects but cannot operate alone. Foreign companies are also subject to the laws governing China's economy, which does not allow for a foreign-owned company to own more shares than its Chinese partner. Currently, hundreds of foreign-owned companies invest with Chinese counterparts, such as IBM in the Chinese computer company Lenovo.

Articles 19–25 detail the responsibilities of the state to the people of China with respect to education, culture, and security. Because little education had been provided during the Cultural Revolution, Article 19 makes primary school education (consisting of nine years of schooling) compulsory and accessible to all. The goal was to bring up literacy rates among the whole population. According to UNESCO (United Nations Educational, Scientific, and Cultural Organization), in 1985 China had a 75 percent literacy rate. By 2008 the rate was approximately 95 percent. The motivation for boosting the literacy rate and expanding education was not only to improve the quality of people's lives but also to enhance China's technological and scientific capabilities. More people entering these fields would help contribute to scientific advances.

Along with improvement of the mind was the call for improvement of medical and health services (Article 21). Since the nineteenth century, traditional Chinese medicine and Western medical practices coexisted. During the Nationalist period (1912–1949), the state regarded Western medical practices as superior to traditional Chinese medicine. The Communist government promoted both types of medicine, believing that a synergy of practices could result. As a result, many Western-style medical doctors in China are also trained in traditional Chinese medicine. The state financially supports schools that offer both programs. In creating more doctors, hospitals, and clinics, the state also hoped to improve health and sanitation. Many mass hygiene and sanitation projects, such as waste disposal and education about infection prevention, were launched during the late twentieth century and beyond.

Prodemocracy demonstrators occupy Beijing's Tiananmen Square in June 1989, during a several-months-long demonstration that resulted in a confrontation with soldiers, leaving hundreds dead. (AP/Wide World Photos)

◆ Chapter II: "The Fundamental Rights and Duties of Citizens"

The articles in Chapter II highlight the duties and responsibilities of citizens. These important articles have to do with personal autonomy and freedom of the press and religion. Article 35 states that all citizens have the freedom to speak out, to put in writing their own ideas and publish them, to call an assembly, and to demonstrate. However, the media censored public criticisms of the Socialist government under Deng Xiaoping. For example, mass demonstrations over the past fifty years have always been staged in Tiananmen Square. In April 1989, Hu Yaobing, a high government official who had pushed for democracy and other reforms, died. Public support for Hu was shown: About a million people gathered in Tiananmen Square over the next few months to mourn his death. Students who joined the crowds called for democratic reforms. In July the government violently suppressed the demonstrators, resulting in arrests and hundreds of deaths. The coverage of the 1989 protests and their brutal suppression was not broadcast, demonstrating that the right of the citizens to assemble and protest was not an infallible right in China.

Another freedom afforded by the 1982 constitution was freedom of religion (Article 36). Marxist Socialist doctrine deemed that religion was destructive and should not be encouraged. All religion was banned. However, the 1978 constitution allowed for religions sanctioned by the state, including Buddhism, Taoism, Catholicism, Protestantism, and Islam. The 1982 constitution further amended this article by stating that no religion could compel people to join: No evangelism or forced conversions would be allowed. The state is officially atheist, which means it has no attachment to any religion.

◆ Chapter III: "The Structure of the State"

Chapter III is divided into several sections that deal with the NPC, the presidency, the State Council, the Central Military Commission, local government, and self-government in autonomous provinces; a section about the judiciary is not reproduced.

The articles in this chapter define the workings of the state structure in the PRC. The NPC is the governing body of the state, which meets every year with other government organizations to make political decisions, including electing a president. The president serves as the head of the NPC. At the time when the 1982 constitution was written, the role of president had been abolished. The constitution reestablished the office and named Li Xianian as president. The NPC is made up of delegates elected by every provincial congress, who in turn are appointed or elected by officials from municipalities. In almost all municipalities, the

"*Taiwan is part of the sacred territory of the People's Republic of China. It is the lofty duty of the entire Chinese people, including our compatriots in Taiwan, to accomplish the great task of reunifying the motherland.*"

(Preamble)

"*All nationalities in the People's Republic of China are equal. The state protects the lawful rights and interests of the minority nationalities and upholds and develops the relationship of equality, unity and mutual assistance among all of China's nationalities.*"

(Chapter I, Article 4)

"*The state promotes family planning so that population growth may fit the plans for economic and social development.*"

(Chapter I, Article 25)

"*Citizens of the People's Republic of China enjoy freedom of religious belief. No state organ, public organization or individual may compel citizens to believe in, or not to believe in, any religion; nor may they discriminate against citizens who believe in, or do not believe in, any religion. The state protects normal religious activities.*"

(Chapter II, Article 36)

"*Citizens of the People's Republic of China have the right to criticize and make suggestions to any state organ or functionary. Citizens have the right to make to relevant state organs complaints and charges against, or exposures of, violation of the law or dereliction of duty by any state organ or functionary.*"

(Chapter II, Article 41)

people elect a representative to send to the provincial meetings in local elections. The power of the NPC cannot be ignored: It has the duty to call elections and remove heads of state such as the president and premier (Article 63).

There are special autonomous regions in the PRC, however, that function differently from the provinces (Article 59). An autonomous region is a minority area, such as Tibet and Inner Mongolia, where most people are non-Han Chinese. They have a local government but have the right only to appoint their governor. Currently there are five autonomous regions. CCP officials and ethnic Han Chinese dominate the politics in these autonomous regions, which has been met with resistance by the local ethnic groups. For example, riots and protests in the Xinjiang Autonomous Region are on the rise as the dominant Muslim Uygur peoples oppose Han political rule.

The Standing Committee, chaired by the premier, is part of the NPC and is responsible for decisions made when the NPC is not in session. The acting premier in 1982 was Zhao Ziyang, a close associate of Deng Xiaoping's. The tasks of this committee range from making ministerial appointments to effecting economic reforms (Article 67). Other committees, similar to ministries, also fall under the NPC and have defined responsibilities. However, all organs of the NPC are protected from litigation. All members, including the committees, can be called to account for criminal actions only by the NPC itself. The NPC cannot be called to legal account on any action taken at its meeting (Articles 74 and 75). This was to have consequences later on with respect to corruption in the NPC.

The State Council is the main administrative branch and is made up of all the heads of every government department. It is directed by the premier and is given numerous administrative powers (Article 89). Interestingly, the 1982 constitution gives the State Council approval to act independently; that is, it does not need approval from the NPC or Standing Committee for any action. As a result, the council is subject only to the constitution itself and is to maintain the constitution at all times.

◆ **Chapter IV: "The National Flag, the National Emblem and the Capital"**

The flag of the PRC consists of one large yellow star and four smaller stars on a red background. It was designed by Zeng Liangsong, a young Communist Party member, and adopted in 1949. The red symbolizes the revolution, a color that was also used by the Soviet Union as the background of its national flag. The larger star represents the CCP, with the four smaller stars standing for the unity of the people. This pattern is also on the national emblem, which includes the Tiananmen (the gate leading into the Forbidden City, the Chinese imperial palace), encircled by grain symbolizing growth and a cogwheel to stand for the work of the proletariat.

Audience

The importance of the constitution as a guide to all Chinese people cannot be overly stressed. People looked upon it as their personal call to change and to help modernize their country while maintaining Socialist morals and beliefs. Another audience was all levels of government officials. Chapter III, which details the state apparatus, dictates in clear terms how the government system would work. Outside China, the 1982 constitution was translated and made available to all governments. The constitution, then, can be seen as China's calling card to world governments, reintroducing itself and its position on many matters of state, including Taiwan.

Impact

The impact of the new constitution is difficult to measure. The document is more of a presentation of ideas and policies than a strictly legal document that changed precedent. The constitution informs the law, but the constitution itself does not have a separate legal status that is enforced. Changes have been introduced, however. Obviating the need for a new constitution every time a new leader

---

Questions for Further Study

1. The People's Republic of China made several attempts to create a constitution dating back to the 1950s. Why did those efforts fail? Why do you think the 1982 constitution succeeded?

2. What social and economic changes in China led to the need for a new constitution in 1982?

3. One characteristic of Western democracies is that they have many political parties. In contrast, the People's Republic of China is a one-party state. How would China reconcile this one-party system with its avowed intent of placing more power in the hands of the people?

4. The Chinese constitution recognizes the right of the Chinese people to dissent. What evidence suggests that dissent is stifled in Communist China?

5. Compare this constitution to any of the other constitutions in this set. Possibilities include the Athenian Constitution, Constitution Act of Canada, Constitution of Carthage, Constitution of Haiti, Constitution of India, Constitution of Sparta, and Prince Shōtoku's Seventeen-Article Constitution. To what extent do the constitutions emerge from similar needs? To what extent do they differ?

---

gained power, the 1982 constitution allowed for amendments to be made while leaving the basic structure intact, and the constitution was indeed amended in 1988, 1993, 1999, and 2004. All of these amendments, passed in NPC sessions, were enacted to address economic changes in China as it became an open market—a capitalist economy in a Socialist state. Changes to articles reasserted the role of the state in managing and controlling the market and labor. The articles regarding owning private property were also changed to allow private ownership in a previously collectivized land system. The constitutional amendment in 2004 guarantees the legal right to own property. This right cannot be violated, meaning that the state can no longer seize land unlawfully.

Since the creation of the 1982 constitution, the lack of constitutional guarantees of human rights and growing government corruption have become major issues. Under Deng Xiaoping, the government became increasingly oppressive, and with the rise in corruption among party officials, such as acceptance of bribes for rewarding building contracts, the Chinese people again called for reforms. The Tiananmen Square demonstration in 1989 called for a crackdown on corruption as well as for democratic reforms. While the demonstration was suppressed, the plea for reform was partly answered. In early 2000 the NPC demanded the removal of many corrupt officials. With regard to the constitution, a 2004 amendment makes the claim that the state "respects and protects human rights." The definition of "human rights," however, has yet to be determined, as have the legal and social implications that will arise with enactment of this amendment to the constitution.

Further Reading

■ Articles

Weng, Byron. "Some Key Aspects of the 1982 Draft Constitution of the People's Republic of China."*China Quarterly* 91 (September 1982): 492–506.

Schwarcz, Vera. "Behind a Partially-Open Door: Chinese Intellectuals and the Post-Mao Reform Process."*Pacific Affairs* 59, no. 4 (Winter 1986–1987): 577–604.

■ Books

Fenby, Jonathan. *The Penguin History of Modern China: The Fall and Rise of a Great Power, 1850–2008*. London: Allen Lane, 2008.

Folsom, Ralph, and John H. Minan, eds. *Law in the People's Republic of China: Commentary, Readings and Materials*. Boston: M. Nijhoff Publishers, 1989.

Hsu, Immanuel Chung-yueh. *China without Mao: The Search for a New Order*. New York: Oxford University Press, 1990.

Schoppa, R. Keith. *Revolution and Its Past: Identities and Change in Modern Chinese History*, 2nd ed. Upper Saddle River, N.J.: Pearson Prentice Hall, 2006.

Sun, Yan Y. *The Chinese Reassessment of Socialism, 1976–1992*. Princeton, N.J.: Princeton University Press, 1995.

UNESCO. *Literacy Situation in Asia and the Pacific: Country Studies—China*. Bangkok, Thailand: UNESCO Regional Office for Education in Asian and the Pacific, 1984.

■ Web Sites

"Freedom of Expression, Speech, and the Press." Congressional-Executive Commission on China Virtual Academy Web site.
  http://www.cecc.gov/pages/virtualAcad/exp/.

"Deng Xiaoping: 1904–1997." Society for Anglo-Chinese Understanding Web site.
  http://www.sacu.org/dengxiaoping.html.

Education for All: The Year 2000 Assessment Final Country Report of China. UNESCO Web site.
  http://www.unesco.org/education/wef/countryreports/china/contents.html.

—Tereasa Maillie

CONSTITUTION OF THE PEOPLE'S REPUBLIC OF CHINA

Preamble

China is one of the countries with the longest histories in the world. The people of all nationalities in China have jointly created a splendid culture and have a glorious revolutionary tradition. Feudal China was gradually reduced after 1840 to a semi-colonial and semi-feudal country. The Chinese people waged wave upon wave of heroic struggles for national independence and liberation and for democracy and freedom. Great and earth-shaking historical changes have taken place in China in the 20th century. The Revolution of 1911, led by Dr Sun Yat-sen, abolished the feudal monarchy and gave birth to the Republic of China. But the Chinese people had yet to fulfil their historical task of overthrowing imperialism and feudalism. After waging hard, protracted and tortuous struggles, armed and otherwise, the Chinese people of all nationalities led by the Communist Party of China with Chairman Mao Zedong as its leader ultimately, in 1949, overthrew the rule of imperialism, feudalism and bureaucrat capitalism, won the great victory of the new-democratic revolution and founded the People's Republic of China. Thereupon the Chinese people took state power into their own hands and became masters of the country.

After the founding of the People's Republic, the transition of Chinese society from a new democratic to a socialist society was effected step by step. The socialist transformation of the private ownership of the means of production was completed, the system of exploitation of man by man eliminated and the socialist system established. The people's democratic dictatorship led by the working class and based on the alliance of workers and peasants, which is in essence the dictatorship of the proletariat, has been consolidated and developed. The Chinese people and the Chinese People's Liberation Army have thwarted aggression, sabotage and armed provocations by imperialists and hegemonists, safeguarded China's national independence and security and strengthened its national defence. Major successes have been achieved in economic development. An independent and fairly comprehensive socialist system of industry has in the main been established.... Both the victory of China's new-democratic revolution and the suc-

cesses of its socialist cause have been achieved by the Chinese people of all nationalities under the leadership of the Communist Party of China and the guidance of Marxism-Leninism and Mao Zedong Thought, and by upholding truth, correcting errors and overcoming numerous difficulties and hardships.

The basic task of the nation in the years to come is to concentrate its effort on socialist modernization. Under the leadership of the Communist Party of China and the guidance of Marxism-Leninism and Mao Zedong Thought, the Chinese people of all nationalities will continue to adhere to the people's democratic dictatorship and follow the socialist road, steadily improve socialist institutions, develop socialist democracy, improve the socialist legal system and work hard and self-reliantly to modernize industry, agriculture, national defence and science and technology step by step to turn China into a socialist country with a high level of culture and democracy. The exploiting classes as such have been eliminated in our country. However, class struggle will continue to exist within certain limits for a long time to come. The Chinese people must fight against those forces and elements, both at home and abroad, that are hostile to China's socialist system and try to undermine it. Taiwan is part of the sacred territory of the People's Republic of China. It is the lofty duty of the entire Chinese people, including our compatriots in Taiwan, to accomplish the great task of reunifying the motherland. In building socialism it is imperative to rely on the workers, peasants and intellectuals and unite with all the forces that can be united.... The People's Republic of China is a unitary multi-national state built up jointly by the people of all its nationalities. Socialist relations of equality, unity and mutual assistance have been established among them and will continue to be strengthened. In the struggle to safeguard the unity of the nationalities, it is necessary to combat big-nation chauvinism, mainly Han chauvinism, and also necessary to combat local-national chauvinism. The state does its utmost to promote the common prosperity of all nationalities in the country. China's achievements in revolution and construction are inseparable from support by the people of the world. The future of China is closely linked with that of the whole world. China adheres to an independent foreign policy as well as to the five principles of mutual respect for sovereignty and territorial integrity, mutual non-aggression, non-interference in each other's internal affairs, equality and mutual benefit, and peaceful coexistence in developing diplomatic relations and economic and cultural exchanges with other countries; China consistently opposes imperialism, hegemonism and colonialism, works to strengthen unity with the people of other countries, supports the oppressed nations and the developing countries in their just struggle to win and preserve national independence and develop their national economies, and strives to safeguard world peace and promote the cause of human progress. This Constitution affirms the achievements of the struggles of the Chinese people of all nationalities and defines the basic system and basic tasks of the state in legal form; it is the fundamental law of the state and has supreme legal authority. The people of all nationalities, all state organs, the armed forces, all political parties and public organizations and all enterprises and undertakings in the country must take the Constitution as the basic norm of conduct, and they have the duty to uphold the dignity of the Constitution and ensure its implementation.

◆ **Chapter I. General Principles**

Article 1. The People's Republic of China is a socialist state under the people's democratic dictatorship led by the working class and based on the alliance of workers and peasants. The socialist system is the basic system of the People's Republic of China. Sabotage of the socialist system by any organization or individual is prohibited.

Article 2. All power in the People's Republic of China belongs to the people. The organs through which the people exercise state power are the National People's Congress and the local people's congresses at different levels. The people administer state affairs and manage economic, cultural and social affairs through various channels and in various ways in accordance with the law.

Article 3. The state organs of the People's Republic of China apply the principle of democratic centralism. The National People's Congress and the local People's congresses at different levels are instituted through democratic election. They are responsible to the people and subject to their supervision. All administrative, judicial and procuratorial organs of the state are created by the People's congresses to which they are responsible and under whose supervision they operate....

Article 4. All nationalities in the People's Republic of China are equal. The state protects the lawful rights and interests of the minority nationalities and upholds and develops the relationship of equality, unity and mutual assistance among all of China's nationalities. Discrimination against and oppression of any nationality are prohibited; any acts that undermine the unity of the nationalities or instigate their secession are prohibited.... All the national autonomous areas are inalienable parts of the People's Republic of China. The people of all nationalities have the freedom to use and develop their own spoken and written languages, and to preserve or reform their own ways and customs.

Article 5. The state upholds the uniformity and dignity of the socialist legal system. No law or administrative or local rules and regulations shall contravene the constitution. All state organs, the armed forces, all political parties and public organizations and all enterprises and undertakings must abide by the Constitution and the law. All acts in violation of the Constitution and the law must be investigated. No organization or individual may enjoy the privilege of being above the Constitution and the law.

Article 6. The basis of the socialist economic system of the People's Republic of China is socialist public ownership of the means of production, namely, ownership by the whole people and collective ownership by the working people. The system of socialist public ownership supersedes the system of exploitation of man by man; it applies the principle of 'from each according to his ability, to each according to his work'.

Article 7. The state economy is the sector of socialist economy under ownership by the whole people; it is the leading force in the national economy. The state ensures the consolidation and growth of the state economy.

Article 8. Rural People's communes, agricultural producers' co-operatives, and other forms of co-operative economy such as producers' supply and marketing, credit and consumers co-operatives, belong to the sector of socialist economy under collective ownership by the working people. Working people who are members of rural economic collectives have the right, within the limits prescribed by law, to farm private plots of cropland and hilly land, engage in household sideline production and raise privately owned livestock....

Article 9. Mineral resources, waters, forests, mountains, grassland, unreclaimed land, beaches and other natural resources are owned by the state, that is, by the whole people, with the exception of the forests, mountains, grassland, unreclaimed land

and beaches that are owned by collectives in accordance with the law. The state ensures the rational use of natural resources and protects rare animals and plants. The appropriation or damage of natural resources by any organization or individual by whatever means is prohibited.

Article 10. Land in the cities is owned by the state. Land in the rural and suburban areas is owned by collectives except for those portions which belong to the state in accordance with the law; house sites and private plots of cropland and hilly land are also owned by collectives....

Article 11. The individual economy of urban and rural working people, operated within the limits prescribed by law, is a complement to the socialist public economy. The state protects the lawful rights and interests of the individual economy. The state guides, helps and supervises the individual economy by exercising administrative control.

Article 12. Socialist public property is sacred and inviolable. The state protects socialist public property. Appropriation or damage of state or collective property by any organization or individual by whatever means is prohibited.

Article 13. The state protects the right of citizens to own lawfully earned income, savings, houses and other lawful property. The state protects by law the right of citizens to inherit private property.

Article 14. The state continuously raises labour productivity, improves economic results and develops the productive forces by enhancing the enthusiasm of the working people, raising the level of their technical skill, disseminating advanced science and technology, improving the systems of economic administration and enterprise operation and management, instituting the socialist system of responsibility in various forms and improving organization of work. The state practises strict economy and combats waste. The state properly apportions accumulation and consumption, pays attention to the interests of the collective and the individual as well as of the state and, on the basis of expanded production, gradually improves the material and cultural life of the people.

Article 15. The state practises economic planning on the basis of socialist public ownership. It ensures the proportionate and co-ordinated growth of the national economy through overall balancing by economic planning and the supplementary role of regulation by the market. Disturbance of the orderly functioning of the social economy or disruption of the state economic plan by any organization or individual is prohibited.

Article 16. State enterprises have decision-making power in operation and management within the limits prescribed by law, on condition that they submit to unified leadership by the state and fulfil all their obligations under the state plan. State enterprises practise democratic management through congresses of workers and staff and in other ways in accordance with the law.

Article 17. Collective economic organizations have decision-making power in conducting independent economic activities, on condition that they accept the guidance of the state plan and abide by the relevant laws. Collective economic organizations practise democratic management in accordance with the law, with the entire body of their workers electing or removing their managerial personnel and deciding on major issues concerning operation and management.

Article 18. The People's Republic of China permits foreign enterprises, other foreign economic organizations and individual foreigners to invest in China and to enter into various forms of economic co-operation with Chinese enterprises and other economic organizations in accordance with the law of the People's Republic of China....

Article 19. The state develops socialist educational undertakings and works to raise the scientific and cultural level of the whole nation. The state runs schools of various types, makes primary education compulsory and universal, develops secondary, vocational and higher education and promotes pre-school education. The state develops educational facilities of various types in order to wipe out illiteracy and provide political, cultural, scientific, technical and professional education for workers, peasants, state functionaries and other working people.... The state promotes the nationwide use of Putonghua (common speech based on Beijing pronunciation).

Article 20. The state promotes the development of the natural and social sciences, disseminates scientific and technical knowledge, and commends and rewards achievements in scientific research as well as technological discoveries and inventions.

Article 21. The state develops medical and health services, promotes modern medicine and traditional Chinese medicine, encourages and supports the setting up of various medical and health facilities by the rural economic collectives, state enterprises and undertakings and neighbourhood organizations, and promotes sanitation activities of a mass character, all to protect the People's health. The state develops physical culture and promotes mass sports activities to build up the People's physique.

Article 22. The state promotes the development of literature and art, the press, broadcasting and television undertakings, publishing and distribution services, libraries, museums, cultural centres and other cultural undertakings, that serve the people and socialism, and sponsors mass cultural activities. The state protects places of scenic and historical interest, valuable cultural monuments and relics and other important items of China's historical and cultural heritage.

Article 23. The state trains specialized personnel in all fields who serve socialism, increases the number of intellectuals and creates conditions to give full scope to their role in socialist modernization.

Article 24. The state strengthens the building of socialist spiritual civilization... The state advocates the civic virtues of love for the motherland, for the people, for labour, for science and for socialism; it educates the people in patriotism, collectivism, internationalism and communism and in dialectical and historical materialism; it combats the decadent ideas of capitalism and feudalism and other decadent ideas.

Article 25. The state promotes family planning so that population growth may fit the plans for economic and social development.

Article 26. The state protects and improves the living environment and the ecological environment, and prevents and controls pollution and other public hazards. The state organizes and encourages afforestation and the protection of forests.

Article 27. All state organs carry out the principle of simple and efficient administration, the system of responsibility for work and the system of training functionaries and appraising their work in order constantly to improve quality of work and efficiency and combat bureaucratism. All state organs and functionaries must rely on the support of the people, keep in close touch with them, heed their opinions and suggestions, accept their supervision and work hard to serve them.

Article 28. The state maintains public order and suppresses treasonable and other counter-revolutionary activities; it penalizes actions that endanger public security and disrupt the socialist economy and other criminal activities, and punishes and reforms criminals.

Article 29. The armed forces of the People's Republic of China belong to the people. Their tasks are to strengthen national defence, resist aggression, defend the motherland, safeguard the People's peaceful labour, participate in national reconstruction, and work hard to serve the people. The state strengthens the revolutionization, modernization and regularization of the armed forces in order to increase the national defence capability.

Article 30. The administrative division of the People's Republic of China is as follows: (1) The country is divided into provinces, autonomous regions and municipalities directly under the Central Government; (2) Provinces and autonomous regions are divided into autonomous prefectures, counties, autonomous counties and cities; (3) Counties and autonomous counties are divided into townships, nationality townships and towns....

Article 31. The state may establish special administrative regions when necessary. The systems to be instituted in special administrative regions shall be prescribed by law enacted by the National People's Congress in the light of the specific conditions.

Article 32. The People's Republic of China protects the lawful rights and interests of foreigners within Chinese territory, and while on Chinese territory foreigners must abide by the law of the People's Republic of China. The People's Republic of China may grant asylum to foreigners who request it for political reasons.

◆ **Chapter II. The Fundamental Rights and Duties of Citizens**

Article 33. All persons holding the nationality of the People's Republic of China are citizens of the People's Republic of China. All citizens of the People's Republic of China are equal before the law. Every citizen enjoys the rights and at the same time must perform the duties prescribed by the Constitution and the law.

Article 34. All citizens of the People's Republic of China who have reached the age of 18 have the right to vote and stand for election, regardless of nationality, race, sex, occupation, family background, religious belief, education, property status, or length of residence, except persons deprived of political rights according to law.

Article 35. Citizens of the People's Republic of China enjoy freedom of speech, of the press, of assembly, of association, of procession and of demonstration.

Article 36. Citizens of the People's Republic of China enjoy freedom of religious belief. No state organ, public organization or individual may compel citizens to believe in, or not to believe in, any religion; nor may they discriminate against citizens who believe in, or do not believe in, any religion. The state protects normal religious activities....

Article 37. The freedom of person of citizens of the People's Republic of China is inviolable. No citizen may be arrested except with the approval or by decision of a People's procuratorate or by decision of a People's court, and arrests must be made by a public security organ. Unlawful deprivation or restriction of citizens' freedom of person by detention or other means is prohibited; and unlawful search of the person of citizens is prohibited.

Article 38. The personal dignity of citizens of the People's Republic of China is inviolable. Insult, libel, false charge or frame-up directed against citizens by any means is prohibited.

Article 39. The home of citizens of the People's Republic of China is inviolable. Unlawful search of, or intrusion into, a citizen's home is prohibited.

Article 40. The freedom and privacy of correspondence of citizens of the People's Republic of China are protected by law. No organization or individual may, on any ground, infringe upon the freedom and privacy of citizens' correspondence except in cases where, to meet the needs of state security or of investigation into criminal offences, public security or procuratorial organs are permitted to censor correspondence in accordance with procedures prescribed by law.

Article 41. Citizens of the People's Republic of China have the right to criticize and make suggestions to any state organ or functionary. Citizens have the right to make to relevant state organs complaints and charges against, or exposures of, violation of the law or dereliction of duty by any state organ or functionary;... No one may suppress such complaints, charges and exposures, or retaliate against the citizens making them. Citizens who have suffered losses through infringement of their civil rights by any state organ or functionary have the right to compensation in accordance with the law.

Article 42. Citizens of the People's Republic of China have the right as well as the duty to work. Using various channels, the state creates conditions for employment, strengthens labour protection, improves working conditions and, on the basis of expanded production, increases remuneration for work and social benefits. Work is the glorious duty of every able-bodied citizen. All working people in state enterprises and in urban and rural economic collectives should perform their tasks with an attitude consonant with their status as masters of the country....

Article 43. Working people in the People's Republic of China have the right to rest. The state expands facilities for rest and recuperation of working people, and prescribes working hours and vacations for workers and staff.

Article 44. The state prescribes by law the system of retirement for workers and staff in enterprises and undertakings and for functionaries of organs of state. The livelihood of retired personnel is ensured by the state and society.

Article 45. Citizens of the People's Republic of China have the right to material assistance from the state and society when they are old, ill or disabled. The state develops the social insurance, social relief and medical and health services that are required to enable citizens to enjoy this right. The state and society ensure the livelihood of disabled members of the armed forces, provide pensions to the families of martyrs and give preferential treatment to the families of military personnel. The state and society help make arrangements for the work, livelihood and education of the blind, deaf-mute and other handicapped citizens.

Article 46. Citizens of the People's Republic of China have the duty as well as the right to receive education. The state promotes the all-round moral, intellectual and physical development of children and young people.

Article 47. Citizens of the People's Republic of China have the freedom to engage in scientific research, literary and artistic creation and other cultural pursuits. The state encourages and assists creative endeavours conducive to the interests of the people made by citizens engaged in education, science, technology, literature, art and other cultural work.

Article 48. Women in the People's Republic of China enjoy equal rights with men in all spheres of life, political, economic, cultural and social, and family life. The state protects the rights and interests of women, applies the principle of equal pay for equal work for men and women alike and trains and selects cadres from among women.

Article 49. Marriage, the family, and mother and child are protected by the state. Both husband and wife have the duty to practise family planning. Parents have the duty to rear and educate their minor children, and children who have come of age have the duty to support and assist their parents. Violation of the freedom of marriage is prohibited. Maltreatment of old people, women and children is prohibited.

Article 50. The People's Republic of China protects the legitimate rights and interests of Chinese nationals residing abroad and protects the lawful rights and interests of returned overseas Chinese and of the family members of Chinese nationals residing abroad.

Article 51. The exercise by citizens of the People's Republic of China of their freedoms and rights may not infringe upon the interests of the state, of society and of the collective, or upon the lawful freedoms and rights of other citizens.

Article 52. It is the duty of citizens of the People's Republic of China to safeguard the unity of the country and the unity of all its nationalities.

Article 53. Citizens of the People's Republic of China must abide by the constitution and the law, keep state secrets, protect public property and observe labour discipline and public order and respect social ethics.

Article 54. It is the duty of citizens of the People's Republic of China to safeguard the security, honour and interests of the motherland; they must not commit acts detrimental to the security, honour and interests of the motherland.

Article 55. It is the sacred obligation of every citizen of the People's Republic of China to defend the motherland and resist aggression. It is the honourable duty of citizens of the People's Republic of China to perform military service and join the militia in accordance with the law.

Article 56. It is the duty of citizens of the People's Republic of China to pay taxes in accordance with the law.

Chapter III. The Structure of the State

◆ Section 1. The National People's Congress

Article 57. The National People's Congress of the People's Republic of China is the highest organ of state power. Its permanent body is the Standing Committee of the National People's Congress.

Article 58. The National People's Congress and its Standing Committee exercise the legislative power of the state.

Article 59. The National People's Congress is composed of deputies elected by the provinces, autonomous regions and municipalities directly under the Central Government, and by the armed forces. All the minority nationalities are entitled to appropriate representation. Election of deputies to the National People's Congress is conducted by the Standing Committee of the National People's Congress. The number of deputies to the National People's Congress and the manner of their election are prescribed by law.

Article 60. The National People's Congress is elected for a term of five years....

Article 61. The National People's Congress meets in session once a year and is convened by its Standing Committee. A session of the National People's Congress may be convened at any time the Standing Committee deems this necessary, or when more than one-fifth of the deputies to the National People's Congress so propose. When the National People's Congress meets, it elects a presidium to conduct its session.

Article 62. The National People's Congress exercises the following functions and powers:

(1) To amend the Constitution;

(2) To supervise the enforcement of the Constitution;

(3) To enact and amend basic statutes concerning criminal offences, civil affairs, the state organs and other matters;

(4) To elect the President and the Vice-President of the People's Republic of China; (previously translated as Chairman and Vice-Chairman of the People's Republic of China—translator's note.)

(5) To decide on the choice of the Premier of the State Council upon nomination by the President of the People's Republic of China, and to decide on the choice of the Vice-Premiers, State Councillors, Ministers in charge of Ministries or Commissions and the Auditor-General and the Secretary-General of the State Council upon nomination by the Premier;

(6) To elect the Chairman of the Central Military Commission and, upon his nomination, to decide on the choice of the other members of the Central Military Commission;...

(14) To decide on questions of war and peace;...

Article 63. The National People's Congress has the power to recall or remove from office the following persons:

(1) The President and the Vice-President of the People's Republic of China;

(2) The Premier, Vice-Premiers, State Councillors, Ministers in charge of Ministries or Commissions and the Auditor-General and the Secretary-General of the State Council;

(3) The Chairman of the Central Military Commission and others on the commission;

(4) The President of the Supreme People's Court; and

(5) The Procurator-General of the Supreme People's Procuratorate.

Article 64. Amendments to the Constitution are to be proposed by the Standing Committee of the National People's Congress or by more than one-fifth of the deputies to the National People's Congress and adopted by a majority vote of more than two-thirds of all the deputies to the Congress. Statutes and resolutions are adopted by a majority vote of more than one half of all the deputies to the National People's Congress.

Article 65. The Standing Committee of the National People's Congress is composed of the following: The Chairman; The Vice-Chairmen; The Secretary-General; and Members. Minority nationalities are entitled to appropriate representation on the Standing Committee of the National People's Congress. The National People's Congress elects, and has the power to recall, all those on its Standing Committee. No one on the Standing Committee of the National People's Congress shall hold any post in any of the administrative, judicial or procuratorial organs of the state.

Article 66. The Standing Committee of the National People's Congress is elected for the same term as the National People's Congress; it exercises its functions and powers until a new Standing Committee is elected by the succeeding National People's Congress. The Chairman and Vice-Chairmen of the Standing Committee shall serve no more than two consecutive terms.

Article 67. The Standing Committee of the National People's Congress exercises the following functions and powers:

(1) To interpret the Constitution and supervise its enforcement;

(2) To enact and amend statutes with the exception of those which should be enacted by the National People's Congress;

(3) To enact,when the National People's Congress is not in session, partial supplements and amendments to statutes enacted by the National People's Congress provided that they do not contravene the basic principles of these statutes;...

Article 74. No deputy to the National People's Congress may be arrested or placed on criminal trial without the consent of the Presidium of the current session of the National People's Congress or, when the National People's Congress is not in session, without the consent of its Standing Committee.

Article 75. Deputies to the National People's Congress may not be called to legal account for their speeches or votes at its meetings....

◆ **Section 2. The President of the People's Republic of China**

Article 79: The President and Vice-President of the People's Republic of China are elected by the National People's Congress. Citizens of the People's Republic of China who have the right to vote and to stand for election and who have reached the age of 45 are eligible for election as President or Vice-President of the People's Republic of China....

Article 80. The President of the People's Republic of China, in pursuance of decisions of the National People's Congress and its Standing Committee, promulgates statutes; appoints and removes the Premier, Vice-Premiers, State Councillors, Ministers in charge of Ministries or Commissions, and the Auditor-General and the Secretary-General of the State Council; confers state medals and titles of honour; issues orders of special pardons; proclaims martial law; proclaims a state of war; and issues mobilization orders.

Article 81. The President of the People's Republic of China receives foreign diplomatic representatives on behalf of the People's Republic of China and, in pursuance of decisions of the Standing Committee of the National People's Congress, appoints and recalls plenipotentiary representatives abroad, and ratifies and abrogates treaties and important agreements concluded with foreign states.

Article 82. The Vice-President of the People's Republic of China assists the President in his work. The Vice-President of the People's Republic of China may exercise such parts of the functions and powers of the President as the President may entrust to him.

Article 83. The President and Vice-President of the People's Republic of China exercise their functions and powers until the new President and Vice-President elected by the succeeding National People's Congress assume office.

Article 84. In case the office of the President of the People's Republic of China falls vacant, the Vice-President succeeds to the office of President. In case the office of the Vice-President of the People's Republic of China falls vacant, the National People's Congress shall elect a new Vice-President to fill the vacancy....

◆ **Section 3. The State Council**

Article 85. The State Council, that is, the Central People's Government of the People's Republic of China, is the executive body of the highest organ of state power; it is the highest organ of state administration.

Article 86. The State Council is composed of the following: The Premier; The Vice-Premiers; The State Councillors; The Ministers in charge of Ministries; The Ministers in charge of Commissions; The Auditor-General; and The Secretary-General. The Premier has overall responsibility for the State

Council. The Ministers have overall responsibility for the respective ministries or commissions under their charge. The organization of the State Council is prescribed by law.

Article 87. The term of office of the State Council is the same as that of the National People's Congress. The Premier, Vice-Premiers and State Councillors shall serve no more than two consecutive terms.

Article 88. The Premier directs the work of the State Council. The Vice-Premiers and State Councillors assist the Premier in his work. Executive meetings of the State Council are composed of the Premier, the Vice-Premiers, the State Councillors and the Secretary-General of the State Council. The Premier convenes and presides over the executive meetings and plenary meetings of the State Council.

Article 89. The State Council exercises the following functions and powers: ...

(9) To conduct foreign affairs and conclude treaties and agreements with foreign states; (10) To direct and administer the building of national defence; (11) To direct and administer affairs concerning the nationalities and to safeguard the equal rights of minority nationalities and the right of autonomy of the national autonomous areas....

Article 90. The ministers in charge of ministries or commissions of the State Council are responsible for the work of their respective departments and convene and preside over their ministerial meetings or commission meetings that discuss and decide on major issues in the work of their respective departments....

Article 91. The State Council establishes an auditing body to supervise through auditing the revenue and expenditure of all departments under the State Council and of the local governments at different levels, and those of the state financial and monetary organizations and of enterprises and undertakings....

Article 92. The State Council is responsible, and reports on its work, to the National People's Congress or, when the National People's Congress is not in session, to its Standing Committee.

◆ Section 4. The Central Military Commission

Article 93. The Central Military Commission of the People's Republic of China directs the armed forces of the country....

Article 94. The Chairman of the Central Military Commission is responsible to the National People's Congress and its Standing Committee.

◆ Section 5. The Local People's Congress and the Local People's Governments at Different Levels

Article 95. People's congresses and People's governments are established in provinces, municipalities directly under the Central Government, counties, cities, municipal districts, townships, nationality townships and towns. The organization of local People's congresses and local People's governments at different levels is prescribed by law. Organs of self-government are established in autonomous regions, autonomous prefectures and autonomous counties. The organization and working procedures of organs of self-government are prescribed by law in accordance with the basic principles laid down in Sections V and VI of Chapter Three of the Constitution.

Article 96. Local People's congresses at different levels are local organs of state power. Local People's congresses at and above the county level establish standing committees.

Article 97. Deputies to the People's congresses of provinces, municipalities directly under the Central Government, and cities divided into districts are elected by the People's congresses at the next lower level; deputies to the People's congresses of counties, cities not divided into districts, municipal districts, townships, nationality townships and towns are elected directly by their constituencies. The number of deputies to local People's congresses at different levels and the manner of their election are prescribed by law.

Article 98. The term of office of the People's congresses of provinces, municipalities directly under the Central Government and cities divided into districts is five years. The term of office of the People's congresses of counties, cities not divided into districts, municipal districts, townships, nationality townships and towns is three years.

Article 99. Local People's congresses at different levels ensure the observance and implementation of the Constitution....

Article 100. The People's congresses of provinces and municipalities directly under the Central Government, and their standing committees, may adopt local regulations, which must not contravene the Constitution, the statutes and the administrative rules and regulations, and they shall report such local regulations to the Standing Committee of the National People's Congress for the record.

Article 101. At their respective levels, local People's congresses elect, and have the power to recall, governors and deputy governors, or mayors and deputy mayors, or heads and deputy heads of counties, districts, townships and towns. Local People's congresses at and above the county level elect, and have the power to recall, presidents of People's courts and chief procurators of People's procuratorates at the corresponding level. The election or recall of chief procurators of People's procuratorates shall be reported to the chief procurators of the People's procuratorates at the next higher level for submission to the standing committees of the People's congresses at the corresponding level for approval.

Article 102. Deputies to the People's congresses of provinces, municipalities, directly under the Central Government and cities divided into districts are subject to supervision by the units which elected them....

Article 103. The standing committee of a local People's congress at and above the county level is composed of a chairman, vice-chairmen and members, and is responsible, and reports on its work, to the People's congress at the corresponding level. The local People's congress at and above the county level elects, and has the power to recall, anyone on the standing committee of the People's congress at the corresponding level. No one on the standing committee of a local People's congress at and above the county level shall hold any post in state administrative, judicial and procuratorial organs.

Article 104. The standing committee of a local People's congress at and above the county level discusses and decides on major issues in all fields of work in its administrative area; supervises the work of the People's government....

Article 105. Local People's governments at different levels are the executive bodies of local organs of state power as well as the local organs of state administration at the corresponding level. Local People's governments at different levels practise the system of overall responsibility by governors, mayors, county heads, district heads, township heads and town heads.

Article 106. The term of office of local People's governments at different levels is the same as that of the People's congresses at the corresponding level.

Article 107. Local People's governments at and above the county level, within the limits of their authority as prescribed by law, conduct the administrative work concerning the economy, education, science, culture, public health, physical culture, urban and rural development, finance, civil affairs, public security, nationalities affairs, judicial administration, supervision and family planning in their respective administrative areas....

Article 108. Local People's governments at and above the county level direct the work of their subordinate departments and of People's governments at lower levels, and have the power to alter or annul inappropriate decisions of their subordinate departments and People's governments at lower levels.

Article 109. Auditing bodies are established by local People's governments at and above the county level. Local auditing bodies at different levels independently exercise their power to supervise through auditing in accordance with the law and are responsible to the People's government at the corresponding level and to the auditing body at the next higher level.

Article 110. Local People's governments at different levels are responsible, and report on their work, to People's congresses at the corresponding level. Local People's governments at and above the county level are responsible, and report on their work, to the standing committee of the People's congress at the corresponding level when the congress is not in session....

Article 111. The residents' committees and villagers' committees established among urban and rural residents on the basis of their place of residence are mass organizations of self-management at the grass-roots level. The chairman, vice-chairmen and members of each residents' or villagers' committee are elected by the residents....

◆ **Section 6. The Organs of Self-Government of National Autonomous Areas**

Article 112. The organs of self-government of national autonomous areas are the People's congresses and People's governments of autonomous regions, autonomous prefectures and autonomous counties.

Article 113. In the People's congress of an autonomous region, prefecture or county, in addition to the deputies of the nationality or nationalities exercising regional autonomy in the administrative area, the other nationalities inhabiting the area are also entitled to appropriate representation. The chairmanship and vice-chairmanships of the standing committee of the People's congress of an autonomous region, prefecture or county shall include a citizen or citizens of the nationality or nationalities exercising regional autonomy in the area concerned.

Article 114. The administrative head of an autonomous region, prefecture or county shall be a citizen of the nationality, or of one of the nationalities, exercising regional autonomy in the area concerned.

Article 115. The organs of self-government of autonomous regions, prefectures and counties exercise the functions and powers of local organs of state as specified in Section V of Chapter Three of the Constitution. At the same time, they exercise the right of autonomy within the limits of their authority as prescribed by the Constitution, the law of regional national autonomy and other laws, and implement the laws and policies of the state in the light of the existing local situation.

Article 116. People's congresses of national autonomous areas have the power to enact autonomy regulations and specific regulations in the light of the political, economic and cultural characteristics of the nationality or nationalities in the areas concerned....

Article 117. The organs of self-government of the national autonomous areas have the power of autonomy in administering the finances of their areas. All revenues accruing to the national autonomous areas under the financial system of the state shall be managed and used independently by the organs of self-government of those areas.

Article 118. The organs of self-government of the national autonomous areas independently arrange for and administer local economic development under the guidance of state plans. In developing natural resources and building enterprises in the national autonomous areas, the state shall give due consideration to the interests of those areas.

Article 119. The organs of self-government of the national autonomous areas independently administer educational, scientific, cultural, public health and physical culture affairs in their respective areas,

sort out and protect the cultural legacy of the nationalities and work for the development and prosperity of their cultures.

Article 120. The organs of self-government of the national autonomous areas may, in accordance with the military system of the state and concrete local needs and with the approval of the State Council, organize local public security forces for the maintenance of public order.

Article 121. In performing their functions, the organs of self-government of the national autonomous areas, in accordance with the autonomy regulations of the respective areas, employ the spoken and written language or languages in common use in the locality.

Article 122. The state gives financial, material and technical assistance to the minority nationalities to accelerate their economic and cultural development. The state helps the national autonomous areas train large numbers of cadres at different levels and specialized personnel and skilled workers of different professions and trades from among the nationality or nationalities in those areas....

◆ **Chapter IV. The National Flag, the National Emblem and the Capital**

Article 136. The national flag of the People's Republic of China is a red flag with five stars.

Article 137. The national emblem of the People's Republic of China is Tian'anmen in the centre illuminated by five stars and encircled by ears of grain and a cogwheel.

Article 138. The capital of the People's Republic of China is Beijing.

Glossary

dictatorship of the proletariat	an allusion to the socialist state that Karl Marx saw as the transitional phase between a capitalist class society and a Communist society without classes
Han chauvinism	the bias of the Han Chinese, the country's majority ethnic group, against minority ethnic groups
Mao Zedong Thought	Maoism, as derived from the teachings of Mao (1893–1976)
Revolution of 1911	the struggle that resulted in the end of the Qing Dynasty, which had ruled China since 1692

AGREEMENT ON RECONCILIATION BETWEEN SOUTH AND NORTH KOREA

"South and North Korea shall permit ... visits between dispersed family members."

Overview

On December 13, 1991, high-ranking representatives of the Republic of Korea and the Democratic People's Republic of Korea signed the Agreement on Reconciliation, Nonaggression, and Exchanges and Cooperation between South and North Korea, to become effective on February 19, 1992. Composed of four chapters, it addressed the nations' mutual intentions to engage in multifaceted exchanges to end the ongoing state of political and military confrontation between them, setting forth the principles that would be involved in unification.

Prepared by the delegates to the South-North High-Level Negotiations, the agreement was foremost designed to bring about an end to the hostilities that had begun before the outbreak of the Korean War (1950–1953). It was seen by many as a major breakthrough in the long-term suspicions between the two Koreas, but it has not lived up to expectations. Although it was negotiated and initialed by both parties, each nation was soon afterward beset with distracting problems, such that neither side sought progress toward fulfilling the tenets of the agreement. As of the start of 2010 it had not been implemented, nor had the more significant provisions been followed. Despite these shortcomings, the agreement at least provides a definition for the potential relationship required for Korean reunification and outlines the primary steps necessary for a peaceful unification process. The agreement has also encouraged positive actions and sporadic efforts toward further diplomatic considerations. Somehow, through the ensuing two decades of political discord between the two countries, economic concerns, and even nuclear crisis, both sides have held on to the document as worthy of implementation.

Context

In November 1943 at the Cairo Conference, representatives from the United States, the Republic of China (now known as Taiwan), and Great Britain provided for the division of Korea along latitude 38° north as a means of accept-

ing the surrender of Japan. To end World War II, Japan, which had occupied Korea since 1905, would be required to surrender to the Soviet Union north of the thirty-eighth parallel and to the United States to the south. This somewhat arbitrary division separated a nation that had, through centuries and in the face of numerous foreign interventions, managed to keep its national character intact. The division eventually led to the formation of two separate nations: the Democratic People's Republic of Korea, or North Korea, under the Communist leadership of Kim Il-sung, and the Republic of Korea, or South Korea, under President Syngman Rhee. The division did little, however, to separate the strong ethnic ties among the nation's peoples. In June 1950, North Korea invaded South Korea and set off a war that eventually also involved the United States, the People's Republic of China, and the United Nations. The long and costly war concluded with a cease-fire on July 27, 1953, but this did not resolve the primary cause of the war: the desire for reunification. For over half a century since then, no peace settlement has been reached. Nonetheless, the desire to unite the Koreas has never diminished among the people, and numerous efforts have been made to form some basis for accomplishing this goal.

Indeed, almost immediately following the war, efforts were made by both sides to bring about some sort of reconciliation. But both countries were plagued by debts and the destruction of infrastructure as well as political unrest, economic uncertainty, and military paranoia. The first indications of significant progress occurred from May to July 1972, when talks were held in the nation's capitals of P'yŏngyang and Seoul. The talks were mediated by Kim Young-ju, the North Korean delegate and director of the Organization and Guidance Department in P'yŏngyang, and Li Hu-rak, the South Korean delegate and director of the Korea Central Intelligence Agency. The statement that was finally initialed on July 4, 1972, acknowledged that reunification of the nations was a basic and significant priority for both countries. It provided seven points by which reunification could be accomplished. It also established the North-South Coordination Committee to promote implementation of the agreement. In accordance with the proposal, both sides promised to refrain from any action that might lead to further controversy and to seek an inde-

1943

■ **November 22–27**
The Cairo Conference is held in Egypt, during which the Allied powers decide to arbitrarily divide Korea at the thirty-eighth parallel.

1950

■ **June 25**
The Korean War begins with North Korea's invasion of South Korea.

1953

■ **July 27**
The Korean War concludes with an armistice agreement signed by North Korea, China (the People's Republic of China), and the United Nations Command, promising continued talks leading toward reconciliation.

■ **October 1**
The United States and South Korea sign the Mutual Defense Treaty, which enters into force November 17, 1954.

1972

■ **July 4**
The South-North Joint Communiqué is issued, delineating essential principles for reunification.

1986

■ **June 23**
North Korea proposes making the Korean Peninsula a nonnuclear peace zone.

pendently achieved reunification—that is, one not dictated by any third-party nations or international organizations. This last intention, which would keep reappearing among like documents for the next forty years, remains a pivotal aspect of the Korean desire to reunite.

The 1972 agreement failed to be fulfilled for a variety of reasons, but most significant among them was the North Korean assumption that the call for freedom from foreign interference meant that the United States would be leaving South Korea altogether. The response from the Republic of Korea was that the U.S. presence was yet a matter between South Korea and the United States and not subject to negotiation. Consequently, the agreement essentially became a dead letter. Both nations then turned their focus to the domestic expansion of economic and national power.

Nearly twenty years later—some forty years after the armistice that concluded the Korean War—high-ranking delegates from both Koreas met once more to try to reach an agreement on reconciliation of the nations. During these forty years both countries had struggled with the effects of the hostilities dividing them. They had tried to bring about such reconciliation as was spelled out in the 1972 document but had failed to achieve its rather lofty affirmations, and now they saw fit to make a renewed effort. There seems little doubt that at this point, South Korea was intent on working out a meaningful relationship with North Korea. There was nothing to be gained, and a great deal to be feared, if hostilities got out of hand.

Thus, following long discussions, in 1991 both parties signed the Agreement on Reconciliation, Nonaggression, and Exchange and Cooperation between South and North Korea. The preamble of this document relates the continuing impact of the 1972 document, for it reaffirms the principles enacted in the South-North Joint Communiqué of July 4, 1972, and acknowledges the desire to avoid aggression and establish peace. Along with this document, and equally significant to the future of both nations, was the Joint Declaration of the Denuclearization of the Korean Peninsula, which was likewise implemented on February 19, 1992.

As with the 1972 communiqué, the primary problem with the 1992 Agreement on Reconciliation was the lack of any external guarantors, and thus the agreement was at the mercy of inter-Korean relations. In fact, soon afterward, North Korea admitted to the pursuit of a nuclear weapons policy, and with the United States expressing its opposition, other aspects of the agreement were sidetracked.

About the Author

The Agreement on Reconciliation was the work of the staffs of the attendees at the South-North High-Level Negotiations of 1991. It was signed by Chung Won-shik, prime minister of the Republic of Korea, and Yon Hyong-muk, premier of the Administration Council of the Democratic People's Republic of Korea. The two men were their nation's chief delegates to the negotiations and fully representative of their nation's wishes and policies. Chung Won-shik had a long history within the inner circles of South Korea's government. After serving in a number of highly sensitive posts, including as minister of education from 1988 to 1990 and as the nation's envoy to Africa, he became prime minister at the age of sixty-two in 1991. Yon Hyong-muk was born in November 1931 and rose to become prime minister of North Korea (1988–1992) and an alternate member of the Political Bureau of the Central Committee of the Workers' Party of Korea; with these roles his was a highly respected and powerful position. Well educated, he spoke several languages and had the reputation of bearing wide knowledge of international affairs.

Explanation and Analysis of the Document

The tenets of the Agreement on Reconciliation, Nonaggression, and Exchanges and Cooperation between South and North Korea came into effect on February 19, 1992. As signed, the document consists of a preamble and four chapters, each with a number of articles. The preamble presents the primary focus, stating the longing of the Korean people to arrive at a peaceful reunification of the two nations. It thus reaffirms and elaborates upon the South-North Joint Communiqué of July 4, 1972, expressing determination to eliminate the state of political and military hostilities yet separating the Koreas. The 1992 agreement asserts that in order to accomplish this goal, the nations should avoid armed aggression and establish widespread societal exchanges to promote the interests in prosperity common to them both.

During the 1972 talks the two Koreas had agreed on the principles of unification—to be achieved independently and peacefully so as to produce one nation transcending the differences of ideology. The 1972 document had remained unimplemented as the result of the onset of a variety of domestic issues on both sides as well as a state of military paranoia—primarily in North Korea, which feared aggression on the part of both South Korea and the United States. That document outlined seven points necessary for reunification to be achieved, and none of these points lost their appeal or their promise of pragmatic results in the ensuing twenty years. The points included the beliefs that reunification needed to be achieved independently, without outside interference, and by peaceful means, without force; that the resulting union should be promoted above all as one nation; and that it would be essential to transcend differences in ideology and systems, to avoid slanderous disputes, to realize active interchanges in various fields, to resolve the ongoing Red Cross negotiations, and to establish direct telephone lines between the capitals to avoid unforeseen incidents of miscommunication. In the end, the 1972 document called for the creation of a North-South Coordination Committee to promote implementation. This committee failed to fulfill its mission owing to extenuating circumstances, but its mantle was taken up by the delegates to the South-North High-Level Negotiations of 1991.

Time Line

1991

■ **December 13**
The two Koreas sign the Agreement on Reconciliation, Nonaggression, and Exchanges and Cooperation between South and North Korea, to take effect on February 19, 1992.

1992

■ **January 20**
The Joint Declaration of the Denuclearization of the Korean Peninsula is signed by North and South Korea, effective February 19, 1992.

1998

■ **August**
North Korea tests a two-stage Taepodong-1 rocket.

2000

■ **June 13–15**
The North Korean leader Kim Jong-il and the South Korean president Kim Dae-jung convene a historic summit in P'yŏngyang and issue a joint declaration on cooperation.

2007

■ **October 2–4**
A second summit of the two Koreas is held in P'yŏngyang.

◆ **Chapter 1: Articles 1–8**
The first chapter addresses reconciliation between the nations in eight articles. These articles acknowledge the differing character and systems of the separate nations and the need to avoid interference in the internal workings of the respective systems. There is no suggestion that reconciliation would necessarily alter or affect the existing governments. The nations agree to avoid actions of hostility, from simple slander to acts of sabotage or insurrection, and

North Korean leader Kim Jong-il (left) and South Korean President Kim Dae-jung shake hands at the start of a summit between the two countries in June 2000. (AP/Wide World Photos)

recognize the need to conform to the existing Military Armistice Agreement until such time as a true peace could be affirmed. On several occasions North Korea had suggested it might no longer honor that agreement.

Being aware of the need to maintain an attitude of agreement, both parties acknowledge the need to cease any confrontations (primarily raids across the border) and to promote the racial dignity of the Korean people within the international community. To ensure this cooperation, a South-North Liaison Office would be opened at the old 1953 treaty site of Panmunjom, in the demilitarized zone, within three months of the agreement. Moreover, a South-North Political Committee would consider valid and pragmatic means to implement reconciliation.

◆ Chapter 2: Articles 9–14

Chapter 2, consisting of six articles, addresses problems of aggression between the nations. Significant border clashes had begun shortly after the post–World War II division of Korea and continued after the Korean War. Significant to working out any agreement was the need to end such clashes, and Article 9 states that neither side would thenceforth use force or attempt military aggression. While the precise natures of prohibited acts are not

described in detail, both sides were well aware of specific incidents and realized the mutual costs if exaggerated military preparations were to continue. Such disagreements as might be bound to occur would be dealt with by negotiations. For the purpose of definitively identifying their respective territories so as to avert territorial military actions, the nations agreed to accept the Military Demarcation Line set up by the Military Armistice Agreement of July 27, 1953.

To monitor the proposed nonaggression, a South-North Joint Military Commission would be set up to discuss problems as they might arise. Paramount would be mutual notification of military movements, exercises, and utilization of the Korean Demilitarized Zone. Reductions in arms and armaments, including the elimination of weapons of mass destruction and the verification of such reductions, are a stated priority. Communication would be maintained by the installation of a telephone line between the military authorities, so as to prevent accidental clashes or escalation of unexpected events. Associated with this link would be the creation of a South-North Military Subcommittee to further discuss and implement the agreements on nonaggression and to resolve the state of military confrontation.

◆ Chapter 3: Articles 15–23

The nine articles of Chapter 3 concern exchanges and cooperation between South and North Korea. Seeking to balance the national economies, the nations agree to economic exchanges, trade agreements, and the joint development of resources, with overall focus on inter-Korean commerce and joint ventures. Exchanges would be carried out in the fields of science, technology, education, literature, the arts, health, sports, the environment, journalism, and the media, including print, radio, and television.

Perhaps most important to the people of the two nations, the agreement calls for the implementation of inter-Korean travel and contact among the Korean people, allowing for the possible unification of families that had been separated for decades. In particular, freedom of correspondence and the movement of individuals between states would be allowed, and reunions among families would be promoted. Along these lines, the agreement calls for the reconnection of railways and roads previously closed and for the opening of sea and air routes. Link facilities for post and telecommunication would be established, and the confidentiality of inter-Korean communications would be ensured. The united Koreas would together be involved in international economic, cultural, and societal activities.

As with the previous chapters, the nations seek a means to implement this chapter's aspects of the agreement and so call for the establishment of a joint commission in each significant field, including, within three months, a Joint South-North Economic Exchanges and Cooperation Commission. A Subcommittee on South-North Exchanges and Cooperation, to operate within the extended framework of the South-North High-Level Negotiations, would be set up to discuss concrete measures to achieve the implications of this part of the agreement.

◆ Chapter 4: Articles 24–25

In the last chapter, made up of just two articles, the signing parties acknowledge that the agreement could be amended or supplemented by mutual agreement. The agreement would be enforced from the date that both sides complete the respective procedures necessary for its implementation.

Audience

There appear to have been at least three audiences for which this document was designed. The degree to which any might have been more significant in certain respects than the others is hard to determine, but the two nations had definite expectations. The first audience was the governments themselves, the second the Korean people in both nations, and the third the international community.

Through the negotiations the governments involved were trying to work out their own policies, to see what the other nation was willing to consider, and to test the limitations on what they might gain from a closer relationship. Nothing about the armistice settlement of 1953 provided guidelines for reconciliation, and both nations—essentially wanting

A North Korean soldier looks at the South Korean side through a telescope at his checkpoint near the truce village of Panmunjom in the demilitarized zone that separates the two Koreas. (AP/Wide World Photos)

the same conclusion but on the basis of different agendas—were still trying to define their diplomatic stances.

Thus, the agreement that resulted was part posturing, part instructing, and part pacifying, all directed toward the Korean people. In terms of posturing, the primary delegates from the two nations saw the need to present themselves as reasonable men in search of a meaningful solution to a mutual problem. As such, the agreement was designed to instruct the populace on what they might expect from any reconciliation agreement, perhaps dampening any expectations for too much while softening any potential disillusion over what could be perceived as too little. Indeed, both nations were concerned with rising feelings among their own people. People in the south—perhaps more than in the north—were tired of family separation and fearful of yet another peninsula war. North Korea needed to take into consideration the high proportion of its people living in poverty, imposed at least in part by military expenditures and left unresolved owing to military paranoia, which left the nation isolated in the international community.

The third audience would have been the international community. For North Korea, there was a need to present rational desires and peaceful intents, to agree to limitations on military aggressiveness, to suggest an opening up that would encourage fewer international restraints, and to gain access to markets for both imports and exports. North Korea especially needed to maintain relations of some sort with neighboring Communist China and Russia, for otherwise it would risk enduring a problematic degree of isolation. In South Korea, the government and people were concerned with maintaining a balance between national and Pan-Kore-

"South and North Korea shall recognize and respect the system of each other."

(Chapter 1, Article 1)

"In order to implement and guarantee nonaggression, the South and the North shall establish a South-North Joint Military Commission within three months of the entry into force of this Agreement. In the said Commission, the two sides shall discuss problems and carry out steps to build up military confidence and realize arms reduction."

(Chapter 2, Article 12)

"South and North Korea shall permit free correspondence, movement between the two sides, meetings, and visits between dispersed family members and other relatives, promote their voluntary reunion, and take measures to resolve other humanitarian issues."

(Chapter 3, Article 18)

an loyalties and with retaining friends in the West; the nation esteemed its role as arbitrator and peacemaker.

Impact

It might be easy to downplay the significance of this agreement since, in reality, as of early 2010 the agreement had not been officially implemented and had meanwhile been violated on numerous occasions by both North Korea and South Korea. But the agreement has served other purposes and, most important, remains as concrete evidence of a basic desire on the part of the Koreas to find some means for the unification of their nations. As such, it has played a key role in sustaining the desire, if not the immediate intention, to work toward such reconciliation.

Produced in association with the agreement signed in December 1991 was a second document on denuclearization, which in the main seemed to be advancing significant goals of the initialed agreement but at the same time turned out to be a major blockage of the implementation of the preceding document. This was the Joint Declaration of the Denuclearization of the Korean Peninsula, signed on January 20, 1992, and designed to become effective along with the earlier agreement as of February 19, 1992. Its purpose was to eliminate the danger of nuclear war through denuclearization of the Korean Peninsula, which was to be

accomplished by the mutual promise that neither side should test, manufacture, produce, receive, possess, store, deploy, or at all use nuclear weapons. It reaffirmed that nuclear energy was to be used solely for peaceful purposes, with neither side possessing nuclear-reprocessing or uranium-enrichment facilities. The declaration also carried with it the requirement that both sides should be able to inspect areas in the other nation to ensure agreement; this provision would be carried out by the establishment and operation of a South-North Joint Nuclear Control Commission, to be put in place within one month of the implementation.

This declaration, too, was signed by Chung Won-shik, prime minister of South Korea, and Yon Hyong-muk, premier of the Administration Council of North Korea. But even as it was signed, there were reasons to believe that North Korea was involved in some form of nuclear weapons production. The United States declared its suspicion of this intention, particularly after North Korea announced its intention to withdraw from the Nuclear Non-proliferation Treaty on March 12, 1993. North Korea subsequently linked the issue to national pride, causing both Koreas to pull back from the agreement they had reasoned through together and raising questions once again about foreign interference.

A serious change occurred in South Korea during the launching of the Kim Dae-jung administration in February 1998. The new administration signaled a rather drastic change in the Republic of Korea's policy toward its neighbor to the north, an approach that became known as the Sunshine Policy. The policy was based on three principles—ones that had been worked out in the 1992 Agreement on Reconciliation—that went a long way toward addressing diplomatic concerns on both sides. They included the deterrence of armed aggression, the rejection of any reconciliation based on the idea of absorption (that is, that the south would somehow absorb the north), and the realization of reconciliation and cooperation.

There were some responses to this policy on the part of North Korea and even a meeting between Kim Jong-il, chairman of the National Defense Commission, and President Kim Dae-jung on June 15, 2000, from which was issued a joint declaration outlining plans to reunite separated families and to engage in inter-Korean exchanges and cooperation. This announcement suggested that the 1992 agreement was still a significant basis for political consideration. Furthermore, in 2000 North Korea issued a brief pledge to work toward implementation of the 1992 agreement. Mention of the agreement was significant, since such a reference had been conspicuously absent for several years. Some hope was rekindled—but by 2001 North Korea began to slow the pace of inter-Korean talks once again.

An interesting aside to the existence of the 1992 agreement and its provisions came out of May 2002 meetings of the North Korean leader Kim Jong-il and the Chinese leadership. For years North Korea had been calling for reunification on the basis of a "one nation, one country, two states,

two governments" formula for a north-south confederation. However, a presentation held after Kim Jong-il's visit to China made reference to "one nation, one state, two systems, two governments," a subtle and interesting difference. Some commentators believe the revision might be nothing more than Chinese editorial difficulties—but if any nation is going to have an impact on North Korea's willingness to discuss reconciliation further, it will be the Chinese. Much of China's previous two-Koreas policy was based in part on keeping North Korea as a viable buffer state.

In the wake of the first years of the Sunshine Policy, hopes cooled considerably, and tensions increased dramatically. North Korea's apparent efforts to develop nuclear weapons—and its successful test launch of a two-stage rocket capable of carrying a nuclear weapon in August 1998—in the wake of the 2000 inter-Korean summit undermined much of the hope for success. Most significant, however, appears to be the fact that the nuclear crisis has brought the United States back as a critical partner in the debates, which, owing to North Korean objections, may actually make it more difficult to bring about more talk of reconciliation.

The 1992 agreement and much of the language since have focused on the basic principle of one people, not one state. For some, this suggests that the ultimate solution, if one is to be found, will come from the people. The disunity of the Korean family is a force with pragmatic implications that may well be more powerful than the individual nations. Addressing that disunity, the South Korean president Lee

Questions for Further Study

1. Using this document in combination with the Korean Declaration of Independence, trace the history of Korea in the twentieth and twenty-first centuries with emphasis on its role in world affairs.

2. Like Korea, Vietnam was divided between a Communist North and a (supposedly) democratic South. Compare the circumstances surrounding the divisions of the two countries, using this document and the events surrounding the Declaration of Independence of the Democratic Republic of Vietnam. Why has Vietnam become a single (Communist) nation, while Korea has remained divided?

3. South Korea is regarded as a leading democratic nation and growing economic powerhouse, while North Korea is widely regarded as a rogue nation where people live in poverty under a secretive and erratic Communist dictatorship. What, then, explains the desire of the South Koreans to achieve some sort of reconciliation with the North? Do you think that North Koreans share similar aspirations?

4. Why, specifically, does the West, along with South Korea, oppose the presence of nuclear weapons on the Korean Peninsula? How has North Korea, in the view of the West, disrupted the balance of power in the region by testing nuclear weapons?

5. What role have the United States and China played in Korean affairs in recent decades? Why do these two nations play such a role?

Myung-bak reaffirmed in May 2008 that his nation would continue honoring existing inter-Korean projects and delivering shipments of humanitarian aid to North Korea, without regard to the ever-present nuclear controversy. North Korea, despite its public belligerence, remained desperately poor and could only profit from the easing of tensions and the improvement of relations. While neither the 1972 communiqué nor the 1992 Agreement on Reconciliation has ever been implemented—and, in fact, both have been blatantly violated on numerous occasions, fomenting intense rivalry—North and South Korea have at least remained at peace for more than fifty years. It has been a difficult and very nervous peace, but it has been peace nonetheless.

Further Reading

■ Articles

Kim, Jong-bae. "A Critique of the Chinese Theory of 'One History Shared by Two States' as Applied to Koguryo History." *Journal of Inner and Eastern Asian Studies* 3, no. 1 (June 2006): 5–26.

Kim, Kook-shin. "Political Future of the Korean Peninsula: A New Challenge to Unification." *International Journal of Korean Studies* 5, no. 2 (Fall/Winter 2001): 141–156.

Snyder, Scott. "South Korea's Squeeze Play." *Washington Quarterly* 28, no. 4 (Autumn 2005): 93–106.

■ Books

Cumings, Bruce. "Division, War, Reconciliation." In *Modern Korean Society: Its Development and Prospect*, eds. Hyuk-rae Kim and Bok Song. Berkeley: Institute of East Asian Studies, University of California, 2007.

Oberdorfer, Don. *The Two Koreas: A Contemporary History*. New York: Basic Books, 2002.

Oh, Kongdan, and Ralph C. Hassig. *Korea Briefing, 2000–2001: First Steps Toward Reconciliation and Reunification*. Armonk, N.Y.: M. E. Sharpe, 2001.

■ Web Sites

Feffer, John. "Progress on the Korean Peninsula?" *Foreign Policy in Focus* 5, no. 41 (2000). Foreign Policy in Focus Web site. http://www.fpif.org/briefs/vol5/v5n41korea.html.

—Paul Edwards

AGREEMENT ON RECONCILIATION BETWEEN SOUTH AND NORTH KOREA

South and North Korea,

In keeping with the longing of the entire Korean race for the peaceful unification of our divided fatherland;

Reaffirming the three basic principles of unification set forth in the South-North Joint Communiqué of July 4, 1972;

Determined to end the state of political and military confrontation and achieve national reconciliation;

Also determined to avoid armed aggression and hostilities, and to ensure the lessening of tension and the establishment of peace;

Expressing the desire to realize multi-faceted exchanges and cooperation to promote interests and prosperity common to the Korean people;

Recognizing that their relationship, not being a relationship as between states, is a special one constituted temporarily in the process of unification;

Pledging themselves to exert joint efforts to achieve peaceful unification;

Hereby agreed as follows:

◆ Chapter 1. South-North Reconciliation

Article 1
South and North Korea shall recognize and respect the system of each other.

Article 2
South and North Korea shall not interfere in the internal affairs of each other.

Article 3
South and North Korea shall not slander or defame each other.

Article 4
South and North Korea shall refrain from any acts of sabotage or insurrection against each other.

Article 5
South and North Korea shall together endeavour to transform the present state of armistice into a firm state of peace between the two sides and shall abide by the present Military Armistice Agreement until such a state of peace is realized.

Article 6
South and North Korea shall cease to compete with or confront each other, and instead shall cooperate and endeavour to promote the racial dignity and interests of Korea in the international arena.

Article 7
South and North Korea shall establish and operate a South-North Liaison Office at Panmunjom within three months of the entry into force of this Agreement to ensure close liaison and consultations between the two sides.

Article 8
South and North Korea shall establish a South-North Political Committee within the framework of the South-North High-Level Negotiations within one month of the entry into force of this Agreement to consider concrete measures to ensure the implementation and observance of the agreement on South-North reconciliation.

◆ Chapter 2. Agreement of Nonaggression between South and North Korea

Article 9
South and North Korea shall not use force against each other and shall not undertake armed aggression against each other.

Article 10
South and North Korea shall resolve peacefully, through dialogue and negotiation, any differences of views and disputes arising between them.

Article 11
The South-North demarcation line and the areas for nonaggression shall be identical with the Military Demarcation Line provided in the Military Armistice Agreement of July 27, 1953, and the areas that each side has exercised jurisdiction over until the present time.

Article 12
In order to implement and guarantee nonaggression, the South and the North shall establish a South-North Joint Military Commission within three months of the entry into force of this Agreement. In the said Commission, the two sides shall discuss problems and carry out steps to build up military confidence and realize arms reduction, in particular, the mutual notification and control of large-scale movements of military units and major military exercises, the peaceful utilization of the Demilitarized Zone, exchanges of military personnel and information, phased reductions in armaments including the elimination of weapons of

mass destruction and attack capabilities, and verifications thereof.

Article 13

South and North Korea shall install and operate a telephone line between the military authorities of each side to prevent the outbreak and escalation of accidental armed clashes.

Article 14

South and North Korea shall establish a South-North Military Sub-Committee within the framework of the South-North High-Level Negotiations within one month of the entry into force of this Agreement to discuss concrete measures for the implementation and observance of the agreement on nonaggression and to remove the state of military confrontation.

◆ **Chapter 3. Exchanges and Cooperation Between South and North Korea**

Article 15

In order to promote the integrated and balanced development of the national economy and the welfare of the entire people, the South and the North shall engage in economic exchanges and cooperation, including the joint development of resources, the trade of goods as intra-Korean commerce and joint ventures.

Article 16

South and North Korea shall carry out exchanges and promote cooperation in various fields such as science and technology, education, literature and the arts, health, sports, the environment, journalism and media including newspapers, radio, television broadcasts, and other publications.

Article 17

South and North Korea shall implement freedom of intra-Korean travel and contact among the members of the Korean people.

Article 18

South and North Korea shall permit free correspondence, movement between the two sides, meetings, and visits between dispersed family members and other relatives, promote their voluntary reunion, and take measures to resolve other humanitarian issues.

Article 19

South and North Korea shall reconnect the railway and the previously severed roads, and shall open sea and air routes.

Article 20

South and North Korea shall establish and link facilities for exchanges by post and telecommunications, and shall guarantee the confidentiality of intra-Korean mail and telecommunications.

Article 21

South and North Korea shall cooperate in the international arena in the economic, cultural and other fields, and shall advance abroad together.

Article 22

In order to implement the agreement on exchanges and cooperation in the economic, cultural, and other fields, South and North Korea shall establish joint commissions for each sector, including a Joint South-North Economic Exchanges and Cooperation Commission, within three months of the entry into force of this Agreement.

Article 23

A Sub-committee on South-North Exchanges and Cooperation shall be established within the framework of the South-North High-Level Negotiations within one month of the entry into force of this Agreement, to discuss concrete measures for the implementation and observance of the agreement on South-North exchanges and cooperation.

◆ **Chapter 4. Amendments and Effectuation**

Article 24

This Agreement may be amended or supplemented by agreement between the two sides.

Article 25

This Agreement shall enter into force from the date the South and the North exchange the appropriate instruments following the completion of the respective procedures necessary for its implementation.

Signed on December 13, 1991

Chung Won-shik

Chief Delegate of the South delegation to the South-North High-Level Negotiations

Yon Hyong-muk

Head of the North delegation to the South-North High-Level Negotiations

Premier of the Administration Council of the Democratic People's Republic of Korea

TREATY ON EUROPEAN UNION

"This Treaty marks a new stage in the process of creating an ever closer union among the peoples of Europe."

Overview

Upon its signing in 1992, the Treaty on European Union, also known as the Maastricht Treaty, provided the framework for the multinational polity called the European Union (EU). The treaty was a pivotal effort by the European nations to unify politically so as to increase the region's economic integration and establish joint policies on the environment, defense, citizenship, justice, health care, transportation, and the like. The treaty called for the creation of a single currency, originally the European Currency Unit, which was later reborn as the euro, and for the establishment of a central bank that would coordinate monetary policies among the member nations. By eliminating tariffs on goods imported from one EU country to another and by relaxing border and immigration policies, the treaty—in line with its predecessor treaties—made Europeans freer to work, live, study, travel, and purchase goods and services in any of the EU's member states.

In late 1991 the heads of government of the EU's twelve original member states approved the treaty, which was then signed in early 1992 in the Dutch city of Maastricht. The twelve founding nations were Belgium, Denmark, France, Germany, Greece, Ireland, Italy, Luxembourg, the Netherlands, Portugal, Spain, and the United Kingdom. The treaty required the approval of voters in each of the member states, and while there was widespread support for the treaty's goals, many European voters were reluctant to give up control of their economies. Voters in Denmark initially opposed the treaty by a narrow margin, but in a later vote, in May 1993, they reversed course and approved it. Britain, too, proved resistant to some of the treaty's provisions, and that nation, along with Sweden, did not support a common currency; while the euro was in use in sixteen EU nations as of 2010, Britain continued to use the pound, while Sweden retained the krona.

After the ratification process was complete, the EU, with headquarters in Brussels, Belgium, was established in late 1993. From its original membership of twelve nations, the EU expanded to twenty-seven nations over the ensuing fifteen years. Austria, Finland, and Sweden joined in 1995.

In 2001 the Treaty of Nice (France), addressed issues related to the expansion of the union. Accordingly, ten more countries—Cyprus, the Czech Republic, Estonia, Hungary, Latvia, Lithuania, Malta, Poland, Slovakia, and Slovenia—joined in 2004, and Romania and Bulgaria joined in 2007.

Context

For some fifteen hundred years, beginning with the collapse of the Roman Empire and culminating with World War II, the nations of Europe were intermittently at war with one another. Throughout that span of time, such historical figures as Charlemagne, Napoléon Bonaparte, and Adolf Hitler tried to unite Europe into a single political entity, but these efforts failed in part because they were based on force rather than cooperation. In the first decades of the twentieth century, European powers such as the Austro-Hungarian Empire, Germany, England, and France remained distrustful of one another and would have rejected out of hand the notion of ceding authority to a supranational body.

The horrors of the twentieth century's two world wars, however, led to changes in thinking. National leaders finally accepted that some sort of political union would be necessary to eliminate future wars. They also recognized that Europe, fragmented into numerous small nations, all with different policies, currencies, and so forth, would be unable to compete economically with the United States unless the nations pooled their resources. Among the first countries to recognize the potential benefits of political unity were Belgium, the Netherlands, and Luxembourg, three smaller nations in northwestern Europe that agreed to cooperate in matters of trade, tariffs, and economics through the formation of the Benelux Customs Union in 1948 (with the word *Benelux* coined from the opening letters of the three nations' names). This union evolved into the Benelux Economic Union in 1960.

In 1950 proposals for the formation of a unified coal and steel community were made, to join the coal and steel industries of France and West Germany. (Communist East Germany would not be included.) The motives were as much political as economic, for as the West German econ-

1948

- **January 1**
The Benelux Customs Union is formed by Belgium, the Netherlands, and Luxembourg.

1952

- **July 24**
The European Coal and Steel Community (ECSC)—encompassing France, West Germany, the Benelux countries, and Italy—is formed.

1957

- **March 25**
The Treaties of Rome are signed, forming the European Atomic Energy Community (Euratom) and the European Economic Community.

1967

- **July 1**
The ECSC, Euratom, and the European Economic Community are merged into a single organization, the European Community.

1986

- **February 17**
The European Council signs the Single European Act, which takes force in 1987.

1992

- **February 7**
The Treaty on European Union is signed.

omy revived after World War II, France wanted to keep an eye on its neighbor and former enemy, especially since coal and steel are central to the armaments industry. West Germany eagerly joined with France and also the Benelux nations and Italy, and the treaty forming the European Coal and Steel Community (ECSC) was signed in 1951, with the organization beginning operations the following year. The formation of the ECSC was a crucial step; for the first time, major European powers submitted themselves to a supranational body of ministers and a court of justice that would adjudicate disputes.

A breakthrough step occurred in 1957, when the ECSC nations signed the Treaties of Rome. These treaties formed the European Atomic Energy Community, or Euratom, and, most important, the European Economic Community, informally referred to as the Common Market. The chief feature of the Common Market was that it sharply reduced tariffs and import duties on products shipped from one member nation to another. It also allowed the member nations to create common policies on a range of matters, including transportation and agriculture. Other nations were invited to join, but Great Britain expressed reluctance and instead persuaded Norway, Sweden, Denmark, Switzerland, Austria, and Portugal to join it in the formation of the European Free Trade Association. In 1961 Great Britain reexamined its position and sought membership in the European Economic Community, but its membership was blocked by the French president Charles de Gaulle, who objected to England's close ties with the United States.

Yet another step toward European integration was taken in 1967 when the ECSC, Euratom, and the European Economic Community merged into a single organization, the European Community (EC). The EC featured a common financing system and developed a framework for cooperation in foreign policy. Discussions were soon held about expanding membership, and in 1973 the United Kingdom, Ireland, and Denmark joined, though the people of Norway rejected membership.

Despite the enhanced degree of economic and political cooperation of the EC, it faced numerous problems. The admission of Greece, Spain, and Portugal proved problematic because those nations were not as economically advanced as the original members. Britain was not always an especially cooperative member of the EC because it was unwilling to cede its independence to an international body. Additionally, questions were raised about the funding of the EC and how its resources were to be distributed. Accordingly, in 1986, the European Council, consisting of the EC nations' heads of state, signed the Single European Act, which took force in 1987. The purpose of this act was to amend earlier treaties to create a single economic market, form common economic and fiscal policies, and adopt shared policies on taxes, health, employment, and the environment.

The most significant step yet in the process of European integration was the signing of the Treaty on European Union and the formation of the EU. This step was taken in response to the massive changes in Europe of the late 1980s and early 1990s. Chief among these changes were the collapse of the Soviet Union, the fall of the Berlin Wall (which had divided East and West Berlin) and reunification of Germany, and the gaining of independence by the Eastern European nations that had been part of the Soviet bloc. Many of these latter nations were economically underdeveloped, so they immediately looked to the European Community for financial help. As all these developments progressed, France and West Germany called for a conference to propose ways to augment European unity. The result of their deliberations was the Treaty on European Union and the consequent formation of the EU. The treaty was approved in December 1991; signed on February 7, 1992; and, after being ratified by the member states, took effect on November 1, 1993.

About the Author

No individual, or even any small group of individuals, wrote the Treaty on European Union. The treaty is a lengthy legal document that consists in large part of revisions and amendments to earlier agreements, particularly that of the ECSC. Many of these revisions are minor, involving the insertion or alteration of words and phrases, while others are more substantial. These revisions and amendments, as well as new provisions, were negotiated among the member nations, with government officials, jurists, trade negotiators, and their staffs meeting and agreeing on the revisions and new policies falling within their various areas of expertise. All of this activity took place under the authority and supervision of the heads of state (either monarchs or presidents) of each of the member countries. These heads of state designated plenipotentiaries, or diplomats empowered to conduct business, who signed the treaty. In every case, the diplomat was a minister of foreign affairs, a minister of finance (or the treasury), or a secretary of state.

Explanation and Analysis of the Document

The Maastricht Treaty is not easy reading. It functions in part as a constitution for the EU, laying out goals and principles that govern the union's operations. It also functions as a kind of handbook, specifying policies and procedures, though in most cases the details of these policies and procedures still had to be worked out by the EU's agencies. Much of the treaty consists of amendments to earlier treaties, such as the one governing the ECSC, and a number of its provisions simply incorporate other agreements and treaties signed earlier by the member nations. Thus, it is a document that few people would actually read from beginning to end; rather, it is the type of document that people would consult, if necessary, to seek guidance on particular issues that might arise.

It is nonetheless possible to discern certain themes and principles in the document. Its early portions focus on the

Time Line

1993

■ **November 1**
The Treaty on European Union takes effect.

1995

■ **January 1**
Austria, Finland, and Sweden join the EU.

1997

■ **October 2**
The Treaty of Amsterdam, revising the Treaty on European Union, is signed.

1999

■ **January 1**
The Economic and Monetary Union of the European Union begins to take effect, with the euro replacing the currencies of most of the EU's member nations.

2001

■ **February 26**
The Treaty of Nice, addressing procedure for enlarging the EU, is signed, to take effect on February 1, 2003.

2004

■ **May 1**
Cyprus, the Czech Republic, Estonia, Hungary, Latvia, Lithuania, Malta, Poland, Slovakia, and Slovenia join the EU.

2007

■ **January 1**
Romania and Bulgaria join the EU.

Time Line

2009

■ **December 1**
The Treaty of
Lisbon, amend-
ing the Treaty
on European
Union, takes
effect.

overarching goals of the treaty. The opening resolutions and commitments enumerate these goals as they apply to member nations: "the ending of the division of the European continent," "the strengthening and the convergence of their economies," the promotion of "economic and social progress," the implementation of "a common foreign and security policy," and the creation of "an ever closer union among the peoples of Europe." These and similar goals all emphasize the commonality of purpose among the member states.

In sum, the provisions of the Treaty on European Union provide a framework for the establishment of what is often called the "pillar system." This system consists of three "pillars," or areas in which EU members cooperate. Central to the system is the European Community pillar, with its supranational functions and variety of institutions that govern the EU. The second pillar is the Common Foreign and Security Policy, and the third pillar was originally known as Justice and Home Affairs but is now called Police and Judicial Cooperation in Criminal Matters. Above these three pillars sits the European Council, through which leaders of EU member states meet, although the council is not an EU institution. The council is rather a negotiating body that shapes the policies that the union adopts. It thus fosters the process of integration in allowing member nations some say over the EU's decisions.

◆ **Title I: "Common Provisions"**
Under Title I, the treaty enumerates more particular goals of the union. Among these goals are promoting economic and social progress through high levels of employment, achieving "balanced and sustainable development," strengthening "economic and social cohesion," asserting the EU's position "on the international scene," introducing union citizenship as a way of protecting people's rights and interests, and allowing "free movement of persons." Another goal is that of maintaining the union's *acquis communautaire*—a French term meaning "that which has been acquired by the community." This refers to the total body of EU law, organized into thirty-one chapters for the 2007 accession of Romania and Bulgaria (and later into thirty-five chapters for negotiations for the future accession of Croatia and Turkey), with titles such as "Free Movement of Goods," "Free Movement of Persons," "Science and Research," "Energy," and "Environment."

The first title goes on to specify the mechanisms by which the EU will operate. Among these mechanisms are

the European Council (consisting of the heads of state of the member nations), the European Commission (the executive arm of the EU, responsible for proposing laws, implementing policies, and supervising the ongoing functions of the EU), the Court of Justice, and the Court of Auditors. Acting as a constitution, the treaty specifies the voting procedures of the European Council. Although the council has no formal executive or legislative powers, it is the highest-ranking body with respect to the EU and advises the union on any issues that come before it.

◆ **Title V: "Provisions on a Common Foreign and Security Policy"**
Title V deals with security and foreign policy issues. As the key purpose of the treaty is to promote common interests and common policies, Title V begins with a statement of overarching goals: "to safeguard the common values, fundamental interests, independence and integrity of the Union"; "to strengthen the security of the Union"; "to preserve peace and strengthen international security"; "to promote international cooperation"; and "to develop and consolidate democracy and the rule of law, and respect for human rights and fundamental freedoms." The treaty is not a defense pact, as is the North Atlantic Treaty Organization, but it leaves open the possibility that such a pact may be formed in the future. Here, the treaty calls for joint consultation and the adoption of common strategic policies with regard to security threats and foreign policy issues. Again, the treaty functions as a kind of constitution by outlining the specific procedures, particularly voting procedures, that will be followed by the European Commission in connection with any issue that has security or foreign policy implications. The treaty does not preclude any member nation from forming defense or security pacts with other member nations or with nations that are not part of the EU. It does, however, require that any such pact adhere to "the interests of the Union as a whole" and respect "the principles, objectives, general guidelines and consistency of the common foreign and security policy and the decisions taken within the framework of that policy, the powers of the European Community, and consistency between all the Union's policies and its external activities."

◆ **Title VI: "Provisions on Police and Judicial Cooperation in Criminal Matters"**
Title VI addresses criminal matters, where again a primary goal is to achieve higher levels of cooperation and information sharing among member states. A particular goal is the establishment of more uniform and consistent criminal codes, so that, for example, an action that merits a certain prison term in one nation will merit a similar prison term in all others. This title further expresses the intent of the union to combat "racism and xenophobia"; "crime, organised or otherwise"; terrorism; human trafficking; offenses against children; illicit drug and arms trafficking; corruption; and fraud. Prior to the Treaty on European Union, each nation was responsible for its own criminal investigations (though nations cooperated through such

The signing, on March 25, 1957, of the Treaties of Rome, creating the European Economic Community, the forerunner of the European Union (AP/Wide World Photos)

agencies as Interpol), and criminals could escape one jurisdiction by simply crossing a border. Enhanced cooperation would mean that criminals could not hide behind borders, for national police forces would have the ability to investigate crimes throughout the union, as supported by enhanced mechanisms for sharing information.

◆ Title VII: "Provisions on Enhanced Cooperation"

The last title excerpted here, Title VII, takes up the issue of member states that wish to establish any kind of agreement among themselves, outside the framework of the Treaty on European Union and the EU. Such an agreement "may be undertaken only as a last resort" and only when the objectives of such an agreement cannot be met by the EU. The treaty states that "Member States which intend to establish enhanced cooperation between themselves may make use of the institutions, procedures and mechanisms laid down by this Treaty and by the Treaty establishing the European Community." The treaty specifies that such cooperation must be "aimed at furthering the objectives of the Union and of the Community, at protecting and serving their interests and at reinforcing their process of integration." Such cooperation must also respect

the treaty and "the single institutional framework of the Union." It must likewise respect the *acquis communautaire* and cannot involve a matter outside "the limits of the powers of the Union or of the Community." It may not "undermine the internal market ... or the economic and social cohesion" established by the treaty. Any such agreement would also have to be open to all member states.

Audience

The Treaty on European Union is a legal document, so from its inception, its primary audience has consisted of government officials, government agencies, and their attorneys and advisers in each of the member states. Thus, for example, if the treasury of a member state wishes to propose a monetary or fiscal policy, it is obligated to consult the treaty to ensure that the proposal is consistent with the terms of the treaty—and only by adhering to the terms of the treaty can that nation realize the financial benefits the treaty offers. Another audience is the business and corporate community within the EU. A business proposing an expansion that would, for example, have a potential impact

Performers in front of the golden-domed cathedral Alexander Nevski in the Bulgarian capital Sofia, during the celebrations marking the country's accession to the European Union (AP/Wide World Photos)

on the environment would have to ensure, in consultation with the government and with its lawyers, that the expansion is allowable under the terms of the treaty and that all environmental concerns are met. In a larger sense, the treaty's audience was and is all of Europe and indeed the world. The treaty announced to the peoples of Europe and the world that EU nations were to be regarded no longer as a fragmented collection of nations, each pursuing its separate interests, but instead now as a larger, supranational entity with common goals and common policies. In relation to the global community, then, the treaty makes clear that the EU's purpose is, among other goals, "to assert its identity on the international scene, in particular through the implementation of a common foreign and security policy including the progressive framing of a common defence policy, which might lead to a common defence."

Impact

The path to the signing of the Treaty on European Union was not entirely smooth. Negotiations were often contentious, and while the majority of Europeans favored in principle the concept of greater cooperation, in practice many were reluctant to cede national autonomy, so the ratification votes tended to pass by narrow margins. Great Britain's refusal to adopt the euro, for example, was in part

the result of rational self-interest—Britain, with its robust economy, did not want its economic policies dictated by bureaucrats in Brussels—but also in part by sentiment and tradition, for it was thought that by relinquishing the pound as its currency, Britain would be relinquishing a portion of its identity. Some of the fears of the treaty's opponents were partially realized in the late 1990s when evidence came to light that the European Commission was not holding itself accountable to the people of Europe. Widespread charges of corruption, cronyism, and incompetence were leveled at the commission. Furthermore, the European Parliament, which, in contrast to the commission, is democratically elected by the people of Europe, came to be seen as a weak organization. In turn, many have objected to the power of the Court of Justice of the European Union, for in the application of law, EU law supersedes the laws of individual member nations. The upshot is that many Europeans feel that the Court of Justice can be heavy-handed in effectively crushing the laws and legal traditions of member nations.

Other observers have pointed to the weakness of the EU as established by the treaty. They note that the foundation of the treaty lies on such idealized concepts as "cooperation," but the effect of this emphasis on cooperation, for example, is that decisions often need to be unanimous. For instance, the Common Foreign and Security Policy pillar provides a forum in which foreign policy is discussed and proposals are

"*Recalling the historic importance of the ending of the division of the European continent and the need to create firm bases for the construction of the future Europe.*"

(Preamble)

"*By this Treaty, the High Contracting Parties establish among themselves a European Union, hereinafter called 'the Union.' This Treaty marks a new stage in the process of creating an ever closer union among the peoples of Europe, in which decisions are taken as openly as possible and as closely as possible to the citizen.*"

(Title I, Article 1)

"*The Union is founded on the principles of liberty, democracy, respect for human rights and fundamental freedoms, and the rule of law, principles which are common to the Member States.*"

(Title I, Article 6)

"*Enhanced cooperation ... shall be aimed at safeguarding the values and serving the interests of the Union as a whole by asserting its identity as a coherent force on the international scene. It shall respect: the principles, objectives, general guidelines and consistency of the common foreign and security policy and the decisions taken within the framework of that policy, the powers of the European Community, and consistency between all the Union's policies and its external activities.*"

(Title V, Article 27a)

"*The Union's objective shall be to provide citizens with a high level of safety within an area of freedom, security and justice by developing common action among the Member States in the fields of police and judicial cooperation in criminal matters and by preventing and combating racism and xenophobia.*"

(Title VI, Article 29)

made for united actions that enhance security and defense. The problem is that this pillar often fails in its endeavors. Some Europeans would like for the EU to develop its own common defense pact, but many argue in response that Europe is already protected by the North Atlantic Treaty Organization and that U.S. participation is needed for any defense posture to have teeth. This argument gained force when the nation of Yugoslavia disintegrated. Yugoslavia, which had been under the influence of the Soviet Union, was in many senses an artificial country, forged out of six republics: Bosnia and Herzegovina (often referred to simply as Bosnia), Croatia, Macedonia, Montenegro, Serbia, and Slovenia. Additionally, two autonomous provinces, Vojvodina and Kosovo, existed within Serbia. Ethnic tensions divided the country, and four of its six republics declared their independence in 1991–1992. The result was a period of civil warfare, and the EU seemed unequal to the task of confronting the crisis. The EU member states were unable to reach agreement on a course of action; some did not want to be drawn into a war against other Europeans. The international community intervened only when the United States and the North Atlantic Treaty Organization, acting under UN authority, conducted military operations in Bosnia. The 1997 Treaty of Amsterdam attempted to resolve the EU's inability to act, but again the union was expressing intent rather than taking concrete action.

Despite these weaknesses, the impact of the Treaty on European Union nd the formation of the EU was—and continues to be—profound and far reaching, particularly in the economic sphere. It has turned Europe into a single major trading bloc of nearly five hundred million people—a bloc whose size makes it more than able to compete effectively with similar trading blocs in North America and Asia. Collectively, the nations of the EU produce roughly 30 percent of the world's gross domestic product. The reduction of trade barriers and tariffs, the adoption of a common currency and common central bank policies, and the opening of borders have reduced frictions and inefficiencies, thus enabling Europe to make its voice heard in world affairs.

Supporters of the treaty and of the EU point to numerous advantages afforded by the treaty. They note, for example, that the Common Agricultural Policy created as a result of this and earlier treaties has benefited farmers and consumers by creating a single market for farm products and by protecting European farmers from external competition. The Common Fisheries Policy helps to prevent the overfishing of common waters. The European Investment Bank offers loans that promote economic development. Various agencies use pooled funds to help level out some of the economic disparities between the richer nations of northern and western Europe and the poorer nations of southern and eastern Europe.

Most important, the EU's Economic and Monetary Union led to the integration of monetary and budgetary policies, stabilizing currency values and interest rates. Prior to the introduction of the euro, considerable inefficiencies abounded, such as where currencies had to be constantly converted into one another. A corporation in France, for example, denominated its activities in the French franc. If the corporation had a factory in Germany or sold its products in Germany, it had to deal with fluctuating exchange rates between the franc and the German deutsche mark. And if that French-owned factory exported its German-

Questions for Further Study

1. What historical and economic factors motivated the nations of Europe to form the European Union?

2. By joining the European Union, nations give up some of their sovereignty in exchange for certain benefits. What do they give up, and what do they gain?

3. Some critics of the European Union argue that nations are forced to cede authority to "bureaucrats" in Brussels, Belgium, who may be insensitive or indifferent to the needs and traditions of member nations. Do you think this is so? Why or why not?

4. Assume that you are an average person who lives in one of the European Union's member nations. What do you think your attitude toward the treaty and the union would be? What personal circumstances might influence your attitude?

5. The European Union is in part a defense pact, but many observers suggest that as such it is ineffective. Why do they make this argument? If it were in your power, how would you change the EU to make it more effective as a means of defense?

made products to Italy, now the Italian lira and its fluctuating value in relation to both the franc and the deutsche mark introduced additional measures of uncertainty. The common currency of the euro, along with policies designed to curb inflation and stabilize interest rates across Europe, has eliminated many of the inefficiencies that sapped value from Europe's economies. It has also reduced the instability of currency speculation, whereby financial agents direct large currency flows across borders to take advantage of changes in exchange rates and interest rates. The process of introducing the euro was gradual. It was a "virtual" currency used for cashless transactions and accounting purposes beginning in 1999. Euro coins and banknotes were introduced in 2002. As of the end of 2009, sixteen nations were using the euro: Belgium, the Netherlands, Luxembourg, Finland, Ireland, Portugal, Spain, France, Italy, Germany, Austria, Slovakia, Slovenia, Greece, Cyprus, and Malta. Britain and Sweden opted out of using the euro, while the remaining EU members will adopt the euro after they have met certain economic conditions. At the end of 2009, one euro was worth about $1.50.

Other aspects of the EU benefit citizens more directly. A student from Germany who wishes to study in France or the Netherlands can do so without having to undergo time-consuming procedures allowing him or her to gain admission to a university in another country and, especially, to live there. People who live near borders can freely pass into neighboring countries for recreation or to shop without having to worry about exchange rates or carrying passports. And to the benefit of the European economy and world travelers alike, tourism has been greatly facilitated. Prior to the Treaty on European Union, a tourist traveling from country to country in Europe had to deal with a wallet or purse full of different currencies and had to constantly convert one currency into another. Delays were common at border crossings as passports had to be examined. Today, a tourist can fly into, say, Munich, Germany, rent a car, and pass into Austria on the way to Salzburg in much the same way that tourists in America can drive from state to state. Only one currency is necessary, and armed border guards are a thing of the past.

In December 2007 the member states of the EU signed the Treaty of Lisbon, which entered into force on December 1, 2009. The Treaty of Lisbon is an amendment to the Treaty on European Union intended to boost efficiency.

Among other changes, it gives a larger role to the European Parliament in the EU's legislative process and makes the EU human rights charter, the Charter of Fundamental Rights, binding on EU member states.

Further Reading

■ Articles

Garrett, Geoffrey. "The Politics of Maastricht." *Economics and Politics* 5, no. 2 (1993): 105–124.

Pollack, Mark A. "The End of Creeping Competence? EU Policy-Making since Maastricht." *Journal of Common Market Studies* 38, no. 3 (2000): 519–538.

■ Books

Bomberg, Elizabeth E., John Peterson, and Alexander Stubb, eds. *The European Union: How Does It Work?*, 2nd ed. New York: Oxford University Press, 2008.

Corbett, Richard. *The Treaty of Maastricht: From Conception to Ratification.* London: Longman, 1993.

Dinan, Desmond. *Europe Recast: A History of European Union.* Basingstoke, U.K.: Palgrave Macmillan, 2004.

Hix, Simon. *The Political System of the European Union*, 2nd ed. Basingstoke, U.K.: Palgrave Macmillian, 2005.

Hoebink, Paul, ed. *The Treaty of Maastricht and Europe's Development Co-operation.* Brussels, Belgium: European Union, 2005.

Urwin, Derek W. *The Community of Europe: A History of European Integration since 1945*, 2nd ed. New York: Longman, 1994.

■ Web Sites

"Europa: Gateway to the European Union." EUROPA Web site. http://europa.eu/index_en.htm.

"The World Bank and European Union." World Bank Web site. http://www.worldbank.org/eu.

—Michael J. O'Neal

TREATY ON EUROPEAN UNION

HIS MAJESTY THE KING OF THE BELGIANS, HER MAJESTY THE QUEEN OF DENMARK, THE PRESIDENT OF THE FEDERAL REPUBLIC OF GERMANY, THE PRESIDENT OF THE HELLENIC REPUBLIC, HIS MAJESTY THE KING OF SPAIN, THE PRESIDENT OF THE FRENCH REPUBLIC, THE PRESIDENT OF IRELAND, THE PRESIDENT OF THE ITALIAN REPUBLIC, HIS ROYAL HIGHNESS THE GRAND DUKE OF LUXEMBOURG, HER MAJESTY THE QUEEN OF THE NETHERLANDS, THE PRESIDENT OF THE PORTUGUESE REPUBLIC, HER MAJESTY THE QUEEN OF THE UNITED KINGDOM OF GREAT BRITAIN AND NORTHERN IRELAND,

RESOLVED to mark a new stage in the process of European integration undertaken with the establishment of the European Communities,

RECALLING the historic importance of the ending of the division of the European continent and the need to create firm bases for the construction of the future Europe,

CONFIRMING their attachment to the principles of liberty, democracy and respect for human rights and fundamental freedoms and of the rule of law,

CONFIRMING their attachment to fundamental social rights as defined in the European Social Charter signed at Turin on 18 October 1961 and in the 1989 Community Charter of the Fundamental Social Rights of Workers,

DESIRING to deepen the solidarity between their peoples while respecting their history, their culture and their traditions,

DESIRING to enhance further the democratic and efficient functioning of the institutions so as to enable them better to carry out, within a single institutional framework, the tasks entrusted to them,

RESOLVED to achieve the strengthening and the convergence of their economies and to establish an economic and monetary union including, in accordance with the provisions of this Treaty, a single and stable currency,

DETERMINED to promote economic and social progress for their peoples, taking into account the principle of sustainable development and within the context of the accomplishment of the internal market and of reinforced cohesion and environmental protection, and to implement policies ensuring that advances in economic integration are accompanied by parallel progress in other fields,

RESOLVED to establish a citizenship common to nationals of their countries,

RESOLVED to implement a common foreign and security policy including the progressive framing of a common defence policy, which might lead to a common defence in accordance with the provisions of Article 17, thereby reinforcing the European identity and its independence in order to promote peace, security and progress in Europe and in the world,

RESOLVED to facilitate the free movement of persons, while ensuring the safety and security of their peoples, by establishing an area of freedom, security and justice, in accordance with the provisions of this Treaty,

RESOLVED to continue the process of creating an ever closer union among the peoples of Europe, in which decisions are taken as closely as possible to the citizen in accordance with the principle of subsidiarity,

IN VIEW of further steps to be taken in order to advance European integration,

HAVE DECIDED to establish a European Union and to this end have designated as their Plenipotentiaries:

[List of plenipotentiaries not reproduced]

WHO, having exchanged their full powers, found in good and due form, have agreed as follows.

Title I. Common Provisions

◆ Article 1

By this Treaty, the HIGH CONTRACTING PARTIES establish among themselves a EUROPEAN UNION, hereinafter called "the Union."

This Treaty marks a new stage in the process of creating an ever closer union among the peoples of Europe, in which decisions are taken as openly as possible and as closely as possible to the citizen.

The Union shall be founded on the European Communities, supplemented by the policies and forms of cooperation established by this Treaty. Its task shall be to organise, in a manner demonstrating consistency and solidarity, relations between the Member States and between their peoples.

Article 2

The Union shall set itself the following objectives:

—to promote economic and social progress and a high level of employment and to achieve balanced and sustainable development, in particular through the creation of an area without internal frontiers, through the strengthening of economic and social cohesion and through the establishment of economic and monetary union, ultimately including a single currency in accordance with the provisions of this Treaty,

—to assert its identity on the international scene, in particular through the implementation of a common foreign and security policy including the progressive framing of a common defence policy, which might lead to a common defence, in accordance with the provisions of Article 17,

—to strengthen the protection of the rights and interests of the nationals of its Member States through the introduction of a citizenship of the Union,…

—to maintain and develop the Union as an area of freedom, security and justice, in which the free movement of persons is assured in conjunction with appropriate measures with respect to external border controls, asylum, immigration and the prevention and combating of crime,

—to maintain in full the *acquis communautaire* and build on it with a view to considering to what extent the policies and forms of cooperation introduced by this Treaty may need to be revised with the aim of ensuring the effectiveness of the mechanisms and the institutions of the Community.

The objectives of the Union shall be achieved as provided in this Treaty and in accordance with the conditions and the timetable set out therein while respecting the principle of subsidiarity as defined in Article 5 of the Treaty establishing the European Community.

Article 3

The Union shall be served by a single institutional framework which shall ensure the consistency and the continuity of the activities carried out in order to attain its objectives while respecting and building upon the *acquis communautaire*.

The Union shall in particular ensure the consistency of its external activities as a whole in the context of its external relations, security, economic and development policies. The Council and the Commission shall be responsible for ensuring such consistency and shall cooperate to this end. They shall ensure the implementation of these policies, each in accordance with its respective powers.

Article 4

The European Council shall provide the Union with the necessary impetus for its development and shall define the general political guidelines thereof.

The European Council shall bring together the Heads of State or Government of the Member States and the President of the Commission. They shall be assisted by the Ministers for Foreign Affairs of the Member States and by a Member of the Commission. The European Council shall meet at least twice a year, under the chairmanship of the Head of State or Government of the Member State which holds the Presidency of the Council.

The European Council shall submit to the European Parliament a report after each of its meetings and a yearly written report on the progress achieved by the Union.

Article 5

The European Parliament, the Council, the Commission, the Court of Justice and the Court of Auditors shall exercise their powers under the conditions and for the purposes provided for, on the one hand, by the provisions of the Treaties establishing the European Communities and of the subsequent Treaties and Acts modifying and supplementing them and, on the other hand, by the other provisions of this Treaty.

Article 6

1. The Union is founded on the principles of liberty, democracy, respect for human rights and fundamental freedoms, and the rule of law, principles which are common to the Member States.

2. The Union shall respect fundamental rights, as guaranteed by the European Convention for the Protection of Human Rights and Fundamental Freedoms signed in Rome on 4 November 1950 and as they result from the constitutional traditions common to the Member States, as general principles of Community law.

3. The Union shall respect the national identities of its Member States.

4. The Union shall provide itself with the means necessary to attain its objectives and carry through its policies.

Article 7

1. On a reasoned proposal by one third of the Member States, by the European Parliament or by the Commission, the Council, acting by a majority of four fifths of its members after obtaining the assent

of the European Parliament, may determine that there is a clear risk of a serious breach by a Member State of principles mentioned in Article 6(1), and address appropriate recommendations to that State. Before making such a determination, the Council shall hear the Member State in question and, acting in accordance with the same procedure, may call on independent persons to submit within a reasonable time limit a report on the situation in the Member State in question.

The Council shall regularly verify that the grounds on which such a determination was made continue to apply.

2. The Council, meeting in the composition of the Heads of State or Government and acting by unanimity on a proposal by one third of the Member States or by the Commission and after obtaining the assent of the European Parliament, may determine the existence of a serious and persistent breach by a Member State of principles mentioned in Article 6(1), after inviting the government of the Member State in question to submit its observations.

3. Where a determination under paragraph 2 has been made, the Council, acting by a qualified majority, may decide to suspend certain of the rights deriving from the application of this Treaty to the Member State in question, including the voting rights of the representative of the government of that Member State in the Council. In doing so, the Council shall take into account the possible consequences of such a suspension on the rights and obligations of natural and legal persons. The obligations of the Member State in question under this Treaty shall in any case continue to be binding on that State.

4. The Council, acting by a qualified majority, may decide subsequently to vary or revoke measures taken under paragraph 3 in response to changes in the situation which led to their being imposed.

5. For the purposes of this Article, the Council shall act without taking into account the vote of the representative of the government of the Member State in question. Abstentions by members present in person or represented shall not prevent the adoption of decisions referred to in paragraph 2. A qualified majority shall be defined as the same proportion of the weighted votes of the members of the Council concerned as laid down in Article 205(2) of the Treaty establishing the European Community. This paragraph shall also apply in the event of voting rights being suspended pursuant to paragraph 3.

6. For the purposes of paragraphs 1 and 2, the European Parliament shall act by a two-thirds major-

ity of the votes cast, representing a majority of its Members....

Title V. Provisions on a Common Foreign and Security Policy

◆ **Article 11**

1. The Union shall define and implement a common foreign and security policy covering all areas of foreign and security policy, the objectives of which shall be:

—to safeguard the common values, fundamental interests, independence and integrity of the Union in conformity with the principles of the United Nations Charter,

—to strengthen the security of the Union in all ways,

—to preserve peace and strengthen international security, in accordance with the principles of the United Nations Charter, as well as the principles of the Helsinki Final Act and the objectives of the Paris Charter, including those on external borders,

—to promote international cooperation,

—to develop and consolidate democracy and the rule of law, and respect for human rights and fundamental freedoms.

2. The Member States shall support the Union's external and security policy actively and unreservedly in a spirit of loyalty and mutual solidarity. The Member States shall work together to enhance and develop their mutual political solidarity. They shall refrain from any action which is contrary to the interests of the Union or likely to impair its effectiveness as a cohesive force in international relations. The Council shall ensure that these principles are complied with.

◆ **Article 12**

The Union shall pursue the objectives set out in Article 11 by:

—defining the principles of and general guidelines for the common foreign and security policy,

—deciding on common strategies,

—adopting joint actions,

—adopting common positions,

—strengthening systematic cooperation between Member States in the conduct of policy.

◆ **Article 13**

1. The European Council shall define the principles of and general guidelines for the common for-

eign and security policy, including for matters with defence implications.

2. The European Council shall decide on common strategies to be implemented by the Union in areas where the Member States have important interests in common.

Common strategies shall set out their objectives, duration and the means to be made available by the Union and the Member States.

3. The Council shall take the decisions necessary for defining and implementing the common foreign and security policy on the basis of the general guidelines defined by the European Council.

The Council shall recommend common strategies to the European Council and shall implement them, in particular by adopting joint actions and common positions.

The Council shall ensure the unity, consistency and effectiveness of action by the Union.

◆ Article 14

1. The Council shall adopt joint actions. Joint actions shall address specific situations where operational action by the Union is deemed to be required. They shall lay down their objectives, scope, the means to be made available to the Union, if necessary their duration, and the conditions for their implementation.

2. If there is a change in circumstances having a substantial effect on a question subject to joint action, the Council shall review the principles and objectives of that action and take the necessary decisions. As long as the Council has not acted, the joint action shall stand.

3. Joint actions shall commit the Member States in the positions they adopt and in the conduct of their activity.

4. The Council may request the Commission to submit to it any appropriate proposals relating to the common foreign and security policy to ensure the implementation of a joint action.

5. Whenever there is any plan to adopt a national position or take national action pursuant to a joint action, information shall be provided in time to allow, if necessary, for prior consultations within the Council. The obligation to provide prior information shall not apply to measures which are merely a national transposition of Council decisions.

6. In cases of imperative need arising from changes in the situation and failing a Council decision, Member States may take the necessary measures as a matter of urgency having regard to the general objectives of the joint action. The Member State concerned shall inform the Council immediately of any such measures.

7. Should there be any major difficulties in implementing a joint action, a Member State shall refer them to the Council which shall discuss them and seek appropriate solutions. Such solutions shall not run counter to the objectives of the joint action or impair its effectiveness.

◆ Article 15

The Council shall adopt common positions. Common positions shall define the approach of the Union to a particular matter of a geographical or thematic nature. Member States shall ensure that their national policies conform to the common positions.

◆ Article 16

Member States shall inform and consult one another within the Council on any matter of foreign and security policy of general interest in order to ensure that the Union's influence is exerted as effectively as possible by means of concerted and convergent action.

◆ Article 17

1. The common foreign and security policy shall include all questions relating to the security of the Union, including the progressive framing of a common defence policy, which might lead to a common defence, should the European Council so decide. It shall in that case recommend to the Member States the adoption of such a decision in accordance with their respective constitutional requirements.

The policy of the Union in accordance with this Article shall not prejudice the specific character of the security and defence policy of certain Member States and shall respect the obligations of certain Member States, which see their common defence realised in the North Atlantic Treaty Organisation (NATO), under the North Atlantic Treaty and be compatible with the common security and defence policy established within that framework. The progressive framing of a common defence policy will be supported, as Member States consider appropriate, by cooperation between them in the field of armaments.

2. Questions referred to in this Article shall include humanitarian and rescue tasks, peacekeeping tasks and tasks of combat forces in crisis management, including peacemaking.

3. Decisions having defence implications dealt with under this Article shall be taken without preju-

dice to the policies and obligations referred to in paragraph 1, second subparagraph.

4. The provisions of this Article shall not prevent the development of closer cooperation between two or more Member States on a bilateral level, in the framework of the Western European Union (WEU) and NATO, provided such cooperation does not run counter to or impede that provided for in this title.

5. With a view to furthering the objectives of this Article, the provisions of this Article will be reviewed in accordance with Article 48.

◆ Article 18

1. The Presidency shall represent the Union in matters coming within the common foreign and security policy.

2. The Presidency shall be responsible for the implementation of decisions taken under this title; in that capacity it shall in principle express the position of the Union in international organisations and international conferences.

3. The Presidency shall be assisted by the Secretary-General of the Council who shall exercise the function of High Representative for the common foreign and security policy.

4. The Commission shall be fully associated in the tasks referred to in paragraphs 1 and 2. The Presidency shall be assisted in those tasks if need be by the next Member State to hold the Presidency.

5. The Council may, whenever it deems it necessary, appoint a special representative with a mandate in relation to particular policy issues.

◆ Article 19

1. Member States shall coordinate their action in international organisations and at international conferences. They shall uphold the common positions in such forums. In international organisations and at international conferences where not all the Member States participate, those which do take part shall uphold the common positions.

2. Without prejudice to paragraph 1 and Article 14(3), Member States represented in international organisations or international conferences where not all the Member States participate shall keep the latter informed of any matter of common interest. Member States which are also members of the United Nations Security Council will concert and keep the other Member States fully informed. Member States which are permanent members of the Security Council will, in the execution of their functions, ensure the defence of the positions and the interests of the Union, without prejudice to their responsibilities under the provisions of the United Nations Charter.

◆ Article 20

The diplomatic and consular missions of the Member States and the Commission delegations in third countries and international conferences, and their representations to international organisations, shall cooperate in ensuring that the common positions and joint actions adopted by the Council are complied with and implemented. They shall step up cooperation by exchanging information, carrying out joint assessments and contributing to the implementation of the provisions referred to in Article 20 of the Treaty establishing the European Community.

◆ Article 21

The Presidency shall consult the European Parliament on the main aspects and the basic choices of the common foreign and security policy and shall ensure that the views of the European Parliament are duly taken into consideration. The European Parliament shall be kept regularly informed by the Presidency and the Commission of the development of the Union's foreign and security policy. The European Parliament may ask questions of the Council or make recommendations to it. It shall hold an annual debate on progress in implementing the common foreign and security policy.

◆ Article 22

1. Any Member State or the Commission may refer to the Council any question relating to the common foreign and security policy and may submit proposals to the Council.

2. In cases requiring a rapid decision, the Presidency, of its own motion, or at the request of the Commission or a Member State, shall convene an extraordinary Council meeting within 48 hours or, in an emergency, within a shorter period.

◆ Article 23

1. Decisions under this title shall be taken by the Council acting unanimously. Abstentions by members present in person or represented shall not prevent the adoption of such decisions. When abstaining in a vote, any member of the Council may qualify its abstention by making a formal declaration under the present subparagraph. In that case, it shall not be obliged to apply the decision, but shall accept that the decision commits the Union. In a spirit of mutual solidarity, the Member State concerned shall

refrain from any action likely to conflict with or impede Union action based on that decision and the other Member States shall respect its position. If the members of the Council qualifying their abstention in this way represent more than one third of the votes weighted in accordance with Article 205(2) of the Treaty establishing the European Community, the decision shall not be adopted.

2. By derogation from the provisions of paragraph 1, the Council shall act by qualified majority:

—when adopting joint actions, common positions or taking any other decision on the basis of a common strategy,

—when adopting any decision implementing a joint action or a common position,

—when appointing a special representative in accordance with Article 18(5).

If a member of the Council declares that, for important and stated reasons of national policy, it intends to oppose the adoption of a decision to be taken by qualified majority, a vote shall not be taken. The Council may, acting by a qualified majority, request that the matter be referred to the European Council for decision by unanimity. The votes of the members of the Council shall be weighted in accordance with Article 205(2) of the Treaty establishing the European Community. For their adoption, decisions shall require at least 62 votes in favour, cast by at least 10 members. This paragraph shall not apply to decisions having military or defence implications.

3. For procedural questions, the Council shall act by a majority of its members.

◆ Article 24

1. When it is necessary to conclude an agreement with one or more States or international organisations in implementation of this title, the Council may authorise the Presidency, assisted by the Commission as appropriate, to open negotiations to that effect. Such agreements shall be concluded by the Council on a recommendation from the Presidency.

2. The Council shall act unanimously when the agreement covers an issue for which unanimity is required for the adoption of internal decisions.

3. When the agreement is envisaged in order to implement a joint action or common position, the Council shall act by a qualified majority in accordance with Article 23(2).

4. The provisions of this Article shall also apply to matters falling under Title VI. When the agreement covers an issue for which a qualified majority is required for the adoption of internal decisions or

measures, the Council shall act by a qualified majority in accordance with Article 34(3).

5. No agreement shall be binding on a Member State whose representative in the Council states that it has to comply with the requirements of its own constitutional procedure; the other members of the Council may agree that the agreement shall nevertheless apply provisionally.

6. Agreements concluded under the conditions set out by this Article shall be binding on the institutions of the Union.

◆ Article 25

Without prejudice to Article 207 of the Treaty establishing the European Community, a Political and Security Committee shall monitor the international situation in the areas covered by the common foreign and security policy and contribute to the definition of policies by delivering opinions to the Council at the request of the Council or on its own initiative. It shall also monitor the implementation of agreed policies, without prejudice to the responsibility of the Presidency and the Commission. Within the scope of this title, this Committee shall exercise, under the responsibility of the Council, political control and strategic direction of crisis management operations. The Council may authorise the Committee, for the purpose and for the duration of a crisis management operation, as determined by the Council, to take the relevant decisions concerning the political control and strategic direction of the operation, without prejudice to Article 47.

◆ Article 26

The Secretary-General of the Council, High Representative for the common foreign and security policy, shall assist the Council in matters coming within the scope of the common foreign and security policy, in particular through contributing to the formulation, preparation and implementation of policy decisions, and, when appropriate and acting on behalf of the Council at the request of the Presidency, through conducting political dialogue with third parties.

◆ Article 27

The Commission shall be fully associated with the work carried out in the common foreign and security policy field.

◆ Article 27a

1. Enhanced cooperation in any of the areas referred to in this title shall be aimed at safeguarding

the values and serving the interests of the Union as a whole by asserting its identity as a coherent force on the international scene. It shall respect:

—the principles, objectives, general guidelines and consistency of the common foreign and security policy and the decisions taken within the framework of that policy,

—the powers of the European Community, and

—consistency between all the Union's policies and its external activities.

2. Articles 11 to 27 and Articles 27b to 28 shall apply to the enhanced cooperation provided for in this article, save as otherwise provided in Article 27c and Articles 43 to 45.

◆ Article 27b

Enhanced cooperation pursuant to this title shall relate to implementation of a joint action or a common position. It shall not relate to matters having military or defence implications.

◆ Article 27c

Member States which intend to establish enhanced cooperation between themselves under Article 27b shall address a request to the Council to that effect. The request shall be forwarded to the Commission and, for information, to the European Parliament. The Commission shall give its opinion particularly on whether the enhanced cooperation proposed is consistent with Union policies. Authorisation shall be granted by the Council, acting in accordance with the second and third subparagraphs of Article 23(2) and in compliance with Articles 43 to 45.

◆ Article 27d

Without prejudice to the powers of the Presidency and of the Commission, the Secretary-General of the Council, High Representative for the common foreign and security policy, shall in particular ensure that the European Parliament and all members of the Council are kept fully informed of the implementation of enhanced cooperation in the field of the common foreign and security policy.

◆ Article 27e

Any Member State which wishes to participate in enhanced cooperation established in accordance with Article 27c shall notify its intention to the Council and inform the Commission. The Commission shall give an opinion to the Council within three months of the date of receipt of that notification. Within four months of the date of receipt of that notification, the Council shall take a decision on the request and on such specific arrangements as it may deem necessary. The decision shall be deemed to be taken unless the Council, acting by a qualified majority within the same period, decides to hold it in abeyance; in that case, the Council shall state the reasons for its decision and set a deadline for re-examining it.

For the purposes of this Article, the Council shall act by a qualified majority. The qualified majority shall be defined as the same proportion of the weighted votes and the same proportion of the number of the members of the Council concerned as those laid down in the third subparagraph of Article 23(2)....

Title VI. Provisions on Police and Judicial Cooperation in Criminal Matters

◆ Article 29

Without prejudice to the powers of the European Community, the Union's objective shall be to provide citizens with a high level of safety within an area of freedom, security and justice by developing common action among the Member States in the fields of police and judicial cooperation in criminal matters and by preventing and combating racism and xenophobia. That objective shall be achieved by preventing and combating crime, organised or otherwise, in particular terrorism, trafficking in persons and offences against children, illicit drug trafficking and illicit arms trafficking, corruption and fraud, through:

—closer cooperation between police forces, customs authorities and other competent authorities in the Member States, both directly and through the European Police Office (Europol), in accordance with the provisions of Articles 30 and 32,

—closer cooperation between judicial and other competent authorities of the Member States including cooperation through the European Judicial Cooperation Unit (Eurojust), in accordance with the provisions of Articles 31 and 32,

—approximation, where necessary, of rules on criminal matters in the Member States, in accordance with the provisions of Article 31(e).

◆ Article 30

1. Common action in the field of police cooperation shall include:

(a) operational cooperation between the competent authorities, including the police, customs and other specialised law enforcement services of the Member States in

(b) the collection, storage, processing, analysis and exchange of relevant information, including information held by law enforcement services on reports on suspicious financial transactions, in particular through Europol, subject to appropriate provisions on the protection of personal data;

(c) cooperation and joint initiatives in training, the exchange of liaison officers, secondments, the use of equipment, and forensic research;

(d) the common evaluation of particular investigative techniques in relation to the detection of serious forms of organised crime.

2. The Council shall promote cooperation through Europol and shall in particular, within a period of five years after the date of entry into force of the Treaty of Amsterdam:

(a) enable Europol to facilitate and support the preparation, and to encourage the coordination and carrying out, of specific investigative actions by the competent authorities of the Member States, including operational actions of joint teams comprising representatives of Europol in a support capacity;

(b) adopt measures allowing Europol to ask the competent authorities of the Member States to conduct and coordinate their investigations in specific cases and to develop specific expertise which may be put at the disposal of Member States to assist them in investigating cases of organised crime;

(c) promote liaison arrangements between prosecuting/investigating officials specialising in the fight against organised crime in close cooperation with Europol;

(d) establish a research, documentation and statistical network on cross-border crime.

◆ Article 31

1. Common action on judicial cooperation in criminal matters shall include:

(a) facilitating and accelerating cooperation between competent ministries and judicial or equivalent authorities of the Member States, including, where appropriate, cooperation through Eurojust, in relation to proceedings and the enforcement of decisions;

(b) facilitating extradition between Member States;

(c) ensuring compatibility in rules applicable in the Member States, as may be necessary to improve such cooperation;

(d) preventing conflicts of jurisdiction between Member States;

(e) progressively adopting measures establishing minimum rules relating to the constituent elements of criminal acts and to penalties in the fields of organised crime, terrorism and illicit drug trafficking.

2. The Council shall encourage cooperation through Eurojust by:

(a) enabling Eurojust to facilitate proper coordination between Member States' national prosecuting authorities;

(b) promoting support by Eurojust for criminal investigations in cases of serious cross-border crime, particularly in the case of organised crime, taking account, in particular, of analyses carried out by Europol;

(c) facilitating close cooperation between Eurojust and the European Judicial Network, particularly, in order to facilitate the execution of letters rogatory and the implementation of extradition requests.

◆ Article 32

The Council shall lay down the conditions and limitations under which the competent authorities referred to in Articles 30 and 31 may operate in the territory of another Member State in liaison and in agreement with the authorities of that State.

◆ Article 33

This title shall not affect the exercise of the responsibilities incumbent upon Member States with regard to the maintenance of law and order and the safeguarding of internal security.

◆ Article 34

1. In the areas referred to in this title, Member States shall inform and consult one another within the Council with a view to coordinating their action. To that end, they shall establish collaboration between the relevant departments of their administrations.

2. The Council shall take measures and promote cooperation, using the appropriate form and procedures as set out in this title, contributing to the pursuit of the objectives of the Union. To that end, acting unanimously on the initiative of any Member State or of the Commission, the Council may:

(a) adopt common positions defining the approach of the Union to a particular matter;

(b) adopt framework decisions for the purpose of approximation of the laws and regulations of the Member States. Framework decisions shall be binding upon the Member States as to the result to be achieved but shall leave to the national authorities the choice of form and methods. They shall not entail direct effect;

(c) adopt decisions for any other purpose consistent with the objectives of this title, excluding any approximation of the laws and regulations of the Member States. These decisions shall be binding and shall not entail direct effect; the Council, acting by a qualified majority, shall adopt measures necessary to implement those decisions at the level of the Union;

(d) establish conventions which it shall recommend to the Member States for adoption in accordance with their respective constitutional requirements. Member States shall begin the procedures applicable within a time limit to be set by the Council. Unless they provide otherwise, conventions shall, once adopted by at least half of the Member States, enter into force for those Member States. Measures implementing conventions shall be adopted within the Council by a majority of two thirds of the Contracting Parties.

3. Where the Council is required to act by a qualified majority, the votes of its members shall be weighted as laid down in Article 205(2) of the Treaty establishing the European Community, and for their adoption acts of the Council shall require at least 62 votes in favour, cast by at least 10 members.

4. For procedural questions, the Council shall act by a majority of its members.

◆ Article 35

1. The Court of Justice of the European Communities shall have jurisdiction, subject to the conditions laid down in this article, to give preliminary rulings on the validity and interpretation of framework decisions and decisions, on the interpretation of conventions established under this title and on the validity and interpretation of the measures implementing them.

2. By a declaration made at the time of signature of the Treaty of Amsterdam or at any time thereafter, any Member State shall be able to accept the jurisdiction of the Court of Justice to give preliminary rulings as specified in paragraph 1.

3. A Member State making a declaration pursuant to paragraph 2 shall specify that either:

(a) any court or tribunal of that State against whose decisions there is no judicial remedy under national law may request the Court of Justice to give a preliminary ruling on a question raised in a case pending before it and concerning the validity or interpretation of an act referred to in paragraph 1 if that court or tribunal considers that a decision on the question is necessary to enable it to give judgment; or

(b) any court or tribunal of that State may request the Court of Justice to give a preliminary ruling on a question raised in a case pending before it and concerning the validity or interpretation of an act referred to in paragraph 1 if that court or tribunal considers that a decision on the question is necessary to enable it to give judgment.

4. Any Member State, whether or not it has made a declaration pursuant to paragraph 2, shall be entitled to submit statements of case or written observations to the Court in cases which arise under paragraph 1.

5. The Court of Justice shall have no jurisdiction to review the validity or proportionality of operations carried out by the police or other law enforcement services of a Member State or the exercise of the responsibilities incumbent upon Member States with regard to the maintenance of law and order and the safeguarding of internal security.

6. The Court of Justice shall have jurisdiction to review the legality of framework decisions and decisions in actions brought by a Member State or the Commission on grounds of lack of competence, infringement of an essential procedural requirement, infringement of this Treaty or of any rule of law relating to its application, or misuse of powers. The proceedings provided for in this paragraph shall be instituted within two months of the publication of the measure.

7. The Court of Justice shall have jurisdiction to rule on any dispute between Member States regarding the interpretation or the application of acts adopted under Article 34(2) whenever such dispute cannot be settled by the Council within six months of its being referred to the Council by one of its members. The Court shall also have jurisdiction to rule on any dispute between Member States and the Commission regarding the interpretation or the application of conventions established under Article 34(2)(d).

◆ Article 36

1. A Coordinating Committee shall be set up consisting of senior officials. In addition to its coordinating role, it shall be the task of the Committee to:

—give opinions for the attention of the Council, either at the Council's request or on its own initiative,

—contribute, without prejudice to Article 207 of the Treaty establishing the European Community, to the preparation of the Council's discussions in the areas referred to in Article 29.

2. The Commission shall be fully associated with the work in the areas referred to in this title.

◆ Article 37

Within international organisations and at international conferences in which they take part, Member States shall defend the common positions adopted under the provisions of this title. Articles 18 and 19 shall apply as appropriate to matters falling under this title.

◆ Article 38

Agreements referred to in Article 24 may cover matters falling under this title.

◆ Article 39

1. The Council shall consult the European Parliament before adopting any measure referred to in Article 34(2)(b), (c) and (d). The European Parliament shall deliver its opinion within a time limit which the Council may lay down, which shall not be less than three months. In the absence of an opinion within that time limit, the Council may act.

2. The Presidency and the Commission shall regularly inform the European Parliament of discussions in the areas covered by this title.

3. The European Parliament may ask questions of the Council or make recommendations to it. Each year, it shall hold a debate on the progress made in the areas referred to in this title.

◆ Article 40

1. Enhanced cooperation in any of the areas referred to in this title shall have the aim of enabling the Union to develop more rapidly into an area of freedom, security and justice, while respecting the powers of the European Community and the objectives laid down in this title.

2. Articles 29 to 39 and Articles 40a to 41 shall apply to the enhanced cooperation provided for by this article, save as otherwise provided in Article 40a and in Articles 43 to 45.

3. The provisions of the Treaty establishing the European Community concerning the powers of the Court of Justice and the exercise of those powers shall apply to this article and to Articles 40a and 40b.

◆ Article 40a

1. Member States which intend to establish enhanced cooperation between themselves under Article 40 shall address a request to the Commission, which may submit a proposal to the Council to

that effect. In the event of the Commission not submitting a proposal, it shall inform the Member States concerned of the reasons for not doing so. Those Member States may then submit an initiative to the Council designed to obtain authorisation for the enhanced cooperation concerned.

2. The authorisation referred to in paragraph 1 shall be granted, in compliance with Articles 43 to 45, by the Council, acting by a qualified majority, on a proposal from the Commission or on the initiative of at least eight Member States, and after consulting the European Parliament. The votes of the members of the Council shall be weighted in accordance with Article 205(2) of the Treaty establishing the European Community. A member of the Council may request that the matter be referred to the European Council. After that matter has been raised before the European Council, the Council may act in accordance with the first subparagraph of this paragraph.

◆ Article 40b

Any Member State which wishes to participate in enhanced cooperation established in accordance with Article 40a shall notify its intention to the Council and to the Commission, which shall give an opinion to the Council within three months of the date of receipt of that notification, possibly accompanied by a recommendation for such specific arrangements as it may deem necessary for that Member State to become a party to the cooperation in question. The Council shall take a decision on the request within four months of the date of receipt of that notification. The decision shall be deemed to be taken unless the Council, acting by a qualified majority within the same period, decides to hold it in abeyance; in that case, the Council shall state the reasons for its decision and set a deadline for re-examining it. For the purposes of this Article, the Council shall act under the conditions set out in Article 44(1).

◆ Article 41

1. Articles 189, 190, 195, 196 to 199, 203, 204, 205(3), 206 to 209, 213 to 219, 255 and 290 of the Treaty establishing the European Community shall apply to the provisions relating to the areas referred to in this title.

2. Administrative expenditure which the provisions relating to the areas referred to in this title entail for the institutions shall be charged to the budget of the European Communities.

3. Operating expenditure to which the implementation of those provisions gives rise shall also be

---

charged to the budget of the European Communities, except where the Council acting unanimously decides otherwise. In cases where expenditure is not charged to the budget of the European Communities, it shall be charged to the Member States in accordance with the gross national product scale, unless the Council acting unanimously decides otherwise.

4. The budgetary procedure laid down in the Treaty establishing the European Community shall apply to the expenditure charged to the budget of the European Communities.

◆ **Article 42**

The Council, acting unanimously on the initiative of the Commission or a Member State, and after consulting the European Parliament, may decide that action in areas referred to in Article 29 shall fall under Title IV of the Treaty establishing the European Community, and at the same time determine the relevant voting conditions relating to it. It shall recommend the Member States to adopt that decision in accordance with their respective constitutional requirements.

Title VII. Provisions on Enhanced Cooperation

◆ **Article 43**

Member States which intend to establish enhanced cooperation between themselves may make use of the institutions, procedures and mechanisms laid down by this Treaty and by the Treaty establishing the European Community provided that the proposed cooperation:

(a) is aimed at furthering the objectives of the Union and of the Community, at protecting and serving their interests and at reinforcing their process of integration;

(b) respects the said Treaties and the single institutional framework of the Union;

(c) respects the *acquis communautaire* and the measures adopted under the other provisions of the said Treaties;

(d) remains within the limits of the powers of the Union or of the Community and does not concern the areas which fall within the exclusive competence of the Community;

(e) does not undermine the internal market as defined in Article 14(2) of the Treaty establishing the European Community, or the economic and social cohesion established in accordance with Title XVII of that Treaty;

(f) does not constitute a barrier to or discrimination in trade between the Member States and does not distort competition between them;

(g) involves a minimum of eight Member States;

(h) respects the competences, rights and obligations of those Member States which do not participate therein;

(i) does not affect the provisions of the Protocol integrating the Schengen *acquis* into the framework of the European Union;

(j) is open to all the Member States, in accordance with Article 43b.

◆ **Article 43a**

Enhanced cooperation may be undertaken only as a last resort, when it has been established within the Council that the objectives of such cooperation cannot be attained within a reasonable period by applying the relevant provisions of the Treaties.

◆ **Article 43b**

When enhanced cooperation is being established, it shall be open to all Member States. It shall also be open to them at any time, in accordance with Articles 27e and 40b of this Treaty and with Article 11a of the Treaty establishing the European Community, subject to compliance with the basic decision and with the decisions taken within that framework. The Commission and the Member States participating in enhanced cooperation shall ensure that as many Member States as possible are encouraged to take part.

◆ **Article 44**

1. For the purposes of the adoption of the acts and decisions necessary for the implementation of enhanced cooperation referred to in Article 43, the relevant institutional provisions of this Treaty and of the Treaty establishing the European Community shall apply. However, while all members of the Council shall be able to take part in the deliberations, only those representing Member States participating in enhanced cooperation shall take part in the adoption of decisions. The qualified majority shall be defined as the same proportion of the weighted votes and the same proportion of the number of the Council members concerned as laid down in Article 205(2) of the Treaty establishing the European Community, and in the second and third subparagraphs of Article 23(2) of this Treaty as regards enhanced cooperation established on the basis of Article 27c. Unanimity shall be constituted by only those Council members con-

cerned. Such acts and decisions shall not form part of the Union *acquis*.

2. Member States shall apply, as far as they are concerned, the acts and decisions adopted for the implementation of the enhanced cooperation in which they participate. Such acts and decisions shall be binding only on those Member States which participate in such cooperation and, as appropriate, shall be directly applicable only in those States. Member States which do not participate in such cooperation shall not impede the implementation thereof by the participating Member States.

◆ Article 44a

Expenditure resulting from implementation of enhanced cooperation, other than administrative costs entailed for the institutions, shall be borne by the participating Member States, unless all members of the Council, acting unanimously after consulting the European Parliament, decide otherwise.

◆ Article 45

The Council and the Commission shall ensure the consistency of activities undertaken on the basis of this title and the consistency of such activities with the policies of the Union and the Community, and shall cooperate to that end....

IN WITNESS WHEREOF the undersigned Plenipotentiaries have signed this Treaty.

Done at Maastricht on the seventh day of February in the year one thousand nine hundred and ninety-two.

[List of signatories not reproduced]

Glossary

Helsinki Final Act	the Helsinki Accords, signed in 1975
Paris Charter	also called the Charter of Paris for a New Europe; adopted on November 21, 1990, with the purpose of strengthening the collective security of Europe by inviting Eastern bloc nations to join with the West

Nelson Mandela (AP/Wide World Photos)

> *"Never again shall it be that this beautiful land will again experience the oppression of one by another."*

Overview

On May 10, 1994, Nelson Mandela was sworn in as president of the Republic of South Africa. The moment was a triumphal celebration of the transition from apartheid rule to a democratic South Africa and from white minority rule to black majority rule. Mandela, who had led the resistance to white rule and who had been imprisoned for that resistance from 1962 to 1990, became the first black man to become South Africa's head of state. His inaugural address was a conciliatory, forward-looking celebration of the changes that had taken place in South Africa.

In the 1980s, when white minority rule was still strong and the apartheid policy still tried to separate whites and blacks, few could have predicted that within a decade apartheid legislation would be repealed and all citizens would be able to vote freely for a new head of state. At that time, most commentators predicted that South Africa would descend into a bloody racial civil war. But that racial war did not come to pass. Instead, after a gradual dismantling of the apartheid system, Mandela became president through a relatively peaceful democratic process. Many spoke of this as a miracle. The new leader was a man who had endured imprisonment for more than a quarter of a century and had emerged from that imprisonment without bitterness toward those who had imprisoned him. His reconciliatory attitude and remarkably open and charismatic personality gave him a saintly aura, and his inauguration as president of the country that only a few years earlier had been despised for its apartheid policies was celebrated around the world. It was on the occasion of his inauguration that Mandela delivered this speech.

Context

South Africa had a long history of racial segregation before the National Party government's adoption of a policy of apartheid in 1948. Black Africans had always formed a majority of the population of the area that in 1910 became the Union of South Africa, a nation that comprised Cape Colony, Natal, Transvaal, and the Orange Free State, under primarily British dominion. The borders of the state formed in 1910 are virtually coterminous with those of the modern state. But the white population had conquered the indigenous peoples and dispossessed them of their land, and though whites wanted to use black labor, they kept blacks in subordinate positions.

Black challenges to colonialism had been in vain, and it was only gradually that new forms of resistance emerged. In the cities, members of the black African elite began to organize politically and to campaign for equal rights. To that end, the South African Native National Congress was formed in 1912, and in 1923 it changed its name to the African National Congress (ANC). The ANC went through a period of decline in the 1920s and 1930s, but under the influence of its Youth League, of which Mandela was a member, it revived in the 1940s.

The Afrikaner National Party came to power in 1948 on a program of rigid and more extensive racial segregation than before, known as apartheid. ("Afrikaner" refers to an ethnic group descended from seventeenth-century settlers from northwestern Europe.) In response, the ANC launched a new campaign involving civil disobedience and strike action. In 1952, for example, the ANC joined with the South African Indian Congress to embark on the Campaign of Defiance against Unjust Laws, a passive resistance protest launched on June 26 in which more than eight thousand people, including some whites, defied key racial laws. Many were imprisoned, including Nelson Mandela. The campaign lost steam after the government banned all meetings of more than ten Africans. Further, the Public Safety Act suppressed future campaigns by allowing the government to declare a state of emergency in response to threats to the public peace, and the Criminal Law Amendment Act imposed severe penalties, including fines, imprisonment, and whipping, for publically protesting a law. During the campaign, the ANC attracted more members, growing to more than one hundred thousand, but the organization's leaders were unsure how to maintain the momentum of protest action.

One step taken to continue the momentum was the drafting of the Freedom Charter of South Africa, which became a key document in the struggle against apartheid. It was drafted by a small committee, on the basis of a large

Time Line

1912
- **January**
  The South African Native National Congress is founded.

1923
- The South African Native National Congress changes its name to the African National Congress.

1948
- **May**
  The white National Party comes to power and begins to introduce apartheid.

1949
- **December 17**
  The ANC conference adopts a program calling for direct action against apartheid.

1952
- **June 26**
  The Campaign of Defiance against Unjust Laws begins.

1955
- **June 25–26**
  The Congress of the People convenes and adopts the Freedom Charter.

1990
- **February 2**
  President F. W. de Klerk announces the unbanning of the ANC and other organizations and the impending unconditional release of Nelson Mandela.

number of submissions, and during the Congress of the People, held at Kliptown outside Johannesburg on June 25–26, 1955, the charter was adopted. It became a document of immense symbolic importance, for it embodied a vision of a future democratic South Africa that was not organized around distinctions of race. It would later become significant in the 1980s, when "charterists," or those whose philosophy was based on the charter, dominated resistance to apartheid; after apartheid had come to an end, the nation's new constitution, adopted in 1996, was in part based on ideas in the Freedom Charter.

The apartheid regime retaliated against this and other instances of activism with more brutally repressive policies, and in March 1960, in the township of Sharpeville, south of Johannesburg, the police shot dead sixty-nine black Africans who were engaged in peaceful protest against the law that required them to carry identity books, which prevented them from moving around the country freely.

After that, Mandela and others in the ANC decided that they had to take up arms to challenge the state. Mandela himself became the commander in chief of a new organization formed to lead the armed struggle. Known as Umkhonto we Sizwe (MK), meaning "Spear of the Nation," this group became the armed wing of the ANC. Within a few years, however, the leadership of MK had been arrested, and Mandela and others were imprisoned on Robben Island in Table Bay, off the coast of Cape Town. After Mandela was released on February 11, 1990, South Africa went through a turbulent period in which there was considerable political violence, but eventually the government of President F. W. de Klerk agreed to meet in a negotiating forum in Cape Town with leaders of the ANC to hammer out a settlement. The settlement took the form of an interim constitution and provision for the election of a new parliament, comprising the Constitutional Assembly and the National Council of Provinces. The democratically elected parliament was to be responsible for drawing up a final constitution. The interim constitution specified that the head of state was to be elected by the parliament for a five-year term. In May 1994, Mandela became that president.

About the Author

Nelson Rolihlahla (meaning "troublemaker" in the Xhosa language) Mandela was born in 1918 in the rural Transkei in what is now the Eastern Cape province of South Africa. He attended a leading missionary school in that region and then the University College of Fort Hare before he moved to Johannesburg, the largest city in South Africa, where he became active in the ANC in the early 1940s. In the 1950s, based in Johannesburg, he was one of the leading figures in the ANC's resistance to the apartheid state. The ANC was banned in 1960, and the following year he and others formed MK to challenge the state by violent means, first sabotage and later guerrilla war.

As commander in chief of MK, Mandela left the country in 1962 to organize military training for guerrillas from

South Africa in other African countries. On his return to South Africa, he was arrested and jailed. Then, on June 12, 1964, he and his colleagues were given a life sentence for their involvement with MK. Mandela's statement in court before he was sentenced was widely quoted as a classic explanation of why he and others had chosen to adopt the armed struggle in resisting apartheid. He ended by saying,

> I have fought against white domination, and I have fought against black domination. I have cherished the ideal of a democratic and free society in which all persons live together in harmony and with equal opportunities. It is an ideal which I hope to live for and to achieve. But if needs be, it is an ideal for which I am prepared to die. (Karis and Carter, p. 796)

In 1982 he was moved, in part because of his growing international fame as a political prisoner, from Robben Island to Pollsmoor Prison on the mainland. It was there, a few years later, that he began discussions with government ministers about the possibility of a negotiated end to the conflict in the country.

By the late 1980s Mandela was the world's most famous prisoner and an icon of resistance to apartheid. The apartheid government knew that there would be an outcry if he were to die in prison, and its officials came to see him as a man with whom they could arrange a negotiated settlement, for unlike most of his close colleagues in the ANC, he was not a member of the Communist Party. All who met him recognized him as a potential future leader of the country. He was therefore moved to a house on the grounds of another prison, Victor Verster, where he was able to receive guests and conduct business.

By the time he became president in late 1989, F. W. de Klerk, the head of the National Party, had realized that apartheid had to go and that the enormous pressure to release Mandela could be resisted no longer. No one knew what Mandela's release would lead to, but de Klerk was prepared to take the risk. Lacking bitterness, Mandela was able to engage with his former enemies and work for a successful transition to a new society. He traveled extensively after his release, was elected president of the ANC at the first congress after it was unbanned, and took a leading role in the subsequent negotiations. In December 1993 he and De Klerk were jointly awarded the Nobel Peace Prize in Oslo, Norway, for their efforts to bring peace to South Africa. Mandela then campaigned for the ANC in the first democratic election, after which he was elected the first president of the democratic South Africa. Little more than four years had passed since he was Prisoner 466/64, the number he received on arrival on Robben Island and which he retained until his release from Victor Verster.

Mandela made it clear that he would serve only one term as president. He hoped his example would be followed by other leaders on a continent where most remained in power for very long periods of time. In retirement, Mandela remained active on both the local and the world stages. He set up three foundations bearing his name, to do mostly

Time Line

1990

- **February 11**
  Mandela walks out of Victor Verster Prison outside Cape Town and is driven to Cape Town, where he addresses the crowd gathered on the Grand Parade in the center of the city.

- **May**
  The ANC and the government hold their first formal bilateral meeting at Groote Schuur, an official government residence in Cape Town.

1991

- **December**
  The Convention for a Democratic South Africa meets at the World Trade Center in Kempton Park to begin the drafting of a new constitution.

1992

- **September**
  Mandela and De Klerk sign the Record of Understanding, which paves the way for the resumption of constitutional negotiations after the breakdown of the Convention for a Democratic South Africa.

1993

- **November 18**
  The Multiparty Negotiating Forum completes the drafting of the new interim constitution for a democratic South Africa.

1993

- **December**
  The draft constitution is approved by the South African Parliament.

1994

- **April 27**
  The first democratic general election is held, relatively peacefully. Mandela casts his vote at Ohlange High School, outside Durban, in honor of John Dube, a cofounder of the ANC, who is buried in a nearby cemetery.

- **May 2**
  The results of the election are declared, and the ANC celebrates its victory.

- **May 9**
  The new parliament elects Mandela president.

- **May 10**
  Mandela gives his inaugural address to a crowd gathered in Pretoria after having delivered a similar address in Cape Town the previous day.

1997

- Mandela hands over the presidency the ANC to Thabo Mbeki.

1999

- Mandela's five-year term as president of South Africa comes to an end; Mbeki succeeds him.

educational and charitable work: the Nelson Mandela Foundation, the Nelson Mandela Children's Fund, and the Mandela-Rhodes Foundation. In the 2009 election campaign, a frail Mandela appeared in support of the new ANC leader, Jacob Zuma.

Ten years after Mandela had left office, little of the dream for a new South Africa contained in his inauguration address had been realized. South Africa remained a democracy, but there was little of the optimism and hope and idealism that Mandela had spoken of in his inaugural address fifteen years earlier.

Explanation and Analysis of the Document

Mandela's inaugural address was highly symbolic. The very fact that he, a black man and former prisoner of the apartheid regime, was delivering it before a large crowd in which there were representatives of most of the countries in the world, demonstrated that South Africa had rejoined the world community after a long period of isolation under apartheid. Mandela speaks of humanity having "taken [South Africa] back into its bosom" and remarks, "We, who were outlaws not so long ago, have today been given the rare privilege to be host to the nations of the world on our own soil." Mandela was acknowledging that apartheid South Africa had long been isolated and treated as a pariah nation because of its racial policies, and he was celebrating that now South Africa had become a model for others to follow, a land in which it seemed that racial reconciliation had triumphed. And so Mandela thanks the guests from all over the world for attending and hopes that they would "continue to stand by us as we tackle the challenges of building peace, prosperity, non-sexism, non-racialism and democracy." He was very conscious of the fact that South Africa was emerging from decades of conflict, isolation, and economic decline, and he knew that it would need much help from others if it was to overcome the challenges it faced.

In the first sentence of his address Mandela speaks of newborn liberty, referring to the fact that South Africa was experiencing a new dawn of democracy after the long night of apartheid. His references to "an extraordinary human disaster that lasted too long" and to South Africa tearing "itself apart in a terrible conflict" point to apartheid and to the struggle against it, in which many had died and millions had suffered. For although far fewer people died in the South African conflict between 1948 and 1994 than in other conflicts on the African continent, such as in neighboring Zimbabwe in the 1970s or in the war for independence in Algeria in the 1950s and early 1960s, the policy of apartheid had trampled on the dignity of black people.

In speaking of apartheid in this way, Mandela addressed not only the black majority who had suffered under it but also those whites who had supported apartheid until recently and who had served the apartheid state. Of course, he was speaking as well to the whites who had opposed apartheid. Mandela's general attitude of reconciliation ensured that he did not arouse antagonism among those

A crowd gathers at the township of Sharpeville, south of Johannesburg, South Africa, on March 21, 1960, a few hours before white police opened fire on marchers. (AP/Wide World Photos)

who had supported the old apartheid order. Although Mandela continued to fear a far-right backlash against his new government from Afrikaners who were not reconciled to the new order, no serious resistance occurred. This was in large part due to Mandela's personality and policies of reconciliation. Mandela here speaks inclusively. All South Africans, he says, were attached to the soil of their particularly beautiful country, and he specifies some of these beauties in his references to "the famous jacaranda trees of Pretoria and the mimosa trees of the bushveld." His speech anticipated the reconciliatory spirit of his presidency, in which he would reach out to his opponents and do all he could to enhance nation building.

In his address, he singles out "the masses" for their role in bringing South Africa to the present moment. Most historians would agree that apartheid had been brought down by internal resistance in the 1980s rather than by the armed struggle waged mainly from outside or by the sanctions that other countries had imposed on South Africa. On the other hand, the masses had played very little part in the negotiated settlement, which had been reached by elites of the old apartheid order and the ANC leadership.

Mandela also singles out his second deputy president, F. W. de Klerk, who had been responsible for Mandela's release. Mandela had become disillusioned with De Klerk, whom he blamed for not acting to end the political violence that had plagued the country during the years of transition and in the campaign leading up to the general election. As leader of the National Party, De Klerk had been Mandela's chief opponent, but Mandela chose to credit De Klerk with what he had done to help bring about the new order and to accept him as a colleague in the new government of national unity.

Mandela also pays tribute to the country's security forces for helping secure the election and for defending against the "blood-thirsty forces which still refuse to see the light," a reference to those far-right whites who rejected the transition and from whom Mandela continued to fear violence might come. He reminds his listeners that the country had taken its "last steps to freedom in conditions of relative peace." He himself had long talked of walking to freedom, and his autobiography, published later that year, was titled *Long Walk to Freedom.*

In the remainder of the address, Mandela looks forward to the future. He talks of healing wounds, bridging the

"We dedicate this day to all the heroes and heroines in this country and the rest of the world who sacrificed in many ways and surrendered their lives so that we could be free. Their dreams have become reality. Freedom is their reward."

(Paragraphs 21–22)

"We know it well that none of us acting alone can achieve success. We must therefore act together as a united people, for national reconciliation, for nation building, for the birth of a new world."

(Paragraphs 25–26)

"Let there be justice for all. Let there be peace for all. Let there be work, bread, water and salt for all. Let each know that for each the body, the mind and the soul have been freed to fulfill themselves."

(Paragraphs 27–30)

"Never, never and never again shall it be that this beautiful land will again experience the oppression of one by another and suffer the indignity of being the skunk of the world. Let freedom reign."

(Paragraphs 31–32)

chasms of racial division, and building. He pledges that the new government will continue the process of emancipation by liberating the people from poverty, deprivation, and discrimination and by "the construction of a complete, just and lasting peace." In calling for unity among blacks and whites in South Africa, he refers to the nation by the common image of a rainbow, where all colors merge to form a thing of beauty—perhaps an allusion to the "Rainbow Coalition" formed by the civil rights activist and Baptist minister Jesse Jackson in the United States. As a gesture of good faith, Mandela indicates that the new government will address the issue of granting amnesty to people in prison, probably referring both to those who were imprisoned for activism and protest and more important, to those who perhaps took part in human rights violation against blacks but had come forward to confess.

The final paragraphs of the address consist of a series of short, inspirational sentences. Mandela acknowledges that there is "no easy road to freedom," but he expresses hope that if South Africans act as a "united people," there can be justice and peace, as well as "work, bread, water and salt for all." He looks forward to a future without oppression and indignity, where freedom reigns and where the sun will "never set on so glorious a human achievement."

Audience

Mandela's May 10 inaugural speech was directed at both a South African and an international audience. In what was in a sense a state-of-the-nation address, Mandela wanted both audiences to recognize the importance of the turning point that his address represented in the country's history. He wanted the international community to see the new South Africa as a model state, which could teach others how to reconcile and overcome conflicts of the past. He hoped that South Africans would accept his message of the need to move away from the past and look to the future as a newly united people, who should work together to overcome the legacies of the past.

Never before had so many heads of state and other dignitaries assembled on South African soil as gathered for Mandela's inauguration—nor have so many ever gathered in South Africa since. Vice President Al Gore and Hillary Clinton, wife of President Bill Clinton, came from the United States; from the United Kingdom came Prince Philip; from Cuba, Fidel Castro; Yasser Arafat of the Palestinian National Authority also came. There was an atmosphere of great excitement as the crowd that had gathered at the impressive Union Buildings, the seat of government overlooking Pretoria, awaited the arrival of Mandela. The most emotional moment came when helicopters of the South African air force flew overhead displaying the new multicolored South African flag. For many people, not only within South Africa but also in the neighboring countries, those helicopters had previously represented the repression of apartheid and the threat of attack. Now, however, they stood for the victory of liberty and the commitment of the armed forces to the new democracy.

Impact

While it is difficult to assess the precise impact of any speech, Mandela's inaugural address helped to promote the reconciliation agenda that was to be the hallmark of his presidency. Both blacks and whites were uplifted by his explicit commitment to bridging the chasms that had divided the two communities. In the course of his address, he made clear that as a "token of its commitment to the renewal of our country, the new Interim Government of National Unity will, as a matter of urgency, address the issue of amnesty for various categories of our people who are currently serving terms of imprisonment."

This was done: The first parliament of the new democratic South Africa passed the Promotion of National Unity and Reconciliation Act in 1995. That act provided for the setting up of the Truth and Reconciliation Commission. The commission addressed the issue of amnesty not only for people imprisoned but also for perpetrators of gross violations of human rights who came forward to avoid being sent to prison. In terms of the mandate given the commission, if they made full disclosure of what they had done, they would receive amnesty.

Mandela did not deliver his inaugural speech with the soaring oratory displayed by Barack Obama at his inauguration in Washington, D.C., in January 2009. Mandela's delivery was fairly matter of fact, except when he placed special emphasis on the word *never*. The timing of the flyby meant that he had to pause in his speech because of the noise they made. But his speech was well received and is generally regarded as both highly appropriate and inspiring. It went around the world and has often been quoted and cited. When Obama delivered his inaugural address, many commentators in South Africa referred it to a "Mandela moment" and reminded their readers of Mandela's speech.

In the years that followed Mandela's inauguration as president, the nation has only partially delivered on the promises he made in his address. On the one hand, the country is relatively high on an index called the Ibrahim Index of African Governance. This index examines and ranks the nations of sub-Saharan Africa along five dimensions: safety and security; rule of law, transparency, and corruption; participation and human rights; sustainable

Questions for Further Study

1. The inauguration of Nelson Mandela as president of South Africa was celebrated worldwide as a historical event of major importance. Why do you think this was so?

2. For more than four decades, since the passage of apartheid laws in 1948, the South African authorities resisted calls for a democratic form of government. Why do you think that resistance broke down? What factors led to the emergence of a democratic form of government and the election of Mandela as president?

3. Examine the rhetoric of Mandela's speech. What images does he create? How does the "poetry" of the speech add to the spirit of reconciliation that Mandela strove for?

4. What economic interests did F. W. de Klerk and his administration have to overcome to effect a fundamental alteration in South Africa's government?

5. Some form of racial prejudice and discrimination exists in virtually every country in the world, or at least is perceived to exist. Why do you think such prejudice and discrimination specifically in South Africa became the focus of worldwide attention?

economic opportunity; and human development. As of 2008 South Africa ranked fifth (behind Mauritius, the Seychelles, Cape Verde, and Botswana). The nation ranks very highly on rule of law and participation and human rights but less highly in the other three measures. Since the mid-1990s employment has remained high for blacks, and the number of whites living in poverty has increased. As of 2009 the overall unemployment rate was 23 percent. As of 2006 the nation ranked 125th on the United Nations Human Development Index, representing a decline from previous years and particularly from the mid-1990s. Reasons given for this lack of progress include the legacy of apartheid, but many observers question government policies, particularly undisciplined economic policies. Meanwhile, in 2009, rioting broke out across the nation in response to the government's inability to deal with the more than a million people who continue to live in shantytowns, or settlements, often on the edges of cities, where people live in improvised shelters made of scrap materials and lack such basic services as clean water, sewage facilities, and garbage collection.

Further Reading

■ Articles

Nasson, Bill. "The Was, the Is and the Might-have-been: Political Leadership in Post-Apartheid South Africa." *Journal of African History* 49, no. 3 (2008): 467–474.

■ Books

Boehmer, Elleke. *Mandela: A Very Short Introduction*. Oxford, U.K.: Oxford University Press, 2008.

Callinicos, Luli. *The World That Made Mandela*. Johannesburg, South Africa: STE Publishers, 2001.

De Klerk, F. W. *The Last Trek—A New Beginning: The Autobiography*. London: Macmillan, 1998.

Gevisser, Mark. *Thabo Mbeki: The Dream Deferred*. Johannesburg, South Africa: Jonathan Ball, 2007.

Karis, Thomas, and Gwendolen Carter, eds. *From Protest to Challenge. A Documentary History of African Politics in South Africa 1882–1964*. Vol. 3: *Challenge and Violence 1953–1964*. Stanford, Calif.: Hoover Institution, 1977.

Limb, Peter. *Nelson Mandela: A Biography*. Westport, Conn.: Greenwood Press, 2008.

Lodge, Tom. *Mandela. A Critical Life*. Oxford, U.K.: Oxford University Press, 2006.

Mandela, Nelson. *Long Walk to Freedom: The Autobiography of Nelson Mandela*. London: Abacus, 1995.

Moriarty, Thomas A. *Finding the Words: A Rhetorical History of South Africa's Transition from Apartheid to Democracy*. Westport, Conn.: Praeger, 2003.

Salazar, Phillipe. *An African Athens*. Mahwah, N. J.: L. Erlbaum, 2002.

Sampson, Anthony. *Mandela: The Authorised Biography*. London: Hamish Hamilton, 1990.

—Christopher Saunders

NELSON MANDELA'S INAUGURAL ADDRESS

Your Majesties;

Your Highnesses;

Distinguished Guests;

Comrades and Friends:

Today, all of us do, by our presence here, and by our celebrations in other parts of our country and the world, confer glory and hope to newborn liberty.

Out of the experience of an extraordinary human disaster that lasted too long must be born a society of which all humanity will be proud.

Our daily deeds as ordinary South Africans must produce an actual South African reality that will reinforce humanity's belief in justice, strengthen its confidence in the nobility of the human soul and sustain all our hopes for a glorious life for all.

All this we owe both to ourselves and to the peoples of the world who are so well represented here today.

To my compatriots, I have no hesitation in saying that each one of us is as intimately attached to the soil of this beautiful country as are the famous jacaranda trees of Pretoria and the mimosa trees of the bushveld.

Each time one of us touches the soil of this land, we feel a sense of personal renewal. The national mood changes as the seasons change.

We are moved by a sense of joy and exhilaration when the grass turns green and the flowers bloom.

That spiritual and physical oneness we all share with this common homeland explains the depth of the pain we all carried in our hearts as we saw our country tear itself apart in a terrible conflict, and as we saw it spurned, outlawed and isolated by the peoples of the world, precisely because it has become the universal base of the pernicious ideology and practice of racism and racial oppression.

We, the people of South Africa, feel fulfilled that humanity has taken us back into its bosom, that we, who were outlaws not so long ago, have today been given the rare privilege to be host to the nations of the world on our own soil.

We thank all our distinguished international guests for having come to take possession with the people of our country of what is, after all, a common victory for justice, for peace, for human dignity.

We trust that you will continue to stand by us as we tackle the challenges of building peace, prosperity, non-sexism, non-racialism and democracy.

We deeply appreciate the role that the masses of our people and their political mass democratic, religious, women, youth, business, traditional and other leaders have played to bring about this conclusion. Not least among them is my Second Deputy President, the Honourable F.W. de Klerk.

We would also like to pay tribute to our security forces, in all their ranks, for the distinguished role they have played in securing our first democratic elections and the transition to democracy, from blood-thirsty forces which still refuse to see the light.

The time for the healing of the wounds has come.

The moment to bridge the chasms that divide us has come.

The time to build is upon us.

We have, at last, achieved our political emancipation. We pledge ourselves to liberate all our people from the continuing bondage of poverty, deprivation, suffering, gender and other discrimination.

We succeeded to take our last steps to freedom in conditions of relative peace. We commit ourselves to the construction of a complete, just and lasting peace.

We have triumphed in the effort to implant hope in the breasts of the millions of our people. We enter into a covenant that we shall build the society in which all South Africans, both black and white, will be able to walk tall, without any fear in their hearts, assured of their inalienable right to human dignity— a rainbow nation at peace with itself and the world.

As a token of its commitment to the renewal of our country, the new Interim Government of National Unity will, as a matter of urgency, address the issue of amnesty for various categories of our people who are currently serving terms of imprisonment.

We dedicate this day to all the heroes and heroines in this country and the rest of the world who sacrificed in many ways and surrendered their lives so that we could be free.

Their dreams have become reality. Freedom is their reward.

We are both humbled and elevated by the honour and privilege that you, the people of South Africa, have bestowed on us, as the first President of a united, democratic, non-racial and non-sexist government.

We understand it still that there is no easy road to freedom

We know it well that none of us acting alone can achieve success.

We must therefore act together as a united people, for national reconciliation, for nation building, for the birth of a new world.

Let there be justice for all.

Let there be peace for all.

Let there be work, bread, water and salt for all.

Let each know that for each the body, the mind and the soul have been freed to fulfill themselves.

Never, never and never again shall it be that this beautiful land will again experience the oppression of one by another and suffer the indignity of being the skunk of the world.

Let freedom reign.

The sun shall never set on so glorious a human achievement!

God bless Africa!

Thank you.

Glossary

bushveld	grassland with copious shrubbery and thorny vegetation

Osama bin Laden (AP/Wide World Photos)

OSAMA BIN LADEN'S DECLARATION OF JIHAD AGAINST AMERICANS

"The blatant imperial arrogance of America, under the cover of the immoral United Nations, has prevented the dispossessed from arming themselves."

Overview

The Declaration of Jihad on the Americans Occupying the Country of the Two Sacred Places, issued in August 1996, was Osama bin Laden's first call for jihad against the United States. Also known as the "Ladenese Epistle," it can be taken to represent al Qaeda's declaration of war on Washington. In the context of debates among Muslim militants, it called for adjusting strategy so that instead of fighting local battles, they would wage a global-scale jihad against the Western superpower in response to its assaults on Muslims. The declaration also addresses issues specific to Saudi Arabia, asserting that American forces on Saudi soil constitute a military occupation and that Muslims should expel them.

In terms of Bin Laden's career, the declaration marked a turning point. As a young man in his twenties, he joined the Afghan struggle against Soviet forces by 1984. In the early 1990s, he became active in Saudi Arabia's dissident religious current. The Saudi government cracked down on the dissidents, however, imprisoning some and driving others, like Bin Laden, into exile. In 1992 he found refuge in Sudan. The United States and Saudi Arabia suspected him of plotting terrorist activities, so they put pressure on the Sudanese government to expel him. In 1996 he moved back to Afghanistan; shortly after arriving there, he published the Declaration of Jihad. Two years later, al Qaeda carried out its first major terrorist attack on American targets with truck bombings of the U.S. embassies in Nairobi, Kenya, and Dar es Salaam, Tanzania. There followed the 2000 attack on the USS *Cole* in the port of Aden, Yemen, at the southern tip of the Arabian Peninsula, and the attacks on the United States of September 11, 2001.

Context

Bin Laden's Declaration of Jihad reflects the intersection of several currents in late-twentieth-century Muslim politics, including the evolution of Islamic revivalist ideologies, the aftermath of the war in Afghanistan of the 1980s, and the emergence of religious dissent in Saudi Arabia. By

the 1970s, Islamic revivalist organizations like the Society of the Muslim Brothers, or Muslim Brotherhood, had become influential actors in Arab and Muslim countries. Such organizations sought to make Islam the central principle of politics and society in the belief that doing so would improve moral and material conditions and strengthen society against Western powers. In Egypt, the Society of the Muslim Brothers was the largest and most influential revivalist organization. The Muslim Brotherhood was generally inclined to consider gradual reform the surest path to realizing its vision of a true Islamic social order. In the mid-1970s, however, radical splinter groups jettisoned the gradualist approach and adopted a revolutionary attitude toward the Egyptian government, deeming its leaders to be apostates—renouncers of Islam—and therefore legitimate targets for religiously sanctioned warfare, or jihad.

Throughout the history of Islam from its rise in the seventh century, jihad as a form of military struggle took two forms: either warfare against non-Muslim lands in order to expand the realm of Islam or warfare to defend Muslim lands against non-Muslim aggression. (Jihad as a spiritual struggle to bring one's soul into alignment with divine will is a related but distinct sense of the term, with its own history.) Deeming a Muslim ruler to be an apostate and labeling rebellion against such a ruler to be jihad is a modern development in Muslim thought. In the name of such jihad, militants assassinated the Egyptian president Anwar as-Sadat in 1981. His successor, Hosni Mubarak, was obliged to fight militant organizations that attacked government officials, security forces, and foreign tourists. During the 1990s the Egyptian government succeeded in its campaign to suppress the militant organizations, but their ideology of rebellion in the name of jihad spread to other Muslim countries.

Jihad was also invoked in Muslim movements for national liberation and minority rights. In Palestine and Kashmir, for example, the breakup of the British Empire caused Muslim populations to find themselves living under non-Muslim rule—Jewish Israeli rule in Palestine and Hindu-majority Indian rule in Kashmir. In the case of Palestine, national liberation movements from the 1950s to the 1980s generally framed the cause in secular, anticolonial terms, as did the nationalist movements in African and Asian politics. In the 1980s, however, it became increasing-

1957

- **March 10**
Osama bin Laden is born in Riyadh, Saudi Arabia.

1978

- **April**
A Marxist revolution is staged in Afghanistan, with the Marxists seizing control in Kabul.

1979

- **December**
The Soviet Union invades Afghanistan to support the regime against anti-Communist forces, initiating the Soviet-Afghan War, which lasts until 1988.

1984

- Bin Laden goes to Pakistan to support the Afghan cause.

1988

- **August**
Bin Laden forms al Qaeda in Peshawar, Pakistan.

1990

- **August 2**
Iraq invades Kuwait; Saudi Arabia invites U.S. forces in to defend against Iraq, and Saudi dissidents condemn the resort to non-Muslim military assistance.

1991

- **February**
The United States and coalition forces liberate Kuwait.

---

ly common for those involved to frame liberation struggle as jihad to free Muslim land from infidel rule. In historical terms, this form of jihad fit the template of defense against non-Muslim aggression and therefore more readily captured Muslim imaginations than did the notion of rebellious jihad against an apostate ruler.

The idiom of defensive jihad likewise colored the struggle in Afghanistan against a Communist regime backed by the Soviet Union. In April 1978, a Marxist political party seized power in Kabul. In the context of the cold war rivalry between the Soviet Union and the United States, the Afghan coup—called the Saur Revolution—prompted alarm in Washington, which was also preoccupied with events in Iran, where antigovernment protests that year led to the ouster of a pro-Western monarchy. As much of the world's attention focused on developments in the newly proclaimed Islamic Republic of Iran, Kabul's Marxist regime was undermined by disputes between the ruling Khalq faction and the rival Parcham faction. A bloody purge in September 1979, whereby the leader of the Khalq tried to eliminate the Parcham's leadership, threatened to destabilize the government. Moscow responded by sending military forces into Afghanistan to oust the Khalq and install Parcham's leader. Instead of stabilizing the situation, the Soviet invasion initiated the Soviet-Afghan war: The United States, Pakistan, and Saudi Arabia supported the anti-Communist Afghan forces.

Muslim solidarity with Afghans took the form of a transnational volunteer campaign, with headquarters in Peshawar, Pakistan, as thousands of young Muslims from Arab countries and central and southern Asia flocked to fight the infidel Communists. Various Islamic groups operated guest houses that served as centers for recruitment, propaganda, and channels to military training camps. Osama bin Laden founded al Qaeda in August 1988. Al Qaeda originally limited membership to Arab volunteers for the broadly defined purpose of waging jihad on behalf of oppressed Muslims in Afghanistan and elsewhere.

One phase of the Soviet-Afghan War concluded when Moscow decided to withdraw its forces in 1989, leaving its Communist client exposed to Afghan enemies. The ensuing civil war involved the defeat of the Communists in 1992, leaving Afghan forces and the emerging Taliban movement to grapple for power. In the meantime, Muslim volunteers departed for other fronts on the expanding horizon of jihad in defense of Muslims in Chechnya, Bosnia, Kashmir, and elsewhere.

In 1989 and 1990, Bin Laden and other Saudi "Afghans," as veterans of the jihad in Afghanistan were known, returned home as heroes to a country where upholding Islam formed the core of dynastic legitimacy. Some decades earlier, the Saudi Arabian dynasty had demonstrated Muslim solidarity when it admitted Muslim Brothers fleeing persecution under Arab nationalist governments. The Muslim Brotherhood and the Saudi government ostentatiously championed religious causes by cooperating in pan-Islamic organizations to distribute funds for mosques, schools, and publications. The one blemish on

---

the Saudi government's pan-Islamic record was its alignment with the United States, which was unpopular for its
close relations with Israel. Saudi Arabia's delicate balance
between strategic security under Washington's military
umbrella and domestic legitimacy through adherence to
Islamic principles was ruptured in the wake of the Iraqi
invasion of Kuwait.

When Saddam Hussein's forces occupied Kuwait in
August 1990, it was not clear whether he intended to
send his army into Saudi Arabia as well, in order to seize
the world's richest oil fields. Not trusting Hussein's
intentions, the United States dispatched a diplomatic
mission to Riyadh to see whether Saudi leaders would
allow American and allied military forces into the kingdom to deter a possible Iraqi attack. Bin Laden tried to
dissuade the Saudi government from admitting non-
Muslim forces, proposing that Saudi forces and Muslim
volunteers for jihad, on the Afghan model, could protect
the kingdom. The Saudi government nonetheless decided to rely on the massive conventional military power
offered by Washington. The upshot was a severe political
crisis for Saudi Arabia.

The crux of the controversy over hosting American
forces rested on two issues. First, Muslims are not supposed to seek military assistance from non-Muslims. Second, the introduction of non-Muslim troops into Arabia
created the impression that the holy places were under
infidel occupation. Saudi religious dissidents like Safar
al-Hawali and Salman al-Auda emerged as leaders of a
movement known as Sahwa, or "the Awakening." They
argued that the government had effectively surrendered
the country's sovereignty to Washington. When American
troops remained even after the expulsion of Iraqi forces
from Kuwait, the dissidents called for fundamental government reform to curb Western influence, broaden the
scope of Islamic law, and relieve economic distress. By
1994 the authorities had suppressed the movement
through censorship and arrests of leaders such as al-
Hawali and al-Auda. Bin Laden ended up in Afghanistan
by May 1996.

Meanwhile, debate continued among Muslim militants
regarding the strategies of jihad. Until the mid-1990s, the
antigovernment facet of jihad had focused solely on secular authoritarian regimes in Muslim nations, seeking to
destabilize Algeria and Egypt, for instance. These regimes
and others were able to defeat the jihadist rebels, leading
some in their ranks to conclude that it was fruitless to
attack "the near enemy"—the regional regimes—when they
had the powerful backing of the Western powers, "the far
enemy," especially the United States. Proponents of waging
jihad against the far enemy eventually decided to target the
United States, in the belief that only if its forces were
expelled from the Muslim world would jihad against its
local clients be successful. The declaration issued by Bin
Laden in August 1996, then, embodies the mixing of Saudi
religious dissent with the emergence of the notion of fighting a jihad against the far enemy, a struggle that would
become known as global jihad.

Time Line

1991

- **May**
  Saudi dissidents
  present a peti-
  tion to the king
  seeking a
  greater role for
  religion in deci-
  sion making
  and law.

1992

- **Spring**
  Bin Laden
  moves to Sudan.

1994

- **September**
  Saudi authori-
  ties imprison
  leaders of reli-
  gious dissent.

1995

- **November 13**
  A truck bomb-
  ing at a Saudi
  Arabian Nation-
  al Guard build-
  ing in Riyadh
  kills five Ameri-
  cans and two
  Indians.

1996

- **May**
  Bin Laden
  moves to
  Afghanistan.

- **June 26**
  A truck bombing at
  a military complex
  in Khobar, Saudi
  Arabia, kills
  nineteen U.S.
  soldiers.

- **August 23**
  Bin Laden issues
  his Declaration of
  Jihad against
  Americans.

1998

- **August 7**
  Al Qaeda stages
  attacks on the
  U.S. embassies
  in Kenya and
  Tanzania.

Time Line

2000

■ **October 12**
Al Qaeda executes an attack on the USS *Cole* in Aden's harbor.

2001

■ **September 11**
Al Qaeda operatives hijack four passenger jets in a terrorist attack on the United States.

About the Author

Osama bin Laden (1957–) is the Saudi leader of al Qaeda, an organization dedicated to waging jihad against the United States and Western influence in the Muslim world. He grew up in one of Saudi Arabia's wealthiest families in the Red Sea city of Jidda. He was in his early twenties when the Soviet Union invaded Afghanistan in December 1979. Like many idealistic young men in the Muslim world, he went to Pakistan to support the anti-Communist jihad, arriving in Peshawar in 1984. Bin Laden lent his organizing and fund-raising talents to the jihad, and he also fought in at least one battle against Soviet forces. Toward the end of the war, in August 1988, he founded al Qaeda in Peshawar. After the Soviet evacuation, he returned to Saudi Arabia and became active in the religious protest movement against the government's decision to host American military forces in response to Iraq's invasion of Kuwait.

In the early 1990s, Bin Laden was yet a minor figure among religious dissidents, but his opposition to the government resulted in his expulsion from his homeland and resettlement in Sudan. There he expanded his contacts with militants from different countries, building on relationships formed in Pakistan during the 1980s. In May 1996, the Sudanese government succumbed to pressure from the United States and Saudi Arabia to deport him. Bin Laden then moved to Afghanistan, and shortly after establishing new headquarters there, he issued the August 1996 Declaration of Jihad. As long as he resided in Khartoum, he had refrained from issuing inflammatory statements that would complicate Sudan's official relations with Riyadh and Washington. In Afghanistan's anarchic circumstances, he was no longer so constrained. In the next two years he attracted increasing attention as a potential threat to Western interests in the Muslim world. Al Qaeda's attacks on U.S. targets between 1998 and 2001 made him the focus of attention among national security officials and experts in the West. After the attacks of September 11, 2001, the United States invaded Afghanistan, forcing him to flee over the border into Pakistan, where he is believed to have found refuge in the rugged mountains of North-West Frontier Province.

Explanation and Analysis of the Document

The Declaration of Jihad on the Americans Occupying the Country of the Two Sacred Places was published in *al-Quds al-Arabi*, a London-based Arabic newspaper. The purpose of the document was to persuade Muslims that the United States is the primary enemy of Muslims, responsible for oppressing them in numerous lands, and that Muslims therefore have a duty to wage jihad against America. The declaration blends religious texts with descriptions of overall Muslim suffering and the specific suffering of Muslims in Saudi Arabia. In the latter case, the declaration asserts that oppression, corruption, and economic mismanagement are connected to what it calls American military occupation of the heart of the Muslim world. The abridged version of the document reproduced here captures all of the major themes in the original version, which expands on grievances particular to Saudi Arabia and incorporates more citations of classical authorities.

◆ Paragraphs 1–9

Bin Laden opens by addressing Muslims in general and the Muslims of the Arabian Peninsula in particular. The declaration follows the convention of Islamic discourse by providing citations from the two authoritative sources for guidance, the Qur'an and the Sunna. In Arabic, *al-qur'ān* means "the recitation," referring to the recitation of God's revealed word by the prophet Muhammad. The Sunna is the prophetic tradition, Muhammad's words and deeds recorded in hadiths, or reports traced to him. The Declaration of Jihad begins with a hadith in which the Prophet calls for expelling polytheists from Arabia. Bin Laden cites the hadith to remind Muslims of their obligation to rid Arabia of Americans. The Arabic term in the hadith translated as "polytheists" is *kuffar*, which has the general sense of "unbelievers" and can refer to both Christians and Jews.

Five quotations from the Qur'an follow the invocation of God's guidance. They call on the believers (Muslims) to be mindful of God, to trust that obedience to God and the Prophet will lead to success, and to remember that the believers are the best of humankind. The presentation of these verses serves to reinforce the Muslim believer's resolve to undertake a difficult and risky mission. There follows a hadith warning believers of a duty to restrain oppressors, an allusion to the Saudi authorities.

◆ Paragraphs 10 and 11

The declaration proceeds to remind Muslims that they are under wide-ranging assault by Jewish and Christian powers. In April 1996, Israel had attacked Lebanon in an escalation of border clashes with the Hezbollah militia. On April 18 an Israeli artillery shell had struck a UN compound near the village of Qana, killing over one hundred Arab civilians who had sought refuge there. Meanwhile,

Iraq was under UN sanctions that Muslims blamed for shortages of food and medicine, which they considered the cause of many civilian deaths. The list of eleven other regions where Muslims were struggling against occupation or non-Muslim domination illustrates the broad scale of Muslim suffering attributed to the United States and the United Nations for not allowing Muslims to acquire arms to defend themselves. The worst of all offenses against Muslims is cited as the American occupation of Saudi Arabia, because the Arabian Peninsula is the cradle of Islam and site of the holy cities of Mecca and Medina.

◆ **Paragraphs 12–14**

Bin Laden next asserts that despite the Muslim world's dire condition, believers should not despair, as religious scholars were leading an awakening to stir Muslim believers to rise up against their enemies. Islamic religious scholars have been natural leaders against corrupt rulers who collude with infidel enemies, and there are many historical examples of such scholars. Ibn Taymīyah (1263–1328), a fourteenth-century Syrian scholar who has become a significant influence on modern revivalist thinkers, urged the Muslims of his time to rally against a nominally Muslim Mongol dynasty rulership over Iraq and Iran. 'Izz al-Din ibn 'Abd al-Salam al-Sulami (1181–1262) is celebrated for having denounced a Muslim ruler who allied with the Crusaders against a Muslim rival. These two medieval scholars, renowned for standing up to rulers and urging believers to fight infidel enemies, are models for many modern-day Muslims.

Modern heroes include Abdallah Azzam (1941–1989), a Palestinian Muslim Brother whose activities for the Afghan jihad and writings on jihad in general have inspired many Muslims to enlist in the transnational militant movement. Ahmed Yassin (1937–2004), killed by an Israeli missile strike, was the leading religious figure in the Palestinian Hamas movement. Omar Abd al-Rahman (1938–) was the Egyptian leader of the militant Islamic Group. He was not killed by the United States, as the declaration states, but is serving a life sentence there for conspiracy to detonate a truck bomb under the World Trade Center in 1993. Salman al-Auda (1955–) and Safar al-Hawali (1950–) were the two leading figures in Saudi Arabia's Awakening (Sahwa) movement of the 1980s and 1990s. The declaration depicts the Saudi government as an American puppet, claiming that the Saudi authorities arrested al-Auda and al-Hawali at Washington's behest.

Bin Laden proceeds to place himself in the line of brave scholars, from Ibn Taymīyah to the present, who suffered for speaking truth to power and were forced to move from one country to another. Bin Laden found a haven in Khurasan, by which he means Afghanistan, site of the recent Muslim triumph over the Soviet Union. From his haven in Afghanistan, he says, he plans to strive against the alliance of Jews and Christians—in secular terms, Israel and the United States—which was inflicting injustice on *umma*, the worldwide community of Muslim believers. He highlights what are to his mind the two most grievous instances of the Judeo-Christian assault on Muslims: the occupation of Jerusalem by Israel and the takeover of Saudi Arabia by the United States. In his view, they are not discrete, unrelated political events but part of a single plan to oppress Muslims.

◆ **Paragraphs 15–19**

The declaration turns from an overview of the Muslim world to conditions in Saudi Arabia, where every segment of society was suffering the effects of poverty, repression, and injustice. Bin Laden draws attention to anti-American violence in the kingdom and asserts that this was a natural reaction to widespread suffering. The fatal explosions in Riyadh and Khobar were expressions of mounting internal pressures. The Riyadh explosion took place in November 1995, when five Americans and two Indians were killed in a truck bombing against a National Guard building. A connection to al Qaeda has not been established, although the perpetrators were veterans of the Afghan jihad and Bin Laden applauded their deed. The explosion in Khobar, a city in Saudi Arabia's Eastern Province, occurred in June 1996, when a massive truck bomb was detonated near a military complex, killing nineteen U.S. soldiers. This attack was not related to al Qaeda; rather, it was probably the work of Saudi Hezbollah al-Hejaz militants.

The declaration taps the current of Saudi dissent in paragraph 16 by addressing economic and political issues. In the early and mid-1990s, low oil prices, a high rate of population increase, and slow economic growth made citizens' daily lives more difficult. Ordinary Saudis felt the effects of inflation and personal debt. The invocation of usury and foreign debt intimates the moral failings of the government, a point driven home with the complaint that the country abides by man-made laws rather than divine law. Government failure was not limited to the economic and legal realms: It included the fundamental task of defending the country against foreign threat, as posed by Iraq when it invaded Kuwait. That failure was embodied in the decision to allow American troops into Saudi Arabia, a situation considered equivalent to foreign occupation. When courageous religious scholars denounced the government for failing to manage the economy, defend the homeland, and rule according to God's law, the authorities threw them in prison.

To emphasize the Saudi government's most grievous offenses, the declaration states that the government lost legitimacy for two reasons in particular: first, for not ruling in accordance with religious law and crushing the dissent of religious scholars and "pious youth" who supported them and, second, for failing to defend the kingdom and permitting a prolonged Crusader occupation, which became the central factor underlying the country's terrible plight. All of these problems and policies came about despite efforts to offer sincere advice to the king. As early as May 1991 (the year 1411 AH in the Islamic calendar), religious intellectuals signed a petition calling for reforms to address economic problems and to buttress the Saudi government's commitment to Islam rather than paying lip service. Instead of heeding that petition and subsequent calls for reform, the ruling family ignored them and punished their authors.

A United States Marine walks with embassy employees and an FBI investigator in front of the burned-out wreckage of the U.S. Embassy in Tanzania in August 1998. (AP/Wide World Photos)

◆ **Paragraph 20 and 21**

In paragraph 20 the declaration comes to speak more directly to its Muslim audience, first by posing a rhetorical question asking how the Saudi government can be the largest arms buyer and trading partner with a country that occupies the kingdom and props up Israeli control over Palestine, with the accompanying killing and deportation of its Muslims. In order to combat the United States, Muslims in Saudi Arabia should boycott American goods as part of fulfilling the duty to wage jihad.

The declaration then cites authoritative religious texts to summon Muslim youth to wage jihad against the Americans occupying the Muslim holy places. The Qur'an promises heavenly reward to believers who die in the course of waging jihad. Three hadiths describe in detail the heavenly rewards in store for martyrs, such as forgiveness for sins, high standing among the denizens of paradise, marriage to seventy-two virgins, and the right to intercede for seventy kinsmen. Continuing the citation of religious texts in paragraph 21, the declaration cites a hadith in which the angel Gabriel urged the Prophet not to rest after a battlefield triumph against a coalition of Arabian tribes (the *ahzab*, or

parties). Instead, the Prophet was to lead his men against the Banu Qurayza (here spelled Bani Qorayza), a Jewish clan that had not accepted his authority.

◆ **Paragraphs 22–24**

The lesson for today's Muslims is that achieving victory in one quarter, such as Afghanistan or Bosnia-Herzegovina, is no reason to cease waging jihad when Muslims are under occupation in Saudi Arabia and Palestine. Therefore, Bin Laden calls on Muslims not only in occupied lands but, indeed, everywhere to join the jihad against the Americans and the Israelis, the enemies of Muslims.

The language of the declaration provokes the believer's imagination to see the world through the lens of religion rather than nationality: Muslims are brethren and compatriots, not citizens of different nations, and they share the same political and military fortunes regardless of country of origin. Likewise, the enemies of Muslims, be they Israeli, American, or Soviet, are all part of the non-Muslim—that is, Judeo-Christian or Zionist-Crusader—aggression against Muslims. The division of the world into believers and unbelievers is at the heart of global jihad's appeal for recruiting warriors of various nationalities to armed struggle against oppressors of Muslims anywhere. The declaration closes with a summation of the call for Muslims to cooperate for the sake of liberating Islam's holy places—Mecca, Medina, and Jerusalem—as part of the effort to unify all Muslims under allegiance to God.

Audience

The Declaration of Jihad was presented in print in an Arabic daily published in London. It explicitly addresses the entire Muslim world, urging believers to respond to non-Muslim aggression against believers by waging jihad in defense of their rights. It also addresses the Muslims of Arabia in particular and therefore dwells on political and economic conditions in Saudi Arabia. References to dissident Saudi religious scholars and their efforts to persuade the government to undertake sweeping reforms resonated with the influential discourse of religious dissent that arose during the crisis over Iraq's 1990 invasion of Kuwait. A third, implicit audience would have been the regional circles of militants committed to jihad against secular regimes and non-Muslim oppressors. The declaration calls on them to join the fight against the far enemy as a more effective way to turn the tide in local struggles.

Impact

The Declaration of Jihad had limited immediate impact. Bin Laden had recently arrived in Afghanistan, which was witnessing the consolidation of the Taliban regime after years of civil war. The al Qaeda leader had to rebuild his organization in Afghanistan while plotting attacks on Western targets. The declaration's near-range impact, then, was to raise Bin Laden's profile in transnational Islamic militant

"The massacres that have taken place in Tajikistan, Burma, Kashmir, Assam, the Philippines, Fatani, Ogaden, Somalia, Eritrea, Chechnya, and Bosnia-Herzegovina send shivers down our spines and stir up our passions. All this has happened before the eyes and ears of the world, but the blatant imperial arrogance of America, under the cover of the immoral United Nations, has prevented the dispossessed from arming themselves."

(Paragraph 10)

"People are struggling even with the basics of everyday life, and everyone talks frankly about economic recession, price inflation, mounting debts, and prison overcrowding."

(Paragraph 16)

"Brother Muslims in Saudi Arabia, does it make any sense at all that our country is the biggest purchaser of weapons from America in the world and America's biggest trading partner in the region, while at the very same time the Americans are occupying Saudi Arabia and supporting—with money, arms, and manpower—their Jewish brothers in the occupation of Palestine and their murder and expulsion of Muslims there?"

(Paragraph 20)

"I say to our Muslim brothers across the world: your brothers in Saudi Arabia and Palestine are calling for your help and asking you to share with them in the jihad against the enemies of God, your enemies the Israelis and Americans."

(Paragraph 22)

circles. His notions became part of debates among Muslim militants over the scope and targets of jihad. Most militants remained focused on local political struggles rather than converts to global jihad against the United States.

Two years later, al Qaeda's first major terrorist operation, the 1998 attacks on American embassies in East Africa, would thrust Bin Laden to the forefront of the Islamic militant current. The United States reacted by launching cruise missile attacks on an al Qaeda base in Afghanistan and a pharmaceutical company in Khartoum, Sudan, that Washington suspected of manufacturing bio-

logical weapons agents. These attacks failed to deter al Qaeda from pursuing jihad against the United States. In October 2000, an al Qaeda cell in Yemen attacked the USS *Cole* in Aden's harbor by detonating a boat loaded with explosives next to the U.S. warship.

The chain of al Qaeda operations against the United States reached a climax on September 11, 2001, with the hijacking of four civilian airliners. In New York City, al Qaeda's hijackers flew two airplanes into the World Trade Center's twin towers, causing their collapse. In Washington, D.C., the hijackers flew an airplane into the Pentagon.

In the fourth airplane, passengers struggled with the hijackers, resulting in a crash landing in a field in western Pennsylvania. Almost three thousand people were killed in the four attacks, with the largest number perishing as the result of the collapse of the World Trade Center towers. The United States responded by invading Afghanistan a month later to expel al Qaeda from its havens and overthrow the Taliban regime that sheltered Bin Laden. Nevertheless, both groups survived and reorganized in Pakistan, and the idea of jihad against the United States remains a potent inspiration for Muslim militants.

Further Reading

■ Articles

Wiktorowicz, Quintan. "The New Global Threat: Transnational Salafis and Jihad." *Middle East Policy* 8, no. 4 (December 2001): 18–38.

■ Books

Bergen, Peter. *Holy War, Inc.: Inside the Secret World of Osama bin Laden*. New York: Free Press, 2002.

Fandy, Mamoun. *Saudi Arabia and the Politics of Dissent*. New York: Palgrave Macmillan, 2001.

Gerges, Fawaz A. *The Far Enemy: Why Jihad Went Global*. Cambridge, U.K.: Cambridge University Press, 2006.

Hegghammer, Thomas. *Jihad in Saudi Arabia*. Cambridge, U.K.: Cambridge University Press, forthcoming.

Lawrence, Bruce, ed. *Messages to the World: The Statements of Osama bin Laden*, trans. James Howarth. London: Verso, 2005.

Scheuer, Michael. *Through Our Enemies' Eyes: Osama bin Laden, Radical Islam, and the Future of America*. Washington, D.C.: Potomac Books, 2007.

Wright, Lawrence. *The Looming Tower: Al-Qaeda and the Road to 9/11*. New York: Knopf, 2006.

—David Commins

Questions for Further Study

1. In the early 1980s the United States seemed to be allied with Muslim forces in opposing the Soviet invasion of Afghanistan. Yet in the 1990s the United States came to be regarded as the implacable enemy of Islam as conceived by people such as Osama bin Laden. Why did this realignment occur?

2. Many people argue that the concept of "jihad" as practiced by terrorists such as Osama bin Laden is actually a corruption of the concept. What is jihad, and why do some people believe that Bin Laden's vision of jihad is not consistent with the principles of Islam?

3. Compare this document with Ayatollah Khomeini's *Islamic Government: Governance of the Jurist*. To what extent do the two documents express similar—or differing—visions of Islam and its place in the world?

4. Following the 2001 terrorist attacks on the United States, Osama bin Laden became a despised figure in the United States, and U.S. military action in Afghanistan was focused in part on capturing him; as of 2010 he was still at large. Do you believe that if Bin Laden is eventually captured, the dynamic in the Middle East will change? How serious a blow would his capture be to Islamic militancy?

5. Do you believe that Islamic extremism would diminish if the Western powers simply withdrew from the Middle East? Or do you believe that Islamic extremists would simply find another reason to wage jihad against the West?

OSAMA BIN LADEN'S DECLARATION OF JIHAD AGAINST AMERICANS

Expel the Polytheists from the Arabian peninsula.

A Letter from Sheikh Osama bin Muhammad bin Laden to his Muslim Brothers across the world, and particularly those in the Arabian peninsula.

Praise be to God. We beseech Him for help and forgiveness. We seek refuge in God from the evil of our souls and our bad deeds. He whom God guides will not go astray, and he whom He leads astray can have no guide. I testify that there is no god but God alone, who has no partners. And I testify that Muhammad is His Servant and Prophet.

"You who believe, be mindful of God, as is His due, and make sure you devote yourselves to Him, to your dying moment."

"People, be mindful of your Lord, who created you from a single soul, and from it created its mate, and from the pair of them spread countless men and women far and wide; be mindful of God, in whose name you make requests of one another. Beware of the severing of ties of kinship: God is always watching over you."

"Believers, be mindful of God, speak in a direct fashion and to good purpose, and He will put your deeds right for you and forgive you your sins. Whoever obeys God and His Messenger will truly achieve a great triumph."

Shu'ayb said: "I cannot succeed without God's help: I trust in Him, and always turn to Him."

Thanks be to God, who said: "[Believers], you are the best community singled out for people: you order what is right, forbid what is wrong, and you believe in God."

And blessings and peace upon His Servant and Prophet, who said: "The people are close to an all-encompassing punishment from God if they see the oppressor and fail to restrain him."

It is no secret to you, my brothers, that the people of Islam have been afflicted with oppression, hostility, and injustice by the Judeo-Christian alliance and its supporters. This shows our enemies' belief that Muslims' blood is the cheapest and that their property and wealth is merely loot. Your blood has been spilt in Palestine and Iraq, and the horrific images of the massacre in Qana in Lebanon are still fresh in people's minds. The massacres that have taken place in Tajikistan, Burma, Kashmir, Assam,

the Philippines, Fatani, Ogaden, Somalia, Eritrea, Chechnya, and Bosnia-Herzegovina send shivers down our spines and stir up our passions. All this has happened before the eyes and ears of the world, but the blatant imperial arrogance of America, under the cover of the immoral United Nations, has prevented the dispossessed from arming themselves.

So the people of Islam realised that they were the fundamental target of the hostility of the Judeo-Crusader alliance. All the false propaganda about the supposed rights of Islam was abandoned in the face of the attacks and massacres committed against Muslims everywhere, the latest and most serious of which—the greatest disaster to befall the Muslims since the death of the Prophet Muhammad—is the occupation of Saudi Arabia, which is the cornerstone of the Islamic world, place of revelation, source of the Prophetic mission, and home of the Noble Ka'ba where Muslims direct their prayers. Despite this, it was occupied by the armies of the Christians, the Americans, and their allies.

I meet you today in the midst of this gloomy scenario, but also in light of the tremendous, blessed awakening that has swept across the world, and particularly the Islamic world. After the scholars of Islam underwent an enforced absence—enforced due to the oppressive Crusader campaign led by America in the fear that these scholars will incite our Islamic *umma* against its enemies, in the same way as did the pious scholars of old (God bless their souls) such as ibn Taymiyya and al-Izz ibn Abd al-Salam—this Judeo-Crusader alliance undertook to kill and arrest the righteous scholars and hardworking preachers. May God sanctify who He wishes. They killed the *mujahid* Sheikh Abdallah Azzam, they arrested Sheikh Ahmed Yassin in Jerusalem, and they killed the *mujahid* Sheikh Omar Abd al-Rahman in America, as well as arresting—on the advice of America—a large number of scholars, preachers and youth in Saudi Arabia. The most prominent of these were Sheikh Salman al-Auda and Sheikh Safar al-Hawali and their brothers.

This injustice was inflicted on us, too, as we were prevented from talking to Muslims and were hounded out of Saudi Arabia to Pakistan, Sudan, and then Afghanistan. That is what led to this long absence of mine, but by the grace of God there became available a safe base in Khurasan, high in the peaks of the Hindu Kush, the very same peaks upon which were smashed, by the grace of God, the largest infidel military force in the world, and on which the myth of the great powers perished before the cries of the holy warriors: God is greatest!

And today, in the same peaks of Afghanistan, we work to do away with the injustice that has befallen our *umma* at the hands of the Judeo-Crusader alliance, especially after its occupation of Jerusalem and its appropriation of Saudi Arabia. We pray to God that He might bless us with victory—He is our protector and is well capable of doing so.

And so here we are today, working and discussing with each other to find ways of rectifying what has happened to the Islamic world generally and Saudi Arabia in particular. We need to study the appropriate paths to take in order to restore things to good order, and to restore to the people their rights after the considerable damage and harm inflicted on their life and religion. This has afflicted every section of society, whether civilian or military or security personnel, whether employees or merchants, young or old, university students, graduates or the unemployed, who now represent a broad section of society numbering hundreds of thousands. The situation in Saudi Arabia has begun to resemble a huge volcano that is about to explode and destroy unbelief and corruption, wherever it comes from. The two explosions in Riyadh and Khobar are merely warning signs pointing to this destructive torrent which is produced by bitter repression, terrible injustice, and the humiliating poverty that we see today.

People are struggling even with the basics of everyday life, and everyone talks frankly about economic recession, price inflation, mounting debts, and prison overcrowding. Low-income government employees talk to you about their debts in the tens or hundreds of thousands of riyals, whilst complaining that the riyal's value is declining dramatically. Domestic debts owed by the government to its citizens have reached 340 billion riyals, and are rising daily due to usurious interest, let alone all the foreign debt. People are wondering: are we really the biggest source of oil in the world? They feel that God is bringing this torture upon them because they have not spoken out against the regime's injustice and illegitimate behaviour, the most prominent aspects of which are its failure to rule in accordance with God's law, its depriving of legal rights to its servants, its permitting the American occupiers into Saudi Ara-

bia, and its arresting of righteous scholars—inheritors of the Prophet's legacy—and unjustly throwing them in prison. The regime has desecrated its legitimacy through many of its own actions, the most important being:

1. Its suspension of the rulings of the Islamic law and replacement thereof with man-made laws, and its entering into a bloody confrontation with the righteous scholars and pious youth. May God sanctify whom He pleases.

2. Its inability to protect the land and its allowing the enemies of God to occupy it for years in the form of the American Crusaders, who have become the principal reason for all aspects of our land's disastrous predicament.

The voices of the shadows have spoken up, their eyes uncovering the veil of injustice and their noses smelling the stench of corruption. The voices of reform have spoken up, calling for the situation to be put right: they have sent petitions, testimonies, and requests for reform. In the year 1411 AH, at the time of the Gulf War, a petition was sent to the king with around 400 signatures calling for reform in the country, but he made a mockery of them by completely ignoring their advice, and the situation went from bad to worse.

Brother Muslims in Saudi Arabia, does it make any sense at all that our country is the biggest purchaser of weapons from America in the world and America's biggest trading partner in the region, while at the very same time the Americans are occupying Saudi Arabia and supporting—with money, arms, and manpower—their Jewish brothers in the occupation of Palestine and their murder and expulsion of Muslims there? Depriving these occupiers of the huge returns they receive from their trade with us is a very important way of supporting the *jihad* against them, and we expect you to boycott all American goods. Men of the radiant future of our *umma* of Muhammad, raise the banner of *jihad* up high against the Judeo-American alliance that has occupied the holy places of Islam. God told his Prophet: "He will not let the deeds of those who are killed for His cause come to nothing; He will guide them and put them in a good state; He will admit them into the Garden He has already made known to them." And the Prophet said: "There are one hundred levels in Heaven that God has prepared for the holy warriors who have died for Him, between two levels as between the earth and the sky." And the *al-Jami al-Sahih* notes that the Prophet said: "The best martyrs are those who stay in the battle line and do not turn their faces away until they are killed. They will achieve the highest level of Heaven, and their Lord will look kindly upon them. When your Lord looks kindly upon a slave in the world, He will not hold him to account." And he said: "The martyr has a guarantee from God: He forgives him at the first drop of his blood and shows him his seat in Heaven. He decorates him with the jewels of faith, protects him from the torment of the grave, keeps him safe on the day of judgment, places a crown of dignity on his head with the finest rubies in the world, marries him to seventy-two of the pure virgins of paradise and intercedes on behalf of seventy of his relatives," as related by Ahmad al-Tirmidhi in an authoritative *hadith*.

I say to the youth of Islam who have waged *jihad* in Afghanistan and Bosnia-Herzegovina, with their financial, spiritual, linguistic, and scholarly resources, that the battle is not yet over. I remind them of what Gabriel said to the Prophet, after the battle of Ahzab: "When the Messenger of God, prayers and peace be upon him, departed to Medina and laid down his sword, Gabriel came to him and said: 'You have laid down your sword? By God, the angels have not yet laid down their swords. Get up and go with whoever is with you to the Bani Qorayza, and I will go ahead of you to shake their fortresses and strike fear into them.'

So Gabriel went off, accompanied by his pageant of angels, the Prophet, and his holy warriors and helpers." This is as it was told by al-Bukhari.

I say to our Muslim brothers across the world: your brothers in Saudi Arabia and Palestine are calling for your help and asking you to share with them in the *jihad* against the enemies of God, your enemies the Israelis and Americans. They are asking you to defy them in whatever way you possibly can, so as to expel them in defeat and humiliation from the holy places of Islam. God Almighty has said: "If they seek help from you against persecution, it is your duty to assist them."

Cavalry of Islam, be mounted! This is a difficult time, so you yourselves must be tough. You should know that your coming-together and cooperation in order to liberate the holy places of Islam is the right step towards unification of the word of our *umma* under the banner of God's unity. At this point we can only raise our palms humbly to ask God Almighty to provide good fortune and success in this matter.

Lord, bless your slave and messenger Muhammad, and his family and companions. Our final prayer is praise to God, Lord of the worlds.

Your brother in Islam,
Osama bin Muhammad bin Laden

Glossary

al-Bukhari	Sahih al-Bukhari (810–870); compiler of one of the six canonical hadiths of Sunni Islam, the branch to which Bin Laden adheres
al-Jami al-Sahih	the work of Sahih al-Bukhari
Gulf War	in this context, the conflict often called the Persian Gulf War (August 2, 1990–February 28, 1991)
place of the revelation	the cave, located in present-day Saudi Arabia, where the Qur'an is said to have been revealed to Muhammad
Shu'ayb	a Muslim prophet of the BH (before hegira) period
umma	in this context, the community of Islamic believers; the Muslim world

The 1998 Nobel Peace Prize laureates John Hume (right) and David Trimble (AP/Wide World Photos)

"Victims have a right to remember as well as to contribute to a changed society."

Overview

On April 10, 1998, the British and Irish governments, after having participated in the Northern Ireland peace talks, agreed on a document that they hoped would end violence in and bring political stability to Northern Ireland. The Northern Ireland Peace Agreement—or more formally, the Agreement between the Government of the United Kingdom of Great Britain and Northern Ireland and the Government of Ireland—is often called the Belfast Agreement or the Good Friday Accord.

Peace talks had resumed in 1993 after U.S. president Bill Clinton decided to open dialogue with Sinn Féin, the party generally recognized as the political voice of the Irish Republican Army (IRA). This move by President Clinton gave credibility to the IRA's previously announced cease-fire. On April 7, 1998, just two days before the prearranged deadline for concluding the peace talks, the U.S. envoy, George Mitchell, produced a detailed outline for the peace agreement, which included provisions to encourage the British to accelerate the release of political prisoners. Mitchell's outline also proposed the establishment of five to eight British-Irish intergovernmental bodies to deal with agriculture, transportation, and similar issues; a council of ministers to select members of those bodies; and a commission to assist Catholic participation in the Royal Ulster Constabulary. The final agreement, signed at 4:30 p.m. on Good Friday, April 10, 1998, would include all of these proposals.

Context

Animosity between the Irish and British runs deep and can be traced to significant historical events. By 1171 English barons had seized Irish territory around Dublin, and by the fourteenth century all of Ireland was under British control. As the English aristocracy became assimilated into society, actual English control became limited to an area surrounding Dublin. The power shifted again in 1541 when Henry VIII forced the Irish to declare him king of Ireland and introduced new laws as well as the Anglican Church to

the predominantly Roman Catholic country. In the early seventeenth century, James I encouraged Protestant settlement in Ulster in Ireland's north to quell revolt against British rule. In 1649 an army led by Oliver Cromwell massacred a large number of Catholics at Drogheda in eastern Ireland, to avenge a massacre of Protestants in Ulster in 1641.

On July 11, 1690, William III, also known as William of Orange, defeated forces led by the deposed Catholic English monarch, James II, at the river Boyne in northeastern Ireland. This became a landmark event in Protestant-Catholic tensions, and it is still celebrated today in Northern Ireland every July 12 with marches through the Belfast streets that have often agitated Catholic resentment. By the early eighteenth century, Protestant English nobles owned approximately 90 percent of the land in Ireland, and laws restricting the rights of the Catholic majority had been enacted. On January 1,1801, the Act of Union became effective, formally uniting Ireland and Great Britain and renaming the islands the United Kingdom of Great Britain and Ireland. Sporadic revolts against British land policies ensued until yet another landmark event in the history of the Irish people.

Although potatoes are not indigenous to Ireland, the Irish people had gradually become dependent on that crop as a staple. Certainly, other crops were grown, and domesticated animals were in relatively plentiful supply, but British landowners commonly exported and traded the commodities of wheat, oats, lamb, beef, poultry, and pork. Poor tenant farmers and farmhands had no choice but to derive much of their sustenance from the potato. In 1845 a disease overwhelmed the Irish potato crop. The crop failures worsened during the succeeding two years, causing massive starvation. To escape famine, approximately one million Irish emigrated to the United States and Canada, the vast majority without much more than the clothes on their backs. The British government, fearing riots and rebellion, offered no monetary or physical aid to the starving masses. More than 1.5 million Irish died because of the famine. In the decades afterward, already bitter Irish-English and Catholic-Protestant relations would take on more intense levels of distrust and hatred.

By the late nineteenth century, the concept of home rule for Ireland gained popularity and was proposed twice in Parliament, although no pertinent legislation was then

1916

■ **April 24–30**
The Easter Rising takes place; its bloody conclusion and aftermath lead to the formation of the Irish Republican Army.

1920

■ **December 23**
The Government of Ireland Act is passed, legalizing the partition of Ireland into the six counties of Northern Ireland and the twenty-six counties of the Irish Free State.

1921

■ **December 6**
The Anglo-Irish Treaty is signed, ending the Irish War of Independence.

1948

■ **December 21**
The Irish Free State is granted independence from Great Britain under conditions stipulated in the Republic of Ireland Act; however, Northern Ireland remains part of the United Kingdom.

1966

■ **May 21**
The Ulster Volunteer Force declares war on the IRA, saying in a statement that the group included heavily armed Protestants dedicated to their cause.

passed. After the twentieth century dawned, many Irish became convinced that they must take matters into their own hands. On November 28, 1905, the political party, Sinn Féin, officially came into existence. In Gaelic, Sinn Fé means "we ourselves." The party's goal was to form a free and independent Ireland by shaking off British rule from the entire island. In April 1912 the British House of Commons approved the Home Rule Bill, which was scheduled to take effect in September 1914 (but the outbreak of World War I postponed implementation of the legislation). The prospect of home rule led directly to the formation in late 1912 of the Ulster Volunteer Force, whose stated aim was to resist all efforts to initiate home rule in Ireland. In an effort to avoid conflict, Parliament compromised with a solution known as home rule with partition, which divided Ireland such that six predominantly Protestant northern counties—counties that would become Northern Ireland—would remain within the United Kingdom, while the remaining twenty-six counties to the south and west would have home rule. This division of Ireland has since remained the focal point of discontent and violence.

In November 1913, a new group, the Irish Volunteers, formed to counter the threat posed by the Ulster Volunteer Force. After the outbreak of World War I, many Irish Volunteers enlisted in the British military, where they became known as the National Volunteers; however, a smaller anti-war group dedicated to home rule retained the name Irish Volunteers. This group, under the direction of the military council of the Irish Republican Brotherhood and working in concert with James Connolly's Irish Citizen Army, organized the Easter Rising, named for its commencement on Easter Monday, April 24, 1916. Hoping to take advantage of Great Britain's preoccupation with World War I, these rebels took control of Dublin's General Post Office and many other strategic locations and declared a free Irish nation. This action, rather than catching the British unaware, elicited an immediate military response in the form of invasion forces equipped with gunboats and armored vehicles. By April 30, once the last remaining rebels had surrendered, over four hundred people were dead and more than twenty-five hundred wounded; parts of Dublin had sustained extensive damage. Ninety of the 3,509 arrested by British authorities were sentenced to death, and fifteen, including most of the Easter Rising's organizers, were executed within two weeks of the rebellion's end. But those who had participated in the Easter Rising were soon to be known as the IRA (a union of the Irish Volunteers and the Irish Republican Brotherhood, founded in 1867 and committed to ending British rule by force). Resistance had become synonymous with violence.

Forceful opposition to continued British rule began with isolated acts against the police in 1919, escalating into widespread violence in 1920–1921. The IRA, under the leadership of Michael Collins, operated with effective guerilla tactics against the newly constituted British force of former servicemen called the Black and Tans in a harsh and ruthless war that exhausted the Irish forces. In 1920 the Government of Ireland Act created the Irish Free State within the British

Empire. The act also created Northern Ireland. The 1920–1921 violence, often called the Irish War of Independence, ceased with the signing of the Anglo-Irish Treaty in 1921. This treaty, which was more in the nature of a cease-fire, gave Northern Ireland the option of leaving the Irish Free State, an option that it exercised in December 1922. Thus, at this point, Ireland was partitioned. The six counties constituting Northern Ireland remained part of the United Kingdom. Provision was made for Northern Ireland to have its own legislative assembly, called the Stormont, which was to meet in Belfast. The remaining twenty-six counties were the Irish Free State, with its own parliament in Dublin and dominion status in the British Empire. The Irish Free State (later the Republic of Ireland) never officially accepted the division of Ireland and made it a policy aim to restore Irish unity. The IRA continued a long and intermittently violent campaign against both governments, which was condemned and outlawed by both Britain and Ireland.

From 1923 to 1963 discrimination against the Catholic minority in Protestant-dominated Northern Ireland was legally sanctioned. It was not until the advent of the British welfare state in the decades following World War II that Catholics in Northern Ireland received equitable educational opportunities and began to call for change. In 1966 violence erupted when two Catholics and one Protestant were murdered by the Ulster Volunteer Force, which that year declared war on the IRA. Rioting ensued. By 1967 a new organization, the Northern Ireland Civil Rights Association, had emerged. Although it was a predominantly Catholic body, the association was able to pressure the Northern Ireland government into making concessions to improve the situation of Catholics. However, governmental reforms proved to be inadequate, and civil rights marches served only to intensify hostilities.

With a political solution appearing less likely, splinter groups and paramilitary organizations gained new adherents. In August 1969 civil unrest erupted into three days of rioting in Belfast and Derry. Over the next several years, the more militant Provisional IRA and the Ulster Defence Association waged campaigns of violence, with the British army often caught in the middle of hostilities. By March 1971 Northern Ireland had a new prime minister, Brian Faulkner, who reintroduced internment detention without trial for terror suspects. As maintaining order became increasingly difficult, the British army adopted more aggressive tactics. On January 30, 1972, Bloody Sunday was added to the lexicon of Irish struggles, when in reaction to rioting stemming from a civil rights march in Derry, the British army's Parachute Regiment shot and killed fourteen protesters. Edward Heath, the conservative British prime minister, took the extraordinary step of assuming direct rule of Northern Ireland from London in March. The Northern Ireland government resigned en masse.

During 1972 at least 496 lives would be lost in Northern Ireland violence. Renewed initiatives to stem the violence resulted in the Sunningdale Agreement, a British proposal for power sharing between Protestants and Catholics. In the following British general election of February 1974,

Time Line	
1966	■ **June** The Ulster Volunteer Force attacks a number of Catholic civilians in western Belfast.
1971	■ **August 9** The British government initiates the policy of internment, or imprisonment without trial, setting off further violence.
1972	■ **January 30** While responding to rioting in Derry during a march by the Northern Ireland Civil Rights Association, British paratroopers kill fourteen demonstrators in an incident that becomes known as Bloody Sunday. A later British inquiry into the shootings would exonerate the paratroopers. ■ **March 24** The British government initiates direct rule over Northern Ireland. ■ **July 21** Bloody Friday ensues as the IRA sets off twenty-six bombs in Belfast, killing nine and injuring 130.
1974	■ **May 15** The Northern Ireland (Emergency Provisions) Act 1973 is amended to legalize Sinn Féin and the Ulster Defence Force.

Time Line

1975

■ **December 5**
The British government officially ceases the policy of internment.

1985

■ **November 15**
The Anglo-Irish Agreement is signed by Margaret Thatcher, the British prime minister, and Garret FitzGerald, the Republic of Ireland's *taoiseach* (prime minister); the agreement establishes British-Irish conferences to monitor political matters, security, and other issues in a spirit of cooperation.

1988

■ **January 11**
Sinn Féin leader Gerry Adams and Social Democratic and Labour Party leader John Hume meet to discuss possibilities for peaceful settlement of hostilities in Northern Ireland.

1993

■ **December 15**
Talks between British and Irish leaders result in a declaration that the people of Northern Ireland shall be free to decide their own future and that all groups shall be involved in Northern Ireland's government, provided that a cease-fire is observed.

anti–Sunningdale Agreement unionists won eleven of the twelve seats allocated to Northern Ireland in the British Parliament. On May 14, 1974, after the new Northern Ireland assembly reaffirmed their support for the Sunningdale Agreement despite popular opposition, the Ulster Workers Council, a Protestant trade union, initiated a general strike. On May 17, bombs were detonated in Dublin and Monaghan by paramilitary British loyalists, killing thirty-two. Before the month was over, Northern Ireland had virtually shut down. The British hesitated to send in more troops, which could further inflame the situation. Then on July 21, 1972, Bloody Friday ensued when the IRA set off twenty-six bombs in Belfast, killing nine and injuring 130. Tensions, though, were dialed down by two events. In 1974 the Northern Ireland (Emergency Provisions) Act was amended to legalize Sinn Féin and the Ulster Defence Force. In 1975 the British government officially ended the policy of internment. Nevertheless, the IRA continued its campaign of violence throughout the late 1970s.

A new method of protest against direct rule appeared in the form of hunger strikes. Originating in Maze Prison outside Belfast, the method gained widespread notoriety when Bobby Sands led a hunger strike in 1981—and nevertheless won an election. Sands's death on May 5, 1981 was followed by that of nine others before the strike was called off in October. Yet the British government, now led by a new conservative prime minister, Margaret Thatcher, refused to make any concessions. Later that same year, Sinn Féin announced a policy of contesting elections while continuing to support the IRA's use of violence. In 1983 Sinn Féin leader Gerry Adams, a radical voice for Northern Ireland's Catholics, won the Parliament seat for West Belfast. Conciliation with the British government became less likely, and in October 1984 Margaret Thatcher herself narrowly escaped an IRA bomb in Brighton. As Sinn Féin's influence broadened and violence continued, Margaret Thatcher and Garret FitzGerald, the Irish prime minister, arrived at the Anglo-Irish Agreement in November 1985, which stated that Northern Ireland would remain independent of the Republic of Ireland as long as that was the will of the majority of Northern Ireland's people. The agreement also dictated that British authority under direct rule could not devolve to the Northern Ireland government until there was an acceptable agreement for power sharing between Protestants and Catholics. The Anglo-Irish Agreement held until 1998. Meanwhile, in January 1988, Sinn Féin leader Gerry Adams and Social Democratic and Labour Party leader John Hume met to discuss possibilities for peaceful settlement of hostilities in Northern Ireland.

In December 1994, Belfast IRA representatives met with representatives of the Ulster Defence Association and Ulster Volunteer Force, most of whom were Protestant and considered fiercely supportive of Northern Ireland's separateness. The groups wanted to present a united front at peace talks and reached an informal agreement to release prisoners and to disarm, although they remained adamant that disarmament would not be a precondition for negotiations. John Major, the British prime minister, moved cautiously and suggested that the IRA decommission its weaponry, which would be tantamount to disarmament. Fearing an end to the brief respite of violence, British officials in February 1995 produced the "Framework for Accountable Government in Northern Ireland," which did little to inspire the negotiating parties but at least did not antagonize any of them. In March 1995 Sir Patrick Mayhew, the British secretary of state for Northern Ireland, announced that the IRA must begin disarmament procedures before Sinn Féin would be allowed to participate in the talks. The IRA responded that decommissioning of weapons had never been agreed upon as a precondition.

As tensions mounted, President Bill Clinton intervened to keep the process from collapsing. In December 1994 Clinton threatened to withhold the U.S. special envoy George Mitchell, a former Democratic senator from Maine, from the peace talks if the British refused to seat Sinn Féin. To emphasize the U.S. commitment to the peace talks, Clinton announced that he would visit Northern Ireland on November 30, 1995. Clinton's public acknowledgment of the need to include Sinn Féin forced feverish negotiations between the British and the Irish governments. An international committee chaired by George Mitchell was established, and it was to report on the decommissioning of weapons in January 1996. The Clinton visit ended successfully, thus maintaining a fragile peace. The committee headed by Mitchell submitted its recommendations, which advised that weapons disposal should not be a precondition to peace talks. The British continued to hesitate and asked for elections to be held in Northern Ireland. On February 9, 1996, the IRA laid claim to a bombing at Canary Wharf in London that killed two people, injured over one hundred, and caused approximately $215 million in damage. The IRA cease-fire was officially over. The British and Irish governments both condemned the bombing and broke off talks with Sinn Féin. The U.S. government, however, did not follow suit. The IRA's new campaign of violence, though, suffered several setbacks and did not resemble the reign of terror of years past.

The Northern Ireland peace process took another turn in May 1997 when the Labour Party defeated the Conservative Party for the first time since 1979, and Tony Blair became the new British prime minister. Sinn Féin won its highest percentage of votes ever in a parliamentary general election in Northern Ireland, leading to encouragement that the peace process could continue. Blair aggressively pursued peace negotiations and agreed to Sinn Féin's conditions in exchange for a new cease-fire. Sinn Féin would be included in talks within six weeks and the deadline for arriving at an agreement would be April 9, 1998. At this point, those seeking a lasting peace as well those wishing to usurp the peace process stepped up their efforts. Because of scattered incidents of violence, the Ulster Unionist Party refused to negotiate with Sinn Féin unless the IRA immediately disarmed. The hope of dissatisfied extremists on both sides was that the talks would collapse. The tense negotiations became literally a race against mayhem. George Mitchell monitored and coordinated negotia-

Time Line

1994

- **August 31**
  The IRA announces a cease-fire.

1997

- **September 15**
  For the first time since Ireland was partitioned, the governments of the Republic of Ireland, Northern Ireland, and Sinn Féin negotiate.

1998

- **April 10**
  The Northern Ireland Peace Agreement is reached on Good Friday.

- **May 23**
  A referendum in support of the agreement passes with 71 percent in favor in Northern Ireland and 94 percent in favor in the Irish Republic.

- **October 16**
  David Trimble and John Hume win the Nobel Peace Prize in recognition of the roles they played in arriving at the agreement.

tions since the representatives of many groups—nationalists, loyalists, Irish republicans, Sinn Féin, and the Ulster Unionist Party—would not speak directly to one another. The talks often threatened to break down, but in the final days and hours President Bill Clinton made several phone calls to group leaders urging them to reach an agreement. Finally, seventeen hours after the deadline, Mitchell announced that an agreement had been reached. The agreement was signed on Good Friday, April 10, 1998.

About the Author

The Northern Ireland Peace Agreement was truly a collaborative effort. Government officials from Northern Ireland, the United Kingdom, and the United States all had a hand in writing the document. Ulster Unionist Party leader David Trimble and Social Democratic and Labour Party leader John Hume were to win the 1998 Nobel Peace Prize in recognition of their contributions to the agreement, although they did not specifically author it. Among the leaders who made significant contributions to the peace process but did not individually have a hand in writing the agreement were Sinn Féin leader Gerry Adams; Bertie Ahern, the Irish *taoiseach*; Tony Blair, the British prime minister; George Mitchell, U.S. special envoy and former senator; and U.S. president Bill Clinton.

David Trimble was born on October 14, 1944. After earning a law degree, he taught law at the Queen's University of Belfast throughout the 1970s and 1980s. Meanwhile, he was also active in political affairs. He was a member of the Vanguard Progressive Unionist Party and, in 1975, was elected to the Northern Ireland Constitutional Convention. In 1978 he joined the Ulster Unionist Party, and in 1995 he was elected the party's leader, to the surprise of many observers. After successfully helping to broker the Northern Ireland Peace Agreement, he became first minister of Northern Ireland from 1998 to 2002. As of the twenty-first century, he continued to serve as a life peer for the Conservative Party in Ireland.

John Hume, born on January 18, 1937, originally intended to become a Catholic priest but instead turned to teaching early in his career. Throughout the 1960s he was a leader in the civil rights movement and became a leader in the Derry Citizen's Action Committee. He was a founding member of the Social Democratic and Labour Party, serving as its head from 1979 to 2001. In 2004 he announced his retirement from politics but remained active as a speaker and as a proponent of European integration.

Explanation and Analysis of the Document

The Northern Ireland Peace Agreement begins with the "Declaration of Support," which affirms that all the parties involved supported the peace initiative. The sixth and last item recommends that the people of Northern Ireland and the Republic of Ireland vote to approve the agreement. The subsequent section, "Constitutional Issues," assures the people of Northern Ireland that their vote concerning whether to continue to support the Union with Great Britain or opt for a sovereign united Ireland would be binding. It also recognizes the birthright of all people in Northern Ireland to consider themselves British, Irish, or both. Annex A: Draft Clauses/Schedules for Incorporation in British Legislation, includes the official announcement of the repeal of the Government of Ireland Act of 1920, which had legalized the formal partition of Ireland.

Strand One, subtitled "Democratic Institutions in Northern Ireland," outlines provisions for a 108-member assembly and includes a section on safeguards designed to allow equal representation of opposing parties and constituencies. This section also states that an equality com-

mission would have oversight power over the assembly and that neither the assembly nor any other organization would be able to encroach upon the legal authority of the European Convention on Human Rights or "any Bill of Rights for Northern Ireland" that would supplement it. This section includes provisions for the proposed assembly to pass legislation either by a basic simple majority of members present or by a weighted majority vote that would ensure cross-community representation.

Strand Three calls for the establishment of a British-Irish council. The purpose of the council was to promote a harmonious working relationship between the British and Irish governments and thus help overcome the deep animosity between the two nations. Issues to be addressed by the council would include transportation, agriculture, the environment, culture, health, education, and matters related to the European Union. The commission was to operate by consensus and by agreement of all members regarding common actions. The British-Irish Intergovernmental Conference was to be created to bring together the British and Irish governments "to promote bilateral co-operation at all levels on all matters of mutual interest." The decisions of the conference were to be agreeable to both governments, including those made on matters of security. Further, Strand Three specifies that a British-Irish Intergovernmental Conference would meet twice annually at "Summit level": a meeting of the British prime minister and the Irish *taoiseach*. The conference was delegated with responsibility for specific issues of mutual concern, such as prisons and the policing of Northern Ireland.

"Rights, Safeguards and Equality of Opportunity" begins with an affirmation of basic human rights, including freedom of political thought, freedom of religion, the right to seek constitutional change through peaceful methods, and the "full and equal" participation of women in the political process. This section stipulates that the British government would incorporate into Northern Ireland law the European Convention on Human Rights. Likewise, the Northern Ireland Human Rights Commission would be created, independent of the government and able to consult and advise on pertinent legislation concerning Northern Ireland. Also under the New Institutions in Northern Ireland section the new Equality Commission would consolidate four previous commissions, and a Human Rights Commission would monitor progress in Northern Ireland. In the subsection titled "Reconciliation and Victims of Violence," the agreement expresses the pledge of all participants in the peace talks to support existing organizations dedicated to reconciliation as well as to establish new organizations that would address the needs of the victims of violence.

The agreement then takes up the inflammatory issue of decommissioning weapons. This section requires all parties to stand by their commitment to total disarmament of all paramilitary organizations and work with the Independent International Commission on Decommissioning to achieve that goal within two years of the voter referendum about the agreement. The latter commission had been established by treaty between the Irish and British Governments in 1997

British troops fire rubber bullets at stone-throwing Protestant rioters who had set fires in Belfast in March 1972.
(AP/Wide World Photos)

as a prerequisite to peace talks to oversee the decommissioning of paramilitary weapons. The commission would be responsible for monitoring, reviewing, and verifying the decommissioning of weapons and regularly reporting on the process to both the Irish and English governments. The following section, "Security," stresses that the British government must make reasonable progress toward a reduction in deployed military forces in Northern Ireland and that emergency powers were to be relinquished.

The section titled "Policing and Justice" deals with Northern Ireland's internal security. Here the agreement calls for the formation of a police force that could enjoy the support of the entire population. The existence of such a force would be imperative to containing future incidents of violence and addressing past community grievances. Indeed, the agreement acknowledges that "Northern Ireland's history of deep divisions has made it [policing] highly emotive, with great hurt suffered and sacrifices made by many individuals and their families." The agreement, then, promises that the parties will "recognise the full and equal legitimacy and worth of the identities, senses of allegiance and ethos of all sections of the community in Northern Ireland." This statement, in effect, is a promise to end sectarian violence and to enforce laws not on the basis of religious affiliation but in a way that is "professional, effective and efficient, fair and impartial," and "free from partisan political control."

The section titled "Prisoners" discusses five points relating to the release of prisoners and their peaceful reentry into society. The first adamantly declares that "mechanisms to provide for an accelerated programme for the release of prisoners" by both governments are to be put into effect in an attempt to defuse heated passions on both sides. However, the second point states that any prisoner belonging to an organization that is not established or that is not maintaining the required cease fire would not be able to participate in the release program. This point ties release to cessation of violence. This section of the agreement then specifies that the governments would seek appropriate legislation dealing with the release of prisoners and concludes by stressing the importance of the prisoner's reintegration into society through assistance in job training and educational opportunities.

The summarizing articles, under "Validation, Implementation and Review," repeat the call for approval of the agreement by voter referendum and include a declaration that the Anglo-Irish Agreement of 1985 would no longer be in force. It likewise provides for a referendum to be held on May 22, 1998, and stipulates that the respective parliaments would issue supportive legislation should the referendums support the agreement. The section also allows for

"*The Government of Ireland Act 1920 is repealed; and this Act shall have effect notwithstanding any other previous enactment.*"

("Constitutional Issues")

"*The Conference will meet as required at Summit level (Prime Minister and Taoiseach). Otherwise, Governments will be represented by appropriate Ministers. Advisers, including police and security advisers, will attend as appropriate.*"

("Strand Three: British-Irish Intergovernmental Conference")

"*It is recognised that victims have a right to remember as well as to contribute to a changed society. The achievement of a peaceful and just society would be a true memorial to the victims of violence.*"

("Rights, Safeguards and Equality of Opportunity: Reconciliation and Victims of Violence")

"*All participants accordingly reaffirm their commitment to the total disarmament of all paramilitary organisations. They also confirm their intention to continue to work constructively and in good faith with the Independent Commission, and to use any influence they may have, to achieve the decommissioning of all paramilitary arms within two years following endorsement in referendums North and South of the agreement and in the context of the implementation of the overall settlement.*"

("Decommissioning")

review of any problems and subsequent remediation to iron out remaining problems.

Audience

Copies of the agreement were posted to every home in Northern Ireland, since voters were to cast their ballots in a referendum about it on May 22, 1998. Newspapers, official and unofficial Web sites, and the broadcasting media in Northern Ireland, the Republic of Ireland, and Great Britain reported extensively on what was widely considered a historical step toward reconciliation. For this reason, the greatest consideration was given to reaching the target audience, which was, first and foremost, the people of Northern Ireland. Citizens of the Republic of Ireland, as provided in the

agreement, were to have a referendum, and the rest of Great Britain, although they had no referendum to consider, were still affected by the agreement. The intense media coverage of the peace talks, at which leaders from many organizations were present, indicated that another intended audience was the IRA, as well as the other paramilitary organizations, all of which were to begin decommissioning their weapons in the quest for a lasting peace.

Impact

The impact of the agreement was immense. Once all the parties had signed it, centuries of animosity and hate, in theory at least, were to be set aside in the interest of achieving a peace in what was "the longest war the world has ever known"

(Toolis, p. 6). However, questions remained. Chief among these was whether the factions would be able to work together and whether the paramilitary parties would be willing to give up their weapons and, in effect, their purpose for being.

A more immediately pressing matter was the referendum, the results of which proved to be a landslide in favor of the agreement. The hope was that the referendum's outcome would demonstrate to the more steadfast opponents of the agreement that the people were tired of terror and violence. Still, there remained a significant chasm between the opposing sides, particularly with respect to decommissioning the IRA's weapons. By July 1999, Ulster Unionist Party leaders, the most significant Protestant politicians, disputed whether the IRA had actually disarmed. The party leaders then declared that they would refuse to share power with Sinn Féin in the Protestant-Catholic coalition government for which the peace agreement had provided. By 2002 the Northern Ireland government was unable to resolve political discord, and once more the British government assumed direct control of Northern Ireland.

Perhaps the most amazing impact of the agreement was that negotiations have continued since 2002, despite the negotiators' inability to agree on basic conditions. However, on October 13, 2006, British prime minister Tony Blair and Irish *taoiseach* Bertie Ahern persuaded Democratic Unionist Party leader Ian Paisley and Sinn Féin leader Gerry Adams to consent to the Saint Andrews Agreement. This new accord would usher in the Northern Ireland government stipulated in the Northern Ireland Peace Agreement of 1998.

Further Reading

■ **Books**

Brendon, Piers. *The Decline and Fall of the British Empire, 1781–1997.* New York: Knopf, 2007.

Coogan, Tim Pat. *The Troubles: Ireland's Ordeal and the Search for Peace.* New York: Palgrave, 2002.

Hennessey, Thomas. *Northern Ireland Peace Process: Ending the Troubles?* New York: Palgrave, 2001.

Holland, Jack. *Hope against History: The Course of Conflict in Northern Ireland.* New York: Henry Holt, 1999.

Mitchell, George. *Making Peace.* New York: Knopf, 1999.

Moloney, Ed. *A Secret History of the IRA.* New York: W. W. Norton, 2002.

Toolis, Kevin. *Rebel Hearts: Journeys within the IRA's Soul.* London: Picador, 1995.

■ **Web Sites**

"Northern Ireland: The Troubles." BBC Web site. http://www.bbc.co.uk/history/recent/troubles/.

—John Eder

Questions for Further Study

1. Describe the historical circumstances dating back to the twelfth century that led to the tension and violence in Northern Ireland.

2. In the nineteenth century and the early half of the twentieth, Great Britain sustained an empire that stretched around the world. Using this document in conjunction with Queen Victoria's Proclamation concerning India, the Constitution Act of Canada, the Government of India Act (1919), and Gamal Abdel Nasser on the Nationalization of the Suez Canal, trace the history of the dissolution of the British Empire and explain why that empire has largely dissolved.

3. The issues that have divided Great Britain and Northern Ireland are complex and often not well understood by people in other countries. Imagine that you had to summarize those issues in a single paragraph. Compose the paragraph.

4. An old expression says that "one person's terrorist is another person's freedom fighter," meaning that depending on one's perspective, a person who commits acts of violence can be seen as a hero or a villain. Do you believe that those responsible for violence in Northern Ireland were freedom fighters or terrorists? Defend your position.

5. Compare the events preceding the Northern Ireland Peace Agreement with the events surrounding the 1954 Proclamation of the Algerian National Liberation Front. In what ways was the situation in Algeria with regard to the French similar to—and different from—the situation that prevailed in Northern Ireland?

NORTHERN IRELAND PEACE AGREEMENT

Declaration of Support

1. We, the participants in the multi-party negotiations, believe that the agreement we have negotiated offers a truly historic opportunity for a new beginning.

2. The tragedies of the past have left a deep and profoundly regrettable legacy of suffering. We must never forget those who have died or been injured, and their families. But we can best honour them through a fresh start, in which we firmly dedicate ourselves to the achievement of reconciliation, tolerance, and mutual trust, and to the protection and vindication of the human rights of all.

3. We are committed to partnership, equality and mutual respect as the basis of relationships within Northern Ireland, between North and South, and between these islands.

4. We reaffirm our total and absolute commitment to exclusively democratic and peaceful means of resolving differences on political issues, and our opposition to any use or threat of force by others for any political purpose, whether in regard to this agreement or otherwise.

5. We acknowledge the substantial differences between our continuing, and equally legitimate, political aspirations. However, we will endeavour to strive in every practical way towards reconciliation and rapprochement within the framework of democratic and agreed arrangements. We pledge that we will, in good faith, work to ensure the success of each and every one of the arrangements to be established under this agreement. It is accepted that all of the institutional and constitutional arrangements—an Assembly in Northern Ireland, a North/South Ministerial Council, implementation bodies, a British-Irish Council and a British-Irish Intergovernmental Conference and any amendments to British Acts of Parliament and the Constitution of Ireland—are interlocking and interdependent and that in particular the functioning of the Assembly and the North/South Council are so closely inter-related that the success of each depends on that of the other.

6. Accordingly, in a spirit of concord, we strongly commend this agreement to the people, North and South, for their approval.

◆ Constitutional Issues

1. The participants endorse the commitment made by the British and Irish Governments that, in a new British-Irish Agreement replacing the Anglo-Irish Agreement, they will:

(i) recognise the legitimacy of whatever choice is freely exercised by a majority of the people of Northern Ireland with regard to its status, whether they prefer to continue to support the Union with Great Britain or a sovereign united Ireland;

(ii) recognise that it is for the people of the island of Ireland alone, by agreement between the two parts respectively and without external impediment, to exercise their right of self-determination on the basis of consent, freely and concurrently given, North and South, to bring about a united Ireland, if that is their wish, accepting that this right must be achieved and exercised with and subject to the agreement and consent of a majority of the people of Northern Ireland;

(iii) acknowledge that while a substantial section of the people in Northern Ireland share the legitimate wish of a majority of the people of the island of Ireland for a united Ireland, the present wish of a majority of the people of Northern Ireland, freely exercised and legitimate, is to maintain the Union and, accordingly, that Northern Ireland's status as part of the United Kingdom reflects and relies upon that wish; and that it would be wrong to make any change in the status of Northern Ireland save with the consent of a majority of its people;

(iv) affirm that if, in the future, the people of the island of Ireland exercise their right of self-determination on the basis set out in sections (i) and (ii) above to bring about a united Ireland, it will be a binding obligation on both Governments to introduce and support in their respective Parliaments legislation to give effect to that wish;

(v) affirm that whatever choice is freely exercised by a majority of the people of Northern Ireland, the power of the sovereign government with jurisdiction there shall be exercised with rigorous impartiality on behalf of all the people in the diversity of their identities and traditions and shall be founded on the principles of full respect for, and equality of, civil, political, social and cultural rights, of freedom from discrimination for all citizens, and of parity of esteem and of just and equal treatment for the identity, ethos, and aspirations of both communities;

(vi) recognise the birthright of all the people of Northern Ireland to identify themselves and be accepted as Irish or British, or both, as they may so choose, and accordingly confirm that their right to hold both British and Irish citizenship is accepted by both Governments and would not be affected by any future change in the status of Northern Ireland.

2. The participants also note that the two Governments have accordingly undertaken in the context of this comprehensive political agreement, to propose and support changes in, respectively, the Constitution of Ireland and in British legislation relating to the constitutional status of Northern Ireland.

◆ Annex A: Draft Clauses/Schedules for Incorporation in British Legislation

1. (1) It is hereby declared that Northern Ireland in its entirety remains part of the United Kingdom and shall not cease to be so without the consent of a majority of the people of Northern Ireland voting in a poll held for the purposes of this section in accordance with Schedule 1.

(2) But if the wish expressed by a majority in such a poll is that Northern Ireland should cease to be part of the United Kingdom and form part of a united Ireland, the Secretary of State shall lay before Parliament such proposals to give effect to that wish as may be agreed between Her Majesty's Government in the United Kingdom and the Government of Ireland.

2. The Government of Ireland Act 1920 is repealed; and this Act shall have effect notwithstanding any other previous enactment....

Strand One

◆ Democratic Institutions in Northern Ireland

1. This agreement provides for a democratically elected Assembly in Northern Ireland which is inclusive in its membership, capable of exercising executive and legislative authority, and subject to safeguards to protect the rights and interests of all sides of the community.

THE ASSEMBLY

2. A 108 member Assembly will be elected by PR (STV) from existing Westminster constituencies.

3. The Assembly will exercise full legislative and executive authority in respect of those matters currently within the responsibility of the six Northern Ireland Government Departments, with the possibil-

ity of taking on responsibility for other matters as detailed elsewhere in this agreement.

4. The Assembly—operating where appropriate on a cross-community basis—will be the prime source of authority in respect of all devolved responsibilities.

SAFEGUARDS

5. There will be safeguards to ensure that all sections of the community can participate and work together successfully in the operation of these institutions and that all sections of the community are protected, including:

(a) allocations of Committee Chairs, Ministers and Committee membership in proportion to party strengths;

(b) the European Convention on Human Rights (ECHR) and any Bill of Rights for Northern Ireland supplementing it, which neither the Assembly nor public bodies can infringe, together with a Human Rights Commission;

(c) arrangements to provide that key decisions and legislation are proofed to ensure that they do not infringe the ECHR and any Bill of Rights for Northern Ireland;

(d) arrangements to ensure key decisions are taken on a cross-community basis;

(i) *either* parallel consent, i.e. a majority of those members present and voting, including a majority of the unionist and nationalist designations present and voting;

(ii) *or* a weighted majority (60%) of members present and voting, including at least 40% of each of the nationalist and unionist designations present and voting.

Key decisions requiring cross-community support will be designated in advance, including election of the Chair of the Assembly, the First Minister and Deputy First Minister, standing orders and budget allocations. In other cases such decisions could be triggered by a petition of concern brought by a significant minority of Assembly members (30/108).

(e) an Equality Commission to monitor a statutory obligation to promote equality of opportunity in specified areas and parity of esteem between the two main communities, and to investigate individual complaints against public bodies....

TRANSITIONAL ARRANGEMENTS

35. The Assembly will meet first for the purpose of organisation, without legislative or executive powers, to resolve its standing orders and working practices and make preparations for the effective functioning of the Assembly, the British-Irish Council and the North/South Ministerial Council and associ-

ated implementation bodies. In this transitional period, those members of the Assembly serving as shadow Ministers shall affirm their commitment to nonviolence and exclusively peaceful and democratic means and their opposition to any use or threat of force by others for any political purpose; to work in good faith to bring the new arrangements into being; and to observe the spirit of the Pledge of Office applying to appointed Ministers.

REVIEW

36. After a specified period there will be a review of these arrangements, including the details of electoral arrangements and of the Assembly's procedures, with a view to agreeing any adjustments necessary in the interests of efficiency and fairness....

Strand Three

◆ British-Irish Council

1. A British-Irish Council (BIC) will be established under a new British-Irish Agreement to promote the harmonious and mutually beneficial development of the totality of relationships among the peoples of these islands.

2. Membership of the BIC will comprise representatives of the British and Irish Governments, devolved institutions in Northern Ireland, Scotland and Wales, when established, and, if appropriate, elsewhere in the United Kingdom, together with representatives of the Isle of Man and the Channel Islands.

3. The BIC will meet in different formats: at summit level, twice per year; in specific sectoral formats on a regular basis, with each side represented by the appropriate Minister; in an appropriate format to consider cross-sectoral matters.

4. Representatives of members will operate in accordance with whatever procedures for democratic authority and accountability are in force in their respective elected institutions.

5. The BIC will exchange information, discuss, consult and use best endeavours to reach agreement on co-operation on matters of mutual interest within the competence of the relevant Administrations. Suitable issues for early discussion in the BIC could include transport links, agricultural issues, environmental issues, cultural issues, health issues, education issues and approaches to EU issues. Suitable arrangements to be made for practical co-operation on agreed policies.

6. It will be open to the BIC to agree on common policies or common actions. Individual members

may opt not to participate in such common policies and common action.

7. The BIC normally will operate by consensus. In relation to decisions on common policies or common actions, including their means of implementation, it will operate by agreement of all members participating in such policies or actions.

8. The members of the BIC, on a basis to be agreed between them, will provide such financial support as it may require.

9. A secretariat for the BIC will be provided by the British and Irish Governments in coordination with officials of each of the other members.

10. In addition to the structures provided for under this agreement, it will be open to two or more members to develop bilateral or multilateral arrangements between them. Such arrangements could include, subject to the agreement of the members concerned, mechanisms to enable consultation, co-operation and joint decision-making on matters of mutual interest; and mechanisms to implement any joint decisions they may reach. These arrangements will not require the prior approval of the BIC as a whole and will operate independently of it.

11. The elected institutions of the members will be encouraged to develop interparliamentary links, perhaps building on the British-Irish Interparliamentary Body.

12. The full membership of the BIC will keep under review the workings of the Council, including a formal published review at an appropriate time after the Agreement comes into effect, and will contribute as appropriate to any review of the overall political agreement arising from the multi-party negotiations.

◆ British-Irish Intergovernmental Conference

1. There will be a new British-Irish Agreement dealing with the totality of relationships. It will establish a standing British-Irish Intergovernmental Conference, which will subsume both the Anglo-Irish Intergovernmental Council and the Intergovernmental Conference established under the 1985 Agreement.

2. The Conference will bring together the British and Irish Governments to promote bilateral co-operation at all levels on all matters of mutual interest within the competence of both Governments.

3. The Conference will meet as required at Summit level (Prime Minister and Taoiseach). Otherwise, Governments will be represented by appropriate Ministers. Advisers, including police and security advisers, will attend as appropriate.

4. All decisions will be by agreement between both Governments. The Governments will make determined efforts to resolve disagreements between them. There will be no derogation from the sovereignty of either Government.

5. In recognition of the Irish Government's special interest in Northern Ireland and of the extent to which issues of mutual concern arise in relation to Northern Ireland, there will be regular and frequent meetings of the Conference concerned with non-devolved Northern Ireland matters, on which the Irish Government may put forward views and proposals. These meetings, to be co-chaired by the Minister for Foreign Affairs and the Secretary of State for Northern Ireland, would also deal with all-island and cross-border co-operation on non-devolved issues.

6. Co-operation within the framework of the Conference will include facilitation of co-operation in security matters. The Conference also will address, in particular, the areas of rights, justice, prisons and policing in Northern Ireland (unless and until responsibility is devolved to a Northern Ireland administration) and will intensify co-operation between the two Governments on the all-island or cross-border aspects of these matters.

7. Relevant executive members of the Northern Ireland Administration will be involved in meetings of the Conference, and in the reviews referred to in paragraph 9 below to discuss non-devolved Northern Ireland matters.

8. The Conference will be supported by officials of the British and Irish Governments, including by a standing joint Secretariat of officials dealing with non-devolved Northern Ireland matters.

9. The Conference will keep under review the workings of the new British-Irish Agreement and the machinery and institutions established under it, including a formal published review three years after the Agreement comes into effect. Representatives of the Northern Ireland Administration will be invited to express views to the Conference in this context. The Conference will contribute as appropriate to any review of the overall political agreement arising from the multi-party negotiations but will have no power to override the democratic arrangements set up by this Agreement.

Rights, Safeguards and Equality of Opportunity

◆ Human Rights

1. The parties affirm their commitment to the mutual respect, the civil rights and the religious lib-

erties of everyone in the community. Against the background of the recent history of communal conflict, the parties affirm in particular:

—the right of free political thought;
—the right to freedom and expression of religion;
—the right to pursue democratically national and political aspirations;
—the right to seek constitutional change by peaceful and legitimate means;
—the right to freely choose one's place of residence;
—the right to equal opportunity in all social and economic activity, regardless of class, creed, disability, gender or ethnicity;
—the right to freedom from sectarian harassment; and
—the right of women to full and equal political participation.

◆ United Kingdom Legislation

2. The British Government will complete incorporation into Northern Ireland law of the European Convention on Human Rights (ECHR), with direct access to the courts, and remedies for breach of the Convention, including power for the courts to overrule Assembly legislation on grounds of inconsistency.

3. Subject to the outcome of public consultation underway, the British Government intends, as a particular priority, to create a statutory obligation on public authorities in Northern Ireland to carry out all their functions with due regard to the need to promote equality of opportunity in relation to religion and political opinion; gender; race; disability; age; marital status; dependants; and sexual orientation. Public bodies would be required to draw up statutory schemes showing how they would implement this obligation. Such schemes would cover arrangements for policy appraisal, including an assessment of impact on relevant categories, public consultation, public access to information and services, monitoring and timetables.

4. The new Northern Ireland Human Rights Commission (see paragraph 5 below) will be invited to consult and to advise on the scope for defining, in Westminster legislation, rights supplementary to those in the European Convention on Human Rights, to reflect the particular circumstances of Northern Ireland, drawing as appropriate on international instruments and experience. These additional rights to reflect the principles of mutual respect for

the identity and ethos of both communities and parity of esteem, and—taken together with the ECHR—to constitute a Bill of Rights for Northern Ireland. Among the issues for consideration by the Commission will be:

—the formulation of a general obligation on government and public bodies fully to respect, on the basis of equality of treatment, the identity and ethos of both communities in Northern Ireland; and

—a clear formulation of the rights not to be discriminated against and to equality of opportunity in both the public and private sectors.

◆ New Institutions in Northern Ireland

5. A new Northern Ireland Human Rights Commission, with membership from Northern Ireland reflecting the community balance, will be established by Westminster legislation, independent of Government, with an extended and enhanced role beyond that currently exercised by the Standing Advisory Commission on Human Rights, to include keeping under review the adequacy and effectiveness of laws and practices, making recommendations to Government as necessary; providing information and promoting awareness of human rights; considering draft legislation referred to them by the new Assembly; and, in appropriate cases, bringing court proceedings or providing assistance to individuals doing so.

6. Subject to the outcome of public consultation currently underway, the British Government intends a new statutory Equality Commission to replace the Fair Employment Commission, the Equal Opportunities Commission (NI), the Commission for Racial Equality (NI) and the Disability Council. Such a unified Commission will advise on, validate and monitor the statutory obligation and will investigate complaints of default.

7. It would be open to a new Northern Ireland Assembly to consider bringing together its responsibilities for these matters into a dedicated Department of Equality.

8. These improvements will build on existing protections in Westminster legislation in respect of the judiciary, the system of justice and policing.

◆ Comparable Steps by the Irish Government

9. The Irish Government will also take steps to further strengthen the protection of human rights in its jurisdiction. The Government will, taking account of the work of the All-Party Oireachtas Committee on the Constitution and the Report of the Constitution Review Group, bring forward measures to strengthen and underpin the constitutional protection of human rights. These proposals will draw on the European Convention on Human Rights and other international legal instruments in the field of human rights and the question of the incorporation of the ECHR will be further examined in this context. The measures brought forward would ensure at least an equivalent level of protection of human rights as will pertain in Northern Ireland. In addition, the Irish Government will:

—establish a Human Rights Commission with a mandate and remit equivalent to that within Northern Ireland;
—proceed with arrangements as quickly as possible to ratify the Council of Europe Framework Convention on National Minorities (already ratified by the UK);
—implement enhanced employment equality legislation;
—introduce equal status legislation; and
—continue to take further active steps to demonstrate its respect for the different traditions in the island of Ireland....

◆ Reconciliation and Victims of Violence

11. The participants believe that it is essential to acknowledge and address the suffering of the victims of violence as a necessary element of reconciliation. They look forward to the results of the work of the Northern Ireland Victims Commission.

12. It is recognised that victims have a right to remember as well as to contribute to a changed society. The achievement of a peaceful and just society would be the true memorial to the victims of violence. The participants particularly recognise that young people from areas affected by the troubles face particular difficulties and will support the development of special community-based initiatives based on international best practice. The provision of services that are supportive and sensitive to the needs of victims will also be a critical element and that support will need to be channelled through both statutory and community-based voluntary organisations facilitating locally-based self-help and support networks. This will require the allocation of sufficient resources, including statutory funding as necessary, to meet the needs of victims and to provide for community-based support programmes.

13. The participants recognise and value the work being done by many organisations to develop reconciliation and mutual understanding and respect

between and within communities and traditions, in Northern Ireland and between North and South, and they see such work as having a vital role in consolidating peace and political agreement. Accordingly, they pledge their continuing support to such organisations and will positively examine the case for enhanced financial assistance for the work of reconciliation. An essential aspect of the reconciliation process is the promotion of a culture of tolerance at every level of society, including initiatives to facilitate and encourage integrated education and mixed housing....

◆ Decommissioning

1. Participants recall their agreement in the Procedural Motion adopted on 24 September 1997 "that the resolution of the decommissioning issue is an indispensable part of the process of negotiation", and also recall the provisions of paragraph 25 of Strand 1 above.

2. They note the progress made by the Independent International Commission on Decommissioning and the Governments in developing schemes which can represent a workable basis for achieving the decommissioning of illegally-held arms in the possession of paramilitary groups.

3. All participants accordingly reaffirm their commitment to the total disarmament of all paramilitary organisations. They also confirm their intention to continue to work constructively and in good faith with the Independent Commission, and to use any influence they may have, to achieve the decommissioning of all paramilitary arms within two years following endorsement in referendums North and South of the agreement and in the context of the implementation of the overall settlement.

4. The Independent Commission will monitor, review and verify progress on decommissioning of illegal arms, and will report to both Governments at regular intervals.

5. Both Governments will take all necessary steps to facilitate the decommissioning process to include bringing the relevant schemes into force by the end of June.

◆ Security

1. The participants note that the development of a peaceful environment on the basis of this agreement can and should mean a normalisation of security arrangements and practices.

2. The British Government will make progress towards the objective of as early a return as possible to normal security arrangements in Northern Ire-

land, consistent with the level of threat and with a published overall strategy, dealing with:

(i) the reduction of the numbers and role of the Armed Forces deployed in Northern Ireland to levels compatible with a normal peaceful society;

(ii) the removal of security installations;

(iii) the removal of emergency powers in Northern Ireland; and

(iv) other measures appropriate to and compatible with a normal peaceful society.

3. The Secretary of State will consult regularly on progress, and the response to any continuing paramilitary activity, with the Irish Government and the political parties, as appropriate.

4. The British Government will continue its consultation on firearms regulation and control on the basis of the document published on 2 April 1998.

5. The Irish Government will initiate a wide-ranging review of the Offences Against the State Acts 1939-85 with a view to both reform and dispensing with those elements no longer required as circumstances permit.

◆ Policing and Justice

1. The participants recognise that policing is a central issue in any society. They equally recognise that Northern Ireland's history of deep divisions has made it highly emotive, with great hurt suffered and sacrifices made by many individuals and their families, including those in the RUC and other public servants. They believe that the agreement provides the opportunity for a new beginning to policing in Northern Ireland with a police service capable of attracting and sustaining support from the community as a whole. They also believe that this agreement offers a unique opportunity to bring about a new political dispensation which will recognise the full and equal legitimacy and worth of the identities, senses of allegiance and ethos of all sections of the community in Northern Ireland. They consider that this opportunity should inform and underpin the development of a police service representative in terms of the make-up of the community as a whole and which, in a peaceful environment, should be routinely unarmed.

2. The participants believe it essential that policing structures and arrangements are such that the police service is professional, effective and efficient, fair and impartial, free from partisan political control; accountable, both under the law for its actions and to the community it serves; representative of the society it polices, and operates within a coherent and

cooperative criminal justice system, which conforms with human rights norms. The participants also believe that those structures and arrangements must be capable of maintaining law and order including responding effectively to crime and to any terrorist threat and to public order problems. A police service which cannot do so will fail to win public confidence and acceptance. They believe that any such structures and arrangements should be capable of delivering a policing service, in constructive and inclusive partnerships with the community at all levels, and with the maximum delegation of authority and responsibility, consistent with the foregoing principles. These arrangements should be based on principles of protection of human rights and professional integrity and should be unambiguously accepted and actively supported by the entire community.

3. An independent Commission will be established to make recommendations for future policing arrangements in Northern Ireland including means of encouraging widespread community support for these arrangements within the agreed framework of principles reflected in the paragraphs above and in accordance with the terms of reference at Annex A. The Commission will be broadly representative with expert and international representation among its membership and will be asked to consult widely and to report no later than Summer 1999....

◆ Prisoners

1. Both Governments will put in place mechanisms to provide for an accelerated programme for the release of prisoners, including transferred prisoners, convicted of scheduled offences in Northern Ireland or, in the case of those sentenced outside Northern Ireland, similar offences (referred to hereafter as qualifying prisoners). Any such arrangements will protect the rights of individual prisoners under national and international law.

2. Prisoners affiliated to organisations which have not established or are not maintaining a complete and unequivocal ceasefire will not benefit from the arrangements. The situation in this regard will be kept under review.

3. Both Governments will complete a review process within a fixed time frame and set prospective release dates for all qualifying prisoners. The review process would provide for the advance of the release dates of qualifying prisoners while allowing account to be taken of the seriousness of the offences for which the person was convicted and the need to protect the community. In addition, the intention would

be that should the circumstances allow it, any qualifying prisoners who remained in custody two years after the commencement of the scheme would be released at that point.

4. The Governments will seek to enact the appropriate legislation to give effect to these arrangements by the end of June 1998.

5. The Governments continue to recognise the importance of measures to facilitate the reintegration of prisoners into the community by providing support both prior to and after release, including assistance directed towards availing of employment opportunities, retraining and/or re-skilling, and further education.

Validation, Implementation and Review

◆ Validation and Implementation

1. The two Governments will as soon as possible sign a new British-Irish Agreement replacing the 1985 Anglo-Irish Agreement, embodying understandings on constitutional issues and affirming their solemn commitment to support and, where appropriate, implement the agreement reached by the participants in the negotiations which shall be annexed to the British-Irish Agreement.

2. Each Government will organise a referendum on 22 May 1998. Subject to Parliamentary approval, a consultative referendum in Northern Ireland, organised under the terms of the Northern Ireland (Entry to Negotiations, etc.) Act 1996, will address the question: "Do you support the agreement reached in the multi-party talks on Northern Ireland and set out in Command Paper 3883". The Irish Government will introduce and support in the Oireachtas a Bill to amend the Constitution as described in paragraph 2 of the section "Constitutional Issue" and in Annex B, as follows: (a) to amend Articles 2 and 3 as described in paragraph 8.1 in Annex B above and (b) to amend Article 29 to permit the Government to ratify the new British-Irish Agreement. On passage by the Oireachtas, the Bill will be put to referendum.

3. If majorities of those voting in each of the referendums support this agreement, the Governments will then introduce and support, in their respective Parliaments, such legislation as may be necessary to give effect to all aspects of this agreement, and will take whatever ancillary steps as may be required including the holding of elections on 25 June, subject to parliamentary approval, to the Assembly, which would meet initially in a "shadow" mode. The estab-

lishment of the North-South Ministerial Council, implementation bodies, the British-Irish Council and the British-Irish Intergovernmental Conference and the assumption by the Assembly of its legislative and executive powers will take place at the same time on the entry into force of the British-Irish Agreement.

4. In the interim, aspects of the implementation of the multi-party agreement will be reviewed at meetings of those parties relevant in the particular case (taking into account, once Assembly elections have been held, the results of those elections), under the chairmanship of the British Government or the two Governments, as may be appropriate; and representatives of the two Governments and all relevant parties may meet under independent chairmanship to review implementation of the agreement as a whole.

Glossary

existing Westminster constituencies	present election districts (for members of the House of Commons) in the British Parliament, which sits in Westminster
Oireachtas	the national parliament of Ireland
PR (STV)	proportional representation (single transferable vote)
RUC	the Royal Ulster Constabulary; the police force in Northern Ireland between 1922 and 2001

CONSTITUTIVE ACT OF THE AFRICAN UNION

"The Union shall [seek to] achieve greater unity and solidarity between the African counties and the peoples of Africa."

Overview

The Constitutive Act of the African Union, signed at Lomé, Togo, on July 11, 2000, lays out the framework for the African Union (AU). As such, it is in essence a constitution. The AU, which replaced the Organization of African Unity (OAU), is a transnational entity designed to forge and implement common goals on the African continent. Specifically, its purpose is to speed political and economic integration and promote security and peace, human rights, democratic institutions, and common African positions on issues that affect African people. The Constitutive Act established such organs as the Assembly, the Executive Council, the Pan-African Parliament, the Court of Justice, and various other agencies that have more specialized functions. Although it lacks the enforcement authority of the European Union, the African Union bears many similarities to the European Union. Both organizations unite the nations of a continent in the pursuit of shared goals. The AU's membership comprises fifty-three nations, virtually the entire continent; Morocco is the sole African nation that is not a member. From time to time, the AU has felt compelled to suspend members for various reasons. For example, in 2008 it suspended Guinea because of a military coup. In 2009 the AU suspended Madagascar because of a political crisis and Eritrea because of its support of Islamists in the troubled and divided nation of Somalia (though, technically, Eritrea withdrew from the AU under the threat of UN sanctions).

Context

The African Union, which was formally launched on July 9, 2002, represents the culmination of efforts to unite the nations of Africa. These efforts have dated back at least to the eighteenth century and have involved people who were part of the African diaspora—the spread of Africans throughout much of the world because of the slave trade—who collaborated in a unified resistance to the injustice of slavery. Such organizations as the Sons of Africa, formed in London in the 1790s, joined with abolitionists to pressure prime ministers and the British monarchy to end slavery. These antislavery campaigns were the first instances in modern history in which Africans and people of African descent attempted to speak with one voice.

One of the earliest organizations that promoted political unity on the African continent was the Fante (also spelled Fanti) Confederacy, which was formed in 1868 and created its own constitution in 1871. The confederacy attempted to link the numerous Fante clans and states along the Gold Coast of western Africa and thereby achieve self-determination. Although the organization dissolved in 1873, it served as a model for future efforts to break down Africa's tribal and national barriers and resist colonialism. Around 1897, Trinidadian Henry Sylvester Williams formed the African Association, later called the Pan-African Association, which was active in the very early 1900s. In the decades that followed, numerous key figures—including the prominent American intellectual W. E. B. Du Bois, Marcus Garvey (founder of the Universal Negro Improvement Association and African Communities League), and the Ethiopian emperor Haile Selassie—called for greater unity among African nations.

In the second half of the twentieth century, as the nations of Africa were gaining their independence from European colonial powers, serious efforts were begun to promote African unity. Among the first organizations dedicated to that end was the Union of African States, formed on November 23, 1958. Initially, the union consisted of just two members, Guinea and Ghana; Mali joined the union in April 1961. It was led by Kwame Nkrumah of Ghana and Sékou Touré of Guinea, both of whom were revolutionary Marxist heads of state. After Guinea had tried to forge a closer relationship with the United States rather than the Communist Soviet Union, the union dissolved in 1962.

An organization that had more clout and lasted much longer was the AU's predecessor, the Organization of African Unity. This organization was created on May 25, 1963, but only after divisions on the continent had been overcome. Nevertheless, two blocs emerged within the OAU, each espousing a different view of African unity. One, called the Casablanca bloc, was led by Nkrumah and backed by Algeria, Guinea, Morocco, Egypt, Mali, and

1897

- Henry Sylvester Williams forms the African Association, later called the Pan-African Association.

1958

- November 23 The Union of African States is formed, consisting of Guinea and Ghana; Mali joins in 1961.

1963

- May 25 The Organization of African Unity (OAU) is established.

1981

- June 27 The OAU adopts the African Charter on Human and Peoples' Rights.

1991

- June 3 The African Economic Community is formed under the terms of the Abuja Treaty.

1999

- September 9 The OAU issues the Sirte Declaration, which calls for the formation of the African Union.

2000

- July 11 The Constitutive Act of the African Union is signed.

Libya. This bloc called for an immediate confederation of all African countries. The other, called the Monrovian bloc, was led by Léopold Sédar Senghor of Senegal and included Ethiopia, Liberia, Nigeria, and many of France's former African colonies. The Monrovian bloc wanted to take a more gradual approach to economic cooperation and resisted any kind of broader political union. Eventually, Ethiopia's Haile Selassie invited the two groups to a conference in Addis Ababa, which later became the headquarters of the OAU, where he brokered an agreement between the two camps and thirty-two nations signed the OAU's charter. Eventually, membership in the OAU grew to fifty-three nations; Morocco had been a member but withdrew in 1984, making it the only nation on the continent that does not belong to the OAU.

The OAU suffered from limitations that sometimes bedevil international confederations. For example, it had no armed forces and was unable to intervene in conflicts such as protracted civil wars in Nigeria and Angola. It also had no power to prevent or stop human rights violations in countries such as Uganda, which had been under the tyrannical rule of strongman Idi Amin in the 1970s. Critics derided the OAU as powerless, and it often came to be referred to as the "Dictators' Club" and the "Dictators' Trade Union." Further, the organization remained divided, particularly because several nations in the Monrovian bloc remained dependent on France for economic aid. Another source of division emerged between those nations that supported the capitalist model of the West and the United States, such as the Ivory Coast under President Félix Houphouët-Boigny, and those that were drawn to Soviet Communism, such as Ghana under Nkrumah. Rarely were the two camps able to agree on a united course of action.

The OAU's supporters, on the other hand, pointed to its successes. In the United Nations, OAU member states joined together to promote African interests. The OAU worked tirelessly to eliminate colonialism and minority rule, aiding organizations that fought apartheid in South Africa and that strove for an independent Southern Rhodesia. Through the efforts of the OAU, ports and airspace throughout Africa were closed to South Africa, and the World Health Organization expelled that nation. The OAU provided aid for refugees and created the African Development Bank, which enabled former colonies to become less dependent on their former colonial rulers for development loans and markets for their goods.

One other organization bears mention: the African Economic Community (AEC), which was created on June 3, 1991, by the Abuja Treaty signed in Abuja, Nigeria, and is still in operation. Modeled after the European Economic Community, the goal of the AEC has been to establish a monetary and economic union through the creation of a single African market, free trade areas, a common currency, and a central bank. The AEC consists of several overlapping trade and economic-cooperation blocs called Regional Economic Communities, which include the Community of Sahel-Saharan States, the Common Market for Eastern and Southern Africa, the East African Community, the

Economic Community of Central African States, the Economic Community of West African States, the Intergovernmental Authority on Development, the Southern African Development Community, and the Arab Maghreb Union. The ultimate goals of the AEC, which have been projected as far into the future as 2028, are to turn the continent into a free-trade zone with a common currency and to establish a common market for African-made goods.

The perceived inadequacies of the OAU, however, led to its dissolution and replacement with the African Union. The position of Africa in world affairs had changed since the OAU's formation in the early 1960s. During the early decades of the cold war—the state of hostility between the West, led by the United States, and the Communist Soviet Union and its allies—the nations of Africa had acquired some importance, as both the United States and Soviet Union courted support and wanted to expand their spheres of influence. With the end of the cold war in the early 1990s, though, Africa became less strategically important, and many observers came to believe that the only way African nations could survive was by uniting. Further, other regions of the world were forming trading blocs; chief among them was the European Union and NAFTA, or the North American Free Trade Agreement, which brought Canada, the United States, and Mexico into a mutual free-trade zone, in which Chile was later included.

Calls for a new, more competitive African organization began in the mid-1990s under the leadership of Libya's Muammar al-Gaddafi, who has urged the formation of a "United States of Africa." On September 9, 1999, the OAU issued the Sirte Declaration, named for Sirte, Libya, the site of the OAU's Fourth Extraordinary Session of the Assembly of African Heads of State and Government. The intent of the declaration was to create the African Union and to speed implementation of the Abuja Treaty provisions for establishing the AEC in order to foster economic development as well as to create a central bank, a monetary union, the Court of Justice, and the Pan-African Parliament. A chief goal, too, was to call for the writing of the Constitutive Act of the African Union, which was signed in 2000.

From July 9 to July 11, 2001, the OAU's heads of state met at Lusaka, Zambia, to adopt a plan for implementing the AU, which began formal operation on July 9, 2002. Also at the Lusaka conference, the New Partnership for Africa's Development was adopted. This organization merged two previous African economic-development organizations: the OMEGA Plan for Africa and the Millennium Partnership for the African Recovery Programme. The new organization was an outgrowth of a report issued by the United Nations Economic Commission for Africa titled *Compact for Africa's Recovery*. This document, which was combined with resolutions adopted by the United Nation's Millennium Summit in 2000 and backed by the European Union, China, and the G8 (Canada, France, Germany, Italy, Japan, Russia, the United Kingdom, and the United States), was adopted as the New African Initiative. Thus, the African Union was part of a broader set of initiatives for the development of Africa.

Time Line

2001
- **July 9–11**
  The OAU's heads of state meet at Lusaka, Zambia, to adopt a plan for implementing the African Union.

2002
- **July 9**
  The African Union commences formal operations.

2003
- **March**
  The African Peer Review Mechanism is created.

2007
- **January 19**
  The African Union's Peace and Security Council implements the African Union Mission to Somalia.

About the Author

The Constitutive Act of the African Union was a collaborative document prepared by the delegations from the signatory nations. Accordingly, it is difficult to cite a particular author or group of authors. However, the drive for African unity during this period was led by the Libyan leader Muammar al-Gaddafi. The Sirte Declaration had been signed in Sirte, Libya, at the OAU's Fourth Extraordinary Session of the Assembly of African Heads of State and Government. This declaration helped serve as an impetus to the formation of the African Union, so Gaddafi would likely have had major input into the Constitutive Act.

Gaddafi was born on June 7, 1942, and grew up in the desert region of Sirte. In 1963 he entered a military academy, and he received additional military training in England, returning to Libya in 1966. He and a group of officers were opposed to the nation's pro-Western monarchy, and on September 1, 1969, they staged a coup d'état when Libya's king, Idris I, was out of the country. They proclaimed the nation a republic, with Gaddafi as president. In the years that followed, he assumed various positions

Muammar al-Gaddafi meets with African parliamentarians in Tripoli, Libya, on September 9, 2009, the tenth anniversary of the Sirte Declaration.
(AP/Wide World Photos)

and titles, including that of prime minister, but in 1977 he declared that Libya would be known as a *jamahiriya*, a word that loosely translates as "state ruled by the masses." Thus, Gaddafi shed formal titles; he promoted himself to the rank of colonel rather than general, claiming that he did not have to hold grandiose titles, so he is often referred to as Colonel Gaddafi. Although he has no official title such as president or prime minister, he and a close council of advisers hold near-absolute power in Libya.

From his seizure of power in 1969 through the 1990s, Gaddafi was widely regarded in the West as one of the world's most dangerous heads of state. Libya during these years became a haven for terrorists and revolutionary groups committed to opposition to Western imperialism. He was a strong supporter of the pan-Arabism of Egypt's Gamal Abdel Nasser and of the Palestine Liberation Organization. He shipped arms to the Irish Republican Army and supported other "liberation" movements throughout the world. In 1986, U.S. president Ronald Reagan ordered bombing raids on Libya in retaliation for sus-

pected Libyan involvement in a bombing at a nightclub in Berlin, Germany, frequented by U.S. military personnel. Among those killed in the bombing raid was Gaddafi's adopted daughter. Later, Gaddafi was in the headlines again when a jetliner exploded over Lockerbie, Scotland, in 1988; Gaddafi denied Libyan involvement, yet the evidence proved otherwise. Ultimately, in 2003, Gaddafi acknowledged the involvement of Libyan government officials and authorized a large financial settlement to the families of the victims.

Throughout his career, Gaddafi cultivated an image as a flamboyant thorn in the side of the West. The history of Libya under his rule has been a history of economic sanctions, the politics of oil, military skirmishes, denunciations of the West, and Western characterizations of Libya as a "rogue" nation. In the twenty-first century, however, Gaddafi seemed to be trying to improve his image. In addition to the Lockerbie settlement, he opened Libya to weapons inspectors, vowed to support the fight against al Qaeda (the organization responsible for the September 11, 2001, terrorist attacks on the United States), opened diplomatic relations with countries in the West, invited Western leaders to Libya, and in general behaved more like a statesman and less like a revolutionary gadfly.

Explanation and Analysis of the Document

The Constitutive Act of the African Union is not a complex document. It is written in simple, straightforward language that outlines the goals, governing principles, structure, and functions of the AU. It also sets up and defines the administrative functions of the AU.

◆ Preamble and Articles 1–2

Perhaps the most interesting portion of the act is its preamble. It first lists the signatories of the act—virtually all of them presidents, with one king (Swaziland), two prime ministers, and Muammar al-Gaddafi, who goes by the cumbersome title, Leader of the 1st of September Revolution of the Great Socialist People's Libyan Arab Jamahiriya. The last word in his title is an Arabic term that loosely translates as "state ruled by the masses," and "1st September" refers to the date in 1969 when he assumed power in Libya. The preamble then lists the motivations that led to the creation of the African Union. It makes reference to the founders of the organization and Pan-Africanists; the objectives of the OAU and AEC and the need to "accelerate the process" of implementing the AEC; the OAU's emphasis on "collective action"; the "social, economic and political changes taking place in the world"; the "common vision of a united and strong Africa"; the need to reduce conflict and provide for peace, security, and human rights; and finally the need to fulfill the call of the Sirte Declaration for establishing the African Union. The preamble is followed by Article 1, which simply defines terms and abbreviations, and Article 2, which declares that the Constitutive Act establishes the African Union.

◆ Article 3

Article 3 states the fourteen objectives of the African Union, which are listed with little elaboration. The overarching purpose of the AU is to "achieve greater unity and solidarity" in Africa. The act constitutes a defense pact, since it calls for protection of the "sovereignty" and "territorial integrity" of the member states and pledges to promote "peace, security, and stability" throughout Africa. A further goal is to promote "political and socio-economic integration," which is to be achieved by the AEC's regional trade blocs, called Regional Economic Communities; a closely related AU goal is to "harmonize" the policies of these trade blocs. A more general goal is to "promote and defend African common positions on issues of interest," which the African states can accomplish through the United Nations. The union pledges to adhere to the United Nations Charter and particularly to the UN Universal Declaration of Human Rights, adopted in 1948. A further goal is to adhere to the African Charter on Human and Peoples' Rights, adopted by the OAU on June 27, 1981, and entered into force on October 21, 1986.

Article 3 also calls for the promotion of "democratic principles and institutions, popular participation and good governance." In recent years, the AU has attempted to implement this objective through the African Peer Review Mechanism, a voluntary agency of the AU whose goal is to assess the political progress of member states. The mechanism, created in 2003, is an outgrowth of the New Partnership for Africa's Development and its Declaration on Democracy, Political, Economic and Corporate Governance, which was adopted at the same summit that produced the Constitutive Act. The African Peer Review Mechanism has been controversial, as member states and outside observers have contended that it has thus far failed to fulfill its mandate.

Article 3 then specifies another important AU goal as promoting sustainable development and enabling Africa "to play its rightful role in the global economy and international negotiations." Meeting this goal has been elusive because of increasing desertification and water shortages, especially in the Sahel region. Also, by encouraging "cooperation in all fields of human activity," particularly science and agriculture, the Constitutive Act expresses hopes for raising African living standards. A related goal is the eradication of disease and the promotion of good health. Two disease pandemics continue to ravage Africa. One is AIDS; as of the end of 2007 it was estimated that twenty-two million people in Africa were HIV-positive and that during that year some 1.5 million Africans had died of AIDS. As of August 2009, some twenty-five million Africans had died of AIDS-related complications since 1981. The other disease is malaria, which has claimed the lives of nearly one million Africans every year.

◆ Article 4

Article 4 briefly states the sixteen principles that will govern the AU. In many respects, these principles overlap with the AU's goals. Article 4 asserts the principles of "equality and interdependence," respect for territorial borders, participation of the people of Africa in their governance, and the need for common defense and peaceful resolution of conflicts. Each member state is prohibited from using force or the threat of force against another member state or meddling in another state's internal affairs. The Constitutive Act gives the AU the authority to "intervene" in member states under "grave circumstances" that include evidence of war crimes, genocide, and crimes against humanity, and any state has the right to solicit aid from the AU to "restore peace and security." The last principle of Article 4 is a rejection of "unconstitutional changes of governments," an ongoing problem in Africa, where coups (such as the one that brought Gaddafi to power) and attempted coups have been the norm in such countries as Nigeria, Ghana, Togo, Congo, Uganda, and many others, particularly in sub-Saharan Africa.

Article 4 also states social principles, including "self-reliance," gender equality, and respect for "democratic principles, human rights, [and] the rule of law and good governance." It calls for social justice, interestingly linking social justice with "balanced economic development." Additionally, it calls for respect for the "sanctity" of human life and a rejection of terrorism.

◆ Articles 5–9

Article 5 simply lists the official organs of the AU. With Article 6, the Constitutive Act turns to the nuts and bolts of the AU's operations. Articles 6 through 9 deal with the Assembly, which consists of the heads of state of the member nations. It is to meet once a year under the leadership of a chair who is elected annually for a one-year term. Article 7 states that the Assembly will favor reaching decisions by consensus, but in the absence of a consensus, a two-thirds majority vote is required. Article 9 then outlines the powers and functions of the Assembly: to determine "common policies" of the AU, to act on recommendations and reports from the AU's various organs, to consider requests for membership in the AU, to establish additional organs, to implement and monitor policies and decisions, to maintain a budget, to work with the Executive Council in emergency situations, and to appoint judges to the Court of Justice.

◆ Articles 10–13

This sequence of articles deals with the structure and functions of the Executive Council, which is composed of the ministers of foreign affairs of the member states. The council's ordinary sessions are to convene at least twice each year. As in the Assembly, the preference is for consensus, but failing that, a two-thirds majority is needed for decisions. The Executive Council, which is answerable to the Assembly, is given oversight authority on such matters as foreign trade, resources, agriculture, water and irrigation, the environment, transport and telecommunications, insurance, education, science and technology, immigration and citizenship issues, social security, and a system of awards and prizes.

African Union Soldiers patrol Sudanese Liberation Army territory in North Darfur, Sudan. (AP/Wide World Photos)

♦ **Articles 14–22**

Articles 14 through 22 briefly lay out a framework for future AU activities. Article 14, for examples, creates a number of specialized technical committees to oversee such matters as agriculture; monetary and financial affairs; trade, customs, and immigration; industry, science, and technology; transport, communications, and tourism; health, labor, and social affairs; and education, culture, and human resources. These committees are assigned the tasks of gathering information and making recommendations to the Executive Council. They also charged with monitoring any programs that are implemented and ensuring that those programs are in harmony with the AU's goals.

The remaining articles in this group look to Africa's future. They call for the formation of a Pan-African Parliament; a Court of Justice (a protocol for establishing the court already had been developed in 2003); financial institutions such as a central bank, a monetary fund, and an investment bank; a secretariat to administer the AU; the Permanent Representatives Committee; and the Economic, Social, and Cultural Council.

♦ **Articles 23–33**

This group of articles deal essentially with the rules or "by-laws" of the AU. Article 23 outlines sanctions the organization can impose on member states that do not meet their obligations; later, Article 30 notes that members can be suspended if the member's government comes to power through "unconstitutional means." It should be noted, however, that most of the member states have failed to meet their financial obligations to the AU; in 2006, just twelve nations paid their contributions to the organization. Article 24 notes that the AU's headquarters will be in Addis Ababa, Ethiopia, while Article 25 specifies the AU's working languages (as opposed to official languages): Arabic, English, French, and Portuguese, with African languages used whenever possible. Article 26 gives the Court of Justice authority to interpret the act, while Articles 27 through 29 specify issues involving membership in the AU and when the act enters into force. Article 32 outlines procedures for amendment of the act, and Article 33 notes that there will be a transitional period while the functions and budgets of the OAU are being transferred to the AU.

Audience

The Constitutive Act of the African Union is a legal document—in effect, a constitution—so its primary audience consisted of government officials and government agencies in each of the member states, as well as the transnational organizations to which the member states belonged. Anoth-

"*Inspired by the noble ideals which guided the founding fathers of our Continental Organization and generations of Pan-Africanists in their determination to promote unity, solidarity, cohesion and cooperation among the peoples of Africa and African States.*"

(Preamble)

"*The Organization of African Unity has played a determining and invaluable role in the liberation of the continent, the affirmation of a common identity and the process of attainment of the unity of our Continent and has provided a unique framework for our collective action in Africa and in our relations with the rest of the world.*"

(Preamble)

"*The objectives of the Union shall be to: a. Achieve greater unity and solidarity between the African counties and the peoples of Africa; b. Defend the sovereignty, territorial integrity and independence of its Member States; c. Accelerate the political and socio-economic integration of the continent.*"

(Article 3)

"*The Union shall function in accordance with the following principles: a. Sovereign equality and interdependence among Member States of the Union; b. Respect of borders existing on achievement of independence.*"

(Article 4)

er audience was Africa's business and corporate community, as well as the non-African nations with which African businesses conducted trade. In a larger sense, the treaty's audience was all of Africa and indeed the world, for it announced that Africa was no longer to be regarded as a fragmented collection of nations and tribal states, each in pursuit of its separate interests, but rather as a supranational entity with common goals and policies.

Impact

Since its inception, the AU has faced numerous challenges. Chief among them have been disease, famine, civil war, and poverty and low standards of living. The AU has addressed political unrest in Zimbabwe, with some members calling for the ouster of that nation because of the strong-arm tactics and flagrant human rights abuses of its president, Robert Mugabe. After the death of Togo's president in 2005, the AU considered the accession of his son, Faure Gnassingbé, to the presidency a military coup and forced the country to hold elections. Similarly, the AU has had to deal with regime change in Mauritania. It suspended that nation after a military coup in 2005, forcing the new regime to hold elections. Those elections were held in 2007, but in 2008 yet another military coup took place. Once again Mauritania was suspended, but the suspension and AU sanctions were lifted in July 2009 on the advent of new presidential elections.

The AU has been active in peacekeeping missions, particularly after the formation of the AU's Peace and Security Council in December 2003. One of the most critical areas has been Darfur, a region in western Sudan torn by ethnic conflict and genocide since 2003. The AU initially sent in a peacekeeping force of a mere 150 troops, but as the bloodiness of the conflict became more apparent, that number was increased to about seven thousand. The peacekeeping force has thus far been ineffective, since the troops, mainly from Rwanda and Nigeria, have lacked funds, equipment, and training. The AU Mission in Sudan was sustained only with the help of donations from member states in 2005 and a $173 million grant from the United States in 2006. Despite these efforts, the violence has continued. The International Criminal Court indicted Sudan's leader, Omar al-Bashir, for war crimes, but the AU refused to recognize the court's arrest warrant. Nevertheless, the AU has continued to maintain its peacekeeping mission in Darfur in conjunction with United Nations peacekeeping forces—an unprecedented coalition of UN forces with a regional force.

Another hot spot in Africa has been Somalia. Beginning in the early 1990s, Somalia essentially had no functioning government, as the nation was wracked by civil war. On January 19, 2007, the AU's Peace and Security Council, with the backing of the United Nations Security Council, implemented the African Union Mission to Somalia. This mission eventually dispatched some eight thousand troops whose purpose was to impose stable governmental structures and deliver humanitarian aid. As of 2009 the mission's mandate was continuing in the face of resistance from the Union of Islamic Courts, which still held power in the Somalia's capital city, Mogadishu. Besides efforts in Sudan and Somalia, other AU peacekeeping missions have been complicated by tribal and national tensions that have prevented troops from working together effectively. Meanwhile, the continent continues to be ravaged by conflict; nations such as Liberia, Guinea, and Sierra Leone accuse one another of supporting rebel movements. Some observers regard these nations' common borders as among the world's most dangerous places.

African economic progress has been slow in coming. The AU ranks as the world's seventeenth-largest economy, just behind the Netherlands, with a gross domestic product of about $500 billion and a combined debt of some $200 billion. Africa accounts for only about 2 percent of the world's trade, although this figure is misleading. Many nations trade in futures, or financial instruments that represent commodities. Most African nations, on the other hand, trade in the actual commodities themselves, including such vital materials as gold and aluminum.

One of the problems with economic union in Africa is that many nations continue to trade with their former colonizers rather than with one another. Also, fourteen

Questions for Further Study

1. Compare the Constitutive Act of the African Union with the Treaty on European Union, which has attempted to achieve unity among the nations of Europe. How do the African Union and the European Union differ, and how are they similar? What common goals do the two organizations have? To what extent does the African Economic Community fulfill functions in Africa that the Treaty on European Union does in Europe?

2. What were some of the fundamental weaknesses of the Organization of African Unity? How might these weaknesses have contributed to the formation of the African Union?

3. What role have other nations played in Africa's efforts to achieve some measure of unity and economic development? To what extent have the nations of Africa been treated as proxy states in competition between the world's major powers?

4. Why do you think economic development has been slow to come to Africa, particularly in light of the goals of the African Union and the richness of Africa's resources? Is it because of the legacy of colonialism? The fragmentation of the continent? Internal politics? Other causes?

5. Compare this document with the Resolutions of the National Congress of British West Africa, which were signed in 1920. To what extent did the Constitutive Act of the African Union realize goals expressed in the resolutions? How do you think the authors of the 1920 resolutions would have reacted to the Constitutive Act written eighty years later?

nations in western and central Africa, twelve of them former French colonies, use the CFA franc, guaranteed by the French treasury, as their unit of currency—a stable currency they do not want to abandon. (CFA stands for Communauté Financière Africaine, or African Financial Community.) A continuing problem, too, lies in disparities in economic output and standards of living; the economic output of South Africa, for example, is greater than that of Nigeria by a factor of ten, despite Nigeria's membership in the Organization of Petroleum Exporting Countries.

In face of these intractable problems, many observers are not sanguine about the future of Africa. According to a report prepared by the InterAfrica Group and the Justice Africa organization, "There is a high level of political demoralization across the continent and a clear lack of confidence in political institutions and political leaders." Additionally, the report concluded: "Africa's attempts at regional economic integration have so far failed to realize substantial increases in intra-regional trade. African countries started off with lower levels of intra-regional trade and the situation has largely failed to improve" (http://www.uneca.org/adfiii/auissuepn1.htm). Although this report dates from 2002, many observers still believe that numerous obstacles continue to prevent the AU from achieving its goals.

Further Reading

■ Articles
Loots, Elsabé. "Roadmap for Africa's Recovery: Challenges and Recommendations for Structural Reform." *Africa Insight* 36, nos. 3–4 (September–December 2006): 11–25.

■ Books
Dompere, Kofi Kissi. *African Union: Pan-African Analytical Foundations.* London: Adonis & Abbey, 2006.

Heyns, Christof H., and Magnus Killander, eds. *Compendium of Key Human Rights Documents of the African Union.* 3rd ed. Pretoria, South Africa: Pretoria University Law Press, 2007.

Makinda, Samuel M., and F. Wafula Okumu. *The African Union: Challenges of Globalization, Security, and Governance.* New York: Routledge, 2008.

Meredith, Martin. *The Fate of Africa: From the Hopes of Freedom to the Heart of Despair—A History of Fifty Years of Independence.* New York: Public Affairs, 2006.

Murithi, Timothy. *The African Union: Pan-Africanism, Peacebuilding and Development.* Burlington, Vt.: Ashgate Publishing, 2005.

Murray, Rachel. *Human Rights in Africa: From the OAU to the African Union.* New York: Cambridge University Press, 2004.

■ Web Sites
InterAfrica Group and Justice Africa. "The Economic Dimension to the African Union." African Development Forum Web site. http://www.uneca.org/adfiii/auissuepn1.htm.

—Michael J. O'Neal

CONSTITUTIVE ACT OF THE AFRICAN UNION

We, Heads of State and Government of the Member States of the Organization of African Unity (OAU):

1. The President of the People's Democratic Republic of Algeria
2. The President of the Republic of Angola
3. The President of the Republic of Benin
4. The President of the Republic of Botswana
5. The President of Burkina Faso
6. The President of the Republic of Burundi
7. The President of the Republic of Cameroon
8. The President of the Republic of Cape Verde
9. The President of the Central African Republic
10. The President of the Republic of Chad
11. The President of the Islamic Federal Republic of the Comoros
12. The President of the Republic of the Congo
13. The President of the Republic of Cote d'Ivoire
14. The President of the Democratic Republic of Congo
15. The President of the Republic of Djibouti
16. The President of the Arab Republic of Egypt
17. The President of the State of Eritrea
18. The Prime Minister of the Federal Democratic Republic of Ethiopia
19. The President of the Republic of Equatorial Guinea
20. The President of the Gabonese Republic
21. The President of the Republic of The Gambia
22. The President of the Republic of Ghana
23. The President of the Republic of Guinea
24. The President of the Republic of Guinea Bissau
25. The President of the Republic of Kenya
26. The Prime Minister of Lesotho
27. The President of the Republic of Liberia
28. The Leader of the 1st of September Revolution of the Great Socialist People's Libyan Arab Jamahiriya
29. The President of the Republic of Madagascar
30. The President of the Republic of Malawi
31. The President of the Republic of Mali
32. The President of the Islamic Republic of Mauritania
33. The Prime Minister of the Republic of Mauritius
34. The President of the Republic of Mozambique
35. The President of the Republic of Namibia
36. The President of the Republic of Niger
37. The President of the Federal Republic of Nigeria
38. The President of the Republic of Rwanda
39. The President of the Sahrawi Arab Democratic Republic
40. The President of the Republic of Sao Tome and Principe
41. The President of the Republic of Senegal
42. The President of the Republic of Seychelles
43. The President of the Republic of Sierra Leone
44. The President of the Republic of Somalia
45. The President of the Republic of South Africa
46. The President of the Republic of Sudan
47. The King of Swaziland
48. The President of the United Republic of Tanzania
49. The President of the Togolese Republic
50. The President of the Republic of Tunisia
51. The President of the Republic of Uganda
52. The President of the Republic of Zambia
53. The President of the Republic of Zimbabwe

Inspired by the noble ideals which guided the founding fathers of our Continental Organization and generations of Pan-Africanists in their determination to promote unity, solidarity, cohesion and cooperation among the peoples of Africa and African States;

Considering the principles and objectives stated in the Charter of the Organization of African Unity and the Treaty establishing the African Economic Community;

Recalling the heroic struggles waged by our peoples and our countries for political independence, human dignity and economic emancipation;

Considering that since its inception, the Organization of African Unity has played a determining and invaluable role in the liberation of the continent, the affirmation of a common identity and the process of attainment of the unity of our Continent and has provided a unique framework for our collective action in Africa and in our relations with the rest of the world;

Determined to take up the multifaceted challenges that confront our continent and peoples in the light of the social, economic and political changes taking place in the world;

Convinced of the need to accelerate the process of implementing the Treaty establishing the African Economic Community in order to promote the socio-economic development of Africa and to face more effectively the challenges posed by globalization;

Guided by our common vision of a united and strong Africa and by the need to build a partnership between governments and all segments of civil society, in particular women, youth and the private sector in order to strengthen solidarity and cohesion among our peoples;

Conscious of the fact that the scourge of conflicts in Africa constitutes a major impediment to the socio-economic development of the continent and of the need to promote peace, security and stability as a prerequisite for the implementation of our development and integration agenda;

Determined to promote and protect human and peoples' rights, consolidate democratic institutions and culture, and to ensure good governance and the rule of law;

Further determined to take all necessary measures to strengthen our common institutions and provide them with the necessary powers and resources to enable them discharge their respective mandates effectively;

Recalling the Declaration which we adopted at the Fourth Extraordinary Session of our Assembly in Sirte, the Great Socialist People's Libyan Arab Jamahiriya, on 9.9. 99, in which we decided to establish an African Union, in conformity with the ultimate objectives of the Charter of our Continental Organization and the Treaty establishing the African Economic Community;

Have agreed as follows:

Article 1: Definitions

In this Constitutive Act:

"Act" means the present Constitutive Act;

"AEC" means the African Economic Community;

"Assembly" means the Assembly of Heads of State and Government of the Union;

"Charter" means the Charter of the OAU;

"Committee" means a Specialized Technical Committee of the Union;

"Council" means the Economic, Social and Cultural Council of the Union;

"Court " means the Court of Justice of the Union;

"Executive Council" means the Executive Council of Ministers of the Union;

"Member State" means a Member State of the Union;

"OAU" means the Organization of African Unity;

"Parliament" means the Pan-African Parliament of the Union;

"Union" means the African Union established by the present Constitutive Act.

Article 2: Establishment

The African Union is hereby established in accordance with the provisions of this Act.

Article 3: Objectives

The objectives of the Union shall be to:

a. Achieve greater unity and solidarity between the African counties and the peoples of Africa;

b. Defend the sovereignty, territorial integrity and independence of its Member States;

c. Accelerate the political and socio-economic integration of the continent;

d. Promote and defend African common positions on issues of interest to the continent and its peoples;

e. Encourage international cooperation, taking due account of the Charter of the United Nations and the Universal Declaration of Human Rights;

f. Promote peace, security, and stability on the continent;

g. Promote democratic principles and institutions, popular participation and good governance;

h. Promote and protect human and peoples' rights in accordance with the African Charter on Human and Peoples' Rights and other relevant human rights instruments;

i. Establish the necessary conditions which enable the continent to play its rightful role in the global economy and in international negotiations;

j. Promote sustainable development at the economic, social and cultural levels as well as the integration of African economies;

k. Promote cooperation in all fields of human activity to raise the living standards of African peoples;

l. Coordinate and harmonize policies between existing and future Regional Economic Communities for the gradual attainment of the objectives of the Union;

m. Advance the development of the continent by promoting research in all fields, in particular in science and technology;

n. Work with relevant international partners in the eradication of preventable diseases and the promotion of good health on the continent.

Article 4: Principles

The Union shall function in accordance with the following principles:

a. Sovereign equality and interdependence among Member States of the Union;

b. Respect of borders existing on achievement of independence;

c. Participation of the African peoples in the activities of the Union;

d. Establishment of a common defence policy for the African Continent;

e. Peaceful resolution of conflicts among Member States of the Union through such appropriate means as may be decided upon by the Assembly;

f. Prohibition of the use of force or threat to use force among Member States of the Union;

g. Non-interference by any Member State in the internal affairs of another;

h. The right of the Union to intervene in a Member State pursuant to a decision of the Assembly in respect of grave circumstances, namely war crimes, genocide and crimes against humanity;

i. Peaceful co-existence of Member States and their right to live in peace and security;

j. The right of Member States to request intervention from the Union in order to restore peace and security;

k. Promotion of self-reliance within the framework of the Union;

l. Promotion of gender equality;

m. Respect for democratic principles, human rights, the rule of law and good governance;

n. Promotion of social justice to ensure balanced economic development;

o. Respect for the sanctity of human life, condemnation and rejection of impunity and political assassination, acts of terrorism and subversive activities;

p. Condemnation and rejection of unconstitutional changes of governments.

Article 5: Organs of the Union

1. The organs of the Union shall be:
a. The Assembly of the Union;
b. The Executive Council;
c. The Pan-African Parliament;
d. The Court of Justice;
e. The Commission;
f. The Permanent Representatives Committee;
g. The Specialized Technical Committees;
h. The Economic, Social and Cultural Council;
i. The Financial Institutions;
2. Other organs that the Assembly may decide to establish.

Article 6: The Assembly

1. The Assembly shall be composed of Heads of States and Government or their duly accredited representatives.

2. The Assembly shall be the supreme organ of the Union.

3. The Assembly shall meet at least once a year in ordinary session. At the request of any Member State and on approval by a two-thirds majority of the Member States, the Assembly shall meet in extraordinary session.

4. The Office of the Chairman of the Assembly shall be held for a period of one year by a Head of State or Government elected after consultations among the Member States.

Article 7: Decisions of the Assembly

1. The Assembly shall take its decisions by consensus or, failing which, by a two-thirds majority of the Member States of the Union. However, procedural matters, including the question of whether a matter is one of procedure or not, shall be decided by a simple majority.

2. Two-thirds of the total membership of the Union shall form a quorum at any meeting of the Assembly.

Article 8: Rules of Procedure of the Assembly

The Assembly shall adopt its own Rules of Procedure.

Article 9: Powers and Functions of the Assembly

1. The functions of the Assembly shall be to:

a. Determine the common policies of the Union;

b. Receive, consider and take decisions on reports and recommendations from the other organs of the Union;

c. Consider requests for Membership of the Union;

d. Establish any organ of the Union;

e. Monitor the implementation of policies and decisions of the Union as well as ensure compliance by all Member States;

f. Adopt the budget of the Union;

g. Give directives to the Executive Council on the management of conflicts, war and other emergency situations and the restoration of peace;

h. Appoint and terminate the appointment of the judges of the Court of Justice;

i. Appoint the Chairman of the Commission and his or her deputy or deputies and Commissioners of the Commission and determine their functions and terms of office.

2. The Assembly may delegate any of its powers and functions to any organ of the Union.

Article 10: The Executive Council

1. The Executive Council shall be composed of the Ministers of Foreign Affairs or such other Ministers or Authorities as are designated by the Governments of Member States.

2. Council shall meet at least twice a year in ordinary session. It shall also meet in an extra-ordinary session at the request of any Member State and upon approval by two-thirds of all Member States.

Article 11: Decisions of the Executive Council

1. The Executive Council shall take its decisions by consensus or, failing which, by a two-thirds majority of the Member States. However, procedural matters, including the question of whether a matter is one of procedure or not, shall be decided by a simple majority.

2. Two-thirds of the total membership of the Union shall form a quorum at any meeting of the Executive Council.

Article 12: Rules of Procedure of the Executive Council

The Executive Council shall adopt its own Rules of Procedure.

Article 13: Functions of the Executive Council

1. The Executive Council shall co-ordinate and take decisions on policies in areas of common interest to the Member States, including the following:

a. Foreign trade;

b. Energy, industry and mineral resources;

c. Food, agricultural and animal resources, livestock production and forestry;

d. Water resources and irrigation;

e. Environmental protection, humanitarian action and disaster response and relief;

f. Transport and communications;

g. Insurance;

h. Education, culture, health and human resources development;

i. Science and technology;

j. Nationality, residency and immigration matters;

k. Social security, including the formulation of mother and child care policies, as well as policies relating to the disabled and the handicapped;

l. Establishment of a system of African awards, medals and prizes.

2. The Executive Council shall be responsible to the Assembly. It shall consider issues referred to it and monitor the implementation of policies formulated by the Assembly.

3. The Executive Council may delegate any of its powers and functions mentioned in paragraph 1 of this Article to the Specialized Technical Committees established under Article 14 of this Act.

Article 14: The Specialized Technical Committees Establishment and Composition

1. There is hereby established the following Specialized Technical Committees, which shall be responsible to the Executive Council:

a. The Committee on Rural Economy and Agricultural Matters;

b. The Committee on Monetary and Financial Affairs;

c. The Committee on Trade, Customs and Immigration Matters;

d. The Committee on Industry, Science and Technology, Energy, Natural Resources and Environment;

e. The Committee on Transport, Communications and Tourism;

f. The Committee on Health, Labour and Social Affairs; and

g. The Committee on Education, Culture and Human Resources.

2. The Assembly shall, whenever it deems appropriate, restructure the existing Committees or establish other Committees.

3. The Specialized Technical Committees shall be composed of Ministers or senior officials responsible for sectors falling within their respective areas of competence.

Article 15: Functions of the Specialized Technical Committees

Each Committee shall within its field of competence:

a. Prepare projects and programmes of the Union and submit to the Executive Council;

b. Ensure the supervision, follow-up and the evaluation of the implementation of decisions taken by the organs of the Union;

c. Ensure the coordination and harmonization of projects and programmes of the Union;

d. Submit to the Executive Council either on its own initiative or at the request of the Executive Council, reports and recommendations on the implementation of the provision of this Act; and

e. Carry out any other functions assigned to it for the purpose of ensuring the implementation of the provisions of this Act.

Article 16: Meetings

1. Subject to any directives given by the Executive Council, each Committee shall meet as often as necessary and shall prepare its rules of procedure and submit them to the Executive Council for approval.

Article 17: The Pan-African Parliament

1. In order to ensure the full participation of African peoples in the development and economic integration of the continent, a Pan-African Parliament shall be established.

2. The composition, powers, functions and organization of the Pan-African Parliament shall be defined in a protocol relating thereto.

Article 18: The Court of Justice

1. A Court of Justice of the Union shall be established;

2. The statute, composition and functions of the Court of Justice shall be defined in a protocol relating thereto.

Article 19: The Financial Institutions

The Union shall have the following financial institutions, whose rules and regulations shall be defined in protocols relating thereto:

a. The African Central Bank;

b. The African Monetary Fund;

c. The African Investment Bank.

Article 20: The Commission

1. There shall be established a Commission of the Union, which shall be the Secretariat of the Union.

2. The Commission shall be composed of the Chairman, his or her deputy or deputies and the Commissioners. They shall be assisted by the necessary staff for the smooth functioning of the Commission.

3. The structure, functions and regulations of the Commission shall be determined by the Assembly.

Article 21: The Permanent Representatives Committee

1. There shall be established a Permanent Representatives Committee. It shall be composed of Permanent Representatives to the Union and other Plenipotentiaries of Member States.

2. The Permanent Representatives Committee shall be charged with the responsibility of preparing

the work of the Executive Council and acting on the Executive Council's instructions. It may set up such sub-committees or working groups as it may deem necessary.

Article 22: The Economic, Social and Cultural Council

1. The Economic, Social and Cultural Council shall be an advisory organ composed of different social and professional groups of the Member States of the Union.

2. The functions, powers, composition and organization of the Economic, Social and Cultural Council shall be determined by the Assembly.

Article 23: Imposition of Sanctions

1. The Assembly shall determine the appropriate sanctions to be imposed on any Member State that defaults in the payment of its contributions to the budget of the Union in the following manner: denial of the right to speak at meetings, to vote, to present candidates for any position or post within the Union or to benefit from any activity or commitments therefrom.

2. Furthermore, any Member State that fails to comply with the decisions and policies of the Union may be subjected to other sanctions, such as the denial of transport and communications links with other Member States, and other measures of a political and economic nature to be determined by the Assembly.

Article 24: The Headquarters of the Union

1. The Headquarters of the Union shall be in Addis Ababa in the Federal Democratic Republic of Ethiopia.

2. There may be established such other offices of the Union as the Assembly may, on the recommendation of the Executive Council, determine.

Article 25: Working Languages

The working languages of the Union and all its institutions shall be, if possible, African languages, Arabic, English, French and Portuguese.

Article 26: Interpretation

The Court shall be seized with matters of interpretation arising from the application or implementation of this Act. Pending its establishment, such matters shall be submitted to the Assembly of the Union, which shall decide by a two-thirds majority.

Article 27: Signature, Ratification and Accession

1. This Act shall be open to signature, ratification and accession by the Member States of the OAU in accordance with their respective constitutional procedures.

2. The instruments of ratification shall be deposited with the Secretary-General of the OAU.

3. Any Member State of the OAU acceding to this Act after its entry into force shall deposit the instrument of accession with the Chairman of the Commission.

Article 28: Entry into Force

This Act shall enter into force thirty (30) days after the deposit of the instruments of ratification by two-thirds of the Member States of the OAU.

Article 29: Admission to Membership

1. Any African State may, at any time after the entry into force of this Act, notify the Chairman of the Commission of its intention to accede to this Act and to be admitted as a member of the Union.

2. The Chairman of the Commission shall, upon receipt of such notification, transmit copies thereof to all Member States. Admission shall be decided by a simple majority of the Member States. The decision of each Member State shall be transmitted to the Chairman of the Commission who shall, upon receipt of the required number of votes, communicate the decision to the State concerned.

Article 30: Suspension

Governments which shall come to power through unconstitutional means shall not be allowed to participate in the activities of the Union.

Article 31: Cessation of Membership

1. Any State which desires to renounce its membership shall forward a written notification to the Chairman of the Commission, who shall inform Member States thereof. At the end of one year from the date of such notification, if not withdrawn, the Act shall cease to apply with respect to the renouncing State, which shall thereby cease to belong to the Union.

2. During the period of one year referred to in paragraph 1 of this Article, any Member State wishing to withdraw from the Union shall comply with the provisions of this Act and shall be bound to discharge its obligations under this Act up to the date of its withdrawal.

Article 32: Amendment and Revision

1. Any Member State may submit proposals for the amendment or revision of this Act.

2. Proposals for amendment or revision shall be submitted to the Chairman of the Commission who shall transmit same to Member States within thirty (30) days of receipt thereof.

3. The Assembly, upon the advice of the Executive Council, shall examine these proposals within a period of one year following notification of Member States, in accordance with the provisions of paragraph 2 of this Article.

4. Amendments or revisions shall be adopted by the Assembly by consensus or, failing which, by a two-thirds majority and submitted for ratification by all Member States in accordance with their respective constitutional procedures. They shall enter into force thirty (30) days after the deposit of the instruments of ratification with the Chairman of the Commission by a two-thirds majority of the Member States.

Article 33: Transitional Arrangements and Final Provisions

1. This Act shall replace the Charter of the Organization of African Unity. However, the Charter shall remain operative for a transitional period of one year or such further period as may be determined by the Assembly, following the entry into force of the Act, for the purpose of enabling the OAU/AEC to undertake the necessary measures regarding the devolution of its assets and liabilities to the Union and all matters relating thereto.

2. The provisions of this Act shall take precedence over and supersede any inconsistent or contrary provisions of the Treaty establishing the African Economic Community.

3. Upon the entry into force of this Act, all necessary measures shall be undertaken to implement its provisions and to ensure the establishment of the organs provided for under the Act in accordance with any directives or decisions which may be adopted in this regard by the Parties thereto within the transitional period stipulated above.

4. Pending the establishment of the Commission, the OAU General Secretariat shall be the interim Secretariat of the Union.

5. This Act, drawn up in four (4) original texts in the Arabic, English, French and Portuguese languages, all four (4) being equally authentic, shall be deposited with the Secretary-General of the OAU and, after its entry into force, with the Chairman of the Commission who shall transmit a certified true copy of the Act to the Government of each signatory State. The Secretary-General of the OAU and the Chairman of the Commission shall notify all signatory States of the dates of the deposit of the instruments of ratification or accession and shall upon entry into force of this Act register the same with the Secretariat of the United Nations.

In Witness Whereof, We have adopted this Act.
Done at Lomé, Togo, this 11th day of July, 2000.

Correspondence

Boniface VIII's Clericis Laicos (1296) and Unam Sanctam (1302)

Christopher Columbus's Letter to Raphael Sanxis on the Discovery of America (1493)

Qianlong's Letter to George III (1793)

Diplomatic Correspondence between Muhammad al-Kānamī and Muhammad Bello (1810–1812)

Lin Zexu's "Moral Advice to Queen Victoria" (1839)

Balfour Declaration (1917)

Essays, Reports, Manifestos, and Narratives

"Mandate of Heaven: The Numerous Officers" (ca. 475–221 BCE)

Plato's "Allegory of the Cave" (ca. 380 BCE)

Canon of Filial Piety (ca. 300–239 BCE)

Discourses on Salt and Iron (74–49 BCE)

Deeds of the Divine Augustus (14)

Popol Vuh (250–925)

Capitulary of Charlemagne (802)

Han Yu's "Memorial on the Buddha's Bones" (819)

Al-Māwardī's "On Qāḍīs" (1045–1058)

Kai Kaus on the Purchase of Slaves (1082–1083)

Domesday Book (1086)

Niẓām al-Mulk's *Book of Government; or, Rules for Kings* (1091)

Usama ibn Munqidh's "A Muslim View of the Crusaders" (ca. 1185)

Marco Polo's Description of Hangzhou (ca. 1298)

Ibn Khaldūn's "Social Solidarity" (ca. 1375)

Niccolò Machiavelli's *The Prince* (1513)

Requerimiento (1513)

Martin Luther's *Ninety-five Theses* (1517)

Dutch Declaration of Independence (1581)

John Locke's *Second Treatise on Civil Government* (1690)

Declaration of the Rights of Man and of the Citizen (1789) and Declaration of the Rights of Woman and of the
    Female Citizen (1791)

Simón Bolívar's Cartagena Manifesto (1812)

Carlsbad Decrees (1819)

Communist Manifesto (1848)

Theodor Herzl's "A Solution to the Jewish Question" (1896)

Vladimir Lenin's *What Is to Be Done?* (1902)

Emiliano Zapata's Plan of Ayala (1911)

Proclamation of the Provisional Government of the Irish Republic (1916)

Korean Declaration of Independence (1919)

Resolution of the General Syrian Congress (1919)

Resolutions of the National Congress of British West Africa (1920)

Mao Zedong's "Report on an Investigation of the Peasant Movement in Hunan" (1927)

Benito Mussolini's "The Doctrine of Facism" (1932)

Lahore Resolution (1940)

Declaration of Independence of the Democratic Republic of Vietnam (1945)

Declaration of the Establishment of the State of Israel (1948)

Universal Declaration of Human Rights (1948)

Juan Perón's "Twenty Fundamental Truths of Justicialism" (1950)

Fidel Castro's *History Will Absolve Me* (1953)

Proclamation of the Algerian National Liberation Front (1954)

Freedom Charter of South Africa (1955)

"Mao Tse-tung's Thought Is the Telescope and Microscope of Our Revolutionary Cause" (1966)

Arusha Declaration (1967)
UN Security Council Resolution 242 (1967)
Palestinian National Charter (1968)
Ayatollah Khomeini's *Islamic Government: Governance of the Jurist* (1970)
Osama bin Laden's Declaration of Jihad against Americans (1996)

Laws and Legal Codes
Code of Hammurabi (ca. 1752 BCE)
Hittite Laws (ca. 1650–1400 BCE)
Middle Assyrian Laws (ca. 1115–1077 BCE)
Constitution of Sparta (ca. 650 BCE)
Twelve Tables of Roman Law (451 BCE)
Constitution of Carthage (ca. 320s BCE)
Athenian Constitution (ca. 320s BCE)
Law of Caesar on Municipalities (ca. 44 BCE)
Laws Ending Persecution of Christians in the Roman Empire (311 and 313)
Theodosian Code (438)
Code of Justinian (534)
Prince Shōtoku's Seventeen-Article Constitution (604)
New Year's Day Taika Reform Edict (646)
Capitulary of Charlemagne (802)
II Aethelstan, or the Grately Code (924–939)
Russkaia Pravda, or Justice of the Rus (ca. 1019)
Constitutions of Clarendon (1164)
Magna Carta (1215)
Great Yasa of Chinggis Khan (thirteenth through fifteenth centuries)
Laws Governing Military Households (1615)
Ulozhenie, or Great Muscovite Law Code (1649)
Habeas Corpus Act of the Restoration (1679)
English Bill of Rights (1689)
British Regulating Act (1773)
Constitution of Haiti (1801)
Act for the Abolition of Slavery throughout the British Colonies (1833)
Constitution Act of Canada (1867)
Constitution of the Fante Confederacy (1871)
Meiji Constitution of Japan (1889)
Government of India Act (1919)
Nuremberg Laws (1935)
Japanese Constitution (1947)
Geneva Convention Relative to the Treatment of Prisoners of War (1949)
Constitution of India (1949)
Gamal Abdel Nasser on the Nationalization of the Suez Canal (1956)
Palestinian National Charter (1968)
Biological Weapons Convention (1972)
Constitution of the People's Republic of China (1982)
Constitutive Act of the African Union (2000)

Royal Edicts and Proclamations
Reform Edict of Urukagina (ca. 2350 BCE)
Divine Birth and Coronation Inscriptions of Hatshepsut (ca. 1473 BCE)
Rock and Pillar Edicts of Aśoka (257–240 BCE)
Wang Kŏn's Ten Injunctions (943)
Japan's Closed Country Edict (1635)
Queen Victoria's Proclamation concerning India (1858)
Emperor Guangxu's Abolition of the Examination System (1898)
Articles Providing for the Favorable Treatment of the Great Ching Emperor after His Abdication (1912)

Speeches and Addresses

Funeral Oration of Pericles (431 BCE)
Bernhard von Bülow on Germany's "Place in the Sun" (1897)
Sun Yat-sen's "The Three Principles of the People" (1921)
A. B. Xuma's "Bridging the Gap between White and Black in South Africa" (1930)
Adolf Hitler's Proclamation to the German People (1933)
Mahatma Gandhi's Speech to the All India Congress Committee (1942)
Winston Churchill's "The Sinews of Peace" (1946)
Jawaharlal Nehru's Speeches on the Granting of Indian Independence (1947)
Patrice Lumumba's Speech at the Proclamation of Congolese Independence (1960)
Nelson Mandela's Inaugural Address (1994)

Treaties, Agreements, and Military Proclamations

Egyptian-Hittite Peace Treaty (1259 BCE)
Victory Stela of Piankhi (ca. 725 BCE)
Urban II's Call to Crusade (1095)
Treaty of Westphalia (1648)
Treaty of Córdoba (1821)
Treaty of Nanjing (1842)
Treaty of Guadalupe Hidalgo (1848)
Treaty of Limits between Mexico and Guatemala (1882)
D'Arcy Concession (1901)
Treaty of Versailles (1919)
Covenant of the League of Nations (1919)
Treaty of Lausanne (1923)
Japan's Fourteen-part Message (1941)
Geneva Convention Relative to the Treatment of Prisoners of War (1949)
Biological Weapons Convention (1972)
Helsinki Final Act (1975)
Treaty on European Union (1992)
Agreement on Reconciliation between South and North Korea (1992)
Northern Ireland Peace Agreement (1998)
Constitutive Act of the African Union (2000)

Africa

Constitution of Carthage (ca. 320s BCE)
Diplomatic Correspondence between Muhammad al-Kānamī and Muhammad Bello (1810–1812)
Constitution of the Fante Confederacy (1871)
Resolutions of the National Congress of British West Africa (1920)
A. B. Xuma's "Bridging the Gap between White and Black in South Africa" (1930)
Proclamation of the Algerian National Liberation Front (1954)
Freedom Charter of South Africa (1955)
Patrice Lumumba's Speech at the Proclamation of Congolese Independence (1960)
Arusha Declaration (1967)
Nelson Mandela's Inaugural Address (1994)
Constitutive Act of the African Union (2000)

Americas

Popol Vuh (250–925)
Constitution of Haiti (1801)
Simón Bolívar's Cartagena Manifesto (1812)
Treaty of Córdoba (1821)
Treaty of Guadalupe Hidalgo (1848)
Constitution Act of Canada (1867)
Treaty of Limits between Mexico and Guatemala (1882)
Emiliano Zapata's Plan of Ayala (1911)
Juan Perón's "Twenty Fundamental Truths of Justicialism" (1950)
Fidel Castro's *History Will Absolve Me* (1953)

Ancient Egypt

Divine Birth and Coronation Inscriptions of Hatshepsut (ca. 1473 BCE)
Egyptian-Hittite Peace Treaty (1259 BCE)
Victory Stela of Piankhi (ca. 725 BCE)

Ancient Near East

Reform Edict of Urukagina (ca. 2350 BCE)
Code of Hammurabi (ca. 1752 BCE)
Hittite Laws (ca. 1650–1400 BCE)
Middle Assyrian Laws (ca. 1115–1077 BCE)

Asia

"Mandate of Heaven: The Numerous Officers" (ca. 475–221 BCE)
Canon of Filial Piety (ca. 300–239 BCE)
Rock and Pillar Edicts of Aśoka (257–240 BCE)
Discourses on Salt and Iron (74–49 BCE)
Prince Shōtoku's Seventeen-Article Constitution (604)
New Year's Day Taika Reform Edict (646)
Han Yu's "Memorial on the Buddha's Bones" (819)
Wang Kŏn's Ten Injunctions (943)
Marco Polo's Description of Hangzhou (ca. 1298)
Laws Governing Military Households (1615)
Japan's Closed Country Edict (1635)
British Regulating Act (1773)

Qianlong's Letter to George III (1793)
Lin Zexu's "Moral Advice to Queen Victoria" (1839)
Treaty of Nanjing (1842)
Queen Victoria's Proclamation concerning India (1858)
Meiji Constitution of Japan (1889)
Emperor Guangxu's Abolition of the Examination System (1898)
Articles Providing for the Favorable Treatment of the Great Ching Emperor after His Abdication (1912)
Korean Declaration of Independence (1919)
Government of India Act (1919)
Sun Yat-sen's "The Three Principles of the People" (1921)
Mao Zedong's "Report on an Investigation of the Peasant Movement in Hunan" (1927)
Lahore Resolution (1940)
Japan's Fourteen-part Message (1941)
Mahatma Gandhi's Speech to the All India Congress Committee (1942)
Declaration of Independence of the Democratic Republic of Vietnam (1945)
Japanese Constitution (1947)
Jawaharlal Nehru's Speeches on the Granting of Indian Independence (1947)
Constitution of India (1949)
"Mao Tse-tung's Thought Is the Telescope and Microscope of Our Revolutionary Cause" (1966)
Constitution of the People's Republic of China (1982)
Agreement on Reconciliation between South and North Korea (1992)

Classical Greece and Rome
Constitution of Sparta (ca. 650 BCE)
Twelve Tables of Roman Law (451 BCE)
Funeral Oration of Pericles (431 BCE)
Plato's "Allegory of the Cave" (ca. 380 BCE)
Athenian Constitution (ca. 320s BCE)
Law of Caesar on Municipalities (ca. 44 BCE)
Deeds of the Divine Augustus (14)
Theodosian Code (438)
Code of Justinian (534)

Middle East
Al-Māwardī's "On Qāḍīs" (1045–1058)
Kai Kaus on the Purchase of Slaves (1082–1083)
Niẓām al-Mulk's *Book of Government; or, Rules for Kings* (1091)
Usama ibn Munqidh's "A Muslim View of the Crusaders" (ca. 1185)
Ibn Khaldūn's "Social Solidarity" (ca. 1375)
Theodor Herzl's "A Solution to the Jewish Question" (1896)
D'Arcy Concession (1901)
Balfour Declaration (1917)
Resolution of the General Syrian Congress (1919)
Treaty of Lausanne (1923)
Declaration of the Establishment of the State of Israel (1948)
Gamal Abdel Nasser on the Nationalization of the Suez Canal (1956)
UN Security Council Resolution 242 (1967)
Palestinian National Charter (1968)
Ayatollah Khomeini's *Islamic Government: Governance of the Jurist* (1970)
Osama bin Laden's Declaration of Jihad against Americans (1996)

Western World
Laws Ending Persecution of Christians in the Roman Empire (311 and 313)
Capitulary of Charlemagne (802)
II Aethelstan, or the Grately Code (924–939)

Domesday Book (1086)
Urban II's Call to Crusade (1095)
Constitutions of Clarendon (1164)
Russkaia Pravda, or Justice of the Rus (ca. 1019)
Magna Carta (1215)
Boniface VIII's Clericis Laicos (1296) and Unam Sanctam (1302)
Great Yasa of Chinggis Khan (thirteenth through fifteenth centuries)
Christopher Columbus's Letter to Raphael Sanxis on the Discovery of America (1493)
Niccolò Machiavelli's *The Prince* (1513)
Requerimiento (1513)
Martin Luther's *Ninety-five Theses* (1517)
Dutch Declaration of Independence (1581)
Treaty of Westphalia (1648)
Ulozhenie, or Great Muscovite Law Code (1649)
Habeas Corpus Act of the Restoration (1679)
English Bill of Rights (1689)
John Locke's *Second Treatise on Civil Government* (1690)
Declaration of the Rights of Man and of the Citizen (1789) and Declaration of the Rights of Woman and of the
    Female Citizen (1791)
Carlsbad Decrees (1819)
Act for the Abolition of Slavery throughout the British Colonies (1833)
Communist Manifesto (1848)
Bernhard von Bülow on Germany's "Place in the Sun" (1897)
Vladimir Lenin's *What Is to Be Done?* (1902)
Proclamation of the Provisional Government of the Irish Republic (1916)
Covenant of the League of Nations (1919)
Treaty of Versailles (1919)
Benito Mussolini's "The Doctrine of Facism" (1932)
Adolf Hitler's Proclamation to the German People (1933)
Nuremberg Laws (1935)
Winston Churchill's "The Sinews of Peace" (1946)
Universal Declaration of Human Rights (1948)
Geneva Convention Relative to the Treatment of Prisoners of War (1949)
Biological Weapons Convention (1972)
Helsinki Final Act (1975)
Treaty on European Union (1992)
Northern Ireland Peace Agreement (1998)

Volume numbers are indicated before each page number. Bold page numbers indicate the primary entry about the topic.

Baudouin, King (Belgium) 4:1625, 4:1626, 4:1628, 4:1630

Becket, Thomas 2:515–517, 2:519–522

Beer Hall Putsch 3:1357–1359

Begin, Menachem 4:1676

Belfast Agreement. *See* Northern Ireland Peace Agreement.

Bello, Muhammad 2:855–862
> Diplomatic Correspondence between Muhammad al-Kānamī and Muhammad Bello **2:855–866**

Ben Bella, Ahmed 4:1592

Ben-Gurion, David 4:1483, 4:1485–1486, 4:1489, 4:1618

Benito Mussolini's "The Doctrine of Fascism" **3:1336–1354**

Berlin airlift 4:1724

Bernhard von Bülow on Germany's "Place in the Sun" **3:1074–1083**

Bin Laden, Osama 4:1809–1816
> Declaration of Jihad against Americans **4:1808–1819**

Biological Weapons Convention **4:1709–1720**

Bismarck, Otto von 2:638, 3:1075, 3:1076, 3:1077, 3:1081

Blaine, James G. 3:1036, 3:1037

Blair, Tony 4:1825, 4:1826, 4:1829

Bloody Friday 4:1824

Bloody Sunday 4:1823

Boer War 3:1081

Bolívar, Simón 2:868–876
> Cartagena Manifesto **2:868–882**

Bolshevik Revolution 3:1111, 3:1207, 3:1226, 4:1437

Bomilcar 1:182, 1:186

Bonaparte, Napoléon 1:363, 2:840, 2:842, 2:844, 2:845, 2:870, 2:885–886, 2:899, 3:979, 4:1775

Boniface VIII, Pope 2:575–581
> Clericis Laicos and Unam Sanctam **2:575–585**

Borgia, Cesare 2:632, 2:633, 2:635

Borgia, Rodrigo. *See* Alexander VI, Pope.

Boxer Rebellion 3:1075, 3:1080, 3:1091–1092, 3:1142, 3:1266

Brezhnev, Leonid 4:1723

British East India Company 2:795–801, 2:825, 3:917, 3:933, 3:935–936, 3:939, 3:947–949, 3:950–951, 3:997–1001, 3:1233, 4:1471

British North America Act (1867). *See* Constitution Act of Canada.

British Regulating Act **2:795–806**, 3:998

Bronze Age 1:61, 1:75

Brutus, Marcus Junius 1:257, 1:267, 1:273

Buddha 1:379, 1:380, 1:384–385, 1:407–408

Buddhism 1:225–226, 1:227, 1:231, 1:341, 1:342, 1:343, 1:344, 1:347, 1:353, 1:379–387, 1:407–408, 1:410, 1:412, 4:1642

Bukhārī, Ibn Ismā'il Muḥammad al- 1:437, 1:441

Burgoyne, John 2:796, 2:797

Buyid Dynasty 1:439, 2:483

Byzantine Empire 1:329, 1:334, 1:364, 1:417, 2:454, 2:455, 2:497, 2:498, 2:529, 2:617, 4:1697

C

Cabinet Mission Plan 3:1385, 3:1387, 4:1414, 4:1473, 4:1474, 4:1477, 4:1547, 4:1548

Cabrera, Luis 3:1133

Caesar, Gaius Julius 1:186, 1:254–258, 1:267, 1:272, 1:273, 2:635
> Law of Caesar on Municipalities **1:254–265**

Camp David Accords 4:1676, 4:1686

Canadian Charter of Rights and Freedoms 3:1010

Canning, Charles John 3:1000, 3:1001

Canon of Filial Piety **1:209–222**

Canon of the Way. *See* Dao De Jing.

Capitulary of Charlemagne **1:363–376**

Carlsbad Decrees **2:885–896**, 3:979

Carolingian Dynasty (France) 1:363, 1:364, 1:365, 2:501

Casely Hayford, Joseph Ephraim 3:1251, 3:1256
> Resolutions of the National Congress of British West Africa **3:1249–1262**

Cassin, René 4:1496, 4:1497

Castro, Fidel 4:1572–1579
> *History Will Absolve Me* **4:1572–1587**

Celestine V, Pope 2:578

Charlemagne 1:363–369, 2:501, 4:1775
> Capitulary of Charlemagne **1:363–376**

Charles I, King (England) 2:568, 2:667, 2:751, 2:765–770, 2:779

Charles I, King (Spain). *See* Charles V (Holy Roman Emperor).

Charles II, King (England) 2:751, 2:752, 2:754, 2:765, 2:766, 2:767, 2:768, 2:779

Charles V (Holy Roman Emperor) 2:620, 2:631, 2:635, 2:652, 2:666, 2:675–2:676, 2:678, 2:679, 2:713

Charles VIII, King (France) 2:619, 2:632, 2:649

Chelmsford, Lord. *See* Thesiger, Frederic John Napier, 3rd Baron Chelmsford and 1st Viscount Chelmsford.

Chernyshevsky, Nikolay Gavrilovich 3:1111

Chiang Kai-shek 3:1266, 3:1267, 3:1270, 3:1301, 3:1391, 4:1408

Chinggis Khan 2:544–552, 2:587–588
> Great Yasa of Chinggis Khan **2:544–558**

Choe Namson 3:1175, 3:1176, 3:1177

Choe Rin 3:1175

Chosŏn Dynasty (Korea) 1:407, 1:412, 3:1175, 3:1178

Christian IV, King (Denmark) 2:716, 2:717

Christopher Columbus's Letter to Raphael Sanxis on the Discovery of America **2:616–629**

Chung Won-shik 4:1764–1765, 4:1768

Churchill, Winston 3:1188, 3:1238, 3:1319, 3:1369, 3:1393, 4:1408, 4:1428, 4:1437–1445, 4:1486, 4:1495
> "The Sinews of Peace" **4:1436–1451**

Cixi, Empress Dowager (China) 3:1080, 3:1085, 3:1089, 3:1091–1092, 3:1141, 3:1142, 3:1145, 3:1266

Classic of Changes. *See* I Ching.

Claudius, Appius 1:122–123

Clemenceau, Georges 3:1207, 3:1208

Clement VII, Pope 2:632, 2:633–634